Delineating Wales

POLITICS AND SOCIETY IN WALES SERIES
Series editor: Ralph Fevre

Previous volumes in the series:

Paul Chaney, Tom Hall and Andrew Pithouse (eds), *New Governance – New Democracy? Post-Devolution Wales*

Neil Selwyn and Stephen Gorard, *The Information Age: Technology, Learning and Exclusion in Wales*

Graham Day, *Making Sense of Wales: A Sociological Perspective*

The Politics and Society in Wales Series examines issues of politics and government, and particularly the effects of devolution on policy-making and implementation, and the way in which Wales is governed as the National Assembly gains in maturity. It will also increase our knowledge and understanding of Welsh society and analyse the most important aspects of social and economic change in Wales. Where necessary, studies in the series will incorporate strong comparative elements which will allow a more fully informed appraisal of the condition of Wales.

Delineating Wales

CONSTITUTIONAL, LEGAL AND ADMINISTRATIVE ASPECTS OF NATIONAL DEVOLUTION

By

RICHARD RAWLINGS

Published on behalf of the Social Science Committee
of the Board of Celtic Studies of the University of Wales

UNIVERSITY OF WALES PRESS
CARDIFF
2003

© Richard Rawlings, 2003

Published December 2003
Reprinted September 2007

British Library Cataloguing-in-Publication Data.
A catalogue record for this book is available from the British Library.

ISBN 0–7083–1739–1

All rights reserved. No part of this book may be reproduced, stored in a
retrieval system, or transmitted, in any form or by any means, electronic,
mechanical, photocopying, recording or otherwise, without clearance from the
University of Wales Press, 10 Columbus Walk, Brigantine Place, Cardiff, CF10
4UP.
Website: *www.wales.ac.uk/press*

The right of Richard Rawlings to be identified as author of this work has been
asserted by him in accordance with sections 77 and 78 of the Copyright,
Designs and Patents Act 1988.

Library
University of Texas
at San Antonio

Typeset by Bryan Turnbull and at the University of Wales Press
Printed in Great Britain by Antony Rowe Ltd, Chippenham, Wiltshire

History in the hands of lawyers will always turn lawyers into heroes.

Norman Davies, *The Isles*

For Hugh, fraternally as ever

WITHDRAWN
UTSA LIBRARIES

Contents

Figures

Tables

Series Editor's Foreword

The latest addition to the Politics and Society in Wales series is a book about how best to set up a framework for the governance of a small country which has long been dependent on a larger neighbour. Richard Rawlings is a constitutional lawyer who has both good political judgement and a fine appreciation of history. He writes on his chosen subject with unrivalled authority and the conclusions he reaches merit attention and, indeed, demand action. It is a matter of plain fact that we are in a better position to give Wales the governance framework it needs because Professor Rawlings has been able to harness his expert knowledge together with great care, diligence and enthusiasm in this extraordinarily comprehensive and authoritative work. In this case authority does not, thankfully, come at the price of dullness. Reading these pages it might even seem as if many years of devotion to making sense of this particular subject have sharpened the author's sense of humour.

The foreword I wrote for the first volume in this series declared that the series would serve as one of the important arenas where devolution would be discussed. In order to elaborate the point I explained that the series would inform 'ongoing debate about the constitutional settlement'. It is even clearer in 2003 than it was in 2001 that in Wales there is no settlement as yet. Instead it is becoming clear that, over a period of time, Wales is getting a constitution, and a new relationship with the rest of the United Kingdom, while not always knowing it and with little strategic management of the process. To those who are watching closely, and even those most intimately involved, this process can often look confused and chaotic. It resembles the 'milling area' on the ground floor of the National Assembly for Wales at lunchtime on a busy weekday. You might appreciate a pervasive atmosphere of good intentions and good will but you can make little sense of any of the simultaneous presentations and speeches since you cannot make out a word being said above the general hullabaloo.

In the National Assembly's milling area people only communicate when they are standing close enough to shout in each other's ears. *Delineating Wales* shows us the importance of close contact to the whole process of devolution. It is through social networks and informality that many obstacles have been successfully negotiated and potential conflicts avoided. The book also identifies another, perhaps surprising resource: the determination and problem-solving acumen of the civil servants on whose shoulders the burden of devolution has fallen. Professor Rawlings's respect for the way the civil service has coped and innovated as needs must is infectious. Of course there must be caveats, but *Delineating Wales* shows that these men and women are deeply involved in improving public administration in Wales.

It is perhaps harder to win the author's respect if you are a politician, but we can safely conclude that he thinks many of them have done quite well too, in the circumstances. By 'the circumstances' Richard means the Government of Wales Act. He sees the legal kit that Wales was handed when it was granted permission to establish a limited measure of self-government as seriously deficient. In such circumstances it is a wonder the civil servants and politicians have managed to make much of the job they were given. One of the important questions addressed in this book is whether developments in the Assembly since it began its work have consolidated or undermined the arrangement it was gifted by the UK Government. We are asked to consider whether any undermining that has gone on has, in fact, been the outcome of the practical resolution of contradictions and problems that were built into the original 'settlement'. In this respect we are also asked to consider how much was sacrificed in terms of a decent devolutionary start simply in order to get the principle accepted.

It is important for the people of Wales and of the other three countries of the United Kingdom, to understand that what was created by the Government of Wales Act was something new and quite unique. An unsung, but most important, premiss of this legislation was that no lessons could be learnt from established systems elsewhere, especially federal ones. This, and the need to reach many messy, political compromises, and, all the while, nurture a public perception that nothing of any importance was going on, was largely responsible for making this interim stage so weird. What Professor Rawlings calls a framework of governance 'like nothing else on earth' came into being almost overnight and the search for the solutions to the new problems it posed began almost immediately, but who was to be allowed to join in the hunt?

Delineating Wales forces us to consider how open constitution-building has been with Labour in full hegemony and how it might be made a more open process in the future. The Assembly has trumpeted its inclusiveness but how far has this inclusiveness stretched to constitution-building? The book raises many other important questions, for example, if the Government of Wales Act has required a huge amount of muddling through, how much violence has thereby been done to the idea of keeping law making democratic? Is the emerging style of the new governance in Wales distinguished by more trust and less regulation? What happened to the quangos and what happened to civil society? In answering these questions, Professor Rawlings often takes us out beyond the walls of the Assembly and into the wider public sector where we find that devolution has sometimes had a very significant impact.

The biggest question in the book comes in two parts. Is the framework established by the Government of Wales Act stable enough to last in this form and is there anything here that is worth building on? The elaboration of the answers to this question give us the book's big themes. In magisterial fashion, the author tells us exactly what is wrong with the legal, constitutional and administrative aspects of devolution as handed down in the Act. He tells us how it reflects and reinforces a culture of dependency. He sees the first phase of devolution as the product of numerous compromises which was bound to fall down. Yet he argues that in the practical remedies which were resorted to simply in order to govern in such circumstances we can find plenty of reason for praise and cause for hope. Some of the innovations which came with the Act were good (equal opportunities and sustainable development are singled out) but many have rightly been discarded. For Richard Rawlings, the main cause for hope is that the Assembly is moving in the direction of the parliament that it was never meant to be. He turns out to be a lawyer with an almost Marxist view of historical dialectic. Constitutional change will come because there is a force in current arrangements that compels us to break the fetters that bind us – there are historical actors who are their own grave diggers; we see a glimpse of the future in the day to day existence of the present.

Delineating Wales presents a great deal of well-supported analysis about the way governing Wales has turned out. It has felt less and less like either the Welsh Office or the body corporate invented at devolution. Its plenary is its weakest point and its subject committees need to be more involved in scrutiny. There is good news on the way opportunities have been created for lobbying and networking in Europe. But the bit we all really want to read is what should happen next – in particular what powers should the Assembly get next? *Delineating Wales* does not disappoint: the case is closely argued and impeccably supported. When you put this case together with the dialectic of history you might even see a passing resemblance to the style of the *Communist Manifesto*. Of course, that book was a great deal shorter than this one. Marx and Engels only had to unite the workers of the world but Richard Rawlings wants to tell us how best to govern Wales.

The short story of devolution in Wales has already produced a very long book. This is not really to be wondered at because there is an awful lot to fit in. As Professor Rawlings points out, the speed of change has been unbelievable. He entirely captures what this speed feels like as well as all the finer legal details. The book tells us the plenary debates of the Assembly are not (yet) great theatre, and this is true, but the story itself is assuming the lineaments of a minor dramatic classic. It has *plenty* of characters, alarums and diversions, totally unexpected turns of events, farce and comedy and it does have its heroes. Despite what Richard Rawlings says, maybe one or two of these heroes might actually be lawyers.

This book gives us the classification, analysis, constructive critique, diagnosis and prescription you need when you have been landed with an odd, and probably unique, framework of governance. In other words, it makes sense of the mess and unravels the confusion and the result is a superb piece of scholarship. It is amongst the very best work the University of Wales Press has published and it is almost certainly the best book so far produced on any aspect of devolution in the UK. I can take very little credit for the publication of this marvellous book since my colleague on the series editorial board, Richard Wyn Jones, has done almost all my work for me. He knew the value of this book before it was written. The final product exceeds even his expectations, however, so I speak on behalf of the whole editorial board in thanking Richard Rawlings for giving us *Delineating Wales*.

Ralph Fevre
Cardiff, June 2003

Acknowledgements

In the course of writing this book I have incurred many debts of gratitude. Among the politicians, I owe particular thanks to Lord Elis Thomas, Presiding Officer of the National Assembly for Wales, and to Andrew Davies, currently Minister for Economic Development in the Welsh Assembly Government. Among the lawyers, I am especially grateful to Sir John Thomas and Sir David Williams.

Many officials have given cheerfully of their time, including Sir Jon Shortridge, Permanent Secretary to the Assembly, and Winston Roddick, Counsel General. In the Presiding Office, I owe particular thanks to John Lloyd and Paul Silk, the first two Clerks to the Assembly, and Marie Knox and David Lambert. In the Welsh Assembly Government, I am especially grateful to Gary Davies, Elisabeth Jones and Steve Pomeroy.

Among my colleagues at LSE, Carol Harlow has played the major role of sounding board. As ever, my secretary Susan Hunt worked tirelessly on multiple drafts, while my research assistant Katie Pritchard ably coped with the many primary sources. At Cardiff University, I owe special thanks to Barry Jones, Bob Lee, David Miers and Marie Navarro, not least for welcoming me so warmly on a period of study leave. So too, Brigid Hadfield, Robert Hazell, Charlie Jeffery, Alan Page, Keith Patchett and Barry Winetrobe have helped in various ways, including under the auspices of the Constitution Unit's Law and Devolution project for the ESRC's rolling research programme, Devolution and Constitutional Change.

As Editor of the Politics and Society in Wales Series, Ralph Fevre has proved an unfailing source of advice and assistance. Meanwhile, Richard Wyn Jones, of the Institute of Welsh Politics, Aberystwyth, provided much by way of constructive criticism. I also thank Ruth Dennis-Jones and her colleagues at the University of Wales Press for their support – and patience – in bringing an idea to fruition.

Finally, I must thank my brother Dr Hugh Rawlings – currently Director, Open Government and Constitutional Affairs Division, in the Welsh Assembly Government – to whom this book is dedicated. He will happily disagree with much in it, which is as things should be.

Richard Rawlings
London School of Economics and Political Science
May 2003

Acronyms

The UK devolutionary development in general, and Welsh devolution in particular, has quickly generated a suitably mysterious list of acronyms for the general reader. The following list may help in deciphering the text.

ACW	Audit Commission Wales
AM	Assembly Member
AMS	Additional Member System
ASPB	Assembly Sponsored Public Body
DFM	Deputy First Minister
EAW	Environment Agency Wales
ELWa	Education and Learning Wales
GWA (or GoWA)	Government of Wales Act 1998
IGR	Intergovernmental relations
JMC	Joint Ministerial Committee
LHB	Local Health Board
MoU	*Memorandum of Understanding*
OCG	Office of the Counsel General
NAAG	National Assembly Advisory Group
PO	Presiding Officer
WAG	Welsh Assembly Government
WAO	Welsh Administration Ombudsman
WASC	Welsh Affairs Select Committee
WDA	Welsh Development Agency
WEC	Welsh European Centre
WLGA	Welsh Local Government Association

Introduction

The Rebirth of Welsh Legal History

Devolution is not just an act, a phase, it is also a way of organising the governance of a country – or group of countries, if you will – which is as legitimate as federalism or the unitary state.

Alun Michael (first Assembly First Secretary)[1]

In July 1999, the new National Assembly for Wales was formally empowered. Devolution for the first time had given Wales its own democratically elected and accountable government. It represents not only a turning-point in the history of this little country, but also a fascinating development in constitutional law and politics, an important moment in the constitutional and legal history of the United Kingdom.

The pace of events has been extraordinary. In May 1997, the New Labour government entered into office, with a mandate for a wide-ranging programme of constitutional reform. In July 1997, the White Paper *A Voice for Wales* was published, setting out the proposals for devolution. In September 1997, the people of Wales voted – narrowly – in favour. In July 1998, the Government of Wales Act passed into law, so establishing the statutory framework of the new devolutionary scheme.

In May 1999, the first elections were held to the National Assembly, and by July 2000 the first full session of proceedings had been completed, in the course of which the Assembly faced a mounting tide of criticism, and its first leader was driven from office. In the second full session, beginning in October 2000, minority administration changed to coalition and majority government. A major internal review of the workings of the Assembly was inaugurated, which reported in February 2002. The following month something called the Welsh Assembly Government came into being. In July 2002 an independent review (the Richard Commission) was officially launched, with the task of examining the not insignificant questions of the Assembly's powers and electoral arrangements. Due to report at the end of 2003, the commission may well engender a further wave of constitutional happenings.

From basic reform to fundamental review in this time frame is some constitutional record. It is indicative both of major difficulties with the new structures and processes and of a continuing search for an appropriate form of

Welsh governance in the new millennium. Such is the immediate backdrop to this book, which as an essay in contemporary history traces the development of the new Welsh polity to the end of the first term of the Assembly, focusing on the constitutional, legal and administrative aspects.[2]

In tune with the character of the new Welsh constitutional dispensation, close attention will be paid to the dynamics of the devolutionary process as demonstrated in both the design of the scheme and the early operations of the Assembly. More especially, this book seeks to unravel the great, untold story of Welsh devolution – the role of autochthonous (home-grown) development, first in establishing a governmental apparatus in miniature or microcosm, and second in paving the way to a 'devolution settlement' that is worthy of the name. It amounts to nothing less than a form of constitution-building for Wales, in part by stealth or in silence.

1. CLASSIFICATION: OVERVIEW OF THE SCHEME

Devolution is, like federalism, a slippery concept. The one is correctly distinguished from the other in terms of legal theory and constitutional principle. Strictly speaking, devolution involves no divided sovereignty or constitutional guarantee of the division of legislative competence. In practice, however, the distinction may be blurred, even to the extent that *de facto* there is no great difference. Notably, the terminology of 'quasi-federalism', with its connotations of 'a halfway house' and 'no going back', has been applied to at least some aspects of the UK devolutionary development.[3]

Turning to a dictionary of politics, the definition of devolution as 'the process of transferring power from central government to a lower or regional level' is less than illuminating.[4] It is too general, glossing over the fact that devolutionary schemes come in all shapes and sizes. And it is too limited, effectively draining the devolutionary process of social, cultural and economic meaning.

So let us begin with a basic classification of devolutionary form in the case of Wales. A fourfold categorization is appropriate, denoting factors of political geography and the allocation of functions, internal government structure and constitutional or democratic values. It highlights the vital fact of the peculiar or *sui generis* nature of the Welsh scheme of devolution. The way in which, from the comparative viewpoint, the local development further reflects important trends in contemporary constitutional design is also indicated.

(a) National devolution

Nations, it is commonly observed, are not co-determinous with states. As a social phenomenon, they represent in a famous phrase 'imagined political communities'.[5] The United Kingdom is itself often described as a multi-national state,[6] so underscoring the sense of historical diversity, and in particular the concept of dual or overlapping national identities: not only 'British', but also 'English', 'Irish', 'Scots' and 'Welsh'.

Devolution, which presupposes a basis of territoriality at sub-state level, throws this feature into sharp relief. In Wales as in Scotland, the devolutionary scheme is, first, a form of 'national devolution', with all the symbolic capital which this implies. The development has in fact a particular resonance in Wales, historically closely integrated with (and incorporated in) England. The special claim of Wales as one of four countries of the Union is authoritatively recognized.

There are, it has been said, as many 'Welshnesses' as there are Welsh people. North and south, urban and rural, English- and Welsh-speaking, the history of Wales is in so many ways parochial and fragmented.[7] The choice of nomenclature for devolution is here seen as peculiarly apt. A 'National Assembly' is established, 'for' Wales. The new body provides, on the one hand, a focus for Welsh identity and democratic culture. Indeed, to the arch-devolutionist, the development involves 'a normalisation of Welsh politics'.[8] It is, on the other hand, an institution that has self-consciously to stress the constitutional and political values of partnership and inclusiveness. How could it be otherwise, given the many historical divisions of interests?

'When was Wales?' it was memorably asked. 'Wales', the historian said, 'is an artefact the Welsh produce.' 'If they want to'. 'It requires an act of choice.'[9] Now that a choice has been made, there are more opportunities for local creativity in policy-making and administration ('divergence'). Devolution here represents both an energizing element and a challenge to government, not least in establishing an all-Wales perspective. No longer is the basic constitutional model that of the territorial department of central govern-ment, the Welsh Office, headed by a Secretary of State operating within the confines of the strong UK constitutional convention of collective cabinet responsibility. A related aspect is the National Assembly operating as 'a voice for Wales' on the wider stage, most obviously in the counsels of the United Kingdom.

At one and the same time, however, devolution brings into focus other powerful constraints. So there are strong pressures – financial, European, party political, administrative – for uniformity in policy development etc in the United Kingdom ('convergence'). Then there is the inferior kind of law-making capacity that will be seen to characterize the Welsh devolutionary scheme. Difficulty in producing coherent policies for Wales may be one consequence. Also involved is a problem classically associated with the constitutional development of subsidiarity that devolution represents. How to avoid the muffling of a voice for Wales, whereby limited local control is only achieved at the cost of loss of influence at the centre?

The title of this volume, *Delineating Wales*, reflects a national devolution. And in this study of the legal, constitutional and administrative aspects, it is appropriate to stress the broad practical significance of this dimension. Many of the implications are hard to pin down but it would be absurd to ignore them. Take the general field of regulatory politics, a classic one for involvement by a representative body otherwise constrained in its activities by limited financial resources. It is a bold agency that operating in Wales steadfastly ignores the views or moral suasion of the new democratic forum that is the National Assembly, even assuming that the devolved administration lacks the formal legal powers of control or direction.

For the avoidance of doubt, the (unionist) Welsh Assembly Government has been happy to play 'the national card'. The immediate context is the competitive market struggle, and in particular the process of European integration, where a vigorous policy of promoting Wales *qua* Wales – even something called 'Wales world nation' – has been pursued. Again, for those of us who are concerned for the welfare of the Union (state), it would be foolish to overlook the special sensitivities that may be involved here. The prospect one day of political 'cohabitation' – as the French have learned to call it – between Cardiff and London casts an especially long shadow in this regard. To anticipate the argument in this volume, the idea of national devolution gives an otherwise weak form of devolution a special force, and carries the seeds of its destruction in favour of a more advanced devolution settlement for Wales.

National devolution to Wales should not be regarded simply as a parochial development: quite the reverse! Seen in comparative perspective, the arrangements demonstrate the relevance to domestic constitutional design both of supranational modes of ordering and the broad currents in post-modern society of globalization. By this is meant especially the emergence of an intermediate or 'regional' level of government as a major sphere for the management of economic and social change. Wales is more sharply delineated, better to cope with the realities of a harsh world.

The constitutional development in Wales is in fact a paradigm case of the rise of so-called 'meso-government'.[10] It highlights the major role of economic considerations in the contemporary process of UK constitutional reform. How could it be otherwise, given a vulnerable local economy that has consistently lagged behind the rest of Britain, and, further, the memory of huge suffering in Wales during the years of Depression? So too the process of European integration features strongly in the new design. The case for responding at regional level to the demands of the Single Market, and, in particular, for crafting a regional apparatus well equipped to take advantage of European Union initiatives, has been taken on board. In fact, providing 'clear leadership and a strategic direction to boost the Welsh economy' was identified in the White Paper as 'one of the Assembly's most important tasks'.[11] Aside from a stress on regional planning, this necessarily involves close cooperation with local commercial and other interests related to economic development. 'Team Wales' is an unpleasant piece of official jargon, but it perfectly captures the neo-corporatist dimension to national devolution in the competitive or market struggle.

(b) Executive devolution

Welsh devolution is well known to have introduced into Britain a new and untested set of constitutional arrangements: a form of what is commonly called 'executive devolution' that includes the transfer of various subordinate or secondary law-making powers. It contrasts with so-called 'legislative devolution' as in Scotland, the more powerful and straightforward allocation of primary legislative functions to the territory.[12] Once more the nomenclature is significant: an 'Assembly' in Wales, a Scottish 'Parliament'.

In practice, as a method of allocating law-making functions, executive devolution involves from the standpoint of the lawyer four main elements. The first relates to the vertical division of primary law-making powers that is used in both legislative devolution and federal systems. The UK government, in devolving powers to Scotland, Wales and Northern Ireland, has naturally retained core elements of the functions of the state: not least defence and foreign affairs, general taxation and immigration and nationality laws. In the event, reference is made in the Government of Wales Act (GWA) to certain 'fields' or subject areas for the transfer of functions.[13] They include economic development and transport; agriculture and fisheries; health, social and housing policy; local government and education; and planning and the environment. Beyond this range of functions in public law are many parts that Assembly laws cannot reach.

The second main element is the horizontal division between primary and secondary law-making powers that is the hallmark of executive devolution. It is the question not of whether but of how much legislative power relating to a function should be transferred. In the event, a key feature of the implementation of the Welsh scheme is the specific enumeration of the powers devolved statute by statute. There is in other words no general secondary legislative competence for the Assembly in fields of transferred functions. Also relevant is the way in which the dividing line may be blurred by the use of so-called 'Henry VIII clauses', statutory provisions that allow primary legislation to be repealed or amended by means of secondary legislation. The National Assembly is so empowered for certain limited purposes.

The issue arises of overlapping jurisdiction, which is so familiar in constitutional systems of divided competence. Joint and concurrent powers with central government, as well as consultation and consent requirements, are as the third element a significant feature of the new devolutionary architecture in Wales. Not surprisingly, so-called 'cross-border' matters involving England and Wales furnish various examples. But easily the most important in terms of the legal and constitutional development is the supervisory power of central government in ensuring the implementation of European Community legal obligations. It is a necessary consequence of the legal and political responsibility of the UK government in the role of member state of the European Union.

Figure 1 represents this part of the story.

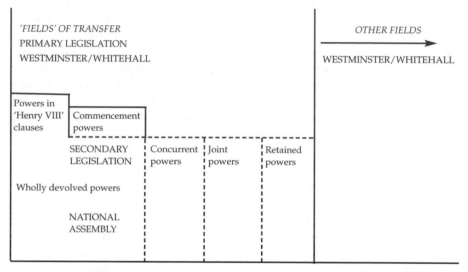

Figure 1: Initial allocation of law-making powers in Welsh devolution

Executive devolution, however, is a moving target. The method implies an ongoing allocation of powers as new statutes come on stream: the fourth element. The Assembly has in this way been a recipient of functions virtually from the moment of its birth. The element of flexibility is further developed in the GWA.[14] The Assembly was first empowered by means of statutory instrument, in the form of a Transfer of Functions Order.[15] As the government had promised in the devolution White Paper, this operated to transfer nearly all of the statutory functions of central government formerly exercised under the auspices of the Secretary of State for Wales. The power exists to make additional orders, in effect transferring functions exercised by other ministers in relation to Wales. Put simply, while the GWA makes reference to the transfer of functions in certain fields, it does not so restrict the process that is executive devolution.

Also involved in executive devolution are the many administrative functions of government. From public information to circulars, and on through grants, contracts and regulatory powers to high-level matters of strategic and regional planning: such are the responsibilities of the Welsh Office that have now been vested in the Assembly. Pride of place clearly goes to the power of expenditure or control over the financial budget for Wales: initially on an annual basis some £8 billion, and happily now hugely increased. At one and the same time, the Assembly is made almost wholly dependent on handouts from central government and exercises discretion to determine and manage spending priorities across broad swathes of public administration.

In turn, in the guise of so-called 'delivery levers', or – as I prefer – carrots and sticks, such functions will be shown to have an added significance in Wales post-devolution. Especially, that is, by reason of the comparative weakness of the local legislative power, and the sense of moral authority and concern for a strategic all-Wales perspective that is associated with the new 'national' democratic mandate.

(c) Institutional design: corporate and flexible

Wales now has a distinctive form of government. The Assembly is in legal terms 'a body corporate' or collective repository of functions.[16] There is in other words no formally empowered and separate executive of the type so familiar in the Westminster parliamentary tradition. Policy leadership by the Assembly cabinet is thus dependent on an internal delegation of powers via the Assembly First Secretary or Minister. It also follows that in administrative terms the Assembly is an expansive institution; nearly all the civil servants previously working in the Welsh Office are now officials of the Assembly.

A statutory framework within which the Assembly can develop organically is at the heart of the constitutional design. Internal architecture is not strongly prescribed in the GWA. Rather, flexibility was built in through broad powers of delegation, both from the Assembly as a whole and as between the diverse actors. So much so, that the character and style of the Assembly is essentially determined by the way in which these powers are exercised.

At the core of the Assembly, government structure takes on a hybrid character. The development reflects the competing claims of a cabinet model versus a committee or classical local government model of administration. In the event, however, the arrangements have now veered sharply in the direction of a parliamentary system, premised first on the operational independence of the presiding chair and clerks, and second on the practice and conventions of cabinet government. A strong 'executive branch', aka the Welsh Assembly Government, thus reflects and reinforces basic constitutional ideas of separation of powers.

How and why this came to pass is of the very essence of the story of Welsh devolution, a firmly autochthonous development that is itself part of a process of maturation of the new territorial polity. As such, it is a chief focus of this volume.

The design of the scheme also has a role to play in helping to create in the theology of New Labour a newly textured democratic culture. In particular, a conscious effort has been made to distance the new representative body from the strong adversarial tradition in British politics that is epitomized by the House of Commons. An all-party committee system, with at least some role in the policy-making process of the Assembly, is one of the most important manifestations of this attempt at democratic renewal. As will be seen, however, it has also been a key battleground in an ongoing struggle over the precise nature and quality of the devolutionary scheme.

(d) Values: inclusiveness, transparency, partnership

The Assembly has the formidable job description of 'a modern, progressive and inclusive democratic institution'.[17] Much has been heard in this context of creating 'a new kind of politics'. Wales might even be considered a testing ground for the so-called 'Third Way' in government: that association of ideas of cooperation, self-government and the search for mutually advantageous, collaborative solutions, which recently has been so fashionable.[18]

Inclusiveness as a constitutional value takes on special prominence in the Welsh devolutionary scheme. At the risk of repetition, the National Assembly was so titled in order 'to stress that it will be for everyone in Wales'.[19] Combating tribalism in local politics is one important connotation, all the more so in light of the Labour Party's long-standing domination of electoral politics in Wales. The system of proportional representation by which Assembly Members (AMs) are elected is clearly vital here. Another major aspect is the place of the Welsh language, notably in former times a divisive political issue inside the territory. Reflecting changing attitudes to the language as part of national identity and cultural heritage, bilingualism is a distinctive feature of the new constitutional development.

Devolution is grounded in territoriality, but must also contend with the contemporary sense of a more cosmopolitan society, whose people have multiple identities. Gender issues for example are rightly seen as a touchstone for a new kind of politics. Coupled with the search for a less confrontational style of politics is a greater involvement by women in the role of representatives in the National Assembly. Welsh devolution in particular suggests a more feminized political culture. Turning the argument round, inclusiveness has also been invoked as a counterpoint or 'important balance' to the sense of national identity that Welsh devolution projects.[20] Reference may here be made to the concept of a civic (and not ethnic) nationalism, residency in Wales being seen as the necessary and sufficient condition for involvement in the new body politic.

A major development is the strong sense of life in a goldfish bowl that now attaches to government work in the devolved territory. The demands of some sixty Assembly politicians who in turn answer to people from all over Wales, coupled with local media glare, represents a qualitatively different experience, at least for senior civil servants, from the traditional or reclusive ways of Whitehall. And in particular, it may be said, from the administrative outpost of central government that was the old territorial department, the Welsh Office. Under Rhodri Morgan, the second First Secretary of the Assembly, considerable stress has been laid on principles of transparency and freedom of information, in contrast that is to the stifling effects of the traditional British approach to official secrecy. The Welsh way is now very much a model of open government, or – to borrow a famous American saying – of 'government in the sunshine'.

Early and sustained input from a welter of interests is developing quickly as a major feature of the policy-making process in Wales. The dominant ideology is one of 'partnership working', collaborative and consensual, or less conflictual, which is seen as particularly well suited in these conditions of small-country governance. Notably, in the view of the White Paper, the Assembly's partners included local authorities and other public bodies in Wales, the voluntary sector, central government in Whitehall, and European institutions.[21] It is an ambitious list, and one that elides some very different kinds of relationship.

Mention must be made of *Putting Wales First: A Partnership for the People of Wales*, the policy manifesto of coalition government in the Assembly, which, consisting of Labour and the Liberal Democrats, was to hold sway from October 2000 to the end of the first term. From aims of openness and consensus, and on through 'a strong Assembly, fully engaged in the examination and development of policy, capable of holding the Executive to account', the manifesto placed great emphasis on novel and collaborative and inclusive ways of working. Not only did 'the people of Wales expect the National Assembly to develop a new kind of politics', they want to see political parties work together to deliver an ambitious programme of reform and renewal, based upon political stability. Such, anyway, was the official view of 'the partnership Government'.[22]

One is entitled to be sceptical. It is one thing to rewrite institutional structures and processes, quite another to promote or achieve basic and lasting change in received forms of constitutional and political culture. Nevertheless, it is appropriate to think in terms of the slow growth of a distinctive Welsh constitutional culture, one that is underpinned by novel institutional developments centred on but also extending beyond the Assembly, and which is both influenced by, and demonstrates variations from, the standard 'British' or Westminster-orientated paradigm. The way in which devolution is so much more than the dictionary definition of 'transferring power' is highlighted here. Values matter, not least in constitutional law!

2. A QUESTION OF DYNAMICS

'Devolution is a process not an event.' This most famous saying of Ron Davies, the former Secretary of State for Wales, serves to highlight the dynamic potential in devolution for adaptation and expansion. So also, in his words: 'Let no-one think that now the devolution genie is out of his bottle he can be forced back in or that he won't want to stretch his muscles . . . Devolution . . . is not . . . a journey with a fixed end-point.'[23] In fact the concept is one that can be used in very different ways. As a process, Welsh devolution can be traced back in time via so-called administrative devolution or decentralization. Most obviously, that is, in the gradual accretion of functions by the territorial department that was the Welsh Office, and which has provided the starting-point for the new constitutional scheme. Then there is that rolling process which is the formulation and administrative and legislative implementation of the policy of executive devolution. It was obviously a huge task in Wales and one as mentioned that was compressed into a short space of time. Looking forward, the process that is devolution may encompass change and development beyond as well as within the existing scheme. And of course, devolution has a potential to be the process that leads to an 'event', in the shape of separate statehood.

There is also ample room for semantics solely in terms of the existing constitutional scheme. The word according to leading Labour Party representatives in Wales has not exactly been universal! A notably conservative or restrictive view was expressed early on by the successor to Mr Davies as Secretary of State for Wales, Paul Murphy: 'We are pledged to make our new democratic achievement a settled question, unlike our opponents who live in a make-believe world of claiming new powers without a people's mandate.'[24] Although exhibiting a cautious attitude when in office, Alun Michael, the first Assembly First Secretary, took as a pet phrase 'dynamic devolution':

> While devolution is a place in its own right, this doesn't mean it is static . . . Devolution is a form of governance which can change and adapt to the changing needs of our country – just as the concept of the 'independence' of the nation state has had to change and adapt over the last decades as globalisation has transformed political realities.[25]

Mr Michael's successor, Rhodri Morgan, has referred in typically colourful language to 'a fragile flower':

> While some people [want] to force feed devolution, to make it grow at an artificial rate with genetically modified democracy fertiliser, I believe that . . . devolution needs to be allowed to develop and grow organically . . . Let's stop talking about

what we can't do and let's get on with what we can do and do it . . . It will [then] be perfectly natural for the National Assembly to grow in status and authority with the full-hearted consent and support of the people of Wales.[26]

Two models

Properly to understand the constitutional development in Wales, it is necessary to look beyond the standard dichotomy with legislative devolution and consider possible variants of – and on – executive devolution. Let us then forsake hindsight and look at the situation as it appeared at the inception of the Assembly. Assuming a Welsh-style system of specific empowerment, and focusing on the constitutional and legal aspects, figure 2 presents the minimal and maximal scenarios. A novel concept is introduced – 'quasi-legislative devolution'. It serves as the counterpoint to a strict or narrow view of what UK ministers have been pleased to call the 'devolution settlement' for Wales.

Aspect	Strict executive devolution	Quasi-legislative devolution
A. Internal architecture		
1. Government structure	Committee or classical local government model	Cabinet model
2. Assembly workings	Corporate form (inclusiveness)	Parliamentary style (oppositional)
B. Secondary legislative powers		
1. Range of transfer of functions	Narrow	Broad
2. Form of delegation	Limited, tight definitions	Framework legislation; Henry VIII clauses
C. Role in primary legislative process	Model of influence	Privileged access
D. Taxing power	None	Tax-varying function

Figure 2: Competing concepts – strict executive devolution and quasi-legislative devolution

This conceptual framework is helpful in a number of ways. As indicated, it serves to highlight the room for manoeuvre or spectrum of possible approaches within, as well as the overarching constraints of, the legislative scheme of the GWA. For example a most important feature is the absence of an Assembly power of taxation. Underwriting the devolutionary process by so providing a measure of fiscal freedom and accountability would obviously require primary legislation. For contrast, reference can be made to the internal rebalancing of roles in terms of the cabinet and committee models of administration that is permissible via the system of broad delegation of functions.

Similarly, a conceptual framework is established with which to measure the trajectory of the current constitutional dispensation. Take for example the idea of the corporate body. One issue fated to arise was the nature of the relationship between on the one hand the Presiding Officer of the Assembly (Lord Elis-Thomas) and his staff, and on the other hand the devolved administration or (now) the Welsh Assembly Government as represented by the cabinet. Speaking more generally, the *de jure* concept that is corporate status cannot be read as exhausting the *de facto* possibilities; as will be seen, quite the reverse.

Certain key factors that go to the substance and workability of a scheme of executive devolution are also identified in the diagram. One clearly is the style or form of the delegation of secondary legislative powers on which this constitutional method depends. Under a strict regime characterized by limited legal autonomy, the devolved administration finds itself curbed by tight restrictions on or definitions of secondary legislative powers; as also perhaps by an increased recourse to primary legislation. In contrast, techniques of legislative drafting may be used which boost the discretionary power of the devolved administration in secondary law making. Framework legislation, whereby myriad rule-making powers are exercised inside the broad parameters of legislative policy, is a potent method. All the more so, if it comes with a liberal sprinkling of 'Henry VIII clauses'. At the extreme end of the spectrum, it becomes necessary to think in terms of quasi-legislative devolution. This would involve a devolved administration in making the kind of policy rules commonly expressed in, but without the proper status of, primary legislation.

Different but related is the question of the general approach to the division of primary and secondary law-making powers. It may (continue to) proceed *ad hoc* in a typical manifestation of the British tradition of constitutional pragmatism. In practice this means the devolved administration exercising law-making powers of uneven width and depth. Or, in recognition of the new devolutionary paradigm, it could involve a serious attempt at developing a set of constitutional principles to guide the division.

In executive devolution, easy and effective access to the primary lawgiver is vital. In terms of the formal parliamentary process, arrangements may on the one hand amount to little more than the standard indirect techniques for exercising influence, and, on the other, involve the concept of privileged access for the devolved administration. This is not to overlook the broader issue of intergovernmental relations, and that access into the central government machine which is so necessary for the efficient and effective operation of devolution, and of executive devolution in particular.

Entirely predictably, all these matters have been brought centre stage in the first few years of the Assembly. Some useful innovations have been made – a typical pattern of incremental change. And, to the greatest extent possible, the constitutional fundamentals have been avoided. Fortunately however – as I think – they cannot simply be wished away.

Suppose that the current devolution statute is still operating in Wales ten years hence. The two models could then be used to track the development. One might envisage, for example, the allocation of law-making functions developing over time as an area of constitutional convention. Changing political hues in Wales and at Westminster, however, may produce substantially different results. The potential in terms of the delegation of functions for a pendulum effect flows directly from the ongoing allocation of powers that is part of the current scheme. More generally, we observe how from a devolutionary viewpoint the existing constitutional arrangement can be operated with more or less enthusiasm. And this, if truth were told, is precisely what has happened.

The many processes of devolution

Let us expand the argument. First, the political convenience of the concept of a devolutionary 'process' should not be overlooked. The familiar phrase has been trotted out – most obviously at the time of the local referendum – to deflect both criticisms of the limited form of devolution and serious questioning of the future path of constitutional development in Wales. That is, why executive devolution and where is it supposed to be leading?

Secondly, 'devolution is a process not an event' has a certain rhetorical appeal. Conveying the sense of a single historical movement – presumably onward and upward – it may even be considered a contemporary Welsh version of the Whig view of history. As this book, which as an essay in contemporary history addresses the constitutional development from a variety of angles, amply attests, Welsh devolution – to put it euphemistically – is a rich tapestry. 'Events' are not unimportant! Especially so for present purposes when they serve to illustrate the growing pains of the infant body. *Pace* 'the new politics', conflict has been a key element influencing the devolutionary development, as most famously in the political butchery of Alun Michael. But further, special emphasis is laid in this book on developments away from the public gaze, the tectonics of institutional and administrative change. As indicated, the construction of a Welsh governmental machinery that at one level can begin to meet the new political and organizational demands, and at another level points in the direction of further constitutional advance, is of the essence of the story.

By its very nature national devolution is apt to have broad 'slop-over' effects. For example, that is, in terms of official relations with, and mobilization of, local elements of civil society, and of a more conscious expression of Welsh identity including in institutional structures. In short, even in terms of the particular focus of this book – the legal, constitutional and administrative aspects – the devolutionary development should be read as a complex and wide-ranging phenomenon.

Better to convey the sense of multifaceted and multilevel developments, as also the cross currents of convergence and divergence, let us speak of devolution not simply as a process, still less as an event, but as involving a series of processes that are more or less closely linked and elaborated. That is, a more generous or plural conception, and one also which does not obscure the failings or false trails.

Devolution and governance

Another angle of approach is in terms of 'governance', a popular if imprecise concept that has largely replaced the word 'government' in the literature of public administration and political science.[27] The change in vocabulary reflects the prevailing sense of erosion of boundaries and hierarchies in state organization, and conversely the increased role of networks and of inter-governmental management in an age of great (regulatory) complexity and (economic and political) interdependence. Viewed in this perspective, the dictionary definition of devolution appears peculiarly narrow. Conversely, a plural conception sits comfortably.

Let us recognize the increased force of models of 'multi-layered governance',[28] the relocation of decision-making powers from central government to supranational institutions and to territories and localities ('internal subsidiarity'). It is, however, one thing to speak of the 'hollowing out of the state',[29] and quite another to subscribe to the thesis that the nation-state is somehow withering away. Greater interdependence across hierarchical state structures, as illustrated by cooperative systems of negotiation and co-ordination, is thus identified in comparative studies as a key feature of the simultaneous processes of European integration and localization or fragmentation.[30] 'Wales in the United Kingdom in Europe': the scheme of executive devolution is itself seen to highlight the need for liaison arrangements etc.

But further, the nature of the internal development makes Wales an especially interesting case. In terms of the theory and practice of governance, the idea of 'team Wales' for example typifies the blurring of the governmental and the non-governmental, as also the multi-polar forms of arrangement in which so many can fairly be viewed as a 'partner'. Then there is what I call 'the closeness of Wales', and more especially the scope for greater flexibility in administrative structures and processes familiarly associated with small countries. A high priority that is afforded such major cross-cutting themes as sustainable development and equality of opportunity further reflects and reinforces this general aspect. Once again, there is more to national devolution than at first meets the eye.

3. PUBLIC LAW AND DEVOLUTION

This volume bears witness to the rebirth of Welsh legal history (after centuries of slumber), which the establishment of the National Assembly (howsoever attenuated in powers) is seen to symbolize and represent. Since this is the first of what I hope will be a new breed of studies in Welsh public law, a special word is in order about the role of legal technique in the new constitutional dispensation. This is a more interesting question than perhaps at first appears.

As a formal constitutional arrangement, devolution itself heralds a greater role for legal considerations and instruments in the conduct of government. This infusion of law is at one with other key elements in the broader United Kingdom process of constitutional reform, most obviously the Human Rights Act 1998. From the standpoint of a constitutional lawyer from a federal tradition, the general phenomenon may seem unremarkable. However it represents a qualitative shift in a constitution and body politic renowned for reliance on informal practices and understandings.

There has, however, been a conscious effort to limit this phenomenon. Especially, that is, in the new and central field of constitutional, political and administrative activity constituted by UK intergovernmental relations.[31] With a view to preserving traditional constitutional attributes of flexibility and scope for evolutionary change, and to promoting values of cooperation and collaboration – more 'partnership working' – a heavy use has here been made of 'soft law', in the broad sense of rules that have limited or no legally binding force. To this effect, the enhancement of the judicial role, which is otherwise reflected in a special jurisdiction for the handling of 'devolution issues', is restrained. It suffices to add that this aspect has a special significance in the case of Wales. The scheme of executive devolution necessarily entails close dependence on Whitehall and Westminster and thus on the political and administrative good will of the central government machine.

What then, it may be asked, of the law and the Assembly itself? One way of approaching this question is in terms of the role and interplay of different modalities of law – a hierarchy of rules – in the new construction. So beginning with the GWA, attention is directed to statutory obligations on the Assembly to promote such good causes as equality of opportunity and sustainable development. The use of legal precept to foster the development of, and establish frameworks for, a reworked form of democratic culture is in fact one of the more striking features of the formal devolutionary architecture in Wales.

Secondary legislation is a *raison d'être* of the model of executive devolution. Rule-making of this kind constitutes an important output function of the National Assembly. The distinctiveness or otherwise of its laws is thus one measure – but only one measure – of the contribution that the new representative institution may be said to be making. In turn, the scope for, and design of, distinctive subordinate law-making procedures in Wales is identified as an important issue.

The broad statutory framework of the GWA also demands much infilling. The internal law of the Assembly, in legal parlance 'practice and procedure', is thus given an extended role in the guise of standing orders. Once again, key provisions reflect and reinforce constitutional values such as partnership and transparency in the structures and processes of the new representative body. There is in turn a raft of codes and statements of principle etc., and of course a burgeoning list of Presiding Officer rulings.

Elsewhere, I have described 'living with the lawyers' as an important part of the Welsh devolutionary experience.[32] The choice for Wales of executive devolution accentuates this feature; and all the more so, by reason of a scheme that would make a virtue out of specification and detail. To this effect, the question of whether secondary legislation properly falls within the four corners of the governing statute, or involves excess of powers (*ultra vires*), is a classic concern of the public law system. In fact, a striking feature of the policy debate in Wales post-devolution is the way in which legal questions of what the Assembly is empowered to do have often taken on great prominence.

Yet there are some powerful cross-currents. Attention has been drawn to the ready availability in this country of only some 3,000,000 people of alternative 'delivery levers' or less hard-edged techniques of governance. First, 'bringing government closer to the people' need not mean slavishly importing into Wales the whole paraphernalia of rules and regulations that central government has deemed appropriate for the governance of a much more populous neighbour. Quite the reverse: the chosen style of administration, as well as particular differences of policy content, may point to a different and more limited use of formal law in matters of internal relations post-devolution. Second, it should not be surprising to find a very limited pathology of court action involving 'devolution issues' in these conditions ('judicial review'). In short, the potential of a distinctive form of Welsh constitutional and political culture is communicated strongly here.

There is also the little matter to contemplate of the long-standing unity of the legal system in England and Wales. Suffice it to note that there is an underlying problem of 'fit' in the Welsh constitutional development between, on the one hand, an explicitly national form of devolution, howsoever limited, and on the other hand, the lack of an indigenous or national legal tradition. It is another way in which the Welsh case is so different from devolution to Scotland. To this effect, one key test of the devolutionary development in Wales is the extent to which it works to generate, and to be properly grounded requires, distinctive legal institutions. Happily, there are now some positive signs.

For their part, public law scholars have generally been slow to respond to the major innovation in constitutional law and politics that Welsh executive devolution represents. One explanation lies in the challenge to a traditional mind-set that is involved here. Reflecting and reinforcing an idea of the unitary state, with its conventional emphasis on (territorial) uniformity in policy and practice, so much of the scholarship has been Anglocentric in character and geared to the metropolis. It is a feature accentuated in the case of Wales, precisely because of the overarching unity of the English and Welsh legal system. A different but related point, a 'top-down' focus has predominated in the public law literature, one that concentrates on the relevant aspects of (Welsh) devolution from a United Kingdom perspective. This obviously is both necessary and valuable, but it is hardly sufficient for evaluation. A 'bottom-up' perspective, one that looks to the constitutional development inside the newly delineated (national) entity, is part of the intellectual effort of devolution. Both kinds of approach are reflected in this volume.

4. DELINEATING WALES

A thematic approach

As indicated, several major and interlocking themes to do with constitution-building inform the discussion in this volume. The fact that all of them find powerful echoes elsewhere in the Union, and possess a particular or distinctive resonance in Wales, is itself a useful reminder of the basic character of the contemporary UK devolutionary development: overarching and strongly asymmetrical.

Centre stage throughout is the interplay of the twin elements of continuity and change that lies at the heart of all basic constitutional development. It is a theme highlighted by the *sui generis* nature of the Welsh scheme and the way in which this reflects a distinctive territorial history. An Assembly, not a Parliament as in Scotland, has been justified on two related grounds. One was lack of consensus for change, the sense that – in a famous phrase – the settled will of the people was missing. The other one, which is symbolized in legal history by the formal incorporation of Wales as 'a very member and joint of the English realm' under Henry VIII,[33] is closer integration with England.

The matter can be approached in another way: by reference to the various geographical paradigms in domestic public law and policy. UK and also GB, and in particular 'England and Wales': it is necessary always to keep in mind the great swathes of uniformity that envelop Wales. Devolution, as for example Alun Michael was so keen to stress, is not separation.

Welsh executive devolution is thus seen in this book to present a dual character. It is limited or gentler devolution, when viewed in terms of the asymmetrical redistribution of powers that is involved in the current United Kingdom devolutionary development. It is transformational, when read in light of the retarded development of a distinctive national polity in Wales. It is then both a small step and a giant leap, as was famously said on another excursion into the unknown.

The second major theme is highlighted: the strong dose of contingency and lack of route maps. The UK government's radical programme of reform is correctly seen to release new constitutional dynamics, operating in cumulative as well as interactive fashion.[34] Like most human endeavours, these pressures are apt to lead in unforeseen directions. To give a single example, the outcome of debate over reform of the upper chamber of the UK Parliament – a potential venue for explicit forms of territorial representation – remains obscure at the time of writing.[35]

Local actors have had – in a very real sense – to make things up as they go along. How could it be otherwise, given that the Assembly was originally designed as a unique constitutional body or hybrid? A different but related point: the uncharted nature of the territory is important to bear in mind in evaluation. In view of the sharp learning curve confronting the various actors, it would be extraordinary if mistakes had not been made in matters of institutional and administrative design and in the early working of the devolutionary scheme. Although much of the pain has been self-inflicted, by virtue of the choice of scheme, let us remember that hindsight is a wonderful thing, including in Wales.

The European dimension is especially relevant. Although much was made of 'Wales in Europe' in the devolution White Paper, the official architects of the scheme were hardly able to second-guess subsequent debates on 'European governance' and 'the future of Europe', both of which are seen to raise the prospect of enhanced activity at the 'regional' level. It is not only the local constitutional development that is fast-moving! Cardiff of course should not wait on Brussels. Yet looking forwards, there is potential here for feeding back into the Welsh autochthonous process.

The way in which the dynamics of devolution operate at various levels is another recurring theme. So for example, a broad statutory framework that facilitates an evolutionary approach to the internal structures of government in Wales has also left space for competing visions or ideas. A space, it was mentioned, that has now been exploited to quite devastating effect. That the devolution of today is not the devolution of tomorrow is itself guaranteed by the ongoing distribution of powers via primary legislation. And – winding the clock back – why in the face of legislative devolution operating elsewhere in the UK would Wales be immune from the pressures for advancement familiarly associated with variable geometry or asymmetry in constitutional systems?

So very 'British': the UK government has been feeling its way through a process of *ad hoc* or incremental change. For example, 'suck it and see' was the language chosen by cabinet minister Margaret Beckett to describe the government's approach to procedural reform at Westminster in the light of devolution.[36] Like the saying that 'devolution is a process', it should not be allowed to obscure the costs and uncertainties associated with this general method of proceeding. Nowhere in fact is this point better illustrated than in the often unimaginative and highly variegated treatment of Wales in primary legislation post-devolution, an arcane exercise it will be seen in 'learning by doing'.

By way of a bottom-up perspective, this book further elaborates the different roles played in the ongoing constitutional development by local actors. Not – it is worth re-emphasizing – that the record of autochthony is necessarily a distinguished one. To anticipate the discussion in the following chapter, the closed or elite nature of the initial burst of constitution-building in Wales, whereby matters were seen as essentially the preserve of the dominant political party, has proved an effective recipe for problems and defects in the devolutionary scheme.

Elsewhere I have used three titles designed to convey the general flavour. The first – 'The New Model Wales' – highlights the administrative, legal and political creativity associated with the devolutionary scheme.[37] In particular, it is indicative of what I call 'the closeness of Wales' as demonstrated in the politics and administration of small country governance. The second title, 'The Shock of the New', was introduced in the context of the United Kingdom process of devolution.[38] It appropriately captures the strong sense of contingency, reflexivity and experimentation in the development, together, that is, with the mediating effects of an old mind-set. 'Histories', Robert Hughes has written, 'do not break off clean, like a glass rod.'[39] Nor do constitutions: least of all in Britain!

The third title is 'Taking Wales Seriously', which perhaps speaks for itself.[40] While there is too much about the Welsh devolutionary scheme that disappoints, the profound and wide-ranging processes that are taking place under the general devolutionary rubric should not be discountenanced. It would be absurd to speak at this point of a flowering of Welsh constitutional, political and administrative culture, as defined in terms of the complex webs of beliefs and values, practices and understandings. However, it would be equally absurd to ignore the seeds of indigenous development that have now been planted in the context of the GWA; and, further, the process of nurturing that is already under way.

An interim constitution

This, I suggest, is how future historians will view the current Welsh dispensation. And for my beloved Wales, it should be considered no great source of embarrassment. So many other lands have travelled this broad path, often as in Africa to independence, sometimes (and far more likely in this case) to a more generous and comprehensible set of arrangements for local autonomy. In the matter of Wales, the thing to fear is fear itself.

This book gives full attention to the basic defects of the Welsh model of executive devolution. By which is meant especially, an underlying lack of stability and an excessive fragmentation of powers. Other vital matters, such as a strange internal architecture, also fall to be addressed under this broad rubric. Ultimately, there is seen to be a failure of constitutional vision, even of understanding.

Yet there is more to the idea of an interim constitution than the negative sense generally conveyed. As indicated, this book also directs attention to the more positive dimension of a framework for organic change, a not unfamiliar concept in comparative politics. From developments in budgetary process to local experiments in law making, and on through the fact of extended accountability to much closer engagement with elements of civil society, there are many important aspects to consider. This, it should be stressed, is not to commend the often-tedious path of legal and institutional development to which Wales has been subjected. There was much to be said for going direct to a form of legislative devolution. But that is another story. Wales – the Assembly – is where it is.

This book is consciously designed to promote a broader perspective: one in particular that extends beyond the formal question of powers to the internal constitutional and administrative arrangements of the new Welsh polity. The upcoming report from the Richard Commission should have some profound things to say about the situation of Wales in the United Kingdom in Europe. But let us not forget the importance of the 'artefact' that people in Wales themselves produce.

Marking out and building up, specifying local methods and venturing new possibilities (if timidly): such are the qualities of constitutional life that are highlighted in this volume. Wales is not only reborn, but also – like Thursday's child – has far to go. Such, anyway, is the idea of *Delineating Wales*.

1

Conditions of Change

It would be extraordinary if a Union of such diverse parts as the United Kingdom could yield to a uniform pattern of powers devolved from the centre . . . The National Assembly for Wales . . . will serve an executive function . . . There was no popular demand in Wales for more . . .

Then Lord Chancellor, Lord Irvine[1]

Whereas attempts at devolution are now crowned with success, some twenty-five years ago they signally failed both in Scotland and Wales. Much has been made in this context of changing views of national identity and attitudes to Britain, including in terms of such distinctively 'British' institutions and experiences as world war, the welfare state and the nationalized industries.[2] Centrifugal forces have also been said to fit with the broad sweep of historical development. Protestantism, wars with France, the Empire: factors that 'provided for the forging of a British nation in the past have largely ceased to operate'.[3]

Be that as it may: what of the considerations – including the historical – that work to influence the design of the new constitutional and legal architecture? How is it for example that Wales currently has a framework of government that may safely be described as like nothing else on earth?

Typically, the Welsh arrangements are shaped by many diverse factors: a mix of the positive and responsive, some general in character, some particular to Wales. For comparative purposes, a convenient angle of approach to the subject is provided by the three central elements in constitution-building of policy, process and people.

In relation to policy, a failure of constitutional vision will be shown to characterize the Welsh devolutionary development. One way of analysing the scheme is in terms of the lowest common denominator; that is, not so much a clearly articulated institutional and administrative policy for Wales, as a set of uneasy compromises between competing wings of the dominant political party. The development is also a classic case of 'back to the future', with policy formulation through strong reliance on a previous (failed) scheme, and of 'making it up as you go', with delivery of that policy being characterized by substantial changes to the scheme.

A closed and elite form of constitution-making has already been mentioned. Old governmental assumptions held true in the initial stages of
design; a rich constitutional discourse was not given the opportunity to
develop. This aspect of the process is the more striking, given New Labour
rhetoric of inclusiveness, transparency and democratic renewal. The new
model Wales is very much a product of the 'old politics', and in this way has
been deeply prejudiced.

The third strand is introduced: the role of the people of Wales, or more
accurately the lack of it, in the constitutional development. Rarely can a
'national' democratic authority have started life with less evidence of popular
legitimacy than in the case of the National Assembly for Wales. Building on
the criticisms of policy and process, it is in many ways a miracle that the
existing Welsh devolutionary scheme came to pass.

While much in the design has been politically and administratively driven in
autochthonous fashion or 'from the periphery', it is important always to keep in
mind the place of Wales in the broader UK process of constitutional
development, and, further, in the rise of regional government in Europe. Cross-
fertilization of ideas and techniques, competing pulls and pressures, interdependence: all these are critical elements in the new form of multi-layered
democracy in the United Kingdom. Wales is *sui generis* but it is not an island.

1. GHOSTS IN THE MACHINERY

As 'an imagined political community', the Welsh 'nation' has been more
imagined than most! Wales after all occupies a very special position in the
historical development of the so-called common law globe. As England's first
colony, nowhere has the process of legal, political and administrative
assimilation been deeper or more thoroughgoing.

It is not fanciful to see the Statute of Rhuddlan (1284) as the original model
for the centuries-long process of common law expansion on the back of
military conquest and commercial endeavour, culminating with the Victorian
splendour of the British ('outer') Empire. With the completion of the
Plantagenet conquest of Wales under Edward I, the statute – 'a dictated peace
par excellence'[4] – provided for the importation of English criminal law and
extension of the shire system. In the words of the Welsh historian writing in
1990, with the death of its last prince – Llywelyn II – 'the Welsh polity which
he and his ancestors had fostered was uprooted, a polity which, as yet, has
had no successor'.[5]

Then there is the way in which the great rebellion of Owain Glyndŵr from
1400 to 1409 echoes down the ages. His failure is seen in particular to have
hastened the increasing integration of the social elite in Wales into the English
state, an aspect of the first importance in the history of the territory.[6] 'But he

was also a hero at the popular and local level over the centuries . . . a truly national hero.'[7] The historical fact of Welsh 'parliaments', however attenuated, and for the cognoscenti, his so-called 'Pennal project' (the aim of an independent Welsh state complete with re-established Welsh church and university institutions), further represents the vital constitutional dimension. That in Arthurian fashion 'he disappeared in the mists of the mountains, his fate unknown',[8] could hardly be bettered in terms of iconology, myth-making and the idea of 'Wales'.

In the words of the 'Act of Union' 1536: 'His Highness therefore, of a singular zeal, love and favour that he beareth his subjects . . . of Wales . . . established that this said country . . . shall be . . . incorporated, united and annexed to and with this realm of England . . . ' Such was the Tudor policy of an integrated Wales, that which, splendidly envisioned, was once called 'the experiment of killing "Welshery" by trusting Welshmen'.[9] And so to the deep historical overlay that would culminate – notoriously – in the ninth edition of the *Encyclopaedia Britannica*: 'for Wales, see England'.

In the words of the people's remembrancer, following the previous failure of devolution, 'We have no historical autonomy. We live in the interstices of other people's history.'[10] Be this as it may, the extent of the assimilation by a powerful neighbour has been rightly perceived as of the very essence of the Welsh condition.

Given the stress laid in this book on the concept of national devolution, special reference should be made to the historical idea of the 'rebirth of a nation', or the so-called 'awakening of Wales' that dates from the second half of the nineteenth century.[11] Inevitably, the demand for national recognition starts from a low base, given the non-survival of a significant store of Welsh institutions, and is also seen manifesting itself primarily in the social, educational and cultural spheres, as befits the close association with a powerful tradition of (religious) nonconformity. Emblematic developments are thus the creation in 1893 of the University of Wales and the disestablishment of the Anglican Church in 1920. Far from an event, it has also been a long and arduous process. By way of illustration, that essential national symbol of a capital city – Cardiff – was only officially designated in the 1950s.

Significantly, one of the most telling contributions in Wales in recent years has been that of the historians. Reflecting and reinforcing an ongoing debate over the meanings of Wales and Welshness, the basic fact of a distinctive political history has been vigorously reasserted, including in terms of industrial protest and the key tradition of radicalism.[12]

Perhaps a fuller appreciation of this aspect would have underscored the constitutional case for legislative devolution, as in Scotland. Not that Welsh devolution is a new demand, having rumbled on and off for over a century. There are in turn important clues in the historical argument concerning the substance and design of the current devolutionary scheme.

A 'national' tier: two models of representation

Why the Home Rule movements did not get off the ground in Wales has naturally been the subject of intense historical debate.[13] In the 1880s Cymru Fydd ('New Wales') championed the cause of federal self-rule but quickly foundered on the rock of intra-territorial divisions of interest. Splendidly envisioned, constitutionalist ideas of 'Home Rule all round' implied a parliament for Wales, but quickly became submerged in the morass of Irish politics. A Speaker's Conference on devolution in 1919/20 that broke up in personal and political disagreement effectively confirmed the obituary.[14] Ireland was to be dealt with separately.[15]

Overarching all this of course was the development of industrialism, and more especially the sense of the twentieth century in Wales as the century of Labour.[16] On the one hand, as Ron Davies would observe many years later, 'only Labour had the strength and organisation to deliver [devolutionary] change'.[17] On the other hand, the party served in this period as an essential agent not only of centralization, through its programmes of nationalization and economic planning, but also of the maintenance of the British state, through its major presence in the Celtic 'periphery'. It suffices to note that when – following the 'locust years' of the 1930s and the fight against fascism – the devolutionary demand resurfaced in an all-party 'Parliament for Wales' campaign (1950–6), culminating in a mass petition, it was largely ignored both by the Conservative government and the official Labour opposition.[18]

The fact of the language both as 'the most obvious badge of Welsh identity' and 'for many years . . . a deeply divisive force'[19] is clearly of the first importance in the historical development, at one and the same time sustaining and bedevilling the case for devolution. It will also be shown to have powerful echoes in the design of the current constitutional scheme. A different but related point: Plaid Cymru, the Welsh nationalist party founded in 1925, was famously described as operating for many years more as a 'cultural conservationist society'[20] than as a 'national' political party. Conversely, the growth and maturing of Plaid as a political party has clearly been an important catalyst for Wales to secure more control over its own affairs. Whether or not national devolution ultimately serves to blunt the separatist appeal, the suggestion that Plaid Cymru has emerged 'from its humble origins to a pivotal position in Welsh politics'[21] is also an important element in the workings of the new Assembly. A situation where the leading opposition party is seeking after a Parliament is apt to create its own dynamics.

The differences in kind in the schemes involved in this history of devolutionary failure are much less remarked on. Especially today, in the context of the UK devolutionary development, one is inclined to think in terms of a 'top-down' approach, the concept of a mini-parliament more or less closely modelled on Westminster. As regards the comparative dimension, this is the ideal-type that has been exported from the United Kingdom to many state parliaments in countries of the old 'outer' Empire. It has also been ventured from time to time in the Welsh context. A good illustration is the Government of Wales Bill 1914, which was closely influenced by proposals for Ireland. According to its Liberal proponent, 'the devolution of domestic affairs generally [would] be made absolute, effecting thereby a rational division of labour, as between the Welsh Legislature and Imperial Parliament'.[22] The proposed competencies extended to general taxation and insurance and benefits under the then nascent welfare state.

But there is also a 'bottom-up' approach, by which is meant proposals to extend the structures and techniques of local government into the territorial tier of what today would be called multi-layered democracy. This ideal-type is once again traceable to Victorian times, including in the shape of the National Institutions (Wales) Bill 1891, a measure with which the young Lloyd George was briefly involved. A set of miscellaneous proposals, the Bill incorporated the idea of a 'National Council' for Wales, with representation from the local authorities, which would 'discuss and enquire into such matters as they deem of common interest to Wales'. As well as giving powers over private Bills and provisional orders, the Bill would have allowed any statutory and administrative function of a government department relating to matters 'arising within Wales' to be transferred to the Council. It was in other words an early model of 'national executive devolution'.

Notably, this alternative approach was actively pursued in the Welsh Labour Party in the mid-1960s. To this effect, the case for devolution became enmeshed with proposals for reform of Welsh local government on a two-tier basis: a lower tier of district authorities and an upper, all-Wales tier.[23] Indeed, consistent with the logic of a bottom-up approach, the initial proposals were not devolutionary in quality, but involved the sucking up of powers from the lower tier. Subsequently, however, the idea was that the new territorial tier – an elected 'Welsh Council' – would draw in powers from both directions: a curious blend of centralization and decentralization. In the event, irony of ironies, the project became impaled on a UK cabinet policy of no encouragement for a Scottish parliament. Resuscitation in the face of the incoming Conservative government's drive via the Local Government Act 1972 to an upper tier comprised of eight county councils obviously came too late. 'With hindsight', wrote the historian and devolutionist in 1981, it was 'a lost opportunity, perhaps a fatal one.'[24]

Set in this context, the strange constitutional animal that is the National Assembly for Wales is rendered more intelligible. It incorporates a significant element of local government design, as well as (and increasingly) assumptions and methods that are associated with a parliamentary style of government. A touchstone is the legal concept of corporate status, the standard form of the local authority, as against the formal division of executive and legislative powers that is so familiar in the Westminster tradition.

Constitutional template: Kilbrandon and the Wales Act 1978

The historical connections, legal as well as political, are underwritten by other more familiar events in the 1960s and 1970s. There is, first, the establishment by the then Labour government of the Royal Commission on the Constitution (the Kilbrandon Commission), in the light of increased electoral support for the nationalist parties (especially in Scotland).[25] And, secondly, there is the chain of subsequent events that can now be seen to have powerfully influenced the contemporary constitutional development. By which is meant the devolutionary scheme of the Wales Act 1978, a bitter political struggle (especially inside the Labour Party), and the overwhelming rejection of the scheme by the people of Wales in a popular referendum.[26]

On the one hand, it is only natural that major political lessons should have been drawn from the unseemly demise of the 1978 statute, and requisite avoiding action taken. On the other hand, many key elements of the current devolutionary scheme have been lifted from that Act. In other words, much of the constitutional template of the novel development that is Welsh devolution came into being a generation ago.

Kilbrandon was able to reflect on a process of administrative decentralization to Wales. This had been hesitant and intermittent, but significant nonetheless, further evidence of the 'rebirth of a nation'. Almost entirely a twentieth-century phenomenon, the process was characterized by particular spurts of activity, notably under the Liberal administrations at the beginning of the century, and again in the 1940s partly in recognition of the Welsh contribution in the Second World War. Key milestones are the creation in 1907 of the Welsh Department of the Board of Education, the formation (1919) and extension of the functions (1940) of the Welsh Board of Health, and the establishment by 1945 of offices in Wales of some fifteen government departments. It is also appropriate to mention the rise of a distinctive Welsh system of advisory bodies, capped by a Council for Wales (1949), a body charged with making known 'Welsh views' on matters of concern to the government, which lingered on into the 1960s.[27]

There was also the slow growth to contemplate of separate political or ministerial responsibility for Welsh affairs. This too was an old demand, traceable to the National Institutions (Wales) Bill 1891, but it was only in the 1950s that a ministerial office was established, as an appendage first to the Home Office and then to the Ministry of Housing and Local Government. A foretaste of things to come, the concept of the Welsh Office, situated in Cardiff and headed by a Secretary of State with a seat in the (UK) cabinet, involved years of dispute inside the Welsh Labour Party, before finally emerging in the election manifesto of 1959.

Established in 1964 when Labour returned to power, the Welsh Office soon became part of a familiar model of territorial government, which encompassed Scotland, Wales and (latterly) Northern Ireland. Commencing with local government, housing and planning, the story is one of a gradual accretion of functions, which by the 1970s had extended into such fields as education, health and industrial development. By the time Kilbrandon reported in 1973, the staff of the Welsh Office had increased from a few hundred to almost a thousand, though of course the department was still (and always was) a minnow in Whitehall terms.

In view of subsequent events, it is worth emphasizing, first, the way in which Wales typically lagged behind Scotland, the Scottish Office with cabinet representation being a tool of Victorian government, and, second, the constitutional concerns that already were raised with Kilbrandon about the governmental model of territorial central departments. To quote the commission, 'the present system is criticized as not enabling them to develop a distinctively coherent set of policies for their respective countries and lacking in democratic accountability'.[28]

Long on description and analysis, short on agreement, the report of the commission can be seen as historically important for Wales in two main ways. First, the idea that Wales *qua* Wales was somehow different was authoritatively recognized, thus grounding the concept of a national democratic institution. In the words of the report, 'the "Welshness" of the people, though it undergoes subtle changes, persists'.[29] This, it may be noted, notwithstanding the evident social and cultural divisions – an internal fragmentation that would later be summarized in terms of the popular 'three Wales model':

- 'Welsh Wales,' the industrial bastion of the old (south Wales) coal field
- *Y Fro Gymraeg,* the (north-western) Welsh-speaking heartland
- 'British Wales', the surrounding (more Anglicized) parts.[30]

Secondly, the report effectively established the official parameters of the constitutional process – up to and including the present day. The commissioners unanimously rejected not only separatism but also federalism, including on the ground – at a time when the British constitution was still characterized by little in the way of judicial review – that it would imply an excessive legalism.[31]

In the event, the approach that garnered most support in the case of Wales, from six of the thirteen commissioners, was for a model of legislative devolution, drawn up on the basis of responsibility for public law matters such as local government and planning, health and education. Most notably, only two commissioners subscribed to the constitutional and intellectual case for a model of executive devolution, as based on the corporate legal form as well as various subordinate law-making powers.[32]

Suffice it to say that there then took place 'an obscure process of consultation'[33] in the high echelons of the Labour Party, one which led – unlike in Scotland – to official disavowal of legislative devolution. To push home the point, in view of what I have called the constitutional template, the current devolutionary scheme can now be seen as the product of a closed and elite form of constitution-building not once but twice. Evidently, as founded on a singular dominance of Welsh politics, 'the long-standing party orthodoxy . . . that "any kind of devolution required in Wales can be discussed within the confines of the Labour movement" '[34] dies hard.

Why – in 1997 – reinvent the wheel? The provisions of the Wales Act 1978 were after all ready-made and part of the collective memory not only of the Welsh Labour Party but also of senior civil servants in the Welsh Office. But further, there was initially little scope for administrative creativity, given on the one hand the fact that successive Conservative Secretaries of State had kept devolution firmly off the intellectual agenda of the department, and on the other the great hurry that was the incoming Labour government's timetable for reform. Indeed such was the need to cut corners that informal steps were taken by officials to prepare a draft White Paper even before the Conservatives were removed from office in the May 1997 general election. To quote John Lloyd, then deputy permanent secretary in the Welsh Office, 'we went back to our beloved papers from the 1970s'.[35]

Historical influence then is most keenly felt at the baseline of executive devolution. In terms of the constitutional fundamentals, the similarities of the 1978 model and the 1997 version may be summarized as follows:

- corporate legal form
- single chamber
- members elected for a four-year term, with no prior dissolution
- staffed by civil servants transferred from the Welsh Office
- funding via the block and formula system
- continuance of the Office of Secretary of State for Wales

And yet – the interplay of the twin elements of continuity and change – it. goes too far to say, as has Plaid's Lord Elis-Thomas, that there is very little that is new in the 1998 settlement.[36] First, the late introduction of an element of proportional representation has operated to transform the internal situation of the Assembly. Second, an even later shift towards a cabinet model, that is away from the committee or traditional local government model of administration which was posited in 1978, has paved the way for a more effective and authoritative form of administration. Third, there is a dynamic potential in the mechanism for empowerment of the Assembly quite different from the 1978 Act.[37] Indeed, to anticipate much of what follows, it is the tendency of such 'new' constitutional elements to undermine the 'old' ones that lies at the heart of the continuing saga of Welsh devolution.

Unionist folly: Wales under the Conservatives

Immediate historical experience writ large in the legislative and institutional design is a classic theme in constitution-writing. That Wales is no exception is shown by the devolution White Paper *A Voice for Wales*. Constitutional and political problems of accountability associated with the modalities of governance in Wales during the period of Conservative rule from 1979 were thus presented as the chief justification for the proposed devolutionary scheme. 'It is to address this democratic deficit that the Government is now proposing to set up an Assembly for Wales.'[38]

The piecemeal process of administrative devolution or decentralization had continued under the Conservatives, especially in the fields of education and industrial and economic development. By 1996, the Welsh Office was responsible for overseeing annual spending of some £6.5 billion: social security apart, the great proportion of identifiable general government expenditure in Wales.[39] But as highlighted by various comparative studies, it was also a case of limited 'regional' autonomy. The standard view was of a department tightly constrained by the British constitutional framework, engaged for the most part 'in the humdrum business of implementing policies decided elsewhere' and introducing 'modest variations where it can to suit the conditions, needs and idiosyncrasies' of Wales.[40] The high degree of integration with England was also underscored, including in terms of centripetal forces generally associated with the unity of the English and Welsh legal system.

Successive Conservative administrations, juxtaposed with a continuing dominance by Labour in electoral politics in Wales, served to heighten awareness of the democratic deficit implicit in this model of government.[41] It was after all the longest period 'of geographically one-sided government in Britain in the twentieth century'.[42] Economically and in social terms, the early 1980s are a watershed in modern Welsh history, as the traditional heavy industries of coal and steel experienced the full force of Thatcherite policies. A sense of political disenfranchisement could only be sharpened by the paucity of local Conservative representation, as the government in London was largely and increasingly sustained by electoral success in southern England. Suitably symbolic was the (colonial) image of the 'governor general', the UK cabinet being represented in Wales from 1987 by a succession of Secretaries of State drawn from English constituencies (Peter Walker, David Hunt, John Redwood and William Hague). What, the question was raised, of the conventional understandings of respect and restraint familiarly associated with British constitutional culture and the Union state?[43] It suffices to add that during this period the special machinery associated with parliamentary accountability for Wales, such as the Welsh Affairs Select Committee, proved largely ineffective.[44]

Concern at a lack of accountability was fostered by the 'onward march of the quangos'.[45] This both echoed broad themes in public administration, the fashion for 'reinventing government' and New Public Management, so familiar under the Conservatives, and took on special prominence in Wales. A model of indirect administration operating outside the traditional lines of democratic control and oversight thus became increasingly standard inside the territory. By 1995 the Welsh Office was devoting over a third of all expenditure to non-departmental public bodies (NDPBs). Leading players such as the Land Authority for Wales and Tai Cymru (Housing for Wales), and most obviously the Welsh Development Agency (WDA), had a major role in the local economy. 'Vice-regal' is one description of the extensive powers of patronage exercised by the Secretary of State for Wales. There were said to be more power-wielding appointees or 'new magistracy', with a disproportionate Conservative representation, than there were local councillors. Nor was legitimacy enhanced by a series of financial scandals, centred in particular on the WDA.[46] In historical terms Kenneth O. Morgan spoke of democracy in Wales 'from dawn to deficit'; an 'insidious web of influence which has resulted from institutional decline', an 'insensitive state [which] has become insulated from the people it serves'.[47]

Here as elsewhere in the Union state, much of the development came at the expense of local government. Thus key functions were transferred, as in housing and education; in conjunction that is with the various regimes of 'contracting out', tough financial constraint and evaluative audit to which local authorities were made subject under the Conservatives.[48] Aside from the obvious party political dimension, perhaps there was in Wales a special sensitivity to the general development, given the historical importance of local government as the only home-grown tier of democratic authority. The significance for the devolutionary project was made clear by the Welsh Local Government Association (WLGA), representing the interests of the local authorities, at the advent of the new Labour government:

Welsh local government has for the last decade committed itself in support of the establishment of an elected Welsh Assembly. [This is] because of its commitment to developing democracy in Wales. We believe that the existing institutions of all-Wales government ought to be subject to the popular control of the people of Wales . . . Welsh local government looks forward to working in partnership with a Welsh Assembly . . .[49]

In paradoxical fashion, Conservative reforms in this period are seen in institutional terms to have eased the passage of the new devolutionary structures. Abolition of the upper tier of local government took place under the Local Government (Wales) Act 1994 (which introduced a system of twenty-two unitary authorities). A historic centre of opposition to devolution was thus removed, which had been highly visible in the sorry saga of the Wales Act 1978.[50] A different but related point: abolition worked to create institutional space for the new form of territorial government, drawing the sting of objections of over-government to which developments in multi-layered democracy are naturally vulnerable.

Again, 'the march of the quangos' led to greater institutional differentiation between Wales, Scotland and England. 'Being a nation rather than a region, and increasingly conscious of the fact, Wales had benefited from a process of administrative devolution which spawned a wide array of bodies to cater for Welsh national aspirations.'[51] Here was an increasingly well established Welsh governmental machinery on which a devolution statute could build. Then there was the idea of the 'hidden' layer of territorial government. A new construction could plausibly be presented as part of a long-established process of devolution, in effect a catching-up, a democratization of existing powers. As will be seen in the next chapter, reform of major quangos is a distinguishing feature of the devolution statute.

In summary, 'unaccounted and unaccountable' is a fair description of much of the governance of Wales in the immediate pre-devolutionary period. Labour in *A Voice for Wales* was thus able to lay claim to the constitutional high ground. Expressed slightly differently, the democratic deficit grounded the case for reinventing a polity in expressly Welsh terms. Unionism, to borrow a historical theme made famous in Ireland, had proved its own worst enemy.

2. LABOUR'S WELSH ODYSSEY

Centralism, pluralism and exclusivity

To understand the Welsh devolutionary scheme it is also necessary to understand the historical role and development of the Labour Party in Wales. And, in particular, the 'contrary pulls of country and cause',[52] which is one facet of the classic conflict between the centralist and pluralist visions of socialism in the labour movement. That is – famously in Wales – the ideological, parliamentary and tactical question of 'The Red Dragon and the Red Flag'.[53]

It is hardly surprising, in the face of successive Conservative administrations, that the bureaucratic centralist tradition in Welsh Labour 'suffered a crisis of confidence [and] found itself labelled as . . . anachronistic'.[54] There was in turn an element of historical revisionism, with appeal to the roots of the labour movement and a more tolerant view of socialism and national identity being a feature of the rebirth of devolution as a policy option inside the party in the early 1990s.[55] What for the comrades of previous generations had commonly seemed backward-looking, and in particular as 'pandering to the nationalists', was now rebranded as a progressive form of politics, intended 'to establish the idea of Wales as a vibrant, diverse, tolerant and outward looking country with an internationalist spirit'.[56]

Nonetheless, various accounts confirm the very great difficulty of selling the constitutional policy inside the party.[57] It was after all that great socialist icon of the Valleys, Aneurin Bevan, who expressed the view that 'devolution of authority would divorce Welsh political activity from the mainstream of British politics'.[58] As indicated, the political humiliation of Welsh Labour in 1978/9 also cast the longest of shadows. The pro-devolutionist wing might temporarily be in the ascendant, but it was only natural that the chief political concern should be to avoid the party in Wales being torn apart over the issue of constitutional development, as had happened previously. Internal compromise was thus the order of the day, with an absolute prohibition on being seen in any way to be engaged in the 'contracting-out' of policy formulation and development.

Ron Davies was first given the responsibility for developing Labour's policy in opposition in the early 1990s. In his words:

> I was guided by the need to be pragmatic. It was all very well for academics and armchair critics to devise grandiose schemes which satisfied constitutional theories but unless there was support for the proposals within the Labour Party . . . then such schemes . . . were pretty futile. The policy making process in the Party was less than ideal. There was insufficient open and informed debate. As a result the formation of policy was left to manoeuvring and compromise within the innermost circle.[59]

Such was 'the Labour veto', as also a form of constitution-making that was premised on exclusivity. This is the more striking in view of the role in Scotland of the unofficial but highly influential Constitutional Convention, a forum in which Labour was engaging not only with other political parties but also with parts of civil society in the search for an appropriate scheme of Scottish devolution.[60] In fact, the party leadership in Wales headed off moves to establish this kind of forum,[61] which had previously gained some support among the trade unions, in favour of an internal process involving a policy commission and Labour's Welsh Executive. The defining feature of central party control of a process of decentralization was thus made manifest.

From the constitutional standpoint, the argument can be pursued in various ways. The lack of a Scottish-style convention did not only mean avoiding 'grandiose schemes' and 'constitutional theories', let alone a Welsh 'claim of right' or assertion of popular sovereignty. It also meant that the detail of Labour's policy proposals was never seriously honed and tested before the die was effectively cast. In particular, the exercise skated over the many technical and other complexities of executive devolution that had been raised by experts[62] at the time of Kilbrandon, and which – entirely predictably – will be seen to have haunted the early operations of the Assembly.

The closed and elite process denied Wales a clear mechanism not only for building cross-party consensus but also for raising public awareness and debate of the opportunities and challenges presented by devolution, and, further, for generating a sense of popular legitimacy. An exercise, it may be suggested, that was even more pressing than in the case of Scotland, precisely because of the greater hesitancies or divisions, the less developed sense of 'nation' and national institutions.[63]

The Welsh development can be seen as doubly pragmatic, by reason of the 'external' as well as internal considerations. The Scottish question is thus a familiar theme in modern Welsh history: that is, the dominance of Scotland in Britain's constitutional debate, the related sense of devolution to Wales as a useful add-on which enables Scottish devolution to be presented in terms of 'internal subsidiarity'. John Smith, the late Scottish leader of the party who famously saw devolution as Labour's 'unfinished business', is quoted as asking Ron Davies to 'develop the same policies for Wales as we have for our planned Scottish Parliament'.[64]

The contours of the political process naturally shifted over time. Especially, it should be noted, when in the light of political pressures in Scotland the devolutionary schemes were declared by Labour to be subject to popular referenda, and not simply constitutional validation via a general election, a 'U-turn' in party policy that clearly took the Welsh leadership by surprise.[65]

In terms of understanding the devolutionary development in Wales, it is thus necessary to grasp the importance of another complicated political balancing act. At one and the same time, local Labour had not to be (too) divided, and, with a view to winning the referendum, sufficient had to be on offer in pro-devolutionary terms for the purpose of an informal 'bargain' with both Plaid Cymru and (the pro-federal) Liberal Democrats. Conditions were ripe for a greater emphasis on 'inclusiveness', leading eventually to the addition of an element of proportional representation. A different but related point: there was a call to genuflect in the direction of various interest groups. To this effect, the new constitutional framework of the devolution legislation would take on a somewhat more distinctive and prescriptive character.[66]

Shaping the Vision

It was in fact the bottom-up approach to Welsh devolution that resurfaced first. In the wake of the hated community charge or 'poll tax', introduced after the 1987 general election, local government reform took on a new prominence in Labour's British agenda, being reworked in Wales to incorporate the idea, approved at the Welsh Labour Party conference in 1990, of 'an all-Wales elected body'. Typically, however, the general commitment was tepid and cautious. A formal commitment to establish the new 'national' institution in the party's 1992 general election manifesto proceeded on the basis that the pace of reform in Wales should parallel progress towards regional government in England.[67]

The internal policy commission, which was subsequently established to review and update key areas of Labour policy in Wales in time for the next (1997) general election, naturally had devolution as its main topic of conversation. In the event, *Shaping the Vision*, its report 'on the powers and structures of the Welsh Assembly', was to be formally approved by the Welsh Labour Party conference in May 1995.

Seen in retrospect, this is a key moment in the contemporary history of Wales. Although the document was by no means the final version, it does contain much of the blueprint of the current constitutional scheme, both the basic concept of executive devolution and a whole series of additional features. Examples include the power 'to debate and make recommendations on any matter relating to Wales', the Assembly to take 'responsibility for all quangos under the authority of the Welsh Office', and the Secretary of State 'to consult with the Assembly' on the UK legislative programme.[68]

Let us introduce the idea of 'devolution on a shoestring', which serves to highlight the political sensitivities. In terms of delivery of the constitutional policy, there was an evident need to combat the cry of 'expensive bureaucrats' that had typically been raised in the referendum of 1979. *Shaping the Vision* happily declared that 'these proposals would not entail any additional costs being imposed upon the Welsh people'.[69] Only slightly less economical, the explanatory memorandum to the Bill later stated that the devolution legislation would only 'require an estimated 100 extra civil servants': a nice round number! The principle that 'the devolved administrations will meet all the operational and capital costs associated with devolution from within their allocated budgets', it is important to add, is now established as a cardinal provision of 'the fiscal constitution' as it has emerged in the reinvented Union state.[70]

Policy then was effectively in favour of postponing the evil day. Devolution is supposed to involve diversity, which is clearly indicative of new resources especially for policy development. All the more so, it may be said, given the major historical role of the Welsh Office as an instrument for the executing or 'topping and tailing' of Whitehall policies. In turn, problems associated with 'devolution on a shoestring', and action to address this, will emerge as a critical feature of Assembly workings in the first few years.

The constitutional basis – or lack of it – of the allocation of powers is a matter that has plagued the Assembly. *Shaping the Vision* was once again deceptively straightforward:

> We propose that the Welsh Assembly should take responsibility for the existing budget of the Welsh Office and its functions. These responsibilities are primarily in the fields of agriculture, industry and economic development, employment and training, education, the Welsh language, arts and recreation, transport, local government and housing, environmental services, and health.[71]

The question is sharply posed: why ground the (new) Assembly in this (old) legal and constitutional form? Especially when, as will be shown in the next chapter, the functions of the Welsh Office were higgledy-piggledy in nature, the typical product of informal compromises and understandings that had happened over three decades inside central government.

The answer brilliantly illustrates the general theme of continuity and change in Welsh devolution. Highly pragmatic: this particular approach represented the line of least resistance. Clearly implicit in the political compromise inside the Welsh Labour Party was a determination to hold back the powers. At the same time, a derived or equivalent set of functions fitted with the accountability argument, or the drive for democratization of the 'hidden' processes of Welsh governance. Who, it is tempting to add, could possibly object? Again, this approach was a useful way of streamlining the process or avoiding arguments with Whitehall departments over appropriate allocations of functions, and so maintaining the momentum of the quick drive to devolution.

So in terms of the delivery of something called 'devolution', the policy of 'back to the future' made practical sense. However, in terms of the quality of the product, it was remarkably naïve, by reason of the technical and other complexities involved in formally dividing existing (central government) powers. In summary, there were two problems with *Shaping the Vision*. It was not shaping. And it lacked vision.

3. WALES IN THE UNITED KINGDOM IN EUROPE

Democratic and economic renewal

Constitutional reform was the most radical aspect of New Labour's election manifesto in 1997, and it has now produced a welter of legislative activity:

from human rights to freedom of information legislation, and on through operational independence for the Bank of England to major revision of the House of Lords. Devolution is at the heart of the affair. Indeed, to quote the Prime Minister in the preface to *A Voice for Wales*, 'This Government is pledged to clean up and modernise British politics . . . This White Paper marks a major step forward in the achievement of our proposals.'[72]

So great are the changes that many speak of a 'constitutional revolution'. It is inaccurate because there is clearly no break in legal continuity. In fact, in paradoxical fashion, nothing better illustrates the extreme flexibility of the informal British constitution than the manner and form of its transformation. By this is meant the passage of 'ordinary' legislation on the back of an election victory, coupled only with an adventitious use by government of the advisory referendum in the case of devolution. A general air of docility has surrounded the process of reform: in what other country has constitutional change of such magnitude taken place other than in conditions of independence or immediate national crisis?

The programme has been criticized in many quarters for lacking coherence, and rightly so, being 'shot through with inconsistency and hesitations'.[73] To this effect, devolution to Wales lays bare a general tendency to the *ad hoc* and piecemeal. Yet it would be absurd to overlook some basic connections between various elements of the reform programme, as also the way in which fashionable themes of modernization and democratic renewal both cut across and are mediated by local conditions and historical experience.

The quest for 'a new kind of politics' is hardly confined to Wales. A now familiar concept, 'bringing Government closer to the people', thus found powerful expression in the New Labour election manifesto in 1997: 'Subsidiarity is as sound a principle in Britain as it is in Europe.'[74] Reference has also been made to writings on the 'Third Way', which – if typically lacking in practical content – have at least provided an intellectual gloss to the UK government's reforms including in the devolutionary process. To reiterate, because it is so important, the Welsh scheme highlights the appealing nostrums of cooperation and collaboration, especially internally in terms of small-country governance.

Again, in the White Paper *Rights Brought Home*, the government promised that 'the Welsh Assembly will not have power to make subordinate legislation or take executive action which is incompatible with the [European Convention on Human Rights]'. 'It will be possible to challenge such legislation and action in the courts, and for them to be quashed, on the ground that the Assembly has exceeded its powers.'[75] While this may sound dry and technical, nothing better illustrates how the constitutional reforms intersect than the dual workings of devolution and human rights law. The latter after all is of the essence of a reworked democratic culture for the United Kingdom, on the one hand demonstrating in the protection of minorities the constitutional value of inclusiveness, and on the other being part of a continuum of citizen empowerment. For reasons that will be explained, the new (incorporated) body of human rights law is only now beginning to achieve major prominence in Wales. But it will surely have a significant to role to play, not least in terms of the political and administrative discourse, and all the more so should the Assembly gain substantial additional powers.[76]

Devolution has often been advocated as a tool of more effective government. Given the comparative weakness of the local economy, a strong linkage in the government's programme between economic reconstruction and democratic renewal has special resonance in Wales. Previously, in opposition, Ron Davies had pressed 'the economic case for a Welsh Assembly':

> An Assembly will only succeed if it can deliver a better quality of life and higher living standards . . . We need an Assembly to shape a new economic agenda for Wales . . . An Assembly will allow Wales to pick the policies and priorities, within the framework of UK macroeconomic policy, best for the Welsh economy. An Assembly will additionally bring together the key players in the Welsh economy to construct a common economic agenda . . . Without raising economic prosperity other social aspirations . . . cannot be achieved . . . An Assembly will be an 'investment' in the Welsh economy.[77]

Especially noteworthy is a clear recognition in the devolution White Paper of the processes of economic globalization, and of the need to identify local strengths, establishing conditions for indigenous industries with a comparative advantage.[78] Again, to jump ahead, the general sense of demands for economic regeneration and development as a major driver of the contemporary Welsh constitutional development is today underwritten by the Welsh Assembly Government's new 'national economic development plan' – *A Winning Wales*.[79]

Reinventing the Union: symmetry and asymmetry

The multifaceted relationship of Wales with the other territories of the Union, underwritten in the shifting constitutional scene by considerations both of architectural design and possible future development, is clearly a vital topic. It both goes to the heart of the character of the reinvented UK polity, and is constituted in terms of an approach to reform that (as Lord Irvine has explained) is explicitly one of 'differential devolution' or 'variable geometry'. Especially in the case of Wales, however, attention is drawn to the interplay in the territorial reforms of the twin elements of symmetry and asymmetry.

The territorial constitution of the United Kingdom has typically been analysed in terms of two comparative concepts. The Anglo-Scottish settlement of 1707 exemplifies the idea of the 'union state': a result not of straightforward dynastic conquest but of bargain or compact, and involving the 'survival of pre-union rights and institutional infrastructures which preserve some degree of regional autonomy'.[80] In contrast, that is, to the historical experience of 'colonial' and 'incorporated' Wales. However this sense of the constitution, familiar up to the late nineteenth century, was itself increasingly overlaid by the competing notion of a 'unitary state', with its emphasis on uniformity in policy and practice, as also (especially with the Welfare State) on the demands of equity in place of diversity.[81] That strand of socialist politics familiarly associated with bureaucratic centralism, which became so dominant in Wales, reflected and reinforced this development.

This is not the place to go once again through 'parliamentary sovereignty', that most famous of constitutional doctrines, whereby the Westminster Parliament may do all that it will, save to bind a successor. As propounded by the great Victorian jurist A. V. Dicey, a more powerful tool of the concept of a 'unitary state' it is hard to imagine. Suffice it to make two general points. There is, first, the way in which parliamentary sovereignty reflects and reinforces the notion of an Anglocentric state, as with the strong historical sense of 'the English constitution extended to the other parts of the union'.[82] And further, it may be said, a state that is geared to the metropolis: not least at the high noon of Empire when Dicey was active. In turn, the powerful challenge posed by the UK devolutionary process to the old political and constitutional orthodoxy, including by reason of its (original) centring in the three Celtic lands, is thrown into sharp relief. Wales is, to this effect, junior partner in a broad gravitational development.[83]

Second, the doctrine has occupied space that in other jurisdictions would be the subject of great constitutional and political exegesis. In Britain, the historian Maitland famously argued, the authority of Parliament has been substituted for a theory of the state. In this regard the current UK devolutionary process is Janus-like. On the one hand, the nature of state forms is thrown into sharper relief than has been the case for generations previously. On the other hand, the New Labour government in carrying through its constitutional reforms has commonly sought to avoid articulating or addressing the basic concepts or theories.[84] Welsh devolution is the perfect example.

Asymmetrical government is hardly a novel concept in comparative constitutional studies. The question, it is rightly observed, is not whether asymmetry is possible, but rather 'just what degree and type of asymmetry is tolerable'.[85] The case of the UK is a particularly striking one, not only because the devolutionary schemes are highly differential, but also because the position of the dominant territory remains largely unresolved. Again, from a Welsh perspective, developments in all three other countries of the Union have a particular role or influence in terms of the local system of devolved government.[86]

Implicit in the model of asymmetrical devolution is a continuing pull from Scotland: enhanced pressures in Wales to move to a more advanced form of devolution. The Parliament after all is afforded primary law-making powers across a wide range of domestic policies. Among the devolutionary schemes the Scottish model of government is also the easiest to operate, it being the most conventional in UK terms: a separate executive drawn from and accountable to the Parliament.[87] Again, although the two schemes are appropriately considered 'chalk and cheese', the Scottish influence will be seen to manifest itself in such important aspects of the Welsh constitutional arrangements as the electoral system and judicial process.

'Power-sharing plus' is an apt description of the 'Belfast Agreement' on the future of Northern Ireland.[88] Compulsory coalition government in the new Assembly, a 'balanced' representation in the executive, elaborate protections in the voting rules, a separate bill of rights to reflect principles of mutual respect: such is the salve for a divided community. The Agreement of course is not only about legislative devolution in the United Kingdom, the Irish dimension in the politics of Northern Ireland being explicitly recognized and with elements of confederation between the UK and the Irish Republic. Co-operation on matters of common interest, including both economic and social matters, is made the task of the new North–South Ministerial Council. Especially noteworthy for present purposes, the Belfast Agreement not only assumed Welsh and Scottish devolution but also envisaged the development of multilateral and bilateral arrangements at UK territorial as well as national level under the auspices of the British–Irish Council.[89] To this effect, a novel political and administrative space have been opened up for relevant (Welsh) actors.

Cautious, complex and evolutionary: such has been the Labour government's approach to the poor relation that is English regionalism. The model is thus one of an institutional chain of development, which is designed to culminate in directly elected regional government 'where there is a demand for it'. The first links in the chain are now in place: a system of regional development agencies matched via consultation requirements with regional chambers operating on a voluntary, non-statutory basis. It is important to stress, however, that what is currently on offer – some extra accountability and responsibility for resources, an 'influencing role' – falls far short even of the Welsh model of executive devolution.[90] The realm of 'block and formula' and significant law-making powers, and – of course – of national devolution, this is not.

But what, it may be asked, of 'the English Question'?[91] Not only are there competing regional models in play, most obviously the 'city region' and that further innovation in the constitution and politics of Britain, first adopted in London, of the directly elected mayor. But also, although the New Labour government has studiously avoided it, the question of England *qua* England will surely run and run. After all, its dominance with 85 per cent of the population is one reason why the UK is ill suited to a model of classical federalism. How far is it 'tolerable' for a government to go, on the one hand effectively promoting the 'national' identity of Scotland and Wales, and, on the other hand, treating with England by segmentation? At the risk of stating the obvious, this is a paradigm example of the contingent nature of the general devolutionary development. Suffice it to add that Wales cannot be other than closely affected by the trajectory of constitutional and administrative development for England. Such is the history and the geography.

Complexity and uncertainty, 'comparative grievance' or complaints of 'unfairness', the potential for 'leap-frog': all are features commonly associated with the constitutional model of asymmetrical devolution. Mediating the tensions will clearly require considerable cooperation and good will among the different administrations. It marks a leap of faith in a constitution renowned for the adversarial nature of its politics.

Turning the argument round, enough has been said to demonstrate significant demands for greater symmetry in the UK devolutionary process. A related factor is the constraints on institutional learning. The immediacy as well as the novelty of the various devolutionary schemes has underscored the need for a cross-fertilization of ideas and techniques. Wales is a good source of examples, precisely because of political and administrative demands for 'parity' in the light of weaker devolution, as also a general sense in the reform process of Wales riding on the coat tails of Scotland. In short, there being some important parallels or equivalencies in the devolutionary schemes, the model of asymmetrical devolution should not be allowed to obscure the interplay in the UK constitutional development of the twin elements of commonality and diversity.

Meso-government in Europe

In terms of public administration in western Europe, the rise of regional or meso-government is one of the most significant phenomena of the last half-century. Experience varies, with a range of types of regional government among and within states, but certain main factors are typically identified: the needs of economic development and competition, administrative and political overload of the central state, demands for democratization and participation, minority nationalism, and European integration.[92] Notably, a strong regional focus has developed inside the European Union, which has in turn generated interest in creating regional administration to respond to schemes.[93] Under the Conservatives, the United Kingdom emerged as the odd man out, alone among the larger EU states in lacking elected regional government. In turn, the UK devolutionary development can be seen as bringing a 'region' like Wales more into the mainstream of European political and constitutional development.

Viewed in comparative perspective, Wales is an especially interesting example of sub-state restructuring, networking and response to forces of European and global market integration.[94] The challenge is clearly an enormous one, which, splendidly envisioned, involves reinventing a territorial society in the role of competitive entity (so-called 'Team Wales'), and is very pressing, not least in view of the fundamental economic and political development that is EU enlargement. Opportunities must be generated and grasped: a 'Euro-region' like Wales, incorporated not only in the Union state but also in the Single Market, cannot bury its head in the sand.

The devolved administration had some initiatives to build on. One reason why the Welsh Office tended to take on a more distinctive 'national' identity was in order to respond to the opportunities presented by UK membership of the European Union.[95] There is for example a significant history of EU 'structural funding' for the territory, some £1,250 million in the five years to the millennium. Again, some steps had been taken in terms of direct representation and regional networking in the Community, but subject to the strict constraints associated with a strongly centralized state apparatus. Turning this round, the fact of devolved government has itself generated new possibilities for so-called 'paradiplomacy', the conduct of foreign relations at sub-state level. The Welsh Assembly Government will be seen working hard to exploit this space.[96]

Power devolved may in the famous phrase be power retained, but much in the substance is no longer in the gift of the national parliament. As an instrument of territorial autonomy the current devolutionary scheme is in some respects more limited than the design model of executive devolution first established for Wales in the 1970s. Such is the knock-on effect of the widening and deepening of EU competencies in the intervening period, in respect of such major fields of devolved activity as agriculture and the environment, as also of burgeoning EU rules and regulations in matters like public procurement. It has evidently come as a shock to some Assembly Members, but this too is of the essence of devolution in an era of supranational ordering and market liberalization.

4. LABOUR IN GOVERNMENT

The unexpected margin of Labour's victory in the general election of May 1997 – a majority of 179 seats in the House of Commons – clearly signalled an easier passage for the devolution legislation. In sharp contrast, that is, to the events of the 1970s, when a minority Labour administration had to struggle on in the face of incessant attack and disruption involving its own anti-devolutionist backbenchers. Yet there was obviously still much to do before devolution was safely delivered in Wales: not least since the government was now committed to holding a popular referendum. The role in the process of the introduction of an element of proportional representation for Assembly elections, so controversial inside the Welsh Labour Party that it was only agreed a couple of months prior to the general election, deserves a special emphasis. It is a classic illustration of the way in which the new constitutional dispensation for Wales has been deeply influenced by the problems of delivery.

Official inputs

Perhaps it is not surprising, such have been the qualities of a political thriller, that the published accounts of 'redesigning democracy in Wales' should have concentrated so heavily on party politics in general, and the internal Labour Party machinations in particular. This kind of approach, however, is apt to be misleading, not least in airbrushing from history the vital role played by Welsh Office and Assembly officials in the establishment and design of the devolutionary scheme. While such involvement may sound unexceptional – a case of civil servants providing advice and working up the detail – matters were greatly accentuated on this occasion.

There is a variety of reasons: the lack of hands-on ministerial experience after eighteen years in the political wilderness; the often vague and incomplete character of the policy proposals developed by Labour in opposition; and the highly technical nature of a scheme of executive devolution. It is thus appropriate to think in terms of a parallel administrative process, matching and buttressing the more visible political element in the development and implementation of the new Welsh constitutional policy.

Pride of place goes to the elite Devolution Unit of the Welsh Office, formally established within days of Labour coming to power, and in operation until after the first Assembly elections in May 1999. Never more than ten to fifteen strong, the Unit supplied an essential element of continuity in the shaping and delivery of the policy, as also coordination and much of the later strategic thinking. Effectively, it was the driving force in the middle. The Unit was thus responsible for preparing and drafting the White Paper, including negotiating it through Whitehall; organizing the referendum; preparing the instructions on the Bill jointly with the Welsh Office lawyers; managing the Bill through Parliament; overseeing the process of creating the standing orders; and organizing the Assembly elections.

Also working against the clock, other dedicated groups of officials tackled more specialist or practical matters, ranging from discussions with Treasury officials over funding arrangements, or negotiations across Whitehall over the delineation of Assembly powers, to such important domestic matters as accommodation, broadcasting and translation requirements. A different but related point: the strong leadership role exercised by the Permanent Secretary in public administration, in the person first of Rachel Lomax and then of Jon Shortridge, came to public prominence with Labour back in the Welsh Office. The sense of 'life in a goldfish bowl' that increasingly would overtake the higher echelons of the civil service in Wales following on devolution was clearly signalled.[97]

Other actors

There were other players in the game. Established by the Secretary of State in December 1997, the National Assembly Advisory Group (NAAG) was a non-statutory body charged with assisting the preparatory work on the Assembly's standing orders. It was 'to produce recommendations on which consensus has been developed and which contribute to the establishment of an Assembly which is democratic, effective, efficient and inclusive'.[98]

NAAG is particularly significant in the devolutionary process in two main ways. First, it reflected and reinforced the concept of a new kind of politics. To this effect, notions of inclusiveness are the common thread, beginning with the very inception of NAAG as a political response to the renewed divisions that were associated with a close result in the Welsh devolution referendum.[99] The membership was carefully balanced in terms not only of the political parties but also of gender and geography, and of business, voluntary-sector and local government interests. The group then took great care in conducting various consultations across Wales. And, typical of the age, its recommendations placed great emphasis on the style or feel of government. As well as family-friendly working hours, useful suggestions were made on such matters as flexible working practices via the new technologies and the avoidance of very formal language.[100]

Second, in making recommendations on Assembly procedures, committee structures, etc., NAAG provided useful 'cover' to ministers and officials in moving towards a more dynamic model of administration. This refers to the substantial shift in the parliamentary proceedings on the Bill, previously mentioned,[101] in the direction of a cabinet-style form of executive authority or more top-down conception of representation in the new national tier of government.

In fact NAAG was closely entwined with the Devolution Unit, which both prepared the factual and policy papers for Members' consideration and helped in the drafting of the consultation documents and the final report.[102] The group was very much a Whitehall-style advisory committee, with all that this implies in terms of the location of the decision-making power. Operating to strict parameters, agenda and time scale, it was emphatically not the equivalent of the Scottish Constitutional Convention.

Turning to the devolution statute, this provided for the appointment by the Secretary of State of standing orders commissioners to prepare a draft of the Assembly's internal law: in practice, now building on the work of NAAG.[103] This part of the process was carefully scripted. Independent office-holders, the work of the commissioners was the subject of statutory guidance; also, it was for the Secretary of State to make the standing orders 'either in the form of the draft or in that form with such modifications as he considers appropriate'. In fact, the work of the Standing Orders Commission, as it came to be known, was far from technical. The commission, it will be seen, came to a series of policy decisions that would closely affect the practice of raw politics in the Assembly.

Once again, to anticipate the discussion, there was a certain naivety in the work of NAAG – a function perhaps of the emphasis on representativeness at the cost of much in terms of Westminster or equivalent experience. The contribution of the commission struck a different note, with the statutory guidance from the Secretary of State signalling a greater emphasis on the need for the Assembly to operate effectively and efficiently.[104] And of course the Devolution Unit was there to supply draft versions of standing orders for consideration by the commissioners.

So the parallel administrative process never ceased to operate. And subsequent chapters will demonstrate how it has gone on operating, for example in the vital spheres of Assembly empowerment and intergovernmental relations. Just as the politicians have set about working the new constitutional system for Wales, so behind the scenes and operating under broad political direction Assembly officials have continued the work of developing the system. Such are the many processes of devolution!

Key compromise: composition and electoral system

Predictably, the electoral system proved one of the most difficult matters to resolve in the design and implementation of the Welsh devolutionary scheme. It went straight to the heart of the character of the constitutional development. Put simply, would the system be an instrument for continuation of Labour's long-standing dominance in Wales, or a potential vehicle for a new form of multi-party politics? And the issue was clearly enmeshed in the general debate in the United Kingdom over proportional representation, with more pluralist approaches in the devolutionary schemes naturally being seen by opponents as the thin end of the wedge.

In the event, Labour's internal Policy Commission in Wales quickly discounted systems of proportional representation such as STV (single transferable vote), effectively narrowing the debate inside the Party to two options:

- Westminster-style 'first past the post' – eighty Assembly Members, two each from the forty parliamentary constituencies in Wales;
- A German-style additional member system (AMS) – incorporating a further twenty 'top-up seats' allocated on a proportionate basis.

Essentially the design of the Wales Act 1978, the first option was then reinvented in *Shaping the Vision*. This, however, was hardly a subtle approach, being liable, with Labour capable of winning over 50 per cent of the vote in Wales, to produce an overwhelming majority in the new democratic institution. Emphatically not the stuff of a new kind of politics, for Labour's pro-devolutionary wing it also threatened to capsize the campaign in any referendum, both in terms of the necessary tactical alliances with Plaid and the Liberal Democrats, and by reason of a proper democratic concern about permanent one-party domination. A concern, it may be said, that has special resonance in Wales in view of some of the least attractive practices of Labour in local government (or popularly, the 'Taffia').[105]

Perhaps then it is not surprising to learn that at the prompting of Ron Davies the Prime Minister intervened, to the effect that the party in Wales look again at a system of AMS. The upshot was *Representing Wales*, a further report from the Policy Commission that duly recommended AMS, but on the basis of a shrunken Assembly of sixty Members. In a remarkable volte-face the document was then approved unanimously at the Welsh Labour Party conference in February 1997 (just in time for the General Election). As the Secretary of State would later tell the House of Commons, it was another 'long and complicated story about internal Labour Party politics'.[106]

And so it is that the people of Wales are currently represented in the Assembly by forty Members elected by 'first past the post' from constituencies identical to the parliamentary constituencies, and twenty Members elected under AMS from five electoral regions.[107] 'Straightforwardly obscure' is an apt description of the element of proportional representation, which turns on the well-known d'Hondt formula, non-transparent and complicated for voters.[108] A further significant twist is that – as had been recommended in Scotland – electors have two votes, one for the 'Assembly constituency' and one for the 'Assembly electoral region'. Initially the idea in Wales was for a single vote, but such different versions of AMS clearly proved too distracting for the UK government – a good illustration of the cross-fertilization of ideas and techniques in the general devolutionary development.[109]

In *A Voice for Wales* the government was at pains to stress how the d'Hondt formula compensates for electoral imbalances created in the first past the post section. The system 'will ensure, as far as possible, that the Assembly reflects the diversity of modern Wales geographically, culturally and politically'.[110] But this is not the whole story. First, the d'Hondt formula is recognized to favour major parties by reason of the numerical progression that is adopted.[111] Secondly, the Welsh scheme provides for a less proportionate outcome than, say, in Scotland, because there are fewer additional members with whom to 'compensate' for first past the post. A ratio, that is, between the sections of 33:67 in Wales, as against 43:57 in Scotland.[112] Alternatively, the Greater London Assembly for example consists of twenty-five members: fourteen directly elected and eleven 'list' members. 'As far as possible' is itself an elastic concept.

In summary, the introduction of AMS was another carefully contrived political balancing act. The precise choice of electoral system not only demonstrates a concern for inclusiveness but also exhibits a desire to stack the cards in favour of the Labour interest. It is to this effect the archetypal internal party deal. A series of attempts in Parliament to establish greater proportionality were predictably rejected by the Secretary of State. The calculations had been done, the projections made.

Let us be more explicit. Underlying the devolution statute is an assumption that was never publicly articulated. To wit: the Assembly electoral system must be one which both offers the dominant party the prospect of forming a majority government and the other parties a plausible prospect of preventing this. For Labour, it was a worst-case scenario of thirty-one or thirty-two seats in the first elections – a narrow but working majority. Needless to say, such historic Labour bastions as the Rhondda had been factored into the equation. How could it be otherwise?

Flanking features

Two related elements merit special attention. At the risk of stating the obvious, the sudden reduction – by a quarter – of the proposed membership is of the first importance in the design and operation of the Assembly. The new Welsh polity may not be overly empowered, but basic issues of institutional capacity and effectiveness are raised in this situation. Once again, this element exemplifies the triumph of delivery over product in the Welsh constitutional scheme. In turn, it has been high on the agenda of the Richard Commission.

As enacted in the devolution statute, the Assembly works on the basis of a fixed term of four years – with no provision for dissolution.[113] Another carryover from the Wales Act 1978, this element is familiarly associated with the local government model of democratic authority. Although bearing directly on the canons of constitutional and political responsibility in the new Welsh structures, as also – at least when combined with AMS – representing something of a prod towards more collaborative forms of government, it was barely discussed in *Shaping the Vision*. Hubris: within the first year of the Assembly, such considerations would be seen centre stage.[114]

Referendum: assent and division

The central role in the Welsh constitutional process of cold political calculation is further illustrated by the approach to the popular referendum. Unlike in 1978/9 and the so-called 'winter of discontent', the immediate political context could be accounted very favourable. There was not only the local legacy of what I have called 'unionist folly', but also the fact of a fresh, newly elected government, with a popular and energetic Prime Minister and a clear mandate, and a demoralized Conservative Opposition (with parliamentary representation confined to England). In the words of a leading 'No' campaigner, 'the principal protagonists were in a state of almost surreal *vice versa*'.[115]

The government took elaborate precautions to ensure a positive result. First, unlike in 1979 it was a choice of pre-legislative referendum, a useful technique for directing attention to the principle as opposed to the content of the devolutionary scheme, or for maintaining the political momentum of the project as opposed to the corrosive effects of Westminster-style trench warfare. Second, the referendum was timed for September 1997, not only in the new government's honeymoon period but also in the slipstream of the Scottish referendum vote. All this goes to explain the breakneck speed of the Welsh constitutional development now that Labour was returned to office. The enabling legislation, the Referendums (Scotland and Wales) Act 1997, was the first measure introduced by the new administration.

Most important were the rules of the game. As in 1979 it was a case of self-determination, with the poll (as in Scotland and latterly in Northern Ireland) restricted to people living in the territory. If there was one thing that could not be countenanced in a context of national devolution, not least in terms of the health of the Union, it was the exercise of an English veto. There was however no equivalent of the threshold requirement or 'fancy franchise' – 40 per cent of those eligible to vote in favour – that had been forced on the previous Labour government and which had famously served to postpone Scottish devolution. Turning the argument round, there was to be no restriction on campaign expenditure, etc. Given the gross disparity of resources in favour of the government and the 'Yes' campaign, this was hard ball.[116] Not least since in retrospect it probably made the difference.

Constitutionally speaking, the recourse to a pre-legislative referendum is significant in two main ways. There is, first, the chilling effect of a device long seen as hostile to parliamentary government. Legislative scrutiny – and indeed the government's subsequent freedom of manoeuvre in redesigning the scheme[117] – was necessarily constrained by this manifestation of popular democracy. Ministers, when it suited in the parliamentary proceedings on the Bill, could plead the text of the White Paper as the 'manifesto' on which the people had voted. Second, as a tool of (political) entrenchment, the referendum is the best available means within the Westminster tradition of sovereignty. It plays in this case in various ways: to blunt any lingering unionist ambitions of policy reversal, and to highlight the absence of any popular mandate for bringing into the scheme primary legislative or tax-varying powers.

To this effect, the precise terms of the referendum question are still very relevant, in view of the ongoing constitutional debate in Wales. The voters were empowered, but only on the restrictive terms dictated by Labour's local trials and tribulations. Hence, a fine example of the structuring and confining of popular discretion, the referendum question was effectively take it or leave it ('I agree/do not agree that there should be a Welsh assembly'). Whatever Lord Irvine for example believes to be the answer, the people of Wales have never been asked about legislative devolution.

The referendum campaign is aptly called a muted affair. Especially note-worthy for present purposes is the nature of the 'Yes' campaign.[118] Non-party and all-party, the one thing it was determined not to be 'is . . . a forum for debate on the merits of different forms of devolution . . . Its sole purpose is to secure a yes-vote in the referendum on the terms offered.'[119] So far from being opened up, the constitutional project was driven forward in what amounted to a conspiracy of silence. Again, the fact that Labour found it difficult to enthuse the troops was hardly surprising, in view of the inward-looking approach to policy-making of the local party elite. Ron Davies, the prime mover in this, would later aver that the 'basic failure in political education nearly cost us dear in the referendum'.[120]

Yet perhaps what is most surprising about the referendum is the surprise that the result was so close. Seen in historical perspective, the pro-devolutionists had a proverbial mountain to climb. In terms of the psephology, the 'swing' required from the previous referendum was some 30 per cent. That it was achieved with nothing to spare – a margin of some 7,000 votes out of 1,110,000 – demonstrates, at one and the same time, the continuing tensions and divisions, and a sea change in Welsh opinion since 1979.

Table 1: Welsh devolution referendum results

1979 referendum		1997 referendum	
Yes:	20.3%	Yes:	50.3%
No:	79.7%	No:	49.7%
Turnout:	58.8%	Turnout:	50.1%

Electoral analysis of the referendum result has served to confirm the many complexities of the Welsh condition. There clearly was some correlation with the 'three Wales model': the more affluent and Anglicized parts that make up 'British Wales', including the capital city, being in the 'No' camp. Yet more striking was the level of disagreement demonstrated in all parts of the country – substantial minority votes in very many of the twenty-two electoral areas, which were themselves divided equally 'Yes' and 'No'.

Typically, the personal sense of 'national identity' – Welsh, British, etc. – has been suggested as a chief factor overlying the cues given to voters by the political parties. In this regard, another significant feature was the much higher participation rate of Welsh-speakers as against the many people in Wales born in England.[121] It has further been suggested on the basis of survey findings that the result was effectively determined by the turnout, and in turn by the failure of the 'No' campaign to play its part in mobilizing anti-devolution opinion. 'By a small majority, the Welsh electorate actually preferred the pre-devolution constitutional *status quo.*'[122]

However that may be, from the constitutional viewpoint of the Assembly securing a broad measure of popular legitimacy and democratic authority, it was an inauspicious start. Embodying and imbuing a new Welsh civic identity 'based on identification with institutions and place, and the values that they represent', could now be seen as a major, ongoing challenge for the infant body.[123] At the same time, a general sense of alienation from the political process is hardly confined to Wales. A case not so much of antipathy, as of apathy, towards the Assembly, is the most plausible interpretation of a modest turnout.[124]

Nonetheless, however grudgingly, the people of Wales had officially signified assent. The litmus test is the response of Her Majesty's Opposition at Westminster: which exemplifies the customary pragmatic style of the Conservative Party in accommodating unwanted constitutional development. To quote the Conservative Assembly Member David Melding, 'in its movements and mannerisms the Conservative Party was rapidly learning the steps for the new devolution dance'.[125] To push home the point, national devolution to Wales was now for the foreseeable future an accomplished political fact. But this, it is important to say in view of the following fourteen chapters, is not the same thing as saying that the constitutional fundamentals of national devolution for Wales have been settled.

The personal is political

This is not a book about political parties, still less is it political biography. One could hardly ignore, however, the remarkable turn of individual events[126] that attended the birth of the National Assembly; not least since this bears directly on the subsequent constitutional and political development in Wales.

September 1998 thus saw another significant milestone in the processes of devolution as broadly conceived. The first leader of the Welsh Labour Party was elected, so providing an alternative or separate mandate. In contrast, that is, to the situation which has obtained under the classical UK cabinet model, whereby the authority of the Secretary of State (for Wales) stems from the patronage of the Prime Minister. In the event, Ron Davies secured a decisive victory over his fellow MP Rhodri Morgan.

In the annals of Welsh history, the following month will also deserve a footnote. Such was the so-called 'moment of madness', with Ron Davies resigning as Secretary of State and prospective Labour leader in the National Assembly in the wake of an encounter with strangers on Clapham Common. The scene was set for the protracted and bitter contest that was the second Labour leadership election in Wales: in the one corner, Rhodri Morgan, and in the other corner, Alun Michael, now appointed by Mr Blair as the Secretary of State for Wales.

For our purposes, this contest, and Mr Michael's narrow victory courtesy of the delivery by the party machine of trade union block votes, is important in two main ways. First, much was heard of 'the London connection'; and in particular, however unfairly, of the 'parachuting' into the Assembly of Alun Michael. Convergence: the potential of party political constraints on devolved government, and strong pressure for uniformity in policy-making in the United Kingdom, is writ large here. Second but related, the seeds were being sown for Wales's own first constitutional crisis: the driving of Alun Michael from the office of Assembly First Secretary. Once again, internal Labour Party strife is seen colouring the path of the devolutionary development in Wales.

Elections: the vagaries of constitution-building

And so – finally – to what was dubbed 'the quiet earthquake' in Welsh politics: the unheralded result of the first Assembly elections in May 1999. The dominance of the Labour Party in Welsh electoral politics that had lasted for almost a century was now put in issue.

Three defeats in its erstwhile strongholds of the Rhondda, Llanelli and Islwyn deprived the Labour Party of a majority. To place matters in context, the Labour vote in the constituencies section fell by 17 per cent from its vote in the UK general election two years earlier, and by up to a third in its old heartlands of 'Welsh Wales'. Plaid Cymru was the direct beneficiary, but also advanced at the expense of all parties across Wales.[127]

Fixing the future is never easy. But to reiterate, the election result is not what was calculated to happen. The voters in 'Welsh Wales' had effectively trumped a key internal party compromise. Expressed slightly differently, an

Table 2: Result of first Assembly elections – May 1999

	Labour	*Plaid*	*Conservatives*	*Liberal Democrats*
Constituency seats (40)	27	9	1	3
Additional Members from regional lists (20)	1	8	8	3
Total (60	28	17	9	6
% vote in constituencies	37.6	28.4	15.8	13.5
% vote in electoral regions	35.5	30.6	16.5	12.5

Turnouts: constituencies 46.3%, electoral regions 46.1%.

implicit or automatic assumption that the so-called 'new kind of politics' would operate, at least initially, under Labour Party tutelage, had been falsified. Such it may be said are the vagaries of constitution-building!

There is further a strong sense of this set of 'national' elections being of a lower, second-order significance for the voters of Wales. The low turnout serves once again to underscore the profound challenge faced by the devolved administration in generating popular enthusiasm. More specifically, and illustrating a well-known phenomenon in comparative politics, the evidence from survey findings is of Plaid Cymru prospering in the light of the specifically Welsh dimension of the Assembly elections.[128]

More immediately, the advent in a very real sense of multi-party politics served to unleash unforeseen dynamics in terms of the constitutional trajectory and administrative practices of the Assembly. As documented in the pages of this book, the unitary concept that is the corporate body would soon be shaken to its core.

CONCLUSION – A POOR BEGINNING

Viewed in terms of the historical development of Wales, devolution amounts, if not to an act of creation, then to a political metamorphosis. Typically there are many layers of explanation, political and sociological, legal and admin-istrative, for the peculiar nature of the constitutional innovation. Under-writing some general themes, this chapter shows how the Welsh scheme both fits with broad contemporary developments in comparative public admin-istration, most obviously regional and economic restructuring inside the

European Union, and demonstrates strong elements of continuity, in both the substance of the scheme and the process of delivery.

The chapter also serves to underscore the strong role in the policy-making of responsive factors. Important here is the extreme political nervousness in view of 1979 – 'no hostages to fortune'; the recent experience of governance in Wales under the Conservatives; and the subsidiary place of the territory in the UK constitutional process, emblematic of a high degree of contingency and reflexivity in the Welsh development. Hardly visionary in nature, or highly pragmatic, incremental and eclectic in character: the initial design work has typically involved a very 'British' way of doing things.

For the avoidance of doubt, constitutional design is rarely an exercise in rational decision-making. But set in terms of mature liberal democracy, the exercise in Wales has been less rational than most. Conflict – or the fear of it – inside the Welsh Labour Party is a pervasive factor, the devolutionary scheme being not so much a matter of internal architectural logic as a set of internal party compromises. Stir in a chief element of political miscalculation and it is hardly surprising that the Welsh development is an odd brew.

It is a story of reform suffering from a poor beginning. The political failure of Labour in opposition to develop robust and credible proposals could not be entirely rescued in government, especially given the speed of process and many complexities involved in executive devolution, notwithstanding the best efforts behind the scenes of senior professionals in the Welsh Office. Later chapters will consider the many improvements that have subsequently been made to the devolved system of government in Wales, both before and after the empowerment of the Assembly. At root, however, constitutional developments of this kind involve mitigating the adverse consequences of an inadequate original design and so are subject to major limitations.

At the heart of the design of the Welsh scheme is a contradiction: on the one hand, the preaching of a new inclusive style of politics, and on the other hand, the practice of constitution-making in (what used to be called) smoke-filled rooms. In terms of buttressing the popular legitimacy of the Assembly, what I have called the triumph of delivery over product or content left much to be desired. Such is the historical legacy of the Labour Party in Wales at the dawn of a new millennium.

2

Building Blocks

The Government of Wales Act contains many provisions about the Assembly. However, the Government believes:

- that devolution is a process that should be allowed to develop in the future, and
- that the Assembly should have maximum flexibility to govern its own affairs.

Accordingly, the Act in many instances merely sets out a framework within which future Government decisions on devolution, and the Assembly's own decisions, are to be made.

Welsh Office Devolution Unit, August 1998[1]

Let us now examine the basic components of the constitutional development in Wales. The arrangements are in fact so complicated that the task is best spread over several chapters. The starting-point obviously is the Government of Wales Act (GWA). Two constitutional fundamentals then demand attention: empowerment or the allocation of legal tasks and responsibilities, and the system of public finance or fiscal transfer from central government. The detail of the internal architecture is a matter reserved for the next chapter, which leads naturally on to the discussion in chapter 4 of the essential historical feature of the Assembly in its first few years: the scale of an autochthonous constitutional transformation.

Two particular ideas underpin the discussion in this chapter. The devolution statute is seen, first, as a written constitution (as well as being legislation subject to revision at Westminster). That is to say, from the bottom-up or Welsh perspective, an overarching and entrenched constitutional instrument, one which establishes, refines and constrains the National Assembly.[2] What then is the quality – drafting and otherwise – of this basic law?

The second idea, already introduced, is that of a complex and diverse hierarchy of rules. It is especially well illustrated in this chapter. The way in which, using secondary legislation, executive functions were originally transferred to the Assembly, says so very much about the Welsh constitutional condition. Meanwhile, territorial finance is the realm of the controversial

'Barnett formula', which in terms of the hierarchy of rules exemplifies the primacy of soft law in the sphere of intergovernmental relations.

1. THE WRITTEN CONSTITUTION

Two paradoxes

Constitutions come in all shapes and sizes: short and long, general and specific, elegant and ugly. In the light of the previous discussion, it is no surprise to learn that the Government of Wales Act contains no ringing endorsement of constitutional change or general statement of principles. It may be one of the most important constitutional documents in the history of Wales, but – as well as being a statement of limited devolution – it has also been made subject to the usual (traditionally formalistic) canons of the Westminster style of legislative drafting. The Preamble could hardly be more prosaic:

> An Act to establish and make provision about the National Assembly for Wales and the offices of Auditor General for Wales and Welsh Administration Ombudsman; to reform certain Welsh public bodies and abolish certain other Welsh public bodies; and for connected purposes.

Consisting of 7 Parts, 159 Sections and 18 Schedules, the statute is certainly a weighty document. This compares with the Scotland Act 1998, which in delivering a generous measure of legislative devolution is considerably shorter. If we then add in the fact that the basic division of competencies has been set out for Scotland in the Act and for Wales in what amounts to voluminous secondary legislation, the contrast is even more striking.

The first of two key paradoxes in the Welsh scheme is introduced. Namely, the comparative weakness of the devolved powers stands in inverse proportion to the scale of the formal measures adopted to deliver this.

Written constitutions are never entireties and it would be wrong to expect the GWA to be anything different. What is significant is the degree and pattern of the open-ended elements. As indicated, the devolution legislation is on occasion highly prescriptive, reflecting particular policy goals or concerns about the quality of an emergent Welsh polity. But as the opening quotation from the Devolution Unit makes clear, the expansive use of flexible requirements is a defining feature. There is often a disjunction between what is in the statute and what really matters, for example the basic formula for calculating the level of devolved funding. The second key paradox is highlighted. Although the GWA is a long and complicated affair, great silences punctuate the statutory provisions.

The constitution of the constitution

This is not to say that the basic arrangement of provisions is anything other than logical and coherent. As regards the constitutional tasks involved in establishing the scheme, it clearly is, as befits the skilled hand of the parliamentary draftsman.

Part I of the Act begins at the beginning, establishing the Assembly and dealing with the electoral system and with the (disqualification of) Members. Part II makes clear that the Assembly will have something to do, granting it certain functions and – more important – allowing it to acquire other functions, not least those previously exercised by the Secretary of State (for Wales). Part III sets out a framework for the Assembly's operating procedures, which involves repeated references to the need for detailed provision in standing orders ('the hierarchy of rules'). Part IV paves the way for the Assembly to have the necessary resources via a mechanism for fiscal transfer, as well as establishing arrangements for audit. Part V tells the Assembly some things that it really cannot do, such as offend Community law or relevant provisions of the European Convention on Human Rights (ECHR), and also has certain things to say about the new Welsh system of governance (partnering etc.). Part VI is the odd one out, being directed to reforms of 'quangoland' prior to the commencement of operations by the Assembly. Part VII is the usual cleaning-up exercise or list of supplementary provisions.

Yet even this brief sketch confirms the general picture, as presented in terms of the two paradoxes. As an organic instrument, the GWA is a statute that more than most must be treated as a starting-point for legal and constitutional analysis. Typically – and helping to explain what I have called the subsequent constitutional transformation of the Assembly – it gave an incomplete picture of the body as a working institution.[3]

Certain considerations shaping the legislative design, or what may now be termed 'the constitution of the constitution', deserve a special emphasis. The first one reflects and reinforces the vital fact of the legal and administrative complexity of the Welsh scheme. Technically speaking, it is the case that doing less is harder, as regards construction of the framework and modalities of this form of devolution. How could it be otherwise, given on the one hand, the disaggregation of the law-making process that is involved ('horizontal' division), and on the other hand, the historical legacy of close integration with England?

Then there is the strong sense of an evolutionary approach, or what was described as a framework for organic development. Let us keep in mind the novelty in Britain of this kind of constitutional scheme, and thus the role for a permissive form of legislation that maximizes the scope for institutional learning. A role for autochthonous development: particularly important in the light of subsequent events is the belief powerfully expressed by the

Devolution Unit of a self-denying ordinance. That is to say, a constitutional understanding expressive of the principle of devolution that prescribing the internal modalities is essentially a matter for the territory and not the centre.

Turning this round, the permissive character of the legislation also fits with Labour's failure properly to plan in advance an appropriate framework for the new Welsh system of government. In this respect too, the statute has provided useful 'cover', not least according to the tried and tested formula of 'devolution is a process not an event'.

Whereas the GWA has been designed as a flexible instrument for other purposes, statute law has generally been considered too rigid a framework for the many political and administrative subtleties of the new forms of intergovernmental relations – and understandably so.[4] Once again there is a premium on administrative and constitutional values of cooperation, co-ordination, and partnership: which – at the risk of repetition – is the more significant in the Welsh case by reason of the exceptional measure of interdependency between the central and territorial layers of government implicit in executive devolution. Such is the idea of legislative 'silences' writ large.

What, it may be asked, of the so-called 'bonfire of the quangos'? Extravagant version of the central idea in the local constitutional development of curing a 'democratic deficit', much was heard of this phrase prior to the devolution legislation – at least in Labour Party circles.[5] As indicated, a concern to tackle the sprawling system of Welsh public bodies does find expression in the GWA, being illustrated by lengthy provisions on the winding-up of such quickly forgotten bodies as the Land Authority for Wales or Tai Cymru (Housing for Wales).

Let truth be told, however. The statute points firmly in the other direction; towards the rise of Welsh governmental machinery that is now ongoing in the context of national devolution, and – as this book argues – rightly so.[6] On the one hand, and all at one with the role of economic considerations as a driver of the local constitutional development, the powers of the Welsh Development Agency (WDA) were substantially increased.[7] On the other hand, new Welsh bodies or agencies were brought into play: as mentioned in the Preamble, separate offices for redress of grievance (the Ombudsman[8]) and for financial accountability (the Auditor General[9]). The fact that – even in strict institutional terms – national devolution to Wales is about much more than the Assembly is thus made apparent on the face of the 'written constitution'.

Particular statutory provisions will naturally be discussed in different chapters of this book. However, better to convey the flavour, it is appropriate at this stage to consider some general powers and duties that demonstrate basic attributes of the constitutional scheme; as also some things which the GWA does not do.

Aspects of multi-layered governance

The major limitations of, the potential for organic growth in, and the constitutional values associated with, the Welsh devolutionary scheme, are all illuminated in the statutory provisions touching on the other tiers or layers of governance. The obvious starting-point is section 33 of the GWA, which represents an advance on the 1978 legislation: 'The Assembly may consider, and make appropriate representations about, any matter affecting Wales.'

This section encapsulates the concept of national devolution, giving practical expression to the title of the White Paper *A Voice for Wales*. As such it has quickly emerged as one of the most significant provisions in the whole constitutional arrangement – precisely because of the comparatively weak set of powers formally associated with the scheme of executive devolution. At one and the same time, the devolved administration has directly within its remit particular matters relating to Wales, and has an indirect or roving role across the broad range of subject matters. That is to say: an inner core of legal and political responsibility, and an outer ring of dialogue, consultation and influence.

'Consider' clearly includes debating and passing resolutions about non-devolved issues. Suffice it to say that much of the Assembly's time in plenary session has been spent doing precisely this.[10] At the same time, section 33 provides a useful legal basis for justifying Assembly expenditure on various types of official inquiry or task force, better to inform the public exercise of a voice for Wales. Perhaps one day it will underwrite official Assembly representations about the need to amend the devolution statute.

Then again anybody can pass resolutions. A special need in executive devolution for additional provision or privileged access to the primary lawgiver has already been highlighted. Much effort has had to be devoted to supplying an appropriate administrative and political gloss on the skeletal linkage that is made in the 'written constitution'.[11]

The relationship with local government is one of the most sensitive aspects of the Welsh constitutional development. On the one hand, by virtue of the general transfer of functions, the Assembly now has responsibility for funding local government, and for much of the strategic direction. On the other hand, the basic structure and functions of local government in Wales remains a matter for Westminster and primary legislation. The devolution statute has here signalled an innovative approach: a special Assembly scheme for promoting and sustaining local government, and a unique institutional framework ('the Partnership Council') for drawing together these two great powers in the land.[12]

Such provision is emblematic of the 'partnership approach' to small-country governance, which it was said characterizes the Welsh devolutionary development. In turn, it is a good example of the clutch of procedural and substantive principles that the GWA mandates as to the workings of the Assembly. There are parallel provisions relating to the voluntary sector and the business community.[13]

Turning to the vital European Union dimension, nowhere is the minimalist tendency of the devolution legislation better illustrated. In sharp contrast to the White Paper, which so trumpeted the opportunities, economic and otherwise, for 'Wales in Europe', the GWA does the bare necessities required to fit a devolved territory like Wales into the EU framework.[14] Transferred functions may empower the Assembly in various Community competencies; the Assembly has no power to act in a way incompatible with Community law; a Community obligation of the UK is also an obligation of the Assembly, if and to the extent that it falls within the Assembly's functions.[15] And of course – reflecting the continuing legal and political responsibility of central government in the role of member state – the Secretary of State is given concurrent powers with the Assembly to make subordinate legislation for the purposes of implementing Community law.[16]

As regards constitutional techniques of control of the subsidiary body, the devolution statute uses both main regulatory models: the 'legal' or 'judicial' model and the 'executive/political' or 'central government' model. For example, on the one hand, in relation to the Human Rights Act 1998, section 107(1) of the GWA provides: 'The Assembly has no power – (a) to make, confirm or approve any subordinate legislation, or (b) to do any other act, so far as the subordinate legislation or act is incompatible with any of the Convention rights.'[17]

On the other hand, as regards the wider world, that is to say international obligations other than obligations to comply with Community law and Convention rights, for example obligations arising under the UN Convention on the Rights of the Child, section 108 of the GWA provides:

> If a Minister of the Crown considers that any action proposed to be taken by the Assembly would be incompatible with any international obligation, he may by order direct that the proposed action shall not be taken . . .

> If a Minister of the Crown considers that any subordinate legislation made, or which could be revoked, by the Assembly is incompatible with any international obligation, he may by order revoke the legislation . . .

In fact, these provisions mark a significant change in constitutional style from the Wales Act 1978. Reflecting and reinforcing the advance of the judicial role in the constitution in the intervening period, it is the legal model that is now prioritized as a way of regulating the outputs of the new devolved institution(s). Whereas the previous devolution statute contained broad governmental override powers,[18] the 'international' power of section 108 – foreign relations – is now the only major survivor. Independence and impartiality: the role of the courts as an authoritative way of settling controversies has a particular appeal in the potentially sensitive context of national devolution.[19]

The Welsh difference

There is now a sense in which Welsh public law is qualitatively different from the public law that exists in England. This is by virtue of the inclusion in the GWA of a series of general principles or legal precepts that serve to guide or constrain the discretion of devolved government in Wales in matters of policy development, establishment and implementation.[20] It is worth adding that this feature is not replicated in Scotland, where the Parliament *qua* Parliament is left more to its own devices.

A bilingual approach is made an article of faith in this Celtic land.[21] The Assembly must treat the English and the Welsh languages equally in the conduct of business, so far as is appropriate and reasonably practicable, and the bilingual texts of Assembly instruments are afforded equal legal status.[22] Such statutory provision is familiar in other jurisdictions, but it marks a new departure in the legal and constitutional history of the United Kingdom. It has already proved a useful peg on which to hang certain practical initiatives.[23]

Again, in what was a constitutional development unique in Western Europe, the GWA has required the devolved administration to make a statutory scheme setting out how it intends, in the exercise of its functions, to promote the good cause that is sustainable development.[24] In the event, a broad approach has been taken: one that encompasses the environmental, economic and social aspects.[25] From the viewpoint of the lawyer, there are significant implications in terms of potential challenges to the Assembly in such matters as planning decisions. Nonetheless, this statutory provision powerfully demonstrates an alternative approach to constitutional protection based on a justiciable bill of rights, one which both establishes and reserves to the political and administrative process the primary responsibility in a complex and controversial field. It is, in other words, one of the better uses of legal technique in the Welsh constitutional scheme.

As regards non-discrimination, the devolution statute provides: 'The Assembly shall make appropriate arrangements with a view to securing that its functions are exercised with due regard to the principle that there should be equality of opportunity for all people.'[26] The formulation is borrowed from the legislation on race relations, where it has been held to establish a specific obligation in respect of all relevant functions.[27] Although not user-friendly for the individual complainant in a court case, this provision in the current 'written constitution' of Wales is not to be lightly dismissed. Quite the reverse: in terms of the proactive effect designed to be induced, it once again has been taken very seriously, as consideration of the role of the Assembly's Equal Opportunities Committee will serve to illustrate.[28] The provision is the more noteworthy for being all-embracing.[29] To this end, it reflects and reinforces the special premium that has been placed on the value of inclusiveness in constructing the new Welsh polity.

In sum, this is what I call 'the Welsh difference'. The precepts constitute one of the principal ways in which the search for a new kind of politics has been given substance in the formal constitutional scheme. They thus represent a conscious striving to be (seen to be) different, as also – of course – political commitments given in the cause of the devolutionary struggle. Constitutions, it is commonly observed, reflect the values or obsessions of their age. In this regard the GWA may be accounted the very model of a postmodern constitution.

Missing links

The nature of the Welsh constitutional scheme is thrown sharply into focus by two particular elements that are missing from the devolution statute. The first one is simply stated: the lack of a fast-track procedure – in the guise of that otherwise very fashionable constitutional device, the Henry VIII clause – for amending the new 'written constitution' of Wales. This is all at one with the minister-speak of a 'devolution settlement' – a practical working-through of the idea of political entrenchment that was established via the devolution referendum.

More specifically, tangible expression is given to the idea of the devolution package as a political compromise or careful balancing act. At one and the same time, the legislative scheme offers some room for growth in powers, as also for substantial internal reordering, but cannot easily be restructured to convert the Assembly into a full legislature.[30] The major practical connotations, especially in terms of the review by the Richard Commission of the powers and electoral arrangements of the Assembly, are self-evident.

Secondly, the GWA does not contain special constitutional provisions or locks designed to secure the 'devolution settlement', and in particular to anchor Wales firmly inside the Union. The legal situation is different from Scotland not only because of legislative devolution to the Parliament but also by reason of the powerful Scots tradition of popular sovereignty.[31] Whereas this has never been entirely overlaid by the (English) doctrine of parliamentary sovereignty, a legal and political concept of this kind has never surfaced to any serious effect in Wales, such is the historical legacy of close amalgamation with England.[32]

On the one hand, the Scotland Act contains a battery of devices, both substantive and procedural, designed to secure constitutional compliance by the Parliament, and which effectively includes a continuous process of pre-legislative scrutiny of *vires*.[33] Nor is parliamentary sovereignty, howsoever wounded by European integration and the rise of multi-layered governance, about to go gently into the night. Legislative devolution, it is bluntly stated, 'does not affect the power of the Parliament of the United Kingdom to make laws for Scotland'.[34] So too the original Acts of Union 'have effect subject to this Act', a provision obviously intended to neutralize the (Scottish) idea of a constitutive law of the United Kingdom to which appeal might be made.

On the other hand, a combination of standard internal machinery for checking *vires*, including a legislation committee, and the ordinary principles of judicial review, is more than sufficient in the case of Wales.[35] Perhaps it is worth adding that attempts by the Conservatives to incorporate assurances about parliamentary sovereignty in the GWA were rejected by the government.[36] The correct response is 'why bother?' The subordinate law-making body that is the Assembly is easily accommodated within the traditional doctrine. Special constitutional locks are a sign of (potential) strength, not of weakness.

2. ALLOCATION OF FUNCTIONS[37]

Turning to the subject of empowerment, section 21 of the GWA establishes some basic ways in which the Assembly gains its functions: either by transfer under the Act or directly by primary legislation. In turn, section 22(1) has provided the machinery by which the government's promise to transfer responsibility for policies and public services exercised by the Secretary of State for Wales could be implemented. Her Majesty may by Order in Council

(a) provide for the transfer to the Assembly of any function so far as exercisable by a Minister of the Crown in relation to Wales,

(b) direct that any function so far as so exercisable shall be exercisable by the Assembly concurrently with the Minister of the Crown, or

(c) direct that any function so far as exercisable by a Minister of the Crown in relation to Wales shall be exercisable by the minister only with the agreement of, or after consultation with, the Assembly.

This is carefully crafted. On the one hand, section 22(1) is not in terms limited to the previous activities of the Welsh Office. Emblematic of the idea of the devolution statute as a framework for organic change, the door was thus left open here for further transfers. On the other hand, the strong measure of interdependency between the central and territorial layers of government is demonstrated in a continuum of possible arrangements: the exercise not only of wholly devolved powers, but also of concurrent powers, and further of reserved powers subject to consultation or Welsh veto.

Beyond a boundary

Turning the argument round, the GWA typically provides little guidance about what functions may be exercised by the Assembly. Very much the exception that proves the rule, section 32 gives the Assembly a general power: to do anything which may assist matters relating to culture, recreation, and – of course – the Welsh language. Otherwise, aside from the special powers relating to its ability to reorganize public bodies in Wales,[38] the Assembly was only directly empowered under the GWA to carry out functions which are supplementary or incidental to (whatever are) its substantive functions.[39]

This unique form of devolutionary technique is of the first importance. In contrast, say, to the Scottish scheme of legislative devolution, where the Parliament's legislative competence is in general terms co-determinous with the devolved subject areas, there is no clearly defined statutory or constitutional boundary in Welsh devolution.[40] Rather there exists what is variously described as a 'jigsaw' or 'kaleidoscope' of powers, the convoluted 'zigzag' of a dividing line between devolved and non-devolved functions – 'ragged edges'. To this effect, the core idea in executive devolution of the 'horizontal division' of powers (with Westminster) is deceptively simple.[41] In the case of Wales, the picture is far more variegated.

The closest that the GWA comes to establishing a boundary is Schedule 2. This lists some eighteen 'fields' or subject areas of competence where in making the first general order the minister was required to consider transferring functions. All at one with the general policy of the statute, the list duplicates the areas of public law and policy where the Secretary of State for Wales was exercising functions.

• Economic development	• Industry
• Agriculture, forestry, fisheries and food	• Transport
• Highways	• Town and Country Planning
• Education and training	• Health and health services
• Social services	• Housing
• Local government	• The environment
• Water and flood defence	• Tourism
• Culture (including museums, galleries and libraries)	• The Welsh language
• Sport and recreation	• Ancient monuments and historic buildings

Figure 3: Initial fields of devolved competencies

The approach is an advance on the Wales Act 1978. An excessive rigidity involved in listing transferred functions in a schedule to the statute[42] has thus been avoided by a creative use of secondary legislation. The change can be explained by reference to the continuing accretion of powers by the Welsh

Office in the intervening period, which would have rendered a detailed statutory formulation even more unwieldy. In turn, this more flexible approach requires some kind of constitutional lock in order to protect the position of the subordinate law-making body. Section 22(4) provides that a transfer order can only be varied or revoked under the GWA with the approval by resolution of the Assembly.

With no clearly defined boundary in view, the ongoing allocation of functions implicit in the model of executive devolution is essentially the product of an administrative and political dialogue or negotiation with central government. That Welsh officials originally saw the listing of the fields in Schedule 2 as a useful resource for these purposes, effectively providing a set of benchmarks or administrative presumption to which appeal could be made, is itself a telltale sign of the likely difficulties.[43]

As indicated, for reasons of speed and avoidance of conflict, it made sense – politically and administratively speaking – to base the initial transfer of functions order on the delegated powers that over the years the Welsh Office had come to exercise.[44] Constitutionally and legally speaking, however, or in terms of the effective and efficient operation of the new representative body, this was a flawed approach that can now be said to have haunted the devolved administration. Let us look more closely.

A Wales of bits and pieces

One of the recurring themes in this book is the way in which the fundamental democratic reform that is devolution has been bolted onto the pre-existing administrative framework. It is illustrated in this sphere both in terms of the distinction between primary and secondary law-making powers and the division of functions between the Welsh Office and the other central government departments.

In turn, the initial allocation of functions in Welsh devolution could not be coherent simply because it was predicated – following that misnomer of a policy document *Shaping the Vision* – on the incoherent, in the sense of a mass of statutory powers not drafted or allocated with devolution in mind. As Rachael Lomax, the then Permanent Secretary, was to observe ruefully:

> The . . . present powers [of the Secretary of State for Wales] have accumulated piecemeal over a long period of time, and the distinction between matters that are dealt with in primary and secondary legislation has reflected pragmatic considerations as much as principle.[45]

The lack of clear general principles governing the respective uses of primary and secondary legislation is in fact a familiar feature of the hitherto strongly unitary British constitution. In the words of the Kilbrandon Commission in 1973, 'the division between [legislative and executive powers] is not a precise one, and under the present arrangements they are not clearly separated'.[46] To this effect, in the absence of general clauses giving the Assembly subject area competencies in the prescribed 'fields', a major element of zigzag was part of the price to be paid for Welsh constitutional advancement. Many examples could be given, ranging across the broad spectrum of devolved powers: from the very important, for example the power to set NHS prescription charges, to the many minor or technical items with which secondary legislation so commonly deals.[47]

In the language of administrative law what is in issue here is the nature of the discretion to engage in formal rule-making (subordinate legislation).[48] Assembly discretion to legislate has thus constituted a patchwork, ranging from 'strong' discretion, the exercise of power couched in subjective terms, to the 'weak', the exercise of the power tightly confined and structured by provisions in the governing statute. And of course in the absence of statute there is no discretion, the Assembly being unable in the words of the minister 'to conjure legislation from the air and call it secondary legislation'.[49]

The scale of the variation and constraint evidently came as a shock to many Assembly Members.[50] Perhaps this is not surprising. The government propaganda that was the White Paper and associated documents served to foster a myth of broad policy autonomy. *Make your Mark on Wales* for example was a leaflet aimed at encouraging people to vote in the Assembly election. Typical is the following sentence: 'The National Assembly for Wales is your Assembly, with *the* power to decide what happens to education, health and jobs in Wales' (emphasis supplied).[51] Such statements were seriously misleading. The reality is a Wales of 'bits and pieces'.

A triumph of particularity

Yet this is only the half of it. Although section 22(1) of the GWA does not in terms prescribe the specific enumeration of powers for the purpose of transferring functions, this was the technique adopted: field by field, statute by statute, section by section. The method was one with which officials were familiar, being used not only in the Wales Act 1978 but also in the gradual expansion of Welsh Office responsibilities. The approach in other words exemplifies the general theme of administrative continuity in a changed constitutional landscape.

In the words of David Lambert, former Senior Legal Advisor at the Welsh Office, prior to devolution: 'It was never necessary to set out in a comprehensive legal document the exact powers of the Secretary of State for Wales. Officials and Ministers in Whitehall and Cardiff had acquired an understanding of these powers over the years . . . '[52] This lack of formality relates to the legal concept of the Office of Secretary of State as a collective body, one and indivisible, and in turn to the constitutional practice whereby statutory powers are typically conferred on 'the Secretary of State' as distinct from a named one.[53] As part of central government the Welsh Office thus acquired its responsibilities via a number of routes. A series of transfer of functions orders transferred specific functions from other ministers;[54] specific provisions in some Acts of Parliament enabled powers to be exercised differently in Wales;[55] and administrative agreements were made as to which minister would exercise powers given to the generic office of 'Secretary of State'. The general development can once again be seen as typically 'British' in character: *ad hoc* and piecemeal, with a strong dose of pragmatism. On the one hand, this was no passing phenomenon: by 1998, the Welsh Secretary was responsible for exercising by agreement some 5,000 ministerial powers. On the other hand, it remained the case that not all 'Secretary of State' powers were handled in Cardiff even in areas like transport that were primarily the responsibility of the Secretary of State for Wales. Furry edges however, could be the more easily accommodated inside the central government model precisely because of the administrative and political flexibility associated with the generic rubric of Secretary of State.

Since, however, devolution is predicated on the legal division of powers between different layers of government, there was now required – for the first time – a complete legal statement of what powers the Secretary of State for Wales was actually responsible for exercising prior to devolution. The result is an extraordinary document – the National Assembly for Wales (Transfer of Functions) Order 1999.[56] Some thirty pages long, it represents the results of a detailed trawl through some 350 Acts of Parliament: roughly a third of the statute book.

Nothing better illustrates the important role of law and lawyers in the Welsh model of devolution. A good measure of the scale and difficulty of the exercise is the *Technical Guide to the Transfer of Functions Order* produced by the Devolution Unit. Intended as an aid for 'those with a close and/or professional interest in policy areas where the Assembly will have functions', the *Guide* sought to provide Act by Act a brief description of each of the transferred functions. It was a most laborious task, involving a series of drafts and consultation exercises, and taking almost a year to complete. The final version weighed in at some 500 pages. Yet even this could not suffice, as the wording of the disclaimer made painfully clear:

> Where a discrepancy is apparent between the Guide and the Order or an Act of Parliament, the Order or the Act, as the case may be, has precedence. Users who require a definitive interpretation of the Order, or of any of the Acts of Parliament referred to below, should seek legal advice.[57]

In fact a clean-up exercise in the form of another general transfer order proved necessary, soon after the Assembly began operations. It also involved transfers in both directions: the Assembly losing powers as well as gaining them.[58] Those involved in the original drafting, however, can scarcely be blamed. Such was the unspeakable nature of the task that no team of lawyers could have produced the perfect result first time round.

At this point there is no substitute for looking at some of the transfer provisions. If what follows seems tedious then it will have served a purpose. The uncomfortable truth is that the Welsh scheme of devolution is founded on a tedious approach to constitution-building. It is why I call the original allocation of functions 'a triumph of particularity'.

Transfer in practice

The 1999 transfer order effectively elaborated on the framework for the allocation of functions established in section 22(1) of the devolution statute. Article 2 of the Order provided both for the ministerial functions under the statutes listed to be transferred, so far as exercisable in relation to Wales,[59] and for various categories of exceptions. The latter included reserved functions, joint powers (where the Assembly and a minister must act together to exercise a specific function), the concurrent powers ('where *either* the Assembly *or* a Minister may exercise the power in Wales'[60]), and requirements of approval or consent powers (typically exercised by the Treasury). In practice, although it was the declared policy to free the Assembly from the constraints of joint powers and consents as far as possible, the provisions of the Order showed only limited achievement.[61]

In sum the powers originally devolved were not inconsiderable, but the picture presented lacked all perspective or clarity. It was pragmatism carried to excess. The Order could thus hardly be described as user-friendly. Set out in chronological order and not by subject headings, the list of statutes contained in the Order was bewildering in its variety. Legislation such as the Race Relations Act 1976, the Local Government Finance Act 1988 and the Education Act 1996 jostled for attention with the likes of the Corn Returns Act 1882 and the Public Lavatories (Turnstiles) Act 1963, as well as some private and local statutes.

Again, in two-thirds of the Acts listed, only some powers were transferred. Literally abounding, the proviso was also expressed in many different forms. The extreme case was the Environment Act 1995 where the reader was treated to a page and a half of numerical and verbal exceptions. Once again, in David Lambert's words, the Order 'has had to dismember many Acts of Parliament which were not designed for such severance'.[62]

Two examples will suffice. The Road Traffic Regulation Act 1984, as its title suggests, is a statute of some consequence. So when are powers devolved to the Assembly? According to the Order:

Road Traffic Regulation Act 1984 (c.27) except –

(a) section 17(2) and (3) with respect to special roads generally;
(b) sections 20, 21 and 23;
(c) section 25 (other than subsection (4) together with the other provisions of section 25 so far as relating thereto);
(d) section 28;
(e) section 64 other than so far as it confers the power to – (i) prescribe a variant of any sign of a type prescribed by 'the Ministers' and carrying words in English, being a variant identical with a sign of that type except for the substitution or addition of words in Welsh (and any increase in size needed to accommodate the substituted or added words); and (ii) authorise signs not otherwise prescribed;
(f) section 65 so far as it relates to the giving of general directions;
(g) section 81;
(h) section 85(2) so far as it relates to the giving of general directions;
(i) sections 86, 88, 95 to 97, 99 to 106, 130 to 132, 136 to 140, 141A and Schedule 6.

It is directed that the function under section 128 shall be exercisable by the Assembly concurrently with the Secretary of State.

Clearly this is impenetrable unless one happens to have to hand the text of the statute. The treatment of section 64 is wonderfully convoluted. A portion of statutory power is excepted or reserved; a slice of that portion is devolved to the Assembly. What this actually means is that the Assembly is prevented from changing the shape of road signs but may enlarge them in accordance with language policy. Such have been the minutiae of Welsh executive devolution.

A personal favourite is the allocation of functions under the Destructive Imported Animals Act 1932. Transfer was secured by the Order:

except that the functions under sections 1, 2, and 10, so far as they relate to the importation of the types of animals to which this Act relates, are transferred to the Assembly so far as they have been transferred to the Secretary of State by the 1969 transfer order.

How should this be translated? The statutory purpose is in fact to prohibit or control the importation into and the keeping within Great Britain of animals like muskrat and for exterminating those that may be at large. Although not apparent on its face, the effect of the Order was to give the Assembly sole powers of licensing and destruction in Wales.[63] However, in relation to importation, the designated powers were to be exercisable jointly with the UK minister. Such was the arrangement involving the Secretary of State for Wales that happened to be reached in 1969.[64] And so on and on.

An important variation on a theme was signalled by Article 3 of the Order:

> Any reference in this Order to a function of a Minister of the Crown under an enactment includes a reference to any functions of that Minister which are included in any scheme, regulations, rules, order, bye-laws or other instrument having effect under or in relation to that enactment, and the power to confer functions on that Minister by any such scheme, regulations, rules, order, bye-laws or other instrument shall have effect as a power to confer such functions on the Assembly.

The effect of the provision was to transfer an inchoate mass of ministerial powers in subordinate legislation to the Assembly. Suffice it to say that a mapping exercise of what these powers might be was ongoing three years later.[65]

Administrative and political dialogue

It should not be supposed that the original empowerment of the Assembly was a purely technical affair. The model of executive devolution in fact serves to accentuate the importance of administrative politics in the legal and constitutional construction. Negotiation on the official plane, far from the public gaze: another important strand in the closed and elite form of constitution-building that has characterized the Welsh devolutionary development is identified here.

Insiders attest to the standard Whitehall mixture of give and take, to a heavy emphasis on personal dealings, and – on occasion more virulently than before – to turf wars. An official involved in producing the 1999 Order gives a whiff of the flavour:

> If the . . . process illustrates anything about the way government works it is to do with quite how entrenched ministers' and departments' views can become in interpreting what would appear to be a fairly straightforward construction . . . and quite how many obstacles can be thrown in the way.[66]

Not that central government is a monolith, or that much in the exchanges was other than routine. Notably, the then Department of Environment, Transport and the Regions was generally seen in the Assembly as the least accommodating, not least in its guise as the department that claimed to 'speak for England' in the post-devolutionary counsels of the United Kingdom. A struggle for influence in an administrative terrain characterized by great interfaces of policy management and implementation, and in particular, by cross-border issues, helps to explain what the same official described as 'the black arts of the negotiations'. In his words:

> We started running into difficulties when Whitehall departments made pleas for concurrency not out of any sensible case of 'well we have these distinct operations in Wales' but because 'we don't trust you buggers in Cardiff' . . . The single issue that caused us more problems than anything else was water. Sorting it required about half a dozen meetings between senior officials with the Cabinet Office really trying to knock heads together . . . The extent to which the subject was used as a peg on which to hang suspicions about devolution was really, really striking.[67]

So much, it might be said, for rational decision-making in the allocation of functions. Alternatively it might be asked why the Assembly could not be trusted to act responsibly in the grave matter of the shape of road signs. Whither the assumption of cooperation or 'partnership' between administrations at these initial stages?

Legal complexity: political and administrative difficulties

Returning to Wales, a different type of dynamic has been engendered here, in the sense of dissatisfaction – not least in the local legal community[68] – with the labyrinthine detail of the so-called 'devolution settlement'. In turn, the fact that the Richard Commission on the Assembly's powers and electoral arrangements has now been directed to probe the consequences of the particular allocation of powers in the Welsh scheme says much.[69]

Let us help the commission. First, the evident patchwork of devolved functions serves to fuel demands for additional powers from Westminster. This has been a constant refrain among Assembly Members. Expressed slightly differently, the evident complexity operates to underscore the unstable character of the devolutionary scheme. Or, as one might say, the 'technical' is 'political', being apt to feed back into the ongoing constitutional debate. It suffices to quote the Presiding Officer: 'devolving "secondary legislation", as a category, makes no constitutional sense, because it is itself legislatively various'.[70]

Secondly, the devolved administration may have difficulty in achieving coherent policies when faced with rule-making powers of uneven width and depth. The difficulty is apt to surface in so-called 'cross-cutting issues', where especially by reason of the *ad hoc* historical development a matching division of primary and secondary legislation cannot be taken for granted. The original design of the scheme was not well suited to that most fashionable of official pursuits: 'joined-up government'.

At the risk of stating the obvious, this issue is liable to play differently in different administrative contexts. The mismatch may cut peculiarly deep in the Welsh case of small-country governance, where the flexibility to range across traditional departmental dividing lines is otherwise a particular advantage. Then again, there may be ready recourse to other levers in what in later chapters is called 'the closeness of Wales'.[71] A different but related point: it is only natural that different political actors should seek to maximize or minimize the extent of such difficulty.

Thirdly, the principle of intelligibility, which is considered so important in constitutional documents, is offended. Who other than a lawyer or official could give any meaningful guidance on the legislative competence of the Assembly? This feature is the more striking because of the great stress that has been placed in the devolutionary design on transparency and bringing government closer to the people. Intelligibility of functions or powers is a *sine qua non* of the practice of inclusiveness.

Going on: reality and rhetoric

Part of the logic of executive devolution, the original transfer order is gradually being superseded by statute as the basis of Assembly functions. Suffice it to note at this stage that there has been no great change in approach. On the one hand, substantial additional powers have been given. On the other hand, there has been little consistency in the ways the powers have been conferred, effectively piling complexity on complexity. And sometimes the provision is mean, on other occasions generous to the Assembly.[72] To this effect, a point that has been given insufficient attention in the Welsh devolutionary development is the extent to which the UK legislative programme is driven by individual departments.

All this is the more striking because ahead of the devolution referendum the message was once again decidedly upbeat. Ron Davies may be quoted:

> The devolution now being proposed will undoubtedly have a profound effect . . . on the Westminster legislative process . . . Having created the Assembly, the next Labour Government will want to ensure that in as many areas as possible for which the Assembly has responsibility, power to act is devolved. Increasingly, therefore, legislation framed by Labour governments on matters such as education or the Health Service will allow for maximum discretion at the Welsh level . . . Labour's commitment [is] to ensure all Westminster legislation will, wherever possible, reflect the demands of devolution . . .[73]

The devolution White Paper could also be read in similar vein:

> As a general principle, the Government expects Bills that confer new powers and relate to the Assembly's functions, such as education, health and housing, will

provide for the powers to be exercised separately and differently in Wales; and to be exercised by the Assembly.[74]

After the Welsh Office

In the light of the discussion perhaps one can understand the allure of a single, general principle: the Assembly to have those powers that would be allocated to Wales under the central government model of territorial administration. The principle could clearly be a useful one in dealing with recalcitrant Whitehall departments, most obviously in terms of attempts to whittle down or rein back the Assembly's powers. It could also be said to represent a continuation of the original devolutionary policy – the transfer of powers from the Welsh Office to the Assembly – part of what may now be labelled a primary design feature of substitution.[75] And 'building blocks': its pull inside the devolved administration in the early months is attested by an Assembly official:

> The test we always try to apply and with varying degrees of success with Whitehall departments . . . is if there was no devolution which Secretary of State would you expect to get the power . . . We haven't got much on the statute book so far but what we've got is pretty much what we expected, what we would have had, had there still been a Secretary of State for Wales.[76]

But such a principle will not wash. First, in adopting an essentially static view of the Welsh constitutional development the approach grates with the basic legislative design of the devolution statute. More especially, it is no defence to equate the principle with the model of executive devolution. As this book has already been at pains to stress, there is more than one approach available under that general rubric, and in particular within the flexible framework with an in-built capacity for change that is the GWA.

Second, it does not do simply to read across from one constitutional model to the other. There is now the small fact of a national, representative institution to consider. Let us also keep in mind the loss of administrative and political flexibility that the scheme of executive devolution has entailed, in the sense that powers previously allocated under the general rubric of 'Secretary of State' have now to be identified as the powers or otherwise of the Assembly. To seek to apply the same general principle in such changed legal conditions is a recipe for difficulties, and will tend to err on the side of caution.

Third but related, a historical approach of this kind suggests a clear basis for allocation of powers to the Secretary of State for Wales prior to devolution. However, as Rachel Lomax observed, and the original Transfer of Functions

Order made so abundantly clear, this never happened. Welsh Office powers 'growed like Topsy'. The methodology of the principle is thus flawed from the very beginning. As regards the ongoing allocation of powers, who can say what powers the Secretary of State for Wales would have but for the Assembly? So let us depart this realm of constitutional fiction. Different approaches need to be ventured, and novel procedures tried and tested, with a view to making the best of the allocation of functions – or of a bad job. We leave the point here, to pick it up in chapter 9.

3. THE FISCAL CONSTITUTION

Vital to the successful operation of multi-layered democracy is the financial element, and, in particular, with a view to promoting economic stability and limiting disparities in regional income and spending power, the provisions on fiscal transfer. Viewed in comparative perspective, the UK arrangements for devolved government are once again distinctive.[77] On the one hand, there is an exceptional degree of central control, built up on the reservation of responsibility for UK fiscal policy, macroeconomic policy and public expend-iture allocation across the United Kingdom in the hands of the Treasury. On the other hand, and so very 'British', the fiscal constitution is aptly described as an unwritten constitution. Continuity and change: the current arrange-ments are to this extent another brilliant example of the constitutional development that is devolution being grafted onto the pre-existing political and administrative arrangements.

The degree of fiscal constraint on the policy diversity suggested by devolution is then a vital consideration in evaluating the constitutional design. Assembly discretion to determine and manage spending priorities is effectively confined within the parameters established by the internal budgetary process of the UK government. Much has also been heard of a lack of fiscal accountability: the concept, to adapt a most famous constitutional saying, of 'representation without taxation'. It is the Parliament in Edinburgh, and not the Assembly in Cardiff, that has a modest tax-varying power.[78]

'Money talks.' It is not surprising to learn that the state of the fiscal constitution is also one of the most challenging and contentious issues in the overarching UK devolutionary development.[79] Some parts of the Union would appear to do well, others poorly, so generating complaints of fiscal 'unfairness'. And enter now the English regions into the equation. Vital building block it is, but this matter will run and run.

All these features are highlighted in the case of Wales, not least because of the fragile state of the local economy. Harsh fact: Wales is financially dependent on England and will continue to be so. More precisely, Wales is consistently found at or near the bottom of the UK regional league tables of income and competitiveness. Indeed, over the period since devolution was previously on offer in 1979, Welsh GDP per head has fallen from 88 per cent to some 80 per cent of the UK average. Suffice it to add that the Welsh Assembly Government's own target of raising this figure to 90 per cent over the next decade is stretching credulity.[80]

Treasury principles: block and formula

Devolution throws into sharp relief the structures and processes of the system of territorial finance. Pre-devolution, matters proceeded on the basis of 'a mutual understanding between parties within the policy network, the implementation of which is subject to both sides observing the behavioural "rules of the game" '.[81] The arrangements thus epitomized the British tradition of 'club' or 'group' government. In contrast, there is today much greater openness and transparency. To this effect, a statement of funding policy that was produced by the Treasury on the eve of devolution explicitly recognized the relevance of the constitutional reform to the culture of public administration. Far from 'private' government it is now a case of the 'goldfish bowl', which in turn reflects and reinforces the rise of a fiscal politics:

> The establishment of the . . . devolved administrations creates a requirement to define clearly the new financial relationships to be established in the United Kingdom . . . . Their funding arrangements will be the subject of detailed scrutiny by the elected Members and those whom they represent. It is important, therefore, that the way in which the budget of each of the devolved administrations is determined should be clear, unambiguous and capable of examination and analysis . . .[82]

The Treasury paper is in fact one of the most important constitutional documents in the reinvention of the union state. Key principles of the fiscal constitution have thus been expounded by way of codification:

- All United Kingdom tax revenues and analogous receipts are passed to the UK Consolidated Fund. Decisions about the allocation of UK public expenditure rest with the UK government.
- Changes in the budgetary provision of the devolved administrations funded by UK tax revenues or by borrowing will generally be linked to changes in planned spending on comparable public services by departments of the UK government. This linkage will generally be achieved by means of the population-based Barnett formula.
- Allocation of public expenditure between the services under the control of the devolved administrations will be for them to determine.
- The devolved administrations will be fully accountable for the proper control

and management of their public expenditure allocation and for securing economy, efficiency and value for money, especially through scrutiny by the relevant Parliament or Assemblies.

- Where decisions of UK government departments or agencies lead to additional costs for any of the devolved administrations, or vice versa, the body whose decision leads to the additional cost will meet that cost.[83]

The principles incorporate the so-called 'block and formula' system of territorial finance, which was developed in the late 1970s when devolution was previously in prospect.[84] Briefly, a block of resources is made available by central government, with marginal changes in public expenditure being dealt with on the basis of the mathematical equation that is the 'Barnett formula'. The system has in turn operated in the context of the three-year Comprehensive Spending Review (CSR) of UK public expenditure. Within this structure a territorial administration like the Welsh Office would have had responsibility for the planning and control of spending on all the relevant public service programmes based in the territory. Constitutionally speaking, the major change associated with devolution is that the ordering of territorial priorities is no longer in the hands of a Secretary of State operating within the confines of the strong UK convention of collective cabinet responsibility. The 'power of the block' now exercised by the Welsh Assembly Government is of the very essence of the devolutionary development.

The Barnett formula is best described as rough and ready. In essence, Wales receives a population-based share of changes in planned spending on analogous programmes in England. Post-devolution, the calculation of the population ratios has been conducted on an annual basis – more transparency. The second calculation, of the extent to which the departmental programmes in central government are comparable with the services carried out at the territorial level, is itself an obvious source of controversy.

Convergence and divergence: the fiscal dimension

The block and formula system has offered a number of advantages. Maximum budgetary discretion inside the block clearly fits with the administrative and political value of responsiveness to local needs. This feature is the more notable when read in light of the systems of specific grants familiar in many federal systems, or the broad comparative rubric of hypothecation.

Once again, however, the case of Wales will serve to highlight the countervailing pressures. It is not simply that in the real world of public administration the principle of freedom to allocate the block between programmes is liable to operate only at the margins. A history of close integration with England – a porous border – can here be seen to exacerbate the pressures to follow suit in such important – and sensitive – areas of public spending as health and education. And public pronouncements are but one way by which central government may seek to influence such matters.[85]

The Barnett formula may also be described as an instrument of conflict avoidance. To this end, it substitutes for an annual squabble for funds involving, in the case of Wales, Treasury ministers, the Secretary of State and (now) the Assembly cabinet. Expressed slightly differently, the formula has the virtue of being a simple and practicable means of settling what are essentially political decisions relating to resource allocation. Indeed, the lack of transparency prior to devolution could be described as functional, with the disguise of transfer of resources serving to mediate tensions inside the Union state.

A basic contradiction is that spending decisions for England – taken in the UK cabinet – drive the expenditure levels of the devolved administrations. This is hardly the dispersal of power suggested by the devolutionary slogan of 'bringing government closer to the people'. Viewed in this perspective, there is an underlying lack of fit with a form of national devolution that – even in Wales – confers significant policy-making powers at the sub-state level.

There is further a high price to pay for simplicity: the failure of the Barnett formula to deal with the relative spending needs of the territories or regions. The formula might even be described as a relict, since the baseline expenditure derives from 1979 when the last official needs assessment study was conducted.[86] That the size of the block is in turn the product of incremental changes made under the formula over many years also goes to show the strong pragmatic quality of the fiscal constitution.

The longer-term aim of the formula was to bring about convergence in per capita public spending across the UK. Such is the so-called 'Barnett squeeze', whereby those areas – like Wales – that enjoy higher than average levels of expenditure receive slightly lower proportionate increases in spending. The 'squeeze' is ongoing, an important fact of life for the new representative institution, but has also been slow to take effect, not least because over the years a significant degree of so-called 'formula bypass' has been sanctioned. As the Assembly cabinet has quickly learned, an element of (intergovernmental) bargaining and negotiation is also part of the process, since the formula is not applied rigidly in all circumstances, and some significant budgetary items lie outside its purview.[87]

The soft law option

But what, the lawyer may ask, of the financial provisions in the devolution legislation? On the one hand, the statute elaborates a formidable system of audit.[88] In terms of the Treasury principles, this reflects and reinforces the idea of establishing the financial accountability of the devolved administrations at the territorial level, which itself has been a major constitutional development. So typical of the original design of Welsh executive devolution, the provisions also represent a halfway house. As well as enhancing Welsh governmental machinery – the Auditor General for Wales – the statute has retained a supervisory jurisdiction for that most powerful of Parliament's servants, the Comptroller and Auditor General.[89]

On the other hand, section 80(1), which provides the basic mechanism for funding and so, technically speaking, is one of the most important provisions in the whole statute, states baldly: 'The Secretary for State shall from time to time make payments to the Assembly out of money provided by Parliament of such amounts as he may determine'.

In the words of the Welsh Office Devolution Unit, this is the idea of 'a framework' for 'future Government decisions' maximally applied. At one and the same time, the new representative institution is distanced from the UK Parliament and a pivotal position is established in the devolution settlement for the Secretary of State for Wales. The minister has thus been assigned the not insignificant role of 'commentator' in the annual negotiations between the devolved administration and the Treasury.[90]

For its part, the Assembly, strictly speaking, has no guarantees. A future Conservative minister for example would not be bound to adhere to a policy of only subtracting from the block the cost of running the Wales Office (successor in title to the Welsh Office (and now incorporated in the newly established UK Department for Constitutional Affairs)).[91] Notably, during the proceedings on the Bill the government refused a series of attempts to draw the basis of funding within the ambit of the statute. In the words of the minister, 'The Barnett formula is a complex set of arrangements that does not lend itself to statutory imposition. Doing so would make the legislation – and the funding process – extremely cumbersome.'[92]

Such in essence is the unwritten character of the fiscal constitution. Administrative and political techniques, a non-use or avoidance of formal law: the approach fits the general preference in UK intergovernmental relations, as illustrated now in the system of concordats.[93] To the extent, it is worth adding, of a lack of formal procedural protection: specific statutory rights for the Assembly to be consulted and make representations on matters of territorial finance. Substance and process, the devolved administration may thus be characterized as doubly dependent in financial matters.

Starting out

The Assembly started life on the basis of a population share relative to England of 5.94 per cent. Meanwhile the comparability figures had been calculated as follows:[94]

Department/programme	Wales (%)
Domestic agriculture	100.0
Health	99.2
Culture, Media and Sport	87.3
Education and Employment	75.8
Environment, Transport and the Regions	70.0
Cabinet Office and Parliament	0
Home Office	0
Lord Chancellor's Department	0
Social Security	0

The exercise usefully serves to illustrate the scale and pattern of the devolutionary development. At the risk of stating the obvious, the fact that the Welsh health budget was almost 100 per cent comparable indicates that virtually all of the spending lines of the central government department are devolved. By contrast, the figures for education and employment have reflected the fact of continuing UK, GB and England and Wales administrative paradigms, as well as the 'Wales-only' one.[95] The work of central government's Employment Service is a good example. Again, as the functions of the Assembly expand, so these figures are apt to alter.

At the time of devolution, the size of the annual block stood at some £7.3 billion. Anticipated increases, to some £8 billion in the financial year 2001/2, were larger than in previous years because of extra provision being made available for comparable English programmes, primarily for health and education. The block itself accounted for over 95 per cent of the territorial expenditure.[96]

But what, it may be asked, of the non-devolutionary part of the story? According to the Treasury figures, around half of the public expenditure incurred 'for the benefit' of Wales was on programmes that remained the responsibility of central government. The breakdown (in table 3) of the position immediately prior to the wholesale transfer of functions from the Welsh Office is in turn another very practical measure of the constitutional development.

'The economic case for a Welsh Assembly':[97] once again, the figures serve to convey the scale of the challenge that now confronted the devolved administration. An overall level of per capita public spending in Wales some 14 per cent above the UK average; disproportionate levels of expenditure on social security reflecting the poor economic condition of large parts of the country: this was local financial dependency highlighted. A taste of things to come, conditions were also ripe for covetous eyes in the direction of Scotland. The Barnett formula has in practice preserved a situation where per capita expenditure in the three Celtic lands is above that in England. But there is symmetry, and there is asymmetry, as a later study would show:

Table 3: Identifiable expenditure on services in Wales, 1997/1998 (£m)[98]

	Total	Welsh Office	Other UK govt depts
Agriculture, fisheries, forestry and food	262	212	49
Trade, industry, energy and employment	437	320	116
Roads and transport	442	357	85
Housing	310	304	6
Other environmental services	701	683	18
Law, order and protective services	758	–	758
Education	1,837	1,707	130
Culture, media and sport	95	85	11
Health and personal social services	2,909	2,909	–
Social security	5,583	–	5,583
Miscellaneous expenditure	89	89	–
TOTAL	**13,423**	**6,667**	**6,756**

Following the introduction of the Barnett Formula Wales became less prosperous relative to the rest of the UK, while Scotland's relative position improved notably. Scottish prosperity levels moved close to the UK average, but transfers to Scotland remained substantial. Welsh prosperity levels declined relative to the rest of the UK, but transfer has not become more generous . . . Wales is the least prosperous economic region in Britain and tax per head is only four-fifths of the UK average . . . In spite of distinctly lower levels of public expenditure per head in Wales than in Scotland, the gap between expenditure and tax is greater in Wales . . . By the standards of other countries and given the objective of horizontal equity, the level of transfer to Wales is not over generous. Scotland is different.[99]

Promise or threat: enough has been said to demonstrate both the significance and the contestable nature of relevant statements in the White Paper *A Voice for Wales*:

Annual changes to the Welsh Block will be calculated by the population-based formula used at the moment. These arrangements based on the Block and formula have worked in practice, producing fair settlements for Wales in annual public expenditure rounds and allowing the Secretary of State for Wales to take his spending decisions in accordance with Welsh needs and priorities . . . The formula will be updated from time to time to take account of population changes. Any other changes to the formula will only be on the basis of a full study of relevant spending needs, to be carried forward in consultation with the Assembly.[100]

Notably, a similar commitment was made in the White Paper *Scotland's Parliament*.[101]

To expand the argument, there is a powerful case for basic revision of the fiscal constitution in the devolutionary context; for example along the lines of an independent grants commission with power to determine how much each territory (and English region) should receive to maintain services at the same standard.[102] Experience teaches however that the role of HM Treasury is not readily diminished! Nor can one ignore the force of political entrenchment. In the words of the minister, the 'Government's position was clearly set out in the two White Papers on which the referendum campaigns in Scotland and Wales were fought and won'.[103] The equation is a stark one: the promise that a detailed study of spending needs would precede substantial revision to the block and formula system; the fact that any such study would be highly subjective and potentially politically explosive in Scotland.[104] The Barnett formula may only be soft law, but it is not so easily replaced.

The European dimension

Special reference must here be made to the topic that would dominate much of the first year in the life of the Assembly: the European dimension to public finance in the guise of the structural funds. Wales is in fact one of the largest recipients of structural funding in the current EU programming period (2000–6), with some two-thirds of the territory – west Wales and the Valleys – having been designated for concentrated support as a 'lagging region' under the key European Regional Development Fund (ERDF).[105] As well as highlighting once again the major economic and social problems at local level, this has presented an unrivalled opportunity, including, it may be said, for the new devolved administration to (be seen to) make a difference. An EU allocation of some £1.2 billion – the stakes could not have been higher.

A notable feature is the passage of esoteric concepts into the political lexicon of Wales: not just 'Objective 1', but also 'match funding' and even 'PES cover'. Nothing better illustrates the way in which fiscal politics has moved centre stage post-devolution – a development accompanied by not a little confusion.

Two further Treasury principles are relevant in this context:

- Responsibility for contributions to and distribution of receipts from the European Commission rests solely with the UK government.
- Consistent with the arrangements for departments of the UK government, the devolved administrations will normally be expected to accommodate additional pressures on their budgets.[106]

In fact, right from the outset, the designation of west Wales and the Valleys for so-called 'Objective 1 funding' also presented the devolved administration with a major headache. For the purpose of the structural funds, the spending is supposed to be over and above the resources already deployed by the domestic authorities on regional development: the principle of 'additionality' (and not substitution). But further, and exemplifying patterns of Treasury dominance, there had always been close linkage with central government funding by reason of the channelling of the structural funds through the Public Expenditure Survey (PES) or planning and control process. More particularly, ERDF provision had been included in the block grant and made subject to the operation of the Barnett formula, which meant that changes in the eligibility for ERDF receipts in (more prosperous) England influenced the level of provision made available to Wales. Clearly, however, the scale of the interaction was now greatly increased by reason of the step change in the volume of the structural fund money available. In short, in paradoxical fashion, the great prize of Objective 1 status was bound under the established UK financial system to generate substantial additional pressures on the budget of the devolved administration.

On the one hand, there was the primary problem of 'PES cover' – the total sum of provision within the block to cover expected ERDF receipts. According to established practice, there is some flexibility for underspend and carry-over, but the books should balance over the life of a structural funds programme. On the other hand, there was the issue of 'match funding', which arises from the co-financing rules of EU regional policy; for example under Objective 1, ERDF payments of up to 75 per cent of the total project costs. From where were the extra resources to be found? Central government orthodoxy: the Treasury had prior to devolution effectively maintained its view that the Assembly would have to find cover and matched funding for EU receipts from within the existing block grant.[107] Thus at the outset the devolved administration had little choice but to scrabble around for funds to initiate the programme, while continuing to pursue negotiations with the Treasury for special treatment.

This is the backdrop to a prolonged wrangle in the Assembly, which famously would culminate in the overthrow of Alun Michael as chief minister. The role and relation of the budgetary cycles of central and territorial government are brought sharply into focus here. Effectively, the attempt was being made to second-guess the forthcoming central government process: a territorial politics of pressure or leverage. Mr Michael was thus charged with failing to deliver that which under the ordinary process of UK financial planning and control could not be delivered, namely additional resources from the Treasury prior to its assessment of competing bids. Such it may be said are the new dynamics of devolution; and, in particular, of a novel form of fiscal politics in the constitution.[108]

Greasing the wheels: continuing controversy

In the event, the Comprehensive Spending Review of 2000 was to set the financial tone of the Assembly's early years. Essential fact: courtesy of New

Labour, devolution has coincided with an exceptional period of growth in UK spending on public services. Devolved expenditure in Wales was thus set to be £2 billion higher by the financial year 2003–4, a real-term increase of some 5.4 per cent over the next three years. This was government largess on a huge scale: constitutionally and politically speaking, a greasing of the wheels of the new Welsh representative institution.

Following the demise of Alun Michael, attention naturally focused on the Chancellor's response to the issue of Objective 1 funding. A leading example of 'formula bypass', the Treasury now came up with substantial extra sums for the programme – some £420 million over the three-year period. The general increases in the block also helped to pave the way for additional match funding. The case for differential treatment in respect of a unique set of budgetary circumstances in Wales had been accepted.

The product of an arduous official negotiation behind the scenes, this is aptly described as 'a classic British fudge'.[109] Suffice it to say that the political case for an adequate settlement was compelling, not least in helping to bring some much-needed internal stability to the Assembly. Turning the argument round, it can plausibly be argued that without the Assembly Wales would not have been so favourably treated. A voice for Wales, severe local democratic controversy, shared political sympathies in London and Cardiff: all the major elements were in place.

A different but related point: 'fiscal transparency' should not be taken at face value. In the fashionable jargon, there are 'statistical numbers', and there are 'spun numbers'. Predictably, the trading of different figures on territorial finance has now become part of the staple diet of Assembly debates. From esoteric concepts to proclaimed 'successes' or 'shortfalls', as for example in competing definitions of appropriate levels of match funding, the Objective 1 affair further illuminates this general feature. 'The Barnett formula – controversy': such is the tenor of political life in post-devolutionary Wales.[110]

Table 4 summarizes the CSR out-turn for Wales in 2002. The increase was an average of some 5 per cent a year in real terms over the three-year period. The immediate explanation was the Chancellor's announcement of large increases in government expenditure on health in England, leading through the operation of the Barnett formula to major increases – or in the economists' jargon 'consequentials' – in the Welsh block. In addition, the Assembly will once again be receiving support over and above the territorial allocation under the formula: some £500 million between 2003–4 and 2005–6. More and more grease – at some £7.3 billion, the original Assembly block now seems but a distant memory!

All at one with the new dynamics of fiscal politics, inter-regional comparison is itself something of a growth industry post-devolution. The following snapshot (table 5) will suffice to show the major discrepancies across the UK; and, in particular, the adverse situation of the poorer English regions.

Table 4: Comprehensive Spending Review settlement for Wales – July 2002
(£ million)[111]

£ million	2002–3	2003–4	2004–5	2005–6
Resource budget	8,829	9,655	10,240	11,000
Capital budget	801	830	919	999
Total departmental expenditure limit (DEL)[112]	9,424	10,275	10,941	11,774

Table 5: Identifiable expenditure per head by region/territory (1999–2000)[113]

	Scotland	Wales	N. Ireland	England	North East	North West	Y&H*	East Midlands
Education	126	100	136	96	100	101	96	93
Health and social security services	199	110	111	97	102	100	98	88
Roads and transport	130	112	89	96	96	97	74	85
Housing	176	145	325	82	57	90	71	35
Other environmental services	131	168	106	93	117	106	45	90
Law, order and protective services	96	96	206	97	104	101	93	90
Trade, industry, energy and employment	149	113	255	90	103	94	91	96
Agriculture, fisheries, food and forestry	267	155	283	73	75	73	75	73
Culture, media and sport	99	157	60	99	143	88	87	81
Total	125	112	142	95	102	99	91	88

UK = 100
* = Yorkshire and Humberside

Wales is shown occupying a middling position, with per capita public spending some 12 per cent higher than the UK average, there being little sign here of convergence.

Perhaps then it is not surprising to learn that in the face of growing demands for the introduction of a new fiscal settlement based on a thorough review of expenditure needs, the Assembly cabinet has counselled caution.[114] Under existing conditions of 'formula bypass' as associated with Objective 1, the so-called Barnett 'squeeze' will typically be felt less strongly in Wales than elsewhere. A relatively generous settlement for Wales, the political imperatives of the UK devolutionary development, why would this Labour-led junior partner of the Union seek to make the running?

Yet looking forwards, it is safe to say that Wales has little to fear from a principle of equalization according to spending need. A peculiar geography, high concentrations of socio-economic deprivation, a raft of dismal statistics on such matters as morbidity and mortality: in terms both of the demand for, and costs of supplying, core public services, there clearly is a powerful case to make in terms of so-called 'fiscal fairness'.

In view of the benign financial conditions in which the Assembly has been operating, the constitutional aspect deserves a special emphasis. The conjunction of the devolutionary development with huge injections of public money has thus helped to disguise the strong measure of centralized control or lack of security for the devolved administration(s) in the domestic financial process. This has been 'the happy time'. One day there will be retrenchment.

CONCLUSION – DESIGN PROBLEMS

Examination of the basic building blocks confirms the *sui generis* nature of the Welsh devolutionary scheme. Turning first to the legislation, the design of the GWA was fated to disappoint precisely because of its origins in a set of uneasy political compromises. In functional terms the statute now serves as a written constitution for a 'national' polity, but saying this is not to imply that the GWA represents a full and final settlement, or that it constitutes an appropriate basic law for somewhere called a new model Wales: quite the reverse.

Judged in its own terms as a vehicle for executive devolution, the Act provides a workable though complicated framework. Fortunately, because the United Kingdom has a first-class civil service, some of the detail is excellent. So it is that increased potential has been factored into the scheme, better to allow for an ongoing process of political and administrative maturation at the territorial level. One of the most innovative aspects is the creation of a body of precepts structuring and informing the operations of the Assembly. This however should not be allowed to obscure the basic limitations in terms of institutional and legal capacity.

The empowerment of the Assembly has constituted a legal minefield. Specificity of powers and an absence of guiding principles concerning the allocation of functions, a basic lack of intelligibility: such is the prospect that greeted Assembly Members. Harsh it may be, but constitutionally and legally speaking the initial transfer of functions under the GWA is an object lesson in how not to proceed.

The close link between the process of delivering devolution and the quality of the product is amply demonstrated here. According to Ron Davies, in navigating internal Labour Party politics in favour of executive devolution, he 'did not envisage the administrative difficulties that are now seen to exist'.[115] This is hard to credit. That so many of the problems flow from the political decision to adopt as the template for devolution 'the powers currently held' by the Secretary of State for Wales is one of the basic truths of the constitutional development.

The fiscal constitution is one of the less convincing aspects of contemporary UK devolutionary policy. More especially, the scope for conflict of interest or competition between the territories and regions is graphically illustrated in the operation of the Barnett formula. On the one hand, this is a case where the formal symmetry of the constitutional arrangement should not be allowed to obscure a real or substantive asymmetry. On the other hand, the functional limits to soft law as a flexible or responsive tool of government are underscored by the technique of political entrenchment. As so often, 'for Wales see Scotland'.

Lastly, in terms of the constitutional development, the treatment of European funding illuminates the different modalities of the post-devolutionary system of multi-layered governance. Viewed in comparative perspective, many of the matters raised are familiar from federal systems, but they represent a novel departure in the British system of public admin-istration, which notably involves more transparency now. That the most contentious policy issue in its first year related not to what the Assembly should do, but to what the Treasury should do for the Assembly, is a telling feature. It is all part of an official culture of dependency, financial and otherwise, which the scheme of executive devolution reflects and reinforces.

3

Strange Anatomy

It never ceases to surprise me how few people, outside Wales, have any idea of the nature – and novelty – of the National Assembly for Wales.

Jon Shortridge, Permanent Secretary[1]

It's as well to recall that – as a Corporate Body – it is to the National Assembly as a whole that power has been devolved . . . It was designed as a hybrid – a Cabinet and Committee model . . .

Ron Davies[2]

Constitutional framework, empowerment and finance: what then it may be asked of the internal architecture of the Assembly? A 'national' representative institution and law-making body, but not (yet) a Parliament; a Welsh Assembly Government and a Presiding Officer but no formal legal separation of powers; an ongoing process of practical rearrangement further and faster than could seriously have been anticipated: it is indeed an extraordinary entity.

The surprise is the Permanent Secretary's surprise. As well as the usual geopolitical considerations – Wales the junior partner of the Union state, Wales a peripheral place in the European Union – the internal architecture is sufficiently complex to engender a lack of constitutional understanding – inside as well as outside Wales. Local politicians and officials alike have continued to struggle with the singular nature of the beast.[3]

The uninterrupted nature of the local constitutional debate is a major theme of this chapter. *Pace* the so-called devolution settlement, this was only to be expected, and by reason not only of the major element of innovation, but also of 'the frustrations of a devolution scheme which is neither fish nor fowl'.[4] Basic concerns were raised in the parliamentary proceedings on the devolution legislation, only to be glossed over, and then to resurface inside the Assembly. The major institutional process of reform that has subsequently taken place inside the Assembly – the autochthonous Welsh constitutional development that is the subject of the next chapter – can only properly be understood by reference to the earlier legislative or parliamentary one.

Following the lead of Ron Davies, it is appropriate to begin with the concept of corporate identity, which is both a constitutional fundamental of the current devolutionary scheme and – like much else in that scheme – can be applied with varying degrees of enthusiasm. Also meriting special attention in the first part of the chapter is the shift during the passage of the devolution legislation towards a cabinet-style model of government for Wales, which is itself the precursor of a greater *de facto* separation of roles inside the Assembly.

The topic of the second section is introduced: the internal delegation of functions among the constituent elements of the Assembly. As mentioned in the Introduction to this book, the way in which the system is operated goes to the very character and status of the new representative institution, as well as constituting the essential legal framework for the day-to-day working relationships of ministers, Members and officials.

The third section is of a different order, being directed first to the archi-tectural design of the Assembly's expansive committee system; and, second, to the elaboration of the founding principles or core constitutional values, and specifically to the place in the constitutional scheme of freedom of information. The discussion picks up on a strong internal design feature of checks and balances, as well as on the original justification for Welsh devolution as stated in the White Paper, namely greater accountability in Wales for the workings of the territorial system of government.

1. THE CORPORATE BODY

Dull and technical though it may appear at first sight, the designation of the National Assembly as 'a body corporate' in section 1 of the GWA is a critical feature of the Welsh constitutional development – in political and administrative as well as legal terms. At one and the same time, it stands for the unique character of that development, or as I prefer the 'strange anatomy' of the new representative institution, and has proved a chief bone of contention.

De jure: administrative and political leanings

As the collective repository of legal functions, the Assembly is clearly distinguished in *de jure* terms from, say, the Scottish model of devolution, the pairing of a Parliament with a statutorily empowered administration. The lack in the GWA of a clear legal separation between the executive and the legislative functions of the Assembly was thus seen in the Introduction to this book as being classificatory of devolutionary form in the case of Wales. In turn, it is only natural that Winston Roddick QC, the first Counsel General to the Assembly, should have greatly emphasized this aspect. In his words:

'Because the Assembly is a corporate body with a single legal personality conflicts of interest within it are not legally possible.'[5]

From the viewpoint of the lawyer, the fact of corporate status is the more striking by reason of the different kinds of functions that are devolved to the Assembly. Account must therefore be taken of the bundle of executive and administrative responsibilities previously exercised by the Secretary of State for Wales: from the making of subordinate legislation to local financial provision, and on through a broad representative function[6] to special tasks, for example a quasi-judicial role in planning cases. Again, far from being confined to the core operating arrangements for the Assembly, the legal concept is one that reappears in particular elements of the devolutionary scheme, for example in terms of the constitutional position of the Counsel General, or the definition of so-called 'devolution issues' in the courts.[7]

Constitutionally speaking, the choice of the corporate body fitted with the official aim of devolution as being to democratize the all-Welsh tier of government. The Assembly replacing the Secretary of State for Wales in the exercise of functions, and being regarded as performing them on behalf of the Crown:[8] such is the original design feature of 'substitution'. However, as the Counsel General was quick to observe, 'the direct discharge of [what formerly were] central government functions by an elected body is a novel and challenging concept'.[9]

In view of the efforts that have subsequently been made to limit the consequences of corporate status – which, to anticipate the argument, may be visualized in terms of a parliamentary body struggling to break free – it is worth re-emphasizing the administrative and political factors involved in the original design. First, nothing better illustrates the strong sense of continuity in the Welsh devolutionary development than the reading across of corporate status from the Wales Act 1978. A related failure to think through the implications in contemporary conditions of constitutional and political development has resulted in a peculiarly painful process of delivery and growth of the infant body.

Secondly, there is the way in which, drawing on the 'bottom-up' approach to devolution familiar in Welsh Labour Party circles, or the local government model with which the concept is classically associated, corporate legal status could plausibly be presented as a line in the sand. Constitutionally speaking, it further represents a block on, or distancing from the idea of, a Parliament for Wales.

De facto: minimal and maximal scenarios

Local actors – the politicians and officials as well as lawyers – have had in a very real sense to learn to live with corporate status. While the devolutionary scheme has typically allowed for dealing with the concept in minimalist fashion – so allowing the basic constitutional idea of separation of powers a greater emphasis – the Assembly has at all times to respect or genuflect to the formal legal classification, courtesy of parliamentary sovereignty. Such are the conditions of a *de facto* form of constitutional engineering.

A different but related point: how far in practice the Assembly should operate in a corporate manner, in the sense of consensually and inclusively, has been at the heart of the question of the quality or 'feel' of this novel form of devolved administration. A close linkage between legal form and political culture ('a new kind of politics') was in fact a major element in the approach enunciated by the ministerial architect of Welsh devolution. According to Ron Davies:

> The structure of the Assembly and its the status as a body corporate will require (indeed, it will force) parties to work together. That approach doesn't weaken the political process, it strengthens it. Our new National Assembly will be the stronger for it; politics will be more mature and the electors will have a more informed choice when the rhetoric and posturing is swept away.[10]

An expansive concept of the corporate body was also viewed in a positive light by the well-known pressure group Charter 88. As presented in evidence to the National Assembly Advisory Group (NAAG), the group's vision of the political process was a Utopian one:

> It is important that the National Assembly should have an effective decision-making process, but this should not be to the exclusion of co-operation, deliberation and consensus. National Assembly Members should have an obligation to put aside their sectional and adversarial interests and work together for the common good of Wales.[11]

The *bête noire* obviously was Westminster with its unique brand of formality and convention, strong adversarial tradition – 'government and opposition', and familiar overtones of executive domination. Echoing these sentiments, NAAG set the scene for a considerable effort at breaking the Westminster mould in favour of a more inclusive and participatory democratic institution.[12] More especially, NAAG sought to calm fears made evident in its consultation process of an over-concentration of power at the centre associated with the development of a cabinet-style model of government. It was a case then of proposing effective checks and balances, and in particular of underscoring the ultimate authority of the corporate body:

> Key [features] are: the role of the subject committees; effective support for individual Assembly members; and also the overall authority retained by the full

Assembly. We believe that vigorous debate, across a range of political parties and outside interests, leading to clear decision making, will be an essential and healthy part of the Assembly's proceedings. Otherwise the opportunity for an inclusive, co-operative approach to developing and implementing policies will be lost.[13]

The argumentation betrays in the case of NAAG a certain naivety and lack of constitutional understanding.[14] For example the balancing of competing values was unconvincing. It was suggested that 'without slowing down the decision-making process', minority parties and backbenchers would 'have real opportunities to [exercise] influence'.[15] If only the values of efficiency and effectiveness were so easily incorporated!

The capacity of the Westminster-style parliamentary tradition to reinvent itself in other settings was grossly underestimated. All the more so, it may be said, in a constitutional context of national devolution; coupled with the facts, first, of some of the most senior Assembly Members having substantial Westminster experience, and, second, of the leading opposition party – Plaid Cymru – seeking after a Parliament for Wales.

NAAG also glossed over the question of how far the Assembly would be able to operate on different constitutional assumptions to Westminster and Whitehall when by reason of the scheme of executive devolution it was so heavily dependent on the centre for political and administrative collaboration and support. External constraints of this type can hardly be wished away.

For the avoidance of doubt, it was never a question of importing Westminster lock, stock and barrel. An element of proportional representation and greater gender balance, a less stuffy atmosphere: in various ways the opportunity has been taken to style the Assembly for a new millennium, and rightly so. Nonetheless, it is fair to say that the extravagant version of the body corporate – 'a new kind of politics in Wales' – was always stretching credulity.

The treatment of the corporate concept further exemplifies the uninterrupted or protracted nature of the constitutional argument. Many of the sharpest exchanges in the parliamentary proceedings on the Government of Wales Bill concerned this aspect. In the event, the legislative stage served to mitigate some of the more obvious defects, and to point up future difficulties, as well as demonstrating the initial strength of the commitment to the corporate model. The architects of the devolutionary scheme could not say but that they had been warned.

Towards a cabinet model

Following on the referendum in September 1997, the devolution debate in Wales was largely focused on the major constitutional question of the distribution of powers inside the Assembly. Once again, the Wales Act 1978 had been read across, in the form of proposals for a strong committee model or system of decentralized executive responsibilities inside the corporate shell. However, the devolution White Paper was noticeably vague about many of the details of the recipe,[16] which itself was not surprising given the failure of such party political documents as *Shaping the Vision* to supply major ingredients. There remained much to play for.

In the event, discussion was largely framed in terms of a cabinet versus a local government model of administration. These are ideal types, expressive of competing values in institutional design. The point is worth emphasizing in view of the diversity of local government practice, and in particular of contemporary shifts in that context to more dynamic, executive-led forms of administration, including in Wales.[17] Another paradox of Welsh devolution is introduced: initial adherence in the case of the Assembly to a traditional form of committee system that was based on, but increasingly rejected for, local government. A mark in the internal party compromise of the distance from a 'parliament', this was hardly an example of outward-looking constitutional thinking. The wind of change was blowing, but the Welsh Labour Party set sail against the tide.

So the Government of Wales Bill, as originally drafted, would have seen the Assembly establish a series of all-party subject committees with executive responsibilities across the range of fields of devolved functions.[18] Elected by the Assembly, the First Secretary would have led an executive committee comprised of the leaders elected by each of the subject committees (the Assembly Secretaries). Also reflecting the traditional local government format, legal authority would have flowed primarily through the subject committees, their functions being derived by delegation from the Assembly, and with further delegation to their Secretary as well as to Assembly staff. The executive committee, charged together with the First Secretary with supplying the overall political direction, would also have derived its functions by delegation from the Assembly, and with further delegation to the First Secretary.

Figure 4 represents this design. It serves to highlight, first, the upwards direction in much of the proposed flow of delegation of functions, and, second, the fact that, legally speaking, the First Secretary would not have had the power to appoint his colleagues or to allocate their portfolios.[19] The list of possible subject committees reflects musings by those in the Devolution Unit of the Welsh Office at this time.

Correctly, the strong committee model came to be increasingly criticized in the course of the parliamentary proceedings on the Bill. Participation by minority parties clearly required firm institutional underpinning, given an electoral history of Labour domination in Wales. Yet an argument for inclusiveness could be turned on its head. Informal and closed arrangements,

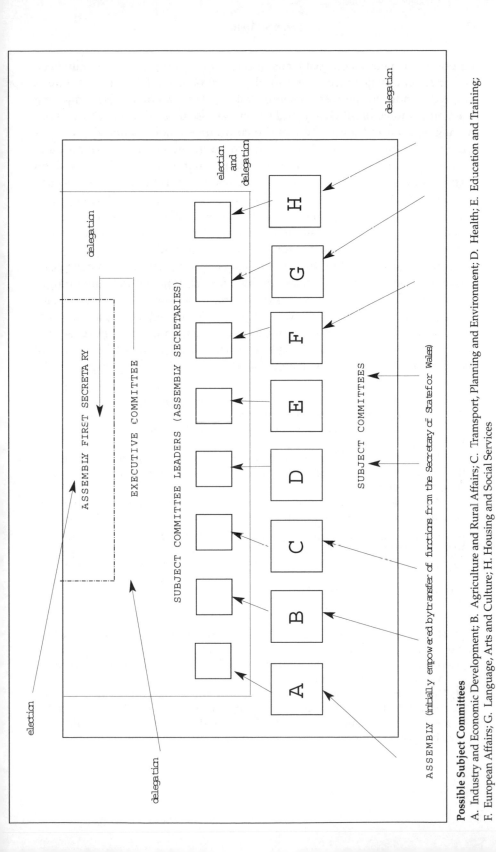

Possible Subject Committees

A. Industry and Economic Development; B. Agriculture and Rural Affairs; C. Transport, Planning and Environment; D. Health; E. Education and Training; F. European Affairs; G. Language, Arts and Culture; H. Housing and Social Services

Figure 4: Assembly mark I or strong committee model

the political caucus as the real locus of decision-making, has commonly been identified as a major vice of the local government model, not least, one is tempted to add, in the case of south Wales.[20] Then there are the competing functional values of efficiency and effectiveness in administrative decision-making, epitomized in the view of the committee model as unduly cumbersome and tending to strategic incoherence. In the event, the case for a more cabinet-style form of government was taken up not only by all the opposition parties, but also by most of the Welsh establishment and interest groups such as the Welsh CBI and the Welsh Local Government Association (WLGA). The development encapsulated the need for sharper lines of accountability in the Assembly; and, further, a desire to cement its status and so avoid the charge, which had echoes of 1978, of 'a glorified county council'.

Operating now with the benefit of officials' advice, Labour was persuaded to move, in the case of the Secretary of State for Wales not entirely unwillingly, towards a more executive-driven form of administration. The change of tack became evident in March 1998, when Ron Davies tabled a complex series of amendments at the Report stage of the Bill. In his words, their purpose was 'to enable the Assembly more easily to establish a Cabinet-style process of decision making'.[21] As now incorporated in the GWA, they included the following provisions:

Assembly First Secretary and Assembly Secretaries
53 – (1) The Assembly shall elect one of the Assembly members to be Assembly First Secretary . . .
(2) The Assembly First Secretary shall appoint Assembly Secretaries from among the Assembly members (and may at any time remove a person from office as an Assembly Secretary).
(3) The standing orders must specify the maximum number of Assembly Secretaries that may be appointed.

Executive committee
56 – (1) There shall be a committee of the Assembly whose members shall be –

(a)   the Assembly First Secretary, who shall chair it, and
(b)   the Assembly Secretaries . . . .

(3) The Assembly First Secretary shall allocate accountability in the fields in which the Assembly has functions to members of the executive committee so that, in the case of each of those fields, accountability in the field is allocated either to one or the Assembly Secretaries or to him.
(4) The Assembly First Secretary need not make an allocation under subsection (3) to every member of the executive committee; but the number of Assembly Secretaries to whom no such allocation is made shall not exceed such number as may be specified in, or determined in accordance with, the standing orders.'

Subject committees
57 – (1) The Assembly shall establish committees with responsibilities in the fields in which the Assembly has functions . . .
(3) There shall be the same number of –

(a)　subject committees, and
(b)　members of the executive committee to whom the Assembly First Secretary allocates accountability in any of the fields in which the Assembly has functions.

(4) The division between the subject committees of the fields in which those committees have responsibilities and the division between members of the executive committee of the fields in which accountability is allocated to members of that committee shall be the same; and the member of the executive committee who has accountability in the field or fields in which a subject committee has responsibilities shall be a member of that subject committee.

Delegation of functions
62 – (1) The Assembly may delegate functions of the Assembly (to such extent as the Assembly may determine) to –

(a)　any committee of the Assembly, or
(b)　the Assembly First Secretary . . .

(5) The Assembly First Secretary may delegate functions of his (to such extent as he may determine) to an Assembly Secretary . . .
(8) The delegation of a function under this section shall not prevent the exercise of the function by the body or person by whom the delegation is made.

There are two main strands in this development. The first one concerns the way in which flexibility is secured through broad powers of delegation, both from the Assembly as a whole and as between the diverse actors.[22] The second one is the strong steer from the centre: effectively a constitutional rebalancing or firm push for the Assembly along the continuum between the local government and cabinet models. On the one hand, the legislation (section 62) would allow the Assembly to gravitate back towards a strong committee system;[23] on the other hand, the Secretary of State made clear his intention to entrench the delegations in a pro-cabinet style in standing orders. In view of later events, this last part of the package deserves a special emphasis. In the Minister's words:

The Assembly's initial standing orders will incorporate a substantial delegation of functions to the Executive Committee and to the First Secretary. The Assembly will therefore begin life with a delegation of functions consistent with a Cabinet model of operation. It would, however, be open to the Assembly subsequently, if it wished, to change those standing orders and instead delegate functions to subject committees, but that would only be possible with a two-thirds vote in favour of such a move.[24]

Flanking measures included the requirement that standing orders restrict the size of the Assembly cabinet (section 53(3)), so deflecting concerns about a sprawling executive power or payroll vote, and a similarly constituted provision for oral and written questions (section 56(7)), a familiar feature of the Westminster parliamentary model. The fact that, legally speaking, Assembly Secretaries are members but not leaders of their subject committees (section 57(4)) also marks the difference from a traditional local government model.

At the same time, coming up short of a full cabinet model, the Assembly had now been established as a 'hybrid body', or, in my terms, given a 'strange anatomy'. A critical feature is the routing of authority via, or concentration of patronage in the hands of, the Assembly First Secretary. Another very significant provision in the light of subsequent events: the appointment of individual ministers or Assembly Secretaries does not require the approval of the Assembly, and it is only the First Secretary who must resign following a vote of no confidence.[25]

In the jargon of the Devolution Unit, 'the driver', or the order in which areas of activity inside the Assembly are determined, had thus been reversed. Whereas it was previously envisaged that the pattern of subject committees would emerge via the route of standing orders and the Assembly, it would now be the First Secretary who determined the pattern by his or her choice of portfolios for Assembly Secretaries. Figure 5 illustrates the change of tack.

Achieving this result involved a singular use in the GWA of the concept of accountability, one that amounted to a sleight of hand. The First Secretary, as well as delegating functions to an Assembly Secretary (section 62(5)), allocates 'accountability' as defined in terms of answering questions, but on the basis that the range of accountability will mirror the range of areas within which the Assembly's functions are delegated (section 56(3)). Then, a second mirroring effect, section 57(4) comes into play, such that the division between the subject committees of the fields in which those committees have responsibilities, and the division between members of the 'executive committee' of the fields in which accountability is allocated to them, is the same.

It is tempting to gloss over these intricacies, but that would be to miss the point. The discussion highlights the fact that the initial choice of constitutional design by the Labour Party in opposition was woefully uninformed. The late shift towards a cabinet model during the legislative process was a major attempt to mitigate the adverse consequences. It is this process of change without abandoning the basis on which a referendum was fought which engendered all the contrivance.

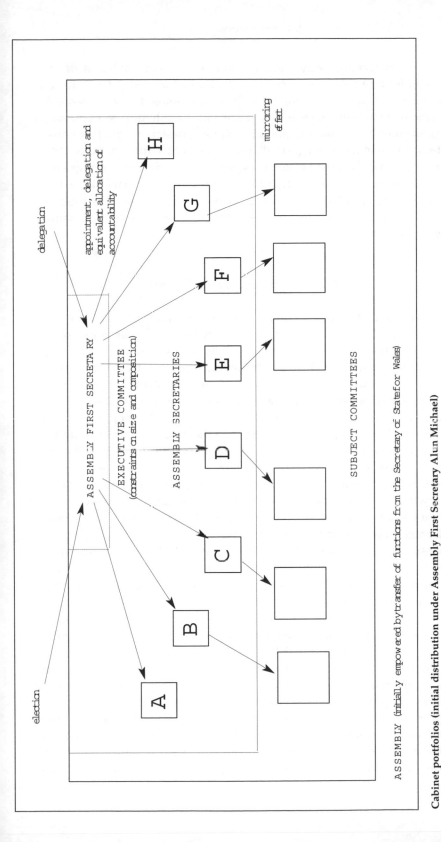

Cabinet portfolios (initial distribution under Assembly First Secretary Alun Michael)
A. Business; B. Economic Development; C. Health and Social Services; D. Post-sixteen Education; E. Pre-sixteen Education; F. Agriculture; G. Local Government and the Environment; H. Finance

Figure 5: Assembly mark II or pro cabinet-style model

Effectively, in tacking away from a committee system redolent of local government in the 1970s, ministers and officials had provided for a stronger political centre inside the corporate body of the Assembly, a considerable improvement. However, despite the brave talk of a hybrid system, major tensions had now been built into the constitutional design, precisely because a cabinet-style system had been grafted onto a model of a different kind.

At the same time, the broad historical significance of the rebalancing should not be underestimated. Effectively, another part of the internal Labour Party deal had become unstitched. For once there was something resembling a cabinet, so there was clear potential for the Assembly to take on a more parliamentary style.

Constitutional pull: separation of powers

The basic dynamic did not go unremarked at Westminster. It was one thing for the minister to declare for a cabinet-style model, but what of the implications of this for the rest of the legislative design? A touchstone is the position of the Assembly staff. Under the statute they are all civil servants,[26] a monolithic approach that follows logically from the substituting idea of the new institution as an executive organ and one operating on behalf of the Crown.[27] However, from whom as individual officials should they take directions, and if working in different parts of the Assembly how should they relate one to another? As a foretaste of more radical developments, staff guidance issued on the eve of devolution serves to underscore the constitutional significance of such nuts and bolts questions. 'Individual civil servants will . . . take their instructions from the Assembly as a whole, or from its committees or the Assembly Secretaries, to the extent that the Assembly has delegated powers to them.'[28]

More especially, in the light of a pro-cabinet model, the issue was bound to arise of the protection of the interests of, and provision of staff and resources for, the rump of this novel representative institution. The constitutional pull of separation of powers, as represented in the UK legislature by the Office of the Speaker of the House of Commons, and further buttressed by a distinctive corps of clerks and system of parliamentary services, is a powerful one. It comes as no surprise to learn that MPs from all parties now fastened on this aspect. In the event, various legislative proposals were presented to and rejected by the government, including that of creating separate categories of Assembly staff (parliamentary, political and executive).

The most far-reaching proposal would have established a very different type of Assembly corporate body, enabling it to employ its own clerks and 'parliamentary' staff, and to enter into contracts. Such is the type of model that now underwrites the doctrine of separation of powers in Scottish legislative devolution.[29] Banished at the time to the backbenches, the mover was none other than future Assembly First Minister Rhodri Morgan. In his words:

> The real problem is that the Secretary of State has expressed a preference for a Cabinet-style model from day one, but without the consequential changes . . . An Assembly separate from the Executive will need a Clerk and a separate staff to protect the interests of Backbenchers and to give them advice on drafting amendments and obtaining information not supplied by the Government or the civil service.[30]

The point was pursued to its logical conclusion, with a call for the abandonment of the general concept of corporate status in the light of the cabinet-style model. While doomed to fail, not least by reason of the pressures on parliamentary time, the argument serves, first, to illuminate the major tensions that were now involved in the constitutional design; and second, it may be ventured, the path of Welsh constitutional development post 2003:

> The Welsh Assembly . . . is referred to as a body corporate. That is fine if we follow the Committee model but not if we follow the Cabinet model, which would give rise to a distinction between the Executive, run by the Cabinet, and the legislature – the quasi-parliamentary body which is to challenge, and occasionally change, what Frontbenchers want to do. That is the whole point of Backbenchers, after all.[31]

The provision that the GWA makes is skeletal in the extreme. Section 52 simply refers to the Assembly electing a Presiding Officer and a Deputy from different parties. Meanwhile, the existence of the Assembly Clerk – a vital post, not least in terms of the ongoing constitutional trajectory of the Assembly – is only made apparent in standing orders. Once again, it was left to NAAG to devise a format, in the guise of an Office of the Presiding Officer (OPO) (now the Presiding Office):

> Those staff working directly in support of the Assembly as a whole and its committees (apart from the Assembly Cabinet) – for example committee clerks, legal advisers, translators, library staff and researchers – should be established in an Office of the Presiding Officer . . . Although these staff would also be civil servants, this Office should be separate from the staff working in support of the Assembly Secretaries and the Assembly Cabinet (executive committee).[32]

So it was to be a case of 'Welsh walls' – not exactly a convincing format for the small village that is the Assembly. For example, what if – perish the thought – actors from the cabinet side of the Assembly sought to apply pressure on the Presiding Officer in the exercise of his core function of interpreting and applying standing orders? Again – parliamentarism writ small – the NAAG format was to be implemented by the Welsh Office in notably austere fashion.[33]

Corporate logic: official secrecy

Bizarre as it may now appear, the Government of Wales Bill as originally drafted would have made Assembly Members Crown servants for the purposes of the Official Secrets Act 1989.[34] Reflecting requirements of confidentiality in a committee model of decentralized executive responsibilities, for example in such matters as EU grants, foreign investments and police investigations, the provision serves to highlight the knock-on effects of the initial design of the Assembly architecture. Another logical product of corporate status, it was explained on the basis that the Welsh Secretary was bound by the Act, and as his functions were to be transferred to the Assembly as a whole, all the AMs should be similarly bound.

Mention need only be made of Article 10 of the European Convention on Human Rights (freedom of expression): such a grave inhibition of the democratic function of individual representatives could hardly be justified. And whither – the critics rightly asked – all those fine devolutionary words about openness and transparency? In hindsight, the eventual abandonment of the provision, in favour of restriction directly targeted on the Assembly cabinet,[35] was one of the first major cracks in the corporate edifice produced by the Welsh Office.

In short, the idea of the Assembly as an executive organ, as distinct from a democratic elected body capable of holding the executive to account, could not be wholly sustained even at this stage. This particular proposal can thus be seen as the high-water mark of a governmental concept of the corporate body, a case of the Welsh Office in the clothes of the Assembly, and as marking the beginnings of revolt.[36]

2. DELEGATION AND MORE DELEGATION

Powers are allocated to the Assembly as a corporate body, but who is to exercise them on behalf of the Assembly? The internal system of delegation of powers may be said to have three main elements. The first one obviously is cabinet formation or the distribution of portfolios, with the resulting changes to the patterns of responsibilities of the subject committees. The second element is the legally prior one, the delegation of functions by the Assembly to the Assembly First Secretary or Minister. As intended, a pro-cabinet dispensation has prevailed, but not without incident! Discussed in more detail in later chapters, delegation to Assembly staff is the third main element.

The system of delegations is a live system, with changes taking place as a consequence not only of revisions to cabinet portfolios and internal or managerial rearrangements but also of the introduction of new legislation and the repeal of existing legislation. The process thus shows the general traits in the Welsh scheme of organic development and of legal and administrative complexity.

Cabinet formation: three administrations

In Welsh devolution, cabinet formation is not only about politics. The First Minister has the power to appoint cabinet members without reference to the Assembly (and the sovereign), but in so doing has to manoeuvre in the light of two major restrictions. As now entrenched in standing orders, the maximum number of Assembly Secretaries is eight; of whom a maximum of two may be freed from subject committee responsibilities.[37] This has effectively allowed for the separate posts of Financial Secretary, essential for proper management of the budgetary process, and of Assembly Business Manager (later called the Minister for Assembly Business), a key figure linked in turn to the Assembly's all-party Business Committee.

So let us consider the shape of the three different administrations formed in the first term of the Assembly, paying special heed to the legal and constitutional aspects.[38] As well as constituting a minority administration, the first Assembly cabinet formed by Alun Michael was notable for being lopsided in two very different ways. First, as regards the workings of cabinet, it never began to give the appearance of being in the famous phrase a case of *primus inter pares*. That the First Secretary was alone in having ministerial experience obviously was influenced by the laudable effort to include in the Assembly a broader range of representatives than typically had been the case at Westminster. But accentuating this feature was the seamless passage of Alun Michael from the post of Secretary of State for Wales to Assembly First Secretary, through whom the internal distribution of power had now been routed.[39]

Secondly, Alun Michael chose to create not one but two education portfolios – pre- and post-sixteen.[40] As well as resulting in two separate subject committees with overlapping interests, this also highlights the restrictions on cabinet appointments in standing orders, the price of 'education, education' being a doubling up of responsibilities elsewhere in the administration. The most visible feature was a sprawling Local Government and Environment portfolio.

The reference to subject area portfolios should not be allowed to obscure the precise contours of the individual ministers' legal and political responsibilities. We are back with the highly specified nature of the Welsh devolutionary scheme: what I called the 'triumph of particularity' or the enumeration of powers statute by statute. So the devolution of functions (from central government) – now usefully termed 'external transfer' – and the delegation of functions (around the cabinet) – 'internal distribution' – can be seen here as two parts of a single overarching process, such that the peculiar quality of the one dictates the strange character of the other. In the words of an explanatory document provided to Assembly Members: 'the First Secretary has delegated functions in a similar way, that is by reference to the Assembly's specific statutory powers'.[41] From a strictly legal viewpoint, the Local Government and Environment portfolio was thus more accurately described in terms of the exercise of certain responsibilities emanating from the Inclosure Act 1845, the Burial Act 1852, the Improvement of Land Act 1864, the Limited Owners Residences Act 1870, and so on.

A complete list of the Acts of Parliament underpinning the then Health and Social Services portfolio for example would have revealed more than fifty statutes. In turn, the list needed to be read in light of the general character of the ministerial portfolio, the various Assembly functions under the statutes being delegated to the minister 'so far as relating to health, the National Health Service and social services'. Then again, reference in the list to an enactment would include not only the functions in that enactment but also functions in any subordinate legislation made under it, this being in line with the approach adopted under the first general transfer of functions order.[42]

The official publication of such details has been made part of the process of delegation by the Assembly to the Assembly First Minister. This is important for defining a minister's accountability to a subject committee and for the purpose of Assembly plenary sessions. The Presiding Officer ruled early on that questions should not be put to the First Minister on detailed matters of policy lying within the delegated responsibility of another member of the cabinet, although the practice has now become more relaxed.[43]

The formation by Rhodri Morgan of the second Assembly administration in February 2000 casts further light on these matters. By keeping the Economic Development portfolio in his own hands, the First Minister was able in compliance with standing orders to break up the unwieldy Local Government and Environment brief in favour of two cabinet portfolios: Local Government; and Planning, Environment and Transport.

But further, there began a development of some significance in the internal constitutional evolution of the Assembly – the creation of deputy or junior ministerial posts. The statutory constraint on the size of the executive core was effectively circumvented, such that the size of the payroll vote was now markedly increased, to a fifth of the size of the corporate body. The development might even be characterized as the Welsh Assembly Government in embryo.

The distribution of the responsibilities also signals a determination to navigate the discernible tension in the devolutionary scheme between the great specificity in powers and the contemporary demands for flexibility and responsiveness more especially in small-country governance. To quote from the official notification of the changes, 'the First Secretary and his colleagues remain committed to working in a coordinated and cross-cutting way, regardless of legal divisions of responsibility'.[44] In assigning to the Finance Secretary coordinating responsibilities on poverty and social exclusion, or the Health and Social Services Secretary responsibility for dealings with the voluntary sector, the new First Minister thus built strongly on foundations first laid by Alan Michael. The creation of junior posts covering such subjects as education and the economy also helped with this aspect.

Coalition-based, the third administration formed in October 2000 obviously looked very different. The creation of the post of Deputy First Minister, held by the Liberal Democrats simultaneously with another ministerial post, lay at the heart of the construction. Also fulfilling the terms of the political agreement between the two parties,[45] the creation of a single education portfolio opened the way under standing orders for the wholly new portfolio of Culture, Sport and the Welsh Language. The number of deputy ministerial posts was further expanded to accommodate the Liberal Democrats. So far had the Assembly already travelled from the agonized debates in Parliament concerning the introduction of a cabinet-style model!

Looking forwards, the argument for a compact Assembly, with substantially fewer members than would have been the case under the Wales Act 1978, has become ever more difficult to sustain. Such is the reality of the increased 'payroll' vote and the greater demand for scrutiny as the Assembly government takes on a more purposeful and confident air. And all those committees are not going to disappear. A projected move to legislative devolution in other words would effectively render an already strong case for an increase in the size of the Assembly overwhelming.[46]

Achilles heel

Now let us backtrack. Ostensibly a technical matter, the way in which the Assembly delegates functions to the First Minister is of the essence of the internal constitutional development. The hierarchy of rules in the design and operation of the scheme is especially important here.

Not surprisingly, in making recommendations the NAAG proceeded on the basis stated by the Secretary of State for Wales, namely that the pro-cabinet form of delegation of functions would be entrenched in standing orders thus requiring the special two-thirds majority for amendment. The statutory commissioners followed suit, as the draft standing orders, published in

The Cabinet

- *First Minister – Rhodri Morgan (Labour).* Responsible/accountable for: exercise of cabinet functions; policy development and co-ordination of cross-cutting issues; co-ordination of government policy in north Wales; partnership with business; European dimension of Assembly policy; intergovernmental and international relations.
- *Deputy First Minister and Minister for Economic Development – Michael German (Liberal Democrat).* Responsible/accountable for: inward investment, promotion of indigenous companies and regional development; European economic issues, including structural funding; industrial policy and business support, including demand-side employment issues; tourism; urban development and regeneration.
- *Minister for Education and Life-long Learning – Jane Davidson (Labour).* Responsible/Accountable for: school education (including curriculum and qualifications); schools administration and organisation; further and higher education; supply-side employment policy; careers services; work-related training.
- *Minister for Assembly Business – Andrew Davies (Labour).* Responsible/accountable for: co-ordinating the business of the Assembly; strategic communications; media planning; corporate image of the Assembly; e-commerce; strategic policy co-ordination.
- *Minister for the Environment – Sue Essex (Labour).* Responsible/accountable for: the environment and sustainable development; water; town and country planning; transport and highways; countryside and conservation issues.
- *Minister for Finance, Local Government and Communities – Edwina Hart (Labour).* Responsible/accountable for: finance and value for money (including local government finance); relations with local government; housing; social inclusion and community regeneration; community safety.
- *Minister for Health and Social Services – Jane Hutt (Labour).* Responsible/accountable for: health and NHS Wales; food safety; social services and social care; children and young people; voluntary-sector partnership.
- *Minister for Rural Affairs – Carwyn Jones (Labour).* Responsible/accountable for: agriculture and fisheries; development and promotion of food production; forestry; development of rural economy.
- *Minister for Culture, Sport and the Welsh Language – Jenny Randerson (Liberal Democrat).* Responsible/accountable for: arts; libraries and museums; sport and recreation; the languages of Wales.

Deputy Ministers

- *Economic Development – Alun Pugh (Labour)*
- *Local Government – Peter Black (Liberal Democrat)*
- *Health – Brian Gibbons (Labour)*
- *Rural Affairs, Culture and Environment – Delyth Evans (Labour)*
- *Education and Lifelong Learning – Huw Lewis (Labour)*

Figure 6: The 'Partnership Government' (as originally constituted in October 2000)[47]

January 1999, make clear: 'Except where the Act or standing orders provide otherwise, the Assembly's powers are delegated by virtue of this paragraph to the First Secretary to exercise on the Assembly's behalf. The First Secretary shall make appropriate arrangements for their effective discharge.'[48]

But in one of those odd twists of history, central government lawyers intervened at this point via the UK Cabinet Office. Since section 62 of the GWA provides for delegation by the Assembly, the appropriateness of delegation via standing orders first made by the Secretary of State was clearly an issue; all the more so, given the entrenching element. In view of possible legal dispute, the preferred route of standing orders was abandoned, in favour of ordinary procedures or delegation to the First Secretary by Assembly resolution when first that body met. All that was left of the original proposal was an official 'note' on the discharge of functions by the Assembly, which set out the arrangements 'assumed by the standing orders': 'Statutory functions of the Assembly will, as the National Assembly Advisory Group recommended, be delegated by Assembly resolution to the First Secretary, who will in turn delegate them as appropriate to other members of the Assembly Cabinet to discharge.'[49]

In terms of the planned constitutional development, the design of the system of delegations had effectively been put out of synch, so underwriting a potential for instability in conditions of minority government. Such was the disparity between, on the one hand, the political and administrative importance of that system in determining the character of the Assembly; and on the other hand, its new lowly position in the hierarchy of rules governing the institution.

In turn, a skilful use of Assembly procedure had been made possible, whereby the routing of the delegations might be altered – even reversed, to the detriment of the First Secretary – by another resolution passed by a simple majority of Members. The not so grand design of the 'devolution settlement' now had an Achilles heel. And it is exactly this that was to be exploited against Alun Michael.

Resolution and reservation

What then were the terms of the resolution that the Assembly was effectively required to make prior to its empowerment? The single most important constitutional instrument passed by the Assembly in its first term read as follows:

1.   The Assembly, acting under section 62(1)(b) of the [GWA], resolves to delegate, subject to paragraphs (2) and (3) and any other resolution of the Assembly, its functions to the Assembly's First Secretary.

2. Paragraph (1) does not apply to any function in respect of which the
    Assembly is precluded under that Act from delegating.
3. Nothing in this resolution will have the effect of either reducing the pre-
    eminence of the authority of the full Assembly, or reducing the role of the
    Assembly Committees in reviewing the effectiveness of policies and in
    developing new policies . . .
4. The First Secretary shall as soon as is practicable lay before the Assembly
    details of all powers he has delegated to the other Assembly Secretaries and
    those which he has kept unto himself.

This too was not the original wording, the resolution itself being something
of a compromise.[50] The new Labour administration had intended the first two
paragraphs, clearly fitting for a more centralized or First Secretary-dominated
form of executive decision-making. However, there was now the unexpected
fact of a 'hung' Assembly. This led naturally on to renewed constitutional
tensions centred on the concept of the corporate body. Liberal Democrat
leader Michael German led the opposition charge, his party being especially
wedded – at this time – to a corporate-style model of inclusive and
collaborative forms of working. Mr German attacked the open-ended nature
of the motion:

> It is not in the power of any one group or party to be able to deliver any one thing.
> However, if you give that power away, you abrogate that responsibility. I worry
> that this Westminster-style motion, which gives all the power to the First
> Secretary, will emasculate this Assembly before it has begun.

The rest of the argument is bizarre, but it usefully illustrates the initial
strength of the appeal of a distinctive approach:

> Those who take the Westminster model are mistaken, as are those who look to
> local government, because this is a new style of government . . . There is no model
> for this anywhere in the British Commonwealth. That makes us a unique branch,
> developing a new constitutional settlement that I hope we will export throughout
> the world.[51]

Paragraph (3) of the resolution thus stood for the hybrid nature of the new
representative institution, at one and the same time expressly reserving the
position of the Assembly *qua* Assembly, and reasserting the importance of the
all-party subject committees in the novel form of constitutional design. It was
an early warning shot across the bows of Alun Michael's administration.

The resolution further serves to demonstrate the artificiality of the system
of delegations. The cabinet-style model clearly depends on delegation to
individual ministers. However, in the words of the official documentation:
'delegation of functions to the First Secretary is the necessary first step, as the

[GWA] does not authorise the Assembly to delegate directly to Assembly Secretaries'.[52] Onward delegation to the appropriate ministers, and where necessary to staff, has to be factored in as a working assumption of the formal Assembly procedure.

Enough has been said to explain one of the regular – and odder – features of Assembly plenary sessions. In light of the controversy, it has been considered necessary to pass a further delegation resolution ('internal distribution') on each occasion that new powers are allocated to the Assembly ('external transfer'). A recipe for excitement it is not.[53]

Further demonstrating the close interplay of the constitutional and political elements, the precise nature of these resolutions has fluctuated with the rise and fall of minority government in the Assembly. At first, under Alun Michael, they were typically bare. Functions were delegated to the First Secretary, in the name of efficient and effective administration, without more ado.[54] However, following his resignation, the fashion developed of the opposition parties attaching specific requirements of openness and account-ability, perhaps an annual report to plenary on the exercise of the delegated functions, or close consultation with the respective subject committees. Such conditions were not exactly necessary, given the legal nature of a power to delegate, but as Michael German explained: 'these amendments are on the agenda . . . because we need recognition, and we want to re-state the recognition, of the minority Government position in the Assembly'.[55]

Latterly, the style of delegation has taken on a more settled air, reflecting the fact of majority government. The following example, which preserves at least the semblance of a corporate style in very different political conditions, gives the flavour:

> The National Assembly for Wales . . . resolves to delegate all the functions of the National Assembly contained in or under the European Social Fund (National Assembly for Wales) Regulations 2001 . . . to the Assembly First Minister, save those which by law cannot be so delegated.

> Nothing in this motion will have the effect of reducing the pre-eminence of the authority of the full Assembly or of reducing the role of the Assembly Committees in the exercise of the above functions.[56]

3. PRESCRIPTION AND BEYOND

For a small body of sixty Members, the Assembly could not be said to be lacking in committees. Many of the most important are prescribed by the GWA, and may therefore be considered part of the devolution settlement. Other committees have been established under standing orders. The burgeoning use of *ad hoc* committees, and in particular of so-called 'task and finish groups', is a separate development, one which exemplifies the continuing rise of Welsh governmental machinery.[57]

The established committees are usefully classified under four main headings.[58] As a core committee, with a central role to play in driving forward the work of the Assembly especially in plenary session, the Business Committee is obviously *sui generis*. Next comes the multi-functional role of the various subject committees, as constituted by a list of responsibilities in standing orders and shaped in turn by the functions delegated to the individual Assembly Ministers. Thirdly, there are the scrutiny committees charged with ensuring compliance with statutory and other requirements or with upholding proper standards of conduct and administration. A fourth category comprises different kinds of advisory committees, including another distinctive Welsh development in the guise of the Assembly's four regional committees.[59]

The following grid demonstrates the basic pattern. Especially however in a new representative institution like the Assembly, the functions are apt to overlap. For example the Business Committee is formally given advisory functions but has also operated as a major forum both for negotiations and for generating conventional understandings between the different political parties.

Check and balance: formal requirements

Committee design is characterized by a high degree of formal constitutional engineering. A defining feature is the principle of party balance.[60] According to standing orders, building directly on the GWA,[61] committee members 'shall, unless the committee exists solely to provide advice, be elected so as to secure that as far as is practicable, the balance of the political groups in the Assembly is reflected in the membership of each committee'. The principle has in practice meant committees of nine–eleven Members; a typical spread in the first ('hung') Assembly being four Labour Members and one Liberal Democrat, three Plaid AMs and one Conservative.[62]

To pursue the theme, the internal architecture of the committee system is one of the areas where the legal framework is highly prescriptive, reflecting concern about the quality of the new Welsh polity. A perceived 'democratic deficit' was emphatically not to be reinvented in the guise of excessive centralization of power, patronage and secrecy, and of lack of oversight. For once the official thinking has been made explicit, courtesy of Martin Evans who as head of the Welsh Office Devolution Unit was one of the main administrative architects of the constitutional scheme:

> The Government of Wales Act . . . recognised that there would be a need . . . to prevent a party or coalition with a majority from making changes which would

	Prescribed under the GWA (ss.56–61) ('statutory committees')	Provided for in standing orders
Executive branch and Assembly business	Cabinet ('Executive committee')	Business Committee
Policy development/scrutiny/law making	Subject committees (7) (linkage via the Panel of Chairs) Agriculture and Rural Development Culture Economic Development Education and Lifelong Learning Environment, Planning and Transport Health and Social Services Local Government and Housing	
Scrutiny	Audit Committee Legislation Committee ('Subordinate Legislation Scrutiny Committee')	Committee on Standards of Conduct
Advisory/review	Regional committees (4) North Wales Mid-Wales South-west Wales South-east Wales	Committee on Equality of Opportunity Committee on European and External Affairs House Committee*

*Now afforded executive powers.

Figure 7: Classification of Assembly committees by function and legal base (July 2002)[63]

rob minority parties of their share of influence or right of legitimate scrutiny. So it was that the checks and balances safeguarding the rights of minority parties were incorporated . . . (e.g. the requirement that any committee that is not purely advisory must reflect party balance) . . .[64]

The statutory design of the subject committees is an acid test, given the special place of these committees in the historical evolution of the Assembly architecture. First, the GWA (section 57(5)) supplies another 'check and balance', the Chairs being selected from a panel composed of Members elected by the Assembly also in accordance with the principle of party balance. In turn, a major forum for senior 'backbenchers' has been promoted, the Panel of Chairs of Subject Committees, which meets on a regular basis and performs a general consultative and networking role.[65]

There is, second, the umbilical cord joining the cabinet and the subject committees in the form of the membership of the individual Assembly Secretaries (GWA, s. 57(4)). This constitutional arrangement is unique to the Assembly. In the guise of a political leadership separate from the role of the Chair, it was designed to provide in the words of Martin Evans 'an immediate and direct link into the decision making process'.[66] Turning the argument round, the potential for executive domination is immediately apparent.

Establishing subject committees was all very well, but what of a firm institutional focus for engaging Assembly Members with overarching or cross-cutting issues seen as fundamental in the new Welsh polity? Once again the strong practical constraint entailed in an Assembly of sixty Members is highlighted. On the one hand, NAAG recognized the need for additional standing committees 'to ensure that a coherent strategic approach is adopted in relation to high profile issues'; and 'to enable the Assembly to ensure consistency of approach across the subject committees, and avoid fragmentation and rigidity'. On the other hand, confronted by the potential for Assembly overload, NAAG recommended that 'the Assembly should as far as possible keep the number of committees it establishes to a minimum'.[67] In the event, NAAG plumped for two cross-cutting committees: the Equality of Opportunity Committee and what is now called the European and External Affairs Committee.[68] Other obvious candidates – sustainable development and human rights – lost out here.[69]

Again, with a view to so-called 'mainstreaming' in terms of policy development and implementation,[70] these cross-cutting committees were given a distinctive architecture under standing orders. First, the idea of 'champions', they were to be elected 'having regard to the desirability of each subject committee being represented on the Committee'. In fact NAAG had envisaged such representation as a requirement, but this was watered down as otherwise unlawfully impinging on the Assembly's choice in the election of members.[71] Second, and in contrast to the subject committees, the Chair was to be a minister. But although there was a case for this arrangement in terms of coordination, official influence and profile-raising, it has presented an obvious difficulty in terms of the committees' scrutiny role. Correctly the Assembly Review of Procedure determined that the arrangement be abandoned.[72]

Another major variation on a theme, the two statutory scrutiny committees – Audit and Legislation – are the most closely regulated ones in terms of their composition. The model is effectively three-pronged (GWA, sections 59–60): the general principle of party balance coupled – in contrast to the subject committees – with a bar on Assembly cabinet members – and – following in the footsteps of Westminster – on the Chair being drawn 'from the largest party with an executive role'.[73] The design feature of checks and balances inside the corporate body is in other words exceptionally well illustrated by these two committees. The Audit Committee for example has operated with a Plaid Cymru Chair, as well as a coterie of senior political figures.

'Unique aspect': the subject committees

One of the main aims in giving the subject committees an extended role was to establish them as a counter-weight to the Assembly cabinet, thus calming fears of over-centralization or Labour domination. In other words, the 'strong committee model' having been abandoned,[74] it was now a case of combining and seeking to balance the strengthened executive core of the Assembly with an entrenched system of portfolio-based and multi-functional committees exercising a strong advisory role.

At the same time, giving the subject committees a proactive role in policy development had positive attractions. Especially so, it may be said, in a small country with no established tradition of policy-making. Again, inclusiveness and partnership working, these committees offered an alternative and more transparent conduit for external inputs – evidence-taking, public consultation etc. A function, it is worth adding, that such organizations as the CBI and the Federation of Small Businesses have considered of particular value.[75]

A 'cabinet and committee model': such was Ron Davies's hybrid. NAAG in particular made much of the argument of checks and balances. The rhetoric was typically high-flown, nothing less than 'a new approach to government' characterized by 'a more consensual approach to policy development', together with 'clear decision-making' and 'a mechanism for effective scrutiny'. Wide-ranging tasks were thus envisaged for these committees:

> Subject committees should have a significant role in reviewing the effectiveness of policies and in developing new policies. They should scrutinise the performance of non-departmental public bodies and other bodies funded by the Assembly,

reporting to the full Assembly on that performance from time to time. Subject committees' role in scrutinising, debating and amending subordinate legislation will equally be of high importance. We recommend that subject committees also discuss Westminster and European legislation which affects their subject area and pass their views on to the Assembly cabinet (executive committee) and the Secretary of State.[76]

It is a measure of the sensitivities that much of this was subsequently entrenched in the standing orders. Most notably, a quadrilateral role in policy development and scrutiny, and in law making and budgeting, each subject committee 'shall':

• contribute to the development of the Assembly's policies within the fields for which the relevant Assembly Secretary is accountable to the Assembly;
• keep under review the expenditure and administration connected with their implementation . . . and the discharge of public functions in those fields by public, voluntary and private bodies;
• advise on proposed legislation affecting Wales; including performing its functions [in Assembly law-making procedure];
• provide advice to the Assembly cabinet on matters relating to the allocation of the Assembly's budget.[77]

Correctly, and of special value in an initial phase of trial and error, the drafting has allowed the subject committees a degree of flexibility in the way they operate. Legally speaking, they are not entirely 'toothless watchdogs', having the statutory powers to summon witnesses and have documents produced relating to public bodies.[78] Clearly, however, while there is a formal guarantee of their role against attack by the cabinet, the extent of their influence very largely depends on how what is now the Welsh Assembly Government behaves towards them.

Especially by reason of their extended remit, and of the immediate problem of the Members' lack of experience, one should beware of rushing to hasty conclusions about the effectiveness or otherwise of the subject committees.[79] At this point some general observations are in order, directed in particular to the main controversy that has arisen concerning their place in the Assembly architecture, namely the balance to be struck between the policy-development and scrutiny functions.

In imagining such an expansive contribution, NAAG – not for the only time[80] – got carried away. Notably little was said about the most obvious internal constraint: the staff and resources that would be required to underpin the successful operation of the subject committees' novel multi-functional role. A brief mention of the possibility of having outside or specialist advisers hardly sufficed. NAAG in short failed to help will the means. Two years of devolution and the Panel of Chairs would lament: 'Tension between the volume of Assembly/committee business and aspirations of committees on the one hand and the availability of resources (which includes numbers of AMs, time, and staff, both within the Presiding Office and policy divisions) on the other hand.'[81]

Famously, Alun Michael once described the subject committees as 'the Assembly's engine room'. 'They have the opportunity to consider issues in detail, to weigh the evidence, and to advise the whole Assembly on the way they should progress on important issues.'[82] However, to pursue the nautical analogy, this kind of characterization – also typical of NAAG – glosses over the crucial role of keeping up the steam of the administrative groups and policy divisions, working of course under the strategic direction of those on the bridge, ministers as well as the Permanent Secretary. This is no idle point. On the one hand, the elected representatives themselves can only do so much. On the other hand, whatever the practical limitations, it reflects the operation inside public administration of the classical feedback loop: policy development and formulation, delivery and implementation, and review and initiative.

In fact, major contours of the subject committees' role in contributing to policy development had been left unresolved in the original design and, in particular, the constitutional implications in terms of the lines of authority and accountability. There was much room for organic development. For its part, the Assembly Review of Procedure in 2001–2 would still be grappling with such basic questions as whether ministers as committee members should be able to reserve their position on certain committee recommendations.[83] Suffice it to add that, as Alun Michael would discover to his cost, such a grey area – the place and force of (all-party) committee proposals – represented a potent source of political tension in the former conditions of minority administration.

A certain kind of insularity has afflicted public discussion of the subject committees' role. 'Strange anatomy': it is undoubtedly the case that the confusion and controversy associated with the concept of the corporate body has not been conducive to the smooth and efficient operation of these committees in these early years.[84] But one should also bear in mind the difficulties or constraints that 'parliamentary' committees commonly confront in exercising authority and influence. Mention need only be made of the tendency to a scattergun approach; of finite resources and insufficient expertise; and of the rigidity of the committee framework: in other words, of the kinds of criticism that are familiarly associated with the work of Select Committees in the House of Commons.[85] In comparative constitutional perspective it is partly a question of careful prioritization and targeting, an avoidance of overload in the exercise of multiple functions.

While much is heard of partnership working, the idea, central to this unique design, of ministers and subject committees working in harness, it remains the case that in some respects the committees' functions in policy development and scrutiny do not sit comfortably together. Obviously much will depend on the relevant topic, as well as on the influence or standing of the Chair. But cooperative and critical modalities: it cannot be expected that combining the two will always be easy.

The argument takes a particular turn in the context of majority government, whether it be coalition or single (Labour) party rule. The issue naturally arises of shifting the balance of the subject committees' functions, policy decisions being the job of the executive part. A shift over time away from the strong role in policy development envisaged by NAAG, in favour of the scrutiny role classically associated with the parliamentary-type system of government, is only to be expected.[86]

But this should not be accounted a zero-sum game. First, it does not follow from a demand to distinguish between the legislative and executive roles of the Assembly that the work of the subject committees should be wholly confined to the exercise of democratic oversight. A contribution to policy development – agenda-setting or feeding in fresh information and ideas – is easily envisaged, as against the specifics of policy formulation or the details of policy delivery and implementation. Secondly, as every student of public administration knows, the scrutiny function broadly conceived is itself part of the continuous process of making and reviewing public policy; such being the standard fare of assessment or evaluation, including via consultation with outside interests, and the making of recommendations. Rhodri Morgan, for one, is apparently convinced: 'subject committees' work in policy development . . . is a unique aspect of the Assembly's working which we should protect jealously'.[87]

To this end, a key design principle is that of complementarity. This entails prioritizing the contribution that the subject committees are best equipped to make as compared with other actors, most obviously the administrative groups and policy divisions. A special emphasis on wide-ranging or groundbreaking inquiries – which is itself appropriate for a new polity charting its way – is thus one way forward. In fact, some of the most important contributions from the subject committees already demonstrate this.[88]

Values again: integrity

In the words of *A Voice for Wales*, the Assembly 'will gain the trust of the Welsh people only if it conducts its affairs openly and properly'.[89] Unexceptional perhaps; but let us remember that the new representative institution was born amidst great public concern about so-called 'sleaze', including – notoriously – in the Westminster Parliament. In turn, the principle of integrity is of the essence of the novel form of constitutional engineering in Wales, as powerfully influenced by the UK Committee on Standards in Public Life,[90] and strongly represented in a detailed framework of norms governing Members' conduct. The Assembly's own standing Committee on Standards of Conduct has an important role.

In architectural terms, the striking feature is the way in which the regulation came to be expanded in the course of constructing the devolutionary scheme. The statutory provision serves to highlight once again the prominent role played by the internal law of the Assembly in the constitutional design. Integrity is one of a series of basic principles – preservation of order, openness, and participation of Members are other ones[91] – to which the standing orders are required to give effect. More especially, the registration and declaration of interests is mandated, underpinned by sanctions not only of suspension and exclusion of Members but also – exceptionally – of the criminal law.[92]

For its part, NAAG emphasized the need for 'the public . . . to feel confident that Members are there as representatives of the public good and not for personal gain'. So it was an occasion for detailed recommendations on conflicts of interest etc., standards of practice at Westminster being regarded as a minimum. An *ad hoc* committee, convened by the Presiding Officer under standing orders, would examine any complaints of non-compliance.[93] Correctly, however, and echoing developments elsewhere in the UK, the Standing Orders Commissioners took the point that establishing a standing committee on standards of conduct would have considerable benefits. As well as encouraging consistency and expertise, there would be room for a more creative function – 'fire-watching' or the proactive exercise of control and influence – together with complaint handling.[94] The opportunity was also taken to bring the conduct of cabinet members within the ambit of the regulation.[95]

Following best practice in local government, an independent external adviser was added to the system. In practice, the adviser has had the twin roles of providing advice and assistance to the Presiding Officer 'on any matter relating' to Members' conduct and of carrying out individual investigations as requested by what is now the Assembly's Standards Committee.[96]

Again, to anticipate the argument, the regulation has gone on expanding under the aegis of the Standards Committee. Suffice it to say that in the rush to empowerment, the guidance to Members was not as clear as it might have been, and the procedures established – especially on determining complaints – were somewhat rough and ready. Much to be applauded, behind the scenes there has been a clean-up operation – yet further evidence of the local official determination to buttress the legitimacy of the Assembly.[97]

'Hallmark': freedom of information

In the words once again of the White Paper: 'The Assembly will operate with maximum openness . . . the Government's proposed Freedom of Information Act will also extend to the Assembly.'[98] Architecturally speaking, freedom of information (FOI) is in fact the one key aspect of the devolutionary development where a formal legal reordering was signalled from the outset.

The devolution statute, in giving effect to openness as a founding principle of the new Welsh 'constitution', establishes some basic norms, for example that all proceedings of the Assembly *qua* Assembly are held in public, and a general presumption that the committees follow suit. A right of public inspection of Assembly documents 'relating to any proceedings of the Assembly' is embedded.[99] Internal law has typically had an extended role, in the guise of exceptions provided for in standing orders, and in particular of the soft law provisions of the Assembly's own administrative guidance.

It is important to stress the substantial gains in terms of access to information that flow generally from the devolutionary development in this small country, not least via the independent representational role of Assembly Members. A major thread is the exceptional use made of the Internet – covering all the Assembly's published documents and encompassing other proactive and innovative developments such as dedicated electronic access via public libraries throughout Wales. In this regard – the modalities of democratic governance in the new information age – the Assembly is appropriately described as a world leader.[100]

Yet it should also be noted that the law which will now bind the Assembly – the Freedom of Information Act 2000 – is not what was on offer at the time of the passage of the devolution legislation. As is well known, a notably liberal White Paper, *Your Right to Know*, has been transformed into a statute as much characterized by discretion and exception.[101] A general right to information held by a public authority is thus matched by long lists of absolute exemptions, and of exemptions that are subject to a test of public interest[102] (which include the development of policy, ministerial communications, and information prejudicial to 'the effective conduct of public affairs'). From a Welsh perspective, a notable feature is the lack of special or territorial provision, the Assembly being treated as separate but equal to a central government department. In sharp contrast, the Scottish Parliament has itself been able to pursue a more liberal statutory regime.

A different but related point: the topic of FOI serves to illustrate the potential, first of internal constitutional and administrative change in the light of the devolutionary scheme, and second of a distinctive Welsh approach in matters of public administration. Under Alun Michael, the Assembly rebadged the code on public access to information previously introduced for central government. Briefly, this meant importing the low threshold test of 'actual harm or prejudice' to justify non-disclosure, as well as some classic 'Yes Minister' exceptions ('information whose disclosure would . . . be likely to inhibit the frankness and candour of internal discussion').[103] FOI now has, however, a very special place in the lexicon of Welsh devolution, being a flagship policy of Rhodri Morgan, a long-term critic of the British tradition of official secrecy. As only he could put it: 'Openness is our hallmark. When the chamois leather of democracy meets the windolene of accountability in the Assembly, it can be said that we have a much healthier politics in Wales.'[104]

A firm statement in favour of greater openness – 'there must be a culture change in favour of making information available' – was one of Rhodri Morgan's first moves on taking office in February 2000. 'Our new democracy in Wales means that this is what people have come to expect, and this is what I would like to deliver.'[105] Headline initiatives, the publication only six weeks in arrears of Assembly cabinet and Business Committee minutes, as also of many cabinet papers,[106] represent a clear distancing from the Whitehall tradition of government.

In approaching the Freedom of Information Act, the devolved administration under Mr Morgan has taken a generous view, reworking its own code in ways that strengthen the right of access.[107] A test of 'substantial harm' has been introduced, which effectively tilts the balance in favour of disclosure in those discretionary categories subject to the test of public interest. As well as some practical measures, a free service in many cases and sharper time limits on dealing with requests, early provision has been made for an (electronically accessible) information register, the condition precedent to an effective system of access. The Assembly in other words has gone further and faster than is strictly necessary. Such is the outline of what I earlier described as the Welsh model of government in the sunshine.

For the avoidance of doubt, there are major limitations. The intriguing question is raised in the context of the corporate body of access to information by opposition or backbench Members. In the first flush of enthusiasm it was officially stated: 'the culture of the Assembly should encourage a free flow of information between the executive and Assembly Members, so that formal mechanisms are not needed simply to acquire factual information'.[108] As one would expect, a more orthodox view has prevailed in relation to official briefings for ministers etc., with direct policy advice remaining confidential. More recently, however, there have been various complaints of the shutters coming down, of a tighter or more rigid approach to the sharing of advice and information across the Assembly.[109] It is a natural concomitant of the rise of the Welsh Assembly Government or the rapid journey of the corporate body towards a parliamentary-type system of government.[110]

Secondly, the Welsh Assembly Government possesses no magic wand. Considerations of 'commercial confidentiality' are apt to blunt the force of FOI, more especially in an era of contracting out or 'outsourcing'. Surprise,

surprise: complaints have already begun to surface in Wales of a lack of openness under the controversial method of public-sector development that is the private finance initiative (PFI). Nor is it remarkable to learn of complaints of delay in dealing with voluminous requests for information.[111] Perhaps in the Welsh model of government in the sunshine expectations have been raised too high.

A third – and crucial – limitation is external in character. Section 28 of the Freedom of Information Act 2000 provides that information is 'exempt information if its disclosure . . . would, or would be likely to, prejudice relations between any administration in the United Kingdom and any other such administration'. In practice, from the time the Assembly was established, confidentiality of Whitehall documents has been maintained in accordance with provisions in standirtg orders. Rhodri Morgan has explicitly preserved this position, noting that 'otherwise, we could become a backdoor route for securing access to material that is lawfully denied under other jurisdictions'.[112] Indicative of the sensitivities, Permanent Secretary Jon Shortridge has also urged staff to reassure colleagues in Whitehall of their continuing commitment to respecting confidentiality in the conduct of intergovernmental relations.[113] Suffice it to note that this issue has special resonance in light of the Welsh constitutional arrangements, by reason not only of the corporate nature of the Assembly but also of the basic model of executive devolution or high dependency on coordination and cooperation with Whitehall. Law making for Wales is seen especially to highlight this aspect.[114]

CONCLUSION – ONLY IN WALES

The corporate shell, the fact that actions taken in its name are legally taken by the Assembly as a whole, cannot simply be wished away. The elasticity of the corporate body as a constitutional concept governing the internal architecture of the Assembly is, however, amply attested. A stretching of the concept ever more thinly will be seen in the next chapter to be of the essence of the major autochthonous constitutional development in Wales post-devolution.

According to Ron Davies the Assembly was designed as a hybrid, and he should know. Less charitably, one may say that the architecture was cobbled together courtesy of the Labour Party in Wales, and in a way that ignored basic laws of physics. To mix metaphors, introducing a cuckoo in the nest in the form of cabinet-style government carried with it the seeds of the destruction of the corporate body. As the following chapter will further demonstrate, the element of surprise is the speed with which the fault lines have split wide open.

An expansive system of internal delegations is the natural concomitant of the Assembly's corporate legal status. In turn, nothing better illustrates the peculiar nature of the 'devolution settlement' than the design and mechanics of this system. It allows great flexibility in the basic contours of Assembly architecture, but fosters an undue legalism in the domestic arrangements of the devolved administration.

The Assembly's subject committees are a unique feature, a talisman of concerns about the undue concentration of power. They have in turn been caught up in the stresses and strains associated with the ongoing constitutional development inside the Assembly. The fact that typically the subject committees have been oversold should not, however, be allowed to obscure the potential of their dual role in scrutiny and enhancing policy development.

A better system of public administration is one important test of the devolutionary development. This is reflected in the strong use of legal precept in defence of core constitutional values. FOI is a valuable touchstone, having been given high prominence in the ongoing constitutional development. In fact, FOI provides an excellent illustration of the constraints on and opportunities for the exercise of policy autonomy under the scheme of executive devolution.

To end at the beginning, the Permanent Secretary has rightly drawn attention to the unique constitutional character of the Assembly. This, however, should not be treated as if it were a badge of honour. To reiterate, the internal structures and processes of the devolutionary scheme show many good points. Yet some of the most distinctive elements have increasingly been challenged – even discarded – and, it is argued, rightly so. Whither then what I have called a strange anatomy?

4

Towards a Parliament

The difficult and complex growth of parliamentary-type government in the National Assembly, from within the body of territorial administrative/executive government in the previous system, has provided the main drama of the first year of powers.

Lord Elis-Thomas[1]

The public should see us in a way that perhaps it does not yet. It should see the Cabinet as a government delivering.

Rhodri Morgan[2]

For laboratory testing of a new set of constitutional arrangements, all those experiments with constants and variables, the contemporary Welsh experience could scarcely be bettered. In four short years Wales has seen: (a) minority administration under the pre-existing UK government representative; (b) a constitutional coup and minority administration with a more popular leader; and (c) coalition government with that same leader and the working majority that had been assumed in the original design.[3] A politically circuitous route, it will be seen, that has left deep marks in terms of the Assembly's internal development.

The starting-point for this discussion is the major gaps or silences in the devolution legislation, the fact that so much has been open to contention. The subsequent development is appropriately analysed by reference to three competing constitutional models of the Assembly – ideal types. A conceptual framework is thus put in place for evaluating the ongoing evolution of the internal architecture, most obviously in terms of the title of the chapter, 'Towards a Parliament'.

The first term of the Assembly will commonly be remembered for the overthrow of Alun Michael. Special attention must here be paid to the working and ethos of the Assembly under the former Secretary of State for Wales. Naturally a period of much constitutional housekeeping, the internal elaboration of practice and procedure, these first nine months in the life of the new Welsh polity would also be characterized by increasing tensions, related at least in part to the constitutional question of the nature and style of devolved administration. The political melodrama itself has a strong legal and constitutional dimension in the guise of procedural considerations that reflect the distinctive anatomy of the Assembly. 'Nuts and bolts' questions relating to motions, resolutions, etc., are not only that.

The detail of the fall will no doubt continue to fascinate. Yet there is clearly a wider significance: first, as regards the character or quality of the Welsh devolutionary development, both in general and at a formative period; and, second, in terms of the knock-on effects, institutional and otherwise, and especially for an autochthonous process of constitution-building. According to the Presiding Officer Lord Elis-Thomas, the overthrow of Mr Michael was 'the first day of devolution'.[4] A tendentious view, but one that reflects the competing constitutional models specified in this chapter, it will echo across the pages of Welsh history.

A vital element is introduced: the rise or increased independence and stature of the Presiding Office. For reasons to do with the separation of powers outlined in the previous chapter, the development is both unexceptional when viewed in comparative constitutional perspective, and is of the first importance in terms of subverting the distinctive constitutional model of the Assembly as a corporate body. In fact, nothing in the constitutional passage of the Assembly better illustrates the influence of the (Westminster) parliamentary tradition, as also of personal factors.

Then there is that other chief pole of authority in the Assembly – the cabinet. Although the trend to strengthen the political centre inside the corporate body pre-dates the infant's birth, it was predictable that the coalition between Labour and the Liberal Democrats would enhance it. Not least, that is, by promoting executive rule or dominance, as well as political stability, with all which that implies for policy development and implementation, and for the conduct of Assembly business. From the 'executive committee' of the devolution statute to the self-proclaimed 'Welsh Assembly Government', it is a remarkable journey.

In terms of the constitutional trajectory of the Assembly, the rapid emergence of Welsh canons of cabinet government can be seen running in parallel with the rise of the Presiding Office, serving once again to reinforce the *de facto* separation of the executive and legislative functions in the corporate body. So much so that there exists today all-party agreement by way of formal resolution in favour of 'the clearest possible separation between the Government and the Assembly which is achievable under current legislation'.[5]

Let us not lose sight of the wider picture. While it is possible to argue for a more parliamentary form of architecture but without parliamentary powers in the guise of legislative devolution, it would be foolish to overlook the synergy of style and substance. By which is meant the general sense – or calculation – that expanding the elements of parliamentary-style government in the Assembly helps to ease the path to having an actual Parliament for Wales.

1. THREE FACES OF THE ASSEMBLY

The concept of the 'body corporate' may be likened to a formal legal mask, behind which the Assembly has presented three faces.[6] The interplay between these different constitutional models, their waxing and waning, as well as the interface with the *de jure* concept, with which they fit more or less comfortably, effectively charts the internal development of the new representative body.

This analytical framework builds on the two competing concepts previously introduced of 'strict executive devolution' and 'quasi-legislative devolution'.[7] Whereas those concepts are more broad-ranging, being designed to point up the close linkages in the constitutional design of issues of architecture and powers, and of intergovernmental relations, these models are directly concerned with matters of style and substance in the internal structures and processes in the Assembly.

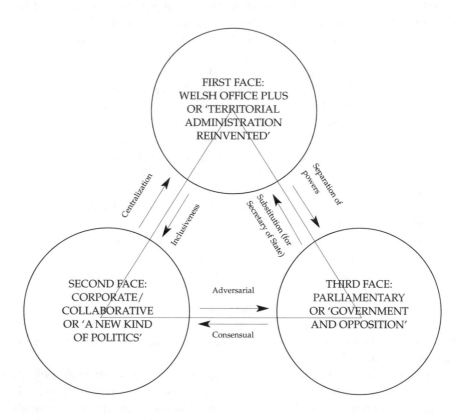

Figure 8: Assembly anatomy – a constitutional triangle

First face: Welsh Office plus

The first face represents a minimalist view of the new constitutional design. The structures and processes are seen as a makeover, so demonstrating much in the way of political and administrative continuity. This is epitomized in the original design feature of substitution, or the grounding of the scheme in the powers and responsibilities of the Secretary of State for Wales. From this perspective, it is a case of the 'Welsh Office plus', the Assembly being treated as an add-on to, or reinvention of, the pre-existing model of territorial administration – a specific cure for the particular malady of a democratic deficit.

A chief characteristic of the model is the powerful role of the Assembly First Secretary (seen here as the lineal descendant of the UK government representative). In turn, the Assembly may be said to have an essentially advisory function, not only in the case of the subject committees, but also in plenary session. Related features are a limited role for cabinet (emphatically not a case of *primus inter pares*) and a strict view of the functions of the Presiding Officer (no great sympathy for separation of powers).

The model can be seen as indicative of the Assembly under Alun Michael. That is to say, cautious and centralist, a very personal or 'hands-on' style of management. But further, it can be seen to fit perfectly well with the formal constitutional design of the devolution statute, for example in terms of the routing of the system of delegations via the Assembly First Secretary, as also in an electoral system that was expected to produce majority government.

One should not underestimate the forces of inertia. That for obvious reasons the model of 'Welsh Office plus' has not been publicly articulated is no measure of its official potency. In practice, the pull or attraction of the model could be expected to fade over time. The key point, to anticipate the argument, is the element of acceleration.

Second face: corporate/collaborative

The second face represents the idea of a newly textured democratic culture: consensual and collaborative, inclusive and cross-party in terms of the structures and processes. As such, it has been seen to feature strongly in the public discussion ahead of devolution, being indicative of the work of the National Assembly Advisory Group (NAAG) as promoted by Ron Davies. It is appropriately labelled the designer-friendly face of the Assembly.

As previously illustrated in terms of minimal and maximal scenarios,[8] the concept of the corporate body is taken most seriously in this model. Whereas with 'Welsh Office plus', the concept is essentially there to fill the (legal) space vacated by the Secretary of State for Wales, great stress is laid here on the role

and authority of the Assembly *qua* Assembly, and on the (policy development) work of the all-party subject committees. Read in conjunction with the
tilt in the parliamentary proceedings on the devolution bill in favour of a
cabinet system, this is the Welsh constitutional hybrid splendidly envisioned.

Third face: parliamentary or 'government and opposition'

The third face is more familiar, that is from the viewpoint of comparative
constitutional design and development. It represents the basic outlines of a
parliamentary system, premised first on the operational independence of the
Presiding Officer and clerks, and second on the practice and conventions of
cabinet government. It is also indicative in the Assembly of an enhanced
scrutiny role for the subject committees, as also an improved range of
parliamentary services for individual Members. A sense of government and
opposition pervades many of the structures and processes.

Emblematic of what I have called the 'strange anatomy', this is also the
model that does not sit easily with the formal constitutional design of the
devolution statute. So to promote it, there is a need carefully to distinguish
the *de facto* from the *de jure*. At the risk of repetition, this face need not be cast
in the particular Westminster mould – as familiarly associated with a largely
adversarial two-party system and by a peculiarly strong form of executive
domination by the party in power. Parliaments come in all shapes and sizes,
including perhaps in Wales.

Constitutional trilemma

Reconciliation of some demands of the competing models is clearly possible.
Rhodri Morgan, while promoting the idea of cabinet 'as a government
delivering', has rightly stressed the need in a small country like Wales to
harness all talents in the political process.[9] That the general contours of a
parliamentary system do not harden into a rigid, formalistic and overly
exclusive system is a vital local concern.

Other tensions between the models are more intractable, such that
accentuating the features or moulding the structures and procedures in the
image of one face serves to disfigure another. One example is the evident
tension between a strong centralized form of decision-making and the more
open and participatory process that people were led to expect in the White
Paper *A Voice for Wales*. So also the parliamentary-style model is indicative of
a restricted role for backbenchers. There has been, to coin a phrase, a
'constitutional trilemma' at the heart of the devolutionary development in
Wales.

The three models further serve to highlight the dynamic or uninterrupted nature of the process of internal constitutional design. The so-called 'devolution settlement' has actually entailed a fluid mix of competing architectural and procedural forms. As indicated, the initial sense of an administrative and political makeover has been successfully – and in my view rightly – challenged. Pressures for change reflect a greater concern for responsible and effective modalities of government, consistent with the ideals of parliamentary democracy.

2. THE FALL OF ALUN MICHAEL

One way of characterizing Alun Michael's approach is in terms of devolution as the done deed. That is to say, an effort to dampen down the ongoing process of devolutionary change or, more positively, a premium on political and administrative continuity justified on the basis of a need for stability for the infant body.[10] Typically, it also involved proceeding inside the Assembly in accordance with a strong hierarchical view of the corporate body ('Welsh Office plus'). Far from exploring the boundaries, it was a case of an already attenuated devolutionary scheme writ small.

The great constitutional and political paradox of this first period is shown. Cautious and controlling, by bearing down so hard or effectively slowing the development of a new Welsh polity above and beyond machinery to implement or manage centrally devised policies, the administration of Alun Michael served to heighten the underlying tensions in Cardiff Bay. Impressionistic perhaps, but the regular visitor to the Assembly at this time could not fail to be struck by the increasingly taut atmosphere among Members and officials. Via a slow-burning fuse, matters would explode in what is aptly called – in the devolutionary sense – the first Welsh constitutional crisis.[11] Who would have believed it?

Threatening skies

Politics, administration and the constitution (of Wales): all three strands are closely entwined in the early meetings of the Assembly. That, following the unexpected results in the elections, Alun Michael chose to spurn overtures from the Liberal Democrats and opt instead for minority government is clearly a factor of the first importance. Constitutionally, as well as politically speaking, it made the idea of a highly centralist regime all the more incongruous. This was naturally underscored by the lingering perception, in light of the mode of his election as Welsh Labour leader, of Alun Michael as the Prime Minister's 'Cymric lieutenant'.[12]

At the same time, the administration was effectively required to limp along; or more precisely, according to Ron Davies, to survive 'day-to-day on the basis of one-off agreements with one or other of the minority parties'.[13] The very first session set the tone. In return for Alun Michael being elected unopposed as First Secretary, the Labour group had to trade the election to the post of Assembly Presiding Officer of the veteran nationalist and former MP, Lord Elis-Thomas.[14] As events would show, there was now a viper in the nest.

Alun Michael may also be said to be the victim of circumstance. Given the small size of the Assembly, there obviously was a limited pool of talent from which to construct the first Welsh administration. In the event, and once again serving to underline the sharp learning curve that so many of our actors have faced, the chief attribute that his cabinet colleagues shared was a lack of ministerial experience. The contemporary jibe of 'the weakest cabinet in Europe' was no doubt horribly unfair, but it may serve to underscore the point. And Alun Michael, successively a minister of state at the Home Office, Secretary of State for Wales, and now of course Assembly First Secretary, certainly had the experience. Conditions were thus ripe for a First Secretary-dominated form of executive decision-making in the initial phase of Assembly workings.

One cannot gloss over the personal factors. In such matters perception is vital and Alun Michael's individual style was clearly seen to exacerbate things. The complaints were not slow in surfacing. An unwillingness to delegate, to the detriment of cabinet colleagues; a painstaking approach, submerged in detail; the failure to articulate an ambitious vision for the Assembly: it was a formidable list.[15] To which may be added key elements of constitutional and administrative practice that fit with the model of 'Welsh Office plus'. Erosion of the (much-vaunted) role of the subject committees, as indicated in the claim by one minister of no greater status for their conclusions than that of public consultees, is but one example.[16]

Conditions were also ripe for little to happen in terms of direct legal and policy outputs. It was not simply the case of an infant body learning to crawl. First, the Labour Party manifesto[17] for the first Assembly elections was notably light in terms of concrete policy proposals, an accurate reflection of the lack of tradition of policy-making in Wales at the political level. Secondly, and also explained by the chief feature of an administration limping along, there was the lack of a clearly articulated government programme of Assembly business. More specifically, there was a dearth of Assembly law making – the subordinate legislation of which so much had been heard in the White Paper *A Voice for Wales*.[18] Liberal Democrat leader Michael German may be quoted: 'we have a car on the road but the handbrake is still on'.[19]

Not that there was a lack of paper: the first Assembly administration effectively inaugurated one of the growth industries of Welsh devolution – consultation papers and more especially strategic or corporate plans stretching over the horizon.[20] A parallel source, already mentioned, was Assembly housekeeping, very necessary but hardly likely to engage the interest of a wider audience. It suffices to add that the discussion in the chamber of the plethora of codes and guidance regulating the new institution was typically lethargic and desultory.[21]

Turning to matters of substance, one of the first issues considered by the Assembly was the lifting of the ban on beef on the bone, a central government measure imposed in response to the BSE crisis but now based on a devolved power.[22] Predictably, the issue was to prove highly contentious, involving at one level complex issues of risk assessment and the general problem of balancing the needs of public health against the demands of hard-pressed (and voluble) local producers, and at another level the various interests of the countries of the UK. In the event, an initial burst of enthusiasm for unilateral action in Wales was tempered by careful deliberations in the relevant subject committee.[23] In particular, there was firm evidence on the precautionary principle from the Chief Medical Officer (CMO) for Wales; and, further, a recognition that – whatever the strict legal position – the UK-wide approach was the best way to gain consumer confidence.

The controversy in the Assembly reflected and reinforced the sense of (Welsh) agriculture in crisis. Given the weight of evidence of difficulties in the rural economy, this was hardly surprising. In turn, it was the perceived failure of the administration to bring forward appropriate measures to help farmers that first occasioned what rapidly became standard fare in the Assembly: censure motions against the then Agriculture Secretary, Christine Gwyther.

Although unsuccessful, this particular motion was, constitutionally speaking, a significant one for being directed, not to some personal mis-demeanour, but to a policy-orientated matter.[24] To explicate, consistent with the distinctive constitutional design of the Assembly as demonstrated in the formal routing of delegated functions, standing orders have only provided for no-confidence motions against the chief minister,[25] so reflecting his account-ability to the Assembly as a whole. In turn, should a censure motion be passed against a cabinet minister, then in the words of NAAG, 'it will be for the First Secretary to decide how to respond and whether to replace that individual'.[26]

For the Assembly, GM (genetically modified) crops, or more precisely the attempt to secure a GM-free environment for Wales, has been a never-ending saga. A resolution to control the commercial release of such crops was passed very early on[27] and then followed by lengthy deliberations in the Assembly's Agriculture and Rural Development Committee. Notably, what was in issue at this stage was not so much the policy but the powers of the Assembly, and not simply under UK law but also under the relevant EU directive.[28] The puzzlement, even bewilderment, of many AMs is amply conveyed by Michael German: 'European law, UK law, Assembly law, devolution law all seem to be at odds on genetically modified crops.'[29] Furthermore, this kind of protracted and convoluted wrangling could not help but fuel the general sense of unease in Cardiff Bay concerning the direction – and worth – of (executive) devolution, something which found tangible expression in the demise of Alun Michael. Such connections were not direct, but it all added up.

Christine Gwyther was successfully censured in October 1999. The catalyst was a calf-processing support scheme, which the Assembly unanimously approved only to discover at a late stage that it fell foul of EU rules. Ms Gwyther blamed her civil servants; the three opposition parties blamed her. In the words of Plaid elder statesman Dafydd Wigley: 'Whatever the situation is, the minister . . . must take responsibility for the failings of her department.' On the contrary, said Alun Michael, far from inclusive politics, cooperation and partnership, 'this looks like politicians squabbling among themselves, [which] does nothing to enhance the Assembly's image'.[30]

The scene was set. Act One: Mr Michael holds the line, to the effect that there is no obligation on Ms Gwyther to resign, nor will he dismiss her. In the First Secretary's words: 'I have the responsibility for appointing members of my Cabinet and they have to have my confidence.'[31] Act Two: the Conservatives move a motion of no confidence in Mr Michael, and on grounds that amount to a rejection of the constitutional model of 'Welsh Office plus'. To quote Conservative leader Nick Bourne, 'This . . . motion . . . is proposed to address how the Assembly is run. [The] minority administration acts and fails to react as if it were a majority administration . . . Ignoring the censure motion was but the latest example of that.' Act Three: the no-confidence motion fails, but on the basis of a not so veiled threat. As Mr Wigley put it: 'A question of confidence will arise if the Government fails to deliver on match funding and on securing European funds for Wales, over and above the Barnett block grant.'[32]

The exchanges neatly convey the increasingly adversarial tone in this formative period: so much for a lack of Westminster-style conflict in Cardiff Bay! But further, the basic constitutional issue of democratic accountability in the new representative institution was now starkly posed. Strictly, when read in terms of the distinctive character of the Welsh scheme, Alun Michael was correct in his formulation. As envisaged by NAAG, a fixed-term Assembly meant very particular responsibilities for the First Secretary, such that consistent with the strong central routing of delegations he had both to retain the confidence of the Assembly and take responsibility for the actions of the individual Assembly Secretaries whom he had appointed.[33] Yet such a formulation was apt to offend received democratic notions of responsible government, not least in the case of those schooled in the Westminster tradition or seeking after a Parliament for Wales. More prosaically, the First Secretary had now raised the stakes on behalf of his minority administration. If a vote of censure was advisory only, this itself suggested further recourse to the so-called 'nuclear option' in the guise of a no-confidence motion.

Hiroshima

And so to the issue that would not go away: the vexed question of Treasury support for Objective 1 funding. The pressure in the Assembly on the administration steadily increased throughout 1999, as the opposition parties hardened their stance, to the effect of requiring an early guarantee of additional funding.[34] As explained, an impossibilist position according to conventional canons of UK resource allocation,[35] it was a most useful pretext for bringing down Alun Michael and with him a particular brand or style of devolved administration. In the event, the three opposition parties fixed on 9 February 2000 for Alun Michael's high noon. 'The National Assembly for Wales has no confidence in the First Secretary.' The clock ticked by.

Alun Michael, however, was not about to roll over. Matters were primed for a major piece of legal and constitutional wrangling in the corridors of the Assembly, centred on the role of the Presiding Officer in interpreting and applying standing orders. The question was sharply posed: assuming the no-confidence motion was carried, procedurally speaking what happened next?

To explicate, the statutory commissioners in designing standing orders had chosen not to follow the practice in some European countries of requiring as part of a no-confidence motion the nomination of an alternative leader (a so-called 'constructive vote of no-confidence'). A form of democratic engineering, it is worth noting, that not only would have made the prospects of the unholy alliance against Alun Michael look very different, but also has particular appeal as machinery for promoting stability or discouraging irresponsible opposition in the context of a fixed-term electoral arrangement. In contrast, the internal law of the Assembly was made typically skeletal:

> A First Secretary may resign by giving notice in writing to the Presiding Officer. If the Assembly resolves that it has no confidence in its First Secretary, he or she shall give such notice immediately.

> Where a First Secretary has resigned (or if the office otherwise becomes vacant), other Assembly Secretaries shall remain in office until the Assembly elects a new First Secretary; and the Assembly Cabinet shall elect one of its members to chair its meetings and discharge the First Secretary's responsibilities until the Assembly elects a new First Secretary.

Lord Elis-Thomas avers that he was put under very great pressure from the highest echelons of the administration to adopt a particular approach to standing orders: from personal entreaties to media briefings and on – fantastically – to suggestions of judicial review.[36] Obviously it suited the First Secretary to say that if the no-confidence motion was carried, and – as was clearly anticipated – Labour renominated him, then the proper course of action – in the light of no alternative nomination – was for the Presiding Officer to disallow or postpone further no-confidence motions.

As a formula for buttressing the legitimacy of the Assembly, or avoiding the worst-case scenario of a constitutional game of 'ping-pong', this had merit. Yet it was not the only possible approach. An alternative and principled view was that the Presiding Officer should not descend into the 'arena' or come down on one side or the other; in other words, he should decline to supply the omission of the statutory commissioners. It was after all virgin territory. And little guidance could be gleaned from precedents established elsewhere precisely because of the peculiar constitutional character of the Assembly.

In the event, Alun Michael was to accuse Lord Elis-Thomas of moving the goalposts, most obviously for partisan advantage. It was said that a 'ruling' in favour of a cooling-off period had been replaced by the procedure whereby any further no-confidence motion would be taken immediately, such that the governing party was effectively deprived of the opportunity to make a full and considered response.[37] It suffices to say, first, that there never was a definitive formal ruling on this point; and, second, that confronted by the corporate body in all its glory, Lord Elis-Thomas took legal advice from other quarters, and so blazed the trail for later developments inside the Presiding Office.

Nagasaki

The motion of no confidence, however, was not the only constitutional challenge that Alun Michael now faced. Plaid's business manager Jocelyn Davies had worked up another devastating motion, once again with legal assistance from outside the Assembly. Primed for action following the no-confidence motion, and so nicknamed for obvious reasons 'Nagasaki', it deserves to be quoted in full:

> This Assembly resolves that all delegations made to the Assembly First Secretary under Section 62(1) of the Government of Wales Act of all the Assembly's functions which the Act did not reserve to the Assembly in Plenary session shall forthwith cease.
>
> The Assembly also resolves in the exercise of its powers under Section 63 of the Government of Wales Act to delegate to the Assembly staff the functions previously delegated to them by Assembly Secretaries.

As a legal ploy, the motion was politically deadly. Assuming that Alun Michael clung on notwithstanding the resolution(s) of no confidence, he faced the prospect of a ghostly existence: the ministerial car but no job content. In turn, because members of the Assembly cabinet derive their functions by means of sub-delegation from the chief minister, they would be similarly embarrassed.

From the constitutional viewpoint, no single document better conveys the distinctive nature of the corporate body that is the Assembly. By invoking the ultimate authority of the representatives in plenary session, the motion effectively threatened the administration with implosion of the internal architecture of the Assembly. Turning the argument round, no such resolution would have been possible had there been a formal statutory separation of the legislative and executive branches of government.

The standard legal proposition that a delegation of powers can also be revoked is underscored in this context by section 62(8) of the GWA, which makes plain that in delegating a function the Assembly retains concurrent power to exercise it.[38] At the risk of repetition, the very idea of providing the Assembly with a broad framework for organic development has depended on this concept. Effectively, its own constitutional design was now being invoked against the Labour Party in Wales.

The motion was skilfully drafted, particularly the second paragraph. To recap, the GWA does not authorize the Assembly to delegate directly to cabinet ministers. How then to circumvent the objection that such a 'reverse-delegations' resolution would effectively bring the government of Wales to a grinding halt, with all functions being concentrated in the Assembly in plenary session? By invoking section 63 and maintaining the delegations to officials, the statutory responsibilities of the Permanent Secretary as the Assembly's principal accounting officer could be satisfied. As against being ruled out of order, the motion was fireproof.

This version of the nuclear option further illustrates the great importance that attaches to the hierarchy of rules in the devolutionary construction. Whereas major players in the administration conceived of the legal and constitutional question in terms of standing orders – no confidence and 'ping-pong' – the 'Nagasaki' motion effectively trumped that line of argument by reference to the statute. The sense of the GWA as 'the written constitution' or 'higher law' of the new territorial polity is communicated strongly here.

It is then this motion that exploited what I identified as the Achilles heel in the official design of the representative body.[39] 'Nagasaki' was clearly dependent for its explosive effect on there being no need for a special majority to reorder the internal architecture. Nine months on, what may have looked like a dry and technical legal ruling, that the system of delegations could not be concretized in standing orders at the behest of Alun Michael as Secretary of State for Wales, had come home to roost. A case, one could say, of London's man undermined by London's lawyers.

Detonation

The debate on the no-confidence motion reinforces how the argument had moved beyond Objective 1 funding to encompass the broad gamut of devolutionist concerns.[40] In view of his later reincarnation as Deputy First Minister in the coalition government, the speech by Liberal Democrat leader Michael German is especially noteworthy:[41]

> We hold the First Secretary to account: not just for the failure to deliver matched funding – as if that were not enough – but failure to deliver for the Assembly and on the very principle of devolution itself. The Objective 1 issue is only the most potent and powerful symbol of the minority administration's failings. It has failed to deliver the principles of devolution and to fight for Welsh solutions to Welsh problems . . .
>
> The Labour minority administration . . . has avoided risk, taken the cautious options and erred towards safety. The result has been unexciting, underwhelming and uninspiring. We must change and must be seen to change, starting with a change of leadership . . .

Alun Michael was naturally unrepentant:

> I have not failed to deliver. I have delivered and I will deliver. I have every confidence that . . . at the end of the negotiating process that is currently under way with the Treasury, we will deliver in full the money that is due to the people of Wales . . .
>
> We must face the reality of our position. Labour is a minority administration . . . We have made enormous progress, despite the difficulties . . . Things will not change overnight. It will take time for us to put in place the building blocks that we need to effect real change in people's lives, whether that be done through European programmes, new youth support services or ways of tackling social exclusion. It all takes time, as it does for a new institution to grow to maturity. Today's motion puts all of that at risk . . .

With that, Alun Michael resigned; or did he? The letter that he now handed to the Presiding Officer said so, while carefully preserving the possibility of his renomination.[42] Lord Elis-Thomas, however, was not to be deflected from proceeding to a vote. And so, by 31 votes to 27, the Assembly formally resolved that it had no confidence in the First Secretary: which in accordance with standing orders also meant his resignation. It was a suitably bizarre ending to an extraordinary moment in Welsh history.

For whatever lingering hopes Alun Michael may have had, they were quickly extinguished. The Labour group in the Assembly had clearly had enough. 'Nagasaki' was never required to happen. Rhodri Morgan finally inherited the leadership. A week later, it was he who was delegating functions. In his words, 'I regard now as the end of the beginning of devolution.'[43]

Fallout

A recurring theme in this book is the way in which the Welsh devolutionary scheme can be operated more or less generously. That Mr Michael's replacement immediately struck a different chord in constitutional and political matters therefore has particular resonance. 'Labour's leader in the Assembly is not there to be a thorn in the side of the UK Labour leader, but not to be a puppet either. Devolution must mean what it says, the defined transfer of power to Wales . . . '[44] And again, in typically colourful language, which notably reflects and reinforces the constitutional fundamental of the Welsh scheme that is 'national devolution': 'If I've got anything to do with it . . . the Welsh Assembly will be flying the flag for Wales. People will look at the Welsh Assembly and they will be as proud to be represented by the Welsh Assembly as they are by the Welsh Dragon.'[45] Meanwhile, his 'first day of devolution', the Presiding Officer rejoiced. His statement is also indicative of the high degree of politicization of his Office that had occurred; and further, of an associated breakdown in personal relations between leading actors in the Assembly, a factor not to be discounted in charting the progress of the new representative institution: 'This is real devolution. The National Assembly said we don't want this style of politics, we don't want these particular things, and we express these views. This was the majority view of the Assembly. This is real democracy.'[46]

In the short term, the advent of Rhodri Morgan heralded a reworked form of (Labour) minority administration in the Assembly: a shift from one-off agreements towards an informal cohabitation arrangement involving Plaid.[47] To quote Mr Morgan, 'The Assembly needs a period of calm and continuity . . . We cannot allow the culling of First Secretaries . . . to become Wales's annual blood sport.'[48] One is tempted to describe this as replacing a 'red light' theory of devolution, minimalist and exhibiting a strong measure of internal hierarchical control, with an 'amber light' view, licence to proceed.

Again, the arrival on the scene some six months later of the coalition government, able to be formed once a generous Treasury settlement had lanced the boil of Objective 1 funding,[49] could be said to have ushered in 'green light' conditions for Assembly policy-making and administration, a more dynamic approach. This is not to overlook the huge constraints entailed in the Welsh devolutionary scheme. Quite the reverse – it is only in this later period that the limitations as well as the many opportunities involved in the devolved system of government could be fully tested.

That Alun Michael's demise was triggered via a classic issue of inter-governmental relations – fiscal transfer or guarantee – gives the affair an extra poignancy. Effectively, his special case for exercising power of a close insider or 'sweetheart' relationship with (Labour) colleagues in London was overborne by expanding forces for increased territorial autonomy. Looked at 'top-down' (from the UK perspective), the constitutional *coup* that overthrew him represents the loss of a measure of control by the centre, while seen bottom-up (in terms of the local constitutional development), it shows the Assembly flexing its muscles as a distinctive polity – less deferential.[50]

Reference here to the three competing models demonstrates how the internal development of the Assembly has been more complicated than first appears. Alun Michael not only practised proprietorial government but also preached the virtues of consensus and inclusiveness.[51] Effectively tarred with the same brush, the designedly friendly model has not had much of an opportunity to shine, the counter-reaction being very much in favour of a parliamentary-style model. Such anyway is the lament of the ministerial architect of the devolutionary scheme.[52]

Put another way, the early quest for a reworked form of democratic culture glossed over the pull not only of the (Westminster) parliamentary tradition, but also, in the Presiding Officer's words, of 'the territorial administrative/ executive government in the previous system'.[53] Or, as I prefer, the model of 'Welsh Office plus'. By in a very real sense reliving the past, the first Assembly administration did little for the idea of a distinctive constitutional future premised on new-style modalities or forms of government. The greatest legacy of Alun Michael is the firm impetus given to the cause of a Parliament for Wales. It is a fine irony.

2. THE RISE OF THE PRESIDING OFFICE

Constitutional matters would take a very practical turn in the period immediately following the demise of Alun Michael. In fact, far from slackening, the pace of constitutional development inside the Assembly was to accelerate sharply in the brief interlude of minority administration under Rhodri Morgan. Post-'crisis', some basic elements of political and democratic legitimacy cried out for attention. Buttressing the role and position of the Presiding Officer (PO) and his office is the most obvious aspect.[54]

The coup gave Lord Elis-Thomas the perfect opportunity to play the parliamentary card. The vision now presented was one of separate budgets, clear procedural and operational autonomy, and discrete control of the 'parliamentary' buildings in Cardiff Bay.[55] Which translated meant a push for the fledgeling institution more into the mainstream of comparative con-stitutional development, not least in the countries of the Commonwealth. Much of this has come to pass.

In the words of the (post-Alun Michael) mission statement:

The Presiding Office exists to serve the Members of the National Assembly for Wales and ensure its successful functioning as a democratic elected body. It will operate without regard to the political affiliations of individual Members under the guidance of the Presiding Officer and in accordance with the Civil Service Code.[56]

To this end, the rise of what was formerly called 'OPO', the Office of the Presiding Officer, involves a series of elements. There is a firmer insistence on the separateness or – as Lord Elis-Thomas would prefer – independence of the Office from what is now the Welsh Assembly Government. An enhanced role and status for the Clerk to the Assembly is, constitutionally speaking, very significant, as is a separate source of legal advice. Organizational change inside the office is a key indicator, not least a more than doubling of the staff complement originally envisaged. The office is seen taking on substantial additional responsibilities or tasks, marking a more expansive approach to the provision of parliamentary-style services. A major flanking development involves a House Committee of AMs: more delineation of a 'legislative branch'.

Stretching matters

The degree of technical difficulty involved in the restructuring is worth emphasizing. A thickening of the 'Welsh walls', the so-called 'separation project' was not only driven by dissatisfaction with the legal corset of the corporate body but also closely structured by it. The mission statement itself serves as a reminder that all the officials involved are civil servants[57] and not employees of the 'House' as in the (Westminster) parliamentary model. Even now, it would be rash to assume that all the i's have been dotted or the t's crossed.

One consideration is the exceptionally thin legal base for many of the activities of the Presiding Office. Since only the bare fact of the posts of Presiding Officer and Deputy is recognized in the GWA, it is largely a case of falling back on supplementary powers. 'The Assembly may do anything . . . which is calculated to facilitate, or is conducive or incidental to, the exercise of any of its functions.'[58] So also the Assembly may incur expenditure 'in connection with' any such exercise of functions.[59] A formulation, the minister explained, that was necessary to permit the Assembly – for which now read the Presiding Office – to pay for running costs, 'as this is not a function *per se* of the Assembly'.[60] Suffice it to add that the House Committee has no specific statutory base.

The ramifications of corporate status go wider still. As a single legal personality, one thing that the Assembly cannot do is contract with itself. The general issue is familiar to public lawyers in the guise of the framework documents of those creatures of central government departments, the Next

Steps Agencies.[61] It is especially noteworthy here, however, given the character of a 'national' representative institution. Much use has been made of soft law in the form of contract-type arrangements that are not legally enforceable – what I call 'pseudo contract'[62] – specifically in order to formalize the administrative relationship – separateness – of the Presiding Office and the rest of the Assembly administration.

Turning the argument round, great ingenuity has been shown in promoting this more 'parliamentary' aspect of the Assembly. Testimony to the strength of local political will to move in this direction, this autochthonous development is the more striking precisely because of the lack of a secure legal base. 'The devolution statute – a framework for organic change': it is a case here of stretching matters.

A matter of principle

The separation project was carried forward by an *ad hoc* committee of officials drawn from the two emerging 'sides' of the Assembly, a notable feature in itself, and ultimately through the political agreement of the First Minister, the Presiding Officer and the different party groups. Where appropriate, the changes are now entrenched in standing orders.

This particular dynamic is the more significant for being founded on something all too rare in the Welsh devolutionary development – clear articulation of a set of constitutional principles:

- The Presiding Officer and his Office are independent of the Assembly's Administration;
- The Presiding Officer has overall responsibility for the conduct of the Assembly business, and for the exercise of Standing Orders;
- OPO is directly accountable to the Presiding Officer and the House Committee, and through them to the Assembly;
- The Clerk to the Assembly and his staff are to have maximum operational independence to carry out OPO's functions in support of Members and the Assembly's business in accordance with the Assembly's wishes and those of the Presiding Officer;
- The staff of OPO will remain Civil Servants, ultimately accountable on staff management matters to the Permanent Secretary. The Permanent Secretary will formally delegate the exercise of those functions within OPO to the Clerk insofar as this is permissible under the law;
- The Office of the Presiding Officer will have its own budget, determined directly by the Assembly.[63]

In turn, there was now to be an agreed statement of the role and functions of this pole of Assembly authority. 'The Presiding Officer holds the position equivalent to the Speaker in Parliament, carrying out his role independently of the Assembly's Executive.' 'His function, and that of his Office (OPO) is to represent the interests of all Assembly Members and to ensure that the business of the Assembly is discharged smoothly and impartially and in keeping with the best traditions of representative institutions.' 'OPO has the role of ensuring that Assembly Members can effectively scrutinise the work of the Assembly's Executive.'[64] The unexceptional character of these proposi- tions – that is, to those reared on basic canons of parliamentary government – makes the point brilliantly.

Implementation of the principles coincided with the arrival on the scene of the coalition between Labour and the Liberal Democrats. In the words of the Partnership Agreement, 'We will secure the independence of the Office of the Presiding Officer and the civil servants that work there.'[65] It is worth noting that no evidence was presented to the subsequent Assembly Review of Procedure in favour of retrenchment.[66] The rise of the Presiding Office is now politically as well as procedurally entrenched.

Pieces in the jigsaw

The establishment of a separate budget for the Presiding Office, covering all the services for which it has direct responsibility, is a development of prime importance in the constitutional life of the Assembly. The provision has in fact been notably generous. This in part reflects the new responsibilities, most particularly the care and control of the 'parliamentary' buildings. But further, in the words of Finance Minister Edwina Hart, it showed acceptance of the need for 'enhancement and development' of the services provided by the Office 'year on year'.[67] The budget was fixed at £24.3 million for 2001–2, with subsequent increases linked to the prevailing rate of inflation.

Standing orders now govern the process. Direct access to the full Assembly is secured via the all-party machinery of the House Committee. Following consideration by the Committee and discussion between the Presiding Officer, the Clerk and the Finance Minister, the draft annual budget is proposed by a member of the committee in a motion that importantly is not subject to amendment. The arrangement is unique, the budget of the Presiding Office being effectively top-sliced and agreed in advance and outside of the Assembly's main budget round. Meanwhile – operational autonomy – there is provision for full end-year flexibility and for virement within the budget at the discretion of the Clerk.[68]

Let us backtrack. Procedural wrangles, exceptional political pressures: the fact that post-'crisis' the Presiding Officer immediately demanded a trusted or separate source of legal advice, not least with a view to the core task of determining the interpretation or application of standing orders, is clearly significant. That previously the PO was required – adapting a famous phrase

– to go naked into the Assembly Chamber is indicative of a lack of constitutional understanding or sense of the democratic proprieties elsewhere in the Administration at the time of empowerment: body corporate or not.[69]

As the first piece in a jigsaw, the post of independent legal adviser has a certain historical significance in the life of the Assembly. A measure of equality of arms was quickly secured by the appointment of David Lambert, former chief legal adviser to the Welsh Office.[70] Latterly in the guise of the Legal Division of the Presiding Office, the input has ranged increasingly widely, once again reflecting the process of maturation of the new representative body. From advice to all and sundry on standing orders, to sensitive matters of registration of interests, and on through assistance to the Library in answering Members' queries, it is the kind of legal support that is so familiar in a Westminster-type system.[71]

Pseudo-contract has served to lessen the dependency of the Presiding Office at bureaucratic level. For the purpose of the separation project, the constitutional issue that fell to be addressed involved the relationship between the Permanent Secretary and the Clerk to the Assembly. That is to say, the striking of a more equitable balance inside the framework of a statutory scheme that – shades of the Welsh Office – has concentrated accounting and staff responsibilities in the hands of the one office-holder and denied recognition to the other. More particularly, the GWA only provides for a single Principal Accounting Officer (the Permanent Secretary) and for the appointment of Additional Accounting Officers (such as the Clerk) to undertake responsibilities on his behalf.[72]

The way forward lay through a revised Accounting Officer Agreement between the two officials. 'The Clerk has personal responsibility with respect to the budgets allocated to [the Presiding Office]; for . . . the propriety and regularity of the management of those public finances; for prudent and economical administration; and for the efficient and effective use of resources.'[73] A parallel agreement then set out the personnel functions under the Civil Service (Management Functions) Act delegated to the Clerk by the Permanent Secretary.[74] The Clerk has thereby had the responsibility for the structure and management of the Presiding Office staff, including on recruitment, grading and training and development, but subject of course to the relevant civil service codes.

A raft of service-level agreements between the Presiding Office and core divisions of the administration has put the flesh on the bones. They have ranged from IT to property services, and on through financial planning to financial services. By way of illustration, an agreement with the Internal Audit Services (IAS) of the Assembly has prescribed in considerable detail the work on financial information and quality control programmes to be done on behalf of the Office. Classic pseudo-contract, it was solemnly declared: 'This Agreement . . . is not intended to be a legal document in that, in the event of a dispute between the parties, it would not be adjudicated in a court of law.'[75]

The House Committee of AMs is a major piece in the jigsaw. Originally a weak and diffuse form of *ad hoc* machinery, it would now be formalized under standing orders as part of the separation project. The design was that of an advisory body, with no executive functions. Legally speaking, this avoided the general requirement for Assembly committees of party balance,[76] so allowing for a small nucleus – modelled on the Business Committee[77] – of one representative from each political group plus the chair (the PO or the DPO).

Advice on the budget, administration, and exercise of the functions of the Presiding Office, including the services and facilities provided for Members, and their fees and allowances: all this quickly became the standard fare.[78] A useful benchmark, the list at this stage did not include staff matters, as well as the more obvious constitutional exclusions such as the conduct of proceedings. Separation was here being engendered but not guaranteed, with the delegation of decision-making powers clearly being considered a step too far.

Triumvirate

Personal factors have once again been important. A year on from the demise of Alun Michael and a powerful triumvirate had formed at the top of the Presiding Office, one that has been mutually supportive in promoting and protecting the *de facto* separation of functions inside the Assembly.

As well as Lord Elis-Thomas there was now John Marek, a Labour AM with considerable parliamentary experience, much of it on the backbenches. The development was the more noteworthy for the manner of its happening: formation of the coalition, a vacancy for the post of Deputy Presiding Officer (DPO) by reason of ministerial appointment, and victory for Mr Marek over the official candidate in the secret ballot that is prescribed in standing orders.[79] No placeman, Mr Marek's mandate was (to be) separate from the Executive. In his words: 'this is a post elected by the Assembly for the Assembly and I hope to carry out my duties impartially and fairly and to be a servant of the Assembly as a whole.'[80]

The DPO quickly came to play an important role in the work of the Assembly. As well as chairing (and making procedural decisions in) the vital Business Committee,[81] Dr Marek was entrusted by Lord Elis-Thomas with chairing the House Committee. He has also chaired the Panel of Subject Committee Chairs, and of course stands in for the Presiding Officer from time to time.

Like Alun Michael, the first Clerk to the Assembly had appeared to move seamlessly from the Welsh Office. As one of two Deputy Secretaries, John

Lloyd was one of the most distinguished and long-standing servants in Wales of the old-style territorial system of central government. So it is also the more noteworthy that following an open competition his successor should have come from a very different hue. Paul Silk – the current Clerk – was a senior and long-standing servant of the House of Commons including as Clerk to the Foreign Affairs Select Committee. Metaphorically speaking, in terms of official versus parliamentary expertise, no single development better illustrates the changing 'faces' of the Assembly.

Attention naturally focuses on the role of the 'Speaker'. Yet the rise of the Clerk epitomizes the rise of the Presiding Office and so also the constitutional trajectory of the Assembly. In the words of the job advertisement:

> The Clerk is a unique appointment in the UK Civil Service, and is equivalent to a Clerk of Parliament. The Clerk is the principal adviser to the Presiding Officer and has management responsibility for all services which are delivered to Assembly Members through the Office of the Presiding Officer . . . The Clerk must at all times uphold the integrity, independence and impartiality of the Office.[82]

To this essentially dual function should be added an important networking role on behalf of the Assembly, especially with other parliamentary institutions including via the Assembly's membership of the Commonwealth Parliamentary Association. It is all grist to the mill in the drive to improve the standing of the new representative body. As a former Westminster insider, Mr Silk has been eminently suited to the task.

A complex web of accountability serves to underscore the pivotal nature of the Clerk's position. That is to say, accountability to the PO and DPO for quality of advice; to the Assembly and Audit Committee for financial regularity and value for money; to the PO, DPO, House Committee and Assembly for efficiency and quality of services; and to the Permanent Secretary for proper staff management. A veritable anchor, the Clerk has clearly been in danger of being pulled in too many directions at once.

So perhaps it is not surprising to learn of a new post of Deputy Clerk to the Assembly. Reflecting and reinforcing the more parliamentary 'face', the Presiding Office as a pole of authority would be further thickened. By early 2003, the trio had become a foursome.

Servicing democracy: after OPO

A snapshot of the Presiding Office (figure 9) following the separation project will serve to illustrate the internal organizational development. It is indicative of the enhanced range of services increasingly on offer.

Briefly, Chamber Services, in the guise of the Chamber Secretariat and the Table Office, are responsible for delivering the classic 'parliamentary'

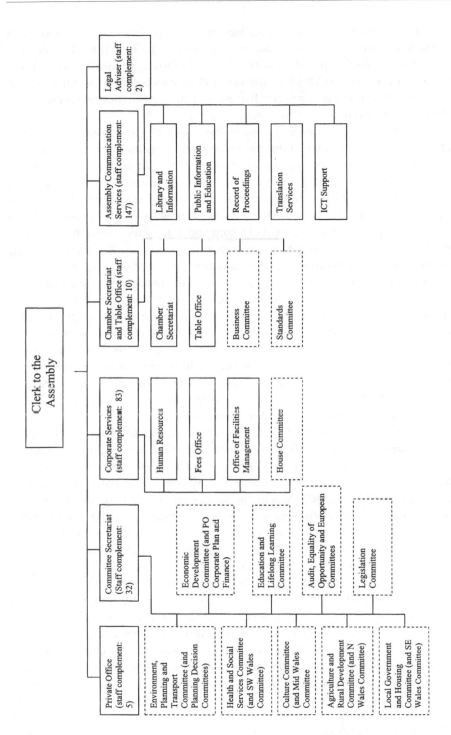

Figure 9: Presiding Office, anatomy and service – July 2001

services: managing plenary meetings and all processes associated with plenary (Assembly questions, motions, debates, etc). Operationally speaking, the team has been flanked by a small Private Office, the source of scripted advice to the PO and DPO on the conduct of proceedings. As the diagram illustrates, Chamber Services has had the additional function of servicing the Business and Standards Committees.

The expansive committee system of the Assembly has obviously meant a challenging task for the Committee Secretariat. Clerking services is the most important task, but one that as the diagram also illustrates has involved a doubling or even trebling up of administrative responsibilities. This has not prevented a strong dose of the management and education of AMs in these early years, better 'to ensure that . . . essential business is processed, and that the [subject] committees effectively contribute to policy development and review'.[83] Direct involvement in the preparation and maintenance of strategic forward work programmes for each committee is but one example.

Corporate Services, responsible for a range of core support functions such as personnel and property management, is very much a creature of the separation project. There was no serious equivalent in the original Welsh Office design for OPO. Acceptance of the fact of matching teams in the Presiding Office – a finance branch here, a dedicated IT unit there, and so on – was to this effect a key feature of the service level agreements. Mundane this may appear, but it has been an essential condition not only of the growth of the Presiding Office but also of the formalization and reworking of its relationship with other civil servants in the Assembly.

The fourth main branch, Communication Services, has continued to employ the bulk of the staff of the Presiding Office. For its part, the Library and Information Service for Members has clearly been stretched. Some 2,500 detailed research requests in a single year: the old territorial system of government, this is not.[84] Much the same may be said of the translation service, which in rendering documents and providing simultaneous translation facilities obviously occupies a very special niche in the new Welsh polity. It is also an exception, with the service encompassing the whole Assembly. The language, it appears, is no great respecter of the separation of powers!

One point deserves a special emphasis in the context of national devolution: an enhanced representational role for the Presiding Office. Via an expansion of Communication Services it has become ever more heavily engaged in the ongoing struggle of the Assembly to win the hearts and minds of the Welsh people. An original objective, 'to make the Assembly accessible by providing information to the public', soon became a more proactive one, 'to raise public awareness and understanding of the Assembly and its work'.[85] From information leaflets abounding to special events, and on through on-line public access to the jewel in the crown, an education and visitor centre adjacent to the Assembly Chamber, it is a remarkable effort. Howsoever attenuated in legal powers, the Assembly should not knowingly be undersold.

In summary, incorporating the Chamber and Committee Secretariats and the Table Office, and now boasting the Corporate Services Division as well as the Assembly Communication Services, the Presiding Office increasingly looks like a professional corps and core of authority for a National Assembly worthy of the title. OPO is no more – long live the Presiding Office! This is another of those name changes that so characterize the early life of the Assembly. As well as deflecting criticism of a personal fiefdom for Lord Elis-Thomas, it stands for the more generous approach to servicing democracy that has now prevailed in the rise of the office.

It does not do to be complacent. Running in tandem, what I call the pursuit of cabinet government is itself seen to generate demands for extra resources in the Presiding Office, better to secure the more 'parliamentary' role of holding the executive to account. Constitutionally speaking, a shift away from the consensual-collaborative 'face' of the Assembly in the absence of effective and efficient means of scrutiny of the increasingly capacious Welsh Assembly Government would represent the worst of both worlds.

At the same time, it is easy to cry wolf. For the Welsh Assembly Government to become the old Welsh Office by another name, with the rest of the Assembly – shorn of resources – being little more than a forum for ministerial pronouncements, the Presiding Officer and his close colleagues would have to go silently into the night. It is not about to happen.

Such is the immediate background to the Assembly Review of Procedure that reported in February 2002. The pressure for more resources was recognized, with the result of some modest proposals aimed at redressing the balance:

> In-house and other resources for committees should be strengthened to enable them to access a greater range of sources of advice and expertise . . . An additional specialist member of staff should be provided to the secretariat of each of the seven subject committees, plus a pool of around three other specialists to serve any of the committees as required . . .
> The Group received various suggestions aimed at improving the services available to individual Assembly Members through the Library, Committee Secretariat, a Vote Office and so on. The provision of high quality, independent support services for Members is vital if individual Members, committees and the Assembly as a whole are to function effectively.[86]

Viewed in terms of the underlying constitutional trajectory of the Assembly, the limited nature of the concessions should not be allowed to obscure the important local precedents that were being set here. Providing alternative and specialist sources in 'the legislative branch' of advice and assistance translates as lessening the committees' dependency on policy officials that was implicit in the model of 'Welsh Office plus'; and, in particular, as direct legal support for the committees, so facilitating Members' inputs especially on legislative matters.[87] From little acorns . . .

Separation project mark II

Emphatically, the rise of the Presiding Office is not complete. In late 2002 what may be described as 'separation project mark II' was inaugurated – a substantial delegation of functions previously routed through the First Minister to a revamped House Committee. Change to a committee with power to take executive decisions: earlier hesitations were once again being overcome, and with unanimous support in the chamber. In constitutional terms, it was in the words of the DPO another 'important step forward'.[88]

The project has entailed reworking standing orders to provide for a larger committee consistent with the statutory principle of party balance. An Assembly resolution exercising its powers under section 62 of the GWA[89] has also been necessary, thereby revoking and reassigning the delegation of relevant functions in favour of the House Committee. Typically, from the legal viewpoint, this has required some very careful navigation of the devolution statute.[90]

RIP 'OPO' – 'the Committee is responsible for':

> the provision to and for Members (including when acting in proceedings of the Assembly) of facilities, accommodation, staff and such other support services as are reasonably necessary for the better performance by Members of their position as Members of the Assembly, including in its capacity as a legislative body.[91]

As one would expect, much of the new remit travels the same ground as for the Committee in advisory mode. But there is also a major expansion, with staffing functions in respect of the Presiding Office and associated services now being delegated, subject to general equivalence in the terms and conditions of employment. Separation writ large: this project could usefully be the launch pad for a new wave of organizational developments, not least in view of the increasingly powerful executive arm of devolved government in Wales.

Speaking more generally, the rise of the Presiding Office shows the common trait in the Welsh devolutionary development of ongoing incremental change, a continuing constitutional negotiation or dialogue between local actors. To this effect, one important test of the local constitutional trajectory over the next few years will be the scale of the infilling in light of the precedents established through the Assembly Review of Procedure. The rise and rise of the Presiding Office: the auguries are good.

Full circle

Looking forwards, the formal legal and constitutional position of the Presiding Office must be high on the agenda of any proper review of the devolution legislation. A minimalist scenario would entail a statutory office of Clerk to the Assembly, coupled with legislative recognition of executive functions for the House Committee. The formal responsibility of the Permanent Secretary would thus be curtailed, or more closely targeted on the Welsh Assembly Government.

Fortunately, in the cause of securing the parliamentary face of the new Welsh polity, a cleaner and more comprehensive solution lies close to hand in the form of a corporate body. Not one hastens to add the 'all-singing and all-dancing' Assembly corporate form, but in the guise for example of the Scottish parliamentary corporation. That is to say, the more familiar constitutional model of a distinct legal entity charged with ensuring the service and support of the parliamentary process and associated activities. Bringing the discussion full circle, it was seen to be the model originally advocated for the Assembly by Rhodri Morgan.[92]

3. ENTER THE WELSH ASSEMBLY GOVERNMENT

On St David's Day 2002, the Welsh Assembly Government was solemnly proclaimed. Not, it should be stressed, by the primary lawgiver that is Westminster but by what according to the devolution statute is the local 'executive committee'.[93] This is autochthonous constitutional development exemplified.

Building on a previous pattern of incremental change, the new invention itself enhances the internal separation of functions. The divide between the executive branch – suitably redefined as 'cabinet ministers and civil servants providing all the normal services of government' – and what is now officially called the 'National Assembly for Wales democratic structure' (Assembly Members, Presiding Office, etc.) grows wider by the day.

The pursuit of cabinet government

One of the many dynamics in the Welsh devolutionary development, what I call 'the pursuit of cabinet government' has typically involved a mix of political, constitutional and administrative elements. Happening largely under the auspices of the coalition inaugurated in October 2000, and effectively paving the way for the Welsh Assembly Government, there is once again special resonance by reason of the strong committee model originally envisaged and the retarded development of a policy-oriented core in the old territorial department.[94] As part of the more parliamentary 'face' of the Assembly, its local significance can scarcely be exaggerated.

A more governmental image was on the agenda of the coalition from day one. A badge of honour, the distinctive Welsh constitutional label emphatically was not. According to the press release:

> The term 'Minister' has now been adopted by the Cabinet in order to distinguish clearly between members of the Cabinet and members of the Civil Service where the term 'Secretary' is a common title. This change will provide clarity for the public about lines of accountability and brings Wales into line with practice in the other devolved administrations in the UK.[95]

Not, it should be stressed, that this has been the comfortable path of 'devolution by evolution'. Cardiff Bay has once again seen more than its fair share of political accidents and imbroglios in the building-up and early operation of a cabinet system. Let us also keep in mind the uncomfortable fit with the formal constitutional design of the devolution statute. Stretching matters: there inevitably is an outer limit.

Majority administration in the Assembly is hardly set in stone. Yet irrespective of how the political cards fall in the future, it can safely be said that the essential features of the new Welsh system of cabinet government are here to stay, such is the force of the underlying constitutional trajectory.

A matter of protocol

The need to clarify structural arrangements, and, further, to formalize political understandings, was clearly articulated in the partnership agreement of Labour and the Liberal Democrats, *Putting Wales First*:

> To work effectively and to deliver this programme, the partners will need goodwill, mutual trust and agreed procedures which foster collective decision making and responsibility whilst respecting the distinct identity of each party within the partnership . . . The Assembly Executive will agree and publish formal documents setting out the principles of collective decision-making and the procedures to be followed to promote the good conduct of business, drawing on those already in place in the Scottish Partnership Government.[96]

In the event, the subsequent *Protocol for Partnership Government in the Assembly*[97] did not so much draw on the coalition agreement between Labour and the Liberal Democrats in Scotland as import large chunks of it. Seen in historical perspective, this is a classic example of Welsh actors following in the footsteps of their (constitutionally more advanced) northern cousins. Yet the Scottish arrangements are obviously a product of, and designed for, a different form of devolution settlement, as epitomized in the formal legal separation of the Parliament and the Executive.[98] Turning the argument round, the invocation of such arrangements in the case of Wales once again reflects and reinforces a move towards parliamentary-type government.

And so are born Welsh constitutional conventions. 'Cabinet members must at all times and in consistent terms support the decisions which other Cabinet Members have made, whether individually (under delegated authority) or collectively.'[99] Conversely, 'the policy-making process must give all Cabinet members with an official interest in an issue a chance to contribute before any decision is taken'. It could have come from the textbook (and probably did).

Nor was the way in which, according to the classical definition, 'the cabinet acts as a political link between the executive and the parliament because ministers are answerable to the parliament',[100] neglected. The *Protocol* listed various mechanisms of individual accountability, some like question time that are mandated in the statute,[101] others – for example ministerial statements or public correspondence – which obviously are not. It all ties up, to the extent of careful avoidance of judicial review on the common law ground of fettering discretion or unlawful delegation of power:

> In accounting for their decisions and policies in these ways, Ministers again remain within collective responsibility. In particular, they do not justify or defend their decisions in ways which might suggest disagreement within the Cabinet, or which suggest that actions they propose are subject to another Minister's agreement.[102]

Traditional constitutional doctrine, however, is made the more intricate in this type of environment. On the one hand, 'collective responsibility applies in its entirety in all cases where the matters concerned are matters of direct Assembly competence'. On the other hand, the *Protocol* was careful to say, in 'matters which remain wholly within the competence of the UK Government, cabinet members from each of the Partnership parties remain free to express the views of each individual Party'. Then again, 'where matters of UK competence impinge directly on matters of Assembly competence', most obviously under concurrent powers, 'cabinet members . . . will strive for agreement in any public comments, in so far as this remains consistent with retaining a respect for the distinctive political views of the different Parties involved'.[103] The many grey areas under the Welsh scheme of executive devolution were thus immediately highlighted.

A formal but living framework, the *Protocol* also cast light on the internal modalities of cabinet government in Wales under a partnership arrangement. Predictably, there was a premium on consensus or non-voting, to the extent of a distinctive interpretation of standard constitutional doctrine:

The Cabinet seeks to operate by discussion and consensus. Political issues arising between the Partnership Parties should, as far as possible, be resolved before an issue reaches Cabinet, either by bilateral discussion or in a cabinet sub-committee . . . Although it is hypothetically possible for the cabinet to take a majority view, this approach is inconsistent with the basic principles of collective responsibility, and it is not used in practice.[104]

Not of course that the cabinet was intended to be the vehicle for general decision-making:

Cabinet discusses any issue at the request of one or more Ministers. In the interests of brevity of Cabinet meetings, though, only the following types of issue should normally feature on the Cabinet's agenda:

(a)   issues which are of general importance to the Cabinet as a whole, whether because they are of major sensitivity or public importance, bear on the overall development of policy or the relationship between the Cabinet and the Assembly, outside bodies such as local authorities or business, the UK Government or the other devolved administrations;
(b)   issues which have not been resolved in bilateral discussions between interested Ministers, and/or a relevant Cabinet sub-committee;
(c)   issues which are of major political significance, including those which impinge upon the functioning of the Partnership.

In addition, each cabinet agenda includes an opportunity for the First Minister and Deputy First Minister to raise late-breaking issues for comment or information, and for the Business Secretary to raise issues relating to the management of Assembly business.[105]

From divided patronage to no monopoly of information, and on through an internal norm of comity or mutual cooperation between the partners, the provisions of the *Protocol* brilliantly illustrate how contrasting leadership styles in the Assembly are the product of political and constitutional circumstance as well as personal factors.[106] Put simply, whereas the first chief minister found himself surrounded by colleagues who were lacking in governmental experience, his successor soon had to navigate the sensitivities familiarly associated with coalition government.

Especially in view of some 'little local difficulties',[107] the prescribed role and position of the Deputy First Minister (DFM) deserves a special mention. Reproducing the Scottish agreement, 'close consultation' between the First Minister and the (Liberal Democrat) DFM was cited as 'the foundation of the Partnership's success'. It thus needed to cover 'all aspects of the conduct of the Assembly Executive, including the allocation of responsibilities, the Assembly's policy and legislative programme, the conduct of its business and the resolution of disputes.'[108] Viewed in comparative constitutional perspective, this is all at one with a genuine coalition arrangement, as distinct from a minority party bolt-on.

The pivotal role that was assigned to the DFM is the more striking in view of the provisions – or lack of them – in the devolution statute. As a purely political invention, one way of dealing with Labour's unexpected shortfall in the first Assembly elections, the post itself could not be a vehicle of formal legal powers since it was never in the contemplation of the parliamentary draftsman. *De facto* and *de jure*: as so often in Wales, 'now you see it, now you don't.'

The growth of the central political apparatus that is represented by deputy ministers has meant exactly the same disjunction in terms of formal legal recognition or delegation of powers, but also one that by definition cannot be 'cured' via the individual responsibilities of a cabinet minister's portfolio. From protocol to special cabinet guidelines, and on now to standing orders, Assembly lawyers have typically had to be busy. Acting in the capacity of a deputy minister only when authorized by a minister, being otherwise an 'ordinary' Member, has been a somewhat curious constitutional existence.[109]

The further twist concerns the doctrine of collective responsibility. Part and parcel of the thickening of the executive core via an increase in the payroll vote, in Cardiff as in other (parliamentary) systems junior ministers are under an obligation. Typically, the distinction has been drawn between matters within the portfolio of a minister whom the deputy minister supports, and matters within the portfolio of another minister where public comment on the basis of a personal or constituency interest is permissible. 'Controversial or outspoken comments' in relation to devolved matters must however be the subject of prior clearance.[110] In the event, Huw Lewis AM has achieved the tiniest footnote in Welsh constitutional history as the first minister compelled to resign for breach of convention. To declaim of the local handling of foot and mouth disease that 'this whole business has been a shambles'[111] was out of order.

'Check against delivery'

In what I have called the 'green light conditions' of the coalition, the political imperative (of being seen) to make a difference was exceptionally strong. How else, that is, to buttress support for the Assembly, and for such 'Lib-Labism'? Coupled with the provision of stable government, policy delivery quickly became of the essence of the Partnership government: even, one could say, its dominant ideology. Hence the First Minister's mantra, 'check against delivery':

> The whole concept of delivery of services to the people of Wales is absolutely fundamental to the Partnership Government . . . What we have to do is to try and

ensure that, having got devolution, we use devolution to try to ensure that we
have a set of policies that are suitable for Wales to try to tackle Wales' particular
set of economic and social problems . . . I want us to be judged upon what we
deliver.[112]

The approach also strikes a chord in the light of survey evidence that while
popular support for the Assembly has increased, only a minority considers
that it has yet managed to improve the quality of public services in Wales.[113]
Putting to one side the limitations of the devolutionary scheme, this would be
strange if it were otherwise. In the exercise of local policy autonomy, the Welsh
Assembly Government obviously needs time to deliver the bigger things.

Constitutionally speaking, the litmus test is the advent of an annual
government business programme in November 2000. The more parliamentary 'face': standing for the serious pursuit of cabinet government, this has also
allowed for a greater measure of structuring and formalizing of Assembly
business in plenary session. Andrew Davies, the minister responsible, may be
quoted: 'Last year we could not produce this sort of speech because we could
have not been sure we could have got its proposals through the Assembly.'[114]

The glib comparison is with the Queen's Speech at Westminster, which by
reason of the firm basis in proposals for primary legislation is obviously
qualitatively different. Emblematic of the Welsh devolutionary development,
the coalition's first effort was at once far more limited in scope and path-
breaking not least in terms of a history of close integration with England.
Reflecting the priorities for government set out in the Partnership Agreement
(and largely extracted from it), it will serve as a benchmark.[115]

Certainly there was guff or propaganda: 'We will ensure that rural
communities across Wales are served by a Government which understands
and responds to their needs.' But there was also a raft of practical ideas: some
for speedy implementation, others not. For example, in the realm of health
and social care, pride of place went to the new NHS Wales Strategy,[116] while
under the environment, planning and transport portfolio matters ranged from
establishing an integrated transport framework – subject to the Assembly's
fragmented powers – to requiring planning permission for telecommunica-
tions masts. Again, in local government and housing, proposals were brought
forward for a national housing strategy, for draft guidance on community
planning, and (a key Liberal Democrat demand) for an independent review of
electoral arrangements for local government in Wales.[117] Notably, a list of
proposed secondary legislation was also included, largely but not entirely the
product of new Westminster legislation allocating functions to Wales, which
itself signalled a significant acceleration in Assembly law making.[118] In
summary, the statement was symptomatic of a new form of government
slowly finding its feet and beginning to push forward.

Welsh mappa mundi

The gradual widening and deepening of the local processes of policy development is best illustrated by reference to what may be appropriately called a Welsh *mappa mundi*. Promulgated by its Strategic Policy Unit, the map has set out the Welsh Assembly Government's main values, strategies and targets, with a view to showing more dynamically the relationships between the various strands. 'If we are going to make a real difference for Wales, every team needs to be thinking of the part it can play in the whole picture – not just in its immediate responsibilities.'[119]

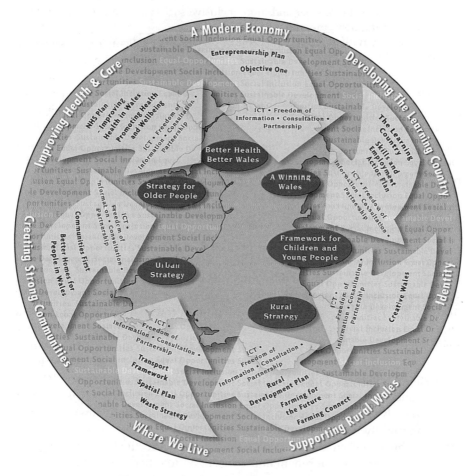

Figure 10: The bigger picture – a policy map

The map draws attention to the drive to inculcate in Welsh policy and administration the three overarching themes of sustainable development, social inclusion and equality of opportunity. Take for example a flagship programme of social and economic measures targeted on the deep-seated problems of deprivation that continue to scar Wales: *Communities First*. The official guidance instructs councils that 'actions should be taken forward . . . in line with the principles by which the National Assembly for Wales works', and enlarges on their meaning:

- Meeting today's needs without compromising the ability of future generations to meet theirs.
- The development of a safer and more inclusive society where everyone has the chance to fulfil their potential.
- The promotion of a culture in which diversity is valued and equality of opportunity is a reality.[120]

Plans galore: the policy map further points up the scale of the commitment to strategies and consultations on the part of the devolved administration. These come in all shapes and sizes: from the short- and medium-term or sector-specific, for example Objective 1 and the Assembly's own Rural Development Plan, to the longer-term and all-embracing, for example the novelty of a spatial plan for Wales.[121] It becomes necessary to think in terms of a hierarchy of plans, culminating in a document like the *Plan for Wales 2001*, which itself integrates the priorities set out in a previous Assembly strategic plan, *Better Wales*.[122]

In suitably uplifting fashion, the *Plan for Wales* has aimed at 'a clear sense of direction for a modern Wales – its economy, its environment, its society', so building on 'Wales' potential as a small, creative, nation'.[123] From long-term vision, extending 'across much of the public sector'; to policy development, 'its own distinctive aims and objectives'; and on through implementation, 'a suitably tailored approach to service delivery':[124] let us hope, in the contemporary jargon, that the 'walk' will match the 'talk'! Suffice it to add that there are already so many plans that one of the tasks of the recently reconstituted Strategic Policy Unit is to combat overlap and confusion.[125]

The policy map also serves to highlight the strategies and concepts adopted by the devolved administration for the purpose of 'check against delivery'. For example, the economic plan *A Winning Wales* is seen to epitomize the effort to break down departmental boundaries, effectively straddling the fields of economic development and education. 'Identity', it is worth adding, translates as various targets in matters of culture, heritage and education, not least in terms of the language.

By way of illustration, the Assembly's blueprint for education policy that is *The Learning Country* features prominently in the pages of this volume.[126]

Demonstrating increased willingness to play a different tune (to England), it has thus occasioned some distinctive law making for Wales, as well as a co-operative or partnership approach across the sector, which is an emergent characteristic of the administrative culture of this little country in the light of national devolution.[127] As for the *mappa mundi*, it is a case of highlighting the targets for policy delivery:

Developing the 'Learning Country'
- Provide free half-time provision for all three-year-olds
- Ensure infant and junior classes contain no more than thirty pupils by September 2003
- Ensure 90 per cent of classes to be of at least satisfactory standard and 50 per cent to be good or very good
- Met the challenging targets endorsed in the Education and Training Action Plan including:

  - Cut by 25 per cent from 1999 levels the number of fifteen-year-olds leaving full-time education without a recognized qualification
  - Reduce proportion of young people and adults without qualifications to 1 in 20 and 1 in 8 respectively
  - Increase proportion of adults of working age with NVQ level 2 qualifications to over 7 in 10; and those with NVQ3 to 5 in 10

- Improve the quality of teaching with the proportion of Further Education courses being assessed as grade 1 and 2 to reach 80 per cent
- Raise universities to their percentage share of UK research council funds from 3.2 to over 4 per cent
- Train 14,000 modern apprentices

Let us be clear. A policy map of this kind is apt to suggest a spurious measure of coherence, a degree of joined-up and interactive government that is beyond organizational capacity to deliver. So also, the very stuff of local political debate, opinions will differ about the feasibility as well as the radicalism of major aspects.[128] Yet the very fact that this kind of document has been produced is significant. At one with a determined pursuit of cabinet government in the Assembly, it reflects and reinforces the fostering of an all-Wales perspective; and, further, the more flexible approach to policy development and implementation which is part of the promise of small-country governance.

Long march

All this activity is relevant to the constitutional development of Wales in another way. It reflects and reinforces the demand for a more developed infrastructure of government in Wales post-devolution. With few exceptions, this was not the way of life in the old territorial department. More and more – to anticipate the title of the next chapter – staffing matters.

The official theme of 'check against delivery' fits with a typically pragmatic approach to formal constitutional change. As the line of least resistance it has obvious attractions, taking into account the political realities of a period of years before a fresh devolution statute, the devolutionary history of division inside the Welsh Labour Party, and the continuing devolutionist struggle for hearts and minds. So far from (in his own words) 'force-feeding devolution', Rhodri Morgan as First Minister has repeatedly stressed the need to achieve effective delivery within the framework of the devolution statute. 'The issue about walking before you run is extremely important. You would hear that . . . in discussions on the Assembly anywhere in Wales.'[129]

Enough has been said to show the synergy of political and administrative factors. Especially through an effort to conjure what Rhodri Morgan has challengingly called 'positive problem-solving political culture of policy-making ability in a Welsh context',[130] the building-up of inner capacities serves slowly but surely to strengthen the case for a more generous devolution. An exemplar, one might say, of constitution-building by stealth, or of the long march through policy development, formulation and implementation.

Going on: subatomics

The politicians themselves cannot be immune. Attempts to make the Assembly cabinet more proactive, and in particular more focused on policy development and longer-term strategic thinking, have gone hand in hand with majority government. Predictably, it is the quest for joined-up government in the realm of cross-cutting policies, and especially the need to provide political and strategic leadership in the face of (ingrained) departmentalism, that has caused ministers most concern.

Shades of Whitehall: another strand in the organizational development is introduced: Assembly cabinet subcommittees. As well as the obvious problem of overload at fortnightly cabinet meetings, the explanation lies in improved methods of working:

> Established to allow Ministers to consider broad policy options and their development in a more reflective and deliberative way, the new sub-committees will work with outside interests as appropriate, bringing a new degree of openness to Cabinet government. While Cabinet remains the ultimate decision-making body, the sub-committees will allow fuller, and more strategic, consideration of policy in the major cross cutting areas.[131]

Four such bodies were inaugurated in May 2001.[132] Supported both by the Cabinet Secretariat and the relevant policy divisions, they have regularly featured the Ministers' special advisers as well as senior management. Legally speaking, the development has necessitated formal exercise of the power given to Assembly committees to establish subcommittees,[133] a most peculiar hangover effect of the statutory classification of the Assembly cabinet as the 'executive committee'.

A subcommittee on sustainable development illustrates the demand for a strong coordinating role: in the words of the mission statement, 'to ensure that the topic is given due priority in all Cabinet and Assembly policy-making'. Meanwhile, a subcommittee on children and young people has been focused on the coordination of activity – or lack of it – among the many other public bodies and agencies working in the field.

The fact of a cabinet subcommittee on 'Wales in the World' is especially noteworthy in terms of the general constitutional development. The Welsh Assembly Government, it will be seen, has set great store on raising the international profile of Wales, and in particular on so-called 'paradiplomacy' or networking with other sub-state authorities.[134] The subcommittee has been charged with identifying and promoting the most fruitful ways of proceeding. Administratively speaking, however, it is the 'Corus' subcommittee, which was set up to ensure the implementation of remedial measures arising from major plant closures in the steel industry, that is the real variation on a theme. Established as a less formal working group, it is a classic institutional response to urgent and politically sensitive difficulties.

Why stop there? The obvious constraint is the small size of the Assembly cabinet as currently prescribed in the devolution statute. Nonetheless, sub-committees on other major cross-cutting areas are easily envisaged: for example on urban regeneration and regional initiatives,[135] on human rights policy and practice across the range of devolved functions, and on the economic and social conditions bearing on the health of the language, to name but a few. By way of practical illustration, a subcommittee on the regeneration of rural Wales was formed in 2002 and one on local government and public services following the May 2003 Assembly elections.[136]

Looking forwards, the pattern of Assembly cabinet subcommittees will be an important litmus test of both the political choice of priorities and the growth of the executive core in Welsh devolution. Especially in the light of comparative constitutional experience, further development may be anticipated.

Taking the temperature: cabinet reshuffle

Ministers come and go, in Wales as in other liberal democratic systems. It is however worth referring to the first cabinet reshuffle of the self-styled Welsh

Assembly Government, which took place in June 2002. This yields some useful clues about the path of the devolutionary development in Wales.[137]

The Assembly thus gained its first Minister for Open Government, with Labour's Carwyn Jones now combining this post with his continuing role as Minister for Assembly Business. In fact, the portfolio would be better described as public or constitutional affairs, since it also included responsibilities for equal opportunities, freedom of information and human rights, as also for the ombudsman system and system of public appointments in Wales. It is to this effect another milestone in the gradual emergence of a distinctive Welsh polity, a firm nod in the direction of local constitutional and administrative culture.[138]

Then there is the propensity for devolved responsibilities to bear increasingly on non-devolved ones. *Pace* the Home Office, the Welsh Assembly Government has given high priority to its responsibilities in crime reduction and creating safer communities. 'Coordination' is once again the name of the game, with Labour's Edwina Hart now adding such matters as drug and alcohol abuse to her existing responsibilities for local government and communities. This political development echoes a series of initiatives in 'joined-up' government at the administrative level.[139] The fledgeling in other words was beginning to spread its wings.

As for the DFM, he could now rejoice in the somewhat odd portfolio of Rural Development and Wales Abroad. 'Foreign Minister', it emphatically was not, but the demarcation of responsibility for coordinating the promotion of Wales abroad was nonetheless a significant one. It points up the way in which Wales has been increasingly delineated for external consumption.

Such is the strange anatomy of the Assembly that there is commonly a twist in the tail. The issue which various Members now took pleasure in raising was the relationship of the concepts of 'responsibility' and 'accountability' in the devolution statute.[140] Correctly, but with a perverse result, the Presiding Officer ruled that the standing orders as they stood did not allow for the questioning of the DFM on his responsibility for promoting Wales abroad since this was not a 'field' of accountability allocated by the First Minister. Constitutionally speaking, the stretching of matters had on this occasion gone too far.[141]

Self-styled

One of the better constitutional arguments against devolution is the potential for confusion or blurring of the lines of political responsibility and accountability by reason of the creation of a new tier of government. A parallel issue has been raised in Wales by the simultaneous use of 'the Assembly' to denote the full Assembly and the Assembly cabinet or administration. On the one hand, this is no different in principle from local government in the guise of 'the council', being at one with the *de jure* concept of a corporate body. On the other hand, and especially in light of the *de facto* separation of functions, it has proved a running sore in the affairs of this infant body, not just for the political parties but also in terms of the (fragile) legitimacy of the devolutionary development. To quote one of the official architects of the scheme:

> A particular and serious problem is that parties not in government need to be able to criticise the cabinet's policies and decisions; but attacks on the failures of the Assembly are all too easily confused – especially in the media – with attacks on the institution as a whole. There's a great difference between arguing that the cabinet's achievements have been unsuccessful and that devolution was a mistake. 'The Assembly has failed' covers both. No prizes for how the media will interpret it – and that reflects on the morale of all those who work here.[142]

The Assembly Review of Procedure was witness to some agonized debates. Perhaps surprisingly, given the headlong rush to the nomenclature of 'minister' etc., a certain constitutional strictness prevailed. The Assembly administration, it was said, should not be called the 'Welsh Executive' on the basis of a scheme of executive devolution. Nor should it be the 'Government of Wales' since Whitehall governed in Wales too.[143] Acting unilaterally, the cabinet eventually plumped for 'Welsh Assembly Government': shame about the acronym![144]

In turn, the local bureaucracy has had another separation project. This one was of a more visual kind, centred on the choice of logos under which the various parts of the corporate body would now communicate, one with another, and externally. In Welsh devolution, however, nothing is ever simple. As well as the National Assembly logo for Assembly Members and officials working in the Presiding Office, and the Welsh Assembly Government logo for ministers and staff from the policy divisions etc., a new National Assembly identification covering an intermediate category was thought to be appropriate. This refers to work otherwise undertaken for the Assembly as a whole, most notably by the Office of the Permanent Secretary, the lawyers in the Office of the Counsel General and the Information Division of the Presiding Office.

In fact, detailed guidance has proved necessary on 'the identity to be used' by individual offices, groups and departments: depending on what they are doing.[145] Viewed in comparative constitutional perspective, it is once again a bizarre feature. But as the Permanent Secretary told staff, the development is invested with great local significance:

> The unveiling . . . of the new logo for the Welsh Assembly Government begins a new chapter in the history of the National Assembly for Wales. This new visual identity for the policies and decisions of the Welsh Assembly Government will

make it easier for the people of Wales – the people we serve – to understand the democratic process that devolution brought about three years ago . . .

This new identity is aimed at making a clearer distinction between the actions and decisions of the Cabinet and the work of Assembly Members as a whole . . . This is an important step in our aim of building a successful Assembly.[146]

The tenor is clear. The civil servants – appointed by the Assembly and still accountable to it under the Civil Service Code – will more and more be dealing across a divide. The Welsh Assembly Government, which most of them will serve to the exclusion of the Assembly as a whole, will be a political and administrative entity of the first importance in the continuing story of national devolution. The internal constitutional dispensation has once again been changed on the basis that it is both possible and legitimate for local actors, while paying homage to the Westminster dictate of a 'body corporate', to distinguish between the constituent parts.

As to the legal position, a title is a title: the Welsh Assembly Government *qua* Welsh Assembly Government can have no statutory functions conferred upon it. In accordance with the devolution statute, the system of internal delegation of functions remains in place, so providing the relevant lines of authority. Then again, it is precisely this distinctive constitutional design that is being obfuscated.

Self-styled – the new visual identity not only marks the general abandonment of what I have called the extravagant version of the corporate body but also signals the way forward: further development of a Welsh system of parliamentary government on more conventional lines; new customs and usages. The Welsh Assembly Government – delineating Wales: the potency of this particular constitutional equation should not be underestimated.

CONCLUSION: A VIRTUAL PARLIAMENT

Confused and contested legal and constitutional framework, policy and politics in a novel devolutionary setting, public administration in the shadow of the (old) central government model: it was a recipe for internal difficulties. Clearly, however, the architects of the scheme could not reasonably have foreseen the crisis that engulfed the Assembly under Alun Michael, at least in terms of the speed and intensity. The shock waves have continued to reverberate.

That its two main poles of authority have grown in stature is of the essence of the constitutional trajectory of the Assembly. Lord Elis-Thomas and his confrères have succeeded in establishing a strong measure of operational autonomy for the Presiding Office. Self-evidently, this too had not been anticipated, and it has created a different dynamic inside the Assembly. Meanwhile, the system of cabinet government prospered under the coalition. The (Welsh) doctrine of collective responsibility, as well the attempts to inculcate a more proactive and strategic approach to territorial government and administration, epitomizes this. And the arrival on the scene of the Welsh Assembly Government serves to confirm and enhance it.

As for the competing constitutional models, it is the way in which the different 'faces' have rubbed up against each other that helps to explain many of the tensions or frictions. In the event, the first face –'Welsh Office plus' – was largely disfigured by the fall of Alun Michael. In paradoxical fashion, the same fate befell the second face, or strong corporate and collaborative model. Increasingly – a *de facto* separation of powers – it is the features of the third or parliamentary face that have been accentuated: which in comparative constitutional perspective represents a flattening of differences. And to reiterate, for those with the strategic vision this appeals as enhancing the prospect of a Parliament for Wales.

In particular, the original design may be said to have underrated the 'background theory' of the British constitution, in the sense of the mind-set or deep values associated with an exceptionally strong tradition of parliamentary government.[147] In the event, the contest between standard constitutional understandings, as expressed in the preference for separate roles and functions, and what I have called the extravagant version of the body corporate, has proved a most uneven one.

A move to legislative devolution obviously is a political question, one on which the people of Wales could reasonably expect to be consulted.[148] Such a question, however, is not asked in the abstract. The developments considered in this chapter can once again be seen to have a broader significance: not only as helping to prepare the (reinvented) devolved administration in case the answer is positive, but also as facilitating the putting of the question.

Perhaps it is the nomenclature that best conveys the flavour. A Presiding Office, not OPO; ministers not Assembly Secretaries; a cabinet not an executive committee; an executive board not a management board; and now the Welsh Assembly Government: one does not have to be a French philosopher to appreciate the symbolism of the change in language. The National Assembly – a virtual parliament: such is the condition of Wales.

Staffing Matters

The main focus of Assembly civil servants has moved to Wales itself and to relations with the wider world. Officials have had to quickly develop new skills and competencies, in particular those concerning policy development, engagement with the Assembly's partners and sensitivity to Ministers' political agendas.

Rhodri Morgan[1]

A picture of an organisation that is under a degree of pressure.

National Assembly Peer Review[2]

Changing public 'faces' is all very well, but for the devolutionary project to flower there needs to be a properly resourced, creative and confident local bureaucracy as part of the self-styled Welsh Assembly Government. To this effect, in tracing the development of national devolution – *Delineating Wales* – the vital happenings discussed in the last chapter should not be allowed to obscure the flanking institutional and administrative ones, more especially in the pursuit of cabinet government. As this chapter will show, there is major synergy.

The core idea of devolution being so much more than the transference of powers is highlighted. Local bureaucratic growth and reordering of a kind that should be happening, that is if one takes the ongoing cause of Welsh devolution seriously, is thus seen as a chief feature of the early years of the Assembly. More precisely, the political quest for ways of 'making a difference' has been working to promote a substantial thickening of the administrative core of the Welsh Assembly Government. And once again, such raising of the inner capacities of the devolved administration has evident potentialities for the future constitutional development of Wales.

This particular devolutionary process is a somewhat painful one, including in terms of political and administrative friction at the heart of the machine. A sharp learning curve is naturally much in evidence, even – one is tempted to add – a sense of culture shock, with officials having to come to terms with a far more demanding environment than the Welsh Office ever was in policy and politics.

The leadership role of the Permanent Secretary and senior colleagues is more than usually important in these conditions. An ongoing process of organizational and managerial reform promoted by them emerges as a vital element. With a view to coping with what in historical terms is a huge new local agenda, the drive has been on to create a higher-performance engine. It might even be described as the brave new world of Welsh public administration.

The early patterns of organization and staffing must also be kept in perspective. 'Devolution on a shoestring': the Assembly was starting from an exceptionally low base, such were the minimalist staffing and resources of the Welsh Office. The devolved administration has been growing very quickly but it is hardly 'big bureaucracy'. At the same time, ministers have hardly been queuing up to publicize this aspect. Especially in light of the history of Welsh devolution, it would be strange if this were otherwise.

The unified Home Civil Service remains in being. This feature is central to the devolutionary development, being part of what I have elsewhere called the 'glue' of a reinvented Union state.[3] Once again then it is a classic case of continuity and change. On the one hand, a unified framework for officials will be seen to have special resonance in the case of Wales, including by reason of the peculiar nature of the corporate body and the particular demands for administrative coordination and cooperation with Whitehall that are engendered in executive devolution. On the other hand, as Rhodri Morgan observes, the focus of the local civil service has already changed, and rightly so in the light of the new constitutional and political dispensation. To this effect, civil service reform and renewal should also be seen as one of the many processes of (Welsh) devolution.

The chapter is in five parts. Special provisions in the devolution statute relating to the civil service in Wales provide the starting-point, whereby a formal constitutional position for the Permanent Secretary to the Assembly is established. The second section focuses directly on the emergent structural patterns of devolved government in Wales, and especially a widening and deepening of the local civil service infrastructure. The way in which the issue of promoting cultural change in the office, and in particular of fostering a more policy-friendly approach, has come quickly to the fore, is considered in the third section. The first of two 'case studies', the fourth section looks to the provision of support for ministers in the guise of the Cabinet Secretariat and a reconstituted Strategic Policy Unit. The second case study completes the chapter, directing attention to an organizational development of the first importance, the construction of a local civil service Executive Board.

1. DELEGATION AND ADMINISTRATION

Life without Carltona

The third main element in the distinctive Welsh system of internal delega-tions,[4] a mix of formal and bureaucratic law provides for the great bulk of Assembly decision-making that goes on at official level – the routine and the not so routine. Famously, in the case of central government – and so previ-ously in the Welsh Office – civil servants are authorized to make decisions on a day-to-day basis in the minister's name without further ado: the 'Carltona doctrine'.[5] However, in the novel circumstances of Welsh devolution, Parliamentary Counsel was apparently not convinced that the doctrine would automatically apply. So, by way of a substitute,[6] Assembly officials were brought inside the special statutory scheme of the GWA on delegations:

> 63 – (1) Each of the following –
> (a)   the Assembly,
> (b)   any committee of the Assembly, apart from the Audit Committee,
> (c)   any sub-committee of a committee of the Assembly,
> (d)   the Assembly First Secretary, and
> (e)   any Assembly Secretary
> may delegate functions of its or his (to which extent as it or he may determine) to the Assembly's staff.
> (2) Where a function is delegated to the Assembly's staff it is for the Permanent Secretary to the Assembly to make arrangements as to which member or members of the Assembly's staff is or are to exercise the function . . .
> (4) The delegation of a function under this section shall not prevent the exercise of the function by the body or person by whom the delegation is made.

Behind the scenes, establishing and maintaining a 'delegation framework' has absorbed significant amounts of bureaucratic time and energy: for no added value. For the avoidance of doubt, this is not the fault of the civil servants, but stems directly from the basic devolutionary design. Rightly, in a missive to staff on the eve of empowerment, Permanent Secretary Jon Shortridge was at pains to stress the importance of the matter:

> Under the Assembly, the exercise of responsibility for Assembly functions by staff can only take place within a formal delegation framework. Otherwise, such exercise by officials will be 'ultra vires' and will carry with it potential legal and financial consequences. Therefore, there must be a delegation of functions in place before the main Transfer of Functions Order comes into effect on 1 July 1999 . . .[7]

The framework has three key parts. The first one obviously is the detailed schedules of statutory functions for each Assembly Secretary, previously discussed.[8] Second, and a product of discussions between cabinet members and senior civil servants, a separate delegation instrument for each Assembly Secretary sets out statute by statute which functions are reserved to the minister and which are delegated – wholly or in part – to the staff. Consistent with the Carltona principle, delegation to officials should not detract from the basic canons of ministerial responsibility. As well as ministers being able to revoke any delegation at any time, this being a live system, section 63(4) of the GWA ensures that they always retain concurrent authority. The legal must be blended with the political:

> Staff will continue to be expected to consider seeking approval from Assembly Secretaries to exercise functions delegated to them where they consider that the Assembly Secretary should be aware of the case so that she/he can make their view known, e.g. novel, contentious, politically sensitive or of national significance.[9]

The staffing arrangements that it is the Permanent Secretary's responsibility to make under section 63(2) of the Act comprise the third part. Typically these operate through the management chain to the heads of division in respect of both the statutory functions and the closely related financial responsibilities (for which the Permanent Secretary is responsible as the Assembly's appointed Principal Accounting Officer[10]). The written delegations have referred in turn to job descriptions and divisional plans for the purpose of definition. Given the scope for organic development, it has been necessary to create no less a thing than the administration's own delegations database, which together with a special delegations manual is the definitive official record of the (latest) state of play.

Such is the exceptional way in which the internal world of the civil service is rendered more legalistic by the Welsh devolutionary scheme. More especially, we see how powerful technical factors lock up together to generate a background to public administration in Wales that is far removed from traditional UK civil service views of law and lawyers as peripheral to the administrative process.[11] The requirement for the Assembly as a creature of statute to demonstrate statutory authority in the exercise of (its highly specified) functions, in other words without the general or prerogative powers that are associated with the office of Secretary of State, is the visible element. The flip side is this need for officials to navigate a formal system of delegations, which substitutes for, but is qualitatively different from, the cosy common law assumption of decision-making implicitly authorized in the name of the minister.

Freedom from political interference: responsibility and management

Section 63(2) may appear prosaic – the Permanent Secretary to organize staff allocation – yet it bears a vital constitutional meaning. An attempt to guarantee the principle of freedom from political interference, the provision stands for the traditional ethos of the UK civil service: professional and apolitical, career-orientated, or serving ministers of whichever political persuasion. At the same time, it has a special resonance precisely because of the distinctive constitutional form of the Assembly.

The provision is an exception to the rule: a formal legal dividing line between two parts of the corporate body. It is a *quid pro quo* for the more complex system of loyalties or less clear-cut line of allegiance to which Assembly staff have been made subject.[12] The protection it provides may be considered especially valuable, in view of the local encouragement for open ways of working for civil servants, or the novel sense of official life 'in the goldfish bowl'. Equally, however – nods and winks from cabinet members etc. – it would be foolish to assume that such a guarantee is watertight.

In the event, a protocol on the working relationships of Members and staff was issued at the start of the Assembly, which fleshed out the internal constitutional implications. As well as illustrating the basic division of activities in the original design, it serves to point up sources of tension with which Assembly watchers would soon become familiar, for example the overarching position of the Permanent Secretary and the contribution of policy staff to the work of committees:

> The Assembly's staff serve the Assembly as a whole. However, different staff have different day to day responsibilities and lines of accountability. Some staff work directly to the generality of Assembly Members in the Office of the Presiding Officer and under the Presiding Officer's direction. Their role will be to support the work of the Assembly in its plenary sessions and committees, and to provide other services to Members to support them in carrying out their roles fully and effectively . . .
>
> The majority of the Assembly's staff – the staff working in policy groups – will work for the Assembly Secretaries and the Assembly Cabinet as a whole. They will:
>
> - provide information and advice to Assembly Secretaries and the Assembly Cabinet as required,
> - advise Assembly Secretaries on their decisions and the execution of their functions, and
> - carry out a range of executive tasks delegated by Assembly Secretaries.
>
> These staff also contribute to the provision of information and briefing to the Assembly and its committees . . .
>
> All staff . . . are managerially accountable to the Permanent Secretary . . .[13]

There is an added potential for boundary disputes. Typically, the best-known example happened in the conditions of minority government. An opposition amendment was passed concerning the Assembly's scheme for sustainable development, to the effect that the relevant civil service unit should be expanded and relocated in the central Policy Unit, so as to ensure a truly cross-cutting approach in the development of policy.[14] The minister opposed this, on the basis that it was not a matter for political determination but one for the Permanent Secretary to decide. Section 63(2), however, being directed to the selection of staff to carry out a function, would not appear to go this far. The Office of the Counsel General (OCG) duly advised that in passing the amended resolution the Assembly *qua* Assembly had acted within its powers.

This was a valuable precedent. Correctly, it is now accepted that the power to direct what should be included in the administrative structures of the Assembly falls within the compass of the elected representatives, and does not lie exclusively in the fiefdom of the Permanent Secretary who is exercising civil service management functions. This sits comfortably with the devolutionary idea of a democratization of an existing tier of government.

The affair also involved a constitutional scuffle between the Presiding Officer and the Permanent Secretary. Lord Elis-Thomas interpreted comments by Jon Shortridge as disputing his right to accept the opposition amendment, thus challenging both his authority as Presiding Officer and the power of the Assembly to instruct the administration.[15] Matters escalated, with complaints to the top of the UK civil service, before a measure of peace was restored.

The imbroglio serves to illustrate once again the underlying tensions associated with the concept of the corporate body, as also the major role for personal factors in the case of a small body still feeling its way. Officialdom has not been exempt from the friction between principal actors that is apt to be generated in conditions of a novel and challenging constitutional scheme, or statutory design of a framework for organic change.

2. ORGANIZATIONAL DEVELOPMENTS

So much for the pathology: as one would expect, organizational questions of this kind have generally been a matter of professional judgement by the Permanent Secretary and senior colleagues. Unlike in the Westminster model, Welsh ministers are not paired with an official departmental head, but are expected – in the name of flexible and cross-cutting government – to work with a range of civil servants on a more informal basis. To do otherwise, in the words of Jon Shortridge, 'would tend to reinforce the compartmentalized mentality, which, in part, the Assembly was being established to break down'.[16]

Although caution at first prevailed, it is now possible to identify a series of major organizational developments, not least at those key pressure points where the new Welsh constitutional arrangements, and in particular the driving force of the Assembly cabinet, have placed novel or greatly increased demands on the office. Continuity and change: while much from the Welsh Office has been carried over, including most obviously in established practices and procedures of the home civil service, increasingly there is a sense of local variation, including Welsh adaptation of general civil service trends or initiatives.

A question of numbers

For once, the bare figures are indicative. On the eve of devolution in 1998 the Welsh Office employed approximately 2,000 permanent staff.[17] In April 1999 the Assembly complement stood at 2,425. This had grown by some 30 per cent to 3,248 two years later and by some 50 per cent to 3,752 in October 2002.[18] Nor, if the weekly raft of advertisements in the *Western Mail* was anything to go by, was retrenchment likely. The mention at the time of the devolution Bill of only 100 additional staff is now another distant memory!

The fact that very many of the new entrants have had little or no civil service experience has also brought a certain freshness to the organization, as well as adding to the many internal pressures in this vital formative period.[19] The 'old' Welsh Office (culture) has in a very real sense been drowning in numbers.

Table 6: Assembly staffing – key growth areas

Group	July 1999	April 2002
Presiding Office	92	204
Cabinet Secretariat	56	120
Office of the Counsel General	40	55
Research and Development Group	–	94
Agriculture and Rural Affairs	487	645
Economic Development Department	198	328
Transport Planning and Environment	232	266
Social Policy	–	251
Training and Education	145	170

As table 6 illustrates, it is a story of expansion on many fronts. As ministers have been keen to stress, part of the growth (roughly one-third of the increase in the first three years) has consisted of mergers with other public bodies. There have in fact been four major clumps: Health Promotion Wales and Health Common Services Agency (135); the Welsh European Programme Executive (44); the Farming and Rural Conservation Agency (100); and the

Care Standards Inspectorate for Wales (204). Building on similar initiatives under the devolution statute, a direct measure of local centralization is one strand in the contemporary Welsh institutional development.

Yet to anticipate the argument, this hardly represents the 'bonfire of the quangos' – a thoroughgoing resettlement in favour of direct lines of democratic authority and accountability under the Assembly – that people were led to expect at the time of the devolution referendum. So let us not lose sight of the many intermediate bodies through which much Assembly spending is channelled, and which have been a particular feature of public administration in Wales.[20]

A related matter: the growth of Assembly staffing is the central element in a more general rise of Welsh governmental infrastructure in the light of national devolution. Flanking developments include the further push to create distinct Welsh public bodies, and what I call the 'Welshifying' – a separate office or unit perhaps – of existing 'cross-border' agencies.[21] The figures in other words only tell part of the story.

Much to be applauded from the devolutionist perspective, such a major enhancement of administrative resources fits with the underlying idea in Welsh constitutional development of the GWA as a framework for organic change. Looking forwards, the extent to which 'people follow powers', that is the scale of civil service transfer from other parts of the government machine as the Assembly gains in authority, will clearly be an important measure of the devolutionary development.

Mapping the administration

A traditional form of central government organization, life in the Welsh Office was characterized by a strong sense of hierarchy, including at the top of the Office.[22] That is to say, a steep departmental pyramid: Permanent Secretary and two Deputy Secretaries (now Senior Directors), and on down via the elite Group Directors to the Heads of Policy Divisions. Set in this context, figure 11 powerfully illustrates the twin elements of continuity and change in the internal organizational pattern of devolved government in Wales.

Continuity: the basic organizational structure remains predicated on two well-established commands centred on economic affairs and on social policy and local government affairs respectively. Such, it may be said, are the essential bureaucratic dimensions to the practice of multi-functional administration within the single territorial entity: past and present. A number of the groups are also familiar from the days of the Welsh Office: most notably, Transport, Planning and Environment, as well as the professional medical groups, Finance, etc.

Aside from the usual advantages of administrative continuity, there is an important political explanation. That is to say, the original design feature of

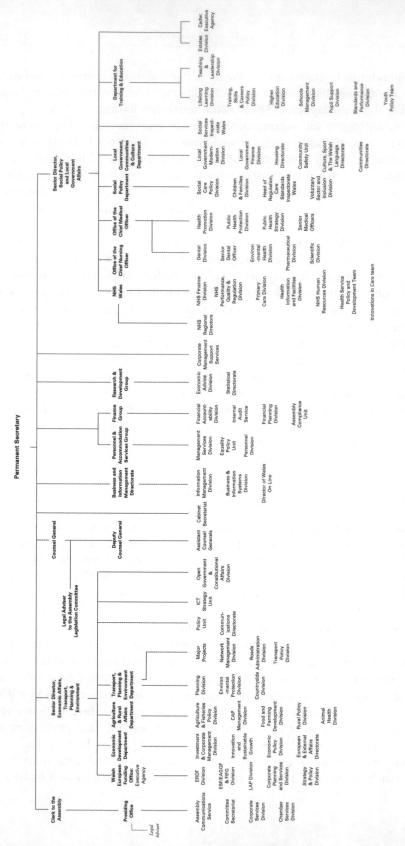

Figure 11: Assembly administrative organization – May 2003

substitution – the allocation of powers to the Assembly cast in the image of the Secretary of State for Wales.[23]

Change: from add-ons to new groups, the ongoing devolutionary process of administrative restructuring has, however, continued to gather pace. For example, expansion of the old Agriculture Department to Agriculture and Rural Affairs itself reflects and reinforces new policy demands and shifting priorities. Another illustration is a mutation of Education to Training and Education in line with a strong political commitment to encouraging lifelong learning ('The Learning Country').[24] Again, a major restructuring of the NHS in Wales has seen a special measure of reorganization at the group level in the guise of a designated programme team.[25]

'One size does not fit all.' The major element of change is clearly shown lower down in the hierarchy, at the level of policy divisions etc. For example, in the guise of Health Service Policy and Development, and Innovations in Care, there are strengthened organizational elements in support of the more holistic approach to public health that has now been taken by the Assembly cabinet.[26] From the constitutional perspective, the establishment of a new European and External Affairs Directorate is another excellent example.[27] At one with the innovative character of Welsh devolution, the various cross-cutting themes are also well represented, from Innovation and Sustainable Growth to the Voluntary Sector and Inclusion Division, and on through to the Equality Policy Unit. And reading the runes, the development of such places in the network as a Community Safety Unit and a Youth Policy Team not only illustrates the administration operating on a close interface with central government, but also points towards an accretion of formal legal powers by the Assembly.[28]

In summary, the all too popular sense of a conservative bureaucracy, one that is effectively in thrall to the UK government, needs to be dispelled. *Delineating Wales*: much of this has been going on in the administrative interstices of the Welsh Assembly Government.

Pressure points

Another way of looking at this is in terms of key pressure points on which the Assembly's scarce administrative resources have had to be targeted. As represented by the Clerk at the top of the office, the servicing of democracy is obviously one, not least as the Presiding Office has increasingly engendered a parliamentary air. Another one, discussed later in this chapter, is the servicing of the executive or ministerial core: the Cabinet Secretariat etc. How else, it may be asked, to begin to develop a more dynamic and responsive style of administration?

In this book, the rise of the lawyers clearly merits special attention. First, the growth of the Office of the Counsel General (OCG) highlights a basic need for enhanced legal resources or capacity if the potential in the devolutionary development for distinctive forms of policy-making and implementation is ever properly to be realized.[29] Second, the OCG has quickly occupied a central place in the local administrative machinery.[30] Nothing in fact better illustrates the strong infusion of law in the conditions of executive devolution than the appearance of so many legal posts in the top echelons of the Assembly, including that of Counsel General next to the Permanent Secretary. Marking a qualitative difference from the Welsh Office, the shift is from a Legal Group that in standard UK civil service fashion was headed by the senior legal adviser to the department.

Then there is the drive – both political and administrative – for a more policy-orientated local bureaucracy: a greater 'thinking' as well as 'doing' capacity. Take for example the sudden appearance of the Research and Development Group in the pantheon of Welsh governance. Reflecting a general trend in public administration, this joining-up of economic advice, statistics, etc. is about developing more sophisticated forms of evidence-based policy-making across the range of devolved functions, including by making the most of small-country governance and promoting links with the external policy community. At one and the same time, this is rightly seen as an essential area of work for the devolved administration, and represents but one in a whole series of related developments, structural and otherwise. Let us look more closely.

3. THE HARDEST NUT: POLICY-MAKING AND CULTURAL CHANGE

The perceived lack of policy-making capacity in the Assembly administration has been a dominant concern in this formative period of Welsh devolution. Such was the historical legacy of the administrative character of the Welsh Office – notwithstanding pockets of creativity in certain fields like education – or what the then Permanent Secretary memorably referred to as its 'colonial' role: transmitting London policy to Wales.[31] Indicative of the internal constraints on the Assembly being able to make the most of its autonomy, the local cadre of senior civil servants with substantial hands-on experience in policy formulation and development has been stretched very thinly.

The civil service has often been singled out for criticism. So it is right to stress the lack of tradition of policy-making in Wales at the political level. There has in fact been a general deficiency: a pervasive sense of pre-devolutionary Wales as a policy-free zone, which is further reflected in the retarded development of much in Welsh civil society.[32] Such it may be said is part and parcel of a history of exceptionally close integration with England. In the words of Rhodri Morgan, himself a former Welsh Office civil servant:

There was no variety and no variegation of the policy-making tools that we could use in Wales. We could do executive decision-making in local government, we could do lobbying the UK Government for more resources, delegations to London we did and delegations to Brussels we did. But distinctive solutions we did not.[33]

In the case of the civil service, the problem has been compounded in various ways. The last years of the Welsh Office under the Conservatives were notable for significant staff retrenchment, not least in the guise of early retirement with all which that implied in terms of loss of official skills and experience.[34] The general practice has also persisted post-devolution of shifting staff across divisions, sometimes at bewildering speed, in the name of career development and multi-functional working, or as a counterbalance to the bureaucratic phenomenon of self-contained silos.[35] A recipe for deep expertise it is not.

Rhodri Morgan has not been shy about highlighting the difficulties:

The Welsh Office had no capability of policy-making at all in the late 1960s . . . You promoted staff . . . on the basis of whether they had kept their nose clean with Whitehall. I hope that's not entirely true today but you are still struggling against a very long tradition where there is not an experience of autonomous policy-making.[36]

Once again longing eyes have turned to Scotland. And this is so by reason not only of the much larger civil service machine available to the Scottish Executive,[37] but also of a historical sense – rooted in a distinctive legal and constitutional tradition – of greater familiarity with the exercise of policy autonomy and administrative confidence in dealing with London.[38] Inevitably, this will take time to promote in the case of Wales. Suffice it to say here, however, that a calculation made by one of Plaid Cymru's constitutional gurus – Jocelyn Davies AM – appears unduly pessimistic: 'In ten years time with a significant increase in staff, we may have accumulated enough legislative experience to be able to claim the expertise possessed by Scotland to successfully operate legislative devolution. At present we cannot make such claims.'[39]

The fact that such questions of institutional capabilities have come to prominence is itself indicative of a growing maturation of the new Welsh polity. A lack of policy-making capacity is not simply the perfect excuse for the politicians, but should also be read in light of the economical approach to building a bureaucracy at the time of the devolution legislation, and the general aim of the devolved administration 'to make a difference'. The local imperative for building up Whitehall-style machinery like a central policy unit, or the politicized concomitant of a system of special advisers, has been a strong one.

As every student of government knows, it is one thing to move chairs round, quite another to alter professional habits and mind-set. Rightly, successive Permanent Secretaries have emphasized the challenges to an administrative culture entailed in Welsh devolution. Not only has it been a question of moving from a departmental ethos to one more appropriate to serving a 'national' representative body, but also the pressures for change have been immediate and by reason of the low profile of the Welsh Office peculiarly intense. Rachel Lomax may be quoted:

> Believe me, a small department that answers to sixty politicians who in turn answer to people from all over Wales is going to respond very differently from one that answers to one Cabinet Ministry, whoever he or she is . . . Our business will be conducted more openly than in the past, and we will almost certainly find ourselves much more actively engaged with other bodies in Wales . . . We will have to listen more actively and respond more fully.[40]

Coincidentally, as Alun Michael fell, so Permanent Secretary Jon Shortridge was beating the drum for new ways of business:

> The process of change is not over yet. Having more or less completed the constitutional and physical changes, we now have to confront the much more complex need for cultural change . . . There is a shared perception that many of our present ways of doing business, which we inherited from our former existence as a government department, are no longer appropriate. They are too laborious, too time-consuming, and do not reflect the political immediacy of the world in which we now live. The degree of scrutiny is intense, and the 'long grass' is not an option.[41]

This is well said. The mistake is to see the devolutionary development as made up of different stages or compartments. As this book demonstrates time and again, the local dynamics of constitutional change have never ceased to operate. And, further, they are inextricably intertwined with the ongoing modalities of cultural change in the administrative branch of the Welsh Assembly Government.

All that jazz

Not that the Assembly administration is an island: quite the reverse. As Permanent Secretary, Jon Shortridge has placed great store on a 'Delivering Better Government' initiative, which is typically a Welsh variant on the contemporary UK civil service reform programme *Modernising Government*.[42] In turn, Wales represents something of a test bed, in novel constitutional and administrative conditions of small-country governance, of the transnational fashion in public administration for so-called 'quality management',[43] and in particular for the emergent twenty-first-century techniques of 'e-government'.[44]

The scale of the ambition could scarcely be faulted. 'The Permanent Secretary is leading a programme to transform the Assembly into "an organisation that sets the standards for public administration in the UK within five years: innovative, confident, open and agile."' 'He intends to do this by "delivering results, valuing people, fairness and equality of opportunity and diversity of contribution" and by engaging in "continuous learning, innovation and improvement, openness and honesty."'[45]

Much is heard in this context of the so-called Excellence Model or framework for quality management – EFQM.[46] Now a common tool for promoting challenge and innovation in the UK public service (and beyond), one that typically emphasizes benchmarking, business planning and internal or staff 'voice', it is now the Assembly's preferred method for driving forward cultural change in the local bureaucracy. To this effect, the EFQM action plan for 2002–3 identified a series of important priorities, from a new performance management framework to streamlined business plans for each division, and on through closer linkage between workloads and staff resources.[47]

A raft of local working groups puts the flesh on the bones: a Human Resources and Diversity project team to deliver better staff appraisal; a Leadership and Teamworking group with a programme of training for all staff; something called a Demonstrating Success team, responsible for regular staff surveys. Not forgetting a Better Policy project group, closely focused on the use of IT, which is one more element in the drive to enhance the thinking capacities of the Welsh Assembly Government.

For their part, Assembly officials are strongly encouraged to act 'as friends of better government', promoting new ideas and spreading the word. It is in fact hard to exaggerate the local fervour of the exercise, including on the individual plane. 'Are you constantly reviewing the way you do your work, always looking for ways to change and improve?' 'Are you constantly thinking: "Is this what my customers want? Is there any way I can satisfy my customers more?" Think Better Government!'[48]

Time will tell. Micro-level and 'soft' initiatives of this kind, however, should not be lightly dismissed. Running alongside the structural changes that are designed to secure fitness for purpose, so much of this is about pepping up performance or greasing the wheels in a new political and administrative environment.

The flavour is perhaps best conveyed by reference to *Cymru Ar-lein*, an information age strategic framework for Wales that focuses on the use of information and communications technologies (ICT) as a tool for organizational development, as well as for economic and social advance.[49] A measure of the local interest in developing advanced techniques of e-government, ICT was incorporated in the *mappa mundi* or overarching policy map of the Welsh Assembly Government. Now given tangible expression in an initial five-year £100 million investment programme to bring greater availability of broadband services across Wales, ICT has thus been prioritized as a way of facilitating the desired future characteristics of the organization, namely:

- knowledge creation and sharing between the Assembly and the community;
- an infrastructure that allows information, knowledge and communications to flow within the Assembly and beyond to communities, business and individuals;
- intelligent use of the organization's knowledge to innovate, act effectively and learn;
- ICT at the heart of delivering new and efficient services internally and externally;
- appropriate ICT practices, in line with the Assembly's commitment to sustainable development;
- exploiting technology to foster social inclusion and equality of opportunity through service-driven action within the Assembly and with communities and business;
- promoting a culture that encourages active acceptance of, and engagement with, ICT.[50]

Some of this no doubt is pie in the sky. ICT 'to foster social inclusion' for example is immediately suspect. The strength of the commitment is if anything slightly scary. 'Information and knowledge management are seen to be strategic drivers for the whole of the public sector in Wales, offering an opportunity to radically alter services and transform relations between government, citizens, businesses, voluntary agencies and elected members.'[51] The dangers and limitations, not least the depersonalizing element for citizens, need to be kept in mind.

But once again: the somewhat sleepy Welsh Office, this is not. Although Whitehall itself has now set demanding targets for public-sector electronic delivery of service as part of the *Modernising Government* programme, the sense of local 'added value' – bringing government closer to the people – is communicated strongly here.

To push home the point, the constitutional development that is national devolution locks up together with these broader trends in comparative public administration, and allows the local administration greater scope for experimentation and innovation in the tools and techniques of (small-country) governance. The public or political face of the Assembly, and in particular the ongoing constitutional argument in Welsh devolution over formal legal powers, has itself tended to disguise the important administrative initiatives that have been happening. The contemporary jazz of New Public Management etc.: little Wales is well to the fore.

Let us also be charitable. That devolution is in part a learning process – and Welsh devolution especially so – is made very apparent in the work of the Assembly staff. At the risk of repetition, it is still early days and there were bound to be mistakes when officials were suddenly called upon to serve the novel and complex constitutional body that is the Assembly. So also continuing calls from the Assembly cabinet for officials to come to terms with their new political environment, to broaden perspectives and not be afraid of failure, and for more ideas and policy input from the lower and middle grades, indicate that the process has far to go.[52] Promoting genuine and lasting cultural change in the administration is the hardest nut to crack.

A Welsh-based civil service

Ultimately, the issue is raised of the position of the Assembly staff in the unified home civil service in Britain.[53] Given such considerations as the limited pool of talent presently available in this small country, and the many other priorities of devolved administration, there is much to be said for proceeding with caution. For his part, Permanent Secretary Jon Shortridge has notably stressed the utility of shared values and professional status in the conduct of intergovernmental relations. 'I think that is very significant in helping to make this particular settlement work.'[54]

Typically, there is a balancing act to perform. On the one hand, application of the Civil Service Code etc. gives assurance as to the quality and the objectivity of officials' work. On the other hand, the peculiar pull or dynamic of national devolution including among the strictly non-nationalist political parties can hardly be ignored. It will be surprising indeed if the Prime Minister's formal powers of patronage over the most senior civil service posts in Wales – and in Scotland – do not come seriously into question. One need only mention the word – 'cohabitation'.

A key section of the Partnership Agreement between Labour and the Liberal Democrats read as follows:

> We seek to move towards an increasingly independent and Welsh-based civil service – investigating ways of introducing an Assembly 'fast-track' programme to attract and retain high quality staff. We will also investigate extending the Assembly's current policies on mature recruitment and secondment.[55]

Enough has been said to show, however, that this demand for distinctive civil service arrangements for Wales should not simply be equated with formal constitutional change. An explicitly Welsh orientation, the emergence of a distinctive working context, efforts to inculcate appropriate skills and a more responsive and flexible local administrative culture: when viewed in a more generous light, much of it is seen to be happening already.

At the same time, one would expect to see a commitment to increasing interchange across the public service inside Wales, in part to assist with career mobility and development inside an emergent system of small-country governance. The Presiding Office is a case in point, both because of the inherently small size of the organization and the constitutional tension that is engendered by close connections with the rest of the Assembly administration.[56] To this effect, a 'bottom-up' approach or promotion of a more integrated approach to staff development and training etc. across the range of Welsh governmental institutions is an obvious way forward, and one that is now being actively pursued by the Permanent Secretary.[57] Splendidly envisioned, this would also gel with the rapid emergence of a so-called 'Welsh way' or distinctive local approach in terms of public law and administration.[58]

4. IN SUPPORT OF MINISTERS

Under the auspices of the partnership government, various steps have been taken to match a political centre more determined and better placed to make a difference with a more integrated and cohesive system of official advice and support for cabinet. This is a happy juxtaposition, but it has also proved to be no easy fix.

At the core: CabSec

Emblematic of the thickening of the executive core, the key component that is the Cabinet Secretariat has kept on growing, not simply in terms of staff numbers but also through a widening and deepening of functions. At the time of writing, it has four branches: the First Minister's Office and the Ministerial Support Branch, the Business Unit and the Cabinet and Constitution Unit. A pivotal position at the interface of political and administrative affairs, it is headed by the First Minister's Principal Private Secretary, who now reports directly to the Permanent Secretary.

A major element in the expansion is the ministers' private offices, which typically now have a staff complement of four or five. The separately designated private office of the Deputy First Minister was another consequence of the Partnership Agreement. Diary secretaries and correspondence management, administrative support and IT: it all abounds.

CabSec's Business Unit plays a vital role. Its work is directed towards, and essentially driven by, plenary session, the Unit being the official link for laying motions, the answering of questions, etc. It is also centrally involved in the many routine and informal discussions with the Presiding Office, with a view to the smooth and efficient operation of Assembly procedures, and supports the Minister for Assembly Business in relations with the all-party Business Committee. Half a dozen officials have been gainfully employed.

Yet the real touchstone is the Cabinet and Constitution Unit. As the name suggests, it has two main sets of functions. On the one hand, it gives direct support to the cabinet, from coordinating papers and agendas, and producing the minutes, to advising on the portfolios of ministers and (in conjunction with the Assembly Compliance Office) the delegation of functions to support them. On the other hand, and far more creatively, the unit has been responsible for giving advice on devolution and constitutional policy in general. The Welsh Office, this is not!

Especially noteworthy, given the special demands for cooperation and collaboration generated by the scheme of executive devolution, is the role of the unit in the sphere of intergovernmental relations. The work has ranged from monitoring the progress of primary legislation affecting Wales and (in conjunction with the OCG and policy divisions) advising on the content, to the coordination of the political and administrative system of concordats, and on through the grounding of relations with the other devolved administrations. Latterly, there has been an increased focus in the unit on internal developments, as in a coordinating role on the Assembly Review of Procedure.[59] All this is a tall order for a unit that has trebled in size but which still consisted in mid-2002 of only six officials. Another significant development: in late 2002 a constitutional affairs division in the Welsh Assembly Government was inaugurated, operating parallel to CabSec.

Communications Directorate

Then there is the Communications Directorate of the Welsh Assembly Government. It is typical of the age that this should have been given high priority. But further, the increased professionalism of the operation itself reflects and reinforces the idea of a governmental apparatus in miniature. From First Minister's media briefings to press statements about individual ministers' comings and goings, and on through formal cabinet statements to strategy for engaging with an Anglocentric media,[60] such is the very public paraphernalia of the Welsh system of cabinet government under Rhodri Morgan.

Not yet, it may be said, London-style spin doctors, but already by 2001 a Press Office with five different teams in support of ministerial portfolios, a Communications Resources Branch incorporating a strategic communications unit, and a Marketing Communications Branch with another five teams to look after different policy divisions. 'Check against delivery'; such is the demand to be seen to make a difference.

'Organisations that invest in effective internal communications do so because it has a major impact on their business effectiveness.' 'Explaining the "big picture" to employees so that they understand the opportunities and constraints facing the organisation makes for greater effectiveness and commitment.' Such is the rationale of a related drive via the Directorate to establish a more developed system of communications for staff, with a view to 'prioritising key messages' and 'listening to structured feedback'.[61] One is entitled to be sceptical. Nonetheless the lesson is clear: no longer will the more informal, village-type ways of the Welsh Office suffice, such is the increasing size and complexity of the organization, and of the political and administrative demands placed upon it.

Apostles: the Strategic Policy Unit

Evidently the First Minister has been dissatisfied. The administration's policy unit has been revamped at his request to incorporate the cabinet's special advisers, another successful breed, and made accountable directly to the First Minister. A closer harnessing of administrative and political machinery in the service of the cabinet, this is another significant development, another strand in the drive to make good a lack of policy-making capacity.

The policy unit was literally a one-man band when first established in the dying days of the Welsh Office. But with the aim of fostering greater creativity in the policy divisions, and in particular a new corporate ethos outside the confines of Whitehall collective responsibility, it soon began to expand, operating to this effect primarily as a facilitator, not as a separate source of policy-making.[62]

A unit of this kind is an especially valuable instrument for promoting joined-up government: that is to say, in the words of the job description, 'overall advice to cabinet and senior management on strategic policy and crosscutting themes'. Notably, in light of the Assembly's special legal responsibility to establish a scheme, considerable time and energy has been devoted here to the 'mainstreaming' of sustainable development.[63]

The development of the ministerial special adviser team, typically operating outside the normal conventions of a professional civil service, itself reflects the changing political and constitutional situation in the Assembly. Originally attached to Alun Michael's private office, the posts were established under Rhodri Morgan as a policy resource for the cabinet as a whole, before being expanded in number for the purpose of the coalition. Another notable innovation in the light of British government practice, the posts have also been made the subject of open competition.

As one would expect, the role is about adding a party political feel or content to material prepared by permanent civil servants.[64] On the other side of the equation, the regular attendance by special advisers at Assembly cabinet meetings alongside the Permanent Secretary further underscores the close political and administrative linkages.

What is now the Strategic Policy Unit (SPU) of the Welsh Assembly Government effectively serves to formalize the close working relationship of the two groups. To this end, the dozen or so officials and advisers that comprise the unit are tasked with joint working on various policy projects, while maintaining separate individual lines of accountability.[65] With a view to reflecting a wide range of local opinion and experience, the unit maintains particular links with representatives of the voluntary sector, business and local government – what Alun Michael once called 'the three golden threads of partnership'.[66] To anticipate the discussion in later chapters, it is all part of 'the closeness of Wales'.

Looking forwards, situated at the heart of what is a relatively small policy community, the unit has important proselytizing and networking functions to perform. Apostles for the development of new policy approaches, and in particular for the importance of overarching strategic frameworks, the unit's responsibilities have included promotion of the *Plan for Wales*, as well as 'overall support for better policy-making, partnership participation and consultation'. And so is created the Welsh *mappa mundi*.[67]

Speaking more generally, the unit is now much better placed, and by reason not only of an enhanced status and unique blend of administrative and political antennae, but also of the various flanking developments inside the administration designed to promote a more outward-looking and policy-orientated bureaucratic culture. The political initiative to create the SPU itself represents the proverbial 'tip of the iceberg'.

5. THE CONSTRUCTION OF THE EXECUTIVE BOARD

One development that merits special attention is the construction of an Executive Board for local civil servants. At one and the same time, this has gone virtually unremarked, and is a most significant feature, the purpose being to align the top corporate management structure of the Assembly more closely to the needs of devolved government in Wales. Correctly, it has been considered necessary to strengthen internal coordination and the corporate focus of the administrative branch.

Bureaucratic reform and renewal: viewed in historical perspective, the Executive Board stands for a more solid core than was ever required in the old, essentially administrative, territorial department. Response to new demands (and criticism), a tooling up: this is a quintessential measure of Welsh administrative reform post-devolution.

Rough stuff

Previously, there was the old-style Management Board inherited from the Welsh Office. Composed of the eight to ten most senior officials, it was charged with advising the Permanent Secretary in his formal and statutory role for the management of the Assembly and as Accounting Officer. As such, it is appropriately described as a somewhat passive body, one that was essentially disengaged from the substance of the work of the Assembly.

Commencing operations in late 2001, and chaired by the Permanent Secretary, the new body is double in size, comprising all group directors, senior directors, the Counsel General and the Assembly Clerk, the First Minister's principal private secretary, and two of the ministers' political advisers as 'observers'. Another 'first', following in the footsteps of some central government departments, the Executive Board now boasts two external or non-executive directors, better to promote 'challenge' to received wisdom and 'an outward looking vision for the Assembly's next stage of development'.[68]

As set out in a classic piece of bureaucratic 'law', a memorandum of governance,[69] the Executive Board has more expansive functions. These notably include advice to the Permanent Secretary on input to cabinet, and managing the delivery of priorities and targets for the Welsh Assembly Government, as well as supporting corporate business plans. Again, in the words of the official documentation, 'the new board must . . . give clear leadership and direction to the staff'. It must 'build closer links with cabinet, providing stronger collective support . . . be proactive and forward looking, not simply reacting to events . . . focus on delivering results and performance . . . address the management of policy as well as resources'.[70] Turning the argument round, if official confirmation is needed that all has not been well in the administrative machine then this is it.

The catalyst for change was a peer review of the effectiveness of the administration's business planning process, with special reference to the implementation framework and policy development. A notable example of intergovernmental networking or the administrative potential post-devolution for the dissemination of best practice, the team was led by the Permanent Secretary to the Scottish Executive and also included representatives from the UK Cabinet Office and the Northern Ireland civil service.

A civil service organization 'under a degree of pressure' was the not so surprising conclusion, but one which served to underwrite calls for both 'a clearer definition of the role of senior staff' and 'leadership from managers'. The review further underlined the essential challenge for the organization of 'growing' its capacity for policy development, as also the need to develop 'a framework for thinking about change' or about where the organization 'is and where it could be going'. By the anodyne standards of civil service language, this was rough stuff.

'The many processes of devolution': typically, the review team saw the staff of the Assembly as having embarked on a journey:

> Eighteen months into the work of the National Assembly some of the initial enthusiasm and excitement has inevitably worn off. We picked up a frustration in some quarters that the organisation didn't yet seem to have 'arrived'. Some people clearly feel the organisation has lost some of its sense of direction. Staff are adjusting to new working relationships and a significant increase in workload. Some people were finding it difficult to see where the additional effort was taking them.
>
> It was clear to us that it was too early to say the organisation has arrived at its destination. It is only yet in the first stage of what will inevitably be a long journey. Senior management will need to demonstrate leadership and commitment to help staff with the realisation that there is still in fact a long way to go.[71]

A subsequent internal review expanded on the need for engagement by the Assembly's top management team:

> Leadership was regarded as the most significant issue in the role of a new corporate structure. We were told that what was required was the development of change of behaviour and a corporate leadership through a board which:

- was able to tell the staff what it was for, what it did, how it added value to their work and what it wanted from them;
- gave strategic direction both in terms of the management and staffing of the Assembly and in the senior management handling of strategic policy;
- had a clear, well understood role and relationship with Ministers and the Assembly as a whole;
- provided communication and clarity throughout the Assembly on the role, decisions and conclusions of the top management board and through the expression of the board's visions and values;
- had a strong performance management function, setting the tone in challenge, giving clarity and authority to the whole performance monitoring system being delivered through operational and policy groups, and using the results in its decisions on oversight of strategy;
- owning and leading jointly the process of continuous improvement set out in *Better Government* and through the EFQM Model; and demonstrating by its own example that it was itself prepared to improve and learn.[72]

So the elite 'top of the office' was not to be spared the more bracing devolutionary air.

Governmental spine

Yet there is more to it than this. As figure 12 illustrates, the Executive Board is at the apex of a revamped pyramidal structure or system of official committees. Its tentacles are thus spread far and wide, and down into those motors of territorial government, the individual policy divisions.

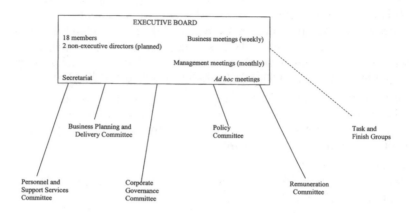

Figure 12: Executive Board and associated committee system – April 2002

The proceedings of the board and its committees are complementary to the delegations made by the Permanent Secretary to senior officials. Authority derives from the Permanent Secretary and the matters he remits to committees. With a view to cementing links with cabinet, the board sits in 'business' format on a weekly basis, tackling current and forward issues and matters emerging from the cabinet, including any strategic policy matters. 'Welsh walls' (1): the political advisers attend these meetings but the Assembly Clerk does not. In 'management' mode the board has been meeting once a month, making decisions on strategic issues about the administration of the Assembly and monitoring overall performance of the office. 'Welsh walls' (2): the Clerk attends but the advisers do not. Additional board meetings take place on an *ad hoc* basis, for more in-depth analysis of particular management issues. Dedicated administrative support serves to underwrite the seriousness of the enterprise. The board has its own secretariat, which serves as a clearing house for papers and communications with staff.

Appointed by the Permanent Secretary, the supporting committees are comprised of a mix of board members and other senior civil servants. All at one with the twin thrusts of greater administrative coordination and policy priority, the committees themselves consider strategic issues. Line management of staff, or making day-to-day operational decisions, this is not. As one would expect, the committees are also designed to operate on the basis of consensus. Strong delegation: whereas the most important corporate management issues are reserved to the board, for example major structural changes to the organization, the committees are generally expected to resolve matters in the areas and issues remitted to them.

Personnel and support services, corporate governance and remuneration: such is the usual paraphernalia of civil service departments. For its part, the Business Planning and Delivery Committee has an especially important and sensitive task in driving forward the work programme of the Welsh Assembly Government. Prescribed areas of interest speak for themselves: systems for planning the delivery of targets and objectives; risk assessment; tracking and measuring performance; identifying corrective action. The general sense of the local bureaucracy seeking to raise its game is communicated strongly here.

Pride of place, however, goes to the new Policy Committee, there notably being no predecessor arrangement. Correctly, given the broad range of fields of devolved functions, the committee has been charged with the management of policy development, including the associated requirements for the evidence base, and not policy-making *per se*. The remit thus includes systems for policy development and the Assembly's research framework; arrangements for the development and management of cross-cutting policies; identification of policy trends and response to policy gaps; and auditing the overall framework and fitness for purpose of major policies. There will clearly be a close interface here with the Strategic Policy Unit.

In summary, the construction of the Executive Board represents a major shake-up, with the scale of the institutional infilling being greater than at first appears. All at one with the overarching constitutional dynamics, the new board and its associated committees give the office a firmer governmental spine. This is not to overlook the genuine difficulties of promoting cultural change in the civil service (or anywhere else). The Permanent Secretary, however, has set out his store. Perhaps hopefully, the Executive Board will prove far more than a rotation of chairs.

CONCLUSION – SECRET HISTORY

In historical terms, the civil service in Cardiff reflected and reinforced what I have called the typically policy-free zone that was pre-devolutionary Wales. The experience of the Welsh Office had done little to prepare officials for the major challenges and opportunities suddenly presented by the arrival on the scene of the new representative institution. Telltale signs have been quick to emerge, not least a sense of political frustration with the lack of a policy-orientated administrative culture.

Necessity is the mother of invention. After a slow beginning, bureaucratic reform has quickly gathered pace at the heart of the Welsh Assembly Government. The Welsh element of the home civil service: it is typically a mix of general trends in public administration, for example in terms of quality management, and of local variations targeted on the fact of small-country governance. Structural and cultural changes have been seen rightly to go hand in hand. Operating directly in support of ministers, the Cabinet Secretariat and the revamped Policy Unit illustrate both the novel pressures on the office and acceptance of the need for effective organizational response. Emphatically, this is not the model of 'Welsh Office plus'.

This chapter has been concerned with developments away from the public gaze, the tectonics of institutional and administrative change. The spur of political and administrative tensions at the heart of the organization, the calm and constructive, or the patient processes of building up a Welsh governmental infrastructure: it is all part of a more rounded picture of the devolutionary phenomenon. The construction of the Executive Board, for example, is the more notable for having happened in silence.

Speaking more generally, the building blocks of a mature Welsh polity are increasingly in evidence, a phenomenon that reflects and reinforces an autochthonous constitutional development, howsoever dimly perceived. The rise of the Presiding Office, the pursuit of cabinet government: local civil service development and growth is the vital third strand in the internal constitutional trajectory of the Assembly, one which further helps to pave the way for a generous scheme of legislative devolution.[73] Such have been the local political sensitivities that it might even be called 'the secret history' of Welsh devolution. Staffing matters.

6

Plenary Business

There is agreement on the broad functions which plenary meetings should fulfil:

- to consider, amend and approve subordinate legislation, the Assembly budget and other formal expressions of policy;
- to scrutinize ministers and their policies;
- to allow 'backbench' Members the chance to influence policy and/or highlight issues of concern to them;
- to act as the most public face of the Assembly's work

However, we are aware that some feel that plenary could discharge these functions more effectively.

Assembly Review of Procedure[1]

An emergent Welsh polity: how then, in the conduct of formal business, has the Assembly been getting on with developing the work of a democratic institution? No fewer than nineteen sets of amendments to standing orders in the first thirty months; and latterly a full-blown review of Assembly procedure generating further changes: clearly something has been up, over and above the initial teething problems normally associated with an infant representative body.

The move to a more parliamentary-type system is once again at the heart of the matter. Major adaptations in the formal framework of Assembly business, and more generally the emerging customs and understandings of the Assembly at work, are part and parcel of the autochthonous Welsh constitutional development that has been happening under the rubric of the devolution statute. So also, the 'secret history' of official growth and development is vital to an understanding of the conduct of formal Assembly business.

The obvious starting place is plenary, the Assembly's highest decision-making body.[2] Typically multi-functional in character, plenary has an especially important role to play as the public face of the Assembly in these early years. In the continuing struggle for hearts and minds in Welsh devolution, a decent set of performances here is not unhelpful! A familiar issue in comparative constitutional design, what then, it may be asked, of the role of the chamber as a cockpit for political debate, or – more grandly – as the 'theatre' of this new manifestation of representative democracy?

Yet it is in plenary that the peculiar character of Welsh devolution comes sharply into focus. At one and the same time, there is an expansive list of topics reserved to the 'full Assembly', as part of the concept of the corporate body, and a hollow core of business, by reason of the absence of primary law-making powers. There are some useful innovations, and a strong sense of aimlessness or lack of purpose.

According to the famous injunction: 'follow the money'. The major stream of Assembly business that is budget-setting clearly demands close attention in this chapter. Locking up with a more effective audit function, it has allowed for a much-improved framework for public discussion and debate under the devolved system of government. But further, the evolution of the budgetary process exemplifies the internal constitutional trajectory of the Assembly. Executive-led by design, it is seen veering further in that direction, including under the tutelage of the coalition government. And correctly so, it may be said, as another nail in the coffin of the concept of the corporate body.

Assembly budget-setting in practice also serves to illustrate how familiar or generalized constraints on the sub-state exercise of policy autonomy have a tendency to bite extra hard in the case of Wales.[3] Especially by reason of a peculiar territorial history, all that glitters in the Assembly is not gold.

As an instrument of management, and of consultation and negotiation, the role and contribution of the all-party Business Committee also needs to be assessed. Much of what happens in plenary is effectively choreographed in this forum: the one cannot be understood without reference to the other. So we shall begin by going behind the scenes.

Assembly business in perspective

In judging performance, let us not impose impossible standards. There may for example be a wealth of experience at Westminster, but the pages of Hansard bear ample testimony to the tedious and irrelevant, the mechanical and the misconceived. Warts and all: such is the great strength of the parliamentary tradition. From the comparative viewpoint, the Assembly falls to be judged on the basis of a greater than usual share of imperfections.

It may sound like a worn record, but these are early days. Even more than the officials, the first Assembly Members have had to struggle to find their feet in the slippery conditions of a novel – and fast-evolving – constitutional and administrative framework. By definition, the strong background of many Members in local government, leavened by a wedge of parliamentary experience at senior levels, could only give partial preparation.[4] A sense of the civil service having effectively to carry elected representatives in the initial phase, and latterly signs of growing confidence and subtlety among Members in operating relevant procedures etc., is only to be expected. It is further the increasing realization among Members in the light of experience that initial procedures were not fit for purpose that helps to explain the volume of amendments to standing orders.

There would obviously have to be major changes in Assembly procedure in a serious case of legislative devolution.[5] Especially, however, in the local conditions of small-country governance, one would not anticipate a clean break. To this effect, some of the innovations discussed in this part of the book – the Business Committee is a good example – may be expected to have a long shelf life. Speaking more generally, much has now been learned of good practice, for example in terms of the greater informality, flexibility and responsiveness that is possible in the workings of a small democratic body. The culture of a parliament for Wales, it may be suggested, is already half-formed inside its virtual one.

1. FORMALIZING THE 'USUAL CHANNELS'

In the process of constitutional design, the Business Committee was something of an afterthought. Perhaps this is not surprising, given that the choice of an appropriate means of coordination machinery to ensure the smooth and efficient flow of Assembly business – clearly depended on the balance to be struck between the cabinet model and the strong committee model of internal architecture. At first NAAG floated the idea of an all-party 'Procedure Committee' operating through agreement, but this was quickly transmuted into a Business Committee with a formally established advisory role, more appropriate to a cabinet or executive-led model.[6]

The Business Committee is a formalized version of the (secretive) 'usual channels' at Westminster, so allowing for the necessary political negotiation about the timetabling of business etc. It is specifically designed, however, to be more open and inclusive, being composed of the business managers of each of the party groups represented in the Assembly, together with the chair, who throughout the first term of the Assembly was the DPO. At one and the same time, the role of the Business Minister (formerly the Assembly Business Manager) is prioritized, and – so typical of the Assembly – some formal checks and balances are incorporated. In short, in devising a functional equivalent, NAAG was very concerned not to replicate Westminster tradition, with a view to better protection of minority party interests.

A degree of give and take, a common acceptance that the Assembly should try to do its best: the Business Committee generally operated in constructive fashion in the first term. Understandings duly emerged governing the timetable and general structuring of Assembly business, although some matters – relating to legislative practice and procedure in particular[7] – proved more intractable. At one with the Welsh model of 'government in the sunshine', the publication of the minutes of these (private) meetings is a notable feature. An insight into the inner world of Cardiff Bay is provided to an extent simply unimaginable at UK level.

The Business Committee offers a broad interface for political, legal and administrative perspectives on the internal workings of Assembly machinery. A variety of actors are in attendance at the regular weekly meetings when plenary is in session. Typically they have included, from the Presiding Office, the Assembly Clerk and the independent Legal Adviser as well as representatives from the Committee and Chamber Secretariats, and, from the administration, the Head of the Business Unit in the Cabinet Secretariat and a representative from the Office of Counsel General.

Situated at the heart of the network for formal business, the Committee is thus an important place where the emergent 'parliamentary' and 'executive' sides of the Assembly meet. In particular, it has provided the Presiding Officer with a formal mechanism by which to ventilate issues about the conduct of business. For their part, the business managers are the essential conduits for consultation with the different party groups. To this effect, there is much use of draft documentation and a kind of 'notice and comment' procedure, in the name of openness and inclusivity. A convention of consultation has also arisen with the Panel of Committee Chairs, which including in its role as a defender of committee prerogatives frequently has an interest in the deliberations.[8]

Standing orders themselves prescribe an extended tripartite function. The Business Committee shall:

- advise the Business Minister on the management of the Assembly's business
- advise the DPO on the exercise of his or her functions under Assembly law-making procedures
- make recommendations to the Assembly on practice and procedure in the conduct of its business, including proposals for revision of standing orders

As for the management of business, the minister alone can timetable motions for debate in government time and also has responsibility for the regular business statements that schedule Assembly business. Check and balance: the statement can, however, be voted down at the instigation of ten Members in plenary if for example the minister chooses to ignore the 'advice' of the Business Committee.

The provisions may appear unexceptional, but they quickly acquired considerable significance in the conditions of minority administration. A few business statements were rejected and the then minister (Labour's Andrew Davies) was required to tread carefully in order to minimize disruption. Since the task was not simply one of internal party management but of managing multi-party relations on a day-to-day basis, this was very much the territory of the Business Committee. In fact, the minister found himself in a unique constitutional position, there being at this time a combination of the roles of government chief whip and functional equivalent of the 'Leader of the House' at Westminster.[9]

It is tempting to describe this period as the heyday of the Business Committee: a necessary instrument for keeping the Assembly show on the road. The unanticipated result of the first Assembly elections thus gave it an unexpected prominence in the conduct of affairs. Its central place at this time as a focus for political negotiations between the parties, that is to say the cobbling together of temporary deals to facilitate the transaction of government business, in particular under Alun Michael, is well attested.[10]

This should not be allowed to obscure the vital ongoing role of the Business Committee in greasing the wheels. Consistent with the greater sense of stability or scope for forward planning introduced by coalition government, the committee's agendas took on a more settled format. 'Forthcoming Business', divided into the immediate and the anticipated, has generally provided an adequate warning system. And 'Matters arising' have been full of reports back on consultations, as well as the procedural detail. Together, that is, with occasional spats in the never-ending negotiation – so familiar in parliamentary systems – about the need of the cabinet to get its business done and the countervailing demands for debate and scrutiny.[11]

The Business Committee, in other words, increasingly assumed a businesslike air: which was also a natural product of the learning process. As discussed in chapter 8, this is well illustrated in the matter of advice to the DPO on the procedural routings of Assembly legislation, the committee's second main function. The fact that there has been an expansive interpretation, so bringing within the remit matters of scrutiny that were originally envisaged to be for the Assembly's Legislation Committee, further underscores the central place of the Business Committee in the Assembly architecture.

Constitutionally speaking, it is, however, the third function – procedural review – which commands attention. The Business Committee may also be seen as the functional equivalent of the House of Commons' Select Committee on Procedure (and on Modernization).[12] Precisely because of the novel institutional setting, and in light of the competing constitutional models that have been in play in the Assembly, the role has taken on great significance.

The internal dynamics are different here. Majority government it may be, but the prospect is raised in a case of serious dispute over revision to standing orders of a sufficient blocking minority.[13] Consultation and expert guidance; negotiation (as appropriate); agreement: there is now a well-established route of procedural reform whereby the committee generates a motion for the Table

Office. Should certain items not have its unanimous support then the minister will be requested to table a separate motion.

Of course many of the recommended changes have been minor, even petti-fogging ones, particular responses to particular realities or realizations. As this book makes clear, however, some of them have been of fundamental import-ance to the workings of the Assembly, for example in the realm of both financial and legislative process. The Business Committee has grappled mightily with the recommendations of the Assembly Review of Procedure, focused on, but not confined to, the formal process of change in standing orders.

The Business Committee has thus been an important agent for the type of internal evolutionary development that is allowed under the broad framework of the GWA. A different but related point: it is seen here as a temperature gauge of party relations in the Assembly. Jostling for advantage; a more febrile atmosphere; nowhere is a lack of political goodwill more likely to be strongly felt.[14] In turn, the abilities – or otherwise – of the Business Minister are a not insignificant factor in this little institution.

2. THE PLENARY QUESTION

Watching the paint dry

It has to be said: Assembly plenary meetings are remarkably tedious. Whereas NAAG had blithely assumed that the meetings would concentrate on the most important issues,[15] there has commonly been a sense of drift and lack of coherence in 'the theatre of the Assembly'. A real depth of concern was made evident on this account in the internal Review of Procedure. To the credit of staff, their evidence did not mince words: 'There is insufficient focus to many plenary debates, and inadequate feedback on their progress and outcome to the officials concerned.'[16] The First Minister gave a damning indictment:

> Perhaps the greatest defect lies in Plenary with Plenary debates resulting in the expression of an opinion rather than making any contribution to concrete policy. That has two major negative effects. On the one hand, it means that the Assembly as a whole is not making an adequate contribution to Welsh policy. On the other, it vindicates the pre-devolution charge that the Assembly would be no more than a talking shop. This diminishes our public standing.[17]

It is, however, the popular caricature of 'watching the paint dry' that has stuck. One explanation concerns the fields of the devolved competencies. Health and education, transport and the environment: of course these are things that 'matter' to people at the local or sub-state level, in accordance with the devolutionary logic of bringing government closer to home. Nonetheless, the high drama of Westminster – controversy over tax and public spending, or foreign affairs and defence – by definition it is not. The Welsh scheme of executive devolution could even be described as 'determinedly micro'.[18]

The sincere efforts that NAAG in particular made to engender under the rubric of a 'new kind of politics' a more friendly – even 'touchy-feely' – style of proceedings inside the Assembly have their downside. Long experience teaches that what is more comfortable for actors may be less than riveting for the audience. Political theatre: a little bit of blood on the carpet from time to time need not be unhelpful! In the event, as the first term progressed, the Assembly in plenary increasingly incorporated more adversarial elements, with meetings being conducted in a spirit of 'friendly partisanship'; that is to say, in an atmosphere which was serious, occasionally combative and party-based, but still relatively informal.[19]

Again, it is one thing to have live broadcasting, even now via the Internet, and quite another to put on a good show. No doubt the eventual provision of a glassy new debating hall, in place of the current subterranean accommodation in a singularly undistinguished office block, will help to improve the atmosphere. But better to engage with the people of Wales, more especially in an age often characterized as one of mass indifference, generally animated and substantial political meetings of the Assembly are what is wanted.

Artificial constraint

Yet there is more to it than this. All parliaments and assemblies have their procedural oddities, but once again the Welsh manifestation has more than most. As well as an excessive number of formal decisions on relatively minor practical and housekeeping matters, the full Assembly has been labouring under the constraints of an overly rigid set of business arrangements. 'The plenary timetable', in the words of the procedural review, 'should be sufficiently flexible to handle high levels of interest in major debates and the pressure of business at particular times of the year.'[20] It should not have needed saying.

The daily template itself appears unexceptional: statements by the Presiding Officer and elections to committees etc.; questions for oral answer; statements by ministers; main plenary business; and the formal opportunity for individual Members to raise issues,[21] short debates prior to the conclusion of plenary meetings. However, research conducted for the review of procedure powerfully illustrated the cluttering effects of a myriad of technical and procedural motions, as well as the ubiquitous points of order.[22] Again, the Standing Orders Commissioners may be said to have treated the Assembly in plenary as something akin to a military operation, the assumption being that the timetable would be more strictly controlled than has proved to be the case. By way of example, a requirement that the minister's business statement specify the period to be allocated 'to any individual item of business' has naturally proved counter-productive, effectively generating further procedural motions to allow unforeseen business to be taken. If this sounds dry and technical then the point has been made! In the event, and a good example of the Assembly taking possession of its own procedures, the review has now instigated a more flexible approach here.[23]

In general, sharp time limits on the length of debates, and thus on the length of speeches, have worked well, at least in terms of the efficient dispatch of business. The Presiding Officer has been notably firm in this respect: 'Members have a responsibility to control the length of their contributions. I want this Assembly to operate effectively, to set good practice and example to other institutions.'[24] Once again, however, there has been insufficient flexibility, a most unfortunate aspect being the curtailment of discussion of contentious and complex issues. A single example will suffice: the main plenary debate on the design of the Objective 1 structural funds programme.[25] Here was a policy of fundamental importance to the economic regeneration of large parts of Wales, one with many different aspects, and on which the officials had laboured long and hard. The debate was crammed into one hour. Far from being, in the famous phrase, 'the Grand Inquest of the Nation', it was 'the theatre of the absurd'.

As well as remarkably long vacations, a feature not exactly designed to endear the new representative institution to the people of Wales, the Assembly in plenary has been operating on the basis of two sessions a week, latterly on Tuesday and Wednesday afternoons. Not surprisingly, the Review Group found it difficult to strike the balance between sufficient time for plenary adequately to discharge its scrutiny and deliberative functions, and the competing demands of Assembly committees and constituency days etc., as also an NAAG-type commitment to so-called 'family-friendly working hours'. The fact that Members months later were still arguing about a proposal to extend closure time to 7 p.m. to allow for exceptional circumstances speaks volumes in this context. In the words of the Review Group, 'more plenary time must be made available'.[26]

A sessional perspective

In contrast, the minimum requirements in standing orders relating to the business that plenary must conduct on an annual basis have been well crafted, not least in terms of the rights of minority parties. In setting the weekly timetables the Business Minister has to manoeuvre within this broad framework.

'Checks and balances': the non-governing parties have thus been guaranteed 'Opposition time' at least once a month when the Assembly is sitting. The natural concomitant of the idea of 'a voice for Wales', there is in practice no restriction on the choice of a non-devolved topic. So for example if Plaid Cymru believes that Members have something important to say about a war with Iraq, then so be it.[27] More especially, it is thus open to the minority parties to explore the Welsh Assembly Government's attitudes to central government policies, a not insignificant constitutional feature in the context of 'national devolution'.

Standing orders also secure a number of 'highlights' that help to relieve the tedium. Time must thus be set aside for debate on the First Minister's annual report on behalf of the administration;[28] for debates on the allocation of the Assembly budget; and for debate with the Secretary of State on the UK government's legislative programme. A useful clue as to the importance and difficulty of the matter, to this list must now be added debate on Assembly proposals for, and subject committees' views of, primary legislation.[29]

Another feature is the long list of annual reports that plenary must debate. Illustrative of 'partnership' and the new Welsh public law, this includes the local government, voluntary-sector and sustainable development schemes, and the arrangements on equality of opportunity and for cooperation with business, as well as audit, (parliamentary) standards and ombudsman matters. So also provision is made for debates on reports submitted by the subject committees. In this way, the Assembly's highest decision-making body is formally connected to distinctive and important elements in the Welsh constitutional scheme, though by no means all of them.[30]

The daily routine obviously adds up in the course of a year. Stiffening democratic accountability: while much can be made of this in a general way, it is also worth rehearsing some hard facts. In the session 2001–2, for example, there were sixty-five plenary meetings. The Table Office dealt with 3,809 oral questions, 1,791 written questions, 384 motions, 423 statements of opinion, and 626 laid documents.[31] There would of course have been much duplication and overlap etc., but if further evidence is required of the immediacy of devolved government, and of official life in 'the goldfish bowl', then this is it.

Collective voice: valuable precedent

An especially noteworthy aspect is the amount of time and energy that goes in plenary on matters for which the Assembly does not have legal and political responsibility. Although the phenomenon is a familiar one in constitutional systems of divided competence, matters are once again accentuated in the case of Wales by reason on the one hand of the strict constraints of the model of executive devolution, and on the other hand of the fact of national devolution.

'Opposition days' are the tip of the iceberg in this regard. Questions to the First Minister about non-devolved matters are par for the course, especially in the context of primary legislation. For his part, the Presiding Officer has encouraged a liberal view of what it is appropriate for the Assembly to discuss, as based on the standing invitation to express a collective view about 'any matter affecting Wales' that is GWA section 33.[32]

One affair stands out, not least in the light of its great political sensitivity. The policy context is the report of the Royal Commission on Long Term Care in favour of free personal care for the elderly funded from general taxation, and in particular the Scottish decision as expressed in primary legislation to go down this path.[33] A major practical example of the asymmetrical nature of the UK devolutionary development, the Assembly now found itself confronted by the UK government's rejection of the principle (effectively for England and Wales), in favour of a limited scheme of free nursing.

In the event, and a good example of the scope for manoeuvre within the official 'England and Wales' paradigm, the Welsh Assembly Government has shown some generosity: enhanced eligibility for free nursing, a period of grace before housing assets are brought into the personal care equation. Notably, however, an advisory committee set up by the minister was less interested in playing at the margins, calling on the devolved administration 'to challenge the UK Government to fund and implement free personal care in the context of UK taxation . . . as the Royal Commission had intended'.[34] Perhaps this was not surprising, since such a policy implemented by the Assembly was (conservatively) costed at £67.5 million a year immediately, rising to £130 million by 2021, which itself serves to underline the awkward issue of competing priorities.

Having duly rejected a Plaid amendment condemning the UK government's stance, the Assembly resolved unanimously in support of the principle of free personal care. The minister would write in these terms to the Secretary of State for Wales, and 'if we are not successful . . . we will press the UK Government for the powers and resources to consider the matter in Wales'. Dialogue and influence: the Assembly had thus expressed its collective voice, effectively as one step in a lobbying campaign. Perhaps, however, the most surprising feature of the affair is the immediate response from the Wales Office: rude and aggressive. Redolent of an official attitude that I have characterized in terms of 'Welsh Office plus', the devolved administration was accused by a ministerial aide of 'an irresponsible approach to politics' in raising its voice. This was manna from heaven for opposition politicians sceptical of the close and collegial collaboration with Whitehall that the First Minister has naturally been keen to trumpet. Suffice it to add that the Secretary of State moved quickly to pour oil on troubled waters. It was in his view 'a regrettable incident', a 'one-off'.[35]

Let us be clear. Whereas it is up to the UK government whether or not it wishes to accede to an Assembly request, in raising this subject Assembly Members were clearly operating within the rubric of the devolution statute. Indeed, it does not go too far to say that so to criticize the Assembly for raising a matter that so closely affected many people in Wales is to put at issue the terms of the so-called devolution settlement. Not for the first time, there has been a certain lack of constitutional understanding in the Wales Office.[36] In the result, the affair can be seen to have generated a valuable precedent.

A more parliamentary play: flexing muscles

It is of course in plenary that the rapid movement towards a more parliamentary 'face' for the Assembly is rendered most visible. Sometimes this is given very tangible expression. For example, once Assembly Secretaries became known as 'ministers', so Plaid Cymru successfully claimed the right to the title 'Leader of the Opposition'. This more parliamentary play is further reflected and reinforced in the increasingly adversarial style of political exchange, not least towards the end of the electoral cycle.[37] The emergent Welsh constitutional conventions of ministerial responsibility also serve to underscore the process.[38]

A useful touchstone is Assembly question time.[39] Imported from Westminster as an essential feature of British constitutional tradition, but freed from some of its more arcane ritual, this is made a weekly event in the First Minister's diary, and a monthly one for other cabinet ministers. Although a lack of clarity in ministerial responsibilities has made the tabling and framing of questions more difficult, the sessions themselves have often been lively and informative, with topics ranging from the determinedly local to the administration's many strategic plans and strategies, and on through to 'Wales in the world'. The practice on the one hand of not allowing 'open' questions such as occur in the House of Commons, and on the other hand of permitting related supplementary questions from other Members, has been helpful in this regard. Consistent with this design, the facility for urgent oral questions, allowed at the discretion of the Presiding Officer on a matter of public importance, has served as an important safety valve.[40]

Then there is the way in which coalition government brought a greater structure and regularity to plenary. Emblematic of 'the green light' conditions of political and administrative stability, the now established custom of the annual government business programme itself implies a major element of planning. In contrast, in the context of an administration unwilling to present opposition parties with opportunities to outvote it, conditions under Alun Michael could not have been riper for generally bland and unfocused plenary meetings, together with the odd loud explosion.[41]

Once again reflecting the depth of concern, ministers themselves took on a responsibility for improving 'the public face' of the Assembly. A conscious effort was thus made to develop a more thematic approach in the timetabling of weekly business, the linking of relevant items under the two main plenary headings of legislative and budgetary decisions. The composite debate or 'wrap round', perhaps a ministerial statement on the policy followed by votes on the various bits of implementing legislation, is but one device that has been tried.[42] At least here the actors are in the same play.

It does not do to overlook the element of friction associated with the autochthonous constitutional development. A good example involves complaints by the minority parties about ministerial statements being used to bypass the normal presumption that Assembly business proceeds on the basis of votable motions subject to votable amendments leading to a resolution of plenary. As the procedural review recognized, statements have a valuable role to play in the policy-making and scrutiny processes, more especially by grounding questions to the minister at the early stages of policy formulation. Nonetheless, 'they should not be used if a formal decision of plenary is more appropriate'.[43]

Again, there has been a dispute traceable to the days of Alun Michael about compliance with plenary resolutions. Whereas the Presiding Office now publishes details of all resolutions passed, the Assembly cabinet likewise publishes material indicating the follow-up action that the administration has taken. So typical of the Welsh model of executive devolution, however, there is something of a 'black hole' concerning primary legislation where the dictates of official secrecy in intergovernmental relations have primacy.[44] In practice, little is apt to turn on these lists in 'green light' conditions, since it will typically be the Welsh Assembly Government reporting on implement-ation of its own resolutions. But much may do so, in terms of the basic constitutional accountability of the 'executive branch' to the 'legislature', in the case of minority government. Perhaps then it is not surprising to learn that the Presiding Office has been most insistent about this matter.[45]

Drawing together the various strands, plenary is seen here changing for the better as the Assembly Government moved up a gear. Then again, the momentum has to be sustained: by definition, it is not sufficient for the popular credibility of the new representative institution that the official machine whirrs away efficiently and effectively in the background. A point, it may be said, powerfully illustrated in the first months of the second term of the Assembly, in the conditions of single-party Labour rule. Procedural wrangling,[46] a sense of drift (in the substantive business), a degree of personal unpleasantness: emphatically it has not been a pretty picture.[47] The new polity, it is worth reiterating, still has far to go.

The hollow core

However, let us not lose sight of the basic structural difficulties. Whereas law making is a touchstone of a parliament, it is precisely in this field that the mimicking by Welsh actors of a system of parliamentary government – 'ministers', 'cabinet', etc. – is apt to lack conviction. Put simply, the general sense of purpose and sharper focus to proceedings that is generated at Westminster around the government's legislative programme is very much harder to achieve in the Assembly. And the more so, it may be said, in view of the many ragged edges or lack of coherence in the devolved competencies. The more developed sense of political and administrative purpose associated with majority government, as also improved techniques in processing secondary legislation, can go some way, but only some way, to filling the vacuum.

As explained in chapter 8, plenary is an important cog in the Assembly law-making machine. It is, however, in the nature of subordinate legislation in general and many of the devolved competencies in particular that large swathes of the material are tedious and technical. Here for example are the items originally listed in the Assembly's 'Votes and Proceedings' for two of the busier days of legislative business.

9 July 2002
Wildlife and Countryside (Sites of Special Scientific Interest) (Appeals) (Wales) Regulations
Plant Health (Amendment) (Wales) Order
Control of Noise (Codes of Practice for Construction and Open sites) (Wales) Order
Feeding Stuffs (Amendment) (Wales) Regulations
Countryside Access (Provisional and Conclusive Maps) (Wales) Regulations
Countryside Access (Appeals Procedures) (Wales) Regulations

11 July 2002
Contaminants in Food (Wales) Regulations
Local Authorities (Companies) (Amendment) (Wales) Order
Local Authorities (Capital Finance) (Approved Investments) Amendment (No. 2) Regulations
Undersized Spider Crabs (Wales) Order
Shellfish (Specification of Crustaceans) (Wales) Regulations
Welfare of Farmed Animals (Wales) (Amendment) Regulations
National Health Service (General Medical Services) (Amendment) (No.3) (Wales) Regulations
Transport and Works (Application and Objections Procedure) (England and Wales) Rules[48]

Some of this material will be of considerable practical importance, not least for those directly affected such as the shellfish and the crabs. But as a recipe for engaging with the people of Wales, it is sadly lacking. 'Legitimacy without power':[49] plenary, in other words, serves to highlight the mismatch in the current Welsh constitutional dispensation between what a 'National Assembly' might reasonably be expected to be able to do, and what the Welsh version can do. It is why I emphasize 'the hollow core' of plenary business.

3. THE POWER OF THE BLOCK: FINANCIAL PROCESS

What then of the most important power transferred to the Assembly at the expense of the Secretary of State for Wales: the so-called 'power of the block' or the discretion (established under the pre-existing system of territorial finance[50]) to determine and manage spending priorities across the range of devolved functions? Assembly financial process is distinctive and must be read in terms of the fixed limits on expenditure associated with the lack of fiscal accountability or taxing powers at territorial level.

As every constitutional lawyer knows, it is in the interstices of financial procedure that so much in representative democracy is won or lost. The Assembly is no exception. Today, the Finance Minister exercises closer control of the process, an efficient part in the effective pursuit of cabinet government. Another major example of constitution-building in silence, the development has gone virtually unremarked. Notably, the Assembly Review of Procedure had nothing to say about financial business. The matter had already been sorted.

Conception

Flexibility for the infant body was established by minimum statutory provision.[51] While section 86 of the GWA requires the Assembly to prepare a statement of its proposed expenditure for the forthcoming year, the mechanics of the formal budget-setting process are governed exclusively by standing orders. So there has been ample scope for revision on a non-contentious basis in the light of experience. The design must also be read in the light of the commitments in the White Paper *A Voice For Wales* that the Assembly would not only have 'maximum discretion' to order its own spending priorities but would also conduct the process of allocating resources 'in an open and transparent way'.[52]

Viewed in historical perspective, the very fact of an Assembly process is a significant achievement. It represents a step change from the secrecy and exclusivity of the previous Welsh Office regime, whereby – in Alun Michael's words – 'the Secretary of State would decide, with officials and with some discussion, and then announce the outcome'.[53] Free of the powerful constraint of the UK convention of collective responsibility, the new dispensation offers much in terms of the principle of subsidiarity – a closer and more responsive targeting of resources, an allocation of the block truly 'made in Wales'. The White Paper drove home the point:

> The Assembly's decisions about how this budget should be spent will determine the range and quality of public services in Wales . . . Putting the spending powers in the hands of an Assembly means that these decisions will be open to scrutiny in Wales . . . A directly elected Assembly will provide opportunities for a fully informed debate in Wales, and will take decisions which can reflect the needs and circumstances of Wales, and most importantly, the views of the people.[54]

At the same time, it is only natural that UK accounting methodology should have been imported, not least by reason of the budgetary dependency on comparable spending in England that the block and formula system of territorial finance represents. So it is that the Assembly's budget has been broken down into two categories for public expenditure purposes. The first one, and representing the 'block', is the Departmental Expenditure Limit (DEL), a fixed limit for a three-year period generated in the usual way as part of the UK government's Comprehensive Spending Review. The second category is Annually Managed Expenditure (AME), which covers items (for example EU Common Agricultural Policy payments) whose provision is volatile, and where – unlike in the case of DEL – there is no flexibility for recycling provision between programmes or across budgetary cycles.

With a view to the effective monitoring and control of expenditure, the Assembly has also adopted levels of budgetary detail familiar from UK government accounting. The highest level of detail – the Main Expenditure Groups (MEGs) – has typically followed the pattern of Assembly cabinet/ subject committee responsibilities. As part of the formal budget process, Members have had to grapple in turn with the designation of Sub-Expenditure Groups (SEGs), which identify important blocks of expenditure, and of Budget Expenditure Lines (BELs), which relate to individual pro-grammes. All this should be set in the context of the Government Resources and Accounts Act 2000, which underpins a new process of preparing departmental estimates and accounts on a resource basis rather than a cash one. Hard to digest, resource accounting has been the subject of not a little confusion in the infant body!

In making recommendations for standing orders, NAAG rightly saw the budget as the plenary Assembly's big decision. The principle that in the exercise of the power of the purse, the formal procedure should reflect and reinforce 'the ultimate authority' of the corporate body 'for everything done in its name', is of the essence of the Welsh constitutional development. Inside this framework, and building on the general move in the parliamentary proceedings towards a cabinet model for the Assembly, NAAG opted for a firm executive-led approach to budget-setting. At the same time, it was keen for the process to be 'as transparent and consultative as possible'.[55]

In putting flesh on the bones, the Standing Orders Commissioners preferred to accentuate the role of the subject committees, especially at the initial stage of establishing priorities for expenditure. According to their draft standing orders, the formal process would begin – in very open fashion – with the Finance Secretary tabling 'any reports received, together with such other documents as he or she considers relevant'.[56] However, by the time the standing orders finally emerged from the Welsh Office, the lead role of the Finance Secretary had been re-emphasized from start to finish. Indicative of the hard-edged character of the design, there was to be no provision for amendment of the budget in plenary, so limiting AMs to the 'nuclear option' of voting it down.

To summarize, the process of conception of this most important of Assembly procedures demonstrates in microcosm, first, the considerable tensions that have existed concerning the respective roles of Assembly actors; and, second, the strength of the dynamic for a more parliamentary-type government in the Assembly at this early stage. Money talks, including in matters of constitutional design.

Crawling

In the words of Assembly Finance Minister Edwina Hart, commending the historic first piece of devolved finance, 'this is an entirely new and radical way of producing a budget. It is designed to promote inclusiveness, accountability and consensus among us.'[57] Once again, however, things were not so simple.

According to the initial design, the budget-setting round consisted of three main phases as punctuated by events in plenary. A 'preliminary draft budget' was tabled by the minister and then debated on a take-note motion. Consistent with the idea of an executive-driven consultative process, this was preceded by representations from the subject committees about their priorities, linked in turn to responses from a public consultation.[58] This supplemented a standard Whitehall-style format of internal, bilateral discussions between the minister and cabinet colleagues about spending priorities. A second formal stage mandated in standing orders, the 'draft budget' had then to be adopted in plenary. Another round of consultation with the subject committees preceded it, concerning the draft allocations at SEGs level. Ratification in plenary of the 'detailed budget' down to BELs level was the third formal stage, which took place after further consultation with the subject committees regarding the allocation of resources within their areas of

Table 7: Welsh budget-setting in transition

A. Planned expenditure (£m) by Welsh Office administrative group, 1998–9*

Agriculture	214.9
Economic Development	279.4
Industry and Training	201.6
Education, Welsh Language, Arts and Recreation	567.2
Transport, Planning and Environment	217.0
Local Government, Housing and Social Services	3032.2
Health	2410.5
Office of HM Chief Inspector of Schools in Wales	10.2
Central Administration including Devolution	86.4
TOTAL	7019.4

B. Planned expenditure (£m) by National Assembly, 2000–1**

	Approved changes to inherited Welsh Office plans	Approved plans
Health and Social Services	12.1	2880.2
Local Government	16.7	2693.3
Housing, Transport and Environment	2.6	714.6
Agriculture and Rural Development	5.9	282.8
Economic Development	−6.2	315.5
(ED including ERDF carried forward)	(49.4)	(371.1)
Education and Training	−12.8	882.7
(E and T budget pre-transfer to Local Government)	(2.3)	(897.8)
Chief Inspector of Schools	0.0	9.5
Auditor General for Wales	1.6	2.0
Assembly Costs	0.0	26.9
Central Administration	0.0	101.9
Capital Modernization Fund/Invest to Save Budget	−17.9	0.1
TOTAL ASSEMBLY EXPENDITURE	2.0	7909.2
Office of the Secretary of State for Wales	0.2	2.9
TOTAL WELSH BUDGET	2.2	7912.1

*Source: *Welsh Office Departmental Report – The Government's Expenditure Plans for 1998–99*, Cm. 3915 (1998), p. 3.
**Draft budget approved by the Assembly, 1 December 1999.

responsibility. It was a decision-making chain that took some eight months to complete (June 1999–February 2000).

There is process, and there is process. In the words of Liberal Democrat leader Michael German, 'sums of money were carved up between parties to meet the political expediency of the moment'.[59] Constructed in the reign of Alun Michael, the first Assembly budget could hardly be immune from the pressures for informal deals associated with the conditions of minority administration. In the event, a concession on free eye tests was apparently sufficient to secure Plaid Cymru's abstention in the crucial vote to adopt the budget.[60] The promise made to the people of Wales of an open and transparent process was here being honoured in the breach.

This first budget round was also happening in the shadow of the controversy over Objective 1 structural funding. It was in fact immediately after the final budget was ratified that Plaid Cymru joined the other opposition parties in taking the 'nuclear option' of the no-confidence motion against Alun Michael. Turning the argument round, the standing orders by excluding the possibility of budget amendment in plenary can be seen to have worked well in fostering the concept of a responsible opposition. In the words of Plaid spokesman Phil Williams, 'this budget has posed us with an acute dilemma . . . We are conscious that a budget must be in place at the start of the new financial year. If we vote against this budget, teachers, nurses and local government staff will be the first to suffer.'[61]

Set in the context of the planned expenditures pre-devolution, table 7 summarizes the outcome of the first Assembly budget. It shows the dominant place of spending on health and social services and on local government and education. As one would expect in this transitional phase, the table mostly shows continuity in the patterns of expenditure. It is nonetheless indicative of the opportunities to make significant changes at the margins within a fixed level of funding.

Walking

Reform of financial procedure ranks high on the list of achievements of the Business Committee. Streamlining and increased flexibility, a distinctively Welsh or internal territorial orientation: such were the chief themes of a reworking agreed to in May 2000 by all the party groups.[62]

Today, standing orders provide for only two formal stages: the draft budget (down to the detailed BELs level) and the final budget. The whole budget-setting round has been pushed forward, which gives the Assembly's official partners in Wales – local government etc. – more time to plan. Although still contributing their views about priorities, and on the draft allocations, the place of the subject committees has also been whittled down. There is now much greater ministerial discretion, via new provisions for control of the setting of the Assembly's budget period, for post-budget changes to the MEGs, and for the tabling of a supplementary budget arising from changes in the UK government's expenditure plans. Considered in the round it is a decisive shift, effectively underpinning a more dynamic form of devolved government in Wales.

The touchstone is the role of the subject committees. Typical of the rhetoric of inclusiveness, much has been made of their input: especially by the minister. The fact of funding nearly all the priorities formally identified by the committees is apt, however, to exaggerate their influence. First, it would be strange indeed – a gross failure of party management – if, given majority government and the political leadership of ministers on these committees, the formal recommendations that are made were not adopted. Second, the subject committees have so operated as to limit their contribution: calling for more but not for less. The difficult choices – balancing the books – have effectively been reserved to the ministers and officials.

Contrary to the general impression, the involvement of these committees is highly managed. Any civil servant worth her salt would recognize the tricks of the trade. In formally setting in motion the annual budget round, the Finance Minister has taken to issuing a commissioning paper that establishes the strategic context or the terms of the discussion.[63] Prepared with the help of the Finance Planning Division of the Assembly government's Finance Group, which is responsible for assisting with the management of the process, it is the key document linking the financial priorities to the policy priorities currently summarized in the Welsh Assembly Government's *A Plan for Wales*. So far from the 'strong committee model' originally envisaged for the corporate body, the role here of the subject committees is an essentially responsive one, with strict parameters.

What then follows is a mass of documentation from ministers and policy divisions in the guise of issues papers covering the different Main Expenditure Groups. That is to say, an assessment of the pressures and priorities specifically designed to focus discussion in each of the committees. From baseline measures to performance indicators, out-turns and targets, it is all very 'New Public Management' or – one is tempted to say – suffocating.[64]

For the avoidance of doubt, this is not to say that committee members are mere pawns in an official game. A high degree of consensus is also indicative of a lack of policy differences about the funding of health and education etc. Enough has been said, however, to demonstrate the role of the all-party subject committees in supplying a gloss of legitimacy to the conduct of cabinet government.

To expand the point, it is not surprising to learn that, freed from the requirement to manufacture a cross-party consensus to pass the budget, the various party groups have slipped easily into the roles of government and opposition. Financial debate in plenary is thus seen to be increasingly adversarial in character, being more geared to the classic modalities of 'scrutiny of the Executive'. Here for example is Edwina Hart commending her third budget to the 'House':

> I believe that these proposals offer a balanced approach, which reflects [the administration's] priorities. They provide the means to take forward our agenda on public services, as well as investing for the long term and building upon the resources that have already been provided to address immediate needs such as the crises in the steel communities and in rural Wales.[65]

In contrast, according to the amendments tabled by Plaid Cymru to the take-note motion: 'The budget is not sufficient to provide the education system that the people of Wales have a right to expect . . . does not recognise the rural crisis . . . nor include all structural funding from Europe as additional resources over and above the Barnett block . . .'[66] That in comparative perspective such exchanges appear unexceptional is precisely the point. *Pace* the corporate body, the Members are doing here what parliamentarians commonly do.

Cross-currents

As the immediate product of the triennial Comprehensive Spending Review, the minister's second budget in 2000 was an especially important one. To coalition government and a revamped procedure could now be added serious money, as the Chancellor of the Exchequer inaugurated what I have called 'the happy time'.[67] With increased freedom of manoeuvre, the Assembly cabinet could begin to order its own priorities.

Table 8 below shows the main allocations. The great bulk of spending on local government and health and social services reflects not only existing commitments but also major increases directed towards front-line services. It could hardly have been otherwise, given an official mantra of 'check against delivery'. Better to convey the flavour, the commitments included a package of measures to support children and youth services (£118 million by 2003–4), extra tranches of money to tackle decrepit school buildings (£43 million), and additional funding (£60 million by 2003–4) for new transport initiatives. Overarching themes included an attack on social exclusion and a substantial push on economic development (an extra £500 million over the three-year period).[68] A different but related point: the table serves to highlight the central role in the Welsh constitutional development of 'indirect administration', or the major dependency in policy delivery on the Assembly's local partners – quangos etc.[69]

Table 8: National Assembly for Wales budget for 2001–2002 by main expenditure groups

Main expenditure group	Amount (£m)	Percentage
Health and Social Services	3243	37.0
Local Government	2866	32.7
Education and Lifelong Learning	930	10.6
Housing	575	6.6
Economic Development	412	4.7
Environment, Planning and Transport	295	3.4
Agriculture and Rural Development	227	2.6
Central Administration	125	1.4
Culture, Sport and the Welsh Language	57	0.7
Assembly Costs, incl. Auditor General for Wales and Welsh Administration Ombudsman	25	0.3
Forestry	3	0.03
Who spends it		
Local authorities	3538	40.4
Health authorities/NHS	3099	35.4
National Assembly	1192	13.6
Assembly-Sponsored Public Bodies	929	10.6

The general pattern has now been replicated. Perhaps not surprisingly, in the light of continuing controversy over the length of NHS waiting lists in Wales, more than half the extra money allocated in the third Assembly budget in 2001 went on health.[70] Again, particular items increasingly illustrate the Administration's 'made in Wales' policies and priorities; for example, the fourth and last budget of the Assembly's first term signals increased efforts to bear down on economic deprivation and the causes of crime.[71] Naturally there is much that is shared (with England), but as compared with the Welsh Office in terms of reflecting UK priorities it would be a calumny to say that nothing has changed.

Finance has been considered 'the spinal cord' of devolution, in the sense of largely determining the degree of autonomy enjoyed by the devolved administrations.[72] The early Welsh experience serves however to confirm the presence of powerful cross-currents.[73] For example, the minister's 'key theme' in the Assembly budget for 2002–3 was 'the urgent need to tackle the problem of under-spending'.[74] Not least, one may say, in order to persuade the Treasury of the Assembly's continuing high spending needs. But further, what to the experienced administrator was a little local difficulty – some £250 million in surplus that could then be rolled over and redistributed across the budget lines – was apt to appear differently in the local press. The affair, in other words, brilliantly illustrates the novel pressures on ministers and

Table 9: National Assembly for Wales budget for 2002–2003 by main expenditure groups

Main expenditure group	Amount (£m)	Percentage
Health and Social Services	3752	36.2
Local Government	2995	28.9
Education and Lifelong Learning	1083	10.4
Environment, Planning and Transport	917	8.8
Housing	583	5.6
Economic Development	536	5.2
Agriculture and Rural Development	227	2.2
Central Administration	144	1.4
Culture, Sport and the Welsh Language	75	0.7
Forestry	31	0.3
Assembly Costs, incl. Auditor General for Wales and Welsh Administration Ombudsman	30	0.3
Who spends it		
Local authorities	3922	37.8
Health authorities/NHS	3579	34.5
National Assembly	1742	16.8
Assembly-Sponsored Public Bodies	1130	10.9

officials that are associated with the reworked processes of territorial government. Such, it may be said, is the visibility and the immediacy of democratic devolution.[75] Suffice it to add that the minister has now instituted more rigorous monitoring and early warning systems.

Edwina Hart also attests the fact of countervailing local pressures for uniformity in patterns of resource allocation. The minister has thus complained of lobby groups seeking to maintain parity with England – when it suits them. In her words, 'we cannot have it both ways. Either devolution has happened or it has not.'[76] Education may be singled out by reason of the local volubility of the teachers' unions, as also a certain penchant for studies berating the Assembly on the basis of cross-border comparison.[77]

To the economist or political scientist this may appear unexceptional, a typical example of so-called 'cherry-picking' or resource maximization by special interests. Of course, local lobby groups will want to have it both ways! All too easily missed, however, is the peculiar intensity of such pressures in the light of the territorial history. The England and Wales paradigm is not about to disappear. In matters of finance, as in the law,[78] a policy of following suit will often be attractive to the Assembly cabinet as the line of least resistance.

There is also the little matter of central government to contend with. Notwithstanding devolution, Whitehall apparently still considers it acceptable for the Secretary of State to pontificate on how the Assembly will spend its resources in the light of the UK budgetary settlement. At one and the same time, a very public intervention to this effect by Paul Murphy on the subject of health care is symptomatic of the many informal pressures in favour of financial uniformity, and risks setting a dangerous precedent.[79] The typically robust statement made by Mrs Hart therefore deserves applause:

> I have no doubt that over the coming days and weeks you will hear a series of spending announcements by Whitehall Ministers; but, as I have said before, initiatives in England will inform our deliberations but not determine our policies. Instead we will conduct our budget planning round in the usual way . . .[80]

Turning the argument round, the fact that so far substantial increases in health and education expenditure in England have led on via the block and formula system to substantial increases in health and education expenditure in Wales tells us little.[81] The fact that the major financial priorities have been shared between centre and territory is scarcely surprising in the conditions of Labour Party hegemony. A case of what political scientists like to call cross-border 'policy spill-over' it may be, but it also represents the express preference of the Welsh Assembly Government.

Looking forwards, a far sterner test of the devolved budgetary process is promised, not only by administrations of different political persuasions in Cardiff and London, but also by retrenchment through reduction in the block via the comparable spending programmes in England. In such conditions, the Assembly's fixed limits on expenditure will naturally serve to intensify the stresses and strains in the local decision-making chain. Let us hope that by then the infant body has learned to run.

CONCLUSION – THE WEAKEST LINK

In the case of plenary, useful lessons have been learned and serious efforts made to sharpen up the proceedings. Formal business became more focused and the debate more lively over the course of the first term. As well as the knock-on effects of 'the pursuit of cabinet government', there was a sense of novel processes bedding in and becoming more productive. Here as elsewhere, the influence of experienced parliamentarians, most obviously the PO and the DPO and the First Minister, was much in evidence.

To understand the workings of the Assembly budget process is to understand much in the nature of the Welsh devolutionary development. The process has itself been a key element in the process of evolutionary change that has so characterized the Assembly in its initial phase. More especially, its workings reflect and reinforce the centrality of the cabinet in the emergent constitutional design and the corresponding limitation of the role of the subject committees. Benign conditions of increased financial largesse and broad policy congruence with central government have allowed for both fine-tuning of the machinery and a smooth passage.

The Business Committee is one of the more notable innovations in Assembly life. Operating in an increasingly businesslike manner in the first term, its changing role also reflects and reinforces the considerable scope for organic change under the auspices of the devolution statute. Large parts of the home-grown constitutional development have been negotiated in this forum.

Reflecting and reinforcing the party-political struggle for advantage in the light of the May 2003 Assembly elections, as also the continuing stresses and strains associated with an emergent system of 'government and opposition', a new low in the formal proceedings could scarcely go unremarked. But further, even assuming the constructive efforts of the various actors, there is no escape from 'the plenary question' and in particular the phenomenon of 'the hollow core'. Constitutionally speaking, this serves to highlight a basic design problem associated with the scheme of executive devolution, the lack of a strong internal legislative dynamic. Theatrical, Assembly law-making rarely is.

A virtual parliament is precisely that: lacking in substance. At one and the same time, plenary stands at the heart of the quest for popular legitimacy on behalf of the Assembly, and is of the essence of the concept of the corporate body. Yet it is also fated to be 'the weakest link'.

Committee Business and Stocktaking

We have a common interest in ensuring that the Assembly works as efficiently as it can.

Rhodri Morgan[1]

This is the first time that we have had possession of our own procedures.

Lord Elis-Thomas[2]

Great store was set in the design of the (peculiar) internal architecture of the Assembly on the role and contribution of its committees. At one and the same time, they were to help with the workload, provide an adequate system of checks and balances (latterly in the context of a cabinet model), and provide a convenient channel for participation by outside interests.[3] So how well have they performed?

The part played by the subject committees obviously is a major test of the constitutional development. Such were the high expectations raised by the National Assembly Advisory Group. However, the fact that reality has not matched the rhetoric should come as no surprise. This is not simply because the subject committees have been inadequately resourced. Their more limited contribution amply illustrates the hardening of the political centre inside the Assembly; and, further, the general problems that parliamentary committees have in achieving a sustained and meaningful interaction with a burgeoning government apparatus.

Turning the argument round, the work of the subject committees in 'big inquiry' mode has proved to be the most valuable aspect, as the case of the Welsh language will serve to illustrate. In fact, this particular policy review – and the Welsh Assembly Government's positive response to it – will also be seen as important for the future course of legal and administrative development in this new devolved polity.

In Euro-speak Wales is a 'region', but what of the 'regions' of Wales? Eyes and ears: the innovative system of regional committees has been specifically designed to help the Assembly engage – and be seen to engage – with all parts of the country. Typically, however, things have proved to be not so simple. In paradoxical fashion, committees that were meant to overcome suspicion in the interior of concentration of power in Cardiff have also served to highlight the difficulties of overcoming the historical and geographical fragmentation of Wales.

As every student of government should know, when it comes to engaging with people, there is manipulation and therapy, informing and consultation, and placation and partnership. By which is meant the different rungs on a famous 'ladder' or typology of citizen participation based on increasing degrees of decision-making clout.[4] The Assembly's regional committees will be seen to be low down on that ladder.

The Assembly, let us remember, is designedly multi-focused. The earnestness of the quest for a reworked form of democratic culture is now amply illustrated in the work of the Equality of Opportunity Committee. Again, while the work of the Committee on Standards of Conduct serves partly to illustrate the constitutional awkwardness of the corporate body, the contribution of the Audit Committee will be seen to bear out the idea of sharper and more regular lines of accountability in devolved government. Whereas many parts of the Assembly have worked less well, other elements have matched and even surpassed expectations.

It is time also to consider the Assembly Review of Procedure. Conducted within the framework of the GWA, it has proved nonetheless to be a worthwhile stocktaking exercise. 'Possession of procedures': Members have had their first real opportunity to reflect on the workings of the new democratic body, in contrast to a process of *ad hoc* or incremental change. The review also provided a useful forum of constitutional dialogue between (and beyond) the political parties in the Assembly, and has served the valuable purpose of further highlighting the limitations of the so-called devolution settlement.

1. SUBJECT COMMITTEES IN SEARCH OF A ROLE

Discretion and routine: complementarity

A defining feature of the subject committees is their diversity. Against the backdrop of the multiple functions specified by NAAG, and of the practical impossibility of achieving them all at once, the individual committees have struck out in various directions, effectively in search of their own particular role.[5] Certain key determinants speak for themselves: the experience of the Chair and the attitude of the minister, the difficulty of the subject and the political context. Again, in the words of the Assembly Review of Procedure, the committees 'must be free to operate in the way which best suits the portfolio they have been given and their priorities'.[6]

By way of illustration, it comes as no surprise to learn that the scrutiny function has bulked large in the work of the Economic Development

Committee as regards implementation of the Objective 1 structural fund programme.[7] Such has been the immense importance as well as the sensitivity of the matter. Again, it is only natural that in the sphere of policy development the Environment, Planning and Transport Committee should have prioritized a review of the Assembly's public transport policies, not least given the evident embarrassment post-devolution of poor north–south links inside Wales.[8]

Members are not always masters: some committees far more than others have been driven by events. The work of the Agriculture and Rural Affairs Committee is the obvious example here: from beef on the bone to BSE and GM foods, and on through the foot and mouth crisis of 2001.[9] Typically, such happenings saw the committee emerge as a major forum of day-to-day scrutiny – questions to, dialogue with, and criticism of the minister – and also gave its more detailed work on the long-term development of the rural economy a sharper focus.[10] It may not be what was intended, but in terms of the constitutional development – the quest for legitimacy of the infant body – the value of Members being seen to engage so directly with public concerns should not be underestimated. Such anyway is the logic of the new form of political responsiveness that devolution represents.

The diversity further reflects the high degree of innovation and experimentation found in the Welsh devolutionary scheme. In the words of an official architect, 'Different committees have different strengths . . . It is still early days and we benefit from trying out approaches and learning from each other's successes and failures.'[11] To this effect, the informal Panel of Chairs has had an important role to play in the dissemination of best practice, as well as working behind the scenes to advance the work of the subject committees generally. Over time, one would expect to see a greater measure of standardization.

An important unifying element obviously is the Committee Secretariat of the Presiding Office. As a source of close and continuing influence on the evolution of the system, not least by the feeding of information and ideas into the Panel of Chairs, it is one way in which the idea of the committees' dual role in policy development and scrutiny has been actively promoted.

As well as the regular cycle of committee meetings when the Assembly is in session, important procedural routines include the maintenance of rolling work programmes and reports to the Assembly on progress in fulfilling them. At one and the same time, a more strategic vision is promoted and the committees gain a (brief) place in the sun. A regular item of business, the minister's report stands out as the product of the distinctive constitutional feature of cabinet representation on these all-party bodies. The best ones are quite illuminating, detailing not only the minister's engagements but also official responses or handling of events, progress on consultations, forthcoming policy initiatives, etc. Subject to the usual time constraints, the reports thus help to anchor exercise of the subject committees' scrutiny function.

It is a measure of the internal constitutional development that whereas in the original design the subject committees were seen primarily as a counter-weight to the 'executive committee', the question increasingly posed is what extra this machinery can bring to a system of cabinet government. Beyond checks and balances to 'adding value': such is the pull of the principle of complementarity. Likewise, a reduction in 2003 in the frequency of subject committee meetings speaks volumes in this context.[12]

Executive dominance

There is moreover no disguising the fact that susceptibility to executive dominance is a particular trait of these committees. Such is the measure of the political leadership that the minister supplies through the medium of party and in particular in the conditions of majority government. Hitherto, the subject committees have commonly been reliant on their ministers for information. The original – corporate body – template that committee clerks would effectively grease the wheels by maintaining close relations with the policy divisions says much.

Self-serving it may be, but the complaint from the leading opposition party serves to highlight the ongoing constitutional dynamics, and especially the sense in which this machinery, originally cast in the mould of one 'face', but now operating in the light of another one, may not be fit for the purpose:

> The Assembly is developing a *de facto* separation of roles between the executive and the legislature, and moving away from the concept of the corporate body . . . Yet the continuing position of the Subject Committees does not reflect this. Briefing papers for the Committees emanate from the Administration. We have very few independent research facilities or resources. The result is that the Subject Committees cannot effectively hold the Administration to account.[13]

Tellingly, the issue of the relationship between subject committees and the cabinet featured prominently in the Assembly Review of Procedure. Perhaps not surprisingly, however, whereas the minority parties advocated stretching matters, for example by separate agendas or careful differentiation of the scrutiny and policy functions with a view to limiting direct ministerial influence, the dominant Labour interest did not see much of a problem.[14] In the event, coupled with the modest increase in resources under the auspices of the Presiding Office, it was a case of change at the edges: ministers to make their officials available to the committees during policy reviews; ministers to make a formal written response to committee reports.[15] For the Review Group itself, offloading was one way forward:

Both subject committees' policy development role and their scrutiny role were seen as valuable – a view we support. There was, however, some discussion as to whether there should be a clearer distinction between the two roles. Effective scrutiny will lead to more effective policy development so at times there will inevitably be some blurring, and even a continuum between the two activities. We recommend that the Panel of Chairs continue to review the operation of the subject committees' policy development and scrutiny roles regularly, preferably annually.[16]

Towards the parliamentary mainstream: here as elsewhere, it is a continuing struggle.

Scrutiny . . .

Members have been encouraged to experiment with various forms of political and administrative scrutiny, from in-depth annual reports to close targeting of issues of implementation. Perhaps this is fortunate, because other aspects of the scrutiny function have remained underdeveloped. To anticipate the discussion in the next two chapters, the role of the subject committees in matters of legislative scrutiny, in the strict sense of oversight of Assembly law making, and further of Welsh inputs into proposals for primary legislation under the scheme of executive devolution, has been dreadfully weak.

Yet even on the administrative front, the contribution of the subject committees has been patchy. Given that one of the original justifications for Welsh devolution was to bring effective accountability to bear on the so-called 'hidden tier' of territorial government, their oversight of the work of the Assembly-Sponsored Public Bodies (ASPBs) is a critical test. In the event, evidence to the Assembly Review of Procedure highlighted the need for a measure of consolidation and greater consistency.[17]

This, it is important to say, is not simply a function of time constraints and of the large number and range of quangos operating in Wales. More cosy dialogue than robust and rigorous scrutiny of agency performance under the rubric of public interest, committee proceedings have been overly imbued with the official ideology of partnership in the political and administrative conditions that I will characterize as 'the closeness of Wales'.[18] To push home the point, whereas devolution holds out the prospect of extended accountability, realizing this demands what the public lawyer would call a policy and practice of 'hard look'.

On a more positive note, the contribution of the subject committees as an agent of transparency in the new Welsh polity should be recognized. From briefing papers to statistical analysis, and on through official documentation to strategic plans, the machinery has helped to generate evidence and information about major policy areas to an extent simply unimaginable in the days of the Welsh Office. Specifically, armed with an expert adviser and making use of the standard techniques of evidence-taking and engagement with external sources such as the universities and specialist interest groups, some committees have already displayed an aptitude for putting in issue official assumptions and methodologies.[19]

As regards the constitutional dynamics, the arrival on the scene of the Welsh Assembly Government is seen to highlight the need for efficient and effective forms of democratic oversight through the subject committees, not least as distinctive 'made in Wales' policies increasingly come on stream. To this effect, greater prioritization of the scrutiny function clearly reflects and reinforces the movement towards a parliamentary-type system. In turn, one would expect to see the inherent tension in these committees that exists by reason of the political leadership supplied by the minister become ever more sharply expressed. 'It is difficult for the Committee to scrutinise the Minister's work while he or she sits as a Member of the Committee':[20] in the interests of the health of the new democratic polity, such plaintive calls from the opposition should not be lightly dismissed.

In the event that the infant body achieves the grown-up status of legislative devolution, one would also expect severance of this so-called 'umbilical cord', better to define the respective constitutional roles of the actors in the absence of a corporate body.[21] The mistake in this context is to consider Westminster a *bête noire*, effectively seeking after different institutional structures for the sake of it. In the conditions of small country governance, it should not be beyond the wit of local Members to secure an effective form of osmosis between ministers and such all-party committees without relying on a formal prop of ministerial presence. Once again, back into the parliamentary mainstream: there is much to be said for it.

. . . and policy development

Subject committees have taken very different approaches to their prescribed role of contributing to policy development. At one end of the scale, a kind of democratic audit or sounding-board function, suggestive of a strong corporate ethos in the Assembly, was fashionable in the conditions of minority administration. As practised most notably by the Health and Social Services Committee, it has entailed short discussions of sets of proposals from a particular initiative or strategy being worked on by the administration.[22]

This sounds well and it may on occasion be appropriate in non-controversial matters. The limitations, however, are all too visible. As well as the problem of overload, keenly felt in the days of Alun Michael, Members quickly discovered the propensity to a scattergun approach that is associated with this essentially reactive form of proceeding. Cross-cutting issues – of which so much is heard under the rubric of the Welsh *mappa mundi* – present a particular difficulty in this regard.

The constitutional and political problem of the blurring of roles and responsibilities is more fundamental. A clue is the difficulty that committees have in this highly collaborate but executive-led process of establishing a visible or discrete contribution to policy development. Once again, the design of the machinery is such that opposition parties have a legitimate concern about the potential for cooption into an administrative process or elongated decision-making chain over which they can hope to exercise only limited influence.

At the other end of the scale, the in-depth investigatory approach or 'big inquiry', whereby a committee generates and examines possible options and then produces general recommendations to the Assembly minister for consideration in plenary session, has rightly proved very appealing. As well as providing for a clearer sense of 'ownership' and of direct engagement with outside interests by the committees, the approach is seen to sit comfortably with a stable or majority government that is actively engaged in policy-making. In fact, given the very many pressures on the local administrative machine post-devolution, the 'space to think' that subject committees in 'big inquiry' mode represent may be considered especially valuable.

Practical illustration: education

In this regard, the role of the subject committee(s) in education can be seen as an exemplar, demonstrating not only much hard work – a veritable mountain of paper – but also the attributes of broad consensus and a willingness to explore or push the possibilities presented by devolution. To this effect, it encapsulates the idea that in a small country beginning to chart a path there is – or should be – considerable scope for cross-party creativity.

As the strategic plan of the Welsh Assembly Government, *The Learning Country* is a vital reference point. Following the lead of ministers, the work of what is now the Committee on Education and Lifelong Learning reflects and reinforces the idea of a single joined-up education system in – and for – Wales. To expand the point, conditions have been ripe for this subject committee to make a significant contribution to policy development. At one and the same time, there has been something to go on, the exceptional legacy of distinctiveness in education policy-making in Wales, and space in which to operate, in light of the bold aim in *The Learning Country* of building one of the best education systems in the world. Suitably encouraged, Members have not been slow to generate ideas and make recommendations via a series of reviews.

The committee has targeted those areas identified by Members as either having no cohesive or 'national' policy or where existing policy needs to be updated. The list includes important and sensitive matters, for example information technology in schools or the supply of school places. Personal factors are especially important here, given the need for a productive working relationship between the minister and the Chair. Suffice it to say that the relevant minister – Jane Davidson – quickly gained a reputation as an active and engaged cabinet member, and that Plaid's Cynog Dafis brought to the committee the experience and networking skills of the senior politician and parliamentarian, as well as engendering a thematic, even visionary approach.[23]

Three reports serve to convey the flavour. The Post-Sixteen Education and Training Committee conducted the first one, a review of education and training action plan (ETAP) proposals that pre-dated the Assembly.[24] In going back over the same ground, or resisting the (minority) administration's attempts to make it a rubber stamp, the committee effectively tweaked the proposals, which were then debated and endorsed by the Assembly before being incorporated as appropriate in the Learning and Skills Act 2000.[25] But further, this review established a template for achieving some of the openness and inclusiveness commonly associated with the birth of the Assembly. In place of the opaque and exclusive modalities that had characterized the approach under the Welsh Office, the committee insisted on wide-ranging consultation, in particular with the schools sector as well as with business, leading on to the accumulation of a substantial body of evidence in the public domain.[26]

A review of early-years provision (pre-school learning), completed by the Education and Lifelong Committee in early 2001, shows the potential of team working between the Members, buttressed by the contribution of a well-qualified outside adviser. Typically, the aim was to develop a national strategic approach ('made in Wales') paying special attention to equality of opportunity. Like the ETAP review, the approach has been innovative and pioneering, for example an interim report to expand dialogue with stakeholders and insistence on a strong comparative perspective. Today, the influence of the committee's work is clearly visible in *The Learning Country*. In summary, to the extent that Wales has now emerged as a leader in this particular field, the subject committee can fairly claim credit for having helped to kick-start a process of reform.

A review of Higher Education in Wales illustrates the in-depth investigatory approach. A yearlong timetable of consultations and deliberations, as also a strong comparative input, has underpinned the process.[27] The fact of the inquiry is the more striking for two reasons. First, although the devolved administration has opportunities to exercise influence in this sector via resource allocation etc., its formal legal powers have been limited especially by principles of university autonomy. It is then another example of Assembly machinery pushing at the boundaries. Second, this was very much new ground, with the Education and Lifelong Learning Committee effectively seeking to fill a historical void associated with the retarded development of policy-making inside the territory. In bringing forward radical proposals or challenging received wisdom, the committee was effectively doing what was it is supposed to do.

So let us be charitable and view a suggestion that the (federal) University of Wales should be broken up as counter-intuitive in the conditions of national devolution. This is no idle point, since other powerful voices then weighed in, on behalf of an institution previously seen to epitomize 'the rebirth of a nation'.[28] Civil society in Wales may be in a retarded state of development, but as the new kids on the block Assembly Members cannot always expect to have it their own way! Even when, as in this case, the minister is fully involved in the deliberations of the committee.

Suffice it to add that *Reaching Higher*, a ten-year strategy for higher education that the minister has now published in response to the policy review, treads more lightly.[29] 'Collaboration' and 'reconfiguration' are now the order of the day, coupled with intended new statutory provision whereby the relevant agency – Higher Education Funding Council Wales (HEFCW) – will exercise planning functions as a last resort.[30] At the same time, the strategy picks up on other more general themes contained in the review, such as expanding the country's share of UK research funding and widening access to higher education across the whole of Wales. In summary, the review and its aftermath brilliantly illustrate the scope for, and limitations on, new ways of thinking in post-devolutionary Wales under the auspices of the subject committees. Constitutionally speaking, the ubiquitous ministerial presence is also highlighted here as a source of confusion.

Infantilism

Two particular controversies cast light on the constitutional development. Under the conditions of minority administration, the work of the Pre-Sixteen Education Committee was dominated by a dispute over performance-related pay for teachers. Whereas the administration cleaved to the view of an England and Wales policy, over which the Assembly had no significant order-making powers, the subject committee sought to promote a distinctive Welsh approach, a majority of its members being opposed to the linkage with pupils' performance. The affair illustrates the element of 'zigzag' associated with the scheme of executive devolution, there being two statutes in play and an uneven devolution of powers between them.[31] In fact, the committee went to the lengths of demanding its own legal advice before acquiescing in the opinion of the Assembly's authoritative legal source, the Counsel General. Eventually there was an element of compromise, the England and Wales policy being adopted but subject to different appraisal methods 'in tune with Welsh needs'.[32]

Shades of the original strong committee model, the members were effectively claiming a direct role in policy-making here. There are parallels too with the series of controversies surrounding the then Agriculture Secretary Christine Gwyther,[33] thus demonstrating once again the general sense of unease in the Assembly under Alun Michael. Turning the argument round, the usual tools of party management and discipline, backed up in this instance by the statutory requirement of party political balance, have effectively ensured a far less challenging approach from this quarter under the firm smack of majority government. So far, it may be said, has the Assembly now travelled from its infantile first period.

A very different kind of dispute has profound implications for the quality of the new form of democracy in Wales. Evidence to the policy review of higher education included the suggestion of an explicit role for the University of Wales in promoting a Welsh(-speaking) elite or 'native governing class'. Provocative certainly, offensive perhaps, it could not seriously be argued that the use of such language was unlawful. Nonetheless, and despite the lack of provision for this in standing orders, Labour Members on the committee moved to have the evidence struck from the record.[34] What price – it may be asked – inclusiveness, in the sense of the Assembly listening to all sides of (lawfully expressed) opinion?

Evidently it is one thing to establish a new 'constitution' for Wales and quite another to engender a mature sense of constitutional culture or understanding. Notably, it was some of the senior parliamentarians in the Assembly who made their dissatisfaction plain, not only Mr Dafis as Chair of the committee but also the Presiding Officer and former Secretary of State Ron Davies.[35] Their influence, together with that of the in-house lawyers operating under the banner of the Convention Rights that bind the Assembly, is clearly visible in the motion eventually adopted by the Panel of Committee Chairs:

> Any interference whatsoever in the process whereby papers are submitted by any contributors is an unacceptable and unwarranted infringement of the principles of freedom of thought and expression especially as defined by the Human Rights Act. Committee members must have the inalienable right to receive and deliberate on any opinion submitted to them and, if deemed appropriate, to comment on, accept or disagree with any such submission.[36]

Let us hope that lessons have been learned and that the subject committees can now proceed unencumbered by thoughts of censorship. The Assembly should take seriously its role as a new bastion of liberal democracy.

The fortunes of the language

Our Language: Its Future, a joint policy review by the Culture and Education and Lifelong Learning Committees, deserves very special attention. The product of over a year of deliberations, and bringing forth a raft of recommendations, as well as important evidence on the fragile state of the Welsh language especially in its rural heartlands, the report is a fine advertisement for the work of the subject committees in 'big inquiry' mode. Let us hope that it marks a turning point in the fortunes of the language.

The vision presented of what a bilingual Wales would be like is a refreshing one. Emphatically, in a situation where only a fifth of the population speaks Welsh, it is not about preserving a cultural heritage in aspic:

> In a truly bilingual Wales both Welsh and English will flourish and will be treated as equal. A bilingual Wales means a country where people can choose to live their lives through the medium of either or both languages; a country where the presence of two national languages and cultures is a source of pride and strength to us all.[37]

History speaks volumes in this context: the language as essential vehicle for the distinctiveness or maintenance of the idea of Wales, the old emphasis on a cultural nationalism, not least in Plaid Cymru's early years.[38] So also, a particular understanding of the Assembly both as an official bastion of bilingualism and new political forum with great power and influence over the fate of the language, which then finds tangible expression in the devolution statute.[39] Self-evidently, there is a limit to what institutional support for the language can achieve. Nonetheless, an important historical step, all-party support has now been declared in that forum for the basic constitutional and political proposition – 'the responsibility for the future of the Language lies with the Government of Wales in partnership with a range of bodies and agencies'.[40]

By reason of the emotions raised, the issue of the language obviously is in a class of its own. The consensus that prevailed in the report is the more striking given the vociferous debates in which Members had engaged, not only in light of conflicting evidence but also in the course of a period when – as so often – the language had appeared as a political football between the parties. In the event, significant compromises were made on all sides in the quest for a practical, challenging and deliverable set of initiatives that would command general support in both the majority- and minority-language segments of the population. A heightened sense of political cooperation on a most sensitive subject in the novel conditions of small-country governance: the fact that leading actors from both Labour and Plaid Cymru could hail the process as an example of the Assembly working at its best also speaks volumes.[41]

'Bringing government closer to the people': this big inquiry further highlights the greater accessibility – and susceptibility – of devolved government to local or grassroots interests. Among the sixty or so organizations that gave evidence, the country's establishment in the form of the Welsh Language Board etc. was naturally well to the fore. But so were schools, universities and individuals, and in particular the language pressure groups such as Cymdeithas yr Iiaith and the new and more radical Cymuned. Upward pressure and responsiveness simply unimaginable for Wales in the Westminster context; it is a very practical rendition of the new opportunities and challenges of interest-group politics post-devolution.

The international perspective is important. A rapid reduction in the number of predominantly minority-language-speaking communities in the rural areas is seen as part of a global trend of population movement and decline.[42] Devolution and the long arm of supranational legal ordering – Members were immediately confronted by the famous 'fundamental freedoms' of EU law. Surprise, surprise: they 'did not believe that it was a practical option (even if it was desirable) to seek restrictions on people's right to move into or within Wales'.[43] Turning the argument round, Wales can once again be seen as a role model here. In terms of language planning and policy-making, what is now in prospect puts the country at the forefront of protection of minority language cultures in Europe:

> During the course of the Review it became clear . . . that the creation of a bilingual Wales could not be achieved solely through the traditional routes for supporting the Language – cultural and educational policies . . . The subsequent evidence brought [us] to the conclusion that any meaningful policy would need to be holistic in nature . . . All of the Assembly's policies should, as a matter of course, include the sustainability of the Welsh Language in their objectives and implementation.[44]

This has major implications for an emergent system of Welsh public law and administration. 'Delineating Wales' – the review is indicative of greater distinctiveness in territorial policy development and implementation and further thickening of the Welsh governmental infrastructure better to deliver the new priorities. In the event, the committees recommended strengthening pre-existing structures such as the Welsh Language Board, and developing new ones, including a high-level cross-cutting policy unit to oversee the 'mainstreaming' of the language.[45]

In terms of the general constitutional development it is interesting to see the Counsel General contributing greatly to the deliberations of the committees. The issue was sharply posed: whether the Assembly could create a bilingual Wales without further primary legislation. Certainly, this is the area where the Assembly's powers are most generously drawn. The words of the devolution statute – 'the Assembly may do anything it thinks appropriate to support . . . the Welsh language'[46] – lock up together with the essential principle of the governing statute that is the Welsh Language Act 1993: 'In the conduct of public business and the administration of justice in Wales the English and Welsh languages should be treated on the basis of equality.'[47] Nevertheless, as the Counsel General was also careful to advise, the Assembly's secondary legislative powers are limited in terms of the transfer orders. Nor is it surprising to learn of other powerful groups – business interests – jibbing at the prospect of additional statutory obligations in the cause of the language.[48]

An important compromise was reached. First, the Welsh Assembly Government should use the existing legislation as fully as the powers in it permit. For example, against a backdrop of 'inward migration' (of non-Welsh-speakers), relevant housing and planning policies in favour of local people could be stretched accordingly. Second, the Richard Commission would be asked to consider the case for so-called 'Henry VIII clauses' to enable the Assembly to amend the 1993 Act by order. That is to say, an example of what I have called 'quasi-legislative devolution'[49] – effectively a patrialization of powers over their language to the Welsh. And the thin end, one is tempted to add, of what constitutionally speaking is a long wedge!

'Policy decisions are a matter for government':[50] so far in the words of the review have we travelled from the extravagant version of the corporate body. A more parliamentary 'face': the 'big inquiry' having run its course, the constitutional and administrative responsibility was correctly seen to be that of ministers. 'The ultimate challenge of creating a bilingual Wales must be taken up by the Government of Wales supported by the goodwill of the people of Wales.'[51]

Maintaining the consensus, the Welsh Assembly Government has responded with alacrity. The policy document is tellingly entitled a *Bilingual Future*:

> The Assembly Government will provide strategic leadership to sustain and encourage the growth of the Welsh language within a tolerant, welcoming and open Wales. The Welsh language will be mainstreamed into the work of the Assembly Government and its agencies. Positive support for communities, including primarily Welsh-speaking communities, will be provided by pursuing policies which seek to create economically and socially sustainable communities. We will ensure that we have effective structures in place to enable individuals to learn the language. We will place greater emphasis on promoting language use and enabling individuals to use the language in all aspects of everyday life.[52]

To this effect, the kinds of administrative tools and techniques that have become so familiar in Welsh governance post-devolution are now to be deployed in what will clearly be a continuing struggle. An action plan, national in character but with major elements of local flexibility, and which the Welsh Language Board will have a major responsibility for implementing, is now being put into effect.[53] Significantly, it encompasses not only individual rights and responsibilities but also 'language and community', by which is meant a blend of policies across the gamut of education and economic development, housing and planning. Following the committees' recommendations, a Welsh Language Unit will be situated at the heart of the administration for the purpose of 'mainstreaming'. Ministers will also be expected to take 'ownership' of the language in their respective portfolios and ASPBs will be instructed to interweave Welsh language considerations. As well as a policy of using existing legislation to its full potential, the intention is gradually to increase the administration's own capacity to work bilingually without relying on translation services.[54] National devolution – an enlarged policy map or Welsh *mappa mundi* that embraces the language: it all adds up.

Bringing the discussion full circle, this major policy development serves to highlight the principle of complementarity in the evolving political and administrative structures of the Assembly. All-party workings to establish parameters and give credibility, clear lines of responsibility, and the increasing weight of the Welsh administrative machine in support of the language: it is on this occasion an appropriate constitutional mix. Credit where credit is due.

2. A STUDY IN FAILURE: REGIONAL COMMITTEES

Rationale and legal base

Like much else in the original design, the Assembly's unique system of regional committees represents a political balancing act. On the one hand, the architects of the scheme were concerned to allay fears that with a 'Voice for Wales' established in Cardiff, other local voices – more especially from north Wales – would lose out.[55] Given the peculiar demography of the country and the strong sense of parochialism in Welsh life, the credibility of the new 'National' Assembly was clearly on the line. Special institutional machinery designed to bring to life the inclusiveness so espoused by the then Secretary of State Ron Davies could be considered useful balm. But then, if north Wales was to have representation, the question inevitably arose of representation for the other parts of Wales.

On the other hand, the important issue arose of political and administrative space in the cramped conditions of small-country governance. A strong model of regional committees, involving the exercise of executive responsibilities, could be seen to threaten local government. So also, a veto power for the committees on Assembly action, as proposed by the Conservatives in

Parliament,[56] was hardly the stuff of a strategic 'National' Assembly. But if this pointed firmly in the direction of advisory committees, the government had then to face the charge of 'waffle shops'.[57] Notably, ministers resisted the idea of a duty on the Assembly to have regard to the advice of a regional committee, as proposed by the Liberal Democrats.[58] Questions of influence were rightly considered a matter for internal organic development or practical workings.

This is all faithfully reflected in the devolution statute. Whereas the Scottish Parliament is typically left to its own devices, Westminster has decreed that Wales shall have regional committees.[59] At the same time, the official preference for framework structures, and so the expanded role of Assembly internal law, is illustrated. It is standing orders that give geographical meaning to the duty to establish committees for 'north Wales' and 'each of the other regions'. Westminster has also provided for the membership, which not unnaturally is comprised of AMs elected from the constituencies and Assembly electoral regions that are 'wholly or partly included' in the relevant geographical areas. The fact that regional committees will not be representative in terms of the party political balance of the Assembly was of course another good argument for their advisory status.[60]

The question of the boundaries of these committees was the issue on which NAAG received the most comments and on which there was least agreement: how very Welsh![61] Precisely because of the multiple divisions of interests inside the country, there were a number of competing models. From the viewpoint of the Assembly as a representative institution, one might have expected five committees, one each for the Assembly electoral regions. In the event, however, a fourfold structure – (a) north Wales (b) mid-Wales; (c) south-east Wales; and (d) south-west Wales – following a pattern previously established for the Welsh Development Agency, won the day. Powerfully illustrating the role of economic considerations – and of official influences – in shaping the new model Wales, this has meant some AMs doubling up, and an unwieldy committee in the case of the south-east – thirty Members or half the Assembly. Suffice it to add that after much navel-gazing in the recent Assembly Review of Procedure, Members have voted for the status quo.[62]

Typically, standing orders have been used to flesh out the committees' role. A statutory function 'to provide advice to the Assembly about matters affecting the region' has thus been recast in tripartite form, with particular responsibilities to advise on 'the effect of Assembly policies in those regions and the work of public bodies there.' Such a prioritization of the issues of implementation and 'democratic deficit' cannot, however, disguise the vagueness of the general mandate.

Disconnected

A lack of clarity and coherence has haunted the regional committees. As well as major inconsistencies in practice and procedure, officially conceded to have sown confusion and to have hindered efforts to 'market' the machinery to the public,[63] the committees themselves have tended to lack focus, a product in part of an annual rotation of chairs. Despite increased stress on thematic approaches,[64] the annual reports speak all too often of a scattergun approach.

It is in fact a catalogue of failings.[65] Perhaps it is reassuring to learn, in the words of one committee Chair, that 'we have succeeded in engaging with the public who attend the meetings'.[66] Commonly, however, this is a story not of crowds but of handfuls of people. Reflecting and reinforcing the low status or priority, little media interest has been generated. Whereas the original annual ration was half-a-dozen meetings, Members' attendance has been very patchy.[67]

Interesting experiments have included open microphone sessions and advertised ballots for short presentations by local groups and individuals. Strict constraints on time and resources and great variation in the scale of the interactivity are factors however that cannot be overlooked. 'Insider' groups and organizations have also featured prominently among the participants; that is to say, the same bodies which already exercise substantial voice in the structures and processes of Welsh governance, from health authorities to quangos, and on through business and the well-established voluntary-sector organizations.[68] In short, in operating in the words of NAAG in 'an open and consultative manner, as befits their position [of] being closest to the people and local areas of Wales',[69] the regional committees have proved not to be so radical or inclusive.

The scrutiny function is singularly inappropriate. In the case of the ASPBs, the regional committees are lacking in information and support, and in expertise and legal powers, properly to perform the necessary monitoring and investigative role. Not so much public accountability as an exercise in public relations, with the quangos commonly playing the lead role or effectively setting the agenda in the hearings, is a natural result. Hard lessons have been learned: the committees' scrutiny function is increasingly consigned to the back burner.[70]

On a more positive note, the Committee Secretariat has made sterling efforts to key the advisory role into (the many) Assembly consultation exercises, including by less formal participatory techniques like road shows.[71] High-profile cross-cutting strategies such as sustainable development have been good choices, not forgetting such matters as the implementation of Objective 1 structural funding. The fact remains, however, that so much in the work of regional committees is decidedly low-key.

In view of the heightened sensitivities, the role of the North Wales Committee deserves a special mention. The committee has in fact adopted a strongly instrumental view of its constitutional purpose as machinery for public participation, 'its biggest task [being] to convince people, particularly in North East Wales, of the relevance of the Assembly to them'.[72] Latterly, it has boasted the attraction of appearances by the First Minister (in view of his special cabinet responsibility for the coordination of policy in the region), and it has also pioneered attempts to feed in the views of participants to the administrative machine. A parallel development is work on establishing relationships with key partners in the region, not least through the North Wales Economic Forum. Who, it may be asked, could possibly object?

This cannot, however, disguise the other classic failure of the system – a type that the celebrated 'ladder' of citizen participation was designed to expose. To this effect, even the official documentation highlights the disjunction between the public face of the hearings and the operation or exercise of power and influence in the decision-making process:

> While AMs and the public value the opportunity for public participation offered by regional committees, it is clear that they feel that regional committees should do more than simply provide a forum for the public to speak to AMs. There is dissatisfaction that members of the public do not get a clear response to their questions and that the regional committees do not seem to be having a clear influence on decisions being made in the Assembly.[73]

Arrangements for feedback from the executive have been exceptionally weak, which is a case at best of a lack of transparency and at worst of an absence of impact or decision-making clout. For example, in the case of the 'flagship' North Wales Committee:

> There is a democratic process, but it seems to finish after the messages or presentations have been given. It is the follow-up that counts, and it is there that the concerns and weakness lie . . . It is important that the democratic cycle is complete and that members of the public feel that they are seriously contributing to the democratic process and that they are part of the process . . .[74]

A case, one could say, of regional voices being disconnected.

Last hurrah

The Assembly Review of Procedure took on board many of these points. Suggesting greater clarity and inclusiveness, and a higher rung on the ladder of citizen participation, the talk now was of the committees acting as 'advocates for the regions' – a vision strongly promoted by officials in the Committee Secretariat.[75] An avowedly functionalist design ('horses for courses'), this meant making the most of the committees' role by building on what is unique about them:

> The strength of regional committees lies in their interest in regional and local issues and their ability to allow the public to participate in an active way in the Assembly's proceedings . . . They should aim to seek out and listen to local views, to identify regional perspectives on selected issues and ensure that these are considered by decision-taking parts of the Assembly.
>
> For this approach to be successful, committees must consider carefully the format, content and output of each of their meetings. In particular, there should be opportunities for public involvement in meetings focused on issues of regional concern. Also, committees should demonstrate more clearly to the audiences they attract how their work can influence the wider business of the Assembly . . .
>
> Committees should encourage the active participation in meetings of individual members of the public and representatives of local, grass roots organisations. The aim should be to reach those people and organisations who do not already have an opportunity to contribute, for example via subject committee meetings.[76]

Warm words, cold comfort: in truth, the Members have voted with their feet. In the words of the Review Group, 'while we would like regional committees to increase their influence . . . we agree that the number of meetings should be reduced from 6 to 3 a year'.[77] So much, it may be said, for the regional committees achieving a clear focus, reaching out and raising their profile, and securing an efficient and effective 'feedback loop'. 'Advocates for the regions', but with less engagement with the public, not more: the equation speaks for itself. In this case, the Assembly Review is likely to be a last hurrah.

For the avoidance of doubt, what may now be called the institutions of the Assembly should actively seek to encourage regional voices. Far more meetings around Wales by the all-party subject committees is one way forward, which has the obvious advantage of specialist focus and more direct links into policy development and legislative affairs. Then there is the not so radical idea of having the full Assembly meet outside Cardiff from time to time: a case truly of 'bringing devolution closer to the people' and a technique of public engagement sometimes practised in other constitutional systems of divided competence. A different but related point: consideration is currently being given to relocating more parts of the growing Welsh administrative machine to the regions.[78]

By reason of the statute, the regional committees will have to struggle on for the next few years, leavened no doubt by the occasional high-profile event or great local crisis. Looking forward, however, to a scheme of legislative devolution, one would not expect them to see them specified in a 'Wales Act'.[79] It would then be open to local representatives to explore other, more effective means for engaging with wider Wales.

3. EXTENDING THE RANGE

'Appropriate arrangements': the Equality of Opportunity Committee

The establishment of this committee reflects the requirements in the GWA that the Assembly make 'appropriate arrangements' with a view to promoting the principle of 'equality of opportunity for all people' in the exercise of its functions and the conduct of its business.[80] According to standing orders, the committee is to 'audit' these arrangements, having 'particular regard to the need for the Assembly to avoid discrimination . . . on grounds of race, sex or disability'.

Another fine example of the political and administrative flexibility in the devolutionary development, a creative interpretation of the formal remit has underpinned the practical workings. The committee has, in its own words, 'taken a multiple approach' to the function of audit. In addition to the annual reporting process, this has included a strong proactive element: for example, raising issues of interest and concern with the relevant policy divisions and commissioning reports on particular issues. The committee has shown a 'strong interest in seeing that a dialogue with organisations representing minority and disadvantaged groups takes place at all levels of the Assembly'.[81] To this effect, it has taken on the role of public forum or conduit, effectively buttressed by standing invitations to the various equality commissions to attend its meetings as advisers.

For its part, the Welsh Assembly Government has increasingly led the way with a string of initiatives.[82] At the same time, this all-party committee has maintained a major role, with most Members giving active and committed support in the attempt to develop a distinctive equality agenda for Wales. Committee meetings have served to illustrate the close working relations with officials that are the particular privilege of small-country governance. At one with the strong cross-cutting theme in the Welsh policy map that is equality of opportunity, the work has thus been conducted in tandem with the likes of the Equality Policy Unit (EPU) in the devolved administration. A good example is the annual equality audits now carried out by the administration, which help to provide the committee with a solid base for its activities.[83]

The committee's role and contribution must also be placed in the broader context of political representation in Wales. The Assembly rightly scores high in terms of gender balance: a fact that has naturally helped to embolden and empower the committee. In contrast, a sea of white faces, the Assembly in its first term scored no points for ethnic minorities' representation, an uncomfortable truth all too easily glossed over.[84]

Turning to the substance of the committee's work, Members deserve praise for not shying away from sensitive or controversial matters. In overseeing a raft of equality reforms, the committee has steadily broadened its scope, moving beyond disability, race and gender, to consider equality of opportunity for groups defined by language, sexuality, age and faith, as well as in relation to those paradigmatic outcasts, gypsy-travellers.

In fact, the work of the committee powerfully illustrates the significance of what I have called 'the Welsh difference',[85] the special quality of local public law and administration, here in the guise of the unique equality clause. All-embracing, determinedly proactive, facilitating a holistic approach to the promotion of equality: the role of this legal precept in underpinning and driving forward a distinctive policy agenda should not be underestimated. It has even been described as 'the most significant factor'.[86]

Deserving of a special mention is *Lifting Every Voice*, a report on institutional racism in devolved government in Wales that was endorsed by the committee in early 2001. Building on the work of the Stephen Lawrence Inquiry, the study focused on staff recruitment, promotion and development, and has in turn paved the way for the implementation of an action plan to address all aspects of inequality in both the Assembly and the ASPBs.[87]

As now included in the Permanent Secretary's 'Delivering Better Government' initiative,[88] there are same major innovations in terms of home civil service practice. Pride of place goes to the rapid development of open, public recruitment to specific posts, in place of the traditional channel of internal recruitment to generic grades. Mandatory equality awareness training has also been introduced, specifically founded on the special statutory imperative. Similarly, the Equality of Opportunity Committee has been pushing hard on greater diversity in public appointments, for example via innovative proposals on remuneration and allowances.[89] Welsh governance in the image of the white, middle-class male, it is not intended to be.

'Mainstreaming' equality of opportunity in the policy process – from formulation of plans to service delivery – is not so easy. Compliance statements and impact assessments, and the development of consultative networks to involve hitherto marginalized groups: such are the administrative techniques that are now being actively promoted across the fields of devolved government in Wales. Assembly-led initiatives to improve equality of opportunity data; measures to tackle inequality as an essential ingredient of local strategies ranging from health to education; improved monitoring and feedback (equality audit): all this too is grist to the mill in 'the new model Wales'.

From the viewpoint of the lawyer, public procurement is an especially interesting case. Here is an area heavily regulated by EU law in the name of the Single Market. Nonetheless, and once again with the active encouragement of the committee, the devolved government has now promulgated a 'voluntary code of equality practice' for suppliers; that is to say, a novel form of Welsh contract compliance, using the equality clause effectively as a peg on which to hang the policy. The practical significance in the conditions of small-country governance may well prove considerable.[90]

Other examples could be given, and still more is in the pipeline. Enough has been said, however, to show not only the range of initiatives but also the beginnings of a more systematic approach under the rubric of a cross-cutting theme. To this effect, what is an increasingly distinctive Welsh equality agenda should be seen as more than the sum of its parts. Pursuing measures designed to make the Assembly an exemplar of good equality practice was an obvious starting-point. Looking forwards, one would expect to see the committee members assisting ministers in further exploring the Assembly's role as regulator and funder of public services.

An air of self-congratulation would be inappropriate. The welter of activity – a singular commitment of scarce political and administrative resources – must itself be read in the light of the depressing facts of socio-economic deprivation in many parts of Wales, and of the historic or deep-rooted patterns of inequality in public employment, pay etc. Devolution clearly has served to put equality of opportunity issues higher up the political and administrative agenda than ever before. But in terms of 'making a difference' detailed evaluation is obviously for the longer term. Suffice it to say that the committee now has an important role to play in 'auditing' for greater uniformity in practice across devolved government in Wales. Delivering the more systematic approach is by definition a complex and continuing challenge.

A sense of quiet satisfaction would be better suited, reflecting the good start that has been made in expanding on the constitutional instruction that is 'the Welsh difference'. To this effect, the cross-cutting approach of the devolved administration in general, and the work of Committee on Equality of Opportunity in particular, suggest a useful role model for developments elsewhere in the Union state.[91] 'Appropriate arrangements': where Wales leads . . .

A sharper light: the Audit Committee

The work of the Audit Committee is especially noteworthy since it illustrates the official purpose in Welsh devolution of securing greater accountability. The model effectively involves patrialization of Westminster-type arrangements, which in turn allows for a sharper and more regular form of financial scrutiny in the conditions of small-country governance. As *A Voice for Wales* explained:

> The Audit Committee will operate in a similar way to the Public Accounts Committee of the House of Commons. It will be able to call the Assembly's Accounting Officer, as well as the Accounting Officers of public bodies it sponsors, to appear before it. It will have a key role in ensuring that money spent

by the Assembly is properly accounted for, properly used, and goes to benefit the people of Wales.[92]

It is no surprise to learn that in the view of Assembly staff 'the Audit Committee has a clearer role and more tangible outputs (in the form of reports to Plenary) than any other [committee]'.[93] Building on the Westminster model, the committee has profited from a close working relationship with the first Auditor General for Wales (Sir John Bourne), as also with NAO Wales, the territorial branch of the National Audit Office (the body responsible for auditing the accounts of UK government departments). The committee, as well as having the statutory responsibility to consider the Auditor General's annual estimates, is largely guided by him, conducting the evidence sessions on the basis of his reports. Belt and braces: the Assembly cabinet is required by standing orders to respond in timely fashion to the committee's findings.

In its own words, 'the Committee's key purpose is to ensure that the Assembly and other public bodies operate to the highest possible standards in the management of their financial affairs'.[94] It is thus a case of the now standard twin-track approach to public audit: a check on probity and regularity, and the more far-reaching technique of 'value-for-money' audit (VFM), examination into the economy, efficiency and effectiveness of the use of resources.[95] The committee and the cabinet agreed early on to give the Auditor General a notably generous budgetary allocation, including some £1 million for VFM examinations. 'It was felt that this would ensure the widest coverage and depth of activity and would demonstrate that the Committee regarded this expenditure as an investment for the longer term.'[96]

The committee has proved to be a strong and vigorous one. As the Assembly's Principal Accounting Officer, the Permanent Secretary in particular has had to endure close and frequent questioning as a witness. A significant feature is the extent to which general party political affiliations have been downplayed in the work of the committee, as befits a body that is specifically enjoined from questioning the merits of policy objectives. For her part, the first (Plaid Cymru) Chair placed great emphasis on unity of purpose, rightly seeing the committee as a useful source of legitimacy for the new – and evolving – constitutional arrangements in Wales:

> I passionately want the Assembly to work, to be accepted and to achieve wider powers for the people in this country. However, it can only do this if the people think that it is run well, openly and efficiently. The Cabinet and the Subject Committees are in the front line, but the Audit Committee is crucial as the backstop and fielders for anything that might go wrong, or might be done better.[97]

At the same time, the committee has been seen to adopt a less confrontational approach to the questioning of witnesses than is famously the case in the Public Accounts Committee.[98] The method sits more comfortably in the political and administrative environment of a little country where so many of the actors are repeat players. It can in fact be seen as part of an emergent 'Welsh way', as illustrated by a more informal and trusting approach to public business.[99] To this effect, the work of the Audit Committee teaches that importing its machinery need not mean the full Westminster style, a not insignificant lesson for the future constitutional development of Wales's 'virtual Parliament'.

The committee has not been completely free of difficulty. Some technical constraints have impeded its operations, both in terms of a lack of power of formal summons and an inability on the part of the Auditor General to audit limited companies which spend public money.[100] In paradoxical fashion, a problem has also arisen by reason of this exercise of financial accountability 'closer to home'. Strict rules in standing orders on the disqualification from participation of committee members, which were clearly designed to underscore the value of integrity, have resulted in poor attendance, which in turn has led to the 'internal law' of the Assembly having to be revised.[101] Such are the growing pains of an Assembly of only sixty Members.

The wide-ranging nature of the committee's work programme, covering several important areas of public expenditure in Wales, is clearly shown in the list of examinations and investigations. It reflects the central place in Welsh devolution of indirect administration, the provision of many services by agencies etc., and thus the Assembly's responsibility not only to account for its own expenditure but also to hold the ASPBs to account for the way in which they spend the monies provided.

The committee's reports have extended from the very specific, and sometimes as in the case of accommodating the Assembly highly sensitive,[102] to the more general forms of inquiry, value for money perhaps in further education, or the official handling in Wales of the growth industry that is clinical negligence litigation.[103] Looking forwards, follow-up examinations and a concern to distil good practice from individual cases will be important to the consolidation of a strategic approach.

In summary, the Audit Committee is another fine example of the interplay of the twin elements of continuity and change in the devolutionary development. The very presence of Sir John Bourne on loan from Westminster has served to underscore the close parallels with the work of the Public Accounts Committee in the UK Parliament. But there is more to it than this, with the combination of established technical expertise and local political representation (and media interest) opening the way to a more effective form of financial scrutiny in practice, a sharper light.[104]

Regulating Members: present and future

Demonstrating the great sensitivities, the issue of how best to regulate (parliamentary) standards in the Assembly has run and run.[105] As well as working and refining the existing system, the Committee on Standards of Conduct has gone to the lengths of commissioning a fundamental review from an expert adviser, Professor Woodhouse.[106] In terms of the Welsh constitutional development, the recommendations represent a breath of fresh air, as being firmly grounded in comparative analysis.

Mercifully, there are no great scandals to report. Indeed, the committee has had few complaints to consider.[107] Nonetheless, its workload has been considerable, precisely because of the need to maintain and refine an appropriate regulatory system including in the special constitutional environment of the corporate body. As well as supervising the Members' Register of Interests, and reporting on ethical standards in the conduct of Assembly business, the committee has thus paid special attention to its function under standing orders of considering matters of principle. A review of arrangements for the registration and declaration of Members' interests, which produced greater clarity in the rules, is but one illustration.[108]

In fact the Assembly, because of its constitutional position, and in particular the need to protect the position of officials inside the corporate body, has an exceptionally large number of documents which prescribe rules of conduct.[109] From codes and protocols of general application to more specific documents, it is a case of soft law abounding. In turn, faced with such a mountain of paper, concerns are naturally raised about the coherence of the regulation, and further of the level of Members' understanding or awareness. All the more so, it may be said, in light of an incremental and piecemeal development that is so typical of Welsh devolution. Three years into the life of the Assembly and it was solemnly reported: 'some Members seem unaware of some guidance and protocols, most notably the rules relating to the use of the Assembly resources, or of changes made to them by Resolutions'.[110] Evidently, the Committee on Standards of Conduct had partly laboured in vain.

Insufficient attention was paid in the original design to the vulnerability of the Assembly to legal challenge in the absence of Westminster-type 'parliamentary privilege'.[111] At one with the retarded development of a public law tradition in Wales, this feature is the more striking in light of the simultaneous application to the Assembly of 'Convention Rights'. Today, it should hardly need saying that rough and ready complaints procedures[112] are a potential source of serious embarrassment, including by reason of (European) requirements of an independent and impartial tribunal.[113]

Such is the immediate background to the Woodhouse Report. Correctly, and marking a new stage in the regulatory development, an overarching code of conduct was recommended, effectively incorporating the multiplicity of guidance. Tighter definitions or more careful wording, drawing in particular on the comparative experience in Scotland and Northern Ireland, is thus the order of the day.[114] A simple point perhaps, but one which has particular resonance in Wales in view of the insular nature of much in the original constitutional design ('strange anatomy').

At one and the same time, the report commended much in the current procedures, and – on the basis of the existing devolution statute – made substantial recommendations on matters of openness, fairness and compliance with human rights. Responsibility for advising Members to pass to the Standards Clerk; the independent adviser to assume total responsibility for sifting complaints; a separate appeals mechanism; the role of the Presiding Officer to be confined to a general oversight of standards in the Assembly: this is how it should be.

Looking forwards, one would expect to see the function of independent adviser, essentially a secondary role, being substituted in favour of a statutory or free-standing Commissioner for Standards. The way would then be open to build on best contemporary practice, functionally tailored to local conditions. Notably, although none of the devolution statutes went down this path, this type of machinery has now been developed in both Scotland and Northern Ireland.[115] With a view both to assuring Members that complaints against them will be investigated in an impartial and non-political way, and to promoting the credibility and the integrity of the investigative process, why should the Welsh wish to be laggards? In the words of Professor Woodhouse:

> A statutory Commissioner may seem like taking a sledgehammer to crack a nut, particularly given the lack of any serious complaints in the Assembly so far. However, the importance of having robust machinery in place in case such complaints arise in future cannot be understated.[116]

Including, one is tempted to add, in a context of legislative devolution.

4. ASSEMBLY STOCKTAKING

The Assembly Review of Procedure was in one sense a victim of timing. Agreed in the brief period of Rhodri Morgan's minority Labour administration, and representing a compromise between the Presiding Office and the cabinet, it clearly bore the marks of the frustrations of Assembly life under Alun Michael. Issues of all-party inclusiveness and the authority of the corporate body were naturally much to the fore. However, by the time the group reported in February 2002, the internal situation in the Assembly obviously looked very different, given the coalition government and the move to a more parliamentary 'face' for the new democratic body. In turn, the review not only reflected but also reinforced this vital constitutional dimension.

Process and delivery

The first achievement was to secure all-party agreement to proceed. More especially to keep the Conservatives on board, this meant acceptance of two key principles in the terms of reference:

> The Review should proceed as far as possible on the basis of all-party consensus. Accordingly, it should focus on the workings of the Assembly rather than on matters of policy.
>   In the interest of producing proposals which the Assembly could implement quickly, the Review should not make recommendations which would require changes to the Government of Wales Act or other legislation which it is beyond the Assembly's competence to amend.[117]

The review was thus immediately directed and confined to two main areas. Essentially a matter for autochthonous constitutional development, the first one obviously was the Assembly's own procedures: from plenary debates to the relationship of cabinet with the rest of the institution, and on through the role and operation of the various committees to the distinctive subordinate law-making process. The fact that much in the standing orders now needed revisiting flowed directly from the decline of the corporate/ collaborative 'face' of the new institution. Such is the import of the Presiding Officer's remark about taking control of the Assembly's internal law.

The second area was constituted in the rubric: 'the Assembly, Wales and beyond'.[118] Essentially this translated as the newfangled modalities of multi-layered governance: the Assembly's relations or so-called 'partnerships' at the local, central and supranational (EU) levels. More especially, it meant the arrangements for the fruitful exercise – or otherwise – of 'a voice for Wales', most obviously in the case of primary legislation. Not only was the Assembly unable to dictate such matters, having instead to exercise voice in the hope of improvement, but it was also here that the most radical proposals for reform and revision were made.[119] Put simply, the constitutional difficulties associated with the model of executive devolution kept resurfacing in the course of the review.

The search for consensus was fully reflected in the composition of the Review Group. As well as the PO and the DPO, with the responsibility for chairing, it included the First Minister and the Business Minister, and the leaders and business managers of each of the other parties in the Assembly. Meanwhile, a measure of the underlying constitutional tensions between the two main poles of authority, there was to be a joint secretariat of Assembly civil servants drawn from the Presiding Office and the Cabinet Secretariat. A different but related point: the conduct of the review was to be firmly 'internal' in character. The appointment of a special adviser, who might after all have had some pithy things to say about the efficiency and effectiveness of Assembly procedures, was evidently considered a step too far.[120] In the instant case, this was probably wise.

A notable feature is the range of organizations submitting evidence. Key players on the local scene, such as CBI Wales and Wales TUC Cymru, the Wales Council for Voluntary Action, and the Law Society for England and Wales, were represented. This is indicative of the developing engagement with the Assembly among relevant policy networks, and of a level of concern about the early practice and performance of devolved government in Wales. According for example to the local representatives of business:

> We believe it is right that the Assembly should be reviewing the way it operates and considering how it could work better at this early stage in its life . . . It has often been difficult to determine the National Assembly's corporate structure, in relation to the authority of the executive Cabinet within the National Assembly. It is not clear whether the initiatives and leadership shown by the Cabinet need to be adopted or endorsed by the National Assembly as a whole. Alternatively, to what extent has the National Assembly the authority to lead and direct the Cabinet? This confusion makes it difficult for interest groups to identify the source and ownership of a particular policy thereby allowing them to direct their efforts effectively.[121]

Across the party groups in the Assembly, there was clear acceptance of basic design flaws in the internal construction. On the point of etching the parliamentary 'face' more firmly in Assembly lore, the evidence from the Conservatives and from Plaid Cymru for example was effectively *ad idem*:

> In the longer term, the [Welsh Conservative] Group would favour a legal separation between a 'Welsh Executive' (established as a Department of State) and the National Assembly which would be a distinct legislative body. However, such a change would require an amendment to the Act and is therefore outside the remit of this review. We would, as an interim measure, favour the establishment of a stronger *de facto* split between the executive and legislative functions of the Assembly.

> The Plaid Cymru Group feels that 'consensus politics' has failed to materialise and that procedures adopted by the Administration are primarily based on the Parliamentary model with a separate Executive. The very concept of the . . . corporate body – as opposed to the legal entity – is therefore challenged. We suggest that the Assembly more clearly define its constituent parts . . .[122]

Of course, the First Minister's perspective was the most significant. Correctly, and in the light of greater internal separation of functions, Mr

Morgan emphasized the need for the Assembly as a democratic body to raise its game in matters of scrutiny and public engagement:

> In political terms, the dynamic within Plenary and elsewhere is for Ministers to be held to account for Cabinet policies and Ministers' executive actions. That reflects the realities of government and the nature of delegated power within the Assembly. Debates also take place within that context . . .
>
> Any move towards a more distinct 'executive' increases the need for effective scrutiny . . . Subject committees provide perhaps the best opportunities for detailed scrutiny of Ministers and their policies . . . Subject committee scrutiny is more successful the more it is integrated into their other work with real dialogue rather than interrogation . . .
>
> Policy-making . . . is the weakest area currently because of the lack of clarity in the Assembly engagement in the . . . process. These weaknesses may also be leading to low public engagement with, and understanding of, the Assembly. The Group should make addressing them its main priority.[123]

Predictably the examination of the Assembly's own procedures coalesced round the twin themes so familiar in systems of parliamentary government of process and delivery. On the one hand, 'protecting the interests of all Assembly Members', 'improving scrutiny' and 'greater focus on legislation'; on the other hand, 'improving policy development', and 'seeking to ensure that the National Assembly for Wales delivers for Wales':[124] this was hardly rocket science. It was, however, concrete evidence of the infant body getting to grips not only with the devil in the detail of its work but also with the essential aims and purposes of this new manifestation of representative democracy. To this effect, the procedural review was also valuable in light of the retarded development of a public law tradition in Wales. The locals were effectively teaching themselves.

Recommendations: a modest affair

The review made some forty recommendations. There were a small number of important ones, especially – and tellingly – on the law-making side.[125] Many other proposals were about crystallizing existing practice in standing orders or about enhancing or streamlining very particular items of Assembly business. Training for Members featured prominently.[126] Perhaps then it is not surprising to learn of a break in the consensus at the end of the process, with the Liberal Democrats joining with the Conservatives and Plaid Cymru to reject the draft report on the basis of excessive tepidity. As brokered in the subsequent political negotiations, the final report was in fact little different, the most significant change being greater resources in support of the all-party subject committees.[127]

As so often in Welsh devolution, the civil servants were blamed for the kerfuffle.[128] No doubt there was an element of self-interest, especially in terms of 'family-friendly' working hours, and, further, a certain attachment to 'the extravagant version of the body corporate' on which officials had laboured.[129] This, however, should not be allowed to obscure the essential points. First, as a product of all-party discussions, the recommendations were naturally inclined towards the lowest common denominator. Second, and more important in terms of understanding the devolutionary development, key procedural elements or sources of friction had effectively been resolved in the course of the review in favour of a more parliamentary 'face' for the Assembly, for example via the 'separation project' for the Presiding Office. The recommendations of the review were in part modest because the process took on an increasingly confirmatory air.[130]

From review to commission

There is once again a broader significance. In suitably paradoxical fashion, the more that the constitutional possibilities under the GWA were fleshed out in the course of the review, the more the essential fault lines of the scheme of executive devolution were highlighted.[131] A powerful local brew, it may be said, in view of the by now familiar idea of a more parliamentary style for the Assembly easing the path to full-blown legislative powers for Wales.

The review is thus best seen as part of a continuing constitutional dialogue, one which had now begun to involve not only the parties in the Assembly, but also some mainstream elements of civil society in Wales. While the review can scarcely be compared with the broad-ranging constitutional convention that Wales had been so conspicuously denied by the Labour Party,[132] it did serve to point up different possibilities in view of what is now the Richard Commission on powers and electoral arrangements.

CONCLUSION – MIXED RESULTS

Looked at in the round, it is pre-eminently a case of mixed results. Statements that the Assembly machinery has or has not been working efficiently and effectively are precisely this: sweeping generalization. It is in the nature of this novel constitutional enterprise – architecturally complex and experimental, a product of compromise and rush – that some of the parts should perform well and others not, and that others again should have played different roles from those originally envisaged.

The subject committees have been oversold. The 'powerhouse' or 'locomotive' of the Assembly they are not, nor were they ever likely to be given the major structural constraints on their role and influence. The unique design feature of the umbilical cord is no substitute for available time and adequate staff resources. An unexceptional conclusion in the light of comparative constitutional experience, the finding is all at one with the movement towards a more parliamentary face for the Assembly, at the expense of a corporate ethos. As the new Welsh polity matures, one would expect to see a clearer recognition of the essential lines of political and administrative responsibility take hold. Why blur the central role of the cabinet and of a professional and full-time civil service?

It does not do to throw out the baby with the bath water. Grounded in the principle of complementarity, it is possible to identify an appropriate set of functions for these committees. As well as agenda-setting, the particular contribution of the in-depth policy reviews, the way forward lies in a more holistic approach to scrutiny and the committees' role in policy development, a continuous loop rather than distinctive processes, and further experimentation with different types of scrutiny. More especially, to anticipate the argument in the next two chapters, one would expect to see increased involvement by them in the various processes of law making for Wales.

The system of regional committees has failed to take off and its days appear numbered. The mistake is to see this as necessarily a bad thing. In terms of the constitutional design, these committees also sit most comfortably with the corporate/collaborative model of the Assembly. With the new institution taking on a more parliamentary style, and more especially the Welsh Assembly Government emerging as the essential policy-maker, so the utility of this formal system of advisory committees was liable to weaken. Their role was destined to be limited, now it is even more so. At worst, it is a case of lip service. In the conditions of small-country governance, more effective and efficient alternatives lie easily to hand.

The contribution of the Equality of Opportunity Committee again serves to illustrate the broader ramifications of the national devolutionary development, and in particular the scope for a distinctive Welsh political and administrative culture. The work has scarcely begun, but the force of 'the Welsh difference' should not be underestimated. At first sight very different, the fortunes of the language are now also seen to reflect and reinforce a general impetus.

The quest for a better standard of public administration has continued to feature prominently in the work of the Assembly. Epitomizing the drive for greater openness and accountability, the contribution for example of the Audit Committee represents a positive argument for the basic project of devolution. Meanwhile machinery such as the Committee on Standards of Conduct has whirred away quietly in the background: a useful reminder that in the continuing struggle to secure public trust and confidence what does not happen in Welsh devolution is also important.

The Assembly Review of Procedure is vital to an understanding of the major autochthonous element of Welsh devolution. At one and the same time, it shows the frictions that are generated when the different constitutional 'faces' of the Assembly rub up one against each other, and has served to underscore the features of the more parliamentary one. Another milestone in the political and constitutional development of Wales, the review has also helped to clear the way for the next stage.

8

Assembly Law Making

> Subordinate legislation represents one of the main tangible products of the Assembly's deliberations. It is a fundamental, though not the only, tool through which Assembly policy is implemented.
>
> Assembly Review of Procedure[1]

At first sight, the arrangement of the next two chapters may appear distinctly odd. Secondary legislation first, followed by the exercise of parliamentary sovereignty in Westminster statute law, offends the standard hierarchy of rules and of rule-making. However, this serves to highlight the way in which executive devolution undercuts the idea of a single process of creating, administering and amending laws, which is of the essence of the current constitutional condition of Wales.

The particular stresses and strains associated with this model have quickly engaged the attention of local actors. Efforts to preserve and reinvent the best of an integrated system of law making have taken up substantial wedges of time and energy, leading in turn to some innovative arrangements designed to grease the wheels or – as I prefer – to paper over the cracks. Meanwhile, the devolved administration has faced the not inconsiderable challenge of building up an efficient and effective system of formal rule-making virtually from scratch, one that pays proper regard to the demands of democratic legitimacy in, and on behalf of, the new national representative institution. The Assembly may only be a virtual parliament but it is a legislature.

Evaluation in this chapter of the Assembly law-making function involves consideration of a series of linked topics. First there comes the original procedural design, and more especially the extent of the departure from the procedural template at Westminster for secondary legislation. Typically it represents a poor beginning, one which local actors have had to try to make good. Warts and all: only in this way can the genuine progress that has now been achieved, as also the major challenges that continue to haunt the Assembly as a legislature, be properly understood.

The second main topic is introduced: the rapid emergence of an internal process of legal and administrative reform, which further reflects and reinforces the ongoing autochthonous constitutional development in Wales. It has taken place both behind the scenes, another example of the important role played by officials, and latterly under the auspices of the Assembly Review of Procedure. A chronological look, one that considers particular stages in the (short) life cycle of the local legislative practice and procedure, will serve to bring this to life, starting from a low point of basic organizational failure that happened under Alun Michael.

As a major stream of Assembly business, the conduct of law making naturally reveals much about the role and relation of the various pieces of internal architecture. For example, the Business Committee and the subject committees will be seen playing a greater and lesser role respectively than was originally envisaged. Plenary meanwhile will be confirmed as something of a vacuum. More important, however, and not before time, the Assembly law-making process will be seen beginning to sit more comfortably with the idea of parliamentary government and separation of functions. Viewed in comparative perspective, legislation as part of an active pursuit of cabinet government, and subject in turn to democratic scrutiny and oversight as appropriate, may be considered unexceptional features. But let us remember that this is Wales, original home to a strange constitutional anatomy.

Then there is the not insignificant matter of outputs: the scale and the distinctiveness (or otherwise) of Assembly legislation. A focal point of local political controversy, this has been prone to exaggeration on both sides: minimalist and maximalist. In fact, after a rocky start, the Assembly as a legislature can be seen making modest waves, as befits a modest scheme of executive devolution. As local capacities continue to grow, and more distinctive 'made in Wales' strategies come on stream, the legislative function may be expected to expand considerably. A point however that has perhaps been underestimated is the continuing pull even in the major fields of devolved functions of the historical geopolitical concept of 'England and Wales'. In this book it is seen to take many forms, valuable and otherwise, including in the legislative sphere.

No discussion of Assembly law making could be complete without reference to bilingualism. A distinctive feature in the UK context, making law in two languages raises intriguing questions of style and substance, which are not confined to the presentation of the Welsh-language text but impact on the whole process and product of the Assembly as a legislature. So typical of much in the local institutional development, the practice is increasingly generous and rubs up against the strict constraints of the model of executive devolution, here expressed in the form of the dominant legal language. It may be an old refrain in Wales, but 'the language and the constitution' is not played out.

Assembly subordinate legislation is hardly the most exciting of subjects, which itself is a major point of criticism of the current constitutional dispensation for Wales. Let us however keep in mind the many processes of devolution, and in particular the way in which the various dynamics are liable to interact. As with the virtual demolition of the corporate body, so with the Assembly law-making function: internal improvement can be seen paving the way and underwriting the demand for a more generous measure of empowerment or local autonomy. The technical is to this end highly constitutional.

Low base: high expectations

Viewed historically, the onset of Assembly legislation represents a quantum leap. Prior to devolution, law making in Wales was very limited, in the sense that subordinate legislation was not generally recognized as a distinctive output function of the territorial department. With some exceptions, for example in the field of education, the common experience was that London led and Cardiff followed, a case of modest local variations and much 'topping and tailing' of Whitehall drafts for aesthetic purposes.[2] An approach, it may be said, which reflected and reinforced the prevailing monolithic view of the 'English' legal system.

Precisely because of the lack of legal formality in this central government system, there is limited information concerning the scale of Welsh Office involvement. It was, however, estimated that in an average year the Secretary of State for Wales might make 150 Wales-only statutory instruments, of which 100 would be local orders, and 400 statutory instruments with other ministers. In 1998, immediately prior to devolution, the Welsh Office actually made ninety stand-alone orders: sixty-six general statutory instruments and twenty-four local ones.[3]

Such then was the legislative inheritance of the Assembly: on the one hand, a substantial responsibility for law making through the transfer of functions, underscored by the restriction of joint and concurrent powers;[4] and on the other hand, comparatively little by way of practical experience in drafting or planning. As well as being a recipe for early difficulties, this is a chief reason why the subsequent expansion of the Office of the Counsel General (OCG) is such a significant development.[5]

Teething problems in the Assembly law-making function were only to be expected, as also a time lag before the new forms of Welsh legislation started to abound. A clutch of organizational failings at the outset will be seen however to highlight the lack of preparedness; insufficient attention having also been paid to the need to develop internal business processes suitable for the new representative institution. In legislative affairs especially, the cosy informality of the Welsh Office could no longer suffice! Another relevant factor here is the very short time frame of the original constitutional construction. In view of the comparative novelty of Welsh law making, and further the many new demands, this was hardly conducive to the effective launch of the Assembly as a legislature.

Meanwhile, the devolution White Paper could once again be found trumpeting the possibilities. Subordinate legislation, it is right to say, comes in all shapes and sizes.[6] But surprise, surprise: the fact that it is apt to amount to a mass of abstruse technicalities was not at all the impression given to the people of Wales at the time of the devolution referendum. The role of subordinate legislation was thus played up, with matching procedures for achieving democratic scrutiny:

> Secondary legislation is concerned with the details of government policy, and is necessary to implement major decisions in many policy areas. For instance, in recent years, the Secretary of State for Wales has signed into law regulations vital to such areas as the National Curriculum in Wales, the major restructuring of Welsh local government and the routes of new trunk roads . . .
>
> The Government's proposals imply a far greater degree of democratic scrutiny of secondary legislation affecting Wales than is possible now. The Assembly's subject committees will be able to consider in detail and amend proposed Orders, and the whole Assembly will have the chance to approve or reject each Assembly Order . . .[7]

As the leading architect of Welsh executive devolution Ron Davies was typically bullish, portraying the ability of the Assembly to influence UK legislation, and the right of implementation if appropriate, as potentially 'the best of both worlds'.[8] A broad hint of generous allocations of legislative power in future statutes reflected and reinforced the idea of the GWA as a framework for organic change.[9] The more immediate challenges, let alone the deep-rooted difficulties that would confront the Assembly in seeking to make good the disaggregation of the law-making process, were effectively glossed over.

Constitution and policy

The Counsel General stated in evidence to the procedural review that legislation was the Assembly's main and most important product.[10] This is not as odd as it sounds, given the particular value – constitutional and symbolic – of this formal legal output to a new devolved administration seeking to secure democratic legitimacy. A key test of credibility and authority, being seen to legislate effectively and efficiently is all part of the building of a mature Welsh polity, not least in terms of national devolution and the growing aura of the Assembly as comprising both a government and a parliament. Such are the special demands on legislation in an interim constitution.

Nonetheless, as the Assembly Review Group observed, 'subordinate legislation should be seen as a tool for implementing the Assembly's policies, rather than as an end in itself'.[11] It was also correct to emphasize the place of formal rule making as a prime but not the sole policy lever that the Assembly government has at its disposal. How could it be otherwise in the contemporary conditions of devolution and governance, the greater sense of interdependency and erosion of hierarchy?

This feature plays in several ways. First, what I have called 'the closeness of Wales', and in particular a local predilection for less hard-edged techniques of government under the rubric of so-called 'partnership working', clearly points to a distinctive use and style of subordinate legislation.[12] The trick in these helpful conditions of small-country governance is to specify the appropriate combinations of actions that can be taken to secure policy objectives, integrating the use of legislative measures as required. While formal rule making carries a certain premium for the Assembly, it should not be allowed to intrude unnecessarily on the development of an administrative and political culture more attuned to local conditions. At one and the same time, the Assembly as a legislature should be seen as a chief component of national devolution, and kept in perspective.

Secondly, the early experience of devolution has apparently brought home to ministers the varying importance of legislation as an implementation tool in particular policy areas.[13] It is not exactly surprising to learn that the power of the purse has figured prominently in matters of economic development, whereas in education for example *The Learning Country* is seen to have spawned a raft of genuinely interesting Assembly law-making activity. Another important trick is ensuring clear and timely links between the policy development process and the production of subordinate legislation, carefully targeted on the key sources of formal business.

Thirdly, the over-optimistic picture painted at the time of devolution should not be allowed to obscure the potential for greater legislative involvement and scrutiny implicit in the idea of 'bringing government closer to the people'. One can readily appreciate the wider sense of 'ownership' of laws and policies able to be disseminated in a little country like Wales via consultation procedures etc. Again, almost any system for democratic oversight of subordinate legislation is liable to be an advance on Westminster, such is the scale of overload at the centre.[14] The trick here is one of proportionality, targeting efforts by separating the (much) mud from the gold, while devising new and more flexible arrangements designed to limit the difficulties of legislative oversight that flow directly from the disaggregation of the law-making process.

All this amounts to a tall order, but one which local actors, stuck for now with executive devolution and having to make the best of it, have not been in a position to duck. Another major arena of constitutional disputation and development inside the Assembly, the local legislative process will now be shown being gradually rendered more tolerable. As much, that is, as the practice of subordinate legislation ever can be.

1. ORIGINAL DESIGN

Classification: Assembly Orders

There is not one Assembly legislative procedure but many: a function, on the one hand, of the disparate types of subordinate legislation arising under the scheme of executive devolution; and, on the other hand, of a choice of procedures for making general subordinate legislation in the guise of 'Assembly Orders'.

Classification of the types of laws thus involves the differentiation of general orders from local ones, separate or autonomous law making from the joint or concurrent exercise of powers, and secondary legislation (statutory instruments) from tertiary rules (including statutory guidance, by-laws and circulars). Initially it was all contained in a single – voluminous – standing order.

Categories of Assembly subordinate legislation
- Assembly Orders
- Subordinate legislation subject to parliamentary procedure
- Subordinate legislation otherwise subject to special parliamentary procedure
- Local statutory instruments
- Subordinate legislation not required to be made by statutory instrument

Defined in the devolution statute as unlike all the rest – statutory instruments free from parliamentary procedure that are not local in character – Assembly Orders represent the lifeblood of a new Welsh administrative law.[15] As the chief legal tool directly available to the devolved administration for implementing distinctive 'made in Wales' policies, Assembly Orders thus serve to highlight how the decoupling from the Westminster machinery for scrutiny of secondary legislation is critical to the Welsh devolutionary enterprise.[16]

A second key feature is introduced: the virtual monopoly on the right of legislative initiative. In the words of standing orders, 'a proposal for an Assembly Order shall be prepared by a Minister'.[17] Opposition Members can huff and puff, but in this respect the flow – or otherwise – of Welsh legislation is firmly in the hands of the executive branch. While this may appear unexceptional in view of Westminster practice and procedure, it once again underscores the shift in the original constitutional design towards a cabinet model.

Mismatch

For the policy-makers, it was both necessary in the devolution statute to create a substitute for Westminster scrutiny, and – as the White Paper had indicated – a tempting opportunity to try, and to be seen, to be 'different'. Reflecting their important role in the devolutionary project, the GWA thus contains a general procedural code for the making of Assembly Orders, which in turn has structured the more detailed procedural provisions in standing orders.[18] So it is that the Minister for Assembly Business proclaimed: 'the new legislative procedures are one of the defining characteristics of devolution in Wales'.[19]

In making recommendations, the National Assembly Advisory Group (NAAG) was properly concerned to strike 'a balance' between 'thorough scrutiny', strong democratic oversight and opportunities for consultation or public involvement, and 'the need to avoid inappropriate delays' in decision-making, efficiency and effectiveness. A twin-track approach was thus proposed: so-called 'full scrutiny' for 'the most high profile pieces of legislation', and 'fast track procedure' for the 'more routine' statutory instruments.[20]

Yet again, however, NAAG showed a weak grasp of the practical realities, both in terms of the likely volume of Assembly Orders, and more especially the large number of boring and technical ones, and of the extent to which Welsh law making will be driven by demands from London and Brussels. It was thus implicit in the recommendations that plenary would deal with each statutory instrument separately, a sure-fire recipe for institutional overload and problems of timing. Again, powers in the devolution statute to disapply procedural requirements, and so produce streamlined methods of working, were essentially disavowed. They were characterized in terms of 'emergency procedures', suitable if for example there was an immediate risk to public health.[21]

So by focusing too much on the 'top end', NAAG failed to elaborate robust and user-friendly procedures for dealing with the great bulk of subordinate legislation through an appropriate variety of channels, more or less 'fast-track'. Furthermore, without proper targeting – 'proportionality' – rightful opportunities for detailed scrutiny might themselves be lost. Precisely this has happened in the early life of the Assembly.

Changing nomenclature is once again a vital clue. A first shot in an ongoing struggle, the technical experts on the Standing Orders Commission tweaked the recommendations – and the statutory code – more in the direction of administrative workability. A somewhat different connotation, 'emergency procedures' now became 'urgency procedure', which in turn would later become 'executive procedure'. Nor would it be long before 'full scrutiny' was replaced in Assembly-speak by 'extended procedure', and 'fast-track procedure' by 'standard procedure'.

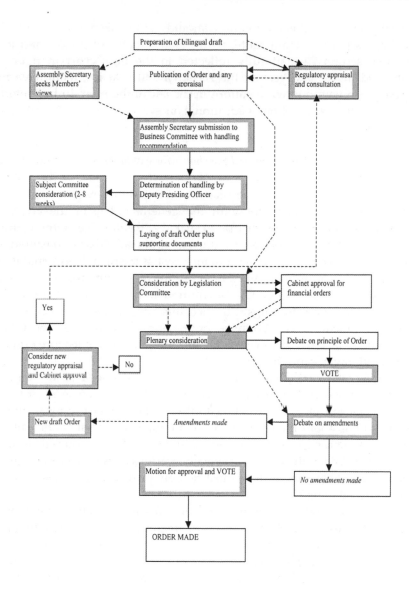

* Source: Cabinet Secretariat

Stages disapplied during urgency procedure

Stages of amended Orders ---------

Figure 13: Procedures for making Assembly Orders – early bird's-eye view*

Equally, however, this terminology should not be taken at face value. The clear impression of a main route, with flanking paths of greater and lesser legislative scrutiny, is faithfully reflected in the flow chart in figure 13, constructed in the first year of the Assembly. In practice, there have been changing priorities, a moving pattern in the use of the procedures, including by reason of the construction of additional ones.

Preliminaries and the channelling of business

Figure 13 serves to illustrate the relevance of statutory requirements at the preliminary stages. Consistent with the general policy of the GWA, the bilingual requirement is sharply drawn such that the devolved administration cannot lawfully designate class or group exemptions.[22] So too the pre-existing UK administrative practice of compliance cost assessment is incorporated in the new Welsh 'constitution' via a demand for regulatory appraisal, another typical example of the delivery of devolution at the price of prescription, the genuflection to interest groups.[23] In fact, this one has tended to be watered down in practice, so avoiding potentially burdensome consultation requirements, an early demonstration of strong executive-led pressures for the streamlining of procedures.[24]

The Business Committee is appropriately characterized as the hinge or buckle of the Assembly legislative process. It is here – 'having regard' to its advice – that the Deputy Presiding Officer (DPO) makes some of the key determinations about the channelling or formal procedural routing of non-urgent draft orders: can they go straight to plenary, or should a subject committee consider them first? Typically, various checks and balances are incorporated in standing orders, most notably provision for a determination to be overruled in plenary.

Of course much of this work is routine, a simple matter of consensus. Consistent however with the pro-parliamentary leanings visible in the Presiding Office, John Marek can be seen using the office of DPO to formalize matters, and to edge the Assembly into closer forms of scrutiny – hard look – as more distinctive 'made in Wales' policies come on stream. An element of friction with the Assembly cabinet is only to be expected! It is not unknown for example for the massed supporters of the Welsh Assembly Government to defeat a planned use of extended procedure.[25]

At the same time, the Business Committee is clearly prone to (legislative) overload, which by inhibiting discussion from the party representatives is apt to favour the minister. Another illustration of the important role of personal factors in this little institution, Dr Marek has been singularly persistent in raising queries on matters of legislative practice and procedure, trivial and otherwise.[26] Had Labour's preferred candidate been elected as DPO in

October 2000, the details of the Assembly as a legislature might well look different.

Starting out: three procedures

In permitting the opening up of the system of making Assembly Orders to various types of legislative scrutiny, the opportunity was created for greatly improving on the working method of the 'Mother of Parliaments' as typified by negative resolution procedure. By which is meant the familiar catalogue of a 'democratic deficit' in the making of subordinate legislation, an essentially reactive model of scrutiny characterized by little debate and no amendment.

The formal design of the Assembly machinery bridges traditional distinctions in Westminster law making. Several features are thus of a kind familiarly associated with the creating of primary legislation, as demonstrated by:

- *Standard procedure*

Hence consideration with debate in plenary, first of the principle of the order and then of possible amendments, which is the hallmark of this procedure, is loosely modelled on the classic parliamentary model of the readings of a Bill.

What then, it may be asked, of the Assembly's much-vaunted subject committees? As the flow chart (figure 13) also serves to illustrate, the litmus test of their involvement at this first stage in the life of the Assembly as a legislature was the use of:

- *Extended procedure*

So prized by NAAG as the way of dealing with the most politically salient pieces of legislation, extended procedure thus involves an additional loop via the relevant subject committee, followed by consideration with or without debate in plenary. It naturally comes equipped with formal powers in standing orders 'to consult or take such evidence as [the committee] considers appropriate'. The working assumption has been two to eight weeks in which to make a report on the draft order, including proposed amendments.

It is one thing to devise elaborate systems, quite another to operate them. An absence of the general kinds of legislative activity implicit in these procedures – formal amendments etc. – would quickly emerge as a major feature.[27] Virgin AMs, little by way of support and guidance for them; the conditions were not yet ripe for creative forms of democratic scrutiny and engagement.

Perhaps it is not surprising to learn that extended procedure has itself scarcely featured. As well as the limited number of high-profile pieces of legislation that have so far been developed, this reflects the costly and cumbersome nature of the routing, extended procedure being of limited utility precisely because it is so extended. In fact much of the difficulty arises from the formal nature of the design, and in particular the need for consideration and determination in the Business Committee before the subject committee starts work. By definition, this is late in the day in terms of the whole business of drafting laws etc., and is apt to involve major difficulties in the typical situation that is thrown up by executive devolution of an enabling legislative process going on (in parallel) at Westminster. The mistake, in other words, is to assume that extended procedure is the only appropriate way of the Assembly securing 'thorough scrutiny' at the 'top end'. One, it will be seen, which happily has now been rectified.

Turning then to the other side of the procedural spectrum, the original design made provision only for:

- *Urgency (executive) procedure*

This translates as elements of 'standard procedure' disapplied by agreement of the cabinet,[28] such as consideration by the Business Committee; consideration in plenary of the report of the Legislation Committee; and the chief requirement of an affirmative resolution in plenary. Not to put too fine a point on it, it means ripping out the guts of a distinctive Welsh way of making subordinate legislation.

Essentially, urgency procedure is negative resolution procedure reincarnate, allowing ministers to make an order that is subject to legislative scrutiny only *ex post facto*. The safeguards, such as they are, comprise the familiar Westminster-style techniques of a subsequent report on legality etc. (by the Legislation Committee), and an opportunity for challenge by Members (in plenary) within forty days.

Perhaps it is not surprising to learn that urgency procedure has been much used, especially at the outset. As an expression of administrative continuity – similar procedure, different fora – it fits with the model of 'Welsh Office plus', the restrictive view of the Assembly as a substitute for the old territorial department. The resort to urgency procedure is also indicative of the extent to which the Assembly as a legislature is driven from elsewhere, especially by UK departments operating by virtue of Westminster procedure on a well-grooved and swift time frame. In turn, the search has been on inside the Assembly for a less brutal form of procedure, a way of preserving at least a modicum of *ex ante* legislative scrutiny while meeting the pressures of business. Away from the original design – progress will also be seen here.

Short straw: the Legislation Committee

Given the decoupling from parliamentary procedure, it was important in the devolution legislation to create a substitute for the Joint Committee on

Statutory Instruments (JCSI) operating at Westminster. That is to say: a (Welsh) 'subordinate legislation scrutiny committee', soon more grandly titled 'the Legislation Committee', tasked with checking on the legality or *vires* of Assembly Orders. The statute requires the Committee to consider draft orders once laid and to report to the Assembly whether or not they demand 'special attention' on any of the grounds listed in standing orders.[29]

At first, the idea of a distinctive Welsh variant tended to be accentuated. Whereas the JCSI is classically an instrument for external oversight of the exercise of ministerial powers, the Legislation Committee was officially explained as 'a species of internal audit',[30] a characterization that fits with the original design of the corporate body. The statute also hinted at the possibility of a broader agenda, empowering the Assembly to give the committee 'other responsibilities relating to the scrutiny' of Assembly Orders, as also 'responsibilities relating to the scrutiny' of the other categories of Welsh subordinate legislation.[31]

In practice, the committee has operated along more conventional lines, which at least sits comfortably with the now developed sense in Cardiff Bay of two sides of the 'House'. Standing orders in particular have restricted the committee to the core remit. A bold proactive exercise in control and influence, it is not.[32]

Yet there are some major differences. Whereas the JCSI is commonly limited to review *ex post facto*, which in turn imports a high degree of formality into the proceedings, the Legislation Committee has the advantage of considering and reporting on *vires* ahead of an affirmative resolution in plenary, unless of course urgency procedure is in operation.

Then there are the all-important conditions of small-country governance. The Joint Committee, which processes each year as many as 2,000 statutory instruments, is naturally dependent for effective scrutiny of *vires* on very careful targeting. Simply by reason of the limited scale of devolved government, the Legislation Committee has enhanced opportunities for the rigorous scrutiny of Assembly Orders. A reading of the committee's reports brings home this point, highlighted by the considerable detail in the papers that relate to each and every piece of Assembly general subordinate legislation.[33]

The conditions are again ripe for a more informal approach, in the sense of expanding on the practices of discussion, negotiation and compromise – redrafting – which take place behind the scenes at Westminster. Standing orders provide a framework: before reporting adversely, the committee 'shall give the Minister an opportunity of giving evidence . . . and answering any questions it has raised, either orally or in writing'. But this is not all. According to the committee Chair, 'we work closely with the Counsel General'.[34] Increasingly administrative practice has taken over in the form of prior consultation. According to the committee's expert adviser, 'all the lawyers know that they have an open invitation to send me any draft when it is pretty well finalised'.[35] Warnings can be issued and suggested amendments made before the instrument is laid. Cooperation across the two sides of the 'House' – one is tempted to say, 'partnership working' – is then much in evidence.

All this is of special importance, given the nature of legislative scrutiny under the scheme of executive devolution. The scope for mismatch between the enabling statutes and subordinate legislation is bound to be increased by the disaggregation of the traditional central government model of doing business, and so calls for even more careful policing in Wales. The greater flexibility can operate to advantage here, not least by relieving the pressure as the formal channels for producing amendments, which tend to be lengthy and time-consuming, are effectively bypassed. The Assembly Review Group agreed: 'the Legislation Committee makes a very valuable contribution to the work of the Assembly'.[36]

As one would expect, the situations for 'adverse reporting' set out in standing orders closely echo the Westminster ones, for instance:

- doubt whether the legislation is within the Assembly's powers
- the legislation appears to make unusual or unexpected use of the powers
- the form or meaning needs further explanation
- the drafting appears to be defective.

The chief addition, naturally, is the bilingual element. The committee thus reports 'if there appear to be inconsistencies between the English and the Welsh texts', which translates as seeking to ensure there are not. Matters of the language have in fact occupied large parts of the committee's time. This is not a ground of criticism, but rather an inevitable consequence of the novel skills required for the drafting of bilingual instruments, coupled with a proper concern on the part of the committee to scrutinize, and promote best practice in, the presentation of Welsh text. The general sense of a creative collaboration with the lawyers in the OCG is communicated strongly here.[37]

As well as being executive-driven, weekly meetings at which it considers anything from two to twenty orders depending on what is in the pipeline, the committee is in a very real sense official-led. The role and remit – law and technique not merits or policy – naturally makes it very reliant for efficient and effective operations on the committee's own independent legal adviser, the first one being a government lawyer of many years' standing.

This is no idle point. While there is an occasional nugget, so much of the committee's business is tedious in the extreme: an ambiguity here, a mistranslation there, and so on. It is worthy and necessary work, but from the viewpoint of the political animal it represents the short straw. Against the backdrop not only of subordinate legislation, but also of laws often driven from elsewhere, this is part of the grim realities of the life of the Assembly as a legislature.

The annual reports serve to confirm the general impression. In the period beginning September 2001, the committee considered 210 Assembly Orders. Comments were made in a majority of cases (121), but many of these raised grammatical and typographical issues. On twelve occasions the committee made its approval conditional on the minister taking action to rectify such errors.[38]

Promoting stand-up fights in plenary on questions of *vires* is not 'the Welsh way' in matters of legislative scrutiny. For the reasons explained, a limited number of adverse reports is apt to convey a false impression of the committee's general contribution. It is, however, an option increasingly used to highlight drafting defects and the need for more elucidation (twenty-four occasions).[39] The Assembly is no exception to the struggle for clear, plain language!

The danger of too cosy an atmosphere was highlighted early on, in a controversy over 'Convention Rights'. While such matters clearly fall under the general rubric of *vires* as a ground of adverse reporting, the traditional formulation adopted – 'if there appears to be a doubt' – takes on new meaning in this context, in view of the strong dynamic quality of the jurisprudence.[40] Calling for a careful exercise of professional judgement, delicate issues of risk assessment are apt to arise here, including on behalf of the Legislation Committee by the expert adviser.

The relevant regulations concerned the system of disabled persons' badges for vehicle parking. In the light of concern that otherwise there would be a breach of Article 6 of the European Convention (need for an 'independent and impartial tribunal'), the issue arose of whether there were powers in the enabling statute to create a right of appeal to the magistrates' court.[41] Correctly, the Legislation Committee declined the minister's invitation to gloss over the matter, despite the fact that the authorities in England and in Scotland had not picked up on it, and – exceptionally – voted by a majority to make an adverse report.[42] A useful illustration of the devolutionary principle, Welsh scrutineers not merely to follow other people's example, the affair was also a valuable warning shot, a reminder to ministers (and the OCG) that collaborative method does not mean taking the committee for granted.

Looking forward, one would hope to see the Legislation Committee making more creative use of its annual reports, with a view to distilling and promulgating good practice in local matters of legislative drafting. To this effect, churning out individual reports on specific pieces of legislation can never be sufficient. Fortunately, the Assembly Review has now encouraged this development,[43] which further highlights the demand for accountability stemming from the major element of informality in the exercise of scrutiny. 'Who guards the guards?'

Useful experience has now been gained. Looking further forward, one can envisage the Legislation Committee taking on additional responsibilities should the Assembly gain primary law-making powers. The Scottish Parliament provides a clue, whereby the equivalent committee also reports on the powers of subordinate legislation contained in Bills, a useful check on the natural propensity of government to generate discretion to make rules. The Legislation Committee has already countenanced the possibility.[44]

2. EARLY STRUGGLES

The Assembly as a legislature did not accelerate into action: quite the reverse. Over the first six months, Assembly Orders were produced at a rate of roughly one a week. Many of the fields of devolved functions, for example the environment and planning and social services, saw little or no legislative activity. It was essentially the UK government that drove Welsh general subordinate legislation, by virtue of requirements to act arising from new primary legislation.[45]

A low-key process: it was all at one with the political style of the devolved administration under Alun Michael.[46] His catchphrase may have been 'dynamic devolution', but the general approach to the exercise of the right of legislative initiative was minimalist in character. Shades of the Welsh Office: the lack of a clearly articulated legislative programme by the incoming administration on the basis of transferred powers says much.

But this legislative hiatus or 'phoney war' also serves to highlight the additional burdens that the devolution statute etc. had placed on Welsh legislators. Coming on top of the detail of the new legislative procedures, one need only mention here compliance with 'Convention rights', the language requirements, and the special duties in respect of equality of opportunity and sustainable development. Critical to the specification of a local administrative and political culture, such elements also greatly sharpened the legislative learning curve for the fledgeling institution. Once again, the OCG in particular has had to grow hard, in order to keep abreast.

In the event, the lack of administrative preparedness was brutally exposed around the time of Alun Michael's resignation. There was thus a failure of legislative planning; the lack of a smooth and consistent flow of draft orders through the Assembly procedures. Limited activity at the beginning of 2000 gave way in mid-March to a rush of orders, partly occasioned by the need to have certain forms of regulations safely completed in time for the new financial year. Yet by definition this was a fixed date in the calendar. The particular rub was the heavy use made of urgency procedure, and so of a reinvention of the 'democratic deficit' apparent at Westminster.[47]

Complaint was also made by the opposition parties of a 'legislative deficit', on the worst-case scenario a separation of laws (from England) by reason not of Assembly creativity but of inactivity. Much of this was exaggerated,[48] but it shows how the general issue of the Assembly as a legislature had begun to take on real salience in the local constitutional and political discourse. Indeed, the very concept of a 'legislative deficit' was eminently contestable, being dependent in part on expectations of Assembly output, not least in terms of generating new policies and initiatives.

Getting a grip

Perhaps, from the viewpoint of the devolutionist, things had to get worse before they got better. In retrospect, March 2000 represents the low point in the fortunes of the Assembly as a legislature. The bulge of orders that had suddenly appeared served to concentrate minds. Behind the scenes urgent action was initiated to improve the internal business processes.

The development further serves to illustrate the important role that the all-party Business Committee has played in the constitutional reworking of the Assembly.[49] Away from the 'theatre' of plenary session, the committee effectively supplied the forum and the continuing impetus for negotiation of the procedural changes.[50]

The establishment of a 'subordinate legislation working party' also shows the facility in the Assembly for collaborative working at the official level. It brought together representatives from various parts of the administrative and legislative machine, from the Office of the Presiding Officer on through the Cabinet Secretariat to the OCG and the policy divisions. A project report was produced in May 2000, which in light of the criticism of the use of urgency procedure laid great emphasis on tighter business processes.

Three related features command attention. The first one concerns the re-equipping of the local civil service better to meet the challenges of national devolution.[51] Centralization in a new unit of the OCG, the aptly named Legislation Management Unit (LMU), of the administrative tasks of co-ordination and use of forward planning information, timetabling and handling of draft orders, was now the order of the day.[52] With the aim of avoiding problems such as policy divisions failing to appreciate the rigours of the formal legislative procedures, or the lack of clear administrative 'ownership' or responsibility for a text, it was not before time.

This feature may be said to exemplify the continuing growth away from the structures and processes of the old territorial department, where a limited legislative output function could be more easily accommodated in a disparate set of arrangements. LMU demonstrates the kind of nuts and bolts arrangement that is so necessary for the Assembly as a legislature to operate efficiently.

Secondly, the idea of a more variegated approach to legislative scrutiny, in particular one that accords more closely with the reality of Welsh legislation often being UK- or EU-driven, can be seen taking root. This is given tangible expression in a more sophisticated classification of proposed statutory instruments – 'routine', 'annual' or 'regular', and 'amending', 'implementing EU legislation', 'matching Whitehall' or 'Wales only' – for the purpose of informing the routing decisions of the Business Committee. It is then a simple illustration of proportionality as a chief business criterion, with the aim of better targeting of Assembly energies and resources.

The regular item of Assembly business that has been changes to standing orders is the third feature. Typically this involved a measure of streamlining, and signalled an ongoing effort to establish greater flexibility in the formal architectural design of the law-making function. In evaluation, it is important to bear in mind the scale of constraint on local actors arising by reason of the detailed procedural code of the devolution statute. This type of reform demands in turn careful manoeuvring through the interstices of the so-called 'devolution settlement'. Fortunately, the Assembly's lawyers have proved up to the task.

One practical example will serve to highlight the excessive rigidity contained in the original version of standing orders, as also the highly technical nature of many of the resulting changes. At first, once a draft Assembly Order was laid the only established machinery for amendment was plenary, with all the delay and inconvenience that this could entail, not least when the text contained the type of minor drafting error which the Legislation Committee routinely identifies as appropriate for correction. The (partial) solution: empowering the relevant minister to lay a memorandum of corrections, so allowing for automatic incorporation when plenary session resolves to approve the order.[53]

In short, by the end of the first full session various steps had been taken to render the Assembly law-making function more efficient and focused. Considered in the round, it represents a more disciplined approach to matters of legislative practice and procedure. Or, as I prefer, getting a grip.

Fourth slip

One set of formal procedural changes deserves a separate mention. Immediately classified as a fourth main type of Assembly legislative procedure, it represents something of a middle way between on the one hand, the rigour of standard procedure, and on the other hand, the Westminster-style connotations of urgency procedure:

• *Accelerated procedure*
This means voting in plenary without debate, a way of short-circuiting the final stage in standard procedure of consideration by the full Assembly.[54] Notably, a single ministerial motion to this effect can encompass any number

of draft orders. 'Checks and balances': use of the procedure is, however, dependent on political agreement in the Business Committee; rightly, in order to protect minority interests, an easy-to-operate blocking mechanism is incorporated.[55] And so it was that the visitor to the Assembly in July 2000 might have been greeted by the spectacle of Members resolving to approve large groups of Assembly Orders, commonly bearing little relation to each other, unanimously and in a matter of minutes.

A procedural innovation of the first importance in the life of the Assembly as a legislature, accelerated procedure thus reflects the need for a light-touch form of scrutiny for routine or uncontroversial matters, while maintaining the skeleton of *ex ante* review including through the Legislation Committee. It has thus filled a gap in the Assembly's procedural armoury traceable to the failure of NAAG properly to comprehend the realities of subordinate law making in the new representative body.

Turning the argument round, little attention had yet been paid in the internal process of reform to buttressing, or giving practical support to, the exercise of democratic scrutiny where it was most likely to be meaningful, as in relation to the administration's 'made in Wales' policies. Perhaps not surprisingly, amid the developing pursuit of cabinet government – 'check against delivery' – the first priority was to secure the law-making function as a slick means of production. Notably, throughout this period, the legislative role of the subject committees remained in abeyance, as reflected in the non-use of extended procedure, and reinforced by an evident lack of technical support.[56] Typically, this was left as a matter for the Assembly Review of Procedure, under the effective chairmanship of the Presiding Officer, to pick up.

Codification, consolidation and constraint

Not, it should be stressed, that the pressures for general business improvements ever ceased. The Legislation Committee quickly compiled a catalogue of concerns, from a certain lack of clarity in drafting to a continued reliance on urgency procedure, and on through to the arrangements for publication.[57] Meanwhile the clearing of the undergrowth via a more disciplined approach has again served the valuable purpose of exposing the basic constitutional constraints on the Assembly.

The obvious next step in the evolutionary development was a codification of the formal legislative procedures: at one level, a tidying-up exercise in the face of a typically *ad hoc* and piecemeal set of changes to standing orders; and at another level, a further opportunity for revision and refinement. As ratified by plenary in October 2000, this involved breaking up the single governing piece of 'internal law' and replacing it with a series of standing orders geared to the different kinds of subordinate legislation that the Assembly makes.[58]

By way of illustration, a special procedure was now instituted for operating the 'constitutional lock' protecting the position of the Assembly as a legislature, the need for its consent before the UK government makes changes by Order in Council to transferred functions.[59] In providing for a minister to propose a motion to approve or reject the changes, the possibility of tabling amendments has been carefully and properly excluded.

For its part, and exhibiting the greater sense of security associated with the advent of the coalition government in October 2000, the Assembly cabinet can be seen in increasingly experimental mode. An especially noteworthy feature is the concern, at least on the part of Rhodri Morgan, to give the new representative body a particular constitutional 'feel'. 'Subordinate legislation of a substantial nature should be debated in plenary on a regular basis to develop the Assembly's legislative character.'[60]

The designation of a 'legislative programme', as part of the new annual government business programme, speaks volumes in this context.[61] Typically it was at first a crude affair, and is in any case highly susceptible to the vagaries of forward planning by reason of the (secondary) nature of the product. Yet happily it came as a shock to the system. In the words of one former insider, the idea 'was quite alien to the officials largely used to following the Whitehall lead'.[62]

Another useful innovation at this time involved composite motions. Whereas accelerated procedure has often been used as a kind of 'legislative vacuum cleaner', collecting up whatever 'rubbish' or routine material happens to be around,[63] it was now seized upon as a vehicle for consolidation, the drawing together of related matters in a thematic way. This was first demonstrated in June 2001, in the context of a raft of Assembly legislation arising from local government reform and modernization. Plenary is seen debating and voting on the policy of a package of measures, via an amendable motion to welcome the regulations, before resorting to accelerated procedure for the purpose of satisfying the legal formalities. At one and the same time, the image of the Assembly as a legislature could be enhanced and some more procedural rigidity bled out of the system.[64]

In fact, on this occasion there was an excess of make-believe. With a view to stressing the importance and coherence, the Assembly cabinet promoted the batch of subordinate legislation as a 'Local Government Bill'. A somewhat desperate measure, this further attempt to recast the Assembly as 'a virtual parliament' proved too much even for the Presiding Officer to stomach. The people of Wales were not to be tricked over the secondary place of the Assembly in the hierarchy of making formal legal rules. In so ruling, Lord Elis-Thomas paid a proper respect to British constitutional tradition and understandings.[65]

What it may be asked of the role of 'private members'? Standing orders have provided for a novel procedure whereby an individual AM can prompt subordinate legislation through a motion instructing a minister to bring forward a draft order to achieve specified objectives. For this purpose, Westminster-type procedure was read across in the form of a ballot of Members, but in notably restrictive fashion. Far from undermining the executive's right of legislative initiative, the design barely dented it. In the event, very little was generated under the procedure in the first few sessions, either by way of legislation or genuine and robust debate. Yet the exceptions which prove the rule, for example a tightening of planning control over the storage of radioactive waste, or an unsuccessful attempt at special duties of consultation relating to school buildings on contaminated land, serve to illustrate the potential.[66] Major local controversy serving to ground legislative activity through the action of individual Members, such is the logic of small-country governance.

Jumping ahead, the Assembly Review Group grappled mightily with this subject. Legislation as a form of political lifeblood for the new representative institution, a vehicle of constructive engagement with interest groups etc.: what could be more appropriate than an expanded Westminster-style element of creativity and polemic from outside the 'machine'? Naturally, however, the Minister for Assembly Business expressed serious reservations about a demand-led system, one that might eat up much time and energy.[67] An uneasy compromise, the final report favoured major expansion of the procedure, so giving every Member in the course of the electoral cycle the right to propose a piece of subordinate legislation, but with little concrete to offer in terms of the necessary technical support.[68]

All this however should not be allowed to obscure the basic constitutional point: the scale of the constraint on individual AMs not least by reason of the scattergun approach to the Assembly's formal legislative powers. Searching the legislation within the fields of devolved functions with a view to bringing about meaningful political objectives through subordinate legislation is a noble vision!

3. BILINGUAL LAW MAKING

The Welsh Office not only made few laws. It also made them in English, a form of linguistic domination that had deep historical roots in the Henrician statutes or so-called Acts of Union.[69] The practice persisted despite the more enlightened attitude shown by the Welsh Language Act 1993 in establishing the general principle of equal treatment of the two languages in the conduct of public business and the administration of justice. In fact at the time of devolution the practical experience of legislative drafting in Welsh was virtually non-existent. Save for some charters and by-laws etc., it had been largely confined to ecclesiastical law in the guise of the Constitution of the Church of Wales.[70]

Welsh as a living language of the law

The provisions of the devolution statute – Assembly Orders normally required to be drawn up in English and Welsh, and the two texts then to have equal legal standing[71] – thus signalled a new beginning, official commitment to the idea of Welsh as a living language of the law.

Implementation further entails a significant policy choice, not least given the many competing administrative priorities. For the purpose of formal legal compliance with the GWA a range of approaches is possible: one that is indicative of greater or lesser respect for the role and place of the minority language. At one end of the spectrum is what can be called the 'cheap and cheerful' method: translation. A creative activity, in the sense of reinvigorating Welsh legal vocabulary after centuries of slumber, nonetheless it clearly assumes the paradigm of a dominant language.[72] At the other end of the spectrum is 'co-drafting', which as the name suggests involves contemp-oraneous drafting in both languages throughout the law-making process. 'Bilingual [laws] will then be the result of integrating two separate texts initially crafted and drafted in a manner sensitive to the contexts and subtleties particular to each language.'[73] A lesser variant, or form of linguistic adaptation, sees the working draft in English but subject to modification in order to accommodate the syntax of Welsh and the range of Welsh con-struction.

The Office of the Counsel General (OCG) has in fact shown great enthusiasm for developing this new language domain. 'This work is highly specialised and groundbreaking: it amounts to nothing less than the establishment of a legal register in the Welsh language.'[74] As an exercise in policy choice, a generous approach to legislative drafting in 'the ancient tongue' further reflects and reinforces the vision of a bilingual Wales now formally embraced by the Welsh Assembly Government.[75] In the light of national devolution, the advancement of the Welsh language as a language of administration and government, but not of legislation, is rightly seen as like Hamlet without the Prince. So also the bilingual drafting of the main Assembly laws is indicative of a more general effort to revivify Welsh as a language of the law, not least in terms of the administration of justice.[76]

The comparative dimension is important. While bilingual law making is a new departure for the United Kingdom, it is a familiar aspect in many other jurisdictions. EU law is an obvious source of inspiration, but for the purposes of the comparative method a legal system steeped in the tradition of the common law – and British methods and techniques of legislative drafting – provides a more comfortable fit. Correctly then the OCG has looked to Canada for instruction, and in particular to New Brunswick where the provincial institutions provide a fully bilingual service of law making and administration of justice for a smaller population than that of Wales.[77] A comparative report, *Bilingual Lawmaking and Justice*, now largely informs the development of Assembly practice and policy.[78] It is a very practical example of 'Wales in the world' post-devolution.

Bilingual law making is in the famous phrase 'a process not an event'. As the report was careful to emphasize, the sophisticated modalities of bilingual law making observed in Canada, which include especially at federal level strong forms of co-drafting, have taken a generation or more to accomplish. The comparative method has then a special instrumental role to play. 'By learning from their experience Wales can hope to accelerate that process.'[79]

The constitutional differences, however, should not be glossed over. On the one hand, Canada is not only a bilingual but also a bijural system (consisting of both civil law and common law jurisdictions). On the other hand, in contrast to a province like New Brunswick which also enjoys primary legislative powers, in the case of Wales it is only one kind of text – Assembly Orders – that has to be in two languages. At one and the same time, the scale of the task is much reduced, and a particular problem of fit with the other (English) legal sources is induced, most obviously in the form of statute.

A further twist to the scheme of Welsh executive devolution is identified. Ideally, the minority language would be considered at the point of construction of any enabling power that is to be exercised bilingually. In a context of particular provisions in England and Wales legislation promoted by and negotiated with different central government departments, this is 'pie in the sky'. Turning the argument round, one point in favour of broad framework legislation on behalf of the Assembly is that this takes into account the necessary requirements of bilingualism by reducing the problem of language fit. A generous scheme of legislative devolution would effectively sidestep the problem.

In evaluation, it is important to keep in mind the knock-on effects. In the case of the Assembly, the logic of the bilingual requirements is that the drafting in both languages will increasingly be affected. A distinctive style of Welsh legislation, one that is more straightforward and less particularistic in nature, could well emerge over time. Self-evidently, however, a natural tendency towards adopting the style of legislation of the UK Parliament is underscored by the current constitutional dispensation, as also by the particular demand for uniformity and consistency that marks the historical concept of 'England and Wales'. For Welsh fully to flower as a language of the law, and to be a main driver of the Assembly's development as a legislature, a much greater measure of constitutional autonomy is required, together with the training of lawyers and linguists to work through the medium of legal Welsh. Looking forward, the idea of a fully bilingual Welsh statute book – primary as well as secondary sources – no longer appears an impossible dream.[80]

On from translation: the language and the constitution

The strength of the local commitment to bilingual drafting was made clear from the outset. Of the 142 Assembly Orders made in the year beginning April 2000, only fifteen were solely in English.[81] A strict interpretation was here being placed on the proviso in the statute that 'in the particular circumstances it is inappropriate or not reasonably practicable for the draft to be in both languages'.[82] The very fact that at this early stage there was generally little or no substantive difference from the delegated laws applicable to England serves to underscore the point. A symbol of national devolution, the local laws were at least to look different.

The potential for legislative delay associated with the use of two languages, which is apt to cause most difficulties where Assembly law making is being driven urgently from elsewhere, is another relevant consideration. The exception that proves the rule, many of the Assembly Orders for combating the onslaught of foot and mouth disease were made in English only, so meeting the vital need to issue identical legislation simultaneously in all parts of Great Britain. Nonetheless, the Legislation Committee was firmly of the opinion 'that for the Assembly to fulfil its commitment and obligations to bilingualism it should establish procedures to enable it to issue legislation in English and Welsh even in urgent situations'.[83] As the devolved administration grows and gains in experience, more especially through additional expert resources, so the proviso in the statute should increasingly appear a last resort.

The distance the devolved administration has to travel in light of the Canadian experience is highlighted by an official description of the making of Assembly Orders:

> Most texts will be produced by lawyers in the relevant subject team in the Office of the Counsel General, in response to written instructions from the policy division. A bilingual text is then prepared by a bilingual lawyer or the Office's specialist bilingual legal texts team . . . The text will then be checked by the originating lawyer (if bilingual) or by the bilingual lawyer in the appropriate team (each team has such a lawyer).[84]

Looking forward, the very fact of a specialist drafting team in the OCG augurs well for the development of Welsh as a language of legislation. To this effect, a formal 'dictionary' power to prescribe Welsh equivalents to established English legal terminology is but one small piece in a general enrichment of the choice of legal Welsh.[85] The OCG itself can already boast of a bilingual atmosphere inside the department, via an active policy of appointing Welsh-speaking lawyers. 'We are now working to develop the process [of bilingual drafting] that works best for us, using the extensive lawyerly and linguistic skills that we have in the Office.'[86]

Co-drafting in the form of pilot projects is an obvious step. The approach has in fact been advocated not only as showing respect for the minority language but also as a method for improving the quality of the law in general. That 'two lawyers . . . are more likely to spot gaps and problems' is one argument against complaints of time-consuming and expensive procedures! Speaking more generally, the practice in New Brunswick involving limited minority language resources, a combination of co-drafting techniques and instructions and meetings in the English medium, has now been assessed as a suitable goal for the Assembly, the achievable best practice at least in the immediate future.[87]

In the case of Wales, matters of the constitution and the language are inextricably linked. Notably, the active pursuit of Welsh as a living language of the law has been officially justified in terms of other possible constitutional developments – a calculation it may be said which brilliantly illustrates the many processes of (national) devolution: 'If the present system achieves bilingualism it will be capable of ready adaptation to ensure that bilingualism will be a feature of any future change in the legislative or judicial structures of Wales.'[88]

The autochthonous development of a Welsh 'state' machinery equipped to meet the particular linguistic needs, as well as the general administrative demands familiarly associated with the allocation of primary legislative powers: it is another piece in the jigsaw of a parliament for Wales.

4. LEGISLATION IN CONTEXT

Bare bones

Table 10 gives the bare bones of the Assembly's legislative output. After the slow beginning, things clearly have warmed up. Setting this in historical context, the devolved administration has for the last two years been making general and local statutory instruments at two to three times the rate for Wales-only orders immediately prior to devolution.[89]

The effect of course is cumulative. A few hundred statutory instruments may not sound very much, but multiplied on an annual basis there rapidly emerges a substantial body – if only in the strict geographical sense – of 'Welsh law'. Also, the large package of measures generated by the foot and mouth crisis in 2001 is the extreme example of a general phenomenon, the tendency of subordinate legislation in particular to be driven by events, as well as by the demands of new primary legislation. The statistics inevitably will fluctuate.

Establishing the difference

To pose the famous question: 'where's the meat?' Putting to one side process and language, how much of this 'Welsh law' has a distinctive content? In

Table 10: Assembly legislation*

Year	General Statutory Instruments (Assembly Orders)	Local Statutory Instruments	Total
1999 (from 1 July)	29	28	57
2000	119	109	228
2001	241**	90	331
2002 (to 3 December)	173	103	276
Total	562	330	892

*Source: OCG. By the end of the first term, the total stood at 697 Assembly Orders.
**The figure for 2001 includes forty-five General Statutory Instruments made by the Assembly in response to the outbreak of foot and mouth disease

some measure, it must be a triumph of form over substance.[90] The very fact of legal delimitation – the transfer of functions orders, etc. – means that the Assembly will be making more 'Wales-only' orders than did the Welsh Office. In the formal legal sense, it typically does not have the option that was generally available to the Secretary of State for Wales of proceeding with colleagues on an England and Wales basis. To secure the legislative and administrative continuity for which there will often be good reason, the option will instead be 'Welsh law – mirroring England'. A case, the non-devolutionist might say, of no added value, at additional cost.

Evidently such matters have touched a nerve. Criticism from the highest levels of the Welsh political establishment, to the effect that in the first year or so the Assembly as a legislature had created virtually nothing that was different,[91] produced from the Counsel General the breakdown given in table 11.

The figures serve to underscore the value of the early organizational reforms of the order-making process. As a legislature, the devolved administration can here be seen to be making a difference. Roughly a third of the regulations were 'either unique to Wales or, where they paralleled similar legislation passed in England, involved significant differences in drafting reflecting Welsh circumstances'.[92]

Once again, let us beware of an exaggerated significance. As every lawyer knows, altering one or two words may fundamentally change the meaning, while lengthy new paragraphs in an instrument may simply reflect bilingual drafting. And reflecting the nature of subordinate legislation, many of the 'distinctly Welsh' orders will themselves be dry and technical, the Beef Labelling (Enforcement) (Wales) Regulations perhaps, or something called the Adjudications by Case Tribunals and Interim Case Tribunals (Wales) Regulations. A significant chunk of commencement orders is included in the category.

Table 11: Assembly orders by subject area – 2001[93]

Subject area	No. of orders with distinctly Welsh content	No. of orders mirroring those for England	Total	% of orders with distinctly Welsh content
Transport, Planning and Environment	10	12	22	45
Education and Lifelong Learning	15	15	30	50
Health and Food Safety	4	34	38	11
Social Care	6	16	22	27
Agriculture, Fisheries and Forestry	12	71	83	14
Local Govt and Housing, Economic and Industrial Development	27	18	45	60
Welsh Language	1	–	1	100
Total	75	166	241	31

The figures usefully highlight the variable legislative demands that arise across the different policy contexts or 'fields' of devolved functions. Whereas the OCG prefers to draft its own instruments, what this actually entails varies considerably. Take agriculture, fisheries and forestry for example. For a large amount of 'mirroring' not to happen would be positively alarming. Such is the looming presence of European law, and further a subject matter that commonly does not lend itself to different regulatory regimes in England and Wales, for reasons of domestic market integration and consumer protection. Here as elsewhere, the trick is then to focus resources on those gaps where there is significant local discretion or 'legislative space'.

Education, naturally, conveys a very different flavour. First, this is an area where there has been some considerable experience of separate drafting and processing of general subordinate legislation to build on, a function of the historical development of differential 'national' policies in the education system in Wales. Second, it is a classic area of 'regulatory politics', one in which the devolved administration has been seen to be very active under the general and distinctive rubric of *The Learning Country*. Examples of education regulations drafted from scratch without seeing an English draft are increasingly many and various.[94] To this effect, far from 'topping and tailing' in Welsh Office style, a proactive approach to legislative drafting, one that in turn reflects and reinforces the enhanced potential in devolution for consultation with local interests etc., is increasingly in evidence here, more especially in the context of new primary legislation. The Learning and Skills

Act 2000 for example produced a bunch of 'distinctly Welsh' regulations on the Counsel General's list.

Not just Assembly law making

The official breakdown is by definition a partial picture. The Assembly, it is important to bear in mind, has no monopoly on secondary law making in respect of Wales. At first glance, this may appear unexceptional, given the many areas of non-devolved functions where executive legislation including on an England and Wales basis is the order of the day, for example in the criminal justice system. But it is a mistake to assume that the Assembly is in a dominant position even in the so-called 'fields' of devolved functions. Statistics produced from Cardiff University (table 12) paint a different picture.

Table 12: General subordinate legislation on health and education applying to Wales – 2000, 2001[95]

Health		
Year	Assembly	Central government
2000	11	72
2001	18	31

Education		
Year	Assembly	Central government
2000	14	41
2001	30	36

Viewed in this comparative perspective, the Assembly as a legislature may now be said to have slipped into second gear. Such anyway will be the long view of the constitutional and political development. The figures are the more striking because of the chosen fields for sampling. At the risk of repetition, health and education are both portfolios where the cluster of devolved functions is seen as more than usually 'complete'. In contrast, table 12 points up the retention by central government – operating on an England and Wales basis – of certain key bundles of functions. In terms of generating subordinate legislation, the most important ones are the regulation – technical and other-wise – of the medical professions, and the regulation of teachers' pay and conditions, respectively.[96]

This aspect deserves a special emphasis, since by reason of the model of executive devolution attention naturally focuses on the so-called 'horizontal' division of functions between primary and secondary legislation. To anticipate the argument in later chapters, one can hardly expect the deeply rooted legal and administrative paradigm of 'England and Wales' to vanish overnight. In fact, the underlying stresses and strains are brilliantly illustrated in this context, with the question of devolving effective control over the teaching profession becoming something of a political football in the Assembly.[97] Is it a prerequisite of a truly radical education agenda or is it not?

Whither, it may be asked, a joined-up approach? The detailed lists behind the figures confirm the patchwork or zigzag of Assembly powers: less principle – more piecemeal. Presumably somebody understands how three sets of regulations, one on a devolved function, the other two not, fit together, on the single topic of roadworthiness.[98] It asks a lot of the locals to ensure requisite knowledge, first, of subordinate legislation made in relation to devolved matters by central government; and second, of subordinate legislation made for England by central government under legislation, the powers of which are exercisable by the Assembly in Wales.

Of course, this may appear less of an issue when looked at through the spectacles of the minimalist devolutionary variant of 'Welsh Office plus'. Assuming, however, a more developed idea of 'democratic devolution', a constitutional sense that Assembly Members at large have a serious role to play, not least in holding ministers to account for both legislative acts and omissions, and further in generating new initiatives, this is not a helpful situation.

Whereas the sense of a jumbled legislative space is a fact of life in constitutional systems of divided competencies, it is apt to be magnified in the case of the Assembly several times over. By reason, that is, of the peculiar historical and constitutional combination of the model of executive devolution and the exceptionally strong geopolitical concept of 'England and Wales'. 'Complexity, what complexity', one hears the Counsel General say.[99] Pity the poor bloody infantry.

5. PROCESS REVISITED: REVIEW AND PROTOCOL

A lack of involvement

Figure 14 confirms that the extended procedure, so beloved of NAAG, has not taken off. Another major indicator of the movement (back) towards a Westminster-type system, the use of accelerated procedure has become increasingly prevalent, alongside executive procedure. In fact on the basis of the figures, the executive, accelerated, standard and extended procedures could be relabelled 'standard', 'common', 'occasional' and 'rare', respectively![100]

The figures clearly are indicative of a lack of involvement by Assembly Members in the formal legislative business. Take for example scrutiny by the

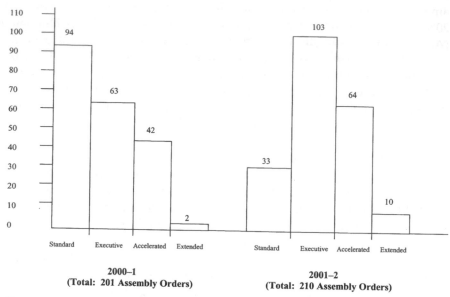

*Source: Legislation Committee annual reports

Figure 14: Assembly Orders – procedural routes*

subject committees. In the period October 2000 to 3 December 2002, they considered a total of 24 draft Assembly Orders, making 1 recommendation for rejection, 3 recommendations for acceptance (of which 2 were accepted), and 20 recommendations for approval without amendment. A total of 24 amendments was tabled, of which 10 were withdrawn, 11 accepted in Committee, and 6 subsequently incorporated into text approved by plenary.

Then there is plenary itself, also seen by NAAG as a vital cog in the formal machinery. In the passage of 562 Assembly Orders, a grand total of six amendments had been formally tabled for debate, with five selected for debate and all defeated. The number of statutory instruments rejected in plenary also stands in zero.[101] Could there be stronger evidence of what I have called 'the hollow core' of plenary business?

One would expect most Assembly legislation to emerge largely unscathed. Such in part is the political and administrative logic since October 2000 of majority government. But it is appropriate to ask once again: where is the essential lifeblood of legislative debate and controversy for this national representative institution? At one level, the limited measure of formal democratic scrutiny can be seen as a function of the lack of experience in the infant body, and in particular of insufficient back-up for Assembly Members at large.[102] At root, however, it does reflect the 'politically lifeless abstruse detail' of much subordinate legislation.[103] Why would one want to move amendments to such 'distinctly Welsh' instruments as the Care Standards Act 2000 (Commencement no. 6) (Wales) Order or the Valuation Tribunals (Amendment) (Wales) Regulations?

Perhaps it is worth adding that the original design of Assembly legislative business has been held up as a possible model for Parliament itself. To quote Lord Dahrendorf, 'the Welsh Assembly has found a way of debating and, if the majority so wish, amending secondary legislation. Should we follow it?'[104] The Assembly itself, however, was still looking.

Redoubling efforts

In fact, local actors deserve praise for redoubling their efforts to bolster the role and image of the Assembly as a legislature in the face of such unpromising material. The 'greater focus on legislation' agreed in the Assembly Review of Procedure has thus given fresh impetus to the internal reform of Welsh law making, as well as to attempts to enhance inputs and influence at Westminster.[105] The details just given conceal a measure of improvement, with much of the legislative scrutiny outlined happening in the last year of the Assembly's first term.

The background here is one of fierce criticism in the evidence generated by the Review of Procedure.[106] The lack of involvement by the subject committees was the obvious starting-point, given the original hybrid model of a 'cabinet and committee' system for the Assembly. But major concerns were also raised about potential overload and lack of information for the Business Committee; and more generally, whether the legislative business was being planned and managed in a way which provided sufficient time and information to enable appropriate and proper procedures to be followed. 'In constitutional terms, the rise of Assembly lawmaking needs to be matched and effectively underpinned by robust machinery for scrutiny.'[107] Simply put, if the Assembly was desirous of increased law-making powers, then it should have its house in order.

The OCG in particular was here being threatened by closer regulation, in the guise of an expanded role for, or relief from the tedium of, the Legislation Committee. It was suggested for example that the committee might usefully check on whether the various legislative procedures were being fully complied with, such as regulatory appraisal and consultation with business.[108] For his part, the Counsel General was less than enthusiastic, adhering not to a broad and facilitative interpretation consistent with the GWA as a framework for organic change, but to a narrow and rigid view of the committee's formal remit.[109] There is however more than one way of skinning a cat. The pressure evidently had the desired effect.

Standing orders have been changed to underscore the contribution that subject committees should consider making on the legislative front. Reflecting a growing awareness in the Assembly of the role and relation of different sources of law, and in particular the importance of the Westminster axis, the framework is now indicative of a more holistic approach to legislative influence and scrutiny. The subject committees are now specifically enjoined to 'advise on proposed primary, secondary and European legislation affecting Wales': which in turn serves to underscore the need for additional resources and a targeted approach.[110] Meanwhile, a technical change serves to free up use of the accelerated procedure, a clear indicator of future intentions.[111]

But why, it has been realized, reinvent the problem of an excessive rigidity by a general resort to standing orders? Especially in the conditions of small-country governance, why not do things a little more flexibly? Soft law, classically a means of administrative experimentation and innovation, has once again a useful role to play here.

One of the better products of the procedural review was thus the elaboration of some nine heads of 'best practice for the management of subordinate legislation'.[112] As now set forth in an informal 'contract', a protocol between the all-party Business Committee and the Welsh Assembly Government, this stands for 'improvement in the procedures for planning, informing Members of, and tracking subordinate legislation'.[113] So typical of the strong organic dimension to Welsh devolution, the protocol itself incorporates practices that were already developing and enumerates new ones.

Fifth man

The protocol gives official sanction to what is effectively a fifth form of Assembly legislative procedure, which although masquerading behind a bland title has considerable potential in the particular conditions of Welsh executive devolution:

- *Initial consideration by subject committee*

It represents a kind of 'pre-secondary legislative scrutiny', grafted onto and operating in tandem with, but also allowing for streamlining in, the formal procedures. To this effect, 'initial consideration by subject committee' coupled with 'accelerated procedure' is an obvious formula. At the other end of the scale, it could even allow in rare cases of great practical importance and controversy for a 'super' form of democratic scrutiny, being coupled then with 'extended procedure'.

Pioneered first by the Health and Social Services Committee, and then by the Agriculture and Rural Development Committee, the procedure effectively took off in 2002. By the end of the year it already accounted for roughly half (eleven) of all the general statutory instruments that had been considered by the subject committees.[114]

The most striking example relates to the passage through Parliament of the NHS Reform and Health Care Professionals Act 2002. In implementation of the Welsh Assembly Government's distinctive health care policies, the statute empowers the Assembly to establish and confer functions on local health boards, and to direct them, in partnership with other public bodies, to prepare health and well-being strategies.[115] The problem was a classic one of timing under the scheme of executive devolution. This clearly was an occasion for significant differences of view concerning the policy content of the relevant subordinate legislation. Yet there was no formal authority for the legislative business to commence under standing orders until the Bill received royal assent and the Assembly received the necessary powers, which in turn would only be a matter of months before the boards were supposed to be up and running.

With a view to effective involvement by the subject committee, what better than to proceed initially on an extra-legal basis, prior to the DPO making a determination about the procedural routing, before going quickly through the legislative formalities specified in standing orders? A special protocol was therefore agreed by the Chair, the minister and representatives of the other political parties allowing for consultation on the terms of 'proposed' draft orders, prior to the royal assent. In the event, this delivered a genuine process of democratic scrutiny, marked by much redrafting.[116]

Two related features stand out. First, the approach parallels general legislative developments at Westminster: greater recognition of the value of democratic scrutiny at the early stages when the details of the policy are not yet set in stone.[117] Second, it can be a useful vehicle for consultation with, and inputs from, outside interests. This happened in the case in question.

There is particular merit in the case of the Assembly. Implicit in the idea of 'bringing government closer to the people' is an increase in the number of levers of influence that local interests and organizations can press to good effect. As well as ministers and AMs, and the local paraphernalia of public consultation and partnership councils, the all-party subject committees – operating in a transparent way – should display this kind of potential on the legislative front. Less rigid and so more timeous in character than 'extended procedure', this additional fifth option holds out the prospect of it actually happening.

Refinement

How then to ensure effective operation of the sifting process, so that individual orders are allowed appropriate amounts of plenary and committee time? In moving to what may now be described as a more orderly and transparent way of conducting legislative business, the Review Group was signalling a greater respect for democratic scrutiny, while seeking to minimize the risk of jeopardizing the timetable for implementation. If in comparative perspective this appears unexceptional, then it marks a real advance in terms of the local constitutional and administrative development.

The need for a rolling programme of legislative business properly advertised and grouped for consideration in plenary is now an accepted part of Assembly culture. 'Having set out a target date for the production of a draft order, the Welsh Assembly Government will strive to maintain that date': so says the new protocol.[118] The role of the Business Committee is further enhanced via a series of notification requirements, including as to the satisfaction of statutory requirements. The use of executive (urgency) procedure in particular should become more strictly disciplined. A requirement in the protocol that reasons be given on an individual basis for the use of the procedure has now been backed up by a legally more secure approach on the part of the Welsh Assembly Government. A written procedure whereby individual cabinet ministers signified assent has been superseded by determinations at meetings of the cabinet or, where necessary, a new cabinet subcommittee on subordinate legislation.[119]

By definition, the Assembly cabinet could not be compelled to follow the new extra-legal procedure. Backed up by a requirement that the minister give reasons in a case of disagreement, the protocol effectively does the next best thing, enshrining the right – and duty – of the subject committees to have a say.

> Each subject committee shall consider the proposed programme of legislation, as updated, as well as any items of proposed legislation noted individually . . . and inform the Minster with subject responsibility as to which draft orders they wish to be subject to initial consideration by the subject committee.

The protocol in other words goes as far as it reasonably can in promoting 'the fifth man'. The executive must have its business; the subject committees should be more proactive. Suffice it to add that the statutorily required ministerial presence on these committees – 'the umbilical cord' – appears even more anomalous in this situation.

The protocol contains a review clause, the necessary tool for pressing the administration to abide by the new rules of the soft law game.[120] But it also signals an ongoing process of procedural change, including in terms of the formal internal law of the Assembly.

> The review of the . . . protocol would be a suitable point for the Business Committee to consider whether there is scope, first, to streamline the subordinate

legislation procedures and, secondly, to re-write the Assembly's standing orders in relation to subordinate legislation in a simpler more user-friendly manner.[121]

The sense of local actors charting their own path within the general framework of the devolution statute is communicated strongly here.

CONCLUSION – DEVIL IN THE DETAIL

It has been a bit of a struggle. The Assembly as a legislature came into this world with some grave disadvantages. The limited capabilities of the Welsh Office, as also a failure in planning and organization in the vital transitional period, showed through in the internal business processes – or rather lack of them – in the first year. Meanwhile, a concoction of cautious political leadership and of AMs generally finding their feet in this strange new body pointed inexorably in the same direction. Overarching all this was a heavy procedural burden – fewer powers, more requirements – which in part reflects the peculiar dominance of delivery over content in the approach of the Labour Party to Welsh devolution. As every lawyer knows, the devil is in the detail.

Law making is not the most important thing the Assembly does, but as a major stream of business its procedural and substantive development once again demonstrates the competing models that have been at the heart of the autochthonous constitutional development in Wales. Reflecting and reinforcing the extravagant version of the corporate body, NAAG especially piled on the procedure in the name of inclusiveness, focusing very much on 'the top end' of the market in statutory instruments. Proper procedures for dealing with the great bulk of orders, including what lawyers like to call the 'dustbin category', were sadly neglected. As the growing number of 'distinctly Welsh' general statutory instruments illustrates, it would be an exaggeration to say that the legislative procedure constituted under the GWA has proved unworkable. Local actors, however, have had to ride especially hard because of the cumbersome nature of the beast, simply to keep up.

At one with the strong political imperative to (be seen to) achieve – 'check against delivery' – the pendulum may be said to have then swung too far in the opposite direction. As well as an internal process of reform, shown in the creative use of some new techniques, there has been much cutting of corners to the detriment of democratic scrutiny. In this sense, coupled with the pursuit of cabinet government, there is a strong whiff of 'Welsh Office plus', with the rest of the Assembly commonly of the status of legislative sausage machine, as is shown by an absence of committee involvement and serious debate in plenary. For a new representative institution, it has been – emphatically – not a pretty picture.

The procedural review and subsequent legislative protocol stand in turn for a constitutional rebalancing, one which aims to expand the potential of democratic scrutiny – where it matters – while paying proper regard to the nature, volume and exigencies of devolved law making. Set in terms of the swing of the pendulum, it might even be called the Assembly's 'third way'.

Some reluctance on the part of the cabinet to have subject committees crawling over important instruments is only to be expected: the exercise would not be worth much if it were otherwise! By now, however, Assembly ministers should have gained a greater constitutional sense and understanding of legislative procedure. The development bears in turn on the broader constitutional dimension – the clearer differentiation of the two sides of the 'House' inside the corporate shell. Welsh Assembly Government-driven, targeted oversight from the Assembly at large: the legislative design shrieks now of 'a virtual parliament'. Pure fiction like government 'Bills' is not required.

There is still more to be done, not least in terms of streamlining or ridding the Assembly legislative procedure of the ghost of pre-devolution politics and administration. The sheer spottiness of Welsh executive devolution – a patchwork of powers – continues to present a formidable obstacle to a coherent and transparent exercise of legislative power by the Assembly, more especially in view of the powerful geopolitical concept of 'England and Wales'.

All the more reason, it may be said, to applaud the considerable ingenuity shown by local actors in circumnavigating some of the difficulties and promoting a more flexible approach better suited to the conditions of small-country governance. This has eaten up valuable time, but the first fruits are now in evidence. The creative and positive approach to the demands of Welsh as a living language of the law – a prevailing concept of cultural opportunity and not of legislative burden – deserves special praise in this context.

Again, part of the argument in Welsh devolution for transferring broad powers in future statutes is precisely that the local legislative procedures are likely to enhance, not curtail, the democratic legitimacy of the law. Whereas suspicion of wide enabling powers for ministers makes perfect sense in a Westminster context of little scrutiny of subordinate legislation, it cuts less ice in Cardiff Bay the more that the local legislative procedures are knocked into shape, so allowing for 'a hard look' where this is appropriate.[122] It is once again in the interstices of documents like the new legislative protocol that Welsh constitutional advance is seen being engineered.

Nor is it fanciful to suggest that future historians will see in this recasting of the local legislative arrangements the green shoots of something much more substantial. Subject committees treating seriously with draft legislation, such is the model of the Scottish Parliament, and in many small jurisdictions (federal and otherwise). Similarly, a cabinet (sub)committee on legislation: it could so easily develop.[123]

It would be a mistake to deduce from the early struggles of the Assembly as a legislature that devolving primary legislative powers would be a step too far, even 'a leap in the dark'. Indeed such a conclusion would be perverse. Provided by Westminster and in standing orders with a poor set of tools, local actors have been seen making up lost ground, seeking once again to make the best of a bad job. There is little here to suggest that given proper tools the devolved administration – elected representatives and local civil servants – could not do a good one.

The devil is in the detail in another sense. Such is the basic lack of constitutional 'fit' between on the one hand secondary law-making powers (howsoever generously conceived), and on the other hand the new political and administrative fact of life of national devolution. Where else, it may reasonably be asked, is a 'National Assembly' directed in such a constitutionally and politically demeaning way to embrace the dull and tedious material so often contained in subordinate legislation? In this sense too, the present configuration carries the seeds of its own destruction. As Churchill might have said, it is something up with which a 'National Assembly' worthy of the name will not long put.

Primary Legislation

The Assembly can neither pass primary legislation of its own, nor simply and passively accept, administer and implement UK Government policy as reflected in new primary legislation; that would be a denial of its separate democratic mandate . . . The Assembly must therefore seek to influence primary legislation so that it reflects its own policy agenda.

Welsh Assembly Government memorandum[1]

The making of primary legislation affecting Wales is already the subject of official inquiry from four directions: the Assembly Review of Procedure; the House of Lords Select Committee on the Constitution; the Welsh Affairs Select Committee; and – currently – the Richard Commission. Luminaries like the Presiding Officer, the First Minister, the Permanent Secretary and the Counsel General, not forgetting successive Secretaries of State for Wales, have moved from one venue to another giving their views and reflections on a fast-changing political and administrative environment, flanked of course by teams of officials. Meanwhile 'the usual suspects' from civil society in Wales have also performed. It has been a bit of a circus.

It is not simply that there is enough paper to fill a small cupboard. The very fact of this not so popular form of entertainment – a rare if not unique series of public investigations in British government – is significant. At one level, it reflects a sense of dissatisfaction in Wales with particular elements of the new arrangements and the search for improvement. At another level, given that the subject is such a critical element of the scheme of executive devolution, this set of inquiries represents a major forum for the ongoing struggle for Welsh constitutional advancement. It is a game played for both low and high stakes.

Of course, the 'official-speak' does not dwell on the disaggregation or fragmentation of the legislative function which lies at the heart of the scheme of executive devolution. Rather, the talk is of 'a law making process which is shared between Cardiff and Westminster',[2] a more soothing prospect. Evaluation in this chapter involves consideration both of a series of developments designed to secure and foster cooperation and coordination between the two centres, including with a view to promoting a 'voice' for

Wales on the London stage, and the major constraints and limitations on this general form of proceeding. So typical of the Welsh constitutional saga, there is much room for improvement, considerable improvement is visible, and such improvement can only go so far in the face of an inherently rickety system.

One concern obviously is to avoid the muffling of a voice for Wales: the bad bargain whereby discrete, local control is achieved only at the cost of much influence in Whitehall/Westminster, on which, in executive devolution, the territory is so reliant. But further, the aim must be to promote a more powerful voice, making use of new opportunities associated with the fact of a national representative institution;[3] not least with a view to underpinning via the primary legislative process local innovations in policy development and delivery. To this effect, many of the procedural developments discussed in this chapter reflect the demand – and need – for privileged access to the machinery of statute-making on the part of the Assembly, in contrast to the ordinary processes of interest representation.[4]

Some scene-setting is in order. The chapter begins by highlighting the variety of ways in which – since the original Transfer of Functions Order – powers and functions have been conferred on the Assembly. Attention is further drawn to the different vehicles for the delivery of primary legislation affecting Wales. By their very nature, some more than others are amenable to local engagement etc. The general development is also seen to be deeply coloured by the practical workings – or otherwise – in the initial period up to and including the Queen's Speech in December 2000; effectively, what I called the 'red-light' and 'amber-light' phases of life in the Assembly, leading up to the 'partnership government'. The sense of a lack of preparedness is pervasive.

The focus then switches to the main actors – ministers and officials – and thus to the design of the system of intergovernmental relations (IGR).[5] At one and the same time, colleagues in the Welsh Assembly Government are distanced from the internal Whitehall processes of preparing primary legislation, and need to be intimately involved, with a view to ensuring that local concerns and demands are taken fully into account. A measure both of the importance of this matter, and of the potential difficulty in maintaining effective forms of communication across the sprawling Whitehall machine, the growth of 'soft law' in the guise of the concordats etc. is shown to be especially thick. So also Wales Office ministers have had an uncommonly large role to play in ensuring collaboration across the different administrations, as well as in fronting up the deliberative stages of the legislative process. Bit by bit, relatively smooth cooperative arrangements on legislative projects affecting devolved matters have been developed over the course of the Assembly's first term.[6] Given the conditions of Labour Party hegemony, it would be truly alarming if this were otherwise.

Turning to the bit players, a suitably provocative characterization of the role of AMs and MPs and peers in the broader legislative process, the arrangements clearly have been less satisfactory. At one level, a series of practical difficulties is seen to arise, ranging from matters of timetabling to the appropriate means for consultation. At another level, there is a basic sense of disconnection: first, AMs with a monitoring role over local policy development and implementation, but little input into the primary law-making process; second, MPs with a role in legislative scrutiny, but no function of democratic oversight of the devolved services. Whither, in the old-style language of government and politics, 'the feedback loop'?

As with Assembly Orders, so with primary legislation affecting Wales: one can hardly overlook the basic legal and political question of (the scale of) the outputs, more especially with a view 'to establishing the difference'. Once again, it is a calumny to say that little has changed in the first term of the Assembly. There already is a significant accumulation of distinctively 'Welsh' statute law, a necessary precursor in many fields to the types of 'made in Wales' policies that the devolved administration has increasingly shown interest in pursuing. Then again, one cannot help but feel that the devolved administration is ever more vulnerable to its own 'success' in terms of policy development, by reason of the eye of the needle through which bids for primary legislation have to squeeze at Westminster. Here, as elsewhere in the chapter, there are seen to be strong pointers to a generous scheme of legislative devolution for Wales.

For its part, the recent report from the Welsh Affairs Select Committee (WASC) is very much in the improving mould, neither criticizing nor endorsing the so-called devolution settlement, 'but taking it as it is'.[7] At one with the general ethos of the Welsh devolutionary development, as also the evident need for a measure of reconnection in the exercise of scrutiny and oversight, WASC has picked up on the idea of developing 'a partnership approach' to primary legislation between Westminster and the Assembly at large.[8] The report also serves to highlight the typically piecemeal nature of the devolutionary development, directly in terms of the problems for scrutiny stemming from the multiplicity of sources of Assembly powers, and indirectly in terms of a cautious approach at Westminster to formal procedural change.[9]

The last section of the chapter is of a rather different order; dealing with a set of principles the Assembly has resolved that it would like to see adopted in government Bills relating to the fields of devolved functions. Picking up on a general lack of consistency in the legislative drafting, the aim has been to establish some understandings and conventions with a view to grounding the intergovernmental exchanges, as well as facilitating a measure of democratic accountability. As their originator, I can also vouch for the fact that the so-called 'Rawlings principles' were so constructed as to give the Assembly space to grow.[10] They are then a useful test of the commitment to devolution as 'a process, not an event', not least on the part of the UK government.

1. LEGISLATIVE LANDSCAPE

A lack of grip

From the viewpoint of the lawyer, one of the more striking features of Welsh devolution is the range of instruments of further empowerment of the Assembly post-devolution. The methods include:

- amendments to the original Transfer of Functions Order (TFO) – further TFOs
- amendments made directly to Acts listed in the TFO
- powers conferred on the Assembly directly by new Acts
- amendments to the Government of Wales Act
- additional functions conferred by delegated legislation made (a) by the Assembly (b) jointly by the Assembly and a UK Government Minister or (c) by a Secretary of State
- designation orders with a view to the Assembly implementing Community Law.[11]

Such are the multifarious legal and policy contexts that a single approach is unlikely ever to happen. Likewise, one could hardly envisage uniformity in the style and substance of post-devolution primary legislation affecting Wales. In particular, whereas distinctive 'made in Wales' policies may well be under-written by new primary legislation, or changes to the devolutionary scheme sensibly accommodated by amendments to the GWA,[12] many matters will be closely integrated with other sets of legal provisions, both pre-existing ones and parallel arrangements (especially for England). 'No clean break': the basic constitutional message of Welsh executive devolution is underscored here.

Yet there is more to it than this. Another example of the way in which national devolution has been grafted onto pre-existing administrative arrangements; the development must also be read in the light of the hitherto highly decentralized legal machinery of the UK government, whereby departments and their legal advisers have enjoyed considerable autonomy.[13] Differential approaches between particular departments, a marked variation in legislative custom and practice: once again, this can be said to fit with a high degree of 'British' pragmatism, a problem solving approach or practical response to immediate difficulties. A different but related point: novel requirements of liaison and cooperation with the devolved administrations, but little in the way of basic organizational change in central government – it is par for the course in the new field of political and administrative activity that is IGR.[14]

So one of the explanatory factors for what – from a bottom-up perspective – appears an unwarranted inconsistency in primary legislation affecting Wales, is the way in which the UK legislative programme is driven by individual departments. In turn, competing pressures are seen being generated, in the guise of new concerns relating to the clarity and structure of legislation from the territorial viewpoint. A decentralized system in central government versus greater demands for consistency in the light of national devolution: it is a fine irony.

Special mention must be made of the role and contribution of Parliamentary Counsel. Given that many of the legal issues will derive from the policy considerations with which a proposed Bill is meant to deal, these highly skilled legal technicians will classically be 'creatures of instruction', courtesy of their 'clients', the policy officials and government lawyers from the individual departments.[15] However, as every public lawyer knows, Parliamentary Counsel also function as 'guardians of the statute book', the voice of authority on the structure and design, and the form and presentation, of legislation. Matters, it should now be clear, which take on a particular prominence and sensitivity in the peculiar constitutional context of Welsh executive – and national – devolution.

In evaluation, one should keep in mind the scale of the challenge that Parliamentary Counsel face in this situation. In drafting Bills and helping to see through their enactment, they also have to operate in a context of competing demands of scarce ministerial time and proper scrutiny in Parliament. Again, they will rarely have the luxury of drafting on a blank sheet of paper, but instead must navigate – more or less boldly – an extant map of laws, including formal usages and technical terminology. First Parliamentary Counsel Geoffrey Bowman, may be quoted:

> Different functions are conferred on the Assembly in different ways because, in some cases, the background is different from the background in other cases; each drafter is not necessarily facing the same problem; he, or she, will adopt the solution which appears to be the most apt in the circumstances concerned.[16]

Nonetheless, as the Welsh Affairs Select Committee has now observed, matters have been taken to excess. One size may not fit all, but there is no requirement to sow additional seeds of confusion on the basis of 'muddling through', and more especially in the case of Parliamentary Counsel of the old-fashioned cult of the talented individual. Likewise, to anticipate the discussion, the different approaches that different draftsmen adopt have been apt in constitutional terms to afford the new national representative institution a greater or lesser measure of respect. Appearing before the Select Committee, Geoffrey Bowman made it painfully clear how little collective thinking had gone on in the Office of Parliamentary Counsel concerning the novel challenges and opportunities for drafting presented by Welsh devolution. It may sound harsh, but there has been an abnegation of professional responsibility at the heart of UK government – a lack of grip.

Legislative options

Let us suppose that the Assembly government wishes to see distinctively 'Welsh' statutory provisions, for example in the guise of legal frameworks supporting its major new policies on the organization and delivery of health services in Wales,[17] and that the UK government is willing to give support. What then are the particular considerations from a territorial perspective of the choice of legislative form?

To the external observer, the obvious option is:

• *Wales-only Bill*
A local sense of 'ownership': using this technique ministers, officials and lawyers in the Welsh Assembly Government are well placed to work in a cohesive way to develop and refine the legislative proposals. At the same time, there may be excellent opportunities for public consultation and debate in the Assembly. Turning to Westminster, the idea of separate 'Welsh Bills' opens up the vista of using the special parliamentary machinery for the representation of Welsh interests – like WASC – for the purpose of detailed scrutiny.

Nor should one overlook the symbolic aspect, as also the general sense of a devolved administration building up inner capacities from a low base. Pre-devolution, it is well to remember, Wales was very different from Scotland with its steady stream of separate statutes. Reflecting centuries of legal history, the Welsh Language Acts 1967 and 1993 were very much the exception that proved the rule. For his part, Rhodri Morgan has naturally stressed this aspect, speaking of a '500% increase' in Wales-only Bills post-devolution.[18]

A technical point, but one that serves to underscore a general theme: Bills or Acts do not apply to Wales only (or England only) in the sense that there is no distinct Welsh (or English) legal system. For instance, the devolutionary device that is the Greater London Authority Act 1999 strictly applies to both countries. Although it obviously produces practical differences in territorial application, a Wales-only Act is, legally speaking, not the same thing as, say, a Scotland-only Act passed at Westminster, because of the fact of a separate jurisdiction 'north of the border'. A brilliant illustration of the question of 'fit' between, on the one hand, national devolution and, on the other, the overarching unity of the English and Welsh legal system, it thus becomes necessary to think in terms of two 'law districts' within an integrated formal whole.[19]

Turning the argument round, reluctance on the part of central government to engage widely in this technique is only to be expected, given the logical corollary of a general need for England-only Bills.[20] The 'Wales-only' option is then a matter for precise targeting by local actors. A different but related point: the exigencies of timetabling will operate as a potent filter here, and no doubt the more so in the case of a substantial and/or controversial Bill. The rough and ready estimate is that two-thirds of the bids for Bills made by government departments do not make it into the Queen's Speech, such is the intense nature of the competition for legislative time.[21]

By way of practical illustration, the major statutory provisions relating to the reorganization of NHS (Wales) represent a variation on a theme. The scheme was originally flagged up in the 2001 Queen's Speech for enactment in a Wales-only Bill. However, in light of the prospect of postponement to a following session, it was agreed in the intergovernmental discussions to incorporate the key provisions in a general 'England and Wales' Bill – the National Health Service Reform and Health Care Professions Act 2002. Not a little local criticism resulted, including on the basis of a loss of 'ownership'.[22]

The second main option is introduced:

* *Combined Bill*

The chief instrument here is the 'England and Wales' Bill, wherein there may be England and Wales clauses, or England or Wales clauses, or Parts containing England-only and/or Wales-only clauses. In fact, the 'Wales-only Bill' should now be considered the proverbial tip of the iceberg, with many more provisions conferring additional powers on the Assembly, or otherwise affecting its functions, being delivered in the traditional 'cross-border' format. Bound up with the idea of a single legal jurisdiction, the dominance of this 'England and Wales' methodology also reflects its continuing pull post-devolution as a geopolitical concept or organizational framework for administrative purposes, as for example in the case of much regulation in matters like the environment.[23]

Typically, this aspect has proved a point of some sensitivity for a Welsh Assembly Government keen to (be seen to) make a difference, in this case by the powerful exercise of a 'voice' for Wales. The then Minister for Open Government, Carwyn Jones, may be quoted:

> Some commentators have . . . argued that, because our proposals have not always resulted in Wales-only legislation, there has been a failure on the Assembly Government's part to secure its objectives. That proposition is incorrect. Securing our requirements through Wales-only Bills is not some kind of test of political virility and only those more interested in presentation than in substance believe that to be the case. Our objective as a Government is to obtain the legislation that Wales requires, whether it is in the form of legislation drafted for Wales alone, or in England and Wales Bills that allow Welsh needs to be distinctively met. The

real test is to ensure that the proposed law promotes the interests of Wales and enables us to better implement our policies.[24]

Combined Bills, it is worth stressing, come in all shapes and sizes. Insiders speak of 'portmanteau Bills', clauses which range across diverse policy areas under a general rubric like 'education', or alternatively of 'Christmas Tree Bills', general legislation on which different players – including the Welsh Assembly Government – may seek to hang their own favourites. At the other end of the spectrum, one finds the clearly designated or technical measure, in which the devolved administration may or may not have a significant interest.[25] Put simply, the opportunities presented to the Welsh Assembly Government for so combining its distinctive legislative proposals will be many and various, but also a bit hit and miss.

To pursue the theme, the attributes are essentially those of the Wales-only Bill – in reverse. Timetabling is the great advantage – and the obvious explanation for the continuing high incidence of this technique post-devolution, even in those cases where the devolved administration has brought forward a substantial and distinctive set of proposals. At least from the viewpoint of UK government ministers and Parliamentary Counsel, it will often make good sense to 'piggyback' territorial provisions in this way, especially when much of the surrounding material is the same.

Then again, from the territorial viewpoint, this may have an unfortunate forcing or twisting effect, wherein the pressures on the draftsman to rewrite novel proposals in the light of the general legal framework are more intense in the context of a combined Bill. 'Second-order' questions of legislative drafting begin to open up here, in the guise of the internal 'separation' – or otherwise – of territorial provisions in combined Bills, with a view to issues like clarity.

The issue of legislative scrutiny is also brought to the fore. How could it be otherwise, given on the one hand, the increased prospect of distinctively Welsh proposals, and on the other hand, a natural proclivity in Parliament to examine the impact of a combined Bill on the predominant part of the legal jurisdiction (or English 'law district'). Again, this choice of legislative vehicle is apt to cause difficulties for the Assembly at large in exercising influence, the more so at the later stages in the context of amendments. To push home the point, the 'England and Wales' Bill is both the chief vehicle for delivering new devolved powers and poses particular challenges as part of the current Welsh constitutional dispensation.

The affair of the Wales-only Bill 'that never was' usefully points up the worst-case scenario from the viewpoint of democratic oversight. Such was the sudden rush of events that relevant Assembly documentation relating to consultation only arrived at Westminster on the day of the Second Reading of the (newly) combined NHS Reform Bill. In turn, the distinctively – and controversial – Welsh provisions received much less parliamentary attention than those for England.[26] Meanwhile, the Assembly was unable to debate the Bill until after the Second Reading.

Exceptional yes, but this affair should not be lightly dismissed. A major policy change for Wales had arguably been the subject of less formal scrutiny than would have been the case prior to devolution. Speaking more generally, the affair exposed the danger of a gap in the arrangements for oversight in the light of executive devolution: the potential of what may now be called 'a scrutiny deficit'. In turn, and so typical of the evolutionary theme, the affair can be seen as a useful prompt for the kind of 'partnership approach' recently envisaged between Westminster and the Assembly at large – new forms of bridging arrangement as a way of limiting such danger.

And so to the third main option, which is different in character: the vehicle of so-called 'pre-legislative scrutiny' which can then result in either a separate or a combined Bill:

• *Draft Bills*
The UK government has moved in recent times to publish more Bills in draft form, as part of a parallel process of modernization of parliamentary procedures.[27] There are solid arguments in favour of this practice: the scope for a wider range of influences on primary legislation, over a longer period; and in particular, for more flexible and – where appropriate – more rigorous forms of scrutiny, freer from timetabling constraints and without matters set in stone.

For the reasons indicated, the technique has special resonance in the case of Wales. For the Assembly at large, operating under the scheme of executive devolution at one remove from the seat of primary legislative power, it offers valuable opportunities, first, to consider the approach of the Bill in the light of local conditions, and second, to raise matters that merit reconsideration. In turn, this opens up the possibility of the Assembly using its own machinery to best advantage: public consultation and local networking in the conditions of small-country governance promoted by, and feeding back into, the relevant subject committee. A 'voice' for Wales, underwritten by the activities of the 'national' representative institution, and less likely to be muffled by the four walls of formal legislative business, it is an enticing prospect.

Again, the technique can be seen as a paradigm for 'partnership arrangements' between Westminster and the Assembly at large. Exchanges of views on proposed legislation at an early stage, whereby on the one hand Welsh MPs are better informed, and on the other hand AMs enjoy a form of 'privileged access' into the primary law-making machine, clearly is one way forward. To this effect, the then Leader of the House of Commons, Robin Cook, signalled at the end of 2001 that Wales-only Bills could undergo pre-legislative scrutiny in parallel both at Westminster and in the Assembly.[28]

The draft NHS (Wales) Bill was the first Wales-only Bill to be so published, in May 2002. Subsequently put before Parliament as the Health (Wales) Bill, it too dealt with distinctive aspects of NHS structures in Wales, the development of Community Health Councils and the establishment of two more agencies (Health Professions Wales and the Wales Centre for Health[29]). A compact and worthy measure, it has been another test bed of the evolving arrangements.

First, the novel idea of dual oversight was now fleshed out, wherein the Welsh Affairs Select Committee and then the Welsh Grand Committee[30] would inquire and deliberate on behalf of Parliament; and the Health and Social Services Committee would conduct an examination on behalf of the Assembly. Second, things did not go entirely well. Not only was there a significant amount of overlap, inevitably so, but also a certain lack of integration, for example little attention given by the subject committee to the public evidence forwarded by the Wales Office, and a plenary debate that lagged behind the work of the parliamentary committees.[31] That said, a number of the MPs and AMs made the effort to attend each other's meetings.

Third but related, there was a significant element of overkill. This modest measure had now been crawled over by various groups of elected representatives, which hardly represents an efficient and effective use of scarce political and administrative resources. Put simply, the idea of dual scrutiny of draft Bills has much to commend it in the peculiar constitutional situation of Welsh executive devolution, but should not disguise the associated costs and difficulties, and thus the practical limitations on the scope of the technique.

This was in fact a major bone of contention in the Assembly Review Group. Robin Cook's initiative was welcome; however:

> We would like to see the UK Government go further than this. We are keen to see maximum possible use of pre-legislative scrutiny of bills in which the Assembly has an interest, although there was disagreement in the Group on the extent to which this is realistic. The Assembly Cabinet felt that pre-legislative scrutiny would be of particular importance for bills proposed by the Assembly. Other Group Members felt that publication in draft format would also be important for other primary legislation relevant to the Assembly's devolved responsibilities.[32]

In the event, the group's recommendation – 'that bills affecting Wales should, wherever possible, be published in draft form' – was successfully watered down by a ministerial amendment to the formal resolution. The Assembly 'encourages the publication of Bills in draft, but recognises scrutiny must, in practice, prioritise Bills proposed by the Assembly and those which significantly affect Wales'. An intervention by Ron Davies neatly conveys the sense of competing pressures:

We must recognise that Assembly resources are scarce in terms of time, people and money. We must concentrate resources to the best effect. [The] amendment is therefore sensible. My only reservation is that I am not sure how practical it would be . . . Most legislation is England and Wales legislation . . . To pretend or delude ourselves that we will have a whole host of draft bills to examine is unrealistic . . .[33]

There are of course lesser alternatives on offer, techniques of 'consultation' of the Assembly that are more akin to the ordinary processes of interest representation as against the idea of privileged access. The case of the Mental Health Bill, published in draft in 2002, is a pertinent example. On the one hand, this is a significant field of devolved functions, one in which the Welsh Assembly Government, with broad support across the Assembly, has developed its own policy approach.[34] On the other hand, this was an 'England and Wales' piece of legislation, and further one that as drafted contained substantial non-devolved matters claimed by that very great power, the Home Office.

The Assembly's Health and Social Services Committee clearly found it more difficult to make an impact. Denied any special status as a body linked to parliamentary scrutiny, Members sought to make good the deficiency by taking evidence from a range of organisations in Wales, and so making representations from the local angle. A consultation period stretched across the Assembly recess was not exactly helpful in this regard. In the event, given a lack of congruence with the local policy (more 'health'-orientated), it is perhaps not surprising that Members now called for a Wales-only Bill, or – if a combined Bill was unavoidable – for 'framework legislation' allowing the devolved admin-istration to do its own thing.[35] A cry, one has to say, in the wilderness!

Speaking more generally, the affair stands for both a wider and a shallower involvement by the Assembly at large in the doing of statute law. It is typical, at one and the same time, of the ongoing organic development, here in the guise of a discrete Assembly development, and of the continued chafing by reason of the operative constraints of the scheme of executive devolution. A subversive thought: it becomes apparent that some clever legislative 'games' can be played in this context by central government, including at the behest of the Welsh Assembly Government.

2. EARLY DOORS

(Welsh) law and politics

Now let us backtrack. It should surprise no one to learn that the qualitative issue of the ongoing legislative treatment of the Assembly, the statutory outputs, and the logically prior matter of access to the central government machine, the legislative inputs, has been centre-stage in plenary from the outset. As Rhodri Morgan wryly observed of the period immediately prior to the Queen's Speech in December 2000:

> During the past few weeks I have answered 23 Assembly questions on what the Cabinet has been doing to influence the process and content of primary legislation. Each time, I have referred to the efforts of the Cabinet and officials to get the best deal in relation to primary legislation.[36]

Likewise, it was only to be expected that different political actors would seek to maximize or minimize the extent of the difficulties. For example, the ministerial architect of Welsh devolution, by then firmly consigned to a backbench role in the Assembly, was not enthused: 'If devolution for Wales were an accepted part of the mindset of Whitehall, it would show. A common approach would inform all departmental legislation and a common principle underpinning the Government's approach would be evident. There isn't and that's worrying.'[37]

A case of general improvement in the light of early difficulties: such was the retort of the then Assembly Business Secretary, Andrew Davies.[38] 'Contrary to what some have said . . . we have an excellent track record in influencing primary legislation . . . However, we cannot take that for granted. The Cabinet will continue to press for legislation that reflects the needs of Wales and respects the Assembly's role.'

Such claim and counter-claim is an endemic feature of life in the Assembly. Whereas the minister at the end of the first term was happy to speak of an 'outstandingly successful' record of achievement, the Plaid Cymru spokesman was exercised by 'a tiny list of minor recommendations'.[39] Given the centrality of primary legislation affecting Wales, first to the perceived performance of the Welsh Assembly Government, and second to the ongoing constitutional debate inside the country, how could it be otherwise?

Some chronology

Once again, a sense of the chronology is important by reason of the strong evolutionary theme or scope for institutional learning and adaptation. What I called 'a triumph of particularity', the original Transfer of Functions Order (TFO) was seen to heighten the sense of a devolved Wales of 'bits and pieces'. In turn, according to a local survey of the UK government's legislative programme for 1998/9 – by which time devolution was an established political fact:

The new legislation shows no overall coherence in either giving functions to the Assembly or retaining them to be exercised in relation to Wales by central government. The functions conferred on the Assembly will be no less complex than the provisions in the existing Transfer of Functions Order. Not all the functions in these Acts will be exercisable by the Assembly as regards Wales, exceptions and provisos will apply to the exercise of these new powers and there is no single method of setting out which powers are exercisable by the Assembly.[40]

Continuity and change: the legislative programme for 1999/2000 – the first full year that the Assembly was up and running – may be said to demonstrate three main traits from the 'bottom-up' or territorial perspective. First, there was a significant increase in the volume of legislation dealing with the transfer of powers to the Assembly. Whereas in the previous parliamentary session only five statutes had made provision for devolved functions, there were fourteen such statutes in this session of Parliament. Second but related, there was an ever more bewildering array of provisions concerning, or references to, the Assembly. Sometimes separate parts of an Act related to Assembly functions, on other occasions the Assembly was given equivalence to a Secretary of State, and on other occasions again parallel powers were set out in particular sections.[41]

A wide spectrum of general legislative approaches to the devolution of powers – more or less generous to the Assembly – was the third main feature. Typically, this can be seen to reflect the scale of policy creativity at the territorial level, decidedly patchy at this initial stage, but is also indicative of underlying tensions, including with individual central government departments, most notably the (then) Department of Environment, Transport, and the Regions (DETR).

By way of illustration, the Transport Act 2000 may be placed at one end of the spectrum.[42] In many parts of the legislation, the rule-making powers were allocated to UK government ministers, and not the Assembly, in relation to Wales. Whereas various functions relating to roads and bus services in Wales were given to the Assembly, there was scarce provision for devolved powers concerning the railways. A theme that notably has continued to run, whither – it was immediately asked – an integrated transport policy or joined-up government?[43]

At the other end of the spectrum, there came several statutes demonstrating a major and genuine attempt to legislate distinctively for the needs of Wales, including by means of generous grants of secondary law-making powers. The vehicle of the reforms to post-sixteen education agreed by the Assembly,[44] Part II of the Learning and Skills Act 2000 established the National Council for Education and Training for Wales (the country's biggest quango[45]), and did so in the form of an entirely Welsh part of the statute. There was also the Care Standards Act 2000, which in the compelling circumstances of a major scandal[46] established the Children's Commissioner for Wales, as well some sixty new formal rule-making powers for the Assembly. In fact, the provisions about the agency were skeletal in nature; a product of the all-party desire in the Assembly to at least get started, in view of that great fact of parliamentary life which haunts the scheme of executive devolution – strict timetabling constraint on the making of primary legislation.

The Local Government Act 2000 deserves a special mention. It raised the not insubstantial constitutional question of the spheres of authority in the post-devolutionary system of Welsh governance. Whereas the devolved administration effectively 'owns' much of this turf, the DETR was successful here in retaining certain key powers on an England and Wales basis, or under the traditional rubric of central–local government relations, in such areas as 'best-value' policy and the modernization of local government. The legislation also occasioned a dispute about the scope of Henry VIII powers by which the Assembly might amend or repeal primary legislation, with the DETR insisting on a conservative approach. This aspect is the more noteworthy, because exceptionally the Assembly cabinet chose to break cover in the official discussions and complain publicly at the turn of events,[47] and further because it highlights an inclination on the part of the UK government to block movement towards the model of quasi-legislative devolution. According to a subsequent Wales Office memorandum:

> As a general rule, powers to make secondary legislation in Wales are conferred on the Assembly where the Bill confers a parallel power for England on UK Government Ministers. The key exception is where the powers allow amendment of primary legislation. Since as part of the devolution settlement Westminster continues to be the principal law maker for Wales, the Government believes it is generally inappropriate for the Assembly to exercise widely drawn powers to amend primary legislation through secondary legislation (so-called 'Henry VIII' powers).[48]

The attenuated programme that was the Queen's Speech in December 2000 also demonstrated some major themes. Five of the sixteen Bills were of particular relevance to the Assembly's responsibilities, on subjects as diverse as health and social care, homes, and regulatory reform. The flagship measure was the Children's Commissioner for Wales Act, which now fleshed out the powers and functions of the agency. Turning the argument round, it represents a paradigm example of how an innovative (home-grown) piece of policy development has had to be fitted into the pre-existing statutory framework, with the constraints on legislative drafting which this implies, even in the context of Wales-only legislation. The form of Henry VIII clause adopted for Assembly purposes was again strictly limited.[49] Put simply, whereas this Act constituted 'go it alone' legislation, it was not 'do as you please'.

In terms of the ongoing constitutional development, the Act also in-augurated a chief political demand of the Welsh Assembly Government under the scheme of executive devolution. That is to say, a convention or under-standing of at least one Wales-only Bill each year as part of the UK government's legislative programme. The First Minister has repeatedly stressed this element, as when appearing in November 2002 before the Welsh Affairs Select Committee:

> In so far as we have been seeking to establish custom and practice by which there is at least one Welsh Bill in draft form, and the one in draft in the previous year is then turned into a real term's bill in the following year after you have considered it in Westminster and we have in the Assembly; it will continue in this year's legislation . . . There will be times when inevitably we will miss out and we thought that if we missed out maybe there would be two or three bills the following year but it all depends because there is no such thing as a typical year. Sometimes we have a short year . . . Last year it was Westminster with a short year because half way through the legislative year there was a Westminster election.[50]

Viewed in retrospect, the Queen's Speech of December 2000 is important in another way: for the reaction it generated in the Assembly. Evidencing a general frustration among members with the patchwork approach to the allocation of powers, plenary unanimously resolved in favour of a broad and generous approach to the allocation of powers:

> The National Assembly . . . calls on the First Minister and the Secretary of State for Wales to ensure that all bills which impact on the functions and responsibilities of the Assembly are drafted in such a way as to permit the Assembly maximum flexibility in implementing their provisions and developing policy in the areas concerned . . .[51]

For his part, the First Minister highlighted the constitutional issue – and the party politics:

> In theory, a future government of another colour . . . could cheat us of our rights by putting almost nothing down for secondary legislation. There is nothing in the British constitution which states what proportion of a Bill confers powers by secondary legislation and when it is all done in the primary legislative Act. One could leave almost nothing to the discretion of the Assembly. There is nothing that lays down any procedure that guarantees powers to the Assembly. It is not a problem provided there is a Labour Government.[52]

To anticipate the discussion in chapter 15, the people of Wales deserve better than a constitutional structure that is so dependent on Labour Party hegemony.

Beginning in this period, Rhodri Morgan has also tried hard to inject a measure of 'realism' into the debate. 'My colleagues and I have frequent discussions with . . . UK Ministers about the terms of primary legislation affecting Wales . . . However, as any devolved administration will know, you win some arguments and you lose others.'[53] But this glosses over the uncomfortable truth that by the very nature of the scheme of executive devolution the Welsh Assembly Government is required to 'win' more often in order to achieve its primary legislative goals. The Scottish Executive has its own ball.

3. KEEPING IT IN THE FAMILY: WHITEHALL AND THE WELSH ASSEMBLY GOVERNMENT

Whereas the Assembly was originally conceived as a corporate body, the exercise of a 'voice' for Wales in the primary legislative process powerfully reflects and reinforces the *de facto* division between the Welsh Assembly Government and the 'other side of the House' or the Assembly at large. Put simply, it does not follow that because the subject committees and individual AMs have trouble accessing the system that Assembly Ministers and officials suffer likewise.

Indeed, the Assembly government is immediately put in a privileged position as against the rest of the corporate body, by reason of the canon of confidentiality that underwrites the conduct of IGR, so effectively shrouding many of the distinctive Welsh inputs into the extended process of statute-making. On the one hand, this should be seen as unexceptional, an 'export' of the Westminster system of parliamentary government that was bound to happen irrespective of the internal legal form of the Assembly. AMs after all could hardly be better placed than MPs to know of the internal discussions taking place under the general rubric of the 'Crown'. On the other hand, it illustrates a difficulty in terms of local political accountability at the heart of the scheme of executive devolution. According to another lament from Ron Davies, 'we do not know whether the Bill reflects the views originally expressed by the Assembly Government or whether the views of [the Department] prevailed. We are prevented from having that debate.'

To reiterate, the ongoing allocation of powers to the Assembly is essentially the product of an administrative and political dialogue or negotiation with the various central government departments. It demonstrates in turn a natural tendency towards the patchwork approach to the allocation of powers – more a matter of immediate responses, less the general sense of constitutional vision. A different but related point: to be properly effective, the Assembly government's voice needs to be heard at the successive stages of the business process: from the selection of Bills for entry into the UK government's legislative programme to the consideration of policy options for Bills affecting the Assembly. And on again, through the fluid and often tortuous stages of working out the preferred option, the legislative approach and the content and form for legislation, to the public face of amendments: with or without the Assembly, it is worth remembering, the making of statutes is commonly a messy affair.

Reflecting the general conduct of IGR, the interaction here will be essentially fluid and informal in character, primarily carried on by officials operating on a bilateral basis, and with little or no recourse to the special machinery for dispute resolution that has been developed as part of the UK development.[54] The general principle being one of good communication with each other, 'especially where the one administration's work may have some bearing upon the responsibilities of another administration', the UK government 'has undertaken to consult the Assembly Cabinet at an early stage on all relevant proposals for primary legislation.'

It obviously is difficult for the onlooker to evaluate the workings of this system, which no doubt is part of the point! Perhaps it is good to know from the Secretary of State for Wales that 'the private discussion is often a lot more lively'.[55] That it has not always been a smooth ride may also be gleaned from the UK government's memorandum to the Richard Commission:

> There are clear mechanisms for consulting the Assembly. However, they will only be effective if operated correctly. Getting this right has been a process of learning for both the UK Government and the Welsh Assembly Government. Although operation of these mechanisms has not always been perfect, the last meeting of the Joint Ministerial Committee in October [2002] agreed that steady progress was being made. It is important though, to ensure that as officials in UK Government Departments and the Assembly who are familiar with operating devolution move on, their knowledge and experience are not lost to their successors.[56]

An element of friction, it is important to say, is all to the good. If there were no differences of view between Cardiff and London over primary legislation affecting Wales, then not a lot would be being achieved! Some of the issues will be politically sensitive, including in the benign conditions for IGR of Labour Party hegemony, and/or technically and financially complex. The question of providing the Assembly with the powers – and money – to follow a distinct policy on student fees and so on in the context of an integrated higher education system in England and Wales, a subject of months of 'detailed discussions' behind the scenes, is a classic case in point.[57]

Surveying the field in late 2002, the House of Lords Select Committee on the Constitution declared itself less than enthusiastic, in terms both of the procedure and the substance:

We are particularly concerned by the unstructured way in which the process of liaison over legislation operates. Liaison is unsystematic, almost random, highly opaque, and hard for lay people, Westminster legislators or Assembly members to follow. It also affords only limited opportunities for the National Assembly's views to be heard in connection with bills affecting the Assembly. Moreover, such opportunities as exist to influence legislation are exercised behind the scenes and are only available to Ministers and the Welsh Assembly Government, not the Assembly as a whole. It appears to us that Wales figures in such arrangements largely as an afterthought appended to a process driven by the UK Government's concerns and priorities rather than those of Wales in general or the National Assembly.[58]

Evidently much of this was news to the First Minister. Along with other Labour Party colleagues, Rhodri Morgan has notably stressed the general smoothness of the operation, the effective exercise in the governmental stages of primary law making of a voice for Wales:

As with the relationship in general, consultation on proposed legislation has broadly worked well. This approach has yielded Bills making significantly different provision for Wales, such as the Education [Act 2002], and the first ever major piece of Wales only legislation for some years (the Children's Commissioner for Wales Act 2001). Again, there are also examples of where the system has worked less well: where a Bill has treated the Assembly less favourably than UK Ministers, particularly as regards 'Henry VIII' clauses. Those are not typical by any means.[59]

A triangular affair

Given the fact of executive devolution, the Secretary of State for Wales has had a significant legislative workload, which in turn has differentiated the role of the Wales Office from, say, the Scotland Office. It has thus been the responsibility of the minister to steer through Parliament any clauses in legislation relating solely to Wales.

For the reasons explained, this means leading on occasion on Wales-only Bills, but more commonly on Wales-only clauses in combined 'England and Wales' legislation. In turn, the territorial department has had to be increasingly octopus-like; such are the many fields of devolved functions and the growing demands from the Assembly for separate provision. In the words of the official guidance: 'with one junior Minister and an interest in most Bills, the Wales Office will need to look for flexibility in membership of standing committees'.[60]

During the first term of the Assembly, the Secretary of State for Wales was aptly described as a pivot of the devolved administration's relationship with Whitehall, a feature that once again was accentuated in matters of primary legislation affecting Wales. The role was not that of an all-embracing channel of communication with Whitehall, but rather one of ensuring that the many bilateral channels were operating effectively, and that any obstacles were removed or circumnavigated as appropriate. To this end, the territorial department has clearly needed to be 'in the loop'. A general request to central government departments for copies of correspondence with Assembly ministers and senior officials has been coupled with a formal commitment on the part of the devolved administration to keep the Wales Office informed about the discussions.[61]

How might this set of relationships be conceptualized? Given the place of the Wales Office as part of the central government machine (since June 2003 under the 'umbrella' of the new Department for Constitutional Affairs[62]), there obviously are strong legal and constitutional elements of a bipolar, arm's-length relationship with the Welsh Assembly Government, not least in view of the powerful UK convention of collective cabinet responsibility. But in a development well illustrated in matters of primary legislation, there has been a thick overlay, an exceptionally close political and administrative nexus. The First Minister and the Secretary of State have even spoken of a new governmental 'triangle' post-devolution: Cardiff, London, and the Wales Office.[63]

Including in matters of primary legislation, the Secretary of State for Wales should not be seen either as a mouthpiece for the Assembly or as a post box. In practice, as Peter Hain makes clear, 'a lot of these things depend on personal relations and working hard at those the whole time'. The more so, since the disaggregation of the law-making process has clearly created additional demands: 'I do not sense any antagonism anywhere in the triangle – it is just that often things are overlooked – so we need to get the message out and continuously do.'[64]

Mr Hain has started from the presumption that 'I am negotiating and representing the Assembly to the extent that it does not represent itself . . . that I want to see the Assembly's wishes carried into practice'. Then 'we seek to bear in mind what interests, objectives and policies there might be in the relevant Whitehall department that need to be adjusted to meet the Assembly's concerns and there is a bit of give-and-take in the negotiations'. Likewise, Mr Hain has described himself as 'a friend and advocate of the Assembly's position in the cabinet'. The question nonetheless refuses to go away: to mix the metaphors, whither this 'triangular affair' in the conditions of 'political cohabitation', including in the light of the fact that the job of the Secretary of State for Wales has now also been rendered part-time?[65]

A wedge of soft law

As indicated, a wedge of 'terms and conditions' on primary legislation affecting Wales are set out in the administrative agreements and sets of guidelines – soft law – that now help to structure the conduct of intergovernmental relations. The provisions are essentially procedural in character, and also allow ample scope for fluid and flexible forms of cooperation on legislative matters between central departments and the Welsh Assembly Government.

The chief document is *Post-devolution Primary Legislation affecting Wales*, a so-called 'devolution guidance note' issued by central government, and updated from time to time. As one might expect, its purpose is 'to facilitate the efficient conduct by the UK Government of its legislative business . . . Disagreements are an impediment to that and it is in the Government's interests that potential disagreements are identified as early as possible through consultation . . . Potential points of disagreement with the Welsh Assembly Government should be fully explored and wherever possible resolved before legislation is introduced or, in the case of Bills which are advance drafted, before Bills are published.'[66] A case, it may be said, of keeping it in the family.

Another key feature is introduced – the requirement of confidentiality. Once again, by the very nature of the executive form that is IGR it will be the Welsh Assembly Government, and not the Assembly at large, which is appropriately placed to influence matters at the vital early stages of Bill preparation. In turn, the special resonance in the Welsh context of publishing draft Bills is confirmed:

Where the possibility of particular legislation has not been publicly announced, information going to the Welsh Assembly Government should be passed in confidence. It will be a matter for agreement whether, and to what extent, confidentiality must constrain wider consultation by the Welsh Assembly Government and in no circumstances will the Welsh Assembly Government circulate or allude to Bill material without the consent of the lead Department.[67]

Limited guidance has been given as to the issues to be attended to by the lead department.[68] 'Commencement provisions in a Bill . . . should normally apply on equal terms to England and Wales, and to Ministers and the Assembly.' 'A Bill should not normally subject the actions of the Assembly to Ministerial consent or approval (or vice versa).' 'New public bodies which fall solely under the Assembly's control should normally be subject to its general powers to reform public bodies in Wales' (which translates as certain limited Henry VIII powers to amend or repeal primary legislation). Such nuggets apart, the guidance has so far not addressed the more fundamental issues of how as a national representative institution the Assembly might reasonably expect to be treated in primary legislation. Put another way, the guidance has tacitly assumed the extent to which the UK legislative programme is driven by individual departments.

In this respect, much may turn on (the shadow cast by) the work of the UK government's Legislative Programme Committee (LP). In the words of the guidance note, 'the essential requirement is that by the time proposals to introduce legislation reach LP, all devolution-related issues are to have been addressed and so far as possible resolved.' In addition papers to LP should:

- explain any provision proposed in respect of Wales which differs from the provision proposed for England or the rest of the UK
- identify any exception to the general rule that a new function created by the Bill will pass to the Assembly in cases where it already exercises similar functions within that subject area and identify the policy clearance for that decision
- identify any change to the existing functions of the Assembly, including any new function being vested in the Assembly which might raise issues of general principle, and the policy clearance for the change
- confirm that the Welsh Assembly Government has been consulted on the draft clauses as necessary [and] summarize the Welsh Assembly Government's view . . .[69]

Proceedings far from the public gaze: we are back here with the role of the Secretary of State for Wales in ensuring what may be loosely called 'fair play' in post-devolution primary legislation affecting Wales.

Consultation – extending the range

The issue arises of the range of this guidance. According to the head note: 'the UK Government has agreed with the Welsh Assembly Government that they will normally consult each other from an early stage on the development of relevant legislative proposals'. But what, it may reasonably be asked, in light of the hitherto patchwork arrangement of Assembly powers and functions, does 'relevant' mean for these purposes? This in turn touches on the general power of the Assembly to exercise voice on 'any matter affecting Wales',[70] which was seen to be a vital element of the so-called 'devolution settlement'.

According to the relevant Devolution Guidance Note, the Welsh Assembly Government should always be consulted on Bills which:

- confer new functions on the Assembly;
- alter the Assembly's existing functions; or
- otherwise affect areas which are the responsibility of the Assembly, including where it will be responsible for implementation in Wales, though policy control remains with the UK government.[71]

This represents an inner core, since in practice, in the words of the Wales Office, 'departments often find it helpful to consult the Assembly on other Bills, although as the guidance makes clear, there is no absolute requirement to do so'. Likewise, 'the Assembly Cabinet may wish to make representations about such bills'.[72]

The soft law 'duty' to consult on the part of central government, however, has been too narrowly drawn. In the spirit of a voice for Wales, a clear commitment to consultation on matters related to or close to a function that has been transferred to the Assembly is the least one would expect. A recommendation by WASC that the requirement should be applied across the fields of devolved functions, irrespective of whether the legislation would have a direct impact on the Assembly's powers, thus deserves applause.[73]

Changing mores

What, it may be asked, of the role of the Assembly's lawyers in the making of primary legislation affecting Wales? On the one hand, the Office of the Counsel General (OCG) will have an increasingly creative role to play in working together with policy colleagues in the Welsh Assembly Government to produce drafts and proposals for central government consumption, the paradigm case being the Assembly-requested Wales-only Bill. On the other hand, the official handling arrangements for Bills obviously have to take account of the fact that the Assembly has no authority to introduce or formally sponsor primary legislation. Indeed, the original soft law provisions were stern, conveying the message that the locals should know their place. 'Parliamentary Counsel is unwilling to accept instructions from lawyers of the Office of the Counsel General of the Assembly.' And again, 'it is not appropriate for Parliamentary Counsel to take instructions direct from Assembly lawyers on provisions for Wales'.[74] Certain habits, it would at first appear, die hard.

Some fine Welsh sidestepping has been in order. According to the Office of the Deputy Prime Minister in late 2002, 'the most effective way of operating has proved to be for Assembly lawyers to provide a draft of instructions for the lead department to approve and then pass on to Parliamentary Counsel.' A useful innovation, it may be noted, but in the guise of a filter also one which reinforces the idea of the devolved administration operating at one remove from Westminster. Meanwhile, Welsh actors were making creative use of the general power in the devolution statute to make agency arrangements between the Assembly and any other relevant authority like a central government department.[75] At one and the same time, the locals could begin to colonize the centre, and bolster the thinly stretched resources of the (then) territorial department. In the case of the combined Bill with substantial distinctive Welsh provisions that was the NHS Reform and Health Care Professions Act, Assembly lawyers thus worked hand in glove with the Wales

Office, carrying out the functions of advising ministers, preparing drafting instructions and supporting debates in the parliamentary stages.[76]

As one would expect, the development has been most pronounced in the case of Assembly-requested Wales-only Bills. It was agreed early on, such has been the paucity of legal resources available to the Wales Office, that in such a case the Assembly would second the department a skeleton Bill team.[77] In the event, the agency arrangements made in respect of the NHS (Wales) Bill provided for Assembly officials to exercise the functions of the department.

Let us be clear: given the spectre of cohabitation etc., the devolved administration cannot expect an unfettered right of instruction. But sending messages via the lead department is no longer officially considered 'the most effective way of operating'. Indeed – changing mores – there is now a distinct sense of unbuttoning. As from early 2003, the guidance states: 'In some cases, it may be appropriate for Parliamentary Counsel to take instructions direct from the Assembly lawyers; but this should be done only where it is the most effective way of operating and the lead departments and its ministers agree to this arrangement.'[78] As a practical example of the evolutionary development in IGR, this represents another tiny victory in the continuing drive by the devolved administration to be taken more seriously. It clearly fits with the idea of close and collaborative working between the two tiers of government. Turning the argument round, it should not have taken four years to produce this arrangement.

The expanding role here of the Assembly lawyers is a classic illustration of what I have called 'constitution-building in silence'. As one in a myriad of micro-level developments, driven in large measure by practical concerns, it merits special attention for helping to fill a large pothole on the road to a scheme of legislative devolution. The Welsh Office, one has to remember, had little direct experience of making statute law to pass on to the Assembly. Then again, a vital strand in the official evidence to the Richard Commission is that, given notice, the devolved administration would be quite capable of managing the enactment of primary legislation.[79] In bridging this historical divide, the increasingly hands-on experience of the Assembly lawyers is valuable.

4. LEGISLATION AND REPRESENTATION

Now let us look at the channels for the exercise of voice available to the Assembly as a representative body. Three main phases of development can be identified: rudimentary provision in the devolution statute; innovative home-grown arrangements developed following the Queen's Speech in December 2000; and a further round of administrative and political initiatives associated with the Assembly Review of Procedure.

Once again, with a view to elaborating and promoting forms of privileged access to the primary law-making machine, and notably with the help of colleagues at Westminster, we see the locals making considerable attempts to combat the difficulty of the constitutional situation. At the same time, the new arrangements are necessarily limited and somewhat artificial in character.

Uniquely late: statutory consultation

In the not so promising words of the devolution White Paper, the Assembly would be able 'to seek to influence' the primary legislative process.[80] In turn, a unique provision, the devolution statute places a duty on the Secretary of State for Wales to consult the Assembly each year about the UK government's legislative programme, principally as set out in the Queen's Speech.[81] To this effect, the minister must attend the Assembly at least once a session. At the risk of repetition, the duty must also be read in the context of the general Assembly powers of consideration and debate, and to make representations, on any matter affecting Wales.[82]

As machinery for maintaining Welsh input into primary law making, such formal provision is typically skeletal. The consultation requirement is itself loosely drawn. The Secretary of State should generally consult 'as soon as is reasonably practicable', but consultation about a Bill need not take place if the minister considers that there are 'considerations . . . which make it inappropriate', the annual Finance Bill being the obvious example. The nature of the consultation is such 'as appears to' the Secretary of State 'to be appropriate'.

This is not to deny the value of the 'consultation' as a (sorely needed) piece of political theatre in the Assembly. It is good knock-about stuff, with AMs debating with the minister on the general direction of, and main planks in, proposed primary legislation affecting Wales, including in relation to non-devolved matters.[83] The scene has also been elongated; whereby the discussion of the programme takes place over two Assembly plenary sessions, one attended by the Secretary of State for Wales, the other by his junior minister.

As every student of the legislative process knows, the Queen's Speech comes late in the day. It is also formally confidential until delivered, and in particular could hardly be made known to AMs ahead of MPs at Westminster. Far from an early or prospective exercise of influence, the Assembly at large is thus seen here in strongly reactive mode, its creativity or 'voice' being effectively circumscribed in terms of the draft legislation. The statutory consultation is not only highly formalized, but much already is set in stone.

A nice historical footnote: the technique immediately proved a recipe for disaster for Alun Michael.[84] In dealing with the first legislative programme post-devolution, the then First Secretary chose the bold course of having a draft consolidated response prepared by officials on the basis of Members' speeches in the two plenary sessions and then presenting it for formal approval by the whole of the Assembly. The document was said to represent a consensus view, a claim vehemently rejected by the opposition parties. In the event, a series of opposition amendments was carried, the final resolution then being passed on the basis of opposition votes, with Labour abstaining. Politically speaking, this was a clear signal that Mr Michael's administration was unravelling – a week later it was defenestration. But further, constitutionally speaking, the affair illustrates the strength of the official ideology of the corporate body in this initial period, and the essential naivety of such thinking. Nick Bourne for the Conservatives rightly ridiculed the administration's method of proceeding. 'We may have individual agreement on some Bills and on some clauses of some Bills but it will not be a surprise that we are diametrically opposed on many of the issues at Westminster.'

Self-help

The Assembly resolution on the Queen's Speech of December 2000 signalled internal changes designed to enhance Assembly inputs into primary legislation. The subject committees, it was said, should become more involved, and the 'Executive' should consult with the Assembly on future bids for Wales-only legislation.[85] Let us take these two strands – in what is yet another significant attempt at autochthonous development – in reverse order.

As the relevant concordat makes clear, the Assembly is free at any time to request primary legislation, which the UK government will then consider in the context of the prospective legislative programme. The First Minister will communicate a formal resolution by the Assembly to this effect to the Secretary of State for Wales.[86] Provision was now being made in the 'internal law' of the Assembly – standing orders – for proactive inputs of this kind to happen on a regular and coherent basis, through an annual debate in plenary.

'A virtual parliament' – 'a shadow Welsh Queen's Speech': it so clearly fits! A parallel process to the statutory consultation has thus been created, whereby each March the Assembly cabinet brings forward a set of proposals for primary legislation in the following session of the UK Parliament. It stands in turn for a more timely system of territorial inputs, one which better accords with the realities of the primary legislative process, or the extended Whitehall modalities of policy development, selection of Bills etc. In this regard too, little Wales was growing up.

The original development also reflected the criticism of a slow start for the Assembly. Clearly one way to (be seen to) make a difference was by 'delivering' some distinctive primary legislation. A more secure planning framework was the natural concomitant at official level, whereby the various policy parts of the Assembly administration would come forward with ideas for Wales-only pieces of primary legislation. An Assembly cabinet shopping list: with the exception of 2002, when eight such requests for primary legislation were made, it has been a standard fare of four bids a session.

By way of illustration, the Assembly cabinet proposed two broadly based Bills, and two specific ones, for inclusion in the 2003–4 UK legislative programme.[87] As the name suggests, the 'Education (Miscellaneous Provisions) (Wales) Bill' could even be described as (shadow) 'portmanteau Bill', ranging across such matters as class sizes and learning grants, and on through reforms to statutory agencies.[88] Meanwhile, the 'Transport (Wales) Bill' would widen and deepen Assembly powers in an important field of devolved functions in a number of ways, for example by enabling the Welsh Assembly Government to establish joint authorities on the lines of passenger transport executives. To anticipate the argument in chapter 11, the bid for a 'Public Services (Ombudsman) Bill' illustrates a major strand of policy development post-devolution, the expansion and reform of separate Welsh 'state' machinery. For its part, the 'Tourism Accommodation (Registration) Bill' is the type of limited measure focused on local conditions that one would expect to see produced in the conditions of small-country governance.

From the viewpoint of the Welsh Assembly Government, the debate and formal resolution has the clear advantage, for the purpose of the negotiation with central government and of any subsequent parliamentary proceedings, of clothing its proposals with the democratic legitimacy of the national representative institution. Such formal procedure, however, also represents something of a tightrope for those ministers concerned to uphold the existing constitutional scheme: on the one hand, the need for primary legislation to secure distinctive 'made in Wales' policies; and on the other hand, the evident difficulty of an accumulation of unsuccessful bids. Even in the favourable political climes of Labour Party hegemony, the practical constraints associated with an overloaded parliamentary timetable are apt to bite hard here. There is a particular problem of perception, which in turn reflects the artificiality of the constitutional design. Understandably, standing orders provide for bids only in the form of separate Welsh legislation. The common translation into 'England and Wales' Bills means that things come not to 'look' so different.[89]

'Shadow private Members' Bills' – individual AMs have been slow to take advantage of the provision in standing orders whereby backbenchers can table a motion proposing a Bill for inclusion in the Assembly's request to central government. This was naturally a point of some concern for the Assembly Review Group, which highlighted the need to build 'awareness amongst Members' regarding the scope, making and interpretation of primary legislation.[90] A harbinger perhaps of events in the second term, the first such proposal was agreed in plenary in January 2003: for a Bill that would enable the Assembly to prohibit smoking in public places.[91] As the thin

gruel of plenary so clearly illustrates, the input of 'private members' into
legislative affairs is a valuable element in the democratic lifeblood of
parliamentary-style institutions. It is hard to think of anything better
calculated to show the relevance of the Assembly to the people of Wales than
the particular suggestion!

The air of unreality in these proceedings is a constant refrain among
Assembly Members. Enough has also been said to demonstrate the acute
political sensitivity of the matter: a dagger at the heart of the scheme of
executive devolution. An intervention from one frustrated Labour AM
brilliantly illustrates the underlying dynamic: the way in which restriction on
meeting its legitimate needs in this way generates more calls for conferring
primary legislative powers on the Assembly:

> As many members have mentioned, in considering these matters we must turn
> our minds to the realities of whether all these bills will become Acts of Parliament.
> We know that that is not the case. We know that they are worthwhile and
> necessary, or they would not have been proposed and we would not be seeking to
> take them forward. However, unfortunately, we know that, such is the legislative
> pressure at Westminster . . . we will certainly not get them all. Given that and
> other reasons, I support the call for the National Assembly for Wales to be given
> primary law-making powers . . .[92]

Turning to the second strand in the Assembly Resolution of December 2000,
a novel process was introduced whereby, following the debate on the Queen's
Speech, the Bills that are of particular relevance to the Assembly's
responsibilities are remitted to the relevant subject committees for
consideration of the Welsh-related provisions.[93] To this effect, it is now a
matter of internal law grafted onto the statutory duty of consultation: a less
skeletal form of provision. In practice, however, it is typically a case of limited
rations.

The first such effort was largely a write-off. Time constraints associated
with the impending UK general election were peculiarly sharp: a graphic
illustration of the practical problems of harnessing together two separate
representative institutions, set up in very different ways, for the single
purpose of making primary legislation for Wales. Indeed, the process failed
for a second time in December 2002, when amid growing political tensions
ahead of the 2003 Assembly elections the relevant resolution was lost.[94]

The strong internal trajectory of the Assembly – the rapid growth and
hardening of the political centre – is very relevant. As part of the maturation
of the new Welsh polity, the central role of the 'Executive' in negotiating with
central government has been further underscored, not least as its own policy
proposals have multiplied in number. In turn, the 'strange anatomy' of the
subject committees, whereby the minister provides the political leadership, is
highlighted yet again. Items of primary legislation discussed publicly in these

all-party fora, and confidentially under the auspices of IGR: with the best will in the world, it is a recipe for ministerial economy with the truth.

The major practical constraints on the role and contribution of subject committees are apt to be accentuated here. The limited number of AMs available to do this work, the various competing priorities, which include Assembly law making, and the difficulty of exercising influence on a dynamic process of formal scrutiny at one remove: such matters cannot simply be wished away. Members' lack of knowledge and experience of the primary law-making process has been underscored by the limited back up, in the form both of technical and professional resources.[95] The fact that some three years into the life of the Assembly the procedural review group was recommending that committees 'receive detailed briefings on the content and progress of Westminster bills'[96] says much.

Not every autochthonous initiative, it is well to remember, is crowned with success. In this instance, confirmation can now be found in the evidence to the Richard Commission. According to the Chair of the Environment, Transport and Planning Committee, for example:

> The Committee has yet to influence primary legislation, and it is unlikely to have the opportunity to do so without draft bills which allow time for meaningful consultation within a more flexible parliamentary timetable. In terms of initiating legislation, the Committee has asked the Minister to take forward its recommendations relating to public transport, but the Assembly Cabinet has thus far not succeeded in securing parliamentary time.[97]

The experience of the Health and Social Services Committee is especially note-worthy, in view of the particular concentration of distinctive Welsh provisions in this policy area. There clearly has been a sharp learning curve, not least in terms of the importance of the form of legislation. According to the Chair:

> The first two Wales only bills since the inauguration of the Assembly have fallen within our field and that has been a huge challenge for us. Nobody on my Committee has previous Westminster experience; so dealing with the legislative process from our perspective as well as learning about how Westminster deals with it has been a real journey of discovery for us. I think we do it better now than we did at the beginning perhaps. There has been quite a contrast also in how we have been able to work, for instance, on the NHS (Wales) Bill where we had the opportunity of pre-legislative scrutiny as apart from the NHS Reform Bill which was going through Westminster already and we had little opportunity to really shape, influence and inform that debate. There has been a stark difference between how we have been able to interact with the legislative process on [the two] things.[98]

Associated with the lack of primary legislative power, a 'freezing effect' on the Welsh body politic is also noted (by reference to the issue of free personal care for the elderly):

There have been discussions in the Assembly, in the Committee and in the plenary session around this important area of policy but the Committee has decided not to pursue it . . . There seems little point in the Committee spending its valuable time, because we do not have much time, actually fleshing out all the in-depth policy discussions because we could not take it forward if we wanted to without Westminster and Westminster has given us a very clear message that they do not want to give us that opportunity.[99]

Looking forwards, one would expect to see further efforts at this form of self-help, most obviously with a view to making the best of a bad job. Yet picking up on the argument in the last chapter, in the broader scheme of things, by which is meant the continuing struggle to achieve a 'devolution settlement' worthy of the name, a developing knowledge and understanding in the Assembly of matters of primary legislation can only be helpful. For those with the strategic vision, this represents another piece of constitution building (in silence), not least because subject committees would most probably have a direct and major role to play in the operation of a scheme of legislative devolution for Wales.[100]

Seeds of partnership

The Assembly Review Group was 'of the strong view that the Assembly needs to have the maximum possible input into primary legislation before Parliament'.[101] In seeking to augment existing procedures, as also to encourage the subject committees in particular to play a greater role, this all-party review was particularly concerned to strengthen 'inter-parliamentary relations' in the guise of Assembly to Westminster contact.[102]

Expressed slightly differently, the procedural review began to articulate the need for a new kind of partnership working. 'We also see the potential for benefits in establishing more formal arrangements for communication and collaboration with colleagues at Westminster.' It was suggested for example that subject committees might liaise with the Welsh Affairs Select Committee when issues of new primary legislation arise in connection with a policy review that a subject committee is conducting.[103] A proposal, it is immediately apparent, which carries the seeds of the idea of collaborative or joint working in other parts of the law-making process.

A variation on a theme: it was recommended that Wales Office ministers should 'attend subject committee meetings to discuss bills affecting Wales'.[104] Later implemented, if only on an occasional basis, this represents another classic example of incremental change: a gloss on the procedure whereby Bills are remitted to the subject committees for consideration, which was itself seen produced on the back of the statutory consultation procedure. For its part, the territorial department has notably stressed the two-way nature of the dialogue: the minister explaining the Welsh aspects of the Bill and updating AMs on progress, and AMs taking the opportunity to make their views known to the minister.[105]

Once again, there is more to the general development than at first appears. At one level, obviously, the fostering of a partnership approach between the Assembly and Westminster holds out the prospect of better primary legislation affecting Wales. As well as it being given a new and enhanced role post-devolution, this no doubt helps to explain why WASC in particular has been enthusiastic.

At another level, the approach fits with the broader autochthonous 'project' of building up the status of the Assembly, including with a view to further constitutional advancement. Given the nature of the subject matter – inter-parliamentary relations – the Presiding Office has been able to make the running here. Lord Elis-Thomas has developed the idea of the Assembly and Westminster as 'co-legislators' – which smacks not so much of the legislative dependency of the one on the other, as of a novel constitutional model in which there are interdependent roles. Notably, the concept has now been used in evidence to the Richard Commission to underpin the case for a more generous allocation of powers to the Assembly. 'If we are co-legislators, then we are equal co-legislators in the sense that we should be able to have our bit of the action in all cases where that is possible.'[106]

So also the development epitomizes the idea of privileged access for the Assembly as a representative institution, with a view to making good the frag-mentation of the primary law-making process. 'Cooperation is growing between our subject committees and the Welsh Affairs Committee, and that Committee at least may be willing to regard the Assembly and its committees as having a different status in respect of primary legislation affecting devolved matters from other bodies wishing to influence the parliamentary process.'[107]

The approach is obviously no panacea. For example, the practical diffi-culties – clearing diaries etc. – that are entailed in close forms of joint working between the two representative institutions should not be underestimated.[108] Likewise, much will depend on the approach taken to the formal handling of business by the different government departments, as in the tabling of amendments. We return to this point.

5. PRIMARY LEGISLATION AFFECTING WALES – OUTPUTS

Whetting the appetite

National devolution has already served to generate a significant amount of new primary legislation of a distinctively Welsh character. As summarized in tables 13 and 14, the output represents a step-change when viewed in the historical perspective of a centuries-old process of legal assimilation (with England). These tables highlight the central place of England and Wales legislation, whereby the 'combined' Acts and Bills listed all contain numerous separate provisions for Wales, often in the form of distinct Parts or Schedules

Table 13: Primary legislation affecting Wales, 1999–2003 – Acts and Bills containing substantially different provisions for Wales*

Care Standards Act 2000	Reforms regulation of social care; establishes Children's Commissioner for Wales
Learning and Skills Act 2000	Reforms structure of post-sixteen education and training, and its inspection
Local Government Act 2000	Reforms local government structures and the associated ombudsman system
Education Act 2002	Reforms school governance and funding; changes structure of National Curriculum
National Health Service Reform and Health Care Professions Act 2002	Changes NHS structures (including, in Wales, establishing Local Health Boards)
**Local Government Bill	*Reforms system of local government finance*
**Planning and Compulsory Purchase Bill	*Establishes new system of spatial development (including the Wales Spatial Plan) and compulsory purchase*
**Licensing Bill	*Removes duty on local authorities to hold polls on Sunday opening*
**Health and Social Care (Community Health and Standards) Bill	*Seeks to raise and coordinate health and social care standards, including via distinctive Welsh administrative machinery*
Draft Housing Bill	Includes provisions for expanded Ombudsman function in Wales

*Source: Welsh Assembly Government. Up to March 2003.
**Bills then before Parliament are shown in italics.

Table 14: Primary legislation affecting Wales, 1999–2003 – Acts and Bills applying substantially to Wales only*

Children's Commissioner for Wales Act 2001	Expands powers of Children's Commissioner for Wales
Health (Wales) Bill*	*Reforms NHS structures in Wales*
Draft Public Audit (Wales) Bill	Creates single audit body for Wales

*Source: Welsh Assembly Government. Up to March 2003. See for an alternative – and compiled on the basis of 'significant' Wales-only provisions – longer list, Wales Office, *Devolution Guidance Note 4.*
**Bills then before Parliament are shown in italics.
***Successor to the draft NHS (Wales) Bill.

to the legislation, flanked in turn by the more specific Wales-only measures. Reflecting and reinforcing key areas of devolved policy-making and service delivery, the lists are also indicative of a quickening tempo.

Not all such legislation will have appeared in the Assembly's annual shopping list. From time to time, it will be a case of official opportunism, such that when Whitehall departments are promoting their own legislation for England, the Welsh Assembly Government is successful in securing separate provision for Wales. The Local Government Bill, in Parliament at the time of writing, is a good example.

As in the case of Assembly law making, the accumulation over time is a significant feature. Perhaps on occasion there will be a measure of retrenchment, whereby distinctive Welsh provisions are replaced. But this hardly represents the prevailing wind! The way in which the devolution of today is not the devolution of tomorrow is liable to be amply demonstrated in 'the Welsh Statute Book' – even in the absence of a scheme of legislative devolution.

Then again, to put this in comparative perspective, the Scottish Parliament has been passing a dozen or more Bills a session. Much of this legislation has been in social policy, in fields of devolved functions in Wales.[109] To anticipate the argument in chapter 15, this is not to imply that legislative devolution for Wales would mean equivalent outputs. In particular, not only is any such scheme liable to be narrower in ambit, but also the pull for uniformity (with England) will commonly be stronger.[110] Equally, however, it would be absurd to overlook the likely energizing effects on the new Welsh polity of primary legislative powers, in the guise both of an enhanced policy space and practical considerations such as local control of the timetable for making statutes.

In this respect too, the current constitutional dispensation can also be seen whetting the appetite. Primary legislation affecting Wales that is newly distinctive in character, and is in turn naturally rationed even in the conditions of party political hegemony by reason of the Westminster bottleneck: there is an in-built frustration.

Table 15, which lists the Acts and Bills that either explicitly convey the same or similar functions on the Assembly as they do on UK ministers, and/or contain isolated provisions which make different provision for Wales, powerfully illustrates the scatter-gun approach to the accumulation of powers. Some thirty measures are listed, roughly a quarter of the public Bills passed at Westminster in the relevant period.[111] Looking ahead, a generous scheme of legislative devolution would reduce – but not eradicate – this phenomenon, such are the many complex and interlocking demands of contemporary governance. In this respect, measures like the Protection of Animals Act, the International Development Act, and the Nationality, Immigration and Asylum Act speak for themselves.

Table 15: Primary legislation affecting Wales, 1999–2003 – Acts and Bills with minor differences for Wales*

Adoption (Intercountry Aspects) Act 1999	Implements Hague Convention on Intercountry Adoption
Food Standards Act 1999	Establishes the Food Standards Agency
Health Act 1999	Reforms NHS structures; establishes Commission for Health Improvement
Local Government Act 1999	Establishes best-value regime for local authorities
Pollution Prevention and Control Act 1999	Consolidates powers to control pollution
Tax Credits Acts 1999	Allows tax credits in relation to child care
Water Industry Act 1999	Reforms law on water charging and metering
Carers and Disabled Children Act 2000	Establishes duty to assess needs of carers and provide assistance to them
Children (Leaving Care) Act 2000	Establishes duty on local authorities to provide assistance to children and young people leaving their care
Countryside and Rights of Way Act 2000	Establishes rights of access to open and common land
Electronic Communications Act 2000	Allows legal documents etc. to be completed in electronic rather than written form
Freedom of Information Act 2000	Establishes new regime for disclosure of official information
Fur Farming (Prohibition) Act 2000	Prohibits the rearing of animals for their fur
Government Resources and Accounts Act 2000	Reforms the structure of, and audit arrangements for, government accounts
Political Parties, Elections and Referendums Act 2000	Establishes the Electoral Commission; regulates the formation and funding of political parties (including funding of party groups in the Assembly)
Protection of Animals Act 2000	Reforms procedures for dealing with animals subject to court proceedings
Race Relations (Amendment) Act 2000	Expands prohibition on race discrimination to the police and Crown bodies (including the Assembly)
Regulation of Investigatory Powers Act 2000	Reforms law on investigatory and surveillance activities
Transport Act 2000	Establishes Strategic Rail Authority; allows charges for road use and workplace parking
Warm Homes and Energy Conservation Act 2000	Establishes regime for providing assistance to those living in fuel poverty
Health and Social Care Act 2001	Reforms NHS structures and funding arrangements
Rating (Former Agricultural Premises and Rural Shops) Act 2001	Changes system of non-domestic rating for rural buildings
Regulatory Reform Act 2001	Allows making of 'regulatory reform orders' to remove burdens on businesses and others
Special Educational Needs and Disability Act 2001	Reforms provision of support for children with special educational needs and prevents disability discrimination in education
Adoption and Children Act 2002	Reforms and consolidates law on adoption
Animal Health Act 2002	Reforms and expands powers to control diseases of livestock
Commonhold and Leasehold Reform Act 2002	Reforms rights of commonhold and leasehold property owners
Homelessness Act 2002	Expands powers to combat homelessness and provide support
International Development Act 2002	Allows public bodies (including the Assembly) to provide non-financial development aid and disaster relief
Nationality, Immigration and Asylum Act 2002	Establishes system for admitting and providing support to asylum-seekers
Travel Concessions and Eligibility Act 2002	Changes eligibility for concessionary public transport
Community Care (Delayed Discharges) Bill	*Establishes system for reimbursing NHS re patients who cannot be discharged due to inadequate social service provision*
Waste and Emissions Trading Bill	*Establishes new regulatory regime for landfill and waste disposal.*

*Source: Welsh Assembly Government. Up to March 2003.

**Bills then before Parliament are shown in italics.

Table 16: Assembly legislative bids 2002–2003 – a year on

Title of Bill	Proposed effect	Outcome of bid
Land Use Planning Bill	Implement proposals on changes to planning procedures. Designed to speed the operation and clarity of the system	Welsh requirements incorporated in Planning and Compulsory Purchase Bill ('England and Wales'), currently in Parliament
Sunday Opening of Licensed Premises Bill	Remove the need for local authorities on request to hold local polls on Sunday opening of licensed premises	Welsh requirements incorporated in Licensing Bill ('England and Wales'), currently in Parliament
Housing Ombudsman Bill	Extend the remit of the local government ombudsman for Wales to enable tenants to make complaints against registered social landlords	Amending provisions included in Housing Bill ('England and Wales') published in March 2003 for pre-legislative scrutiny
Audit (Wales) Bill	Merge the functions of the Audit Commission in Wales and the Auditor General for Wales to create a single audit body for Wales	Draft Bill ('Wales only') published in March 2003 for pre-legislative scrutiny
Passenger Transport Bill	Secure arrangements for structures to support public transport planning and provision, and take direction and appointments powers relating to the Strategic Rail Authority	Bill submitted – response awaited; bid substantially repeated in March 2003
Education Bill	Secure a range of powers necessary for implementation of the Strategic Plan, *The Learning Country*	Bill submitted – response awaited; bid substantially repeated in March 2003
Common Land Bill	Provisions to reform and strengthen the management of common land in Wales	Expectation of inclusion in England and Wales Bill, to be promoted by DEFRA in a later session.[112]
St David's Day Bill	To provide for St David's Day to be a public holiday in Wales	Proposal rejected

Bidding for Wales

Let us return to the novel procedure whereby the Assembly makes a shopping list of bids for primary legislation. Precisely because this is a far more transparent process than the equivalent process in Whitehall, as well as being one that in suitably paradoxical fashion underscores the secondary position of the Assembly, it provides an excellent way of evaluating the statutory outputs from a 'bottom-up' or territorial perspective.

The most recent set of outcomes, for the eight bids targeted on the 2002/3 UK parliamentary session, is summarized in table 16. It is very much a case of mixed results. A year on and two sets of proposals were being taken forward in combined England and Wales legislation. Suffice it to note here that the Welsh requirements in the Planning and Compulsory Purchase Bill represent a more evolutionary approach than the equivalent policy development for England, one example of the capacity of the devolved administration 'to be different' by effectively opting out of, or limiting, a Whitehall reform agenda.[113] Meanwhile, two other bids serve to illustrate the increasingly fashionable technique of draft Bills subject to pre-legislative scrutiny, including one in the scrutiny-friendly format of Wales-only legislation.

Different again: the recent bids for Education and Transport Bills targeted on the 2003/4 legislative session are now seen to be retreads. In turn, they may be said to illustrate the use by the Welsh Assembly Government of the formal Assembly procedure for the purpose of the negotiation with central government. In the words of the minister, 'it is right that we make clear our desire to secure these important proposals'.[114] Meanwhile, the fate of the last two bids brutally illustrates the limitations of the scheme of executive devolution: the lack of control on when primary legislative time will be found and the vulnerability to veto. National devolution, but denial of a bank holiday on the patron saint's day: there is a certain symbolism.

6. IN SEARCH OF IMPROVEMENT: WASC

Such is the background to *The Primary Legislative Process as it Affects Wales*, the recent report from WASC. It elaborated a series of improving themes, from greater consistency in drafting to better public information, as well as enhanced democratic scrutiny through a 'partnership approach' between Westminster and the Assembly. This in turn, however, has now elicited from the UK government a notably lukewarm response, one of great brevity. Conservatism, minimalism and 'muddling through': once again, the countervailing forces at the centre should not be underestimated.

The Select Committee began by focusing on the formal legal methodology of the transfer of functions. In the words of the summary:

Since devolution, additional powers have been conferred on the National Assembly in a number of ways. This has made scrutiny and monitoring of those powers a complex task. Greater consistency would be desirable and we recommend that where possible, powers should be conferred directly by new legislation rather than by amendments to existing Acts or Orders . . . We also recommend that where sensible, Bills should have separate Parts which set out the law as it affects Wales.[115]

WASC then has rightly picked up on the excessively disparate nature of the ongoing devolutionary development; and in particular, the failure of Parliamentary Counsel to develop a conventional approach to the drafting of primary legislation affecting Wales. As the Clerk to the Assembly put it in evidence,

what practitioners here and Members of the Assembly, legal practitioners, interest groups who are affected by Welsh legislation, are concerned about is the absence of clarity. So any means, whether it is a Part in the Bill, a Clause in the Bill or Part of the Explanatory Memorandum which deals with Wales, and which explains with clarity what those provisions are as they affect Wales and their effect, would be welcome.[116]

There is in fact much to be said for developing the idea of 'shadow Welsh statutes' – in the form of internal separation or grouping together of Wales-only provisions in combined England and Wales Bills. As now beginning to be illustrated in measures like the Planning and Compulsory Purchase Bill, where Wales is dealt with entirely separately in Part VI, the practice may be said to reflect and reinforce a less Anglocentric approach to statute-making. National devolution (and evolution): the local demand for a reworked method of drafting, a form of statute law which is explicitly and coherently structured in terms of the territorial policy development, can only increase.

One would thus envisage 'mixed' forms of combined Bills: on the one hand – where this is the policy – uniform England and Wales provisions in some Parts (so avoiding repetition); and on the other hand, separate Parts for Wales and for England in respect of anything other than minor discrepancies. The strong pragmatic approach – in Parliamentary Counsel's terms 'setting out the differences as we came to them'[117] – needs to be tempered if it is not to prove a running sore in the local context. As WASC put it, 'the need for clear, accessible legislation should be a key objective of Government'.[118]

There clearly is some way to go. For example, WASC was referred to the Education Act 2002. Constitutionally speaking this is a significant measure, affording the Assembly important 'Henry VIII'-type powers (to change the national curriculum). However, in terms of its general design, the statute amply demonstrates the diffuse nature of the legislative drafting for Wales. Part 7 applies to Wales only; otherwise it is a case of reading the Act section by section in order to ascertain whether it gives a power to the Assembly or to the Secretary of State to exercise both for England and for Wales. Suffice it to add that the UK government response to WASC offers little by way of practical relief.[119]

The general theme is worth pursuing. There have for example been major differences in the terminology used to refer to the Assembly in combined Bills. One approach smacks of equality: the designation is the 'relevant' or 'appropriate' authority, which is then defined for England and for Wales as the Secretary of State and the Assembly respectively. Another approach sees the Assembly in a secondary position: the designation throughout the Bill is the 'Secretary of State', with a so-called 'glossing provision' at the end to explain that for Wales such references mean the Assembly. An element of farce, both approaches recently featured in the Local Government Bill. The reason, the minister solemnly told MPs, was that two separate Parliamentary Counsels had been involved in the drafting.[120] Let us hope that common sense now prevails, and that the respectful approach is treated as standard.

A word is also in order about the explanatory memoranda that accompany Bills. As a source of public or professional information, and even perhaps as a way of concentrating the mind of the government lawyer, the technique now has a special resonance in the case of Wales. Best practice was illustrated early on in the case of the Special Educational Needs and Disability Act 2001. A section on the territorial coverage of the powers was included, which elaborated the position in the various countries including that in relation to the Assembly.[121] Yet demonstrating once again the disjointed approach, as also the room there has been for improvement in this sphere, the practice was only made standard in January 2003 in the context of the WASC inquiry.[122] The device of a 'Table of the effects of the Bill in relation to Wales'[123] hardly represents rocket science in the light of national devolution. It should have been standard from the outset.

For its part, WASC was greatly exercised by 'the absence of a comprehensive register of the powers of the National Assembly'. In the committee's view, this is 'not merely desirable, it should be a requirement of the devolution settlement'. An admirable sentiment, but the committee's preferred solution – a Consolidation Bill 'by 2008 at the latest' – is likely to prove a non-starter; assuming, that is, the scheme of executive devolution.[124] 'Every Bill a devolution Bill': the codification would be out of date almost as soon as it had been enacted. The inherent difficulties of the current constitutional dispensation cannot so easily be glossed over.

More 'partnership'?

Once again, in the words of the WASC report:

At present, formal joint working between Westminster Committees and the National Assembly is not possible. We state our intention to submit proposals to the [House of Commons] Procedure Committee for formal joint meetings between House of Commons select committees and those of the National Assembly, and for a joint meeting on the legislative priorities for Wales between the Welsh Grand Committee and the National Assembly. We will also explore ways in which the National Assembly and its members can make their views known formally at Westminster on legislation that will directly affect Wales.[125]

WASC then can hardly be faulted for a lack of commitment to the 'partnership approach'. One strand involves draft Bills. The committee looks forward to the day when 'Welsh Parts of draft Bills [are] published in advance of the full draft Bill so that the National Assembly and the House of Commons Committees have sufficient time for pre-legislative scrutiny'. In turn, WASC is determined to promote 'a joined-up approach to legislation affecting Wales'; which translates as joint formal meetings for the purpose of joint scrutiny of draft Bills.[126]

Formal acceptance in Westminster practice and procedure of a right of privileged access for Assembly Members and committees is the second and related strand. WASC has suggested that local actors should have the formal opportunity to register amendments they would like to see made to legislation affecting Wales, which MPs might then take up.[127]

A third strand is introduced, the idea of targeted (Welsh) scrutiny in the House of Commons, and further of 'fast-track' procedure for Assembly-requested legislation. By which is meant the second reading of a Bill in the Welsh Grand Committee, or consideration by a standing committee composed wholly or predominately of MPs with Welsh constituencies. The concept is hardly novel, including in the context of national devolution, but WASC has once again taken a maximal approach. Effectively confirming the link between the form of legislation and the opportunity for scrutiny, the committee has thus recommended that 'the Government, in the spirit of modernisation, experiment with committing a Wales Part of a substantial Bill to a separate Standing Committee'. Likewise, it sees the special standing committee procedures of the House of Commons as one way of allowing 'the National Assembly the opportunity to present formally its views on a Bill before the House'.[128]

Turning the argument round, so much of this recommended practice is dependent on the support of the UK government. And – save for the (inherently limited) proposal of joint meetings on draft bills – the centre has now basically given the 'thumbs down'. 'No current plans', 'a matter for the House', 'not always practical': the language will be familiar to the student of government.[129]

The politics that dare not speak its name

The prospect of 'cohabitation' did not feature in the report of this Labour-dominated committee.[130] So, irrespective of the response from central government, a sense of unreality clouds the recommendations on developing a partnership approach. What happens when the going gets rough? Or more precisely, what does it mean for the Assembly formally to present 'its views' to the House of Commons?

A useful rule of thumb: the level of cooperation which can thus be achieved in matters of legislative oversight will be inversely related to the level of political controversy, as well as to the stage in the timetable at which the clauses become available for democratic scrutiny. Elected representatives of the people of Wales reaching across the legal and constitutional divide, not least with the aim of avoiding a 'scrutiny deficit'; it is a noble vision. But as the Presiding Officer was also careful to point out to the Richard Commission, 'the co-legislator roles of both parties are inherently unstable'.[131]

7. POLICY AND PRINCIPLE

Complaining of inconsistency in the primary legislation affecting Wales is the easy part. Assuming the framework of the GWA, how in substantive terms might the ongoing empowerment of the Assembly be put on a more coherent basis, not least with a view to proper recognition of its constitutional status as the elected representative body of one of the four countries of the Union? Targeted on the wilder excesses of 'British' pragmatism, modest improvement is possible via administrative acceptance of some broad principles for the allocation of powers.

Let us be clear. Primary legislation should essentially be seen as a means to a policy end and not an end in itself. The particular circumstances of each and every Bill need to be carefully reflected in the framing of statute law, which is why for example the way in which the new legislation relates to past legislation will commonly be a determining factor. To this effect, the idea of 'an iron cage' – a detailed set of rules universally worked – is patently absurd. Moving beyond the patchwork approach, characterized by an overwhelming sense of pragmatism, need not, however, entail a rigid framework for the policy for conferring powers on the Assembly. A more sophisticated approach is in order, one that recognizes the primacy of administrative context, the multifarious fact situations of contemporary forms of governance, but also one that reflects and reinforces the not insignificant fact of a new 'national' representative institution. After all, the broad approach to the scope of devolved powers – generous or otherwise – is itself a matter of policy: constitutional policy.[132] Rhodri Morgan may be quoted: 'if the settlement is to remain in robust health, it is important that the primary legislation continues to reflect the Assembly's interests and respect its role.'[133]

A set of principles of this kind should not be seen as antithetical to the processes of administrative and political dialogue and negotiation in IGR. Establishing a firm collaborative basis with sufficient clarity and flexibility to facilitate, on the one hand, the efficient and effective operation of the continuing processes of empowerment, and, on the other hand, ample scope for responsiveness to change or institutional learning, is of the essence of this approach. At the same time, there is a wider purpose: encouragement for those constitutional modes of thought so far sadly lacking in the Welsh devolutionary development. Facilitating a different kind of discourse, one that is not purely 'official' in character or 'policy-oriented' in the narrow sense, is all part of the maturation of the new Welsh democracy. Articulating some broad principles on the allocation of powers should help to provide some answers but also has particular value in the local context in raising questions.

In microcosm: Henry VIII clauses

First, however, a word is in order about 'Henry VIII clauses'. The question of handing the Assembly (secondary) powers to amend and repeal primary legislation has proved a bone of contention between central government and the devolved administration. This is the more significant because a liberal sprinkling of these clauses is emblematic of a strong organic development under the auspices of the devolution statute, such that it was presented in the introduction to this book as a critical element in the maximal scenario of 'quasi-legislative devolution'.[134] In the event, and brilliantly illustrating both the room for manoeuvre within, and the overarching constraints associated with, the legislative framework of the GWA, the UK government has ceded some, but only some, additional ground.

Henry VIII clauses, it is well to remember, come in all shapes and sizes. While many deal with detail and in particular the making of consequential or transitional arrangements in the light of new statutory provision, the more important ones allow a minister to change the substance of legislative policy, according to more or less tightly defined statutory limits. At the latter end of the spectrum, the subject matter drawn within the ambit of a clause may thus allow the alteration of statute law in a wide range of circumstances, perhaps coupled with special procedural constraints to guard against abuse of this formal rule-making power. One aspect of the increasing role played by delegated legislation in modern government, Henry VIII clauses are a species of empowering provision that has multiplied in recent times.[135]

There is also a temporal dimension. Whereas most Henry VIII clauses govern either past Acts or the empowering Act, a major constitutional development has been the rise to prominence of the so-called 'prospective Henry VIII clause', whereby a power is created to change Acts of Parliament passed after the empowering Act.[136] Suffice it to mention here the broad-ranging powers of the executive to alter statutes in the European Communities Act 1972 (compliance with EU obligations), the Human Rights Act 1998 (compliance with Convention rights) and the Regulatory Reform Act 2001 (dealing with the burdens on industry etc.).

A different but related point: in terms of the hierarchy of norms in the British Constitution, the devolution statutes for Scotland and Northern Ireland can themselves be read as conferring delegated legislative power, and so under the traditional (Anglocentric) doctrine of parliamentary sovereignty as embodying very wide Henry VIII clauses.[137] Once again, on this view, the distinction between 'legislative' and (Welsh) 'executive' devolution is not as simple as first appears.

Let us not overlook a substantial (parliamentary) history of antipathy to this form of empowerment.[138] A concern currently given tangible expression in the work for example of the House of Lords Select Committee on Delegated Powers and Regulatory Reform, which is required to report on 'whether the provisions of a bill inappropriately delegate legislative power'.[139] Given the evident potential for circumvention of the standard democratic processes of law making, an expansion of the power of the executive effectively to alter the will of the legislature, this type of scrutiny is very necessary. To push home the point: Henry VIII clauses are now used by central government to an extent that in an earlier age would have been considered blatantly 'offside'.

Reverting to the Assembly, so-called 'tidying up' Henry VIII clauses should pose little difficulty, as the GWA itself serves to illustrate.[140] In turn, when the First Minister boasts of having 'approximately 200 Henry VIII clauses in the bag'[141] it is an essentially meaningless statistic. What matters is not the quantity but the quality of the relevant powers available to the Assembly, wherein a single broad power substantially to change legislative policy counts for more than the myriad opportunities to 'cross t's and dot i's' in the form of incidental, consequential, transitional or supplementary provisions.

Turning then to the more general types of Henry VIII clause, all three basic forms of grading have been contended for in the case of the Assembly. The first one, which sees the devolved administration being treated less favour-ably than central government departments, is appropriately characterized as 'Welsh Office minus'. On this view, the Assembly – emphatically – should not take on airs above its station. As indicated, it held particular sway early on in the life of the Assembly, and is further illustrated in the important matter of the Regulatory Reform Act 2001.[142]

There is something to be said for this view. The UK minister exercising such powers is not only changing statute law but is also answerable to Parliament. In contrast, prospective Henry VIII clauses highlight the disjunction in the case of the Assembly in acute form. Nonetheless, to aver that because Westminster is the principal law-giver for Wales it is generally inappropriate for the Assembly to exercise widely drawn powers to repeal and amend legislation[143] is unconvincing. It is in conceptual terms secondary power that is in issue here, the litmus test being that, technically speaking, the wide Henry VIII-type power can easily be accommodated by the statutory machinery of executive devolution that is the GWA. Marking the difference from legislative devolution, it is not a case of making new statutes from scratch.

The objection also reeks of double standards. It ill behoves a central administration that increasingly resorts to such powers to seek to deny the same facility to the Assembly. In particular, a restrictive approach of this kind is apt to fly in the face of flexible and responsive government on the part of the devolved administration. The Counsel General may be quoted: 'we should be allowed to amend the primary legislation through secondary legislation if that stands in the way of the secondary legislation being made effective. What I do not agree with is the objection to our having [Henry VIII-type powers] based upon some principle.'[144]

Chinks in the armour: central government, it is well to remember, is not a monolith. A rare glimpse of the constitutional debate inside Whitehall: what Peter Hain describes as 'a classic argument' took place in UK cabinet sub-committee in 1999 concerning the propriety or otherwise of the devolved administration having (prospective) Henry VIII-type powers for the purpose of implementing EU obligations. In the event, the practical difficulty of otherwise achieving compliance without trampling on the Assembly carried the day. To quote the minister, 'Wales won.'[145]

The second form of grading is introduced, a principle of equal treatment. This chimes with the initial thrust of the devolutionary development, substitution of the Assembly for the Secretary of State for Wales. As one would expect, it has quickly emerged as a constitutional 'bottom-line' for the devolved administration: the basic idea that in giving Wales its own first-ever democratically elected and accountable government the Assembly should be treated no less favourably than a minister is in respect of England. In the words of the First Minister: 'we would always argue that, whatever power can be conferred on a minister in Parliament to change primary legislation or enact subordinate legislation in any other way, for the same Act it is the Assembly which would have the same power'. Speaking in late 2002, Mr Morgan also felt able to strike an optimistic note, one that is indicative of a greater awareness in central government of the local political and administrative sensitivities in this sphere: 'We believe that with one or two exceptions that are scars as it were . . . that principle is going to be adhered to.'[146]

Allowing for the Assembly to be graded as superior to a central government department: what one may ask of the more radical option? As shown in his words in 'a positive view of so-called Henry VIII powers',[147] the idea is one that has been espoused by the Presiding Office(r). It reflects the view of 'devolution as a process' and, in particular, the expectation encouraged at the time of the devolution referendum that greater scope could be afforded to the devolved administration in policy matters via broad secondary legislative powers.[148] It is then once again a case of stretching matters, and so of helping to maximize the devolutionary dividend from a modest constitutional scheme. In turn, the approach fits with the expansive view of the Assembly and Westminster as 'co-legislators', a less hierarchical relationship or greater sense of democratic 'partnership'.

Constitutionally speaking, there is another important twist. The classic argument against Henry VIII clauses can be stood on its head in the case of the Assembly. Picking up on a theme introduced in the previous chapter, the advanced procedures that the new representative body has at its disposal for dealing with (major forms of) subordinate legislation thus help to underpin the claim for a more generous grading. Changing legislative policy via an 'extended' or Rolls Royce machinery of public consultation and regulatory impact assessment, and subject committee scrutiny and debate and vote (with possible amendment) by the full Assembly (constructed on the basis of AMS); this is hardly the stuff of 'a new despotism'![149] Co-legislation again; to these safeguards may be added the option of subjecting a wide Assembly Henry VIII-type power to parliamentary scrutiny in the guise of negative or affirmative resolution procedure.[150] In the words of the Presiding Officer, never one to understate the argument, there is 'a qualitative difference of democratic principle and of constitutional theory and practice between giving permissive powers of broad legislative remit to an elected body and giving them to ministers'.[151] The Welsh Assembly (Government), it may be ventured, is not about to run amok.

The argument, however, may be expected to meet with limited success. 'Legislative devolution through the back door' is the obvious political and administrative retort. Then there is the no doubt ghastly prospect of the (Welsh) tail wagging the (English) dog. By which is meant the potential knock-on effects on the drafting of statutes for England arising from a permissive use of Henry VIII clauses in relation to Wales. Expressed slightly differently, the powerful geopolitical concept of 'England and Wales' is liable to feature prominently here, most obviously in the context of 'combined Bills'. An unwillingness on the part of central government departments to allow the Assembly wider powers than they themselves can justify, wrapped up in the exercise of parliamentary constraint as through the eagle eye of the Select Committee on Delegated Powers, would be par for the course.

Further, this countervailing demand – 'reverse equal treatment' – sits comfortably with, and no doubt helps to explain, the Assembly administration's adoption of the principle of parity as a constitutional 'bottom-line' or devolutionary minimum. A judicious combination of two forms of grading, it is then a matter of looking at different subject matters, whereby the Assembly may be treated more generously with a view to the effective implementation of policy, safe in the knowledge of delegation to a legislature. To anticipate the discussion, Parliament has its hold by not giving the Assembly *carte blanche* and by, instead, defining inside a box the Henry VIII-type power to change legislative policy.

Enough has been said to convey the flavour of an argument traceable now across four successive public inquiries. The question of the Assembly and Henry VIII clauses demonstrates in microcosm the fact of competing models of executive devolution as reflected in a range of approaches among the different actors to the empowerment of the new representative institution. A constitutional debate, it is important to add, that has been partly disguised by the basic canon of confidentiality in the conduct of IGR.

At the same time, the central place of policy (and legislative) context is underscored. According once again to Peter Hain, 'the question of the legislation providing greater flexibility for the Assembly is really decided on the merits of each case'. So too, in his evidence to WASC, the minister did 'not detect any great struggles of principle or conflicts creating huge momentous issues'.[152] A political and administrative negotiation or dialogue: the constitutional dimension has also been kept determinedly low-key. This is only to be expected in the conditions of Labour Party hegemony.

'Rawlings principles'

As the Presiding Officer tells it:

> Inside the current settlement much more could be done to enhance the Assembly's role. There is no consistency of practice and no clear convention on the drafting of Bills which affect Wales – indeed . . . each new Bill can be seen as re-inventing devolution. That is why the Assembly Review of Procedure endorsed seven principles which Assembly Members unanimously across all parties believe should be adopted in Government Bills affecting functions of the Assembly.[153]

The author had first worked up the idea of a set of principles following the prompt for improvements that was the Queen's Speech in December 2000.[154] Since the allocation of functions to the Welsh Secretary prior to devolution provided no serious guide as to how, once it was determined that a Bill relating to Assembly functions should be prepared, the basis on which Whitehall could reasonably be expected to proceed,[155] this was largely virgin territory. However, behind the scenes in IGR a rudimentary discourse of 'devolution principles' had begun to develop, and so it was a case of working with the grain by means of codification and consolidation. Particular targets at this time were the ungenerous attitude to Henry VIII clauses (the counter-principle of 'Welsh Office minus'), and a wide range of approaches to matters like the allocation of powers to commence primary legislation.[156] Naturally, the design was intended to have broad appeal, both as a kind of constitutional 'hair-comb', a way of pre-empting unwanted tangles in the business of making primary legislation for Wales, and as an encouragement for, and underpinning of, increased legislative 'space' for the devolved administration. Again, in the words of Welsh Labour MP Martin Caton, the principles 'can be embraced by those people who do regard the creation of the National Assembly as an event and those of us who prefer to think of it as the beginning of a process'.[157]

The Assembly Review Group expressed considerable enthusiasm. The principles 'fully and adequately cover all the aspects which we would wish to see in each Government bill, and accordingly we commend them to the Assembly as they stand'. 'Every effort should be made by the Assembly cabinet to impress upon government departments the importance of adopting these principles.'[158] At one with the growing assertiveness of the new Welsh polity, there was also some redrafting of the Rawlings proposals, to the effect of a bolder statement of constitutional policy from the full Assembly:[159]

1. The Assembly should acquire any and all new powers in a Bill where these relate to its existing responsibilities.
2. Bills should only give a UK minister powers which cover Wales if it is intended that the policy be conducted on a single Wales/GB/UK basis.
3. Bills should not confer functions specifically on the Secretary of State for Wales. Where functions need to be exercised separately in Wales, they should be conferred on the Assembly.
4. A Bill should not reduce the Assembly's functions by giving concurrent functions to a UK minister, imposing a requirement on the Assembly to act jointly or with UK government/parliamentary consent, or dealing with matters which were previously the subject of Assembly subordinate legislation.
5. Where a Bill gives the Assembly new functions, this should be in broad enough terms to allow the Assembly to develop its own policies flexibly. This may mean, where appropriate, giving he Assembly 'enabling' subordinate legislative powers, different from those given to a minister for exercise in England, and/or which proceed by reference to the subject-matter of the Bill.
6. It should be permissible for a Bill to give the Assembly so-called 'Henry VIII' powers (that is, powers to amend primary legislation by subordinate legislation, or apply it differently) for defined purposes, the test being whether the particular powers are justified for the purpose of the effective implementation of the relevant policy. Where such powers are to be vested in a UK minister for exercise in England, they should be vested in the Assembly for exercise in Wales.

7.   The Assembly should have powers to bring into force (or 'commence') all Bills or parts of Bills which relate to its responsibilities. Where the minister is to have commencement powers in respect of England, the Assembly should have the same powers in respect of Wales.

Let us call the first one, 'the amoeba principle'. Rightly, the Review Group prioritized this aspect. Emblematic of the idea of the GWA as a framework for organic development, it stands for the gradual widening and deepening of Assembly competencies through new legislation, and more especially for a smoothing of 'ragged edges'. In turn, it picks up on the so-called 'general rule' on the passage of 'similar functions' to the Assembly in the UK government's own devolution guidance note.[160] At the same time, with reference to the central role for political and administrative dialogue, the message is not an unqualified one. Matters which straddle the fields of devolved and non-devolved functions – for example, the environment and energy as in the case of wind farms[161] – obviously present their own difficulties.

Reflecting the fact of, and the need to allow for, the dynamic character of the devolutionary development, the second and third principles build on the first one. The Assembly is thus explicitly confirmed as the prime repository for the ongoing allocation of powers in the fields of devolved functions. On the one hand, it is important to recognize the continuing role of UK ministers not least in terms of the strong 'England and Wales' administrative paradigm. Here, as elsewhere, the wording of the principles should be interpreted flexibly. A practical example: Home Office ministers may exercise their functions differently in respect of police forces in England and Wales although within the same framework of policy. On the other hand, the formulation reflects and reinforces the substitution of the Assembly for the Secretary of State for Wales that lies at the heart of the constitutional design. More especially, it opposes the reinvention of the Wales Office with substantial executive functions – as might conceivably happen in the conditions of 'political cohabitation'. Likewise, it underscores the strong element of consolidation in the design, the sense – to quote Peter Hain – of describing the current process 'rather than prescribing anything totally different'.[162]

A rogue example helps to convey the spirit of these principles. It concerns the not insignificant question of free provision of community care services and the power to prescribe relevant items in regulations under what is now the Community Care (Delayed Discharges Etc.) Act 2003. The Bill as originally drafted provided that the Assembly could make regulations that corresponded to those made in relation to England: that is to say, the Assembly would have had a single legal choice, whether or not to stipulate free provision according to the list determined by the UK minister.[163] Put simply, this type of drafting stands for form not substance in the conduct of devolved government. Resorting to it for a major and sensitive area of policy in the conditions of 'political cohabitation' scarcely bears thinking about! In turn, in the continuing dialogue with Whitehall, Assembly ministers and officials were in a position to mount some powerful counter-arguments. In so constraining devolved competence behind a legal façade, the provision would have blurred the local lines of political and administrative responsibility. It would also have restricted the ability of plenary to amend draft subordinate legislation – a distinctive element of the so-called 'devolution settlement'. And what if the devolved administration believed that proposed regulations were incapable of being funded or even *ultra vires*? In the event, the offending clause was substituted in favour of a straightforward 'parity provision',[164] which in the spirit of the 'Rawlings principles' is as things should be. Speaking more generally, in view of the highly decentralized legal machinery of the UK government, the affair demonstrates not only the difficulty of promoting and policing a set of devolution principles, but also the importance of trying. Three years on from the birth of the Assembly and officials in the UK department were evidently still in need of some basic constitutional instruction.

Further illustrating the interconnected nature of the 'Rawlings principles', the fourth one obviously is protective of the Assembly. Power devolved may, in the famous phrase, be power retained, but it should not generally be called back. As explained, this idea finds limited expression in the GWA, whereby a transfer of functions order can only be varied or revoked under the statute with the Assembly's approval.[165] Underscoring its position as a legislature, the national representative institution is here afforded a more general protection. To repeat, whereas since the Assembly came into being the political focus has been very much on the issue of more generous devolution of powers, this is not the whole story. Of course, an element of flexibility must be factored into the equation, with a view to administrative adaptation in the light of changed conditions. The principle should also be read as operating subject to the consent of the Assembly.[166]

Jumping ahead to number six on Henry VIII clauses, this can now be seen to represent an amalgam of approaches. First, the Assembly is not to be confined to 'nuts and bolts', but may be trusted with broad powers to amend and repeal primary legislation, provided that there are clearly designated boundaries – 'for defined purposes' – and a specified policy need. Second, the devolutionary 'bottom-line' kicks in, such that – in accordance with the declared constitutional policy of the First Minister – the Assembly should not be discriminated against as compared with England. To push home the point, what may at first sight appear a radical formulation is also somewhat modest, especially in view of contemporary central government uses of Henry VIII clauses.

Let us take the case of the national curriculum. In making separate provision for Wales, Part 7 of the Education Act 2002 lists the core and foundation subjects at each of the various 'key stages'. The Assembly, however, is given order-making powers to amend the relevant subsections, as well as to suspend the section on 'key stage four'.[167] At one and the same time, this is an example of 'a parity Bill', there being parallel powers for the Secretary of State in respect of England,[168] and it makes eminent good sense in the (devolutionary) context of a distinctive policy agenda in education, allowing for political and administrative flexibility at the territorial level. Why would one insist that the devolved administration go back into the logjam of legislative business at Westminster in relation to such matters? In terms of the 'Rawlings principles', the legislation thus shows how the sixth one is intended to operate. So too – the many processes of devolution – it shows how the UK government has given some ground on the Assembly and Henry VIII clauses, away from the initial view or counter-principle of 'Welsh Office minus'.

Turning to the last one, the 'Rawlings principles' stand for the basic proposition that commencement should be the responsibility of the body responsible for the execution of the legislation. This is essentially a practical matter, one that is appropriately reserved to the judgement of Assembly ministers and officials in the light of administrative requirements, etc. Once again, the principle may have to yield to particular or special factors, for example a pressing need to guarantee simultaneous regulation across the 'law districts'. So, to the lawyer, it is best viewed as a strong presumption – along with others of the principles. Suffice it to add that, in the period since the 'Rawlings principles' were first devised, the legislative drafting in this respect has become more settled and generous to the Assembly.[169]

Ruffling feathers

The fifth principle on so-called 'framework legislation' merits separate treatment. Included in this book in the expansive model of 'quasi-legislative devolution', it was destined to ruffle feathers. Typically, there are strong echoes here of the controversy over broad Henry VIII clauses and the Assembly. The Presiding Officer may be quoted:

> Of all these principles, the fifth is of particular importance. We need to develop the willingness in Whitehall departments for the Assembly to have greater freedom to make policy decisions and secondary legislation than may be appropriate for a Minister in Whitehall. We readily recognise the problems inherent in giving London Ministers wide powers to make secondary legislation. But what is an appropriate restriction of ministerial freedom in England is a less appropriate restriction when applied to powers exercised by the democratically elected National Assembly.[170]

The major twist in this case involves concern about *vires*, and the tension –
familiar to any student of government – between, on the one hand, conferring
powers in a more flexible way and, on the other hand, ensuring clarity about
what the powers are. For his part, First Parliamentary Counsel has counselled
caution. 'I am not saying it is impossible, or unwise or wrong, to confer wide
powers, it is a matter of policy in the end; all I am saying is that you have to be
careful that the powers are not too vague.'[171]

One is tempted to describe this in terms of 'a storm in a teacup'. The more
frequent and wider use of enabling clauses in Bills to give the Assembly the
power to legislate in respect of a particular function is not – in the words of
Lord Elis Thomas – desperately radical.[172] Trailing the technique in certain
areas like education with a long-standing territorial culture of policy
difference sits comfortably with the underlying constitutional trajectory of the
Assembly – 'towards a Parliament'. Again, the more expansive option of
expressing Assembly competencies by means of specific subject matters –
based on the long title of the Act where this is sufficiently comprehensive or, if
the title is too wide, the subject headings of chapters or parts of the Act[173] –
should be kept in perspective. In deference to the practical concern about
establishing *vires*, one is not talking here about the truly radical option, hinted
at in the devolution statute,[174] of empowerment of the Assembly by reference
to general fields of devolved functions.

It would be a mistake, however, to underestimate the challenge to a mind-
set that is involved here. Legislative drafting in the UK Parliament is famous
for a tendency to dot the i's and cross the t's. Likewise, the legal force of
parliamentary sovereignty exerts a natural pull. 'To be precise and certain
about something, you have to have it in the Westminster legislation' – thus
speaks the First Minister.[175] A different but related point: it is too much to
expect Parliament, the designated 'principal law maker for Wales' in the
devolution White Paper,[176] to content itself with making wholly skeleton
provision on behalf of the Assembly. In the face of the model of executive
devolution, why would Welsh MPs in particular consider themselves mere
ciphers?

For his part, Peter Hain has notably stressed the tension between affording
the devolved administration wide flexibility and 'Parliament's need to
understand how legislation will be applied when it approves that
legislation'.[177] While this so clearly grates with the logic of devolution,
whereby local ministers are responsible to the Assembly for policy development and implementation, a more relaxed approach will not happen
overnight. Likewise it would be absurd to overlook the peculiar territorial
history of close integration with a powerful neighbour. 'We cannot understand why there are different powers of delegated legislation in relation to
Wales from those in relation to England'; this parliamentary refrain has a few
miles in it yet.

Let us beware an 'Aunt Sally' form of argumentation: the setting up of this principle as an iron rule – only to shoot it down. The use of enabling clauses where appropriate, or closely related to distinctive policy contexts and the need for effective means of implementation: this way forward is about the broadening of horizons or, more prosaically, additions to the tool kit of devolved government in Wales. Looking ahead, one would envisage such matters being judged according to the merits of the case and, further, those merits being judged more generously over time, as the Assembly becomes a more familiar part of the political and administrative landscape, at least in the conditions of Labour Party hegemony. Of course 'if you don't ask, you won't get': the constitutional policy or otherwise pursued by the Welsh Assembly Government in the secretive processes of IGR must also be factored into the equation. Meanwhile, the underlying constitutional question will run, precisely because it is so sharply posed here. Why, as the national representative body of one of the four countries of the Union, should the Assembly have powers conferred on it only in the same manner as powers are conferred on ministers in Whitehall?

One practical illustration may suffice. The Waste and Emissions Trading Bill, currently before Parliament, envisages the Assembly exercising wide subordinate law-making powers in a key area of environmental regulation. At one and the same time, the legislation is driven in part by EU requirements,[178] and has to navigate the novel constitutional situation in the reinvented Union state. In turn, it being UK government policy that the Assembly should have the same degree of autonomy here as is accorded in relation to Scotland and Northern Ireland, this effectively means a framework Bill in view of the basic asymmetry associated with the different models of executive and legislative devolution. Notably, the Select Committee on Delegated Powers at first voiced concerns about the extent of the delegation, not least in the case of UK ministers in relation to England, but subsequently concluded that it was 'acceptable in the light of the position under this bill elsewhere in the United Kingdom'.[179] To this end, the Department of Environment, Food and Rural Affairs (DEFRA) was naturally keen to stress that in terms of its enabling nature this was an unusual Bill.[180] In the long view, however, and especially in light of the contemporary dynamics of multi-layered governance and supranational ordering, it may well be seen as an important – and valuable – precedent. Jealous guardian of the prerogatives of Parliament in relation to legislation, the Select Committee has now accepted that different considerations apply in the context of devolution, including in the case of the junior partner of the Union.

Rationale and resource

Let us pull together the various strands. As against the (fundamentally flawed) idea of basing the powers of the Assembly on what the Welsh Office would have had 'but for' devolution, this set of principles is determinedly forward-looking, being targeted on the emergent patterns of allocation of powers. So also, as well as being concerned to protect the devolved administration from a withering of powers, this codification recognizes that a principle of parity or territorial equal treatment in the drafting of primary legislation is necessary but insufficient. The spectre is otherwise raised of an overly Anglo-centric approach to the development of new powers, in line with the prevailing views and concerns of the powerful central government departments in London – in contradistinction, that is, to the devolutionary idea of a territorial government best equipped or specifically empowered for local conditions.

The underlying concept here is one of comity or mutual respect between jurisdictions, one that is familiar in advanced constitutional systems of multi-layered democracy.[181] The devolutionary logic of policy diversity and legal pluralism is seen here to underpin the full Assembly's claim to general or flexible forms of legislative drafting, including in the form of Henry VIII clauses. Again, the criterion of effective implementation clearly has a role to play in the processes of political and administrative dialogue as a basis for determining when special types of powers are allocated to the Assembly. There are conscious echoes here of the familiar (EU) idea of subsidiarity.

At the risk of stating the obvious, 'Rawlings principles' have never been intended as a vehicle for legal action. They were designed as a useful addition to, and to fit with, the general development in soft law techniques that has accompanied the UK devolutionary process. As the first step to a hardening into constitutional convention, their obvious home would be one of the devolution guidance notes promulgated by the UK government, so filling the gap left by the strongly procedural bent of the pre-existing administrative requirements. To reiterate, it was always envisaged that the principles would operate on the basis of 'normal' practice, so maintaining a requisite degree of flexibility, as also that, like any good codification, they would be open to elaboration and refinement in the light of experience.[182]

Of course, principles of this kind can only go so far in promoting the values of rationality and efficiency, and of transparency, in the processes of government. All the more so, it may be said, given the multifarious policy contexts that are involved here, as also the continuing sway of a decentralized form of legal machinery in central government. At the same time, such principles can be seen as a valuable resource for the devolved administration, and – facilitating democratic accountability – as a useful constitutional benchmark for the conduct of central–territorial relations. In terms of the time and energy involved in determining anew specific allocations of powers, and the local demonizing of certain UK departments for an 'uncooperative' attitude, an agreed set of organizing principles to help smooth the ongoing allocation of powers may also be thought to benefit central government.

. . . *Response*

The ringing endorsement of the Assembly Review notwithstanding, the approach of the Welsh Assembly Government to promoting the 'Rawlings principles' around Whitehall is charitably described as 'softly-softly'. According to the First Minister, whereas 'the principles continue to have my strong support and that of my colleagues',[183] Assembly ministers and officials have been able to proceed happy in the belief that all bar the fifth one are generally or universally adhered to in the drafting of legislation post-devolution. 'It was not as though this was something terribly new which, therefore, needed to be put formally to the Wales Office and to . . . other departments because by and large we would have said [the principles] were already being abided by.'[184] Confirmation or otherwise, First Parliamentary Counsel would later cheerfully confess never to have heard of them.[185]

He has now. The 'Rawlings principles' have thus been standard fare in the official 'circus' of inquiries into primary legislation affecting Wales. Adopted by the Select Committee on the Constitution as 'a very useful starting point', they clearly have helped to set the scene for the concession on the part of the UK government that 'greater consistency is desirable in the way in which legislation for Wales is framed'.[186] Likewise, the principles have grounded a forensic interrogation of the Secretary of State for Wales by Lord Richard.[187] So as a means of promoting a form of constitutional dialogue in the context of executive devolution, and in particular of demanding the articulation of key working assumptions in the highly informal practice of IGR that go to shape the Welsh polity, the 'Rawlings principles' have had some impact.

But is this as good as it gets? Eventually published in July 2003, the UK government response to WASC plays a determinedly straight bat. 'Each bill must be drafted in the light of the policy decisions made in that particular case and the Government is not prepared to adopt formally any general set of principles of this kind.' 'Nevertheless', the formulation 'does largely describe the Government's normal practice in considering the powers which the Assembly should be given in primary legislation'.[188] Peter Hain is also worth quoting: 'the general response of the government is we agree with some of the Rawlings principles and not with others.'[189]

Looking more closely, the response illustrates many of the points raised in the discussion. Standard design, but with a measure of flexibility factored into the script, such is the UK government line on number one, the (vital) 'amoeba principle'; on number two, ministers' powers covering Wales; and on number seven, commencement powers. Meanwhile on number three, the position of the Welsh Secretary, the familiar practice whereby functions are conferred on the Secretary of State at large rather than a named Secretary of State is quickly rehearsed. As for (the protective) number four: while not accepting that the requirement to act concurrently or jointly or to obtain consent would necessarily have this effect, 'the Government would not normally reduce the Assembly's functions'.[190]

Surprise, surprise: numbers five and six of the 'Rawlings principles' are the ones that the centre still finds difficult to swallow. On framework legislation, the response is wonderfully spare, simply repeating the gospel according to Peter Hain. 'Each case is decided on its merits. However, in giving the Assembly such powers, Parliament will expect to be informed how the Assembly Government proposes to exercise them in the same way as it expects such information from the Government.' On Henry VIII clauses, the notable feature is a refusal to sign up to the principle of parity favoured by the First Minister. In fact – cogent evidence of the underlying tensions – the wording here is more than usually convoluted. On the one hand – the idea of 'defining inside a box' – number six is declared to be 'normal practice where the exercise of the Henry VIII powers does not change the intention of the primary legislation'. On the other hand – traces of 'Welsh Office minus' – 'secondary legislation made by the Secretary of State is subject to further parliamentary scrutiny while secondary legislation made by the Assembly is not'. And so, it is said, 'a judgement needs to be made as to how wide a latitude Parliament should give the Assembly to amend primary legislation without further scrutiny. For that reason the Government cannot accept [the parity principle] without that qualification.'[191]

Let us be clear. One would not have envisaged the UK government, in the words of Peter Hain, 'just saying "Snap"' to the Rawlings principles.[192] Formal 'response' aside, the critical test is the extent to which, over time, they seep into and become part of the official culture of IGR. Two steps forward, one step back: it is worth stressing once again that the devolved administration has made some headway in terms of the general approach to the allocation of powers. Certain lessons have been learned; much in the situation remains fluid. Executive devolution, it is well to remember, very much involves a continuing negotiation.

Turning the argument round, it is a long way here from the enchanting vision of the roles of 'co-legislators'. And it must be said: the UK government response offers no great encouragement to those like (Labour colleagues on) WASC wishing to pursue the quest for 'improvement'. Not so much 'principle', or even (legislative) 'partnership', as more 'muddling through': it will be interesting to see how the Richard Commission interprets the underlying constitutional message. The case for legislative devolution, it may be said, grows stronger by the day.

CONCLUSION – AFTER HUMPTY DUMPTY

The disaggregation of the legislative function is by definition a central element of the Welsh scheme of executive devolution. In turn, this chapter has highlighted the great and continuing importance for Wales of issues of access to, and influence in, the primary legislative process in London. The various law-making powers of the Assembly, as also the particularistic style in which they are often expressed, brilliantly illustrate this dimension. Likewise, the topic of intergovernmental relations (IGR) takes on in the case of Wales a special legal as well as political and administrative aspect, which now finds increasingly powerful echoes in the development of inter-parliamentary relations. Such is the message of the mantra, 'every Bill a devolution Bill'.

A recurring theme is the importance of the form of legislation. The choice of a combined ('England and Wales') Bill or of 'Wales-only' legislation bears on the general approach to drafting, and underpins issues of democratic scrutiny, both in the Assembly and at Westminster. Likewise, in terms of matters like timetabling, where the technique of pre-legislative scrutiny is again in play, it further serves to illuminate the very practical concerns that go to shape the making of statute law affecting Wales post-devolution.

Separate parts and sections of statutes concerning Wales, clear references to the Assembly and explanation of the territorial dimension to the allocation of powers: such matters may sound dull and technical to the non-lawyer. Yet they help to convey the demand for a broadening of horizons inside government for the purposes of Welsh executive – and national – devolution. This links in turn to the case for a set of principles on the policy for conferring powers on the Assembly: not so much inconsistency (from the generous to the mean), more a general awareness of the constitutional role and position of the new representative institution. In the event, the ritual insistence in the formal UK government response that each case must be decided on its merits does not greatly advance matters. 'Aunt Sally': who thinks otherwise? At the same time it so obviously begs the question of how one tells the merits. The mistake once again is to think that legislative policy does not involve constitutional considerations. In terms of the practical workings, most obviously in the case of legislation to underpin distinctive 'made in Wales' policies, the full Assembly's statement of constitutional policy should continue to resonate. At least it has made one.

Whereas, in the chapter on Assembly law making, we were on 'home turf', the force of the autochthonous constitutional development is obviously more muted in this general area. The devolved administration may exercise 'voice', but is hardly in a position to dictate matters. Likewise, it does not do to underestimate the force of old habits in Whitehall and Westminster, re-inforced here by a peculiar territorial history of close integration with England. For example, this has not been parliamentary counsel's finest hour.

Informal and fluid processes are the general rule in the UK system of inter-governmental relations, and the political and administrative dialogue with Whitehall about primary legislation affecting Wales is no exception. The contribution of the Wales Office at this early stage in facilitating cooperation and collaboration between the two administrations should not be under-estimated, including, as part of a reformed 'Welsh network' in the conduct of public affairs, the likes of WASC. Putting to one side the usual tensions in systems of multi-layered democracy, there are no great alarms to report here. Nor would one expect there to be in the particular conditions of Labour Party hegemony.

The fragmentation of the law-making function has clearly caused consider-able difficulty in terms of the exercise of democratic scrutiny. Notwith-standing the encouragement of the Presiding Office, inputs from the full Assembly into the primary law-making process have been the more notable by their absence. For its part, WASC should be commended for at least trying to redress the constitutional balance, in the form of innovative 'partnership' techniques for legislative scrutiny.

As to the substantive product, the so-called 'devolution dividend' in terms of distinctive provision for Wales, it is in part a matter of spectacles. Viewed through the historical prism of centuries of legal assimilation in the 'English legal system', the primary legislation affecting Wales post-devolution is already seen to mark a transformation. Viewed in comparative perspective, for example in terms of the practice of multi-layered governance in many European countries, it is modest stuff. As one would expect, there is an upward curve reflecting an enhanced policy development at the territorial level, and a depressant effect by reason of the competitive struggle for legislative time in the UK Parliament. Adam Smith and Wales: local legislative demand already is starting to outstrip London-based supply.

In conclusion, the making of primary legislation for Wales demonstrates once again a significant evolutionary development under the auspices of the devolution statute. Improvements have been made, both in terms of the process and the style and substance of the product. At the same time, helping to explain a somewhat patchy and piecemeal development, there are on the UK stage some notable shows of resistance to a more generous allocation of powers to the Assembly. For their part, even supposing broad acceptance by the UK government, determinedly constructive approaches like the quest for a new form of legislative 'partnership' between Westminster and the Assembly, or the attempt to curb the more cavalier legislative forms of 'British' pragmatism via the 'Rawlings principles', can only do so much. They cannot disguise – indeed they also serve to point up – the major structural limitations that are associated with the disaggregation in the Welsh scheme of the legislative function, a fundamental source of instability in the so-called 'devolution settlement'. A bit like Humpty Dumpty, not all the pieces can be put back together again.

The Closeness of Wales (I)

Wales is a small nation with high ambitions facing many challenges. It is only through partnership and joint working with all agencies and spheres of government that Wales will gain the means to innovate and find responses to its distinctive national and local circumstances.

National Assembly, *Local Government Partnership Scheme*[1]

The title of these next two chapters is purloined from the first Assembly Minister for Finance, Edwina Hart.[2] 'Bringing government closer to the people': one of the chief features of the emergent Welsh polity is a greater intensity to political and administrative relationships, outside as well as inside the Assembly. A classic 'little country' syndrome, it typically bears distinctive Welsh characteristics, being partly a product of local history and partly a reflection of the evolving position of the devolved administration in terms of the different sectors and many diverse actors that comprise the Welsh system of governance.

The topic of interior relations merits a special emphasis in this book. First, the model of executive devolution is apt to focus attention on relations with central government, often in the public discussion to the detriment of this aspect. Second, the topic goes to the heart of the character of the new Welsh polity or to the sense of the quality of 'Wales [as] an artefact which the Welsh produce'.[3] It will thus be appropriate to consider two major strands of development. This chapter focuses on the Assembly and local government, while chapter 11 examines the role post-devolution of quangos or semi-autonomous public bodies, and in particular of key agencies for accountability or public-sector regulation.

Prolegomenon: concept and ideology

As explained in chapter 1, the treatment of local government post-devolution has special resonance by reason of its previous role as the only home-grown tier of democratic authority in Wales, and in particular of the sense of constitutional depredation under the Conservatives. Was it to be more of the same, or would national devolution help to provide local government with a fresh impetus, and, further, in tandem with the Assembly, effectively harness its best energies in the service of the people of Wales?

How might our inquiry be conceptualized? A classic point of departure in analysis of (UK) intergovernmental relations, the notion of 'power dependence' directs attention to the different types of 'resources' – constitutional and legal, political and administrative, financial – which are available to, and in play between, the respective tiers of government.[4] Notably, in the case of Wales, the model of executive devolution gives constitutional and legal factors particular salience, by reason of the comparative lack of 'resources' available to the devolved administration.

A strong sense of ambiguity – even a measure of confusion – is another recurrent theme in the study of intergovernmental relations.[5] Multifaceted in terms of the structures and processes, such arrangements are also apt to show a kaleidoscopic quality. The cross-currents are once again brilliantly illustrated in the case of Wales by the particular constitutional and political resource that is national devolution; or the general sense of the Assembly being more strongly placed in matters of interior relations than the emanation of central government that was the Welsh Office.

The related concepts of political, institutional, and regulatory space are particularly useful in this context.[6] A new form of territorial government armed with a democratic mandate: it is easy to spot the potential for crowding. 'Bringing government closer to the people': in suitably paradoxical fashion, the scale of the encroachment by the devolved administration on the local government sphere – or otherwise – is seen here as an important litmus test of the quality of the Welsh constitutional development. Relations, it will be seen, have so far been relatively harmonious; a function in part of fragmented resources. There is not so much a sense of hierarchy, as one of horizontal or negotiated interdependence in this little country. Such, anyway, is the discourse of 'the Welsh way'.

Once again, reference should be made to the concept of 'juridification', in the sense of a move in contemporary public administration from discretion to rules, and in particular of an infusion of law and legal technique.[7] In UK public law, it is familiarly associated with developments in central–local government relations under the Conservatives; an essential vehicle of both centralization and contracting out or market-style disciplines.[8] *Pace* New Labour in London, one would not expect to see this replicated in the emergent forms of territorial–local government relations in Wales. An enticing prospect in the new – and small – Welsh polity, the issue is raised of rolling back the frontiers of 'juridification'.

Taken to excess, power dependence theory is apt to imply a 'battle of resources' or permanent state of war across the tiers of government. In contrast, in considering the case of Wales, it is especially important to keep in mind a sense of shared values and objectives in this new territorial polity. Bank balances of 'resources', it is a necessary but incomplete explanation of an official commitment to so-called partnership working.

The idea of opening the Assembly to, and drawing to it, other interests in society, was seen to be central to the devolutionary design.[9] Hence the statute clearly signalled a series of arrangements designed to foster relations between the Assembly and various public and private institutions in Wales. In turn, and for once waxing lyrical, Alun Michael was to confirm the partnership principle as a dominant value or ideology of the new model Wales:

> There are three golden threads of partnership at the heart of the National Assembly's activities. The partnerships with local government, with business and with the voluntary sector are uniquely enshrined in statute. And they are being transformed into reality, bringing voices from communities across Wales into the heart of government for the very first time.[10]

Constitutionally and legally speaking, the partnering with local government is undoubtedly the strongest 'thread'. Another important factor is the level of organization, as compared for example with the many fragmented or diffuse interests that make up the business sector,[11] let alone the voluntary sector.[12] At the same time, the nature of this broader environment will have a bearing on how the new form of territorial–local government relations evolves. From other (potential) partners, such as the quangos or administrative agencies, to the various institutions of civil society, and on up to Parliament: once again, theirs is not an exclusive relationship.

Mr Michael's comments must now be read in light of the rise of the Welsh Assembly Government. Greater internal stability and experience, the development of a distinctive all-Wales policy agenda: further questions are raised about the nature or equilibrium of partnership in these changed conditions.

The definition of a Welsh official space is itself problematical. Devolution, not separation, and further a distinctive form of devolution steeped in a peculiar territorial history: the strong pull of the 'England and Wales' paradigm should never be forgotten. It is not only that the devolved administration will often have to work within the constraints of 'cross-border' policy systems in the sphere of territorial–local government relations, with the effect of shaping and on occasion overriding its own policy preferences. Attention is also drawn for example to the myriad 'cross-border' bodies – for example inspectorates – that inhabit the local regulatory space.[13]

1. DEVOLUTION AND LOCAL GOVERNMENT

Although glossed over by the typically Anglocentric accounts in public law, central–local government relations in Wales had their own distinctive quality

pre-devolution. A smaller, more personalized set of networks, they were characterized by close working relationships between staff in the Welsh Office and
local authorities, certainly compared with England, as also by less polar-
ization or greater trust and informal understandings even during those heady
days of intra-state conflict in the 1980s.[14] Then again, it may be good to talk,
but Welsh local government was also confronted, on the one hand, by the fact
of limited Welsh Office influence in Whitehall, and on the other hand, by the
remorseless logic of the UK cabinet doctrine of collective responsibility. Such,
precisely, was the complaint of the Welsh Local Government Association
(WLGA):

> Welsh local government has worked hard over the years to build an effective
> partnership with Secretaries of State for Wales. To a large extent it has failed
> because those Secretaries of State have not been accountable to Wales but have
> been accountable to a far wider constituency. All too often when local government
> has made proposals for partnership based on the identified circumstances of
> Wales, the response has been in directions and policies developed elsewhere for
> different interests. All too often the interest of a Secretary of State seeking to
> impose values from outside Wales has been in diminishing the only exercise of
> democratic political power in Wales, diminishing local democracy.[15]

Naturally, in promoting the Assembly, Ron Davies courted Welsh local
government assiduously. The talk was of its place 'at the top table in the
governance of Wales', and in particular of the chief virtue of 'partnership'.[16]
More concretely, an informal Framework for Partnership was quickly
established with the WLGA, which provided for joint working, detailed
consultation and exchange of information in the vital transitional period of
the last days of the Welsh Office. The way in which this vision has now been
carried through, first in the formal language of the devolution statute, and
second in the role and practice of the devolved administration in its early
years, is of the essence of the emergent forms of territorial–local government
relations.

A strategy of promoting collaboration and coordination across the interior
layers of government may thus be said to have infused the devolutionary
development in Wales. How else, from the viewpoint of the architects of the
scheme, to square the circle between a 'national' representative body with
powers across the fields of devolved activities, and a reworked system of
unitary authorities exercising a wide range of functions? A different but
related point: in such a cluttered administrative space, as characterized by
many overlapping powers and responsibilities, more especially in such key
areas (of Assembly interest) as education and social services, the constitutional and political question of mutual respect or comity between jurisdictions
comes to the fore. An obvious touchstone is what commonly matters to local
government – the scope for diversity or the scale of its discretion.[17]

Tensions in this multifaceted relationship are an entirely natural feature. So typical of constitutional systems of divided competencies, the process of dialogue and negotiation or decision will prove an unending one, the two tiers of government being in a very real sense stuck with each other. A sense perhaps in local government of the Assembly as little more than *primus inter pares*, the demand for a strong leadership or directive role at the territorial level: in these early days especially, there is ample scope for competing perceptions of the nature of the 'partnership'. To anticipate the discussion, the devolved administration has thus far proved distinctly simpatico towards local government.

Local government 'modernization'

But what, it may be asked, of the changing face of (Welsh) local government? To pick up on an earlier theme,[18] national devolution in the shape of the Assembly also represents the centrepiece in a more general reform project aimed at developing and revitalizing the governance of Wales, one which encompasses the so-called 'modernization agenda' for local government. The close interweave of the various strands is shown by *Local Voices*, a Welsh Office White Paper promulgated at the time of the passage of the devolution legislation:

> Modernising local government in Wales will be an immense task for everyone involved. The National Assembly will have a key role to play in promoting and helping to implement change . . . This agenda gives councils the opportunity once again to be a force for progress and social justice in their local communities. It opens a future where councils in partnership with the Assembly and others can bring a real difference to the quality of life of the people of Wales.[19]

So once again the vision pre-dates the devolved administration, which effectively – and enthusiastically – has bought into the process. 'The National Assembly', it was soon agreed, 'will encourage councils and other bodies to engage continuously with their local communities, modernise their political management structures, scrutinise their performance and adopt the highest standards of probity.'[20]

Another recurring theme is the close interplay in this devolutionary context of the 'England and Wales' and 'Wales-only' paradigms of official endeavour. The clarion call *Local Voices* was itself a Welsh 'spin' on the modernization agenda then being devised and promulgated for local government in England.[21] Central direction, significant territorial variation: the pair of statutes that have grounded the agenda (the Local Government Acts 1999 and 2000) provide the typical mishmash post-devolution of a legislative framework.

For present purposes, three key aspects of the modernizing programme command attention. The first and most significant one is the creation of new political structures for councils: by which is meant fundamental changes in the way local authorities conduct their business and discharge their functions. As from May 2002, nearly all the unitary councils in Wales operate on the strong centralist basis of 'leader and cabinet' arrangements, while the remainder use a special Welsh option made available under the Local Government Act 2000 of politically balanced 'council boards' for decision-making purposes.

A clear separation of the executive and scrutiny roles has thus been put in place, together with a much greater concentration of decision-making power than was envisaged under the classical local government committee system. The White Paper *Local Voices* had rightly stressed the advantages in terms of efficiency and – via increased transparency and oversight – of political accountability.[22] The lesson for, or parallel with, the Assembly is immediately apparent, such being the essential internal trajectory of that corporate body, first in the parliamentary proceedings on the Bill, second in the ongoing autochthonous constitutional development. Regression to a strong committee model at the territorial level is made here to look even more unlikely.

In suitably tendentious fashion, *Local Voices* had spoken of 'an inward looking culture', decision-taking 'on the basis of what suits the council as a service provider', a relationship with 'essential partners' – local businesses, voluntary organizations and other public-sector bodies – which 'all too often . . . is neither strong or effective'. *Per contra*, 'community leadership' lay at the heart of the role of local government, more especially since concerted action was needed to address the inter-related problems in modern Wales of poor health, low incomes and low skills and qualifications.[23] Major policy-orientated initiatives enshrined in the Local Government Act 2000 were thus clearly signalled – the second main aspect. By which is meant, on the one hand, recourse to (community) planning, a requirement that authorities prepare 'overarching strategies' based on local needs and potential, and, on the other hand, 'an overarching framework for local government' itself, a duty to promote the economic, social and environmental well-being of areas.[24] Once again, the broad and ambitious vision of partnership, now expanded into nooks and crannies across Wales, deserves a special emphasis:

> Fundamental to the strategic role envisaged for councils is the need for an effective relationship between councils and their communities. Many authorities already consult local people about issues affecting them. Some work in partnership with other agencies and organisations to address specific concerns. Too often, these partnerships do not include all the relevant interest groups, and as a result local problems are not tackled in a comprehensive or strategic way, and

there is often insufficient sharing of resources, information and decision making
. . . It is essential that authorities work with the wide range of agencies and
organisations that operate locally.[25]

A revamped ethical framework is the third main aspect. Also mandated by
the Local Government Act 2000, this development is all at one with the strong
emphasis in the design of the Assembly on probity and standards of conduct,
and in turn reflects the contribution made by the (UK) Committee on
Standards in Public Life.[26] It further serves to illustrate the active role of the
devolved administration in promoting the reform agenda for local
government. From elaborate forms of consultation to regulations, guidance
and a model code of conduct for councillors: the development has thus been
seen as one of the early pegs for creative forms of rule-making in the
Assembly.[27]

Pyramid and partnership

Cooperation in achieving reform and a potential for conflict; added
responsibilities for the Assembly in the monitoring and review of councils'
performance; reserve powers etc.: the implementation of the 'modernization
agenda' also serves to highlight the complex interface of these two tiers of
government. The Assembly and local authorities: a simple equation, it is not!
What, it may be asked, of the prevailing political and administrative culture,
especially in terms of the prospects for 'partnership'?

By definition, the new form of territorial–local government relations
represents a qualitative shift. On the one hand, and underwriting the demand
for a 'partnership' approach, a danger of devolution is centralization, the
sucking-up of powers from local government to the territorial level, contrary
to the principle of (internal) subsidiarity.[28] From the viewpoint of constitutional design, there is also a concern about local government being cut off
from central government, still the basic provider in Wales of statutory powers
and public funding. On the other hand, in terms of what is a new pyramidal
model of government authority – 'local government in Wales in the United
Kingdom' – the scheme of executive devolution means that the devolved
administration cannot directly attack local government's statutory powers.
(Unless, that is, it benefits from a generous use of Henry VIII clauses, which
notably has not happened in this sphere of dual democratic mandates.)[29]

At one and the same time, in its dealings with local government the
devolved administration may be said to enjoy a certain form of moral
authority, courtesy of the idea of national devolution, and to be hampered by
the evident fragility of its own political legitimacy. For its part Welsh local
government is hardly a monolith, as table 17 serves to illustrate.[30]

Notwithstanding a distinctive form of symmetry, by which is meant the system of twenty-two unitary or 'principal' councils, there is thus considerable diversity, most obviously in size and density of population and in terms of the local economy, and (increasingly perhaps) in politics. In terms of the nature of the 'partnership', Cardiff and Newport for example are clearly big players, including in the light of a strong Labour electoral tradition.

Table 17: Welsh unitary authorities[31]

Authority	Area (sq km)	Population	Members	Political control* 1995	Political control* 1999
Blaenau Gwent	109	72,000	42	Labour	Labour
Bridgend	246	131,400	54	Labour	Labour
Caerphilly	278	169,600	73	Labour	Plaid Cymru
Cardiff	140	320, 900	75	Labour	Labour
Carmarthenshire	2394	169,000	74	Labour	NOC
Ceredigion	1795	70,700	44	Independent	NOC
Conwy	1130	111,900	59	NOC	NOC
Denbighshire	844	90,500	47	NOC	NOC
Flintshire	438	147,000	70	Labour	Labour
Gwynedd	2548	117,500	83	Plaid Cymru	Plaid Cymru
Merthyr Tydfil	111	57,000	33	Labour	NOC
Monmouthshire	850	86,300	42	Labour	NOC
Neath Port Talbot	442	138,800	64	Labour	Labour
Newport	190	139,200	47	Labour	Labour
Pembrokeshire	1590	113,700	60	Independent	Independent
Powys	5196	126,000	73	Independent	Independent
Rhondda Cynon Taff	424	240,400	75	Labour	Plaid Cymru
Swansea	378	229,500	72	Labour	Labour
Torfaen	126	90,200	44	Labour	Labour
Vale of Glamorgan	335	121,300	47	Labour	NOC
Wrexham	498	125,200	52	Labour	NOC
Ynys Môn	714	65,400	40	NOC	NOC

*NOC = No overall control

Reference has been made to the special local government scheme that the Assembly is required to produce under the devolution statute. It contains a powerful statement of the internal constitutional dispensation in Wales:

> The National Assembly for Wales and local government in Wales are committed to working together in partnership, within an atmosphere of mutual trust and respect, recognising the value and legitimacy of the roles both have to play in the governance of Wales. Subject to the requirements of primary legislation, the National Assembly has a responsibility for setting the framework of policy and of secondary legislation within which local government operates. Local government for its part has a democratic mandate to represent the views of its communities to the National Assembly and to Parliament and to ensure the delivery, within the

legislative and policy framework and the available resources, of services that reflect the expressed needs and priorities of its communities. It also has a responsibility to ensure that local decision making reflects the requirements of the law and priorities determined by the National Assembly.[32]

There is, however, a vital missing piece: the power of the purse, as constituted by the broad discretion to determine budgetary priorities by virtue of the 'block and formula' system, and the sheer scale of the spending channelled through local authorities and into service provision (a system of 'indirect administration'). Put simply, the Assembly cabinet is bound to be concerned about how and to what effect a third of the Welsh 'block' is spent, not least in the case of an administration pinning its colours to the mast of 'check against delivery'.

2. THE 'WELSH WAY'

The rapid development post-devolution of much greater territorial differentiation in the policy and practice of relations with local government is a striking feature. In the words of Edwina Hart, then Minister for Finance, Local Government and Communities, this so-called 'Welsh way' – characterized by a high degree of mutual trust or joint and supportive forms of working – reflects and reinforces 'the closeness of Wales'.[33] In terms of the British contribution to public administration, it thus stands for a partial reversion to so-called 'club' or 'group' government – comfortable with discretion, more informal.

The tight institutional structure of local government in Wales is clearly one factor. As well as drawing on local tradition from the days of the Welsh Office, this Welsh way of doing business is thus usefully underpinned by the move – immediately prior to devolution – to the system of (fewer) unitary authorities. Once again, in the words of Mrs Hart, 'having a national government and twenty two local authorities allows a sharing of objectives which would not be possible elsewhere in the United Kingdom'.[34] Certainly England – a mass of authorities, a patchwork system of local government, and the twin facts of 'London' and 'Whitehall' – this is not!

Then there is the political glue of Labour electoral dominance in (large parts of) Wales. It would be strange indeed if party channels and sense of solidarity did not perform major functions of facilitating and coordinating in the emergent form of territorial/local government relations.[35] In terms of the formal structures, a chief touchstone is the WLGA, essential player it will be seen in the partnership approach and (from its birth in 1996) Labour-led. A different but related point: many of the priorities or policy ambitions – for example in the tackling of socio-economic deprivation – are likely to be shared across the two tiers of government in this left-leaning country. The Assembly, after all, is in a very real sense hewn from a long and powerful tradition of radical democratic politics at the local level.

From the viewpoint of the devolved administration, the sense of mutual dependency is naturally reinforced by a deficit in policy development capacity. 'Administrative' as well as 'constitutional' and 'monetary' resources etc.: one does not have to be steeped in power-dependency theory to appreciate the strong magnetic pull which this exerts in a small country that is still finding its feet. It finds powerful expression in the work of the special Welsh 'Partnership Council', as will be demonstrated.

As so often in the story of Welsh devolution, personal factors are important. That a thick wedge of AMs has direct experience of local government, while many more will be in touch with leading councillors and officials in their area, is all part of 'the closeness of Wales'. Pride of place, however, rightly goes to Edwina Hart. Clearly one of the most forceful and able people in the Assembly, she has emerged as the high priestess of the Welsh way. To the extent, the reader may have noted, of relabelling the devolved administration 'a national government'.

Let us be clear. There is no 'clean break' from the 'England and Wales' paradigm. This, emphatically, is not the way in Welsh devolution! It is more a case of rebalancing in terms of convergence and divergence; or, more precisely, of shifting territorial paradigms across a complex set of structures and processes, public and private, official and unofficial. Such, it may be said, is of the essence of contemporary governance.[36]

By way of illustration, one need only think in terms of the importance of professional ties. Given the chief part that officers play in local government, associations historically constructed on an England and Wales basis, for example the Society of Local Authority Chief Executives (SOLACE),[37] will obviously have a significant mediating role to play. The fact that more autonomous Welsh branches of this type of organization are now appearing reflects at one and the same time the overarching dynamic of national devolution and the evident utility of continuing linkages across wide networks (cross-fertilization of ideas and techniques, as against inbreeding).

Form and substance

How then is the 'Welsh way' manifested? The modernization agenda once again provides an important clue, in the form of the cherry-picking from the UK government White Paper. To the extent that devolution is about policy diversity, it will commonly be shown in the provision of services by local government. This after all is one of the lessons of the education blueprint, *The Learning Country*.[38] Similarly, reference may be made to such valuable – and headline-grabbing – territorial initiatives as free school milk for the under-sevens, special hardship grants for students[39] and free bus passes for the over-sixties and disabled people.

In fact, with a view 'to stating the difference' (that devolution has made), there is an increasingly impressive list of items falling under the purview of local government. It ranges from funding improvements of recreational facilities to new legal duties on housing homeless people, and on through support for major integrated transport projects to the development of a reworked planning law system for Wales.[40] There is to this effect a sense of progression, with the development and implementation of policies at first proceeding in fairly close tandem to those in England, and the devolved administration now beginning to explore what can be done differently within pre-existing powers, as well as pursuing new ones.[41] No doubt some of these things would have happened anyway under the auspices of a (Labour) Secretary of State for Wales, but the liberating effect here of avoidance of UK Cabinet collective responsibility cannot be gainsaid.

Yet once again there is more to it than this. When considering 'devolution in practice' it does not do simply to count up the (more obvious) policy differences.[42] How things get done is also important, including in terms of helping to determine what actually gets done! As Mrs Hart has indicated, the form and substance of delivery run together here. In her words, with reference to the constitutional and administrative canon of mutual respect and joint working:

> You may be asking yourself whether all this closeness and co-operation actually works. I am well aware that there are views that we in Wales are lacking in vigour, in discipline and innovation. I deny that. In working closely together, we will continue to challenge and check each other.[43]

Regulatory technique

One of the more tangible features of the Welsh way is a reworking in terms of regulatory technique. Notwithstanding the view of the Counsel General that legislation is the Assembly's main and most important product, the ministerial approach is indicative of less reliance on the tools of formal law, or in the classic parlance of administrative law on rule-bound techniques of command and control. Here for example is Rhodri Morgan resisting the call to press for new statutory powers: 'There is no need for legislation to allow us to give orders to local government. We should be working with local authorities, supporting them and persuading them to do what we want them to do rather than forcing them.'[44]

A distinct preference is shown for softer or less hard-edged forms of policy instrument. Abandonment of school league tables for example[45] is emblematic of a less coercive or pressurized approach. Put another way, ministers have not been enthusiasts for the more intrusive procedures familiarly associated with the fashionable nostrums of New Public Management:

> Good management, responsiveness to need, fair administration and openness are fundamental to good public services. Too often, good intentions to reinforce these values have led instead to micro-management by central government and an accumulation of requirements whose relationship to each other is not clear. Local authorities' energies are often directed towards dealing with bureaucratic requirements rather than being concentrated on setting themselves clear objectives, taking action and being directly accountable to their electorate. These requirements also result in administrative costs for the Welsh Assembly Government, money which might be better spent elsewhere.[46]

A lighter touch: how then to spread the message? Clearly much will turn on the professional habits and attitudes of the various inspectorates and auditors who inhabit the local regulatory space. So typical of national devolution, and further of the idea of partnership working, an important new network has come into being – the Wales Inspectorate Forum. Armed with a mission statement 'to encourage the co-ordination of inspections', while 'minimising the burden of inspection on local authorities' and 'maximising its added potential', the Forum has brought together all the relevant statutory inspectorates for Wales with local government representatives and Welsh Assembly Government officials.[47]

The theme can be pursued in various ways. Better to underpin 'the Welsh way', one might expect to see the devolved administration press for such agencies to have a discrete Welsh identity. Although a coherent policy has yet to emerge, there being some counter-examples such as Assembly adherence to a new Commission for Health Audit and Improvement in England and Wales (CHAI),[48] there is a growing trend in this direction, as will be illustrated.

It is also interesting to note the firm rejection of a so-called 'metropolitan myth', namely that Welsh local authorities – lacking in managerial and organizational skills – perform significantly less well than their English counterparts. *Per contra*, the sense of 'a commitment to public service' which serves the people of Wales well has been very much the view of the minister.[49]

The significance of this can scarcely be exaggerated. Take the 2002 Comprehensive Spending Review, which was notable not only for the massive increases in public expenditure but also for the close linkage with the reform of public services. By which is meant especially expanded arrangements for auditing by an independent commission – in England.[50] The diversity of devolution: in this instance, it is a case not of what 'Wales' will do, as of what 'Wales' will not do. In the words of Edwina Hart:

In Wales we also believe that reform is essential, but the Welsh Assembly Government is developing its own challenging and robust agenda to deliver reform. We believe that this can be achieved in many areas without introducing a plethora of inspection and audit regimes, because the relationship between the Welsh Assembly Government and those who deliver public services is closer than it is elsewhere.[51]

So also, and despite its close political and administrative interest in service delivery, the Assembly cabinet has thus far avoided the hard-edged tool of hypothecation or widespread use of specific grants, a well-known weapon in the armoury of direct controls over local government. Similarly, the Assembly may have inherited a plethora of default powers etc. from the Secretary of State for Wales, but their usage is the more notable by its absence. To the greatest extent possible, conflict or pathology is not what 'the Welsh way' is about.

Partnership Council

Let us wind the clock back. The authors of the devolution legislation rightly prioritized the issue of territorial–local government relations. So it is, with a view to encouraging cooperation – not conflict and confusion – between the two tiers of government, that the GWA mandates a formal institutional framework of collective representation: the Partnership Council.[52] In turn, this is coupled with an admonition to observe political and administrative space, in the form of a requirement of a statutory scheme setting out how the Assembly intends to sustain and promote local government in Wales. And to quote from that scheme, 'the partnership with local government will be co-ordinated by the Partnership Council but will be conducted by all parts of the Assembly and local government'.[53] Such it may said is the pressing need for effective forms of coordination and collaboration across the new hierarchical structures of multi-layered governance.

The Partnership Council, which comprises representatives of all the parties in the Assembly and from all sectors of local government, as well as from the police, fire and national parks authorities, is a unique institution in the United Kingdom. Emblematic of the concept of close dialogue, it has a broad remit:

- to give advice to the Assembly about matters affecting the exercise of any of the Assembly's functions;
- to make representations to the Assembly about any matters affecting, or of concern to, those involved in local government in Wales; and
- to give advice to those involved in local government in Wales.

The legislative design, at one and the same time prescriptive and entirely flexible in terms of working practice, strikes an appropriate balance. The next step, a statutory duty to have regard to plans and strategies of individual councils, was rightly rejected, by reason of the national character and strategic competence of the Assembly, as also the scope for formal legal conflict.[54] Speaking more generally, recognition of the functional limits of law, the inability of legislation fully to prescribe the tone and substance of the relationship between local government and the Assembly, powerfully influenced the government's approach. The Partnership Council, it could be reasonably be anticipated, would have a useful role to play in grounding the informal 'rules of the game' and conventional understandings historically so important in local government law and practice.[55]

The Partnership Council currently features the minister (in the chair), a clutch of senior AMs, and many of the leading figures in Welsh local government, including the leader of the WLGA, Sir Harry Jones. Predictably, as public occasions, the quarterly plenary meetings tend to be highly formal affairs:[56] full, frank and free exchange between (Labour) colleagues is rare. Never intended to be executive machinery, the Partnership Council is very much an instrument of joint working, and of consensus. Supported by a joint Assembly–WLGA secretariat, and loosely governed by a protocol on the handling of business,[57] the structures provide ample opportunities for informal dialogue and prior agreement, as also for networking activities. So is the closeness of Wales given tangible expression.

Official symbol of the Welsh way, the Partnership Council is also an umbrella organization, providing for, and holding to account, a burgeoning number of working groups or task forces. The story begins with the Standing Consultative Forum on Finance, which makes recommendations on local government finance, not least about the vital distributive formulae. Matters have quickly developed beyond political forms of dialogue or representation and into the sphere of administrative coordination and collaboration. Joint Assembly–local government officer groups established by the Partnership Council have ranged over such diverse topics as performance indicators and the policy and practice of public procurement, and on through the classic subject for joined-up government or coordinated action that is health and well-being.[58]

The potential is well illustrated by one particular sub-group operating in the field of education. The 'Narrowing the Gap' task force has been given the sensitive issue to address of variations in schools' performance, with a view to the dissemination of good practice.[59] A notable feature is the range of representation, which includes the quangos and a catalogue of professional interests. All at one with a drive to build up policy capacity and networks inside the territory, the task force also serves to highlight the flexibility of the structures and processes now developing under the aegis of the Partnership Council.

The emergent machinery can be seen in terms of a search for alignment of the various policy agendas of the different sets of collective interests. On the one hand, local government enjoys privileged access: opportunities to influence territorial policy at the developmental stage, which as every student of government knows is vital. On the other hand, and not least by inculcating a sense of shared ownership, the devolved administration can seek not only to minimize conflict but also to engender a broader vision. Unexciting it may appear, but this is devolution in action.

The Partnership Council obviously is no sure-fire machinery: and thankfully so, in the interests of a vibrant Welsh democracy. Conflict being inherent across governmental systems of divided competencies, the challenge is not to eradicate it, but to minimize and manage it. And a Welsh Assembly Government concerned 'to make a difference' that did not ruffle a few feathers in local government would hardly be worthy of the name! Instructive in this regard is the process of preparing the Wales Spatial Plan. An innovative and very considerable mapping exercise, the plan is designed to help determine the areas of priority for development, including through the prism of the different regions of Wales.[60] For its part, the WLGA has voiced major concerns in the name of a 'bottom-up' approach, that is for firmer grounding of this all-Wales perspective in the councils' own unitary plans.[61] Simply put, there has been ample scope for genuine disagreement, and for a constitutional tug of war, and thence for an accommodation of interests.

Nor should the Partnership Council be considered in isolation. There are instructive parallels with the institutional development in central–territorial relations, not least in terms of specially designed formal machinery as 'the tip of the iceberg', and the firm grounding of many processes at the administrative level, mostly beyond the ken of politicians.[62]

The various linkages now emerging under the rubric of the Partnership Council further represent a widening and deepening of the forms of central–local government relations as these previously existed in Wales. It is not that joint task forces are new, rather that they are proliferating. The development can be seen at one level as a function of the increased search for Welsh policy alternatives, and at another level as seeking to make good the perceived policy development deficit through the pooling of expertise. The pattern of institutional growth is thus once again a significant feature in the story of devolution. In short, serving as a chief reference point in the tangled web of territorial/local government relations, the machinery of the Partnership Council stands for a continuing internal or Welsh constitutional dynamic.

Policy agreements

Turning to the choice of policy instruments, the Welsh Assembly Government has adopted policy agreements as 'the key vehicle for the development of a

more strategic relationship with local government'.[63] Certainly these arrangements have been much hyped; most notably by Edwina Hart as 'an
innovation unique to Wales and a completely new way of improving the
quality of people's lives'.[64] A significant variation on a contemporary theme in
public administration, one that displays some considerable potential in local
conditions, is a more sober assessment. As the nomenclature suggests, we are
back here in the realm of pseudo-contract or non-legally binding contract-
type arrangements, across the tiers of government.[65]

Notably, these arrangements were originally conceived in the WLGA,
before being fleshed out under the auspices of the Partnership Council.
Typically, in this perspective, a key attribute of the policy instrument is the
preservation of local discretion or preference over more intrusive regulatory techniques. By which is meant the aspiration that if the devolved
administration and local government 'can together have trust' in the
effectiveness of an agreement on target outputs, then the Assembly's role in
'prescribing expenditures' through specific grants and hypothecations and
'monitoring processes' through prescribed planning procedures 'could
diminish'.[66]

To the recurrent concept of partnership may now be added that other great
theme of multi-layered governance: coordination. Reference is here being
made to an important bridging role for policy agreements or link between the
local focus of community plans and the national focus of Assembly strategies,
with a view to securing the coherence of priorities. Once again, in the words
of the WLGA, such arrangements 'will reflect the shared aims and objectives
of local government and the Assembly'.[67]

There is also the sense of reworking the fashionable nostrums of New
Public Management. In the guise, that is, of novel or refashioned techniques
of control and accountability, typically as in the case of performance
indicators geared to outputs not inputs, and functioning in part to vindicate
the relevant administrative values of economy, efficiency and effectiveness
('keep it lean and purposeful').[68] How then to avoid the danger, which is
increasingly familiar in an 'audit society', of 'drowning by numbers'?[69] On the
one hand, and so typical of NPM, the policy agreements are framed in terms
of 'contractual' specifications or targets, which in turn provide the basis for
'benchmarking' or comparisons across the sector. On the other hand, 'the
Welsh way', the arrangements may be seen as less prescriptive in character, a
product of both collective and individual negotiations with the local
authorities. Whereas certain ends are specified, it is made a cardinal principle
that councils will the means.

The Welsh Assembly Government has made policy agreements with each
and every principal local authority. Briefly, the instrument consists of two
parts – the written agreement and the schedule of targets or indicators against
which the council's performance falls to be measured.[70] The written agree-

ment is part standard form, part council-specific. In promoting the coupling of national and local priorities, much is made of the three strategic themes of sustainable development, equal opportunities and tackling social disadvantage. The targets are set on the basis of achieving 'a real improvement over existing levels of attainment'. The carrot is tangible if not munificent: a standard share of a £10 million performance incentive grant for making the agreement, a full share of £30 million for achieving the targets. Conceptually speaking, however, this is the 'informal' contract-type arrangement writ large – payment by results.

The $64,000 question is the choice of performance parameters. Thus far, the emphasis has been very much on education and social services: from qualification achievements to improvement in care plans, and on through increased support in the home for vulnerable groups. Other, technically more complex, matters, for example agreed objectives to help build a better, stronger economy, have been avoided. And much ink has been spilt here on the diversity of Wales, specifically the idea that in different local authorities there will be 'different abilities to meet varying targets'.[71]

Policy agreements, it would appear, are here to stay. Covering the three years to April 2004, the first round of policy agreements is officially designated ' "a point of entry" to establish a new way of working'.[72] The Welsh version of pseudo-contract has to this effect considerable potential as an encouragement for partnership working not only between territorial and local government but also between local councils and public and private interests in the context of community planning. After all, many targets cannot be delivered by a council acting alone, but require the active cooperation of many other organizations and groups.

A wider range of targets is envisaged. Broader 'quality of life' indicators are an obvious way forward, not least given a shared commitment in Wales to tackling the many local problems of socio-economic deprivation. Turning the argument round, there is a risk of overload – a multiplicity of targets which serves to over-constrain local choice, even to the extent of skewing the patterns of service provision. Retaining a targeted approach to targets will require considerable self-discipline on the part of the Assembly cabinet, not least one which proclaims 'check against delivery'.

3. GOING ON: GOOD INTENTIONS

The impact of devolution on local government in Wales now falls to be considered in the light of the Welsh Assembly Government's policy statement, *Freedom and Responsibility in Local Government*, published in March 2002. Officially described as a 'milestone document', it too is replete with good intentions:

The aim of the Welsh Assembly Government is to create an environment in which local government will have the freedom and support to work towards the best local solutions, while having agreed national priorities to provide strategic direction. This requires a deliberate effort to create a clear, coherent policy framework which makes government simpler and removes unnecessary bureaucracy.[73]

The fact of the policy statement is itself significant in terms of an autochthonous constitutional development or process of maturation of the new Welsh polity. As the first document in which the coalition government 'set out fully its policies . . . and its vision for the future of local government', it is emblematic of the drive towards bolder and more wide-ranging forms of policy development at the territorial level. The document is also officially described as the Welsh equivalent to a central government White Paper. 'Made in Wales – in the light of England': the Assembly cabinet had thus determined on a discrete approach, once again selecting items from policy proposals made by the Department of Local Government, Transport and the Regions.[74] How, it may be asked, can this be squared with the current constitutional model of executive devolution?

Certain proposals serve to convey the general flavour. For instance, under the rubric of 'community leadership by local government', the devolved administration has laid great store by the development of community strategies. Once again, this is part of the reform agenda in the Local Government Act 2000, whereby county councils in Wales are required to work with others to prepare a strategy for promoting the economic, social and environmental well-being of their areas, and on which the Assembly government has issued guidance.[75] In the words of *Freedom and Responsibility*, 'this model of partnership working is increasingly going to become the norm for local government'.[76]

Then there is information and communication technology (ICT), a hobbyhorse of devolved administration in Wales. So much is made in *Freedom and Responsibility* of so-called 'e-government', using ICT 'to fundamentally change and improve the way public services are delivered and managed'. Notably, this builds on joint work undertaken in the Partnership Council, whereby the local authorities are now encouraged in the style of New Public Management to address targets and such issues as risk assessment in annual 'implementing Electronic Government' statements. For its part, the Welsh Assembly Government is committed to providing additional capital resources. This in turn must be seen as one element in an overarching strategy for delivering the social and economic benefits of the information age in Wales, the Assembly government's *Cymru Ar-lein*.[77]

Local government finance is obviously a crucial issue for the councils and much of *Freedom and Responsibility* is devoted to this aspect. Once again, the aim is to simplify some aspects of what is an extraordinarily complicated system, and 'to give local authorities as much freedom as possible to manage their own resources'. At the same time, and neatly illustrating the never-ending tension between the competing demands of service uniformity and local diversity in this sphere, it is solemnly declared: 'however, there are balances to be struck. There needs to be a balance between the necessary delivery of national priorities and the need for local freedom and respon-sibility.' In the event, pride of place goes to a new revenue formula for distributing funds to local government that the Assembly government has introduced, so achieving a greater measure of fairness and rationality in the system – one which in the official jargon 'better reflects both actual spend and actual need'.[78] Meanwhile – 'cherry-picking' – the specific commitments notably include a more cautious approach to the kind of 'Private Finance Initiative' (PFI) favoured in Whitehall, and a substantial overhaul of the funding arrangements for council housing that is partly the consequence of a new prudential borrowing system for local government developed centrally.[79] As to the future, the devolved administration seeks to ram home the message: 'We will continue to work in partnership with local government to deliver these reforms and build upon the existing, successful and increasingly mature relationship between the National Assembly and local government in Wales.'[80]

All the more significant in light of the discussion is the Wales Programme for Improvement. Developed jointly with the WLGA using the machinery of the Partnership Council, this is officially designed to 'give a fresh impetus to the continuous improvement of local public services in Wales'.[81] At one and the same time, it reflects the changing UK fashions in the regulation of local government, and represents a distinctive Welsh 'spin' inside the constraints of an England and Wales policy framework.

The programme is thus a novel approach – developed in the light of experience – to implementing the so-called 'best-value' legislation, which in turn replaced the more rigid framework of compulsory competitive tendering that grew up in the 1980s and 1990s under the Conservatives. The reference is to the Local Government Act 1999, which established a more flexible require-ment on councils to achieve continuous improvement by reviewing their operations and pursuing the quest for increased efficiency, economy and effectiveness. Coupled, that is, with new monitoring and supervisory powers for the National Assembly and – operating on an England and Wales basis – the Audit Commission. In the event, the Welsh programme stands for an especially heavy emphasis on self-improvement or internal 'ownership' of the policy, via such instruments as corporate or 'whole authority' analysis and regulatory and improvement plans. A contrast is thereby drawn in *Freedom and Responsibility* with the initial approach to implementing 'best value' inside the England and Wales paradigm: 'elected members felt this was something being done to, rather than by, their authorities, with too little return for the effort involved'.

A pure form of self-regulation, it is not. Independent auditors and inspectors such as the local authority external auditors and such specialist bodies as the Social Services Inspectorate Wales (SSIW) will contribute to the process, for example in the difficult areas of risk assessment. A duty to report publicly on such matters as future improvements, as well as on matters of legality and regularity, is secured under a variety of legal provisions. A major element, however, is retrenchment in the role of the Audit Commission in Wales. Audits based on the 'best-value' process are thus replaced by annual health checks conducted by the councils themselves.

To anticipate the argument in chapter 11, the Audit Commission has been seen – especially in Welsh local government circles – as powerful machinery serving the central – and Anglocentric – policy agenda. Perhaps this is not surprising, since the commission has commonly been less than flattering about Welsh performance.[82] More particularly, the agency wears the imprint of a more conflictual approach in territorial–local government relations than the 'Welsh way' would suggest.

It is, however, a bold minister who renounces the use of hard-edged policy instruments. A little sabre-rattling is also in order:

> The Welsh Programme for Improvement is in effect a 'contract' between the Welsh Assembly Government and Welsh local government. Local authorities will have both greater freedom and greater responsibility to lead and manage improvements in public services within this broad framework. The Welsh Assembly Government has confidence in local government's ability to respond to this approach. At the same time, should any authority appear to be failing to meet its legal duties, the Welsh Assembly Government has strong and wide-ranging powers to take action to ensure that services to the public are safeguarded. The Welsh Assembly Government would not hesitate to do so in such circumstances.[83]

Coda

Unlike Excalibur, matters are not set in stone. There remains a potential for the new elected tier of government to crowd Welsh policy space and reduce local discretion, and this may be apt to surface in different conditions. Turning the argument round, the highly collaborative approach to territorial–local government relations in the first few years can in part be explained by local fears of an overweening Assembly, and the concern of the infant body to assuage them.

One test will be the scale of the development of Welsh 'regional' structures and processes at the behest of the Assembly government. The rationale of joint and collaborative forms of working across and above local government areas may be self-evident when addressing such matters as the development of transport systems or the regional impact of steel closures (the 'Five Counties Regeneration Framework'[84]). But there is also the capacity for a creeping institutionalization, or a blurring of local responsibilities in favour most obviously of Assembly-dominated public bodies. The WLGA has made precisely this point in evidence to the Assembly subject committee,[85] and it has clearly touched a nerve. The Welsh Assembly Government, it is solemnly stated, 'will strengthen procedures' to ensure that its emerging strategic policies and approaches 'recognise the role of local authorities as the local democratic bodies with extensive knowledge and understanding of their areas'.[86]

It is important to remember the benign party political conditions in which the new modalities of intra-territorial relations have been operating: broad Labour Party hegemony. There is a conscious echo here of the Assembly's relations with central government, which will be seen in chapter 11 to exhibit many of the same attributes of confidence and trust. Yet even the strong hold of Welsh Labour cannot be assumed for ever and a day (a topic raised in the next section). Again this has been 'the happy time', whereby the new processes of territorial–local government relations in Wales have also been greased with much UK government largess.

Let us hope that 'the Welsh way' serves. A poor performance on the part of the local authorities will inevitably lead to countervailing pressures for increased regulation. Notably, in the view of Edwina Hart, 'the Welsh Assembly Government . . . needs a continued focus on results, for that is what matters'.[87]

4. ACID TEST: ELECTORAL REFORM

Because it casts a long shadow, one development demands special attention. The Commission on Local Government Electoral Arrangements in Wales, an independent advisory body chaired by Professor Eric Sunderland, was asked to consider how existing arrangements 'can be made more effective in helping to bring about councils which are clearly representative of and accountable to their residents'.[88] The suitably bland official language cannot disguise the acute political sensitivities.

The commission was a product of the Partnership Agreement in the Assembly. A chief concession for the Liberal Democrats, it is also one in which the art of political compromise is strongly etched. Whereas the review was specifically to consider electoral systems that 'would achieve greater proportionality in the representation of political parties' – in contrast that is to the current system in Welsh local government of 'first past the post' – there was no clear guarantee of acceptance. In the terms of the agreement, 'we will press

the UK Government to bring forward Assembly sponsored legislation to
implement the Assembly's conclusions from the review'.[89] In the event,
consistent with postponing the day of reckoning, the commission has
proceeded at a leisurely pace. But proceeded it has, leading in July 2002 to a
full and challenging set of recommendations.

A key starting-point is the narrow social base of much local government
representation in Wales. 'Regardless of political affiliation, the typical county
and county borough councillor in Wales is white, male, older than the average
of the population and retired.'[90] First, fewer than 20 per cent of Welsh
councillors are women, and 'unlike other parts of the United Kingdom, there
is no sign of this proportion increasing'. Secondly, less than 1 per cent of
councillors in Wales are from an ethnic minority background, a point which,
given the all-white complexion of the Assembly, is worthy of particular note.
The evidence of systematic exclusion of ethnic minority peoples from the
political life of Wales is compelling.

Then there is the wide disparity between the votes cast and seats won in
certain (typically Labour-dominated) local authorities. At first sight, it is the
familiar controversy over 'first past the post' (FPTP): on the one hand, the
direct linkage or accountability of the member to the electors (as a keystone of
local democracy), and on the other hand, the tendency to produce disproportionate outcomes. There is, however, an additional twist in the case of
Welsh local government, the use in roughly half of the elections of multi-
member divisions. As the commission observes, this compounds the tendency
of FPTP to disproportionality. 'In multi-member divisions where party voting
is strong and also disciplined, the largest party in the division often gains a
considerable advantage.'[91] At the same time, the commission has had especially to keep in mind a tradition in some (rural) parts of Wales of having
independent councillors. Viewed in this light, 'greater proportionality in the
representation of political parties' is emphatically not the whole story. A
different but related point, Wales has had a comparatively high level of
uncontested elections, such that, in the words of the commission, substantial
numbers of electors are 'unable to make use of their right to vote for their
local members'.[92] Speaking more generally, and so typical of our age, low
turnout is a major phenomenon. The commission could scarcely ignore the
evidence of apathy and disenchantment, of a lack of engagement putting in
issue the health of (local) democracy.

There is no magic solution. In the event, many worthy proposals were
made, ranging from greater publicity for council activities to support for
initiatives to improve councillors' terms and conditions, and on through
information campaigns, notably in the context of devolution to explain 'which
tier of authority is responsible for which public services in Wales'.[93] Especially
striking was a proposal to lower the age of entitlement to vote in local
government elections to sixteen: a measure the commission would happily

see applied to Assembly elections. In the event, following on a wide consultation exercise, these various recommendations have been taken up with considerable enthusiasm.[94]

Predictably, however, the commission was divided on the fundamental question of the choice of electoral system. Seven of the nine members opted for a system of proportional representation in the form of the Single Transferable Vote (STV). Preference ranking, redistribution and specified quota of votes: the electoral divisions it was recommended should normally each return between three and five members. With an eye to the future, it is worth underlining the qualitative difference between STV and the counter-balancing arrangement currently used for Assembly elections, the Additional Member System (AMS).[95]

Improving representation and representativeness:[96] it is a convincing case. As the majority opinion noted, STV would allow voters to secure effective representation on each local authority of the diversity of local opinion, and a proper reflection in its composition of the diversity of local people. In conjunction, that is, with maintaining constituency-based representation for local people, offering the prospect of higher turnouts, and enabling independent candidates to continue to have a reasonable chance of success. But further – checks and balances – the link was correctly made with the 'modernization agenda' for local government in Wales. 'The new executive arrangements . . . envisage a strong scrutiny role for non-executive councillors. We believe that scrutiny of the executive may be less effective if there are only a few opposition members on councils to lead or serve on scrutiny committees.'[97]

Notably the view of the Conservative and Labour representatives on the commission, the minority opinion favoured retaining 'first past the post', while doing away with the multi-member electoral divisions. A central plank in the reasoning is worth recording for posterity. 'Any change to the voting system should carry majority support or at least a consensus from those that deliver local government in Wales. This has not been forthcoming.'[98] The councillors' veto: such, it may be said, is the power of vested interest.

In the little world of Welsh politics the stakes are enormous. In the ever-so delicate words of the minister, 'the one recommendation on which there remains no consensus is that regarding the creation of multi-member wards and the election of councillors through a single transferable vote.'[99] Little movement is likely here in the political conditions of Labour Party hegemony.

The issue, however, will not go away. In terms of the autochthonous constitutional development, it goes to the heart of the question of the quality of post-devolutionary democracy in Wales.[100] Put simply, claims by Assembly Members to inhabit and promote a newly textured and progressive polity appear hollow in the face of this unreformed electoral system, not least given the scale of territorial expenditure that is involved in local service delivery.[101]

CONCLUSION – WELSH MULTI-LAYERED GOVERNANCE

Fundamental to the workings of devolution is the state of relations with the other tiers of government. Crafting and operation are required of a whole series of arrangements: in an era of multi-layered governance, at local, central and supranational levels. In the case of Wales, the task has been rightly recognized as all the more important inside the territory, in view of the historical legacy of fragmentation and limited development of a 'national' polity.

If the discussion in this chapter has conveyed a sense of ambiguity and complexity, then it has the considerable merit of accuracy. How could it be otherwise, given the blending of local and territorial perspectives in the face of a very novel form of constitutional arrangement? Expressed slightly differently, it is a mistake to see the rise of territorial government in terms of a zero-sum game at the expense of the local tier of administration.[102] Mixtures of law and administration, which notably include more interdependence across state structures and cooperative systems of negotiation and policy alignment, or of individual and collective forms of partnership working especially with local government, form a key ingredient of the internal Welsh constitutional development post-devolution.

A genuine attempt to preserve and facilitate local discretion, it has been argued, is all the more striking in view of the pressures on political and insti-tutional space that are engendered by the scheme of executive devolution. Juridification, in the broad sense of a move to rule-bound techniques and formal systems of evaluation, has seen its progress checked in Wales. This, it is important to say, is not to hark back to some 'golden age' of local govern-ment. Large parts of the pre-existing regulatory framework remain in place (and may be dusted down). Alternative so-called 'delivery levers' – finance, non-statutory guidance etc. – can be pressed. It is the case, however, that the official notion of 'a trust society' has gained considerable ground in the new territorial polity, by virtue of a mix of local political and administrative imperatives, as mediated through a particular democratic culture in the closeness of Wales.

In this chapter, the value of a 'bottom-up' approach to the story of devolution, one that looks to interior relations and developments, is amply shown. Once again, it is seen to be the autochthonous elements that are so significant in Wales in the context of national devolution. The 'Welsh way': who would have dreamt it?

The Closeness of Wales (II)

There is a greater intensity and proximity politically driven throughout the relevant structures associated with the Assembly.

Jon Shortridge, Permanent Secretary[1]

The rapid if sometimes painful emergence of a governmental apparatus in miniature has been presented as a central theme of this book. To this effect, the trappings of Welsh administrative machinery are increasingly in evidence – alongside the increasingly forceful entity that is the Welsh Assembly Government.

Whereas the Welsh approach to local government is naturally coloured by experience of stringent policies under the Conservatives, the treatment of the quangos post-devolution has special resonance for precisely the opposite reason, namely what was less than lovingly described as their 'onward march' under the Conservatives.[2] Yet in their suitably grand guise of Assembly Sponsored Public Bodies (ASPBs), the question arises not so much of abolition as of closer and more effective forms of democratic oversight or extended accountability.

One way in which the contemporary devolutionary development differs from the model of 1978 concerns the general trend in UK administrative law in the intervening period of 'agencification'.[3] Quangos, or (statutory) bodies operating at arm's length or outside the line of hierarchical control by ministers, are hardly novel. But they have taken on a whole new lease of life, for example as an instrument of managerial reordering under the influence of the New Public Management, or as regulatory agencies designed to monitor and represent the public interest while suggesting a new autonomy from central government. Again, the emergence in (Western) Europe of 'the regulatory state' is an increasingly familiar phenomenon, associated not only with wide-scale privatization but also – in a dynamic, technological age – of the sense of mismatch between pre-existing institutional capacities and the growing complexity of policy problems, such as reducing environmental pollution.[4] From these broad currents little Wales can hardly be exempt. 'Bonfire of the quangos': dream on!

The question of relations between such agencies, not least the many powerful ones operating on an England and Wales or UK basis, and the

devolved administration, is brought sharply into focus. As the Permanent
Secretary has indicated, in the closeness of Wales 'arm's length' may not be
very far. In fact, powerful cross-currents will be seen operating: by reason, on
the one hand, of the sheer range or diversity of these bodies; and, on the other
hand, of divergent pressures in national devolution for the devolved
administration to flex its muscles, and for territorial institutional growth.

In particular, there is that great Welsh passion: the National Health Service.
'NHS Wales' is not a new label but it stands today for an increasingly
distinctive set of territorial arrangements as part of a more diverse
architecture ('the UK's national health services'). Constitutionally speaking,
this trend – which will be seen to involve a major bout of restructuring –
is especially noteworthy because of the high political salience. A chief field
of devolved functions, public health is both a major test bed of 'made
in Wales' policies and a potential hotbed for tensions with central government.

The general institutional growth, it is also important to say, ranges beyond
the quangos as familiarly conceived, to incorporate – for example in the guise
of the new Children's Commissioner for Wales – distinctive machinery for the
redress of grievance.

A comparative perspective is also useful here. Part of a process of
'reinventing government', there is seen to be a growth industry of bureaucratic regulation in the contemporary period, by which is meant the
regulation of government bodies by other government bodies.[5] Audit and inspection, ombudsman and regulatory agency, this too incorporates considerable parts of the machinery of administrative law. So also, to pick up on the
discussion in the previous chapter, much is heard of the so-called 'audit
society', in the sense of the primacy of the three functional values of economy,
efficiency and effectiveness.[6] And in particular of the hard-edged evaluative
techniques associated with value-for-money audit, which in turn sits comfortably with the general phenomenon of juridification. Performance indicators
and benchmarking, targets and league tables: it is all so familiar, including in
such diverse fields (of devolved powers) as education and the environment.
At the same time, the way in which audit shapes the activities that it controls
in significant ways, while tending (like formal legal reasoning!) to insinuate
itself under the guise of neutrality, is increasingly highlighted.

Reverting to Wales, the style and substance of bureaucratic regulation in the
light of national devolution, and further of a preference for partnership
working with local government, was raised as an issue as part of the so-called
'Welsh way'. It is appropriate in this chapter to invert the focus, and to
consider in this context the role and workings of the agencies themselves.
Reworked processes of accountability reflecting local policy priorities; a
moulding of relevant powers and responsibilities in the shadow of the
Assembly; the potential for a lighter touch or more collaborative methods of

improvement: once again, it all bears on the quality of interior relations in the new model Wales.

1. GOING ON: THE CASE OF THE QUANGOS

The map of public bodies in Wales is exceedingly complicated. Perhaps this is not surprising: quangos etc. come in all shapes and sizes, across the range of governmental activities. So very 'British': the development has been almost determinedly pragmatic and piecemeal, including under the rubric of 'administrative devolution'. Nor is the contemporary push for more horizontal forms of networking under the rubric of 'governance' a recipe for simplicity! Yet the special complicating factor is once again the highly variable treatment for historical reasons of 'Wales' as an organizing concept.

In this respect, national devolution is bound to have a knock-on effect. Much is already heard in official circles of 'rebadging': what I will call – in suitably provocative fashion – 'Welshifying'. The concept, however, covers a wide range of institutional responses: from the proverbial change of nameplate all the way to the creation of a Wales-only agency in place of the UK, GB or – by far the most likely – England and Wales paradigm ('decoupling'). Alternatively, there may be enhanced arrangements for territorial representation inside the larger body – 'voices for Wales' – or greater operational autonomy for the local office, perhaps buttressed by lines of reporting to the Assembly, perhaps not. Driven by an enhanced sense of the idea of Wales, the process further underscores the myriad knock-on effects of the 'devolution settlement' – at the micro-level.[7]

A sense of proportion is vital. As mediated by many practical considerations, and operating either in whole or in part, such a process of patrialization will by its very nature be both patchy and gradual. Economies of scale and access to specialist resources, 'cross-border issues' and institutional leverage: there will obviously be many good reasons why post-devolution a separate territorial body or agency is not established.[8] A different but related point: institutional choices of this kind are apt to become more politicized with the advent of the Assembly. Any nationalist party worth its salt will regularly press the case for 'decoupling' – Plaid Cymru has not disappointed!

'Partnership with unelected bodies in Wales (quangos)': thus spoke the devolution White Paper. Here as elsewhere, however, the broad concept cannot disguise the multiplicity of arrangements. To put this in perspective, the Secretary of State for Wales was said to be responsible for over eighty public bodies. They ranged from executive bodies reporting solely to him (19) to health authorities and NHS trusts (no fewer than 36), and on through advisory bodies (19), both statutory and non-statutory, to a clutch of tribunals funded by the Welsh Office (7).[9] And turning the argument round, what it may be asked of 'partnership working' with all those public bodies that are both 'in' Wales and elsewhere? Self-evidently, relationships with the devolved administration are apt to be qualitatively different here – which in turn underscores the issue of more or less 'Welshifying'.

In light of the previous discussion, it is important to stress the contrast with local government. 'Constitutional resources': by definition, even the most powerful quangos lack the democratic mandate or political rooting which the councils can pray in aid in their dealings with the devolved administration. Nor, of course, is there anything equivalent to the powerful machinery of collective representation and collaborative working that is the WLGA. Put simply, in the case of the ASPBs the conditions are ripe for a strongly patriarchal form of 'partnership working', even in truth for a relationship of 'principal and agent'. And the more so, it may be said, given the initial thrust in Welsh devolution against the perceived 'democratic deficit' as constituted by the quangos, and latterly the more assertive stance of a Welsh Assembly Government greatly concerned with standards of service provision.

As creatures of statute, the main Welsh agencies have security of tenure, in the sense that Westminster legislation would be required for their abolition.[10] Looking forward, however, a notable feature is the way in which the grant of very extensive legislative powers to remodel public bodies in Wales has now become administratively entrenched in the organic policy and practice of the devolution settlement. Whitehall has to this extent effectively ceded legal 'ownership' of Welsh interior relations to the Assembly, a singular example of what I called the model of 'quasi-legislative devolution'. In the words of the relevant devolution guidance note: 'new public bodies which fall solely under the Assembly's control should normally be subject' to its Henry VIII clause powers to amend or repeal relevant primary legislation.[11]

Accountability is another concept that needs unpacking here.[12] The distinction is usefully drawn between political accountability, as in the way devolved government produces a new set of politicians more accountable to the electorate, and organizational accountability, for present purposes the accountability of public-sector organizations in Wales to those politicians post-devolution.[13] The extent to which the one fosters the other is of the essence of the local constitutional development. Again, organizational accountability consists of many forms. Reflecting the trajectory of constitution-building in Wales, it is particularly important to distinguish the lines of accountability to the 'executive branch' – the Welsh Assembly Government – and the more general exercise of scrutiny and influence by the Assembly *qua* Assembly including via the all-party subject committees. To anticipate the argument, it is chiefly through the lines of reporting, which are both considerably enhanced and typically in 'the closeness of Wales' do not involve a recourse to formal law, that the Assembly cabinet has pressed its democratic claim to be the dominant partner here.

Welsh agencification

Table 18 below refers to the inner core: by which is meant the key ASPBs with executive functions. With the single exception of Environment Agency Wales, all of them are discrete Welsh public bodies, owing their official allegiance to the Assembly. In addition to the lines of accountability via the individual subject areas or ministerial portfolios, matters affecting ASPBs collectively and in general have been the responsibility of the Minister for Finance.

Table 18: Core Assembly-sponsored Public Bodies – January 2002

Ministerial Portfolio	ASPBs
(I) Culture, Sports and the Welsh Language (5)	Arts Council of Wales National Library of Wales National Museums and Galleries of Wales Sports Council of Wales Welsh Language Board
(II) Economic Development (2)	Welsh Development Agency Wales Tourist Board
(III) Education and Life-Long Learning (3)	Higher Education Funding Council for Wales (HEFCW)* National Council for Education and Training in Wales* Qualification, Curriculum and Assessment Authority for Wales (QCAAW)
(IV) Environment (2)	Countryside Council for Wales Environment Agency Wales
(V) Health and Social Services (1)	Welsh National Board for Nursing, Midwifery and Health Visiting**
(VI) Rural Development (1)	Forestry Commission (including Forestry Enterprise)

*Constituent parts of Education and Learning Wales (ELWa).
**Now abolished, in favour of Health Professions Wales.

The list conveys a strong sense of continuity. Most of the agencies pre-date the Assembly, some by many years. There are also significant elements of growth and adaptation among this species of Welsh governmental machinery. For example, Environment Agency Wales is now added to the list, while the arrival on the scene of Health Professions Wales represents an expanded regulatory remit. The National Council (ELWa) will be seen to be another very significant development post-devolution.

The clutch of agencies in the cultural sphere is significant. A reflection, it may be said, of a historic sense of the distinctiveness of Wales, as also, more prosaically, of the general sense of a 'no-go' area for politicians. In the context of devolution, agencies in the economic field take on a special prominence. At the same time, it is important to avoid too much pigeonholing. The facility for relevant agencies to band together, either in tackling particular issues like major redundancies, or under the banner of a cross-cutting theme such as sustainable development, is one of the advantages of the closeness of Wales.

Speaking more generally, the attributes of specialist and multifaceted agencies operating at arm's length from government are shown to advantage here. Independent and professional judgement is the *raison d'être* of QCAAW. Expertise and an embedded institutional capacity to perform advocacy and networking functions is essential in the case of the Welsh Language Board. Advisory and educational roles, as also an active engagement in rural communities: the Countryside Council itself represents a substantial commitment to sustaining the natural beauty and wildlife of Wales.

From quangocide to quinquennial reviews

It is fortunate then that a sense of realism has prevailed inside the Assembly. The populist idea of 'a bonfire of the quangos', so beguiling in the last days of the Conservatives' rule in Wales, has thus fallen victim to a measured process of review and reform. And this in turn reflects and reinforces the twin aspects of organizational accountability that can now be seen at the heart of Assembly/ASPB relations: expanded democratic oversight intertwined with strategic direction or the leadership role of the Welsh Assembly Government. According to Edwina Hart:

> Our policy is that, subject to the legal frameworks concerned, quangos should only be retained where they are the most appropriate and cost-effective means of carrying out the functions concerned. We have an open mind as to what the right arrangements should be in each case. Organisational options should be assessed on their merits, not according to dogma. Where these point to a sponsored body or an agency as the right solution, the requirement must be to ensure that these bodies are properly accountable to the Assembly and the public. Public accountability is the key area. We must also ensure that the bodies make good use of the funds that they receive, are conducting their business in line with the Assembly's values and principles . . . and are contributing, as appropriate, to the Assembly's vision of Wales. The Assembly must feel confident that it has effective relationships in place which recognise the particular circumstances of each body

and which strengthen the team Wales approach, underpinning the Assembly's strategy.[14]

In fact, as far as general matters of accountability are concerned, the devolved administration has here been following the path carefully sign-posted by the official architects of the devolutionary scheme. In the case of the quangos, oversight was further embedded in the design of the scheme. For example, as well as powers to issue directions and guidance, the Assembly inherited from the Secretary of State numerous powers of appointment and nomination. In the event, and tied to monitoring by the (UK) Commissioner on Public Appointments with a view to bolstering public confidence, a policy of open, fair and equal competition has been vigorously asserted.[15] So far have we travelled from the pre-devolutionary days of close ministerial patronage inside the Welsh Office.

Of course not everything could be anticipated. A variation on a theme, extensive powers to summon witnesses and examine documents were designed to buttress in Westminster Select Committee style the exercise of scrutiny functions.[16] As was noted, however, the performance of the subject committees in this regard has been distinctly patchy.[17] A case, it may now be said, of too much 'sweethearting' and of insufficient forensic analysis in 'the closeness of Wales'. Substance, not shadow, in terms of extended account-ability is what is wanted here.

In contrast, the Assembly's Audit Committee has once again lived up to expectations. Examination of the economy, efficiency and effectiveness with which the ASPBs use their resources has quickly become a staple in the diet of Assembly business.[18] Being 'closer to home', this once again represents a more rigorous form of financial scrutiny than was achievable under the previous central government system, including in the form of detailed investigations into alleged irregularities at the prompting of Assembly Members. Thus far anyway the Audit Committee has been 'satisfied that the financial control environment in the Assembly and its related public bodies is good'.[19]

Arrangements also touch on the complexities of the territorial delimitation of competence. The Assembly's powers of examination are directed – in impeccable constitutional logic – to those bodies for which the Assembly is responsible,[20] which means in practice the WDA but not the Health and Safety Executive and utilities regulators. The Assembly may have to 'invite' agencies with a broad geographical remit to give evidence on their operations inside the territory. Commonly there will be sufficient mutuality of interest, but on other occasions the lack of legal powers could prove a real hindrance. This is a salutary reminder both of the need for good liaison with the UK Parliament and of the jurisdictional divisions in devolution as highlighted in a Wales of 'bits and pieces'.

All at one with the internal constitutional trajectory of cabinet government, it is ministers who have increasingly made the running. And in typically robust fashion, Edwina Hart has once again led the charge:

> The Assembly is a new body that needs to stamp its authority on these bodies because we are the elected representatives . . . We were elected to the Assembly to deal with the democratic deficit . . . The key is the democratic accountability of these bodies. We need to know what they are doing, what their outputs are – we will decide what those outputs are . . . We need to ensure that they are following our agenda.[21]

It is not so much a case of 'corralling the quangos',[22] as if they were some kind of wild beast, as of harnessing them in the service of the new model Wales. The very fact of many more ministers clearly makes a difference here, as compared with the strongly hierarchical but institutionally more limited Welsh Office. But further, the Assembly cabinet is seen making creative use of the various levers available to it: from finance and soft law instruments to the exercise of moral authority through consensus building and the democratic mandate. The development then is far more profound than local tittle-tattle would suggest.[23] It might even be termed 'the smack of firm government'.

At the heart of the process of reform is a system of quinquennial reviews of each and every ASPB. At first glance, this is not unlike the standard type of financial management and performance review that used to happen under the Welsh Office. The relevant guidelines also have a family resemblance to revised Cabinet Office guidelines for executive bodies sponsored by Whitehall departments.[24] However, both the process and the content have been tailored to local conditions, better to reflect the establishment of the Assembly, the interplay of ministers and committees, and in particular – in Edwina Hart's words – 'the need for a strategic approach'. Expressed slightly differently, the demand for organizational accountability post-devolution is writ large here, both in terms of the quest for continuous improvement and of strengthened relations under the tutelage of the devolved administration.

To explicate, there has been a significant acceleration of the programme. Ministers commission the reviews – from outside experts – in consultation with the relevant subject committee. The committee is also consulted on the findings at various stages, before ministers make a final decision on the recommendations. The reviews are open and designed to be inclusive, such that the views of 'stakeholders' are actively sought. 'A successful review requires a partnership approach.'[25] Debate in plenary is the icing on the cake.

It is the heavy emphasis on issues of 'strategic effectiveness' that is so significant in terms of the relationship with ministers. 'What progress has been made with any action plan, targets or objectives' established by the Assembly? 'Is there a need for the connections to be strengthened?' 'To what extent do the ASPB's policies and actions reflect the Assembly's principles and statutory schemes?' The interrogatory nature of the formal quinquennial review, now underwritten by a transparent process, is an excellent source of ministerial control and influence.

Enough has been said to convey the general flavour. Turning to the individual ASPBs, a huge tome could be written, such is the detail of the multiplicity of arrangements; better then to have regard to the three Welsh 'E's – the economy, education and the environment – for some major illustrations.

'It's the economy, stupid': devolution and the WDA

The place of economic considerations as a main driver of – and justification for – the devolutionary development is by now a familiar theme of this volume.[26] So also, a basic fact of constitutional and political life, it is by reference to its performance with respect to the local economy that the devolved administration will commonly fall to be judged. Conditions have been ripe for tensions between a territorial government increasingly keen to assert its authority, and what is aptly called the 'flagship' quango in pre-devolutionary Wales, the Welsh Development Agency, which was itself further empowered in the devolution statute ('a new economic powerhouse'). Then again, if the ambitious targets set out in the National Economic Development Plan, *A Winning Wales*, are to be achieved, it is to this experienced and high-profile agency that the infant body will have to look for a leading contribution.

A lingering hostility to the WDA, at least in Welsh Labour Party circles, was only to be expected, precisely because of its pre-eminent – even buccaneering – role under the Conservatives.[27] Read in this historical context, the fact that the agency has not been committed to the stake, and has instead been subject to close democratic scrutiny, including via quinquennial review, serves to highlight the general trajectory of government/quango relationships in Wales, or – as I prefer – a process of maturation.

What then it may be asked of the concept of partnership working? Typically, prior to the Assembly, the governance of economic development in Wales could be characterized as strongly hierarchical in nature, focused vertically on the Welsh Office and thence the WDA.[28] So a litmus test of changing patterns is the development of horizontal arrangements or interdependent forms of network relations across the devolved administration, other public bodies, and business interests. As explained in chapter 13, this aspect of sub-state mobilization has extra resonance in the case of Wales, being an article of faith of European regional policy (in the local implementation of which the WDA is intimately engaged). Again, the agency is seen as increasingly integrated in the reworked forms of public-sector delivery in Wales, in such fields as the environment and education.[29] In short, the case of the WDA shows how the rise of Welsh government machinery is not simply a matter of new institutions but also of greater width and depth to official relationships inside the territory.

The harnessing of the local executive agencies is further demonstrated. After a slow beginning, there is much closer dialogue with the administration, as also with the Assembly's high-profile Economic Development Committee.[30] But it is not simply a case of more politicians, or of post-devolutionary 'life in the goldfish bowl'. The fact that the Welsh Assembly government now`has a national economic development plan, which by definition means interactive strategies as well as targets, effectively reorders the institutional or regulatory space in which the WDA is operating. The risk in fact is that in this new more politicised environment the agency will become less bold or overly risk-averse. Local representatives are not renowned as a forgiving breed! Ron Davies may be quoted:

> The Assembly must learn to value the agency. We have set ourselves the huge task of improving and transforming the Welsh economy. The WDA will be the principal instrument of that, and if we undermine or hold back that agency, we will have no way of even starting to meet those targets. We must be much more supportive, which means recognising that the agency will fail sometimes. We want it to be enterprising, and if you have enterprise, and are searching for successes, you must sometimes pay the price with failures.[31]

The first quinquennial review of the WDA was completed in March 2001. Happily, the external auditors were able to report 'a sea change in the working relationship' between the agency and the devolved administration: more constructive. Emphatically the WDA was here to stay, and it was time to address the vexed question of the spheres of authority:

> The WDA is regarded as a well-respected and effective organisation with staff whose achievements – particularly in inward investment, land reclamation and environmental improvements – have made a significant contribution to changing the face of Wales . . . In the absence of the considerable efforts made by the WDA, Wales would have fared considerably less well with the fundamental economic restructuring it has undertaken and continues to face . . .
> [There is a need] to clarify and improve the strategic planning relationship between the National Assembly and the WDA which is not as effective as it should be. The underlying problem is that the National Assembly has yet to clarify fully its role in the economic development field and whether that role should extend beyond strategic development into the development and delivery of products. Whilst it is suggested that the Assembly should concentrate on the strategic level with the WDA acting as its implementation arm, the demarcation is unlikely to be straightforward . . .[32]

Quite so: the agency has an important role to play in assisting with the development of strategy – partnership working – while the devolved administration has important executive responsibilities in such overlapping fields as regional selective assistance. There is an evident need carefully to balance between proper accountability to the elected representatives on the one hand and the need to be responsive to market pressures and signals on the other hand. Responding to the review, the minister rejected overly restrictive controls, imposed in the wake of the financial scandals that afflicted the WDA pre-devolution:

> We must now draw a line under history. In broad terms, the Assembly should concentrate on the policy and strategy side of the agency's work. Subject to the usual safeguards of regularity and propriety, I would like to ease, wherever possible, the need for the agency to refer operational decisions on how it deploys its programme budget in-year. We need to be able to update and, if necessary, challenge the agency's plans, and it will, of course, have to account to us for its use of funds. However, I see little value in the Assembly second-guessing day-to-day decisions.[33]

In summary, no public body in Wales better illustrates the twin themes in this volume of continuity and change. The WDA is both a great survivor, even a direct beneficiary of the devolutionary scheme, and epitomizes the extended accountability of public bodies in Wales associated with the devolutionary development. Not surprisingly perhaps, it has taken some time for a supportive attitude to take hold among Members given the agency's previous position of *bête noire*. As to a light touch, strategic direction but not micro-level interventions, the benefits of this arm's-length organization – both in terms of market flexibility and of legitimacy with business – will require considerable self-discipline on the part of the Welsh Assembly Government. A useful start has been made.

A learning country: ELWa – National Council

ELWa – Education and Learning Wales – is the joint name for two ASPBs: the Higher Education Funding Council for Wales, responsible primarily for the universities, and the National Council for Education and Training in Wales, responsible for all other aspects of post-sixteen education and training, including from 2002 school sixth forms. It is also a mix of old and new, with HEFCW being a product of Welsh quangocracy under the Conservatives (Further and Higher Education Act 1992), and the National Council being founded on that great exception, Welsh-inspired England and Wales primary legislation (Learning and Skills Act 2000).[34]

Straddling the creation of the Assembly, the policy development leading to the National Council reflected the view of excessive fragmentation in the sector, both as between vocational training and academic education and structurally in the guise of four Training and Enterprise Councils and the Further Education Funding Council for Wales.[35] Five smaller bodies into one sprawling one: it was hardly, however, 'a bonfire of the quangos'.

Today, with an annual budget approaching £500 million the Council is the largest ASPB of all, with a local presence across the country. Mid-Wales; north Wales; the south-east and the south-west: four regional offices are charged with developing their own objectives and 'critical success factors' in pursuit of the agency's remit, and operate under the guidance of matching regional committees.[36] For their part, the actual service providers are linked together in some twenty newly formed Community Consortia for Education and Training (CCETs). Typically, their main role – as voluntary groupings – is to promote collaboration and best practice.

Much is made in this context of 'partnership working'. The council has both a long list of contributors, or wide agency network that stretches across the public, private and voluntary sectors, and a short list of key partner organizations, which notably includes the WDA and the WLGA. There is in turn a lot of paper flying about, in the guise of informal 'contracts' - memoranda of understanding – between the chief players. The need for complementarity of objectives, and for working together in order 'to avoid duplication and to enhance their joint impacts', is a major concern.[37]

At one and the same time, the council is a repository of the high hopes associated with the strategic plan *The Learning Country*; is emblematic both of the 'all-Wales' perspective and of the strong economic content in the devolutionary development; and faces an enormous challenge. In the words of the minister's remit letter (setting out the devolved administration's vision for the council and the priorities it wishes the council to pursue):

Human resource development is at the heart of the Assembly's modernisation agenda and underpins its economic development strategy . . . Too many young people and adults take little or no part in learning after compulsory education . . . This has contributed directly to social disadvantage and poor quality of life, with low attainment levels of basic skills, and continuing skills shortages and recruitment difficulties for many employers that have hindered the transition of Welsh businesses into the Knowledge Economy.

The Council will bring a strategic perspective to arrangements for lifelong learning. It has the key responsibility for planning, funding and improving the quality of post–16 learning other than within the higher education sector. It must be more than a funding body. The National Assembly wants the Council to build a new learning culture, which will develop individuals' personal prospects, improve the competitiveness of all businesses in Wales, and help build a cohesive and inclusive society . . . The Council will need to promote and judge all that it does by reference to world-class standards for learning. It must be prepared to innovate and promote radical ideas in support of the drive for excellence . . .[38]

The council's immediate priorities also serve to convey the flavour.[39] Explicitly in view of the challenge set in *A Winning Wales* for a dramatic increase in prosperity, the 'first priority must be given to learning which prepares the people of Wales to meet the needs of the local, national, UK and global economies'. A second priority is to drive up the quality of learning in Wales, and more especially 'to reward provision that is responsive to demand'. A third one, directed to stimulating a learning culture, is to develop mechanisms that 'will empower learners by giving them purchasing power'.

The statutory provisions underscore the power of the purse. So as well as duties to secure the provision of proper and reasonable facilities, and to encourage both individuals and employers to participate, the council is given wide powers to fund service providers, including by reference to its own assessment of standards, and to support individuals.[40] In turn, and taking the place of the Secretary of State for Wales, the devolved administration has especially strong powers of strategic direction: in effect the power closely to dictate the policy priorities, to which in exercising its functions the council 'must have regard'.[41]

Minister for Education and Lifelong Learning, Jane Davidson, has made ample use of her powers of instruction. A familiar tool of New Public Management, the formal remit letter has quickly emerged as a linchpin for the disciplining of the quangos by the Welsh Assembly Government. By which is meant, in the case of the council, no less than twelve items of 'vision', sixteen policy priorities, six strategic targets, and nine 'principles' to underpin its work. Similarly, it is of course the minister who sets the budget allocations for particular agency programmes such as youth training or business skills development. A close and continuous dialogue is of the essence of this strong form of policy guidance, from regular meetings to special instructions for urgent or local actions. 'Bringing government closer to the agencies' in Wales: this is it.

There already are some achievements for the minister to report: 'in the first two years since ELWa was established, over 25,000 young people have started work-based learning; some 5,380 adults have begun work-based learning; more than 900 started the new modern skills diploma for adults', and so on.[42] At the same time, enough has been said to demonstrate the particular importance of the National Council having an efficient and effective set of business processes, and of course proper internal financial arrangements etc. in the interest of sound corporate governance.

In the event, there have been major deficiencies. On the accounting side, scrutiny by the Auditor General for Wales has highlighted a series of irregular payments and potential conflicts of interest, as also a general lack of internal rules and regulations – standing orders – in the initial phase of agency operations. 'There was no formal articulation during this period of how business was to be conducted.'[43] In turn, the Assembly's Audit Committee has been much to the fore, not least in quizzing the agency's chief executive (who as the accounting officer has had first responsibility for ensuring a proper form of compliance).[44] The National Council's internal deficiencies have also shown the local machinery of (external) audit working well.

A different but related point: the Education and Lifelong Learning Committee has been slow in becoming engaged. Although members were happy to probe the basic priorities, there was little in this critical early phase by way of in-depth and robust scrutiny of management and implement-ation.[45] It is a further illustration of the general weakness of the subject committees in securing proper accountability of the quangos, a feature that has been accentuated in this case by reason of the novel and wide-ranging nature of the agency's activities. The rise of Welsh governmental machinery – a matching need for democratic oversight by the Assembly in 'parliamentary' guise: it is a lesson that should now be taken to heart.

To pursue the theme, the design of ELWa as an umbrella body was a recipe for administrative difficulties; a point highlighted in an official review of the senior staff structure, commissioned by the minister.[46] A break in the logic: whereas the original ETAP Report[47] had proclaimed its holistic vision for post-sixteen education, the arrangements for close coordination between the National Council and HEFCW were essentially confined to the appointment of a single chief executive. In turn, an overload of work had rapidly developed, not least in the face of the increasing demands on the two agencies emanating from the Assembly. Suffice it to add that the minister was persuaded of the need for additional senior staff, including separate chief executives.[48]

The possibility remains of merging the two agencies under the auspices of statute, but this would no doubt attract considerable opposition from the universities. In the event, a more pragmatic and flexible approach is signalled by the fact of the Education (Miscellaneous Provisions) Bill as one of the Assembly's bids for primary legislation.[49] It would enable the two agencies to act together jointly and on each other's behalf, and to second staff to one another. A 'real' and not a 'virtual' ELWa: it is extraordinary that such arrangements were not put in place at the outset.

In summary, the sense of local diversity is communicated in various ways in the case of ELWa–National Council. The basic policy has much to commend it, not least given the marked concentrations of socio-economic deprivation that remain in parts of Wales. The organizational arrangements, however, may be said to show a lack of legal and administrative awareness in the early days of the Assembly, which has now come to roost. To end on an optimistic note, it would appear in view of the various remedial activities that, in this sense too, Wales is 'a learning country'.

Hybrid: Environment Agency (Wales)

The environment matters: not least to the devolved administration in view of the special Welsh constitutional and policy priority of sustainable development.[50] On the one hand, this is a classic field of overlapping functions and divided powers, more especially in the light of burgeoning EU rules and regulations,[51] as also the obvious relevance of the UK and England and Wales regulatory paradigms. On the other hand, environmental issues are clearly apt to illustrate the new realities of territorial politics, in the sense of Assembly ministers increasingly taking the blame when things go wrong.

At first sight, the Environment Agency typifies the England and Wales paradigm.[52] A board of fifteen members, including the chairman and chief executive, is accountable to UK ministers (and thence to Parliament) for the agency's organization and performance. All are appointed by the Secretary of State, save for the board member for Wales, who is now appointed by the Assembly. A team of directors chaired by the chief executive oversees and coordinates the formulation of 'cross-border' policies ranging from 'environmental strategy' and water management to legal services (including prosecutions). Notably, they are responsible 'for making sure that policies are delivered consistently, while allowing for local differences in environmental, social and economic climate where appropriate'. By way of back-up, some twenty-two specialist centres – for example, the National Laboratory Service and the National Library and Information Service – provide cross-cutting services across the agency. Closer to home, the agency is further divided into eight 'regions' – Wales being one – each with a regional office and regional director. At base, they provide both a focus of coordination and technical and administrative support to some twenty-six area offices across England and Wales which are themselves responsible for day-to-day management and for meeting local needs.

The Environment Agency also epitomizes the rise of the agency model of government regulation in UK administrative law. With some 10,500 staff and an annual budget of £650 million, it is self-proclaimed as the most powerful environmental regulator in Europe. The sense of independence from, or an arm's-length relationship with government, is seen to facilitate the continuity of, and flexibility and responsiveness in, policy formulation and implementation, as also a disinterested expertise. Put another way, the operational design of this specialist, multi-functional agency fits well the theory of regulation as sustained and focused control exercised by a public agency over activities that are socially valued.[53] From lobbying and educational activities, to rule formulation and monitoring and inspection, for example in terms of air, land and water qualities, or in the oversight of waste management through licensing, and on through enforcement and sanctions, the Agency thus stands for a wide-ranging, full-blown and interactive form of regulation.

Yet from the 'bottom-up' or territorial perspective, there is more to it than this. The 'regional office' that is Environment Agency Wales (EAW) is in a special position, being an Assembly Sponsored Public Body as well as part of the corporate cross-border regulatory entity. As an ASPB, it derives much of its funding and direction from the Welsh Assembly Government, and reports back to the minister. In other words, EAW shares with the rest of the agency wide responsibilities for managing the environment, and reflects and reinforces the changed political and administrative climate that is national devolution.

Central to this hybrid arrangement is an annual 'corporate plan Wales'.[54] Typically a product of wide consultation, the priorities and targets have been formulated through discussions with the UK department and the Welsh Assembly Government, and by input from a system of regional advisory committees and other stakeholders. The power of the purse: the devolved administration has also provided funds for tackling some specific priority issues, such as emergency flood defence. The traffic, however, is emphatically not one-way. All at one with the closeness of Wales, EAW has been actively involved in helping to develop many of the Welsh Assembly Government's key policies, including those relating to communities, health and the economy, within the framework provided by the special Welsh sustainable development scheme.

Environment Agency Wales is seriously 'on-message'. Virtually whatever the problem, it is said to be a case for partnership working. As part, it is officially declared, of 'the dynamic Welsh environmental sector', and in pursuit of 'innovative solutions that are specifically tailored to meet the needs of Wales'.[55] More concretely, EAW has a budget of some £60 million and employs roughly 1,000 staff, including those in area offices across Wales. Over half the expenditure goes on flood defence and water resources, and most of the remainder on the suitably miscellaneous category of environmental protection.[56] At one and the same time, the agency has had to face a grim industrial legacy, epitomized by much contaminated land in Wales, and has been confronted by a series of what are euphemistically called 'major environmental incidents', such as foot and mouth. To which might be added – as exemplifying local and political sensitivities – contributing to a major Assembly inquiry into landfill in the Rhondda Valley.[57]

Yet is the element of local design sufficient? The way in which post-devolution this type of organizational question is apt to become more politicized, and in particular to have greater weight attached to the all-Wales perspective, is brilliantly illustrated in the case of the environment. There clearly is an argument, *à la* Plaid Cymru, for a more integrated set of arrangements inside the territory, beginning with the merger of functions of the Environment Agency and Forestry Enterprise. Constitutionally and legally speaking, there is further a growing sense of disjunction between, on the one hand, the formal corporate personality of the Environment Agency, and, on the other hand, the strengthening lines of control and accountability as between the Welsh Assembly Government and EAW.

In the event, and wholly understandably on the balance of the professional argument, the devolved administration has resisted the idea of pressing immediately for legislative changes. EAW itself has notably stressed the value of the current 'cross-border' regulatory paradigm, both in terms of access to the resources and expertise of the larger organization, and a wide view of the environment across England and Wales, and beyond. The door, however, is not closed: it being possible for example to envisage buying-in arrangements for a separate Welsh environment agency, one that is best attuned to local conditions. The first Assembly Minister for Environment, Sue Essex, in fact signalled an intention to revisit the general issue of agency structures.[58] In summary, both the need in devolutionary terms for a sense of proportion – countervailing arguments for 'cross-border' bodies even in certain fields of devolved functions – and the ongoing pressures for Welshifying – the sense that post-devolution the inherited pattern of public organizations will alter over time – are communicated strongly here.

2. RESTRUCTURING: NHS REFORM

No discussion of contemporary Welsh governance can afford to ignore the strategic plan *Improving Health in Wales*.[59] It has heralded the most ambitious restructuring project undertaken by the Welsh Assembly Government, one that has generated much local controversy. And it is emblematic of the major themes in post-devolutionary Wales as set out in the local policy map or 'Welsh *mappa mundi*', not least the fashion for partnership working and the concern with cross-cutting issues such as the tackling of inequalities. So much so that Jane Hutt, the first Assembly Minister for Health, has spoken of something called 'Team Health for Wales'.[60]

Perspectives

The structural change programme should be placed in context. First, there is some history of differentiation in the organization and administration of health policy in what is now sweetly called 'the family of United Kingdom nations'.[61] So it is that the heavy engagement by the Welsh Office and its myriad quangos in this field lay at the heart of the pre-devolutionary criticism of 'a hidden tier' of territorial government. At the same time, Wales as the birthplace of the NHS may be said to demonstrate a particular commitment to the key founding principles: equity, access according to need not income, and public service. Glossing over his strong anti-devolutionist credentials, the Welsh Assembly Government has not been slow to invoke Aneurin Bevan.

Secondly, it would be absurd to suggest that the general themes only feature in Wales. Quite the reverse: the concept of partnership and the reduction of inequalities have both featured prominently in the discourse of UK health policy since Labour returned to office in 1997.[62] Nonetheless, it is right to say that such themes have had a special potency in Wales. To quote the First Minister:

> The Plan is rooted in a series of partnerships. These involve public bodies planning, implementing and working on policies in a joined-up way. More than this, the Plan is rooted in the Partnership Agreement that forms the programme of the Partnership Government. The health of the nation is crucially important and the government is committed to a range of measures to improve it . . .
>
> It sets the policy agenda for the next five to ten years and outlines our commitment to rebuild, renew and improve the National Health Service in Wales; develop effective and innovative ways improving citizens' health; and make primary care the engine which drives constant improvement in the service . . . It lies at the political centre of the Administration which I am proud to lead.[63]

Thirdly, there is the small matter of the legal base. One is back here with the twin poles of primary legislation, the specifically Welsh provisions of the NHS Reform and Health Care Professionals Act 2002, and the stand-alone Health (Wales) Act 2003, and thence a host of relevant Assembly secondary legislation.[64] At the same time, however, it is worth noting the current Health and Social Care (Community Health and Standards) Bill, which in developing for England autonomous and privileged 'foundation hospitals' has already generated much controversy. A classic example of devolutionary difference in the negative sense ('decoupling'), the idea has been ruled out in Wales in favour of 'a health service based on cooperation – not competition – between hospitals'.[65] Why, it may be asked in suitably provocative fashion, would the locals wish to import an English mutant of what – proudly – was born in Wales?

Fourthly, the Plan has been developed and taken forward against the background of unprecedented levels of increase in health funding in Wales: by the end of its first term, some 50 per cent over the £2.5 billion health budget which the Assembly inherited in 1999.[66] Whatever else happens, the NHS in Wales can look forward to a period of rapid growth in which to deliver the new agenda. Let us hope that the hospital trusts and the new local health boards, which will be responsible for the great bulk of the expenditure, prove able to respond in an efficient and effective manner. At the same time, and the pre-eminent example in Welsh devolution of the new immediacy of territorial government and politics, ambitious targets on waiting lists etc. that were set in the early days of devolution have proved elusive, leading in turn to heavy criticism of the minister.[67] In this context, criticism of the restructuring plans for absorbing valuable time and energy, not least in the light of successive rounds of reorganization in the NHS, was only to be expected.[68] Suffice it to add that the reform has been driven forward in remarkably quick time, from major policy consultation through primary and secondary legislation to general administrative implementation in a little over two years.

Virtuous triangle

The main development is the replacement of five regional health authorities with twenty-two local health boards (LHBs), each of which will be co-determinous with its associated unitary local authority. As statutory bodies, they will have powers and duties consistent with their key role as commissioners of health services, and be established with their own representative boards and dedicated management teams. For their part, the pre-existing NHS trusts will continue in their principal role as providers of services 'but will need to be flexible in responding to the new service planning and commissioning arrangements and taking forward the renewal agenda'.[69]

In its determination to place primary care at the core of health policy, the Welsh Assembly Government has thus established a structure very different from England. The programme can further be seen as the Welsh variant in a series of 'Celtic plans' that have now adopted a more holistic approach to matters of public health. It certainly represents a bold vision.

> The National Assembly sees primary care as playing a vital part in the development of a socially, environmentally and economically sustainable Wales and a means by which we might ensure equity of service provision and social justice for all in Wales. Primary care will also in future have a clearer focus on public health and on community health development.
>
> Wales has a very broadly based approach to primary care. It is at the heart of local communities. This reflects a recognition of the importance of meeting people's needs in – or as close as possible to – their homes and in the most practical and effective ways available. This is achieved by using the skills of everyone working in the most practical and effective ways available.[70]

'The Welsh difference': consistent with its all-embracing duty to promote equality of opportunity, the devolved administration has increasingly emphasized issues of equity in health care, to the extent of commissioning a major review on resource allocation from the renowned social policy expert, Professor Peter Townsend.[71] In the words of the strategic plan:

> Developments in primary care are vital for Wales because, despite the targeting of significant resources in the past decade, there are variations in quality and access,

and evidence of service imbalance . . . There is a growing awareness of health
inequalities between communities and between different social groups. Balancing
the concern for the health of the whole population and a concern for the health of
individual patients represents a major clinical and managerial challenge to
primary care and the whole NHS.[72]

The co-determinous element in the new organizational arrangements has
thus been a vital factor for ministers, one that is seen to ground the potential
for a virtuous triangle of cross-cutting policy, 'joined-up government' and a
partnership approach. More plans: the key instrument at local level will be an
individuated 'health, social care and well-being strategy' prepared in accordance with Assembly regulations. Intended to 'span the whole spectrum' from
preventative action to public and private care services, this will also 'reflect
the need to tackle the underlying factors which lead to poor health'. So also, a
legislative underpinning of partnership working, the system will be
distinctive in that the local authority and the LHB will be jointly responsible
for the formulation and the implementation of the strategy. And – of course –
they will be required to cooperate with NHS trusts, the Community Health
Council, and voluntary and private-sector organizations etc. 'to ensure
an inclusive approach'.[73] Such, anyway, has been the gospel according to Jane
Hutt.

A tangled web

Whereas abolition of the five regional authorities suggests clearer lines of
local accountability, the new arrangements are in fact so complicated that a
tome could also be written about them. As well as a complex accountability
framework, there are reworked regional elements, a new element of
agencification, and – so typical of the 'secret history' of Welsh devolution – an
expanded role for the Assembly administration. For her part, the minister has
spoken of a policy 'made in Wales' conducted on the basis of operating
arrangements that are 'cost-neutral'.[74] We shall see.

By virtue of the devolutionary development, all NHS statutory organizations in Wales are accountable to the minister and (that non-legal entity) the
Welsh Assembly Government for the performance of their functions and
financial duties. As the formal accounting officer, the director of NHS Wales
operates as the focal point for accountability for the delegated functions that
are discharged by the chief officers of the local bodies. More precisely, the
Chairs of statutory bodies – NHS trusts and LHBs – will be accountable to,
and act as agents of, the minister; the local accountability of executive
directors is to their boards; and the chief executives will be professionally

accountable to the director. Meanwhile, 'LHBs and local authorities will report to their local communities and the Welsh Assembly Government on the successful implementation of the local Health, Social Care and Well Being Strategy.'[75] To whom they report on unsuccessful implementation is not explained!

Although the co-determinous principle sounds well, the downside is immediately apparent by reason of the great diversity of Welsh unitary authorities, in particular the small size and hence limited resources and administrative capacity of many of them.[76] Left to their own devices, the new LHBs would be severely lacking both in expertise and in the clout to deal effectively with the trusts. So it comes as no surprise to learn that three regional offices are being established, with a view to facilitating and support-ing effective partnerships between particular LHBs to commission services. And further to combat excessive fragmentation and disputing: that is to say, 'brokering strategic and financial solutions as necessary to resolve conflicts and ensure delivery of objectives across local health communities'.[77] As well as internal subsidiarity – local bodies and local strategies – this then is an excellent example of the sucking-up of powers. Whereas the five regional health authorities were arm's-length statutory bodies, the new regional offices will perform their functions on behalf of the director of NHS Wales, in other words the Welsh Assembly Government.

At the same time, the reform could hardly be described as 'a bonfire of the quangos'. A typical point of criticism in the local media, the opportunities for public service of this kind are multiplied tenfold in the new system, such has been the strength of the desire to ensure a balanced representation from all the key stakeholders on the local health boards. But more than this, new ASPBs are being established, either as part of the reform or as flanking machinery.[78] 'Health Commission Wales (specialist services)' in particular will help to fill a vacuum, by providing advice and the guidance to the LHBs etc. on the more difficult issues. As an arm's-length agency, it will have an independent Chair and will also have its own advisory board of representative interests.

The minister has spoken of 'a new pluralism in NHS policy-making in Wales'.[79] Important to the design is the invocation of a by now familiar model in contemporary Welsh governance, in the form of a new national health and well-being 'Partnership Council'. Chaired by the minister, the membership of the council is slated to include 'the broadest possible range of interests', from patients' groups to NHS staff and professional bodies, and from local government to hitherto under-represented groups such as ethnic minorities. Its role serves to underscore the all-Wales aspects:

- support the Welsh Assembly Government in discharging its responsibilities for improving health services;
- engage a full range of stakeholders in the development of policies and plans;

- monitor progress of the implementation of the NHS Plan;
- commission advice from other forums/groups on health and well-being issues;
- provide the Assembly's Health and Social Services Committee with regular reports on progress

Last but not least, there are significant changes to the NHS arm within the Assembly. The director of NHS Wales is a full member of the revamped Executive Board and so 'is in a position to influence policy making in related groups'.[80] In turn, the director chairs a management board that brings together divisional and regional directors within a new structure for the NHS Wales Department (NHSWD), which is comprised as follows:

- Health services policy and development team
- Primary care division
- Performance management, quality and regulation division
- Central support team
- Finance division
- Human resources division
- Health information and facilities division
- Regional office, north Wales
- Regional office, south-west Wales
- Regional office, south-east Wales.

As its name suggests, the policy and development team will be at the heart of the action, addressing key issues across a broad range of clinical services. At one with the underlying philosophy of the restructuring programme, the new primary care division is also seen to have an expanded role to play. 'All that jazz': the performance management division is meant to promote a culture of continuous improvement, including via regular reviews based on something called 'the balanced scorecard approach'. Meanwhile, the central support team will seek 'to achieve better control of all "transient" work falling to the department'; that is to say, ministerial correspondence, Assembly questions and briefing requests.[81] In short, if further evidence is needed of the local civil service tooling up and branching out, then this is it.

Change and controversy

Inconvenient it may have been for Assembly ministers and officials, but it is also a pleasing reflection on the health of the new Welsh polity that the restructuring programme has generated considerable criticism in plenary.[82] Like it or loathe it, this by its very nature has been a controversial reform that should be found at the heart of public debate in the new devolved territory.

Assuming, that is, one sincerely believes in 'bringing government closer to the people'.

And especially, it may be said, because the fact of the restructuring – a unique set of organizational arrangements – sits comfortably with ideas of national devolution and 'Welshifying'. At the risk of repetition, while the rise of Welsh governmental machinery should generally be welcomed as a necessary and valuable part of the devolutionary development, this is not a licence to be uncritical. In fact, in the instant case the point of criticism is one of excess: a jungle of intersecting machinery, a prospective mountain of paper.

A simplistic 'top-down' set of arrangements is out of the question. Such today are the many complexities in health care matters and the many rightful demands for involvement and engagement. Nonetheless, with a view to effective and efficient forms of service delivery, as also to clear lines of democratic accountability, it has to be said. The new arrangements represent an awesome construction for a little country.

3. WIDENING AND DEEPENING

Welsh governmental machinery takes many forms. All too easily overlooked are the many non-executive ASPBs, which may in fact exercise a decisive influence in their particular fields. Statutory and non-statutory, free-standing or Welsh offshoot: these bodies are very diverse. Most were established before the creation of the Assembly, but as well as surviving largely intact, the sector is now showing significant expansion in light of the quest for Welsh policy development and difference, as well as for partnership working.

In the name of increased accountability and openness, the Welsh Assembly Government has once again embarked here on a systematic and wide-ranging programme of quinquennial reviews.[83] A glance at the forty or so public bodies concerned confirms, however, that few are likely to be culled. Many are to be found in the field of health and social services, where for example such bodies as the Welsh Medical, Dental, and Pharmaceutical Committees both perform necessary tasks of self-regulation and bring together professional experts from all parts of Wales. Again, the clutch of Welsh offshoots in the tribunal system, for example in agricultural matters, is surely here to stay post-devolution. Speaking more generally, at a time when the devolved administration is seeking to engage with, and mobilize, civil society in Wales, the demand is for consolidation – and not 'a bonfire' – of existing structures.

By way of new growth, and as illustrating the close interplay with policy priorities, cross-cutting themes, and the ideology of partnership working, one might mention a Transport Forum, an Overseas Trade Forum, and an All-Wales Standing Conference on Community Safety. Now being launched under the auspices of primary legislation, and charged with operating in a most sensitive area, the Wales Centre for Health is an especially noteworthy example. Providing a local forum for multi-disciplinary advice on health hazards, risk assessments and threats to health, it is tasked with disseminating research and other evidence to support decision-making, multi-professional training and something called sustainable health. WCH will thus be a key player in the implementation of the devolved administration's health policy, and clearly requires careful guarantees of its own independence.[84]

ASPBs of the non-executive kind shade off into what is a rapidly increasing number in Wales of more informal advisory groups and committees: some strongly politically driven, others not so. To this effect, the growth of such bodies under the auspices of the Partnership Council with local government can itself be seen as one variant in a more general development. In the first three years, the Assembly government established some eighty new task and finish groups.[85]

Perhaps this sounds unremarkable. 'Government by committee' is an enduring theme in the British constitution, only heightened in Wales. So it is appropriate to stress the dual nature of the phenomenon. By which is meant a 'deepening' in respect of, and a 'widening' beyond, the devolved functions, of this type of local institutional capacity.

A new Welsh Economic Research Advisory Panel for example is all at one with the declared aims of the constitutional development, and further reflects the tooling up or thickening of the executive core of the Welsh Assembly Government. Designedly independent and boasting an impressive mix of public- and private-sector expertise, the panel in the First Minister's words 'marks a maturing of our approach to policy development'.[86] Directly institutionally linked, via a newly created Research and Evaluation Unit within the Cabinet Secretariat, it is thus tasked with advising on economic research, monitoring and evaluation, most obviously in terms of the optimistic vision that is *A Winning Wales*.

In contrast, the fact for example of an Advisory Committee on Criminal Justice to the National Assembly, chaired by a High Court judge, may appear distinctly odd.[87] Although it sits comfortably with the general thrust of the Welsh Assembly Government in terms of key policy areas – most notably, communities and children – it is not at all what was envisaged by the official architects of the devolutionary scheme. Inaugurated in 2001, the committee brilliantly illustrates a propensity for Welsh governmental machinery to range beyond the ambit of devolved powers and into the penumbra of related matters, or topics in which the Assembly (only) possesses the general power of 'a voice for Wales'.

The longer-term implications in terms of the overarching constitutional development should not be underestimated. There is a sense in which the devolved administration has now moved in this direction, as in policies on youth justice and the contemporary (Welsh) scourge of hard drugs, as also in such flanking organizational developments as an Assembly Advisory Body on Substance Misuse and an all-Wales Offending Strategy Group.[88] Not surprisingly, one is tempted to add, given the political salience of such issues. But further, institutional growth or overlapping – the case for a more generous allocation of devolved functions: the equation is easily envisaged. To quote the judge involved, Sir John Thomas:

> It can immediately be seen that a line runs straight through the current devolution structure, because some powers are devolved – health, local government and education – and some are not – the courts, the police etc. Steps towards an interim solution have been made through the Advisory Committee (which brings together all those interested) . . . but there is no body or institution that brings together the necessary powers and functions within Wales . . .[89]

4. BUREAUCRATIC REGULATION

What then, it may be asked, of the main public bodies that are engaged in bureaucratic regulation? As indicated, this is an especially important category of agency in terms of the quality or tone of the devolutionary development. And all the more so, it may be said, in 'the closeness of Wales'.

Gold standard: the Welsh Administration Ombudsman

The ombudsman is an appropriate starting place for two main reasons. First, with the ambition of an accountable and responsive public administration, independent complaint machinery is an integral part of the devolutionary scheme. This refers not only to 'fire-fighting' – redress of grievance – but also to the classic ombudsman role of 'fire-watching' – identifying deficiencies with a view to promoting improvements,[90] and further to the especially important legitimating function in the case of the Assembly of buttressing public confidence. Secondly, the machinery brilliantly illustrates the ongoing dynamic of Welsh institutional development; as marked by the establishment of the Welsh Administration Ombudsman (WAO) in the devolution statute, adaptations to internal working practices etc., and the move towards more fundamental reform – a single public ombudsman system for Wales.

It was originally envisaged that the Parliamentary Commissioner for Administration (PCA) – the central government ombudsman – would have jurisdiction over the Assembly.[91] However, in the course of the proceedings on the Bill, the government accepted the case for a separate office, more in tune with the idea of national devolution.[92] In the event, the WAO has jurisdiction over both the Assembly and many of the local quangos, including the WDA and the Welsh Language Board, as also the functions in Wales of the Environment Agency.[93] The standard of 'maladministration causing injustice', exemptions from jurisdiction such as commercial contracts and personnel matters: naturally much of the framework has been read across from the pre-existing UK scheme of bureaucratic regulation.[94]

There are some significant twists. All at one with the devolutionary idea of 'bringing government closer to the people', the major restriction on access in the central government scheme that is the famous 'MP filter' is not imported. To this effect, it is the ombudsman model for local government, here in the guise of the Office of the Local Commissioner for Wales, which has been read across – direct access. Again, with a view to underscoring the potency of the accountability, there are special provisions relating to the use by the ombudsman of further reports to deal with non-compliance. Publicity – and potential embarrassment – effectively substitutes for the ombudsman's lack of enforcement powers through a requirement that the First Minister propose a motion in plenary accepting the recommendations.[95] As in the case of the Auditor General for Wales, it also made good sense to maintain the guarantee of the 'gold standard' – the great experience and high authority of the PCA – for a transitional period. Sir Michael Buckley was promptly given a new hat.

The parallel system represented by the Office of the Health Service Commissioner in Wales (HSCW) has also undergone some revision. A portent of the developments in legislative drafting, the opportunity was taken in the GWA to disentangle the statutory provisions relating to this Office and to incorporate them in a separate schedule.[96] And a portent of things to come, the Office has become increasingly integrated with the Office of the WAO, with the same staff in a single Cardiff office doing both jobs.[97]

In addition, and once again reflecting comparative trends in administrative law, here in the guise of the Citizen's Charter,[98] there is an appropriate stress on internal procedures for complaints, with special reference to accessibility, speed of process, and feedback into policy and performance. Soft law: the Assembly has now issued a Code of Practice on Complaints to structure this process.[99] In turn, the WAO is in a position to move to the apex of a genuinely pyramidal structure of complaint-handling administered on a territorial basis. Notably, Sir Michael has imported into Wales a wider product range, tailoring complaint-handling to the individual circumstances of the case, which in turn breathes life into the relationship with internal systems of review and redress.[100]

In the event, the WAO has not been overburdened with cases. Perhaps this is not surprising, given that the devolved administration itself has little interface with members of the public. It is rather the key service providers – local government, the NHS and one or two quangos – that will bear the brunt (of complaints). By way of statistics, in the year 2001–2 the ombudsman received fifty-six complaints; concluded fifty-nine cases without investigation (chiefly for lack of jurisdiction or no prima facie evidence of maladministration); and moved to a full investigation in only five cases. Predictably, agriculture (the non-payment of subsidies) and planning have generated the most work.[101] Although much higher (155 new complaints), the caseload as Health Service Ombudsman also appears unexceptional from the comparative viewpoint, both in terms of the rate of complaints and the subject matter (not least 'poor communication'). Obviously these are early days but there is little evidence here of a Welsh virus of maladministration. Constitutionally speaking, it is once more what has not happened in the course of the devolutionary development that is significant.

A consultation paper issued jointly by the Wales Office and the Welsh Assembly Government charts the way forward.[102] Whereas the GWA contained modest provisions on consultation and cooperation between the various public ombudsmen,[103] the choice of option now is 'the full Monty' – merger of the WAO and the HSCW with the local government ombudsman, so creating the single office of Public Services Ombudsman for Wales. This in turn will incorporate an extension of the local government ombudsman's jurisdiction to enable tenants to cover registered social landlords, as previously signalled in an Assembly bid for primary legislation.[104]

Inspiration comes from England, where an earlier review highlighted the many advantages of a unified approach: more flexible service to members of the public – a 'one-stop shop'; a greater breadth of knowledge and experience to underpin the vital fire-watching function; and enhanced visibility and authority.[105] Typically, Wales has also looked to Scotland, where ombudsman offices have already been merged into one (the Scottish Public Services Ombudsman).

But further, the development reflects and reinforces the emergent idea of a distinctive Welsh system of public administration. In the words of the consultation paper, the creation of a single jurisdiction matches 'the emphasis now increasingly being placed on "joined-up" services provided through partnerships between different public bodies and tiers of authority'.[106] To push home the point, the case made for reform in England is even stronger in the context of national devolution and of the 'Welsh way'. 'The closeness of Wales' and the changing face of public-sector service delivery inside the country, external complaint machinery able to range across formal legal divisions: it is an excellent fit.

Flagship: the Children's Commissioner

No serious discussion of the Welsh devolutionary development can overlook the establishment of the special kind of ombudsman that is the Children's Commissioner for Wales. A valuable enterprise in its own right, it has further served as a flagship of territorial initiative and invention, being the first such agency to be established in the UK. Time and again, it is to the commissioner that the local politicians have turned in expounding the Assembly's achievements in its first term.

To recap, there were two stages of statutory reform: first by way of special Welsh provisions tacked onto the Care Standards Act 2000, and then via the Children's Commissioner for Wales Act 2001.[107] A remit that was initially confined to social care services now includes all matters that come within the Assembly's devolved areas of responsibility, such as health, education, the environment and transport.[108] In suitably paradoxical fashion, this non-partisan initiative has also featured prominently in the ongoing constitutional debate inside the territory. Either, that is, as highlighting the limitations of the Assembly – cap in hand to Westminster – or as showing the fine art of intergovernmental working under the model of executive devolution.[109]

The principal aim of the commissioner is to 'safeguard and promote the rights and welfare of children' to whom the statutory provisions apply.[110] The ombudsman role in redress of grievance is defined expansively here: from review and monitoring of internal complaints procedures etc. to assisting complainants, and on through to direct investigation of particular kinds of complaints. The commissioner, however, is also intended to be proactive, in the sense of a general advocacy and lobbying function. He is thus empowered to 'review the effect on children' of 'the exercise or proposed exercise by the Assembly of any function, including the making or proposed making of any subordinate legislation', as also the exercise or proposed exercise of functions by a wide range of other bodies, including ASPBs.[111] Of course, in the case of the Assembly, it will be the elected representatives who have the final say, and in accordance with their constitutional and political accountability rightly so.

Demonstrating a firm commitment to the mainstreaming of children's issues in the local policy process, this is bureaucratic regulation writ large. As such, it is a noble vision: the new representative body effectively promoting oversight of its own work, better to protect the interests of some of the most vulnerable in society. At the same time, this brings into sharp focus the constitutional position of the commissioner, the fact that ultimately he is responsible to the Assembly, to which he reports, and which also has a role in his appointment and the setting of his budget. Once again, there is no obvious way round this difficulty of establishing independence, and so the fact that the processes to date have been demonstrably open and transparent is all the more important.[112] Another first: children were formally involved in the appointment process of this public sector ombudsman. In the event, the selection of the director of Childline Cymru – Peter Clarke – has secured the agency attributes of experience and expertise.

As befits this example of territorial initiative, the legislation was seen to be among the most generously drafted, in the sense of maximizing the decision-making power of the Assembly in subordinate legislation. In turn, in the making of the regulations, the devolved administration has notably built into the regulatory system a participatory process of close dialogue. The commissioner is thus required to take reasonable steps to ensure not only that children in Wales are encouraged to communicate with the agency, but also that their views are sought as to how the commissioner should exercise his functions and as to the content of the annual work programme.[113] At one and the same time, the sense of fit with innovative forms of tools and techniques in the new territorial polity, and the natural advantages that the Office enjoys in a small country with a small population, are powerfully illustrated here. Of course, how far, given a very limited budget – initially, some £1 million per annum – the commissioner is able to go in meeting the many expectations that have been raised, remains to be seen. To strike an optimistic note, his popular appeal – or political capital – should not be underestimated, including as a home-grown source of authority.

It has not been all sweetness and light. The Bill as originally drafted made no provision in respect of policies and activities that do not come within the devolved areas of responsibility, such as youth justice and social security. From a viewpoint in family law this looked distinctly odd, a fragmentation of joined-up government in the case of children, even perhaps in individual cases. To explicate, in terms of a legal and constitutional framework, there were three possible approaches in respect of children in Wales:

- functions for the commissioner across the board;
- full functions for the commissioner in areas of devolved functions; with an additional general power to consider and make representations;
- full functions for the commissioner only in areas of devolved functions.

Although originally favoured in the Assembly,[114] central government had good reasons for rejecting the first option. It would have cut across the basic lines of responsibility and accountability, a creature of the Assembly effectively holding to account UK ministers etc. who are properly under the purview of Westminster. But Wales Office minister David Hanson also rejected the second option – on the basis of inconsistency with the devolution settlement. It was suggested that informal understandings that the commissioner could act more widely would have to suffice.[115]

The junior minister evidently knew little of the nature of the Welsh constitutional dispensation. What was being sought reflects the Assembly's own power in s. 33 of the GWA to operate as a voice for Wales: whether the matter is devolved or not.[116] In the event, under pressure from experienced Welsh hands in the House of Lords, the government backtracked.[117] A neat balancing of constitutional and administrative responsibilities, the legislation has thus produced a two-staged process.[118] The commissioner is explicitly empowered to consider, and make representations to the Assembly about, any matter that affects the rights and welfare of children in Wales; the Assembly can then consider those representations and, if appropriate, make its own representations to central government etc. under s. 33.

All's well that ends well. The significance of the concession, however, should not be underestimated in terms of the general Welsh devolutionary development. Powerful evidence of continuing tensions inside government over the parameters of the new territorial polity, the 'Hanson doctrine' – had it been allowed to go unchecked – would have severely cramped the growth or role of 'Welsh state' machinery, in respect of which the Children's Commissioner is such a leading enterprise. As it is, a major constitutional precedent has been set, all at one with the framework for organic change of the devolution statute.

More 'Welsh way': Inspector Estyn

Estyn, aka the Office of Her Majesty's Chief Inspector of Education and Training in Wales, is another major example of 'rebadging' in the context of national devolution. At one and the same time, it stands for a significant institutional element of Welshifying, here building on the differentiation in education that existed pre-devolution,[119] for territorial policy initiative, as part of a package for more closely integrated educational provision in Wales, and for a reworked style of bureaucratic regulation. Typically, the importance attached to inspection in *The Learning Country* is as a key instrument in promoting a culture of continuous improvement.[120] A different but related point: Estyn illustrates the fact of close and collaborative agency working with the policy-maker that is the devolved administration. The minister has stressed its role, not simply as a means of independent and impartial assessment, but also as helping to enable an evidence-based approach to the review and development of strategy, or in the language of an earlier age, effective operation of 'the feed backloop'.[121]

The creation of ELWa – an extended remit for Estyn: the two developments run in tandem. The Learning and Skills Act has again provided the legal base, empowering Estyn to range beyond primary and secondary schools to all publicly funded learning in Wales, save for higher education ('university autonomy').[122] In the words of its mission statement, the aim is 'to raise standards and quality of education and training in Wales through inspection and advice, in support of the vision and strategic direction set out by the Welsh Assembly Government'. The statute underwrites this in the usual way: on the one hand, requirements to inspect and report to the Assembly on quality of provision, standards of attainment and value for money, as also a general advisory function; and on the other hand, wide-ranging Assembly powers of instruction and guidance. It suffices to add that there are many opportunities for democratic engagement with the inspector in the new devolved system, from discussion in the all-party subject committee to the standard remit letter, and on through debate in plenary on the agency's annual report. That is to say, together with more informal methods.

Happily, Estyn is able to report successive improvement. Better teaching and improved accommodation and training, more effective management and strategic plans: it is an uplifting view of the progress of education in Wales. Public policy – bureaucratic regulation: the new Welsh symbiosis is neatly illustrated in the kinds of matters that Estyn now actively reviews on behalf of the devolved administration. Overarching themes such as equality of opportunity and social inclusion, for example, are increasingly to the fore, including in the dry New Public Management (NPM) form of targets set by ministers, together with such traditional items as the quality of Welsh-language teaching.[123] Turning the argument round, it does not do to gloss over the difficulties and major variations ('narrowing the gap'). The Chief Inspector, Susan Lewis, may be quoted: 'unless learners' ability in the key skills improves a great deal, Wales will not have the skilled workforce it needs to keep its place in the economy of Europe and the wider world'.[124]

All at one with the idea of a Welsh way, the tone or culture of the inspection is subtly – and increasingly – distinct. The touchstone is a new common inspection framework, intended to be fully operational by 2004, whereby procedures piloted in the further education sector will be extended to school inspections. Highly collaborative or soft-edged in flavour, this has naturally gained strong support from the great power in Wales that is the teaching profession. From an obsession with league tables to techniques of 'naming and shaming' – the perceived excesses of the Office for Standards in Education (OFSTED) in England, it is not. Rather, the framework will focus on the needs of learners and 'self-evaluation by the providers', with 'an enhanced role for peer assessors and staff'.[125] A greater element of trust, 'ownership' of the regulatory process is in a very real sense being reclaimed here.

Bringing home audit

But what, it may be asked, of the tough nut – that totem of NPM, or most powerful bureaucratic regulator, the Audit Commission? It goes too far to say that the commission has been in full retreat in Wales. There is, however, a strong sense of the biter bit, or of an element of taming of this England and Wales body in the light of national devolution.

The functions given to the Audit Commission in respect of best value capped a period of extraordinary growth for the institution. As techniques of audit ranged increasingly beyond the traditional issues of probity and regularity, so too the commission's remit was hugely extended. First established in 1983, today its remit covers some 13,000 bodies, which between them spend nearly £100 billion of public money annually. Reeking of cosmeticism, the commission initially responded to devolution by opening a branch office in Cardiff in 1999. Today, however, the discourse is of 'Audit Commission Wales' (ACW) – with its own director. It currently consists of some 200 staff, charged with the major task of auditing the expenditure of some 80 per cent of the funding distributed by the Welsh Assembly Government: in respect, that is, not only of local government, but also of NHS bodies, the police and fire authorities, etc. Put simply, the way in which a body like this proceeds inside the territory, more especially in terms of a distinctive approach tailored to local demand or otherwise, is of the crux of the matter of a new administrative law of Wales.

As so often in the story of Welsh devolution, a vital institutional development has gone generally unremarked. The Audit Commission adopted in 2001 a new strategy, *Delivering Improvement Together*, which incorporated the idea – not before time – that 'in Wales we need to respond to the distinctive Welsh agenda'.[126] The immediate context is the distinctive Welsh Programme for Improvement, and the underlying concern – publicly expressed by the WLGA in the consultation on the commission's draft strategy – that the agency had been overly prescriptive – even jaundiced – in its dealings with public authorities in Wales.[127] 'Struggling to adapt to the changed landscape following Welsh devolution': thus had the constitutional card been played against the commission.

As the title indicates, the new strategy itself implied a cuddlier approach to audit. The commission proposed to 'offer more practical support for service providers in delivering better results for the public'. However, the agency has had to go further in the case of Wales:

> The National Assembly continues to develop ambitious programmes for improving public services within a policy framework that is responsive to Wales' needs and is therefore increasingly divergent from England. It is important that the Commission should respond to this distinctive agenda with distinctive approaches of its own, within a framework that maintains consistent quality and service standards across England and Wales . . .
>
> The challenge for us in supporting improvement is to take account of these differences. We . . . intend to work towards a more seamless audit and inspection service and closer partnership with other regulators in Wales. The overall cost, effectiveness and accountability of regulation are issues that are common to both England and Wales. But they need to be addressed in ways that reflect the differing needs, priorities and resource constraints in Wales.[128]

This – like so much else – would have been unthinkable in the days of the Welsh Office. ACW was now holding out the prospect of both 'a clear "All

Wales" perspective' and 'a suite of Wales specific products'.[129] A measure of the sensitivities, there was suddenly much emphasis on 'representing the Audit Commission in Wales', not least in 'developing relationships with the Welsh Assembly Government and other stakeholders', as also on representing Wales to 'other parts of the Audit Commission family'.

Let us not over-egg the pudding. A recent stocktake by the commission of public services in Wales points up the utility of external comparison (not least with a view to learning from best practice). So for example in local government, a higher proportion of services was considered to be 'good' or 'excellent' in Wales than in England, but fewer services were judged likely to improve. Nor was the agency overly impressed with the state of NHS services in Wales:

> Some services, such as Accident and Emergency, outperform those in England. However, there are particular issues to be addressed in terms of recruitment, retention and sickness rates among staff, reducing waiting times for certain aspects of care and, in some parts of Wales, improving efficiency in day surgery and intermediate care. Social and health deprivation and rurality raise specific challenges for providers in some areas . . .[130]

Nevertheless, the sight of this particular agency genuflecting towards 'a Welsh way' serves to underscore the broad potency of the idea of national devolution. From intrusive regulatory technique to a local re-emphasis on the value of trust, and – against a backdrop of pressures for greater territorial delineation – on through review of agency practice to a special measure of adaptation: it could even be described as a virtuous circle.

Furthermore, this will also come to be seen as a transitional phase. In parallel with the idea of an integrated Welsh ombudsman system, and following the example of Scotland and Northern Ireland, a unified Welsh system of audit is currently in the course of preparation. By which is meant the blocking-up of the functions of the Office of Auditor General for Wales (scrutiny of the Assembly and the quangos) with those of the 'cross-border' Audit Commission in respect of Welsh local government etc.

Indeed, this has been a Welsh Assembly Government priority, the subject of one of its requests for primary legislation.[131] And successfully so: a draft Wales-only bill is now the order of the day.[132] The 'Public Audit (Wales) Act': nothing less than a central arch of Welsh governmental machinery will then be set in place.

CONCLUSION – A NEW ADMINISTRATIVE LAW OF WALES

Post-devolution, much is heard of the competing forces of convergence and divergence. Attention is naturally drawn to the development – or otherwise –

of different policy frameworks or priorities across the four countries of the Union, especially in such vital matters as public health and education or support for the local economy.[133] Yet, to reiterate, there is far more to it than this, not least in the Welsh case of national devolution, as read in terms of the peculiar territorial history of close integration with England. In particular, as this chapter has shown, there are substantial elements of institutional differentiation and cultural diversity inside the system of public administration or world of government. A case it may now be said of *Delineating Wales* – from within.

The point deserves a special emphasis. The quest for local policies as a motor of institutional growth, the local organizational development as an encouragement – even driver – of policy diversity: such, once again, is the strong sense of symbiosis in the new territorial polity. Whereas in chapter 4 – 'Towards a Parliament' – this was approached in terms of the core institutions of Assembly and Welsh Assembly Government, in this chapter it has been taken as a broader phenomenon, present in various guises across the range of Welsh public bodies. For better or worse, the very major restructuring in NHS Wales is in turn seen to exemplify this aspect.

Epitomized in the expansive approach to partnership working, further links are established in terms of that most fashionable concept: civil society. Not so much 'Welsh civil society' as 'a civil society in Wales': such anyway is the idea of the historically retarded territorial development, in the form of private or voluntary as well as public institutions, and in particular of all-Wales bodies.[134] In turn, the way in which the Assembly operates as a catalyst or peak institution to which Welsh society can now respond is highlighted.

It is important to say, however, that banner headlines such as 'education policy breaks loose'[135] are as simplistic as they are absurd. At the risk of repetition, it is not only a matter of content – maths lessons – but of a tangled web of powers and responsibilities, shared values and professional paradigms etc. The twin elements of continuity and diversity: 'Welshifying' is a key element of the contemporary scene, but it is hardly dominant for all purposes and in all sectors. No doubt many patterns of public policy and organization in the fields of devolved powers will go on much as before for the foreseeable future, and from the devolutionist viewpoint rightly so given the many benefits to this small country of close connections and other people's good ideas. In the public administration jargon of the day, 'one size does not fit all'.

The closeness of Wales is seen to offer many advantages. Flexibility: the facility to cut across traditional departmental lines, which is given tangible expression in such cross-cutting themes as sustainable development and equal opportunity. Responsiveness: opportunities to adapt and implement policy more easily, which may then be better suited to local conditions. Conflict-avoidance: an innate capacity to develop more collaborative and constructive forms of relations, which is predicated on regular and personal contact. Inclusiveness: the potential of local or sub-state mobilization, which the devolved administration has been so keen to stress. Solidarity: in the sense that is of 'Team Wales' or of the capacity for concerted actions, under the rubric of national devolution.

Turning the argument round, it is precisely for this reason that the need to build up the organizational – and in particular the policy development – capacity of the devolved administration is so compelling. The devolutionary project effectively demands a critical mass: better to make the most of the various opportunities.

To reiterate, much of this may appear unremarkable when viewed in comparative perspective. As described by the Permanent Secretary, the 'intensity' and 'proximity' of relations, 'politically driven', is so clearly a 'little country' syndrome. Yet such has been the immersion of Wales in the Union, or more precisely in England, that it represents a very profound set of changes.

Another way of expressing these ideas is in terms of a new administrative law of Wales. In respect, that is, on the one hand of the view of law as an instrument of government, and further of the value of alternative techniques or 'levers' in securing government objectives; and, on the other hand, of such democratic virtues as consultation and transparency.[136] Partnership working takes many forms in the new model Wales, and there is seen to be a special distaste for the more intrusive forms of rule and regulation – juridification – as practised in a more populous neighbour.

Simply put, law and legal technique is variously centre stage by reason of the particular Welsh model of executive devolution and cast to the wings in the closeness of Wales. Alternatively, and with a view to highlighting the interplay of the different paradigms – devolution and not divorce – one might speak not of the administrative law of England and Wales, let alone (as has traditionally been the case) of English administrative law, but of the administrative laws of England and Wales.[137]

At the same time, better to secure the good governance of Wales, it is important to be alive to the dangers. First, partnership working is susceptible to drowning under the weight of its own rhetoric. Expressed slightly differently, the prevailing ideology is already taking on a certain formulaic quality (as in the case of the NHS). Let us be clear. More horizontal arrangements – less hierarchy – is all at one with the devolutionary impulse, and is often to be applauded, not least in terms of local and collaborative approaches in the face of entrenched economic problems.[138] Yet the method not only has significant costs, it can also – without careful handling – degenerate into a triumph of process over product, and even be an excuse or buffer against government failure (the blurring of accountability). Partnership working, it is well to remember in the closeness of Wales, is essentially a means and not an end in itself.

Secondly, the values of independence and impartiality, or professional judgement and expertise, that are associated with the design of the arm's-length agency, need to be vigorously asserted. In the case of the Welsh executive agencies, as also the NHS, a firm measure of strategic direction is all at one with the devolutionary project of 'bringing government closer to the people'. Similarly, one cannot but applaud the sincere attempts that are being made in the name of democratic renewal, from public appointments to greater transparency, and on (if more hesitantly) to 'legislative' oversight and influence. It is nonetheless inadvisable to lurch from one extreme to the other.

Thirdly, the extended accountability of public bodies courtesy of the Assembly ought not to be considered a substitute for rigorous systems of external scrutiny. On the one hand, there should be no objection to the 'Welshifying' of such agencies of bureaucratic regulation with a view to enhancing their sensitivity to local conditions, subject, that is, to careful guarantees over comparability and cross-fertilization. On the other hand, a lighter touch in bureaucratic regulation should be seen primarily as a welcome relief from the excesses of centralization under New Public Management. Reducing audit to consultancy, for example, should be regarded as a perversion of the 'Welsh way'.

For the avoidance of doubt, this is not to imply some vast array of nefarious forces. Rather, it picks up on the concern to vindicate the constitutional values of openness and accountability that was uppermost in the minds of the architects of the devolutionary scheme. All at one with the local advantages of the new constitutional dispensation, the closeness of Wales itself demands close vigilance.

Wales in the United Kingdom

There is a close working relationship between the UK Government and the Welsh Assembly Government at both ministerial and official levels. The majority of day-to-day relations are informal and on a bilateral basis.

Wales Office/Office of the Deputy Prime Minister[1]

Devolution, it is worth reiterating, is not divorce. A multiplicity of joint, concurrent and overlapping powers points up the strong measure of interdependency between the central and territorial layers of government; and, in turn, the pressing need for efficient and effective modalities of cooperation and coordination under the general rubric of 'intergovernmental relations'. The more so, it may be said, by reason of the increased complexity and reach of policy problems that is such a feature of contemporary government and regulation.[2]

Matters have once again proceeded in an *ad hoc* and piecemeal fashion. The approach is insular as well as pragmatic – as one might say, typically 'British'. Set against the rich comparative experience in constitutional systems of divided competence, federal and otherwise, of tackling the challenge of accommodating and coordinating state and sub-state interests, there has been a tendency to reinvent the wheel.[3]

The strong asymmetrical element in the UK devolutionary process, including in terms of the novel constitutional imbalance of a Union state characterized by a lack of English political institutions, looms large here. As well as many shared features, there are significant elements in the new structures and processes of intergovernmental relations that are distinctive or unique to Wales, once again reflecting the scheme of executive devolution and the premium on political and administrative goodwill associated with it. Likewise, confronted by the historical and geographical facts of a powerful 'cross-border' paradigm – 'England and Wales', and with limited (if increasing) political and administrative resources at its disposal, this junior partner of the Union has a very special need for close and continuing relations with the central government machine. Such are the ties that bind.

Commonality and diversity; continuity and change

The broad spread and multifaceted nature of intergovernmental relations – IGR – is amply demonstrated in this book: from the block and formula systems (chapter 2) to the arrangements for 'voice' on primary legislation affecting Wales (chapter 9), and on through to central–territorial relations in the context of the EU (chapter 13). Under the general rubric of 'Wales in the United Kingdom', it is convenient in this chapter to consider a set of matters which further serve to highlight the interplay in the (Welsh) devolutionary development of the twin elements of commonality and diversity, and of continuity and change.

There is, first, the strong development of 'soft law' in the guise of concordats. This involves establishing the ground rules for administrative cooperation and exchanges of information between the UK government and the devolved administrations: in lawyer's parlance, a form of 'codification' of the (previously internal) processes of government. For the reasons explained, Wales is a spiritual home of this form of inter-institutional administrative agreement, whose basic concept is 'no surprises'. Constitutionally speaking, the system of concordats is shown to be significant in a number of ways, for example by a conscious effort to limit the role of the courts in the general UK devolutionary development. I have elsewhere used the phrase 'concordats of the constitution' to point up this vital aspect.

A second main feature is introduced: the grounding by concordat of new political machinery to help with the management of IGR. Indeed, if the formal mechanism that is the Joint Ministerial Committee (JMC) did not exist then its functional equivalent would have to be invented. Consisting of UK government, Scottish, Welsh and Northern Ireland ministers, it now inhabits the territory previously governed by the UK government convention of collective responsibility. It will be seen, however, that the full potential of this machinery has yet to be realized. Turning the argument round, there are strong clues here to a distinct preference in official circles for the retention of more informal or fluid and flexible arrangements, including – as the opening quotation says – in the case of Wales.

What, it may be asked, of the recent inquiry by the House of Lords Select Committee on the Constitution into interinstitutional relations post-devolution?[4] The very fact of it being the first substantive investigation by this new committee is significant: testimony to the sudden emergence of a primary field of constitutional, political and administrative activity inside the Union state. In the event, through voluminous evidence-gathering, the inquiry has cast considerable light on the internal structures and processes, as also on the official assumptions behind them; a valuable public service. But further, in challenging the UK government's approach on the basis of insufficient formal working practices, the report has met with a cool response.

To anticipate the argument, who in official circles would want to go down this road in the conditions of Labour Party hegemony?

The thorny question has arisen of the role post-devolution of the Secretary of State for Wales, and of the skeletal remnant of the old territorial department in the guise of 'the Wales Office'. Like his counterparts in Scotland and Northern Ireland, the minister still has a significant role to play in UK or non-devolved matters relating to the territory, and there also remain the special responsibilities under executive devolution on primary legislation affecting Wales. The situation of the Wales Office is in fact a useful barometer of the progress of the so-called 'devolution settlement'. Reinvention, evolution or evaporation: nothing, it may be said, has better illustrated the conjectural quality to the design of the constitutional architecture, as also – it now appears – the 'back of the envelope' approach.

The great importance of IGR should not be allowed to obscure the flanking parliamentary aspect. The issue is naturally raised of the role of Welsh MPs post-devolution, as also of the special institutional arrangements for representation and scrutiny on behalf of Welsh interests – a 'parliamentary voice for Wales' – that had developed prior to the Assembly. A measure of retrenchment, a cautious reworking to take account of the new political and administrative realities: the 'Mother of Parliaments' will typically be found bringing up the rear.

The idea of territorial networks promoting local interests in the United Kingdom is hardly a novel one.[5] A recurring theme of the chapter, however, is the sense in which it has been accentuated in the conduct of Welsh govern-ance post-devolution. It becomes necessary to think in terms of a novel 'Welsh axis', grounded in the devolved administration, and encompassing elements like the Wales Office and the House of Commons committees dealing exclusively with Wales. The conditions of Labour Party hegemony are not exactly unhelpful here! For the avoidance of doubt, this is not to suggest some huge breakdown of the established lines of political and administrative authority, or that the sense of local identity and representation is – or should be – always compelling. Also, many of the connections will be opaque and indirect, and so hard to pin down, as is the way of such networks. To overlook the particular social and cultural content of IGR in the context of national devolution, however, would be absurd.

1. CONCORDATS ETC.: NOT JUST 'ROAD MAPS FOR BUREAUCRATS'

The idea of interinstitutional administrative agreements, better to facilitate harmonious and collaborative working practices across different tiers of government, is hardly a novel concept in comparative public administration. From procedural cooperation to substantive policy coordination, and on through to substituting for more familiar techniques of constitutional reform: such instruments play a variety of roles in federal systems of government.[6] The sheer scale and rapidity of the development in the United Kingdom of such a system of concordats is nonetheless a distinctive feature. Paper has been piled on paper.

The chief purpose, according to ministers, has been 'to preserve the good working relationships' that existed under the old Whitehall model incorporating territorial departments.[7] Indeed, according to the ministerial architect of Welsh devolution, the concordats evolved 'essentially to ensure that the process of government . . . could proceed unhampered by the constitutional change that we were making'.[8] Typically geared towards process and not substance, and often cast in aspirational terms, much of the material is in fact exceptionally tedious: 'roadmaps for bureaucrats'.

But let us keep in mind the constitutional setting, not least the point that almost nothing is said in the devolution statute(s) about the structures and processes of IGR. At one and the same time, the soft law system of concordats can be seen as determinedly low-key, devolution recast in terms of administrative nuts and bolts, and as supplying some major rules of engagement, for example in the EU context.[9] Again, the system effectively depends on constructive political and administrative relations, and has a role to play in facilitating the smooth and efficient operation of a post-devolutionary system of multi-layered governance.

The internal sense of hierarchy is important. The principal agreement is the *Memorandum of Understanding (MoU)*,[10] a multilateral arrangement involving the three devolved administrations and the UK government. It sets out basic principles for the conduct of intergovernmental relations and provides for the JMC. Broadly uniform arrangements are then established in areas of government – coordination of European Union policy issues, financial assistance to industry, international relations, and government statistics – where there are special demands for consistency, courtesy of four separate 'overarching concordats'.

Bilateral concordats between individual UK government departments and their counterparts in the devolved administrations comprise a second level of guidance. The original idea was to lay much of the weight at this level, so disseminating a sense of 'ownership' beyond the political core of government. Predictably, after an initial burst of enthusiasm, which no doubt reflected a certain nervousness about what was then the 'great unknown' of devolution, the flow has slowed to a trickle. Fifteen bilateral concordats involving the Assembly had been produced by the end of 2002, covering most of the key UK actors (table 19).

It may be 'soft law', but from the viewpoint of ministers and officials this type of agreement represents 'one of the most formal mechanisms of intrastate cooperation in the tool-box of intergovernmental relations'.[11] It is not

Table 19: UK departments with concordats with the Welsh Assembly Government, 2002

Cabinet Office
Department of Culture, Media and Sport
Department for Education and Employment (now DFES)
Department of Environment, Transport, and the Regions (now DTLR)
Department of Health
Department for Social Security (now DWP)
Department of Trade and Industry
Forestry Commission
HM Treasury
Health and Safety Executive
Home Office
Lord Chancellor's Department
Ministry of Agriculture, Fisheries and Food (now DEFRA)
Ministry of Defence
Wales Office (now incorporated in the Department for Constitutional Affairs)

surprising then to learn of other, less formal instruments being developed by way of supplement and to maintain flexibility. Working-level and service-level agreements, which deal with day-to-day operational matters and specific issues, will support many of these concordats. For their part, the Devolution Guidance Notes which central government promulgates, both on general matters like ministerial accountability in the post-devolutionary world, and on territory-specific issues such as primary legislation affecting Wales,[12] are now officially categorized as a third level of guidance.[13]

Administrative principles

Of the four key principles set out in the *MoU* good communication takes pride of place, being indicative of the concern to maintain coherent government and close relations. Early warning of policy proposals; the opportunity for administrations to make representations to each other; establishing arrangements where appropriate for joint policy development: such are the requirements that the administrations will seek to observe. Next comes cooperation on matters of mutual interest, which notably extends to agency arrangements and to public bodies dealing with both devolved and non-devolved matters. Then there is the exchange of information on technical, scientific and statistical matters, which is after all the lifeblood of modern government. The administrations will aim to provide each other with as full and open access as possible.[14]

The administrative model that is envisaged here of free flows of policy ideas and information leads directly on to the fourth principle, confidentiality in the workings of the post-devolutionary system of IGR. 'Each administration can only expect to receive information if it treats such information with appropriate discretion.' There is in fact great emphasis throughout the *MoU* on the importance of confidentiality: shades of Whitehall. On the one hand, it will be for 'the administration providing the information to state what, if any, restrictions there should be upon its usage'. On the other hand, and exceptionally, it is recognized that in this sphere the operation of the arrangements may have legal consequences. The administrations thus 'accept that in certain circumstances a duty of confidence may arise and will between themselves respect legal requirements of confidentiality'.[15]

In many ways the provisions appear unexceptional. The values expressed echo those found in other advanced systems of divided competence, as for example in Germany under the (legal) concept of comity.[16] Again, characterized by the central role of intergovernmental relations conducted by ministers and officials, executive federalism is a familiar concept in comparative constitutional studies. The closed nature of the process that is involved has strong parallels in the emergent constitutional architecture of the Union state: a strong executive form of IGR which itself fits with the powerful tradition of executive domination in the British constitution.

Anaesthetizing judges

Strenuous efforts have been made to limit the role of judges in IGR. There are two main strands. First, the *MoU* has grounded an expansive development of machinery for alternative dispute resolution, with a view to restricting confrontation in the courts over the various devolution settlements. Second, the preference for a soft law approach clearly signals a strong aversion to judicial scrutiny of the workings of concordats etc. Put another way, this general development of non-statutory tools and techniques helps to limit the constitutional role played by the judges in the new architecture of the United Kingdom. That the one cannot be understood without reference to the other is all part of the devolutionary design, including in Wales.

The special court jurisdiction that now exists for handling 'devolution issues' is examined in chapter 13. It suffices at this stage to refer to a fast-track procedure, whereby the law officers of the various administrations can go direct to the Judicial Committee of the Privy Council for a decision. The *MoU* makes clear that although the UK government is prepared to use such powers if necessary, it sees them very much as a matter of last resort. The decision-making chain is to this effect elongated, so generating many opportunities for negotiation and settlement, including by the Counsel General operating on behalf of the Assembly. Commitments include direct notification of legislative proposals to the UK law officers; a joint aim of resolving any difficulties through discussion; and early warning by the UK government of an intention to act, so enabling the devolved administration 'to make any representations it wishes, or take any remedial action'.[17]

The concordats themselves commonly disclaim an intention to create legal relations, and on other occasions expressly exclude the creation of legally enforceable rights and obligations. The *MoU* says that it 'is a statement of political intent, and should not be interpreted as a binding agreement. It does not create legal obligations between the parties. It is intended to be binding in honour only.'[18] So there!

A failure to observe the provisions of a concordat could be vulnerable to challenge via the ordinary principles of judicial review. As a judicial tool for entering on soft law territory, the doctrine of legitimate expectation (no reneging on an undertaking) is most relevant. There is also a close fit, given the initial emphasis in the concordats on procedural matters, such as consultation, where the doctrine is most securely rooted.[19] In truth, however, it has never been an issue of total fireproofing. Rather, the aim has been to highlight the sensitive political and administrative aspects of IGR with a view to encouraging judicial restraint.[20]

Concordats and Wales – practical illustrations

By examining particular instruments from a Welsh perspective, one gains an appreciation of both the constraints on and opportunities for territorial initiative in the context of state/sub-state relations. On the one hand, a general understanding of no surprises takes on a whole new meaning in the constitutional situation of executive devolution. On the other hand, when convenient, Welsh actors have practised the familiar art of shadowing their more powerful northern cousins in dealings with Whitehall. The symmetry that now exists in the overarching concordat on European Union issues will be seen to illustrate this.

The legal status of the Assembly as a body corporate has served once again to complicate matters. At first it was assumed that the Assembly as a whole, and not simply the Assembly cabinet, would have to agree the concordats. The fact however that the Members were only invited to 'take note'[21] of the arrangements can now be seen as an early example of the internal development of separation of powers. Today, the strong sense of 'ownership' by the executive branch, in Wales as elsewhere, is symbolized by the listing of the concordats on the cabinet section of the Assembly website.

In fact, the case of the concordats further highlights a basic design fault in the original Assembly architecture: the assumption that notwithstanding the need for close collaboration and coordination with central government, the devolved administration could somehow operate on a different constitutional basis. The new modalities of intergovernmental relations, which obviously cater first and foremost for the Westminster/Whitehall style of government, can now be seen pressing the Assembly in the same direction from day one. Wales, it is well to remember, is not an island.

As for the bilateral concordats themselves, the drafting makes clear the pragmatic approach taken to IGR. As well as a strong contextual element – 'the particular circumstances of the policy area . . . will . . . largely drive the nature of any agreement' – the role of sustaining procedural cooperation was made clear from the outset. The agreements would set down 'common processes' and 'the main features' of working relationships, 'rather than specify substantive outcomes'.[22] Standard items include participation in the Whitehall committee system and territorial inputs on cross-cutting issues, financial arrangements and access to central government services.

So much, it may be said, for the official explanation. A recurring theme in this chapter: central government is hardly a monolith. As with powers, so with concordats: some UK departments more than others have displayed a generosity of spirit. Sometimes the devolved administration appears to be treated as a broadly equal partner, and in particular one that is deserving of trust, and on other occasions less so.

Some examples will help to convey the flavour. The first one concerns the vital matter of relations with HM Treasury, the context being the firm grip that the Treasury retains on macro-management of the UK economy, together with the decentralization of expenditure decisions implicit in the continuing operation of the block and formula system. In light of the general Treasury principles for territorial finance,[23] the concordat echoes the need for some formalization of arrangements post-devolution. Its purpose 'is to set out clearly the relationship' in order to ensure that both parties 'are aware of the requirements of the other' and 'are consequently able to fulfil their responsibilities fully'.[24] It is of course the infant body that is considered in particular need of instruction.

In addition to the information supplied to the Treasury in accordance with the devolution legislation,[25] the Assembly cabinet agrees to respond to all reasonable requests for information on matters ranging from policy on non-domestic rates to the classification of transactions for the purpose of the public expenditure control system. In return, the Treasury takes on some basic commitments, such as early notice of financial allocations in order to allow the devolved administration to manage its resources properly. Typical flanking measures include exchange of documentation on such matters as public procurement and external auditing, and provision for regular consultations between officials. In sum, this concordat brilliantly illustrates the intense interaction of the territorial and central layers of government post-devolution; and, further, the dominance enjoyed by the centre.[26]

Perhaps the Lord Chancellor's Department can afford to be generous, since few of its core activities are directly affected by the devolution of powers. Its concordat is notable for a two-tier approach that fully reflects the constitutional role of the Assembly as a voice for Wales. Arrangements are made for consultation, to the extent of a positive obligation 'to involve each other, as and when appropriate, in policy formulation', in those areas where the respective responsibilities may impinge. Under the rubric of advance notification, the LCD also undertakes to inform the devolved administration of significant policy proposals in such non-devolved fields as legal services, the civil justice system and family law, with a view to enabling comment and due consideration.[27] No surprises etc.: this concordat stands then for best practice.

The concordat originally made with our old friends the DETR is a massive document.[28] As well as providing limited opportunities for making general representations on policy, the sheer detail of the regulation suggests that the virtues of cooperation and consensus may be in short supply. The concordat incorporates a series of annexes containing additional arrangements that relate to specific subject areas or groups of subjects: sustainable development, land use planning and environmental impact assessment are but three examples. A reflection perhaps of the demonstrable tensions in the early days, there is also provision for a forum of senior officials to oversee the bilateral processes of communication and coordination.[29] Put simply, the design and content of this concordat reeks of a lack of trust. At times, it even reads like a commercial contract.

Soft law in context

As the JMC has solemnly recorded, 'formal agreements, while important, can only do so much'.[30] So too it is the nature of IGR that 'the majority of day-to-day relations are informal and on a bilateral basis'[31] between policy counterparts in individual departments. Were it otherwise, much in the system would now be grinding to a halt. The arrival on the scene of e-mail is a suitably fortunate occurrence!

To pursue the theme, 'the importance of continuing informal dialogue between Ministers and officials to promote common understanding and strengthen the relationship between administrations' is rightly emphasized. This 'is vital so that particular issues can be handled in the context of better understanding of each other's position and objectives through the development of a positive relationship, capable of handling specific differences'.[32] Not least, it is worth reiterating, in the case of Wales, by reason of the close interplay with the pre-existing 'cross-border' administrative paradigm.

The work of the Cabinet and Constitution Unit of the Welsh Assembly Government has already been mentioned.[33] In the context of IGR it is one of a set of dedicated units in the four administrations, who are in close and regular contact. According to the UK Cabinet Office, this network forms 'the back-bone of inter-administration relations within the devolved UK'. All at one with a general role of overview and buttering up, as also the sheer range of official contacts across the fields of devolved functions, these units 'usually only get involved with particular topics in order to help resolve bilateral problems'.[34]

Very much a living system, the fluid and flexible nature of IGR is communicated strongly here. At one and the same time, the soft law system of concordats serves to underwrite this feature, militating against rigidities, and must be read firmly in its context. There is merit in the view that if the concordats have to be invoked on a regular basis to ensure good relations, then relations are already bad.

In a system where officials conduct most of the business, the concept of a general framework of reference is important nonetheless. To anticipate the discussion, the golden principle of 'no surprises' will sometimes be honoured in the breach, and perhaps more often in the case of little Wales. Conversely, it is little Wales that by reason of the comparative weakness and dependency of the local political and administrative system stands to gain most from 'no surprises' by way of an official resource and set of expectations. Simply put, where would the Welsh Assembly Government be without the principle?

Waving a piece of paper is not always apt to inspire confidence. Looking beyond the hegemony of New Labour, a far sterner test of this soft law framework is promised by administrations of different political persuasions.[35] It is a system that without the political will to work together could so easily be overwhelmed. Yet for as long as devolution endures large portions of concordatry should endure by reason of the shared interest and common 'ownership' made evident on the official plane. In the complex world of shared and overlapping competencies that the case of Wales high-lights, considerations of administrative necessity or convenience play a major role.

2. POLITICAL COORDINATION: THE JMC (AND WALES)

In grounding the expectation that most business would be dealt with bi-laterally and informally on the administrative plane, the *MoU* recognized the need for some central coordination of the overall relationship.[36] As fleshed out in a supplementary agreement, the JMC was thus established on the basis of a model that in providing for both general and functional formats is not unlike the EU Council of Ministers.

A consultative not an executive body, one that reaches agreements rather than decisions, the JMC has the following terms of reference:

- to consider non-devolved matters which impinge on devolved responsibilities, and devolved matters which impinge on non-devolved responsibilities;
- where the UK government and the devolved administrations so agree, to consider devolved matters if it is beneficial to discuss their respective treatment in the different parts of the United Kingdom;
- to keep the arrangements for liaison between the UK government and the devolved administrations under review; and
- to consider disputes between the administrations.[37]

Stunted growth

This machinery has considerable potential. For example, given that devolution allows for greater innovation in policy-making and delivery, what, it may be asked, of the pooling of those ideas and experiences to mutual benefit? Again, the scope for further incremental development – a greater intensity of such arrangements as the years go by – is attested by a wealth of comparative constitutional experience.[38]

The one clear requirement is an annual 'plenary' meeting of the JMC. As the terminology suggests, this stands for political cooperation and coordination at the highest level. Chaired by the Prime Minister, the meeting is attended by the Deputy Prime Minister, the Chancellor of the Exchequer, the three territorial Secretaries of State, and the First Minister and DFM/senior minister from each of the devolved administrations. Reflecting and reinforcing the model of a strong executive form of IGR, the proceedings of this and other JMC meetings are confidential; in the classic phrase, 'to permit free and candid discussion'.[39] A bland official communiqué typically results.

There was some early growth of the machinery in functional or sectoral format. As well as a JMC on European Affairs for which the *MoU* specifically provides, special ministerial groups were established on major cross-cutting issues such as child and pensioner poverty and preparation of the economy for the digital age. A subcommittee on health was the most active, a classic example in the context of the NHS of the continuing interface in policy-making and implementation of devolved and non-devolved functions. It also serves to highlight the potential value of such intergovernmental machinery, political or symbolic, as well as substantive and procedural. 'Wales leads the way in telemedicine', trumpeted the local press release.[40]

More recently, however, the momentum has visibly slackened. Plenary meetings have simply fulfilled the basic requirement, while the JMC in functional format has commonly been the more notable by absence. Major devolved portfolios like education and the environment have remained outside this loop. Meanwhile a committee of officials (JMC (O)) led by the Cabinet Office, which was created in standard Whitehall fashion to shadow the political machinery, went several years without meeting.

To the external observer, the arrangements also appear haphazard. The Select Committee on the Constitution was unable to find 'any clear criteria to establish whether intergovernmental Ministerial meetings are held, and whether meetings are held within the JMC framework or not'. Again, 'the areas in which "functional" JMC meetings are held, and the frequency with which they are held, do not correspond with the areas of important interaction or overlap of policy between governments'.[41]

This, however, yields some vital clues. One explanation for why there are so few JMC meetings concerns the name on the bottle. The fact that many other meetings bring together ministers and officials from central government and the devolved administrations, sometimes for example in agriculture on a regular basis,[42] is of the essence of the new form of IGR. Why look to back-up from the Cabinet Office when the resources of the individual UK Department are immediately available?

The JMC on Europe is an instructive example. Chaired by the Foreign Secretary, it has been meeting twice a year, as part of the member state's preparations for the European Council held at the end of each EU presidency. But this hardly exhausts the range of contacts designed to incorporate the views of the devolved administrations when formulating the UK line on EU issues. For example, the 'Celtic cousins' are regularly invited to participate in ministerial meetings such as MINECOR, looking at the UK's public diplomacy in Europe. Again, UK ministerial correspondence on EU issues will be dealt with in a cabinet subcommittee ('EP Committee'). Strictly speaking, the deliberations cannot be shared with the ministers from the devolved administrations, but it is common practice for the lead UK minister to invite their comments.[43] Especially for little Wales, this is quite a step up.

Two general observations are in order. The first one concerns the great capacity of the Whitehall machine for regeneration. As well as, and in large measure instead of, recourse to the 'new-fangled' machinery of the JMC, pre-existing or parallel structures and processes have now been harnessed and adapted for the purpose of IGR. The twin elements of continuity and change in the UK devolutionary development: this is another paradigm example.

Secondly, a system of IGR which viewed in comparative perspective was towards the informal end of the spectrum at the outset, more especially by reason of the general recourse to soft law, can now be seen veering further in this direction in the conditions of Labour Party hegemony. This is the reliance on political and administrative good will writ large. Wales of course is no exception. Rhodri Morgan has described the formal aspects as accounting 'for only about 20%' of the relationship between the administrations, and personal chemistry and good will 'as accounting for 80%'.[44]

Political excursus: disputing

Along with Labour colleagues in Whitehall, Mr Morgan has stressed the smooth running of the system:

> By and large the system has worked well to date: communication and consultation routinely takes place on virtually all relevant matters. There have been well-documented cases of it breaking down, but these are very much the exception. Indeed, as understanding of the post-devolution context has grown, relations have become firmer and more productive.[45]

It is, however, in the nature of things that the quality of relationships with individual Whitehall departments will differ. Mr Morgan again:

> There is a kind of notional league table . . . Those Whitehall departments with which we do not compete . . . have a very good relationship with us. [The] Foreign Office as well as the . . . Treasury have been very good to us and they have set out very consciously to be good, and to make it clear to us that we should never entertain ambitions to have our own foreign policy or tax-raising function . . .
>
> Then working through the government departments to those which carry out parallel functions in England, there is always a much greater tension. Finally, you have those bodies where there really is a ragged edge . . .[46]

The exception one hopes that proves the rule, the first Assembly Finance Minister has singled out the Home Office for a lack of communication. In Mrs Hart's experience, 'there are real problems at the heart of the system itself . . . an absolute arrogance about the way they feel about the devolved administrations, particularly in relation to Wales'. According to her senior official, a breakdown 'often proceeds from straightforward ignorance and not really understanding the need to keep us informed and consulted. There are also those who actively resent having to keep us informed and consulted.'[47]

No doubt such things are partly in the eye of the beholder. Even the Select Committee on the Constitution had difficulty penetrating these internal political and administrative systems, properly to evaluate this type of criticism. But then – dense, dark, and tangled, and inhabited by some big beasts – such is the nature of the IGR jungle.

What, it may be asked, of the provision here for dispute resolution? After all, in establishing the new modalities of intergovernmental relations, the challenge for the official architects was not to eliminate conflict, which is inherent especially in systems of multi-layered democracy, but to help devise structures and processes for minimizing and managing it.

The official design is very much one of bilateral settlement and compromise. There is also provision for the exercise of 'good offices' by the Secretary of State (for Wales) in recalitrant disputes, and for the UK Cabinet

Office to play a consultative role in order 'to ensure a consistent interpretation of the devolution settlements'.[48] The presumption is that 'an issue will come to the JMC only when there is an impasse'.[49]

Once again, it is the fact of the dog not barking that is significant. In the suitably comforting language of the UK Cabinet Office, 'the fact that no disputes have so far been referred to the Joint Ministerial Committee for resolution suggests that the existing system of inter-administration relations is working well'.

3. POLES APART

Such is the immediate backdrop to the recent report from the House of Lords Select Committee. In its words:

> The fact that inter-institutional relations in the UK have settled down in a relatively painless manner is . . . attributable in large measure to good will between the different administrations and to the professionalism of the civil service. We have stressed the extent to which issues are discussed and resolved on an informal basis. This extensive informal contact has considerably aided the process of intergovernmental relations. However, in the long term, when administrations are run by different political parties, informal contact will be difficult to sustain . . . We think that preparations for the time when there will be administrations in place of different political persuasions are necessary. In particular, we see the need for relations to be put on a more formal, as well as a more transparent, basis. It is important not to wait. We think it prudent to anticipate and to start taking action now.[50]

And again:

> We recommend that further use should be made of the formal mechanisms for intergovernmental relations, even if they seem to many of those presently involved to be excessive. Formal mechanisms, such as the JMC, are not intended to serve as a substitute for good relations in other respects, or for good and frequent informal contacts, but rather to serve as a framework for such relations and to act as a fall-back in case informal personal relations cease to be sufficient. Such mechanisms are likely to become increasingly important when governments of different political persuasions have to deal with each other.[51]

The Select Committee should be commended for a forward-looking approach. The present high levels of good will clearly are likely to diminish over time, not only for the reason of political 'cohabitation' but also as the de-volved administrations increasingly pursue distinct policies – greater aggre-gate differences – and individual career patterns in public life grow apart. The exceptionally benign conditions of financial largess to date must also be factored into the equation.

Constitutionally speaking, there is much to be said for the argument, including by reference to the diffusion of responsibility that is familiarly associated with the workings of interlocking arrangements in legal and political systems of divided competence.[52] Characterized by a lack of transparency, machinery like the JMC effectively constitutes a 'black hole' at the heart of the emergent constitutional architecture of the Union state. Modest proposals[53] such as substantive press statements and a statement by the Prime Minister to the House after each plenary meeting strike a chord.

Nor can one overlook the attributes of informality as a technique for domination by the centre. A regeneration of Whitehall custom and practice, emblematic of the right of initiative enjoyed by the UK government, may be considered significant here. A different but related point: the report serves to convey the flimsy nature of the present construction. 'We have an unresolved concern that these mechanisms may not prove adequate to the challenges arising from a highly-charged political dispute, especially if the parties are accustomed to informal rather than formal dealings with each other.'[54] Trust in political and administrative quarters is hardly a given; especially, one is tempted to add, in the conditions of national devolution.

Lack of scrutiny

It is worth pausing to note that the existing arrangements for the scrutiny of IGR are limited across the UK.[55] Once again, this is especially noteworthy in the case of the Assembly, not one hastens to say by reason of the 'strange anatomy' of the corporate body, but because of the exceptional measure of the legal, political and administrative (inter)dependency now associated with Welsh devolution. Questions to the First Minister, and consideration by particular subject committees of IGR issues as and when they arise, is hardly a recipe for 'joined-up' and 'cross-cutting' scrutiny.

The matter is also something of a running sore, with Assembly Members voicing concerns about the workings and lack of transparency of IGR on many occasions.[56] As one would expect, the focus has been on the internal processes for the exercise of 'voice' in matters of primary legislation, but not entirely so. Ron Davies for example has suggested that all correspondence between the devolved administration and the Secretary of State for Wales relating to Assembly resolutions should be made available to AMs.[57] A radical proposal, and one which notably the minister did not put forward during the debates on the devolution statute.

Looking forwards, one might think in terms of bringing the topic of IGR and Wales inside the remit of a standing committee, so providing a 'parliamentary' focus on the overall relationship.[58] Such arrangements for monitoring and supervision of the structures and processes would be a novel development among the representative institutions of the Union state, but none the worse for that. For example the Assembly's European and External Affairs Committee, which to anticipate the discussion has been under-employed,[59] could be suitably renamed and its remit extended. Turning the argument round, the very fact that this is unlikely to happen – and would no doubt be regarded as anathema by officials in the Welsh Assembly Government – serves to highlight the general problem of political accountability posed by (the strong executive form of) IGR.

Lead balloon

Likewise, the broad thrust of the Select Committee's findings has not been welcome in the official corridors of power.[60] It effectively contradicts the basic assumptions on which Whitehall in particular has been operating, as the evidence from the UK Cabinet Office also makes clear:

> The Government is committed to making a success of devolution, not just in the early stages but in the long term as well. Not just while there is good will on all sides, but also if relations were to become strained – as at times they might. The Government believes that the formal and informal arrangements established over the past two and a half years provide that robust basis on which successful long-term relationships between the four administrations can be built.
>
> The Government does not believe that the use of such informal arrangements for inter-administration relations has weakened the formal mechanisms . . . On the contrary, devolution is more likely to work if Ministers and officials in all four administrations see such informal contacts as 'second nature'. Whether an issue is resolved by formal or informal means is a matter of choice in individual circumstances.[61]

Consider for example the recommendations for clear criteria on whether ministerial meetings should be JMC meetings; that the JMC in functional format should meet at least once a year in each of the main policy areas of devolved functions; and that the existing agriculture meetings should become JMC meetings.[62] Rationalization, expansion and incorporation: these ideas cut across the attributes of fluidity and flexibility that inform the present arrangements. Suffice it to add that a devolved administration can request a meeting of the JMC if it so wishes.[63]

Alternatively, take the suggestion that concordats should be made fixed-term agreements, with a view to guaranteeing stability for that period and to underwriting a process of 'relearning' on review.[64] This grates with the strong 'soft law' quality of the arrangements, which themselves are open to review to reflect institutional learning. For its part, the JMC in plenary session has been conducting annual stock-takes of the *MoU* and system of bilateral concordats. Surprise, surprise: the political architects have generally given the design a clean bill of health. At worst:

> The new arrangements had not always operated as smoothly as they might. This was understandable given the scale of the constitutional changes and the inevitable learning period . . . But all present stressed their commitment to addressing any weaknesses in order to make a continuing success of devolution.[65]

The theme can be pursued in various ways. Ministers and officials no doubt take considerable pride in 'the extent to which devolution has bedded in with remarkably few problems'.[66] From this viewpoint, increased formality may not only be indicative of conflict but also a potential accelerator of it. Then there are the usual practical concerns – the constraints on ministers' diaries, the inconvenience of officials travelling – which weigh against a more prescribed or clear-cut set of arrangements. Elite, discretionary and closed, in a political and administrative field like IGR the typically 'British' approach to government will have many attractions, for the practitioners.

Things may change – a banishing of the sense of atrophy from the JMC. Highly pragmatic in character and strongly focused on the here and now, the official view of IGR sits comfortably however with so much else in the UK devolutionary development. 'We make it up as we go along.' A different but related point: there is a natural reluctance to second-guess the political and administrative dynamics, and especially in this case how the JMC machinery will respond in bumpy conditions. 'If (it's new and) it ain't broke, don't fix it.'

In summary, 'force-feeding' the formal machinery, which effectively is what the Select Committee recommends, stands to be spurned in favour of a more 'natural' organic development. Not least in terms of the flimsy construction, which so emphasizes the need for political and administrative good will, their noble Lords have made some valid points. But for the time being at least this is lead balloon territory.

4. BAROMETER: THE WALES OFFICE

The Secretary of State for Wales has officially been said to have three main roles post devolution: voice of the UK government in Wales, guardian of the devolution settlement, and voice of Wales in the UK cabinet.[67] The minister has in turn fronted up the Wales Office as a separate and free-standing territorial department. That is, until June 2003, when, as part of a much-criticized UK cabinet reshuffle, the Wales Office (along with the Scotland Office) was incorporated in the new Department for Constitutional Affairs (headed by Lord Falconer).

Focusing here on the situation that obtained through the first term of the Assembly, the first role, representing central government in the political and civic life of Wales, was essentially a carry-over. So for example, with the agreement of ministerial colleagues, the territorial Secretary of State has generally presented the UK government's policy on matters of significance to Wales even when the lead responsibility has lain elsewhere. Then again devolution produced a subtle difference. The minister was immediately made more dependent on the other Whitehall departments, precisely because Assembly officials could not provide him with the relevant policy line. 'Officials from his Department will need to call on colleagues for this more frequently than in the past . . . '[68]

The minister has by virtue of the devolution statute the formal right to attend and participate in Assembly plenary sessions, as also to receive all the documentation made available to the Assembly as a whole.[69] Provisions it may be said that reflect the older and more cautious view of the Assembly as an emanation of central government and therefore properly subject to the formal exercise of UK ministerial influence. In practice, putting to one side the obligatory discussion of the Queen's Speech, it has been a case of the empty chair. In the spirit of devolution, the then Secretary of State for Wales Paul Murphy made clear early on that it was not generally appropriate for him to sit in state.

The second main role, guardian of (executive) devolution, was greatly emphasized by Mr Murphy. In his words, 'by being present as a Member of the Cabinet, as representing Wales, that shows to the world . . . that we are still part of the United Kingdom'.[70] The role has been said to comprise three main elements,[71] the first one being to give advice on the handling of business in the light of devolution. At one with the general approach set out in the concordats, this 'does not mean that the Secretary of State is a channel of communication between the UK Government and the Assembly. Normally Departments should deal with the Welsh Assembly Government direct.' To this effect, much of the work has been done behind the scenes, with a view to greasing the wheels.

Another element, also reflecting the *MoU*, has been to act 'as honest broker' in the event of any dispute between the Assembly and Whitehall or Westminster. In practice, according to the official evidence, 'the political involvement and sensitivity of the Secretaries of State and the expertise in each particular devolution settlement housed within their Offices have played a significant role in defusing . . . issues and preventing them from turning into disputes'.[72] The general sense of fluidity and informality in the conduct of IGR is again communicated strongly here.

Indicative of the many political sensitivities surrounding the so-called 'devolution settlement', the other element apparently entails lectures in civics. The minister and his department 'explain the nature and consequences of devolution to the Assembly on behalf of the UK Government'. Words fail the author!

The major role of 'voice of Wales in the UK cabinet' itself illustrates the twin features in the UK devolutionary development of commonality and diversity. Some elements, chief among them involvement in the discussions on the Comprehensive Spending Review, have paralleled the work of ministerial colleagues in Scotland and Northern Ireland. For his part, Paul Murphy has spoken of 'literally weeks, indeed months, of negotiations' to ensure 'that we get a decent financial settlement for Wales'.[73] So much, it may be said, for the idea of 'block and formula' as a robotic system.

Attention naturally focuses on the special role of promoting and facilitating primary legislation affecting Assembly functions. It is after all the respon- sibility of the (junior) minister to steer through Parliament any clauses in legislation relating solely to Wales. In view of subsequent events, it is worth recording Rhodri Morgan's concerns regarding a potential muffling of 'a voice for Wales'. 'From the Welsh Assembly Government's perspective . . . it is hard to imagine this aspect of the settlement functioning well without a full- time Secretary of State for Wales.'[74]

The workload, shared between the Secretary of State and a single parlia- mentary under-secretary, has not been inconsiderable. Formal parliamentary work in 2001–2, for example, included seven sessions of Welsh questions, four appearances before the Welsh Affairs Select Committee, three Welsh Grand Committees, and four other Welsh debates in the House. Meanwhile, the two ministers were sitting on some twenty UK cabinet committees, an equivalent number of *ad hoc* ministerial committees, and four joint ministerial commit- tees.[75] Let us also keep in mind the complex nature of IGR, and, in particular, the extended nature of the decision-making chain, the sense in which discussion and argument is not confined to a single place or committee room, but flows through the different corridors of power. Working to straddle and help coordinate such dynamic processes of government is both an important and a difficult aspect of the job.

During the first term of the Assembly, a very close working relationship operated inside this little country at ministerial level. In the words of Paul Murphy, 'obviously I talk to Rhodri Morgan almost every day of a working week'.[76] For their part, members of the Assembly cabinet have liaised regularly with the junior minister, as business has demanded. Again, given the general sense of shared experience and common purpose among senior Labour Party colleagues, it is not surprising to hear of 'a huge amount of consensual working'. According to Mr Murphy, 'most of the time, nearly all of the time, we will agree'.[77] Informality premised on the fundamental good will of the administrations to each other; a strong dose of political fixing mediated through the structures of party and government as and when the holes (in the 'devolution settlement') appear: it all adds up.

Harmony and discord

Yet there has been a Janus-type quality to the constitutional situation. On the one hand, in the benign conditions of party hegemony, such arrangements can clearly be seen as part of a new 'Welsh axis' in the British system of government: twin poles of authority, at one and the same time separated and intimately connected ('nods and winks'). On the other hand, this raises concerns for a future where by reason of (party political) hostility or indifference Welsh ministers in Whitehall are much less sympathetic to the demands and needs under the scheme of executive devolution of the Welsh Assembly Government. First Minister and Secretary of State in political 'cohabitation': ultimately, far from a duet, it could be a case of two leading politicians both claiming to represent and articulate the interests of Wales.

The Secretary of State 'will be able to' work in partnership with the Assembly: such was the notably careful wording of the devolution White Paper.[78] The minister, Whitehall colleagues have been told, 'is not a mouth-piece for the Assembly but needs to know the views of the Welsh Assembly Government before coming to a view'.[79] There are in fact two closely related propositions on view. The first one, which properly reflects the role of a cabinet minister in the UK government, is that the Secretary of State for Wales will act as a conduit for the views of the devolved administration but need not press them. Secondly, whatever the Assembly may think, strictly speaking it is in the terms of the White Paper 'a voice for Wales', and not 'the voice of Wales'. In language that may come one day to haunt his Welsh Labour Party colleagues, Paul Murphy has been very clear about this:

> On the question of representing the views of the Assembly, that is not my job. I present the views of the Assembly, which is quite different. The representation of the views is the job of Rhodri Morgan and for the Assembly Government itself, not for me . . . My role is not simply one presenting the views of the Assembly, but one of presenting the views of Wales.[80]

Amid the general harmony, some discordant notes have been struck at the London end. Suggestions about how the Assembly might spend additional government largess, for example, could so easily colour future negotiations on the Comprehensive Spending Review. In the case of care for the elderly, an intemperate response greeted the exercise of voice by the Assembly, one that was shown to display a basic lack of constitutional understanding.[81] It is not simply, however, that the Wales Office has had its own sharp learning curve. As the devolved administration picks up steam and seeks additional powers to promote distinctive 'made in Wales' policies, including ones in areas like health and education which may not sit comfortably with New Labour ideas in London, the role of the Secretary of State is likely to prove increasingly delicate. A proper and effective working of the scheme of executive devolution depends on the minister being prepared to listen.

Lost empire

Devolution resulted in the Wales Office, in its own words, becoming 'a small policy department with few executive functions and work [that] is largely dictated by external demands'.[82] Lost empire: the days when the Secretary of State and a few junior ministers effectively ran Wales, with generous assistance from the many appointees as well as officials, now appear increasingly remote.

The department's annual budget for 2002–3 was just over £3 million – in Whitehall terms, chicken feed. It now employed some fifty staff (up from thirty at the time of devolution).[83] Most of them have been based in the old Welsh Office outpost in London, but there has also been a small presence in Cardiff Bay. Extraordinary as it may seem, given the special role of the ministers in promoting primary legislation, the department has operated on the basis of one and later two legal advisers. For its part, the Select Committee on the Constitution was struck by the general disparity in size with the Scotland Office, which (putting to one side its specialist team of lawyers) has had more than twice the number of officials. 'No cogent explanation' was offered, and – especially given the rather more straightforward devolution settlement for Scotland – the committee could 'not understand' how the discrepancy had arisen.[84] Poor little Wales: it is all at one with the historical fact of junior partner in the Union.

Operating in support of ministers as 'the catalyst in the relationship between the Assembly and the Government', the department has had five main objectives:

- to maintain effective relationships with the Assembly and ensure that the devolution settlement continues to operate in the best interests of Wales, including, where appropriate, exercising the Secretary of State's powers in the GWA
- to work with other Government Departments and the Assembly to ensure that the interests of Wales are fully taken into account in primary legislation which affects the Assembly's responsibilities
- to work with other Government Departments to promote Welsh interests in functions retained by the Government
- to work with other Government Departments and the Assembly to provide effective communication and coordination of policy in areas which straddle the boundary between transferred and retained functions; and
- to keep under review, with Treasury and the Welsh Assembly, the operation of the funding policy for the devolved administration.[85]

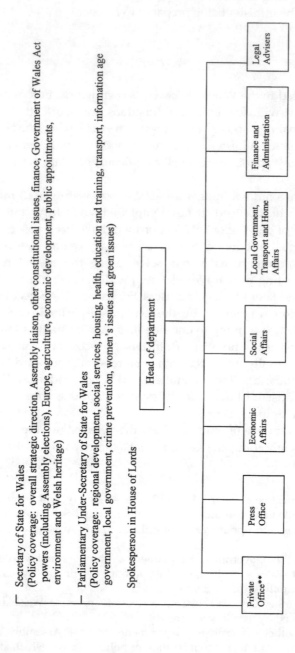

Secretary of State for Wales
(Policy coverage: overall strategic direction, Assembly liaison, other constitutional issues, finance, Government of Wales Act powers (including Assembly elections), Europe, agriculture, economic development, public appointments, environment and Welsh heritage)

Parliamentary Under-Secretary of State for Wales
(Policy coverage: regional development, social services, housing, health, education and training, transport, information age government, local government, crime prevention, women's issues and green issues)

Spokesperson in House of Lords

Head of department

Private Office**

Press Office

Economic Affairs

Social Affairs

Local Government, Transport and Home Affairs

Finance and Administration

Legal Advisers

*   Source: Wales Office, Departmental Report
**   Including special advisers

Figure 15: Wales Office internal architecture – 2002

Given the geopolitical basis of the work – discussions on matters affecting Welsh interests, the potential range of subjects has been enormous. As Figure 15 highlights, the lines of policy advice to Wales Office ministers have had to cover the fields both of devolved and non-devolved functions, as well as the many 'ragged edges' in the scheme of executive devolution. That is to say: all the way from local government affairs (in the case of primary legislation) to vexed issues of 'cross-border' provision in the realm of public transport, and on through to ensuring that Wales receives 'its fair share' in terms of general UK policies. An aspect all too easily overlooked is the potential gap in arrangements arising in those areas where the Assembly does not have powers, and so lacks the focus effectively to buttress the work of a small Welsh representation in Whitehall. Ministers armed with few officials, and without the influence associated with responsibility for major public functions – it was an uphill struggle from the outset. Much has depended on the display of good will – elsewhere in Whitehall – and on the force of personality.

Emblematic of a close and consensus-based set of working relationships, there has been daily contact with the Welsh Assembly Government at official level. Indeed, there has been considerable dependency on Cardiff, given a basic need for information about local plans and developments. A more technical point: service level agreements with the Assembly for the delivery of key services have been a notable feature of the internal administrative organization of the Wales Office: from personnel matters to financial services, and on through to IT, audit and translation. Again the sociology of public administration – it would be absurd to overlook the strong Welsh connections of many of the civil servants in the Wales Office, as also the fact of a strong wedge of experience of working with colleagues inside the Welsh Office and the Assembly. 'Arm's length' and 'hand in glove': let us call it a fluid mix.

The bilateral concordat between the Assembly cabinet and the Wales Office has underscored this general feature.[86] On the one hand, the very fact of its existence, governing relations between two distinct forms of government representation for the territory, highlights the very different contours of the post-devolutionary landscape. On the other hand, the concordat reeks of the central place in the system of IGR of political and administrative good will. Perhaps it is reassuring to know that the parties 'agree that good working relationships between them are vital to the public interest and to the effective governance of Wales'. They 'are committed to working together wherever it is appropriate', and to doing so 'through the agreed processes set out in this concordat'. The parties 'believe that they can benefit' not only from 'familiarity with the other's work and experiences' but also from advance notice of the other's initiatives, proposals and – especially noteworthy – 'developing thinking'. Primary legislation affecting Wales naturally features prominently in this respect.

Behind the scenes, detailed internal guidance has had to be given to local staff on how to respond to requests for briefing from the Wales Office. Correctly in view of the shoestring character of the UK department, the task of providing the basic facts on an issue has been identified as an important one. Then again, unless there is the First Minister's authority for passing on advice,[87] it is for the civil servants in the UK government to assess the facts, set out options, describe the pros and cons and suggest a policy line for their ministers to take. This novel system of 'Welsh walls' has thus had its own constitutional logic.

Incorporation

There has been a good case for retaining in the short term the distinctive territorial representation provided by the Secretary of State for Wales. A recurring theme in this book is the strength of the ongoing or evolutionary character of the constitutional development. The minister has had a valuable role to play in easing or helping to manage the transitions. Not least since, in the cosmos of UK devolution, there is little that is more fluid than the new system of IGR.

Likewise, it can reasonably be argued that the Office of Secretary of State for Wales should endure for as long as the scheme of executive devolution endures. For the reasons explained, simply to rely on bilateral relationships with the various Whitehall departments would be fraught with difficulty for the Welsh Assembly Government, and a recipe for confusion and disappoint-ment in respect of primary legislation affecting Wales. Political hegemony or cohabitation: a continuing role for the minister was very much part of the constitutional deal put to the people in the devolution referendum.[88]

Turning the argument round, a measure of rationalization in the medium term was only to be expected.[89] Why would the so-called 'godfather role' continue undiminished in the face of the growing stature and resources of the devolved administration, as reflected in direct dealings with central government? Likewise, it would fly in the face of the historical evidence if Welsh arrangements were not to be affected by developments elsewhere in the Union. The evident vulnerability of the Scotland Office to 'rationalization' in the light of legislative devolution has cast a long shadow here. For its part, the Select Committee on the Constitution made the case for reform.[90] Whereas Northern Ireland could be expected to retain its own Office, as part and parcel of the Belfast Agreement, a single cabinet minister might job-share Scotland and Wales, with the possibility of appointing separate junior ministers.

It is not a case of all or nothing. As a particular product of a peculiar territorial history, the powerful 'England and Wales' administrative paradigm features prominently in the pages of this book. It will for the foreseeable future continue to generate very special demands for a distinct 'voice' for

Wales at the heart of central government. Again, in constructing arrangements, it does not do to gloss over the potential conflict of interest, not between the centre and the territory, but between two devolved territories. Often there will be consensus here, and sometimes 'alliances', but from time to time there will also be an element of competition. It is also in part a matter of spectacles. Viewed in Anglocentric perspective, or more straightforwardly in terms of the jobs that UK cabinet ministers have to do, the case for rationalization is an especially powerful one. Considered from the 'Celtic periphery', however, things are apt to look somewhat different, at least to those who have a care for the health of the Union.

In the event, Downing Street has come up with an unusual arrangement. According to the press release:

> The devolved administrations have bedded down successfully, and there is no longer a requirement for full-time Cabinet Ministers and free-standing departments to conduct the remaining Scottish and Welsh business within Parliament and the UK Government. The Scotland and Wales Offices will henceforth be located within the new Department for Constitutional Affairs, together with the Parliamentary Under-Secretaries of State for Scotland and Wales. At Cabinet level, responsibility for the conduct of Scottish and Welsh business, and lead responsibility for the representation of Wales and Scotland within the Government and Parliament will lie with Alistair Darling (Scotland) and Peter Hain (Wales) respectively, supported by the staff located within the new Department. They will combine these important duties with their other Cabinet responsibilities.[91]

A measure of confusion: it is not surprising. Put simply, was there still a Secretary of State for Wales (and Scotland), or was there not? Subsequently, a cautious interpretation has prevailed, which sees Peter Hain wearing two hats – as Leader of the House of Commons and territorial Secretary of State – and the Wales Office downgraded but continuing to exist under the 'umbrella' of the new Department for Constitutional Affairs (DCA). Meanwhile the officials in the previously free-standing department support Mr Hain and his junior minister on Welsh affairs but now come under a different set of departmental heads for administrative purposes. Suffice it to add that the DCA, successor-in-title to many of the functions of the Lord Chancellor's Department, will be primarily concerned with legal affairs. A Wales-centred reform, this was not!

For his part, Peter Hain has notably stressed the element of continuity. That is to say, at UK cabinet level, responsibility for conduct of Welsh business and lead responsibility for representation of Wales in government and Parliament, for example answering Welsh questions and taking part in Welsh debates. In his words, 'the settlement is safe'.[92] Meanwhile, the Assembly First Minister has spoken of a 'hybrid' arrangement, one that 'will work extremely well'.[93]

Be this as it may, one can scarcely ignore the wider political and administrative symbolism. In the long view the development will surely be seen as another staging post in a protracted constitutional journey for Wales. It suffices to quote veteran Labour peer, Lord Prys-Davies: 'the loss of a full-time Secretary of State strengthens immeasurably the case for conferring on the National Assembly the power to enact primary legislation in the devolved fields.'[94]

5. WALES AND WESTMINSTER (AGAIN)

'Suck it and see'

As well as the major question of access to, or influence on, the primary lawgiver, the issue arises of the knock-on effects of the Welsh devolutionary development on scrutiny by, and local representation in, the Westminster Parliament. In this instance, the interplay in the UK model of asymmetrical devolution of common elements and separate territorial features emerges in a slightly different form. How will the balance be struck between, on the one hand, considerations of the impact on parliamentary practice and procedure of the UK devolution programme as a whole; and, on the other hand, particular demands placed on Westminster by the *sui generis* Welsh model of executive devolution?

The peculiar quality of constitutional change in this field must be kept in mind. Classically these are matters not of statutory design but of development via the 'internal law' – and lore – of Westminster. At one and the same time, this helps to explain the low salience of the topic in the early stages of the UK devolutionary development, and the tentative and incremental nature of the approach. In fact, the slow rate of formal procedural change at Westminster in the light of devolution deserves a special emphasis by reason of some ambitious predictions to the contrary, including in terms of catering for England.[95] A useful touchstone is a recent report from the (hopeful-sounding) Select Committee on Modernization, which set out a reform programme for the remainder of the 2001 Parliament. Adjustment of the practice and procedure of the House of Commons to reflect the new realities of devolution was notable by its absence from the agenda.[96]

Winding the clock back, a report from the Procedure Committee on the eve of devolution suggested four main principles for relations between Westminster and the devolved territories.[97] Constitutional asymmetry/ procedural symmetry – the last one clearly has particular significance in the case of Wales:

- Parliamentary procedures should not be called in aid to undermine the principle that devolved matters should be dealt with by the devolved administrations.
- There should be as few procedural barriers as possible to cooperation between the two sets of elected representatives.
- The MPs from a territory will have a particular interest in (reserved) business affecting that area.
- Procedures relating to devolved matters should be as consistent as possible across the different countries.

However, when it came to making concrete proposals, the committee was hardly radical. 'Suck it and see': taking a lead from the UK government, here as elsewhere feeling its way forward in matters of constitution-building, Members opted for 'an evolutionary approach', one that was piecemeal as well as highly pragmatic. Round two: the UK government showed little interest in the reforms that the Procedure Committee did suggest, for example standing committees to have a majority of local MPs for Wales-only Bills.[98] Suffice it to add that the committee considered a 'full review' of the procedural consequences of devolution would be necessary 'in the light of experience'.[99] As indicated, there is no sign of it happening.

Comity

Of course some things have had to change. Take for example the issue of demarcation, the sense in which political accountability follows powers. As stated by the *Committee Office Guide*, 'Westminster Committees should respect the spirit of devolution, and should not seek to hold a devolved institution to account.'[100] The comparative concept of comity or mutual respect between jurisdictions thus comes to the fore here.

By reason of the legal and constitutional tradition of parliamentary sovereignty, any such limitations on the part of Westminster must be self-imposed. In the words of the *MoU*, 'the United Kingdom Parliament retains the absolute right to debate, enquire into or make representations about devolved matters. It is ultimately for Parliament to decide what use to make of that power.' Nonetheless, the UK government 'will encourage the UK Parliament to bear in mind the primary responsibility of devolved legislatures and administrations' and 'to recognise that it is a consequence of Parliament's decision to devolve certain matters that Parliament itself will in future be more restricted in its field of operation'.[101]

As one would expect, the *MoU* factors in an element of reciprocity, for example in terms of mutual obligations to provide such information 'as appears appropriate and necessary' to enable a government or administration to meet its responsibilities in terms of scrutiny.[102] Especially, however, in these early days of devolution a tendency at Westminster to stricter adherence to demarcation is not unwelcome[103] – a case for 'the gentle giant'.

The touchstone here is parliamentary questions concerning the devolved territories. Since in principle the subject of a question must be a matter for which ministers have responsibility, their range and frequency was bound to diminish in the wake of devolution. In fact, Speaker Boothroyd began by taking a very strict view of the questions that are in order, an approach reminiscent of famous rulings concerning the Stormont Parliament.[104] In her words,

> where matters have clearly been devolved to the Scottish Parliament or to the Welsh Assembly, questions on the details of policy or expenditure would not be in order. Where [the territorial] Secretaries of State have a residual, limited or shared role, questions should relate to that role.[105]

But what, it was rightly asked, of the new modalities of IGR, and in particular in the Welsh context of the interplay of (the need for) primary and secondary legislation? The House of Commons quickly came to a formal resolution, applicable in respect of all three Celtic lands:

> That subject always to the discretion of the Chair . . . questions may not be tabled for matters for which responsibility has been devolved by legislation . . . unless that question:
> (a) seeks information which the UK Government is empowered to require of the devolved executive, or
> (b) relates to matters which (i) are included in legislative proposals introduced or to be introduced in the UK Parliament, (ii) are concerned with the operation of a concordat or other instrument of liaison . . . or (iii) UK Government ministers have taken an official interest in, or
> (c) presses for action by UK ministers in areas in which they retain administrative powers.[106]

Such are the many ragged edges in Welsh devolution that the Table Office had immediately to be equipped with a lengthy document summarizing the powers of the National Assembly.[107] Nor, in using the open-ended nature of the regulation, should the ingenuity of backbench MPs be underestimated. In practice, however, matters have largely settled down. In the case of the Wales Office, written questions in particular are now much reduced.[108] Activity in the Assembly more than makes up the shortfall.

WASC: another voice for Wales

Turning then to the two parliamentary committees concerned exclusively with Wales, the Select Committee on Welsh Affairs (WASC) was established in 1979 as part of a more comprehensive system of departmental select committees in the House of Commons. One means of targeting the problem of accountability or 'democratic deficit' implicit in the territorial model of central government, the committee was thus empowered to examine the expenditure, administration and policy of the Welsh Office and associated public bodies. Given the demise of the Wales Act 1978, its establishment may also be seen as a centralist alternative to the policy of devolution: at one and the same time, recognition of a distinctively Welsh dimension to British politics, and reassertion of the primacy in Welsh affairs of the UK Parliament.[109]

Since the functions of central government that it was set up to shadow have virtually ceased to exist, this all-party but characteristically Labour-dominated Committee has had to reinvent itself.

> Defining and developing the Committee's role in the light of devolution has been one of the major challenges facing us . . . We felt that there was a danger that Welsh interests might be neglected at Westminster after devolution and that the Committee could act as a voice for Wales and as a bridge between Westminster and the Assembly, though not as the voice of the Assembly.[110]

Again, with more than a hint of self-preservation, 'the Committee is keen to continue to play an active part in post-devolution Wales'.[111]

WASC has in fact declined to be pigeonholed by the 'common objectives' formally recommended for select committees.[112] It is not simply that one objective – the scrutiny of legislation – is particularly important to this committee. Members have taken 'a flexible approach' to the new terms of reference, whereby the role of scrutinizing the Wales Office has included relations with the Assembly.[113] 'A coach and horses' would be more accurate: 'we believe that this gives us a broad remit to examine the impact of UK Government policy in Wales' – and more. During 2002, for example, WASC undertook seven inquiries: into the work of the Children's Society in Wales, Objective 1 funding in Wales, the draft NHS (Wales) Bill, broadband in Wales, transport in Wales, the primary legislative process as it affects Wales, and empowerment of children and young people in Wales.[114] Increasingly then, from controversy surrounding a charity's decision to close its local operations, to issues of disability, race, cultural and sexual preference of importance to young people, the work of this territorial committee appears to know no bounds, save of course for the little matter of devolved functions and policies.

This is not all. The members may not see themselves as the voice of the Assembly, but WASC has proved itself willing and able in the conditions of Labour Party hegemony to supply useful leverage in the context of IGR. The powers of select committees to examine UK ministers and officials, as also the procedural requirement of government responses to reports, can obviously be used to good advantage here. Take for example an inquiry by WASC into European structural funds, and more especially the UK funding aspects. The timing, in the run-up to the Treasury announcement concerning Objective 1 status for west Wales and the Valleys, can hardly be considered coincidental.[115] 'Nods and winks' among local actors, even a political and administrative pincer movement; the affair reeks of it.

In establishing an agenda, WASC has not only been open to, but has also canvassed, the views of Assembly Members. Its recent contribution to the ongoing processes of reform, *The Primary Legislative Process as it Affects Wales*, came out of just such an exercise. In turn, the committee took evidence from the Presiding Office and the First Minister, as well as the Secretary of State for Wales and First Parliamentary Counsel. An open forum session was also held for colleagues in Cardiff Bay. The report itself, in building on and echoing themes first developed in the Assembly Review of Procedure, further illustrates a role for WASC, if not as a megaphone or relay station, then as a close interpreter at Westminster, of the general concerns of the new Welsh polity. Looking forwards, it will be interesting to see what part if any WASC chooses to play in the aftermath of the Richard Commission on the powers and electoral arrangements of the Assembly.

So the idea of 'partnership working' with the Assembly that the committee has been so keen to promote in the legislative process is not confined to that field, but extends more generally to issues of policy development and delivery. WASC now holds various meetings with Assembly committees on an informal basis, and in particular seeks to promote close links with an important counterpart in the Assembly, the Panel of Subject Committee Chairs. More (constitutional) novelties: the devolved administration now comments on WASC reports though it is not under any formal obligation to respond, and also responds locally by means of an oral statement in plenary session. 'We welcome its continued interest in our work.'[116]

In summary, WASC has gone quite some way to reinventing itself as an all-purpose committee, with a wide-ranging Welsh affairs brief. Whereas, generally speaking, formal procedural change at Westminster has been kept to a minimum in the face of devolution, this committee brilliantly illustrates the scope for informal developments of a more political and administrative nature. Moreover, the sense of an expanded territorial axis – Wales in the United Kingdom – is communicated strongly here, not least given the origins of this committee as a limited symbol of the Welsh dimension to British politics. As in the case of IGR, the different voices for Wales will not always be in harmony, including this parliamentary one. But they often will be.

Going on

The advantages of a more radical approach were highlighted in evidence to the Procedure Committee from the Study of Parliament Group.[117] A single territorial committee for Wales at Westminster was thus seen as a way of promoting a more holistic approach to scrutiny at the UK end, one that would encompass the policy-making and legislative functions, and further the liaison role in IGR. So too there would be encouragement for joint scrutiny with other territorial committees of MPs where appropriate, as also for closer links with the Assembly (in 'parliamentary' mode). The topics suggested for inclusion in the remit give the flavour:

- negotiation of the Welsh block grant
- role of the territorial Secretary of State in advancing Welsh interests in Whitehall and in Europe
- impact of Whitehall policies and of cross-cutting strategies on Wales
- assuming the role of a standing committee for the purpose of Wales-only primary legislation
- reviewing the workings of the concordats.

In fact, drawing on the work of the Welsh Affairs Committee and the 'Welsh Grand', this proposal consciously sought the middle way between wholesale structural change and simple reactive pragmatism. Viewed in retrospect, it can also be seen as a useful prompt to the Welsh Affairs Select Committee to reinvent itself as a broad-ranging committee. As the case of the draft NHS (Wales) Bill further serves to illustrate, however – scrutiny not by one but by both these parliamentary 'voices' for Wales[118] – there remains a good case for rationalization.

'Not Welsh, not Grand, not a Committee'

Like most good jokes, this one is no stranger to the truth. The Welsh Grand Committee, first established in 1960, has often been described as a talking shop, and criticized for its impotence to influence policy in Wales, not least during the long years of Conservative government from 1979. In the event, under Prime Minister John Major, the committee's sphere of activity was widened by new standing orders. It now encompassed ministerial statements and general debates on matters affecting Wales, and question times and short debates, as well as debates replacing the second readings of exclusively Welsh Bills on the floor of the House. Splendidly envisioned, this was another version of 'parliamentary unionism', an attempt to resolve the problems of the territorial management of Wales otherwise than through a devolution policy.[119] Consisting of all Welsh MPs and up to five others, it was however destined to founder on the rocks of insufficient Conservative representation.

The devolution White Paper clearly hinted at abolition: for the obvious reason of the committee's deliberative role being overtaken by the new democratically legitimate national forum.[120] On similar grounds, the Procedure Committee in 1999 recommended that the territorial system of Grand

Committees should be suspended, at least for a trial period.[121] Typically, however, the UK government decided that it was too soon to take such a step. In the suitably damning words of the Select Committee on the Constitution, 'the Grand Committees for Scotland, Wales and Northern Ireland . . . remain in existence but they do not figure as significant bodies in discussing issues affecting the devolved areas of the United Kingdom'.[122]

The Welsh Grand thus limps along. Although the UK pre-budget and budget statements and the announcement of the Westminster legislative programmes provide some opportunities for MPs to raise and debate broader issues of particular importance to Wales, there is a demonstrable lack of focus. Few meetings, no forward work plans, a lack of dedicated staffing provision: how could it be otherwise?

If it has one, the future of the Welsh Grand may lie in the legislative field. The idea is not new: the possibility that the committee might act for example as some kind of fast-track machinery for distinctively Welsh primary legislation advocated by the devolved administration was raised on several occasions during the parliamentary proceedings on the devolution Bill.[123] It would also fit with the idea of a 'partnership approach' between the Assembly collectively and the Welsh MPs, the committee then being given prescribed functions in the pre-legislative scrutiny and the parliamentary processing of Bills that particularly affect Wales.[124] Such are the exigencies of the scheme of executive devolution that the committee's consideration in July 2002 of the draft NHS (Wales) Bill could yet prove a significant precedent.

Whatever happens in this regard, one would expect to see some further thickening of relations between the Assembly as a representative body and Westminster. 'Unionists': for constitutional as well as political reasons, that great power in the land the Welsh Labour Party should not object! One would also envisage the style and pattern of these bilateral arrangements being influenced by the more general organic development of inter-parliamentary relations in the UK, as well as by the more mundane if pressing demands of Welsh executive devolution.

The frequency and status of joint committee meetings will be the obvious litmus test. The Assembly Review of Procedure for example proposed annual meetings between AMs and the Welsh Grand and the Welsh Affairs Select Committee, whereby views might be exchanged on the UK government's legislative programme and its impact on Wales. For its part, WASC would like the option of meeting formally with Assembly committees 'when our work and theirs coincides'.[125] Yet let us not expect too much. According to the Presiding Office, timetabling presents real difficulties in this regard, a product both of the demands on Members and basic differences in the organization of the working week between the two representative institutions.[126] Even assuming that Westminster is generally willing to countenance equality and have formal joint inquiries etc., the issue of privilege is apt to surface.[127]

Behind the scenes, there already is much networking among the clerks and officials of the UK parliaments and assemblies, and beyond.[128] At one level, informal meetings of counterparts; at another level, the likes of a Contact Group of finance and administration staff, an Inter-parliamentary Information Services Forum, and an Inter-parliamentary Research Network; and at another level, exchanges, secondments and attachments: it is in fact a bit of an industry. Meanwhile, as well as having membership (and indeed in the case of the Deputy Presiding Officer, chairmanship) of the Commonwealth Parliamentary Association, the Assembly is signed up to the British–Irish Inter-parliamentary Body, an expanded forum since 1999. A practical need for external assistance and support, a practical constraint on the scale of the networking activity: the small size of the Assembly may be said to cut both ways in this broad field of interinstitutional relations.

Yet at the risk of repetition, these kinds of activities and linkages bear a special connotation in the case of Wales.[129] The tapping of a great pool of experience and sharing of resources, the fostering of a more 'parliamentary' ethos, the development of bilateral and multilateral relationships with the wider family of parliaments: it all fits with the idea of further constitutional advancement under the rubric of 'national devolution'. The Presiding Office has been a most willing participant!

Issues of representation

The fact of devolution clearly puts in issue the future role and contribution of Welsh MPs, individually as well as collectively. The White Paper *A Voice of Wales* sought to provide reassurance. As well as being 'involved in considering new primary legislation that applies to Wales', the MPs would 'continue . . . to represent their constituents on all matters'. 'Setting up the Assembly will not reduce Wales's representation at Westminster.'[130] Things, however, could never be so simple. The constitutional and political dynamics now unleashed are far too powerful.

One notable source of tension is the representational roles of AMs and MPs at the grassroots level, as also those of the 'constituency' and 'list' AMs. Individual representatives at Westminster will have a continuing constituency interest in the activities and powers of the devolved administration; different AMs may be jostling for position; all will be in receipt of complaints about local government. For its part, the UK Cabinet Office has issued guidelines. The overlapping interests of Members, government departments are solemnly told, 'can be sensitive for all concerned. The handling of correspondence on constituency cases should respect this.' Ideally the work relating to non-devolved matters should be routed through a Westminster MP, and vice versa: no 'cross-over'.[131] In practice, however, the various groups of elected representatives have largely been left to their own devices. In the case of the Assembly, save for a general insistence by the Presiding Officer that constituency and list members enjoy equal status, there has been little by the way of guidance. Nor has the idea of a parliamentary concordat between different legislatures, which might set out relevant principles and conventions (no 'poaching' etc.), come to fruition.[132]

No doubt much will depend at local level on considerations of party interest and electoral advantage, as also on personal factors. Difficult relations between Members in at least a minority of cases are only to be expected, especially in this formative period.[133] From time to time individual arrangements on passing on cases, or not as the case may be, will have to be hammered out. Let us also keep in mind the demand-led nature of this machinery for the redress of grievance. Past experience suggests both widespread public ignorance of, and healthy disregard for, the jurisdictional map devised by those in authority. 'Every bill a devolution bill': by its very nature, Welsh executive devolution will tend to accentuate these features. Elements of cooperation and interplay, friction and overlap: such is the complex nature of grievance handling in a multi-tiered democracy. Local politicians must learn to live with it.

Reverting to Westminster, a general weakening of the influence of Welsh MPs is easily envisaged; and this may, over a period of years, further strengthen the case for a general scheme of legislative devolution.[134] Partnership working of the kind advocated by WASC itself implies a certain loss of status! A parliamentary career will inevitably appear less inviting to aspiring Welsh politicians as the local focus of attention shifts more in favour of the Assembly. There already is a suggestion of some MPs feeling overshadowed, in the light of media coverage.[135] Meanwhile, so-called 'dual mandate' members are firmly out of fashion.[136]

The Richard Commission has been consulting on 'how Welsh interests would be affected if the role of Welsh MPs were to be reduced' as a consequence of legislative devolution.[137] Given the high degree of conjecture that surrounds the UK government's constitutional programme in the medium term, one is tempted to answer: 'who knows?' More concretely, while (the) individuals may protest, a proportionate reduction in the number of Welsh representatives at Westminster should be no great cause for alarm. A proper representation of local interests and a span of party representation across Wales are not seriously in issue here. Again, the work of WASC illustrates what is now required by way of a special parliamentary 'voice' for Wales; there would be more than sufficient backbench Members for the purpose of staffing. As well as a reduction in the role, one would envisage a further element of reinvention. A key test would be the scale of the working – or otherwise – in tandem with colleagues in the Assembly. Given the strength of the 'England and Wales' administrative paradigm, there could well be greater pressures here for partnership working than is commonly imagined.[138]

The House of Lords has on occasion done the Assembly valuable service. As a revising chamber, it clearly has a particular role to play in the context of executive devolution, as the affair of the Children's Commissioner highlights.[139] As well as providing a parliamentary bolt hole or network for the Presiding Officer, and supplying the machinery of the Select Committee on the Constitution, their Lordships' House has allowed for a kind of genteel guerrilla warfare in the service of Welsh constitutional advancement.[140] Logic, after all, is not the current scheme's strong point.

What then, it may be asked, of the seemingly never-ending saga of House of Lords reform? A classic expression of federal-style principle, the idea of designated territorial representation in a revamped upper chamber, designed both to protect local interests and to combat centrifugal forces, has surfaced from time to time, including in the report of the recent Royal Commission chaired by Lord Wakeham.[141] In turn, various schemes have been floated for linking in the parliaments and assemblies of the UK, perhaps a system of indirect elections to the centre, or powers of nomination of appointed members. Worthy but uninspiring, it must be said: save to the dry constitutionalist. As subsequent events have demonstrated, such issues come second best to the vexed question of a popular mandate, given the primary claim to constitutional legitimacy of the House of Commons.[142] At the time of writing, matters are stalled with no political majority for any particular option.[143] We are, in short, a long way here from the grand vision of a House of Nations and Regions; and in the light of British constitutional method and tradition, predictably so. Suffice it to add that the Assembly at large has shown no great enthusiasm for going down this route.

CONCLUSION – CHALLENGE AND OPPORTUNITY

A highly informal approach to IGR, with great weight placed on bilateral relations, reflects and reinforces the administrative and constitutional values of cooperation, coordination and partnership that have been trumpeted by New Labour. From a Welsh viewpoint, it also parallels many of the political and administrative developments inside the territory post-devolution ('the Welsh way' etc.). 'Law', in the traditional formal sense, does not feature centre stage, and designedly so.

In suitably paradoxical fashion, continuity is a pervasive element in the new modalities of IGR. Expressed slightly differently, the emphasis in the design on flexibility and responsiveness is indicative of an evolutionary approach to basic constitutional and administrative development: New Labour, new conservatism! The general approach also sits comfortably in the current conditions of Labour Party hegemony, with much scope for the internal mediation of tension and conflict. Turning the argument round, the democratic prospect of political cohabitation is seen to cast an especially long shadow here. Concordats and more especially the JMC: it is a bit flimsy. Meanwhile – in the nice Irish phrase – formal procedural change at Westminster 'comes dropping slow'.

Commonality and diversity – matters concerning Wales in the United Kingdom are typically designed at two main levels: as part of the wider set of arrangements, where local policy is classically to keep up; and as part and parcel of the peculiar place of Wales in the British system of government. A recurring theme is the double bind of the Welsh constitutional situation. There is, first, a very special need for close working relations with many central government departments. Secondly, there is added potential for executive domination from the centre, conscious or otherwise, which the lack of transparency in the new modalities of IGR does nothing to dispel. Emphatically, for this purpose, Cardiff Bay is not Holyrood.

The emergence of a novel 'Welsh axis', not one but several connected 'voices for Wales' in the corridors of power, is then the more significant. Once again, the fact on occasion of, and evident potential in different political circumstances for, conflict, should not be allowed to disguise the many new opportunities for promoting Wales in the UK, nor – in the positive sense – the great capacity of the civil service to carry on regardless. At one and the same time, the demise of the Wales Office as a free-standing department, and in particular the allocation of the role of the Secretary of State for Wales as part-time, promises a new and critical test of the political and administrative arrangements, and sends a powerful constitutional message.

Looking forwards, a generous scheme of legislative devolution could be expected to improve matters, both by reducing the scale of political and administrative dependency on the centre, and by heightening the status of the Welsh polity inside the Union. It does not do, however, to overlook the powerful 'England and Wales' administrative paradigm. For reasons of history and geography – the many intimate connections – special demands are bound to arise for close interaction between Cardiff and London. For this junior partner of the Union, it is all part of a continuing challenge.

13

Wales in Europe

The Assembly shall not in the exercise of its functions conduct relations with any country outside the United Kingdom.

Wales Act 1978, section 28

Wales needs a strong voice in Europe . . . The Assembly will need to be involved as closely as possible in developing UK policy on European matters . . . It will be open to the Assembly to decide the form of its own presence in Brussels.

A Voice for Wales (1997)[1]

Evidently things have moved on a little. The difference in approach fits with the great expansion in EU competencies in the intervening period and so with the increased knock-on effects of supranational ordering on the practice of sub-state government. By which is meant, at one level, a burgeoning EU regulation that impacts on local or regional autonomy, the limitation of scope for difference, and, at another level, increased recognition of the important role for regional or meso-government in securing an effective mix of economic and social policies ('internal subsidiarity').

'Wales in Europe' is a chief mantra of the contemporary devolutionary process. Once again, the local constitutional phenomenon may look different, but it also stands for an underlying process of convergence. The idea repeatedly stressed in the devolution White Paper of reinventing the territory as a 'Euro-region' was thus firmly grounded in comparative developments in policy and politics. 'Experience elsewhere shows that effective regional government can bring additional gains both for member states and for areas such as Wales.'[2]

This chapter tests the extent to which the rhetoric is made good. The fact that it is pre-eminently a case of mixed results is only to be expected. By reason, it is important to say, not only of the short time span of the Assembly, the subject of 'Wales in Europe' being a quintessential learning experience for the infant body, but also of the increasingly complex and dynamic world of 'multi-layered governance' that the Assembly now inhabits. That is to say, a world characterized by constitutional and administrative forms of coexistence, concurrency and overlap, or novel paradigms of interdependence across hierarchical structures of government.

In this chapter a novel conceptual framework is utilized, a fivefold model of engagement with Europe at the regional or meso-government level that can also be used as a tool for comparative analysis and evaluation.[3] Reflecting and reinforcing the local experience, it is specifically designed to highlight both the opportunities and the constraints on sub-state creativity in a contemporary era characterized by the broad currents of market liberalization and supranational modes of ordering. Closer to home, the formal legal weakness of the devolutionary scheme is powerfully illustrated in this sphere, and yet should not be allowed to obscure the expanding patterns of the territorial engagement in Europe, which are multi-functional and multifaceted.

It was further suggested in the Introduction to this book that national devolution to Wales exemplified major contemporary strands of development in public administration, typically associated with the effects of globalization and in particular the rise of continental trading regimes like the EU Single Market. By which is meant especially the simultaneous processes of integration and fragmentation in Europe, including in terms of their interaction or the way in which a re-emphasis on territoriality reflects the competing stresses and strains generated by a widened and deepened market economy. It is time in this chapter to make good the claim.

Globalization and integration

How to engage in this context with the deeply contested concept that is globalization? The definitions provided often contrast the 'global' with the 'national', for example seeing globalization as 'the intensification of economic, political, social and cultural relations across borders'.[4] Such an approach is necessary and valuable, the increased permeability in so many ways of the state being at the heart of contemporary developments in comparative public administration. It is also, however, insufficient, and may in particular obscure the way in which integration into global economic arrangements may occur at sub-state level, including in diverse forms inside a single state entity.

It has been said that globalization, which 'in one sense erodes territorial distinctiveness', in other ways 'enhances the importance of territory and gives impetus to the construction of territorial societies'.[5] There is more to this than the idea of 'the safe haven', whereby the individual and the community are (somehow) sheltered from the shrill and homogenizing blast of global forces. It may be 'a runaway world'[6] in which the autonomy of sub-state as well as state government is eroded, but it does not follow that regions and localities have no scope for policy initiative and response, better to harness the economic and other opportunities.[7] In particular, globalization is seen as underscoring the need at sub-state level to identify and develop economic strengths, on the one hand establishing conditions for indigenous industries with a comparative advantage; and, on the other hand, engaging successfully in the competitive struggle to attract (and maintain) major inward investment.[8]

The reference in the subheading to 'integration' denotes two different but related processes: the peculiarly intense growth of 'relations across borders' represented by European integration, and the more diffuse forms of integration into global arrangements. The 'Euro-region' obviously has to contend with both processes. At the same time, and with reference to the parallel processes of EU integration and fragmentation, the rise of regional or meso-government should not be seen as a zero-sum game in which the central tier of government necessarily loses out. A key to this is the idea of sub-state mobilization in terms of EU policy-making primarily through rather than beyond the established central government structures of the member state.[9]

Considerations of economic regeneration were previously identified as a key driver of the new Welsh constitutional dispensation. Indeed, according to Ron Davies, 'an Assembly will only succeed if it can deliver a better quality of life and higher living standards'.[10] The territory has a creditable record in attracting inward investment, but it has continued to struggle in the wake of the decline of heavy industry, as also now of the rural economy. A low GDP is typically a product both of low economic participation rates and low levels of productivity.[11] Looking forwards, the economy of the region clearly faces formidable challenges, but especially so in terms of the intensifying competitive pressures that mark the trajectory of the European legal and political construction. By which is meant not only the creation of the Euro-zone (from which – at least for the moment – the territory is excluded) but also the geographical tilt eastwards that now constitutes EU enlargement. For many years a low-wage economy inside the continental trading regime, the territory must now contend with the labour pool of the many new entrants or 'accession states', and do so as a 'peripheral region' or from a position on the Atlantic shore.[12]

In Alun Michael's words, 'the correct response to globalisation cannot be to look inwards', as if it was somehow possible to build new economic and social barriers with the outside world. On the contrary, 'the progressive response to globalisation must be to reach out, to work with others, to pool our talents, so that we are stronger and fitter and better equipped to meet the challenges of tomorrow.'[13] In achieving an effective mix of economic and social policies, regional or territorial activity is thus 'a necessary complement to the macro-economic and structural reforms which are applied at Member State and European levels'.[14]

1. INTERNAL ARRANGEMENTS: THE STANDING COMMITTEE

Although not specified in the devolution statute, the case for a specialist Assembly committee on European matters was accepted early on in the design of the internal architecture. Typically, however, NAAG provided little guidance about the role, and that which it did – a coordinating function to ensure 'a consistent and coherent approach' to EU matters 'in each of the subject committees'[15] – now looks outdated in view of the fact of the Welsh Assembly Government. In the event, and indicative of the major challenges entailed in devolved administration in the face of the intensive process that is European integration, the committee has struggled to carve out an effective role.

This is the more striking in view of the membership. A measure of the (political) importance attached to it inside the Assembly; the committee has been composed of senior AMs including the First Minister as chair and the other party leaders. In addition, illustrating the concept of 'partnership' in the devolutionary design, the five Welsh MEPs together with Welsh represent-atives on such European bodies as the Economic and Social Committee (ECOSOC) and the Committee of the Regions (CoR) have received standing invitations to attend the meetings. To which may be added various local experts, co-opted from time to time in order to assist in the committee's deliberations, as well as relevant officials from the Welsh Assembly Government. Formally 'connected' this standing committee most certainly is.

Reflecting the many and various dimensions of the European enterprise, the committee has been presented with a broad-ranging mandate under standing orders. By virtue of its original designation as the 'Committee on European Affairs', it must 'keep under review' (a) the Assembly's relations with the EU institutions; (b) the liaison arrangements with the UK government on European issues; and (c) the Assembly's methods and procedures for the consideration of European documentation etc. It is also 'to monitor the general impact and consequences for Wales' of EU policies, as well as assist and supplement the work of the subject committees most obviously as regards cross-cutting issues. At the same time, both the political and administrative resources are obviously in short supply – the committee only meets six times a year – and so there is an exceptional need for prioritization.

Like so much else in the Assembly, the committee made a slow beginning. It was in part a reflection of the very limited involvement in EU affairs of the Welsh Office. New structures had to be developed and administrative processes and relationships elaborated and extended across the post-devolutionary system of multi-layered governance. Not only was much of this work (politically) unexciting, but also much of it was rightly put in train ahead of the first Assembly elections.[16] Conditions were thus ripe for the

Committee to appear as a legitimating agent. Official reports came and went; members were invited 'to take note'. In turn, the committee was an easy target for criticism on the ground of passivity.[17] Notably, the concern was not confined to Plaid Cymru, which obviously has a particular interest in maximizing the Assembly's presence on the European stage, but was shared among the political parties.[18]

In terms of the engagement with Europe, one important clue is the difficulty that the committee quickly encountered with formal *ex ante* scrutiny. As should have been obvious from the outset, 'the volume of legislation and other information coming from Europe is too great for systematic scrutiny by the Committee, particularly in light of the lack of relevance of much of that material to Wales'.[19] So, following the lead clearly given in standing orders, 'the Assembly would be best served by the Committee facilitating the effective handling of European legislation and policies throughout the Assembly'. To this effect, 'the House of Commons' and Scottish Parliament's procedures for detailed legislative scrutiny were examined and found not to be practical for application in Wales'.[20] In practice, and typical of the scheme of executive devolution, the Assembly has to lean on the well-developed machinery in Westminster, both the European Scrutiny Committee of the House of Commons and the House of Lords Select Committee on the European Union. A welcome innovation is that of regular meetings between the Chairs of European committees across the UK, an early illustration of the practical demand for inter-parliamentary networking and coordination inside the reinvented Union state.[21] Once again, Wales as the junior partner has much to gain.

Another clue is identified: the way in which the indirect route to Brussels via London has featured prominently in Members' deliberations. It is the logical product of a devolutionary schema of shared and concurrent competencies in the face of supranational ordering. In the words of the committee, 'it is therefore vital that the Assembly maintain close links with lead Whitehall Departments in respect of both domestic and European policies'.[22] Standing orders serve to push home the point, singling out adequate liaison with the UK Permanent Representation (UKRep) for special attention. At the same time, the work of the all-party committee is inevitably constrained in light of the principle of confidentiality attaching to the new modalities of intergovernmental relations. Keeping such arrangements 'under review' can only extend so far.

One might have expected this committee to feature prominently in the report of the Assembly Review of Procedure. In fact, a measure of pre-emptive corrective action had been taken. Better to avoid the problems of overload, and sensitive to the criticism of a lack of focus, the committee agreed to focus more strongly on strategic, coordinating and networking functions; and in particular:

- monitoring the mechanisms by which Wales pursues its interest in Europe and promoting new initiatives as required;
- contributing to defining a Welsh position on strategic European issues;
- ensuring that relevant European issues are addressed in Wales, including outside the Assembly.[23]

A key test is the relationship with the subject committees. That all has not been well was made abundantly clear in the course of the Assembly Review. 'The Committee has expressed concern that subject committees are sometimes not aware of issues on the European agenda which fall within their remit and it intends to further explore methods for improving coordination of European issues.'[24] Improvements include a system of specialist rapporteurs for each subject committee and annual meetings with the subject committee Chairs. Standing orders have also been amended to allow the committee to consider matters falling within the remit of a single-subject committee (and not just cross-cutting issues).[25] Objective 1 funding is the obvious example, previously being under the exclusive purview of the Economic Development Committee. There is then welcome acceptance of the need for flexibility and for improved communication across the Assembly: or less 'silo mentality', more 'joined up thinking'.

Notably, the opportunity has also been taken to expand the geographical range. As well as 'Wales in Europe' it is now a case of 'Wales in the world'. Such anyway is the message of the relabelling of the committee as the 'Committee on European and External Affairs' (EEAC), with the function of keeping under review 'the Assembly's relations with nations external to the European Union' now being added to the list of requirements in standing orders.[26]

In fact, this change in the formal committee structure of the Assembly was triggered by an administrative reorganization, in the guise of expansion of the relevant policy division. At the same time, and pointing up the close symbiotic relationship with the administrative branch, that reorganization – from 'European Affairs Division' to 'European and External Affairs Directorate' (EEAD) – fitted with the emergent sense of priorities in this committee chaired by the First Minister. To quote from the official briefing paper, 'such a change . . . would be a natural extension of the Committee's work on [EU] enlargement where it has been looking at options for extending the economic and social relations with countries currently outside the Union'.[27]

Promotional activity; overseas events and trade missions; inward visits and international relationships (not least in the image of a Welsh diaspora): such is the non-EU agenda that the committee is now expected to oversee and facilitate.[28] This is yet another clue, being all at one with greater ambition in, and a sharper business edge to, the conduct of Welsh paradiplomacy; and, further, reflecting the twin processes of global and European integration.

Constitutionally and legally speaking, 'Wales in Europe' obviously is the essential aspect, but there is now this wider perspective. To quote Paul Murphy, 'Devolution has added a huge new dimension to our relationship (in Wales) with the rest of the world.'[29] So far have we travelled from the manifest insularity of the Wales Act 1978!

Enough has been said to show that EEAC has a useful role to play, not only as an (all-party) totem of broader horizons, but also as a tool of formal networking and coordination of regional interests and on occasion of strategic direction. At the same time, it is important to recognize that this committee in particular can only do so much, by reason of the peculiarly dynamic and diffuse nature of the subject matter, or external environment.

2. ENGAGING EUROPE: A FIVEFOLD MODEL

It is appropriate to stress the strong Euro-phile flavour of the National Assembly in general and the Welsh Assembly Government in particular. Especially, that is, under the stewardship of Rhodri Morgan, a former European Commission representative in Wales. In his words, 'it is vitally important that the National Assembly does all that it can to make sure that Wales is able to play a full and creative role in Europe'.[30] We are a long way here from past patterns of UK Conservative Euro-scepticism.

So what might this 'full and creative role' entail? The work of EEAC effectively hints at the possibilities, which can now be illuminated by reference to our conceptual framework. The comparative element demands a special emphasis here. Territorial, functional, political spaces: Euro-regions, it is commonly observed, come in all shapes and sizes. As indicated, however, Wales is already something of a showcase of the opportunities for, as well as the constraints on, sub-state mobilization in the light of supranational ordering.[31]

Easily recognizable by the lawyer, the first concept is that of 'the implementing region'. Reference is here being made to the legislative space available to the territory in the implementation of EU requirements. EC directives obviously provide the litmus test, according to the classic treaty formula of domestic choice of forms and methods.[32] How substantial is this space, or to what extent is the Euro-region allowed – and equipped – to go it alone? The question is sharply posed in the Welsh case, in view of the lack of British constitutional tradition in such matters of divided competencies, and of the retarded administrative development of the territory in historical terms, a feature already powerfully illustrated in terms of solely domestic forms of law making. From civil service outpost of London to creative and major user of European legislative space, it is another quantum leap.

The second concept – 'the partnering region' – relates to the novel forms of local democratic governance, including in terms of appropriate models of

CONSTITUTIONAL REGION
(Regions with Legislative Power
(RegLeg))

IMPLEMENTING REGION
(legislative space (via 'designation')

PARTNERING REGION
(local forms of democratic governance; structural funds etc.)

Committee on European and
External Affairs (EEAC)

NATIONAL ASSEMBLY

WELSH ASSEMBLY
GOVERNMENT

European and External Affairs
Directorate (EEAD)

NATIONAL REGION
(accommodation and co-ordination of state and sub-state interests;
political and cultural capital)

LOBBYING AND
NETWORKING REGION
(paradiplomacy)

Figure 16: Wales in Europe – a conceptual framework

regional economic development, as well as to the tools and practices of administrative and political cooperation across the various layers of government. It thus sits comfortably both with the White Paper *A Voice for Wales*, which was seen to illustrate the contemporary search in comparative public administration for collaborative or mutually beneficial solutions, and the partnership approach now widely adopted under the auspices of the Welsh Assembly Government.

The particular twist involves EU regional policy in the guise of the structural funds: the designation of 'West Wales and the Valleys' as a lagging region in the current programming period. As well as sitting comfortably with the strong economic orientation of the Welsh devolutionary development, this brings into play the newly strengthened 'partnership principle' of the EU policy. By which is meant the legal requirement of shared responsibility between the different layers of government and the public and private sectors in the name of solidarity and democratization, efficiency and self-government or non-hierarchical forms of coordination.[33] Wales is once again a key testing ground; and all the more so, it may be said, by reason of the synergy involving the domestic or devolutionary aspect of 'the partnering region'.

The concept of 'the national region' is obviously bound up with the title of this volume, *Delineating Wales*. It serves to underscore the multifaceted nature of the legal and constitutional position of the territory: the conceptualization in terms of a 'nation', and the firm anchoring – as a 'region' for EU purposes – inside the Union/member state. A new representative focus for Welsh identity and democratic culture, special cultural and political forms of capital: far from downplaying this 'national' element, the Welsh Assembly Government has been notably keen to exploit it in the European context.

The way in which central government has to learn to live with shared roles and responsibilities is highlighted by the rise of meso-government in an environment of intensifying supranational ordering and global forces. Attention is thus drawn to the key element in the novel UK system of intergovernmental relations that is the *Concordat on Co-ordination of European Union Policy Issues*.[34] Once again, this choice of soft law technique is seen to fit with the idea of expanding patterns of interdependence and collaborative forms of decision-making across state structures, as well as illustrating the administrative and political values of flexibility and responsiveness. Proper accommodation and coordination of state and sub-state interests in EU affairs: such are the concerns of 'the national region'.

'The lobbying and networking region' is another closely related concept. It serves to highlight the fact of Welsh 'paradiplomacy', the international activities of the sub-state government. Notably, a strong growth in paradiplomacy in recent years is typically associated in comparative studies with the effects of globalization and in particular the rise of continental trading regimes like the EU Single Market.[35] A critical test of sub-state mobilization is the responsiveness of paradiplomacy to changes in the opportunity structure or policy-making environment, for example in terms of the evolving constitutional architecture of the EU. This is not to overlook formal scrutiny, consideration by the regional representative body of draft European legislation. The formidable obstacles to a sustained and effective input from Wales of this type have already been underscored.

The Welsh case is the more notable for illustrating a diverse range of contacts, dedicated first to raising the international profile, and second to grasping the competitive opportunities. The identity of a 'national region' may be used to great advantage here. Regional associational networking at the pan-European level, a familiar feature in paradiplomacy, is one aspect. Another one is the establishing of close bilateral relationships targeted especially on the (more dynamic) economies in the accession states. Neatly illustrating the broad knock-on effects of EU enlargement, this development exemplifies the potential for sub-state initiative in the harsh light of intensifying market forces, and thus the concept of 'the lobbying and networking region'.

The concept of 'the constitutional region' is the fifth one. Recently, the term has been used in the EU context to denote entities such as internal or stateless nations and (federal) lands or provinces with substantial (constitutionally) guaranteed legislative powers.[36] Politically speaking, it stands for the demand of certain significant and clearly delineated territories, such as Catalunya in Spain and Scotland in the UK, for closer parity with member states inside the EU umbrella or supranational framework. A demand, it is observed, which is felt all the more keenly in view of enlargement, the imminent prospect of privileged status for more small states. On the one hand, this serves to highlight the lack of 'fit' in the European construction between the unitary conception of member states as found in major elements of EC law and the domestic political realities of divided competencies as signalled in the rise of meso-government.[37] On the other hand, it clearly implies a process of differentiation from other 'Euro-regions': or, as one could say, not so much 'the third level'[38] as 'two-and-a-half'. A venture, it is immediately apparent, in which Wales is somewhat awkwardly placed by reason of the limited scheme of executive devolution.

In this chapter, the concept is afforded a wider meaning: the region as an actor in the major processes of constitutional and administrative reform in the EU. The new Welsh polity has thus contributed to the wide-ranging debate on 'European governance' initiated by a European Commission White Paper,[39] and to the more fundamental 'future of Europe' debate, which has now been pursued via a European – Constitutional – Convention.[40] Founded on, but not confined to cooperation with central government in the role of member state, this activity is the more striking when read in terms of the territorial history of a low profile.

3. THE IMPLEMENTING REGION

The Welsh Assembly Government has quickly grasped the truth of the matter.

> Generally, then, the effect of the European Union is to limit the scope for separate policy-making by the devolved administrations, at least in (currently) the fields of agriculture, fisheries and the environment. This broadly reflects the experience of the Länder in Germany and the autonomous regions in Spain.[41]

Naturally the upbeat message about 'Wales in Europe' retailed in the White Paper *A Voice for Wales* touched lightly on this aspect. Indeed, in his role of ministerial advocate of the scheme, Ron Davies stressed the margin of appreciation that the Assembly would have in putting into effect Community policies: implementation (of EU directives) 'in a way that [the Assembly] considers best takes account of Welsh interests'.[42] Typically, however, this has so far borne little fruit in the policy and practice of Assembly law making – for a whole battery of reasons.

Transmission belt

A generous and principled allocation of legislative implementing powers to the Assembly, it is not. Under the scheme of the devolution statute, the power to designate a minister of the Crown under section 2(2) of the European Communities Act 1972, so allowing the minister to make regulations 'for the purpose of implementing any Community obligation', may be exercised to designate the Assembly.[43] By spring 2003 nine such Orders in Council had been made, but far from dealing in a generic way with such subjects as the environment, they constituted a ragbag of specifications. On one occasion the Assembly gained powers to implement directives in relation to such diverse activities as keeping wild animals in zoos, the management of hazardous waste, and the deliberate release of genetically modified organisms.[44]

On the one hand, this lack of pattern – especially striking from the viewpoint of federal systems of divided competencies – is all at one with the particularistic or highly pragmatic approach to the allocation of law-making powers in individual Westminster statutes that is the hallmark of Welsh devolution. On the other hand, such cautious use of the designation power is indicative of a concern in central government to maintain a dominant position in this important legal field of member state responsibility, at least on an England and Wales basis. It is worth adding in this context that by the very nature of the beast a designation order is apt to confer 'Henry VIII'-type powers on the Assembly.

The Assembly had made some seventy orders under designated powers by March 2003.[45] Reflecting the substance of the designations, however, the vast majority of these statutory instruments were in the fields of agriculture, fisheries and food.[46] Further, much of the output has been driven by events, with a good third of the orders being directed to the handling of foot and mouth disease, and another ten orders stemming from the earlier BSE crisis in Britain. Other instruments again were largely technical in character or were part of EU-wide forms of (disease) control allowing for no local discretion. Turning the argument round, only a small group of orders – to do with financial support for organic farmers for example[47] – demonstrate any real creativity at the territorial level.

The devolved administration, a transmission belt: such then is the dominant model. Procedurally speaking, a notable feature of EU-inspired legislation in the Assembly has been the common recourse to executive or urgency procedure, the Westminster-type form of secondary legislative process that involves little formal scrutiny.[48] The practice reflects and reinforces the fact that there is little substantive difference from the comparable orders produced for England by the UK central government departments. Constitutional change – political, administrative and legal continuity: the product of devolution, it is well to remember, need not be diversity; and all the more so, under the long shadow of supranational ordering.

As well as a subject matter that frequently does not lend itself to different regulatory regimes, relevant 'European' factors include the incentive to play safe in view of the potential for compensation claims for wrongful implementation under the doctrine of state liability.[49] Especially noteworthy in the context of devolution is a 'grey area' of EU law, which relates to the possibility of differential implementation of EC legislation by the different administrations in the UK for reasons of policy choice. Suffice it to say that the vulnerability to challenge on the basis of the general principle in EC law of equal treatment has been officially noted at the highest level of the Welsh Assembly Government.[50]

Once again on the domestic front the historical legacy of the Welsh Office cannot be ignored: the perceived lack of official policy-making capacity in Wales and the hitherto limited practical experience of law making. So also, exploration of the EU 'margin of appreciation' – and indeed expansion of devolved powers in areas where there is little or no scope for member state discretion – is apt to appear an unnecessary luxury for a new governing entity concerned to (be seen to) make a difference. The initial fact post-devolution of Labour Party hegemony at the central and territorial levels may be said to have underwritten an argument that the Whitehall machinery should take the strain.

A long tradition of legislation on a joint England and Wales basis is further underscored in this context by the provisions of the EU concordat. Reflecting the close interest of central government in its role as the responsible member state, the concordat thus builds in a raft of notification, consultation and liaison requirements in the case of the devolved administration minded to implement differently.[51] A case, one could say, of establishing an administrative disincentive; that is, over and above the standard considerations of official convenience and limitation of legislative complexity which favour matching drafts. In sum, despite Ron Davies's apparent optimism, it would have been remarkable if the Assembly had departed quickly and radically from the English/UK EU template.

All this takes on additional relevance by virtue of the contemporary preference for framework directives, at least as articulated by the Commission White Paper on European governance. The Commission, as part of a less top-down approach, thus aims to 'bring greater flexibility into how Community legislation can be implemented in a way which takes account of regional and local conditions'.[52] Perhaps it comes as no surprise to learn that the assembled Welsh polity has declared itself in favour of this proposal.[53] Enough has been said, however, to demonstrate the distance between local aspiration and practical experience. First, much bargaining with central government over the terms of the relevant designation orders may be anticipated: not obviously to the Assembly's advantage. Second, putting framework directives to distinctive use for Wales inside Wales would require something of a revolution in the making of EU-inspired Assembly legislation. Such change may happen, and of course is liable to be prompted by new opportunities. However, at this stage of the post-devolutionary development of this 'Euro-region' the prevailing forces point firmly in the opposite direction. The administrative 'glue' of the Union state is not about to come unstuck here.

Against the Commission

What, it may be asked, of the statutory provisions on compliance? The devolution legislation solemnly records that the Assembly has no power to act in a way incompatible with Community law. It is further stated that any relevant Community obligation of the UK is an obligation of the Assembly.[54] Given the general dictates of EC law, by which is meant especially the duty of loyal cooperation operating across all tiers of government, this is aptly described as having 'a quality of belt and braces'.[55]

By way of practical illustration, one affair stands out, seeing the Assembly at odds with the Commission in its familiar role as 'the guardian of the treaties'.[56] The policy context is Welsh opposition to the development of genetically modified plant varieties, as encapsulated in the all-party preference for a 'GM-free territory'.[57] Contrary, that is, to the tide of EU legislation, seen (at least in the Assembly) as successfully influenced by the biotech companies through the United States. In the event, an Assembly debate in late 2001 saw the minister seeking approval of secondary legislation designed to secure compliance with the EU regulatory framework. Infringement proceedings had by now been launched against the UK for failure – by reason of Welsh obduracy – to transpose the relevant directive. And the Commission had threatened the Assembly with the prospect of penalty proceedings under Article 228 in the case of non-compliance. To quote the minister, 'the wolves are at the door'.[58]

To the lawyer, this was a case of clear and manifest breach: the Assembly had already delayed for some eighteen months beyond the due date for implementation. Whereas under the scheme of the treaties the penal jurisdiction involves sanction on the member state, the true 'bite' or dissuasive effect largely depends on the domestic arrangements for transfer (or otherwise) of the sanction. Attention is thus drawn to the words of the EU concordat: 'to the extent that financial costs and penalties imposed on the UK arise from the failure of implementation or enforcement by a devolved administration . . . responsibility for meeting these will be borne by the devolved administration'.[59]

The region against the Commission: typically it was no contest. For Plaid spokesperson Jocelyn Davies, it was a painful lesson in the powerful constraints on territorial government under the long shadow of supranational ordering. In her words, 'why vote . . . if we cannot reject?'[60] Nor is it surprising to learn that the UK government was in these conditions prepared to stand back and allow the Assembly to make its 'own' decision.

One aspect of the affair deserves a special mention – the scale of the threat. To explicate, in the only case so far decided by the Court of Justice under Article 228, Greece was fined some EUR 20,000 per day from the date of judgement for continuing failure by the regional authority in Crete adequately to deal with a problem of toxic waste.[61] While the Welsh case is appropriately labelled a more serious breach, the failure to transpose directives being a chief target for Commission enforcement action, this should not be allowed to obscure the stark differential in the approach to sanction. By the time of the Assembly debate, Commission representatives were indicating a fine of up to £300 million; that is, a potential daily charge – levied from the due date for transposition – some twenty-five times the rate eventually imposed on Greece. So much, from the viewpoint of this little country, for equality of treatment!

Alternatively, the scale of the threat could be said to be wholly disproportionate: that is, from the regional or 'bottom-up' perspective. Its draconian nature thus reflects and reinforces the lack of 'fit' in the formal EU constitutional construction with the burgeoning process of regionalism or internal subsidiarity. To this effect, the current penalty system as devised by the commission is explicitly predicated on the ability to pay of the member state,[62] as against in the case of the Assembly a juvenile delinquent.

4. THE PARTNERING REGION

Much has been heard in this context of so-called 'Team Wales'. There are significant elements here of a neo-corporatist strategy of economic development, predicated upon close linkages between the public and private sectors, as well as the assertion, bound up with the concept of national devolution, of a common territorial interest.[63] It has thus been seen as 'imperative that the opportunities and needs of Wales are tackled from an all-Wales perspective, through a strong commitment by the Assembly to mobilise the range of organisations'.[64] Together with the strong economic element in the territorial constitutional construction, the idea of the region as a player in the competitive (single and global) market struggle is clearly shown.

As explained in chapter 4, one of the growth industries of Welsh devolution is strategic planning. Originally it was *An Economic Strategy for Wales* and the happy-sounding *Pathway to Prosperity*. Then it was a *National Economic Development Strategy* and – the Assembly corporate plan – *A Better Wales.*[65] Today it is the optimistic vision of *A Winning Wales* that the economy of this peripheral Euro-region is about to be transformed.[66] Both the scale and trajectory of the planning process are all at one with the strong collaborative theme. 'If the people, businesses and communities of Wales can work together, within an integrated framework agreed by the Government of the National Assembly, the job can be done.'[67]

What then of EU regional policy, traditionally defined in terms of reducing or mitigating geographical and social disparities in the face of market forces?[68] Viewed in comparative perspective, the development in Wales brilliantly illustrates the elasticity of the concept of a 'region' in the European construction.[69] The typical characterization of the territory in terms of 'north' and 'south' constituted a major problem, because so defined neither of the 'regions' of Wales qualified for Objective 1 funding, on the basis of the threshold of per capita GDP less than 75 per cent of the EU average. The internal geography of Wales had therefore to be reinvented, in the guise of the peripheral 'region' of a peripheral region that is 'West Wales and the Valleys'. The case was thus successfully made for its delineation as 'a lagging region' under the key European Regional Development Fund (ERDF) in accordance with EU statistical policy and practice.[70] Not least, it may be noted, on the basis of rendering public policy more effective, since one aim of the most recent reform of the structural funds has been to concentrate resources for greater effect.[71] As an example of sub-state mobilization in the face of supra-national ordering and intensifying market forces, this kind of 'creative geography' could scarcely be bettered!

Turning to the substance, the local action priorities include developing and expanding the SME base, developing innovation and the knowledge-based economy, community economic regeneration, and rural development and the sustainable use of natural resources.[72] All this is sorely needed in light of the low GDP of an especially deprived region inside Wales. In the dispiriting words of the programming document: 'The resulting combination of poor housing, ill health, low educational achievement and skills levels, and low disposable incomes has led to some areas experiencing social exclusion.'[73] The extent to which the large-scale injection of funds can generate sufficient 'compensation' as the EU expands east remains to be seen. That it will surely be a continuing struggle is already reflected in efforts to extend support into the next programming period.

In this classic field for theories of multi-layered governance the 'partnership principle' takes on a special prominence, as not only involving a wide range of actors but also signalling techniques of coordination and collaboration across the many stages of the development planning process. Typically, the Commission has seen it as 'a powerful means of increasing the effectiveness, visibility and democratic acceptance of the Structural Funds', and even – with a hint of desperation – as 'an excellent way of making Europe better known to Europeans'.[74] Yet the provisions of the relevant Council Regulation are wonderfully ambiguous, wearing all the characteristics of intergovernmental bargaining and compromise:

> Community actions . . . shall be drawn up in close consultation . . . between the Commission and the Member State, together with the authorities and bodies designated by the Member State within the framework of its national rules and current practices, namely:
>
> - the regional and local authorities and other competent public bodies
> - the economic and social partners
> - any other relevant competent bodies within this framework . . .
>
> In designating the most representative partnership at national, regional, local or other level, the Member State shall create a wide and effective association of all the relevant bodies, according to national rules and practice, taking account of the need to promote equality between men and women and sustainable development . . .
>   All the designated parties . . . shall be partners pursuing a common goal . . . Partnership shall cover the preparation, financing, monitoring and evaluation of assistance.[75]

On the one hand, a widening and deepening of the legal obligation is in part a response to the mediating of EU policy by national constitutional and administrative traditions such that prior observance of the partnership principle has been patchy, to say the least.[76] On the other hand, the individual member states clearly retain considerable discretion or room for manoeuvre in the ordering of arrangements inside the domestic framework.[77] It is, in other words, a case of mixed messages.

So it is all the more striking that the partnership principle has been taken extremely seriously in Wales. Once again, there is good fit, since the particular references in the regulation to gender equality and sustainable development echo the general provisions in the devolution statute.[78] The obvious touchstone, however, is that major local instrument of structural funds administration and implementation, the Programme Monitoring Committee.[79] The regulation may be silent about composition, but the Assembly in close dialogue with the Commission established a strict tripartite framework, consisting of equal representation from the public sector, the 'private/social sector' (business, farmers and the trade unions), and the voluntary/community sector. This key partnership has in turn given strategic direction to the Welsh European Funding Office (WEFO), a body responsible for performing the important day-to-day activities of managing authority and paying authority under the EU regime.[80]

This is the proverbial 'tip of the iceberg'. The Objective 1 programme in Wales has been implemented through partnerships operating at three further levels: local, regional and strategic.[81] To explicate, the first level is geopolitically structured: fifteen local partnerships, each covering one local authority area. The second level is thematic in character, ten regional partnerships each covering individual topics, from infrastructure to human resources, and on through countryside and forestry to tourism. Typically, the main role of these two levels is to identify, support and assist the development of projects. The third level consists of four strategy partnerships, designed to provide an overview of activity in the different parts of the programme, specifically so-called 'business assets' and 'human assets', and 'rural assets' and 'community assets'. Naturally, all these various bodies must have 'an agreed strategy framework' for their area of responsibility and also 'a lead body' to provide logistical support. In a word, partnership has been piled on partnership.

It is obviously too soon for proper empirical assessment. There clearly were considerable difficulties at the early stage in the policy implementation and delivery: all grist to the mill in the intense political disputation that has marked this programme.[82] Some teething problems were inevitable, being part of the necessary process of sub-state mobilization, and reflecting both the size of the programme and the novelty of devolved administration. The programme – gradually – has gathered speed.[83]

Yet enough has been said to demonstrate the funding for west Wales and the Valleys as a flagship enterprise for contemporary canons of European regional policy. Put simply, if structural funding cannot be made to work efficiently and effectively in Wales, in conditions of happy juxtaposition with the domestic devolutionary development of the national region, then where can it be?

For the avoidance of doubt, there is clearly much to be said for the types of involvement especially at grassroots level that the partnership principle is designed to encourage and promote. The energizing element of committed and innovative partnerships between the public, private and voluntary sectors at the local level, not least in releasing untapped potentials, is rightly seen as of the very essence of this regenerative programme. However, it is not surprising to learn of complaints from the coalface not only of cumbersome process and lengthy delays – an elongated decision-making chain – but also of elements of incoherence and duplication of activity across the range or different levels of partnerships.[84] There is, too, evident tension between, on the one hand, a programme objective of 'developing the skills and attitudes to allow the region to compete as a modern advanced economy', and on the other hand, limited or small minority representation of business in the formal structures of partnership. Whither, it may be asked, the entrepreneurial spirit in a body like the Programme Monitoring Committee? Politically incorrect this may be, but it can plausibly be argued that in the case of Wales the EU partnership principle has been taken too seriously.[85]

5. THE NATIONAL REGION

In the words of Rhodri Morgan, 'The European Union is large and Wales is small. The UK is a large and influential Member State. It makes sense for Wales to work with the UK so that we can punch above our weight.'[86] The quality of central–territorial relations in the light of supranational ordering is to this effect a chief test of the devolutionary development.

The constitutional problem of overlapping jurisdictions that is associated with the rise of multi-layered governance in Europe is once again a defining feature. On the one hand, central government will commonly retain legal and political responsibility in the role of member state, precisely because many of the devolved competencies are ones where EU law and policy apply.[87] On the other hand, and almost by definition, devolution will from time to time serve to heighten tensions between the UK and territorial interests in matters of EU policy and law making. As comparative constitutional experience well illustrates, there is thus a strong demand for robust procedures of communication, cooperation and accommodation between the different governing entities.[88]

Also important is the traditional view of European integration as a subject of foreign policy, which so defined comes under the prerogative of central government (in the guise of 'the Crown'). Prior to devolution this was made evident in the procedures for taking account of distinctive Welsh interests in the UK negotiating position, which developed naturally as part and parcel of the Whitehall arrangements. It was the familiar catalogue of UK cabinet and interdepartmental committees, and of the collective policy line, both in UKRep and the EU Council of Ministers. In turn, inside government, the prospect of devolution raised the by now familiar issue of the scale of adaptation or change to existing administrative arrangements.

In fact, this is one of those areas where a significant shift of thinking took place during the construction of the devolutionary scheme. In more traditional fashion, the White Paper *A Voice for Wales* suggested a strong central government model for the representation of Welsh interests in Brussels. This would have entailed participation by the Secretary of State for Wales in, and the Assembly only advising, United Kingdom delegations; representatives of the Assembly confined to the advisory Committee of the Regions; and UKRep continuing 'to represent the Secretary of State' and 'other Welsh interests'.[89] It hardly needs saying that the White Paper *Scotland's Parliament* was very different, signalling opportunities for attendance by representatives of the Scottish Executive at the Council of Ministers, as also secondment at official level to UKRep, and with no mention of a role here for the territorial Secretary of State.[90] In turn, the cession under much parliamentary pressure of basic parity for Wales in matters of EU representation, notwithstanding the standard dichotomy between legislative and executive devolution, was a step of first-class constitutional importance for the nascent Assembly.[91]

The EU Concordat

As set out in the *Concordat on Co-ordination of European Union Policy Issues*, the formal institutional framework for accommodating territorial interests presents a dual character. On the one hand, in contrast to certain advanced federal systems such as Germany, there is no element of constitutional guarantee and veto power: a weak formulation. Such is the way in which the British constitutional tradition has been reworked including via the system of concordats.[92] On the other hand, many of the individual provisions are welcoming or generous to the devolved administration(s): especially when viewed in terms of the insubstantial history of Wales in the counsels of the Union state.

Once again to quote the First Minister, 'it is difficult to measure objectively how effective [the] mechanisms are for influencing policy.'[93] The situation in terms of 'the national region' is in fact very fluid, which is hardly surprising given the hitherto highly centralist form and culture of government as epitomized in the case of England and Wales, and the strong asymmetrical element in the general devolutionary development. Officials from the Welsh Assembly Government have now actively to explore the boundaries. Informal alliances between what are sometimes referred to in Whitehall as 'the Celtic Cousins' – Scotland, Wales and Northern Ireland – are but one way forward.

Good communication and cooperation on matters of mutual interest, exchange of information and confidentiality: the EU Concordat may be read as the principles of IGR writ large. The provisions thus reflect and reinforce the special demands for internal coordination and collaboration that arise by reason of the sophisticated and dynamic bargaining process operating among the member states. The title is something of a misnomer, since the concordat covers not only policy formulation and representation but also such basic matters as enforcement and compliance. Reference has already been made to the provisions on allocation of legal risk – firmly geographically based – and on consultation over differential implementation (dissuasive). At one and the same time, the EU Concordat is part of administrative procedure and has a substantial constitutional and legal edge.

The sea change in attitudes since the Wales Act 1978 is once again apparent. The words of the overarching *Memorandum of Understanding* best convey the positive flavour. Whereas 'as a matter of law' international relations and relations with the EU 'remain the responsibility' of the UK government and Parliament:

> The UK Government recognises that the devolved administrations will have an interest in international and European policy making in relation to devolved matters, notably where implementing action by the devolved administrations may be required. They will have a particular interest in those many aspects of European Union business which affect devolved areas, and a significant role to play in them.[94]

Devolution should not come at the price of a loss of input capacity into the formulation of the UK policy line. The concordat rightly envisaged that consultation and the exchange of information 'will continue in similar circumstances to the arrangements in place prior to devolution'. But just in case, the Joint Ministerial Committee (JMC) has been made available in special 'European format' as a mechanism for simultaneous consultation by the lead UK minister. A battery of supplementary pledges, for example on the supply of 'full and comprehensive information, as early as possible', or the 'full and continuing involvement' of the devolved administrations as matters progress, indicates a careful hand played in the drafting by officials in Scotland.[95]

The *quid pro quo* is 'mutual respect for the confidentiality of those discussions and adherence to the resultant UK line, without which it would be impossible to maintain such close working relationships'.[96] Holding the whip hand in the role of member state, the UK government could threaten withdrawal of collaboration in a situation of non-compliance. The requirement of confidentiality has further resonance in the European context, effectively denying the devolved administration a valuable source of political leverage in cases of competing interest. So a coda is in order: the evident good intentions must not be allowed to obscure the potential for central domination, for example in the situation of political 'cohabitation'.

In sum, the provisions are appropriately read in terms of a bargain. At one and the same time, a national region like Wales has broad access in terms of policy inputs and is effectively constrained from operating outside agreed channels. Nationalists may rail at this but it reflects and reinforces the essential character of the constitutional development that is devolution. In the words of Assembly cabinet minister Andrew Davies:

> The UK, not Wales, is a member state of the European Union, so it is ultimately for the UK Government to determine European policy. That is not to say that it will ride roughshod over the wishes of Wales or, indeed, of Scotland. The UK line will be stronger when it is apparent that it represents the agreed views of all parts of the country. The concordat recognises that reality and gives it practical effect.[97]

In the case of the national region, the issue of representation in the EU Council of Ministers has a special symbolism, the Maastricht Treaty having opened the way to the representation of member states by ministers from regional governments in accordance with domestic constitutional norms.[98] In the words of the EU Concordat, 'Ministers and officials of the devolved administrations should have a role to play in relevant Council meetings, and other negotiations with EU partners.'[99] After a slow beginning, Assembly cabinet ministers now frequently appear on the UK team, and have even led from the front. The development is all at one with the local policy of raising Wales's profile. The domestic arrangements have in this respect proved sufficiently responsive.

At the same time, the UK government's position is carefully preserved. As well as no legal guarantees of national regional representation, the composition and negotiating tactics of the UK team are presented as essentially a matter for the lead UK minister. In turn, and representing a limited partnership function, 'the role of Ministers and officials from the devolved administrations will be to support and advance the single UK negotiating line which they will have played a part in developing'. The model, in other words, is a logical extension of the arrangements on policy formulation. As the Concordat solemnly records:

> In appropriate cases, the leader of the delegation could agree to Ministers from the devolved administrations speaking for the UK in Council, and that they would do so with the full weight of the UK behind them, because the policy positions will have been agreed among the UK interests.[100]

Soft law: flexibility and constitutional development

Speaking more generally, the idea of expanding patterns of interdependence and cooperative forms of decision-making across state structures is clearly illustrated in the design of this concordat. A paradigm example of the kind of intrastate collaboration that one would envisage in advanced systems of multi-layered governance, more especially in the context of the simultaneous processes of integration and fragmentation, is thus provided in the shape of the constitutional 'bargain'.

As Rhodri Morgan observes, size matters. The EU Concordat further serves as a reminder – if such is needed – that the indirect route to Brussels via London will remain of chief importance to Wales for the foreseeable future. Closer to home, it makes good practical sense for the Assembly admin-istration to lean on the powerful and well-oiled UK central government machine in the specialist areas of EU policy-making. How could it be other-wise, given on the one hand the limited resources available to the Assembly both at the political and civil service levels, and on the other hand the nature of the European agenda: diffuse and complex, or voluminous and elongated? The trick is to identify the critical issues for Welsh interests and to deploy the local political and administrative capital accordingly, using the Whitehall networks. This is more easily said than done, but it nonetheless represents the essential fact of life for the national region.

The famed flexibility of the British constitution can operate to advantage in this realm. The fit of these political and administrative arrangements – concordats as 'soft law' – with a fast-changing environment, not least in terms of the ongoing process that is the European political and constitutional construction, is a good one.[101]

Notably, the recent report from the Select Committee on the Constitution contains little by way of criticism about these arrangements, save on the general issue of transparency. In the committee's words:

> Like the conduct of many other aspects of intergovernmental relations, they rest on a high level of co-ordination at official level and a high level of good will at political level . . . The process is not an open one, for the devolved administrations let alone the general public and it is one in which the UK government retains a high level of control . . . We find it hard to see how matters could be otherwise. The true test of whether the process is the right one will ultimately be in its outcomes. But there is a problem, as the obligations of confidentiality imposed on the devolved administrations mean they cannot tell anyone, including their own assemblies or legislatures, when the outcome of the process has been unsatisfactory.[102]

6. THE LOBBYING AND NETWORKING REGION

The devolved administration has naturally been keen to explore the potential of direct linkages, first with the EU institutions, by way of supplementing and reinforcing the inputs into member state policy formation, and second with other official actors in the European political space, most obviously at the same regional level. In fact, so rapid is the development in this field that it is already possible to speak of two main phases.

Starting out

The first phase sees the Assembly overwhelmingly focused on the Objective 1 programme, and as seeking to make good a history of little engagement by the old territorial department in EU affairs. Further reflecting the sense of a 'Team Wales' approach, the wider effort is strongly focused on the Wales European Centre (WEC), a pre-existing partnership (which the Assembly quickly joins) involving the local authorities, the many Welsh quangos, and elements of civil society. A sensible and pragmatic approach at this initial stage, the infant body is thus seen tapping into an established pool of experience and contacts in Brussels, while also establishing a small Assembly office at the heart of the Union, with direct links into the diplomacy via UKRep. 'It is not a matter of choosing one or the other, but of finding ways of maximizing the benefits which both organizations can offer the Assembly.'[103]

WEC's mission has been 'to give Wales an edge in Europe'. To this end, four main objectives have been pursued: to provide information and intelligence on funding opportunities and relevant policy developments; to present Welsh needs and proposals to the EU institutions; to raise the profile of Wales in Brussels; and to encourage and assist in creating strategic transnational partnerships.[104] On the one hand, the work echoes much in the growth industry that is regional representation in Brussels.[105] On the other hand, as a service organization or channel for the promotion of the policies of its different member organizations or 'clients', WEC has constituted a distinctive model of regional activity at the heart of the Union.

As one would expect, the scope of WEC's work expanded considerably post-devolution, neatly illustrating the way in which diverse patterns of regional representation in Brussels reflect variant domestic constitutional traditions or practices. At the same time, there was clearly an increased demand for an effective advocacy and lobbying function, over and above the kind of information-gathering or intelligence work that had characterized the Welsh effort in Brussels prior to devolution. With some ten staff, and an annual budget of £1 million, there was clearly more than enough for WEC to do.[106]

Welsh paradiplomacy has also been responsive to the changing constitutional architecture of the European Union. WEC, it was declared, 'will need to give more attention in future to the Parliament, its Committees, working groups and political groups'.[107] To explicate, the region that once could reckon on its interests being represented through the member state in a context of unanimous decision in the Council of Ministers, has to focus on the fact that its 'host state' can often be overruled and that the European Parliament is increasingly powerful. There is then greater emphasis on the need for the networking and lobbying region to concentrate on the EU institutional triangle (Council–Parliament–Commission), and not simply an institutional axis (Commission–Council), including of course through its MEPs.

EU enlargement brings a fresh impetus to inter-regional activity. In the case of Wales, better to grasp the opportunities or – more bleakly – to mitigate the adverse economic consequences, an active engagement in key accession states is demanded.[108] An obvious peg has been the Community Phare programme for eastern Europe, as also the accession instruments ISPA (environment and transport projects) and SAPARD (agriculture and rural development). Welsh actors have thus been involved in a range of contacts, from technical exchanges to consultancy and twinning. Pride of place goes to the Welsh Development Agency (WDA). Self-proclaimed in fact as 'Europe's most successful economic development agency', it has a wealth of experience and expertise to offer prospective regional partners.

Thus, as boldly conceived in a strategy document produced by WEC:

Vision
To make Wales a valued player in central and eastern Europe
By contributing to the enlargement of Europe, Wales' expertise, experience and unique and diverse identity can realise mutual economic benefit and sustainable development for itself and the countries concerned.

Overall Objective
To increase Wales's involvement in central and eastern European countries through interregional cooperation and trade.

Specific Objectives
1. increase the visibility of Wales and its unique, diverse identity to regions in central and eastern European countries;
2. position Wales to gain economic advantage from the enlargement process;
3. build strategic relationship with regions in enlargement countries through high quality collaborative projects;
4. create a sustainable Team Wales framework for delivery.[109]

Such activity further illustrates what the first chief minister called 'the progressive response to globalization'; more especially with a view to achieving concentration or multiplier effects, or – as the lawyer might say – to a form of 'relational contracting' predicated on careful selection of priority countries and regions. In this way, 'scarce resources in Wales can be optimised, the impact in the countries will be maximised and the added value from synergies created.'[110] Latterly, these ideas have been taken forward under the direct political guidance of the European and External Affairs Committee.[111] In turn, the establishment of a special working group on enlargement, chaired by Rhodri Morgan, underlines the seriousness with which the devolved administration now takes this kind of activity. In the event, certain regions most notably Silesia in Poland have now been identified as suitable partners for Wales.[112] Such, it may be said, is the regional beauty contest in today's Single Market.

Wales of course must flaunt its own attractions. The local policy has been to exploit an abundant cultural capital with a view to promoting and cementing new official and economic linkages, while at the same time striving to update the image of Wales in Europe (and the World). 'We recognise that to be successful on the world stage we must have a clear vision that informs and inspires our global audience. We must develop a strong brand to support this aspiration.'[113] A region that is diverse and innovative, not simply interested in handouts, and which is willing and able to engage with partners, even to play a part (however small) in the progress of Europe: it is all part of the idea of 'the new model Wales'. The fact of such individual Welsh 'assets' in Brussels as Neil Kinnock, vice-president of the Commission, obviously is useful in this context. In summary, as a lobbying and networking region, a territory like Wales is – and now takes care to be – much better placed than, say, in the UK context a 'non-national region' such as the North East of England.

This is not to underestimate the many obstacles that the territory faces, not least in central and eastern Europe. Apart from the evident lack of contiguity, the basic duality of inter-regional relations – competition as well as coopera-tion or collaboration – is illuminated here. Thus the difficulty arises of balancing the benefits from productive partnerships with a concern to protect the position of the territory as an attractive destination for direct foreign investment.[114] There is also the problem for a fragile local economy of securing and then focusing resources for the purpose of engagement. In the event, however, the devolved administration has not been dissuaded from also developing the broader 'diplomatic' dimension: quite the reverse. The local preference in dealings with the accession states has thus been to estab-lish relationships early or ahead of enlargement, such that economic partner-ship serves to lay the groundwork for future political cooperation inside the EU.[115]

What, it may be asked, of the constraints imposed by the system of concordats? In practice the type of activity that is increasingly standard in the case of Wales – work related to economic development or regeneration in a

European context – is unlikely to be hindered. It is thus open to the devolved administration, in cooperation with the UK Foreign and Commonwealth Office (FCO), to make arrangements or agreements with foreign subnational governments etc. in order to facilitate cooperation between them on devolved matters.[116] Put another way, the constitutional and political idea of reinventing a territory like Wales as a 'Euro-region' is given ample expression here, with specific provisions allowing for regional offices overseas and for the separate promotion of trade and inward investment.[117] For its part, the Assembly Representation in Brussels is formally obliged to 'work closely with, and in a manner complementary to, UKRep', which 'remains responsible for representing the view of the United Kingdom to the European Institutions'.[118] Once again, however, there is little to suggest other than positive encouragement on the part of the FCO. In the words of the Select Committee on the Constitution, 'whatever the shortcomings of the ability of the devolved administrations to affect UK policy at EU level . . . there is no doubt that the devolved administrations have better access to EU institutions, both formally and informally, than their counterparts elsewhere in Europe'.[119]

Reorientation

The beginnings of a second main phase of activity are made apparent. The devolved administration is seen taking an increasingly multi-focused approach, engaging both with the main institutions and other actors in the Community, and one that is expressly geared towards securing access and influence. To this effect, the changing opportunity structure, including in terms of the constitutional architecture of the EU, is underscored.

The synergy of the different types of initiative is worth underlining. The hard-nosed business perspective – the region as competitive entity – is thus coupled with the general aspiration of Wales being more visible;[120] as also the constitutional dimension of a Welsh voice in Europe. At the same time, the development is predicated on a strong leadership role for the Welsh Assembly Government. This reflects the internal dynamic of the devolutionary scheme, the emergence of a separate government machine inside the legal framework of the corporate body, as well as the increased confidence of Assembly politicians and officials in treating with Europe. Put another way, the trajectory of Wales as a lobbying and networking region is in part a product of the autochthonous process of constitution-building that has quickly gathered pace.

All this is highlighted in the expansion of the policy division previously mentioned. By 2002 the European and External Affairs Directorate (EEAD) boasted a fivefold branch structure, which ranged from European Policy, Enlargement and the Euro to Interreg[121] and State Aids, and on through the

Assembly Representation in Brussels to Wales Trade International and International Relations. This, it can safely be said, would have been unthinkable in the time of the Welsh Office.

Official questioning of the design and orientation of WEC is another important clue. Constitutionally speaking, the strong partnership model of this organization, whereby the Assembly as one of a number of 'clients' lacked effective control of the machinery, has appeared increasingly at odds with the political and administrative position inside Wales. It was to this effect an obvious source of frustration for a newly delineated Welsh Assembly Government concerned to exercise strategic political direction at the territorial level.

In the event, the Assembly Cabinet has now withdrawn from WEC, as has the Welsh Local Government Association (in favour of its own dedicated non-stakeholder presence in Brussels).[122] The Centre has in turn reconstituted itself on a much-reduced basis, with a few core members (WDA, ELWa, the environment and university sectors) and offering services to a number of other bodies. The development is in fact a mark of the gradual maturation of the new Welsh polity: acceptance of the view that a single body served too many masters, growing experience in the Assembly of EU matters. Rhodri Morgan may be quoted: 'we believe that there would be greater clarity if we expanded our presence in Europe and made it clear who was speaking for Wales'.[123]

The touchstone is the upsizing of the Assembly Representation in Brussels. At one and the same time, this is a natural progression, expansion of official support beyond occasional attendance at the Council of Ministers to the conduct of (Welsh) government business in Brussels, and reflects and re-inforces the distinctive trajectory of the Welsh Assembly Government. First, the advantage to the devolved administration of the linkage into and through UKRep is prioritized. To this effect, the Assembly's Representation may be considered part of UKRep's 'extended family', whereby its officials have diplomatic status, and easy access to all the official documentation, while at the same time working unambiguously for the Assembly. It is after all these parts that the WEC model could not reach. Second, specialist Assembly representation across the chief fields of devolved powers, better to generate information flows and early inputs into the decisional processes of the Union, is the order of the day. The development is already well under way, beginning with agriculture. In short, the Welsh presence in Brussels is emerging as more akin to the Scottish model of functionally separate representation for the executive and for other actors.[124]

Another strand is introduced, in the form of inter-regional networking at the pan-European level. As well as the formal linkages, Assembly represent-ation on the Committee of the Regions (CoR) and (under the aegis of the Council of Europe) the Congress of Local and Regional Authorities, the territory has been actively engaged in forging new multilateral alliances. Better that is, in the words of the First Minister, 'to exchange ideas on policies and, where relevant, to develop common approaches'.[125] To which might be added the prospective gain in access and influence from associational inputs in the decisional processes of the EU. Delegations, the Assembly government has quickly learned, are apt to open doors including in the Commission.

In fact Wales was involved pre-devolution in an association with the four so-called 'motor' regions of Europe (Baden Württemberg, Catalunya, Lombardy and Rhones-Alpes). Significantly, however, this arrangement, big on 'hands across Europe' or less hard-edged, is now largely overshadowed. Wales has for example recently joined the large and well-established association that is the Conference of Peripheral Maritime Regions (CPMR). As the name suggests, this represents a good fit in terms of the policy orientation. CPMR thus offers the new devolved administration valuable connections and considerable representational experience in such important matters to Wales as Interreg and the structural funds, coastal issues and transport policy.

It is worth adding that the Assembly is somewhat spoiled for choice. It has chosen for example not to join the Assembly of European Regions (AER), another well-established grouping. Such it may be said is the attractiveness of the national region, and such is the growth of this paradigmatic form of paradiplomacy across Europe. The trick for this small country is once again to be highly selective, not dissipating too much effort in multitudinous places.

7. THE CONSTITUTIONAL REGION

It is then all the more striking that Wales has become involved in two further inter-regional networks, which are explicitly focused on constitutional and administrative reform in the EU. The development is at one and the same time a mark of the seriousness with which the territorial entity now takes itself, and a natural extension of its situation as a national lobbying and networking region.

The first such network is the large and diverse grouping comprised by the Regions with Legislative Power (RegLeg). Putting this in context, there is a wide constituency: within the EU, eight out of fifteen member states have regions with legislative power; some seventy regions amounting to approximately 55 per cent of the total EU population.[126] Somewhat optimistically perhaps, the Welsh Assembly Government has concluded not only that 'Wales fits comfortably into the group' but also that measured in terms of powers the Assembly features in 'the top half'.[127]

First established ahead of the Nice Intergovernmental Conference, and latterly concerned with the Convention on 'the future of Europe', this network has a convoluted history – as befits a 'bottom-up' initiative.

Essentially, however, RegLeg serves to underscore as a political phenomenon, and seeks to make good, the evident tension between the classical conception of the EU as a constitutional order of states, and the rise of meso-government across Europe.[128] More especially, the perceived inadequacy of the Committee of the Regions as an instrument of representation – most obviously for the most advanced 'constitutional regions' – is a clear prompt.[129] The Welsh Assembly Government is once again pleased to be involved, and further, it may be said, to exercise a moderating influence in this most sensitive area of constitution-building for Europe.

The 'Flanders Declaration', promulgated in May 2001, was the product of a self-selecting working group or inner core, comprised of seven of the most important 'constitutional regions'.[130] 'In order to ensure due compliance with the principle of subsidiarity and therefore guarantee full respect for the constitutional regions' own areas of competence, the political role of these regions has to be strengthened within the European Union.' Other demands have included direct participation in the recent European Convention[131] and privileged access to the Court of Justice.[132] Successively, however, the net-working process has been broadened – in the form of a RegLeg steering group now sufficiently large to include Wales; and (some of) the language tempered – as in the 'Liège Resolution' of November 2001.[133] 'The application of the principle of subsidiarity should not be restricted to relations between the European Union and its member states, but should be affirmed at every level, including relations between states and regions in particular, but not only with regions that have legislative power.'[134] It suffices to add that Welsh Assembly Government officials have been actively engaged in the working group on the political declaration from RegLeg to the European Convention. Such, it may be said, is the early success of the Welsh paradiplomatic effort.

Latterly, and once again reflecting and reinforcing the visibility of Wales in Europe, the territory has been invited to join a highly selective inter-regional grouping, the so-called Emilia-Romagna network. Expressly targeted on issues of European governance, this grouping is the more notable for benefiting from the personal interest of Commission President Romano Prodi. A fact, one could say, which in the finest traditions of paradiplomacy has not gone unnoticed in Wales.[135] In the event, the network has produced one of the few inter-regional responses to the Commission White Paper.[136] Not, it should be said, that the content is anything other than bland, being indicative like so many such common declarations of the lowest common denominator. The White Paper was solemnly welcomed as 'an important basis for discussion'. The standard pleas were made for a more inclusive model of EU policy-making as well as for the greater use of framework legislation.

The new Welsh polity has also been keen to engage on its own account in the debate on European governance. This is an early example of the more strategic approach to issues of European integration signalled by the

European and External Affairs Committee. Indeed the range of territorial
involvement, from committee hearings in Cardiff and in Brussels to an
Assembly plenary debate, and on through discussions with leading Commission officials to an all-Wales forum incorporating elements of civil society,
has been described by the chief author of the White Paper as almost unique.[137]
A case, one could say, of the new devolved entity wishing to be (seen to be)
'good Europeans'. The process is part of the story in another respect, since the
White Paper has offered a route into dialogue inside the territory on 'Wales in
Europe' – aspirations, expectations, options. In the event, the response from
the Assembly represents a consensual position, as well as being notably free
from direct UK government interference.

The White Paper has elsewhere attracted severe criticism:[138] not least for
being high on sentiment and low on practical proposals, and for prioritizing
Commission-dominated processes of public 'involvement' in EU decision-
making at the expense of more concrete forms of national political and
administrative representation. More particularly, whereas the White Paper
correctly pointed up the positive role that meso-government can play in
bringing the EU closer to its citizens, it was singularly lacking in detail or
specific ideas for charting a way forward.[139] So, for example, a suggestion of
'target-based, tripartite contracts' involving the Commission, member states
and sub-national governments, one that in the process of consultation on the
White Paper provoked more questions than answers, has been slow to come
to fruition.[140] Meanwhile, other proposals to enhance the role of the
Committee of the Regions, and to underpin processes of 'involvement' via a
code of consultation,[141] are seen to gloss over the heterogeneity and lack of
democratic legitimacy of CoR, and application and differentiation in the case
of the regions, respectively.[142]

The official response from Wales skipped lightly over such concerns. The
tone was unremittingly positive. The Assembly welcomed 'the spirit of the
Commission's initiative' and encouraged the exercise 'as a way of bringing
about early improvement'. There was support for increased involvement by
CoR, keenness to explore the 'intriguing idea' of tripartite contracts, 'strong
support' for a code of consultation, and so on.[143]

Would one expect much else? Far from an academic discursus this obviously was a political response, and one that was naturally imbued with the
institutional self-interest of the Assembly. Not only are local actors still feeling
their way, but also why offend the ultimate 'repeat player' in EU affairs that is
the Commission? Similarly, while there may be scratching of heads over the
meaning of 'target based, tripartite contracts', there is good reason to become
engaged at an early stage, better to fashion the initiative in a way that suits
British administrative traditions and Welsh interests, even to curry favour.

What then, it may be asked, of the individual Welsh perspective on 'the
future of Europe' debate? The full territorial position will no doubt prove

elastic in light of the deliberations of a Convention that is itself a precursor to an Intergovernmental Conference. Notably, however, the Welsh Assembly Government has been an enthusiastic participant in discussions on the UK policy line that have taken place in the JMC machinery and elsewhere.

Some preliminary observations are in order. First, along with colleagues in Scotland, the Assembly cabinet has been successful in persuading the UK government to promote a series of pro-regional initiatives in the Constitutional Convention, which link in turn to a general re-emphasis of the principle of subsidiarity. From a treaty reference acknowledging the role of regions in the EU to mandatory consultation by the Commission of regional authorities on matters for which they have responsibility for implementation, and on through institutional reform of the Committee of the Regions: in the words of the First Minister, this UK initiative represents 'a major achievement for Wales in taking forward our European agenda'.[144]

Second, with regard to the idea that is sometimes floated of delineating regional (as well as member state and EU) competencies in a 'Constitution of Europe',[145] the type of concern familiarly expressed in other constitutional systems through the concept of 'the open flank' still lacks salience in this domestic context. A tendency to (internal) centralization via the force of (supranational) integration, as constituted by member state responsibility for EU affairs, is apt to appear less of a problem when the region is newly constituted. At least that is to say in the case of Wales, only now awakening from a history of exceptional dependence on England and the powerful UK central government machine.

Third but related, the First Minister has notably stressed the advantages accruing to Wales from the unwritten British constitution. Its innate flexibility is thus seen as facilitating the growth of territorial activity on the European stage, including by reference to the comparable position in certain federal states. In Rhodri Morgan's words, 'in terms of expanding Wales' role and what we can contribute, we have already achieved a great deal in ensuring that our voice is heard'.[146] To this effect, whereas Wales may prove a useful ally in the pursuit of greater recognition for regions in formal legal terms, the Welsh Assembly Government will happily leave it to the likes of Catalunya to lead the charge.

Bringing the discussion full circle, there is evident potential here for linkage with the autochthonous process of constitution-building now taking place in Wales. Increased recognition of the role of the regions in bringing the EU closer to its citizens, even if limited; internal movement at territorial level towards parliamentary government and legislative devolution: it would be a case of mutually reinforcing pressures on central government for greater constitutional generosity to Wales. For his part, the First Minister has made this precise calculation.[147] It would be a suitably novel Welsh form of convergence.

CONCLUSION – WALES IN THE UNITED KINGDOM IN EUROPE

The effort that will be required to ensure the 'mainstreaming' of Community policies and opportunity structures in the new Welsh administrative process should not be underestimated. A specialist division and committee, the horizontal effects of the EU integrative process: it is a familiar but formidable challenge of dissemination. The struggle to have 'a voice for Wales' heard amid the cacophony of voices in Europe is an unremitting one, and will no doubt intensify in the light of enlargement. The need for a careful prioritization, or the importance of the search for 'added value' when engaging with Europe, is a recurring theme. Local enthusiasm has to be tempered, in favour of a tight quality threshold.

Many useful steps have been taken. The subnational response in the light of supranational ordering and (global) forces of market liberalization is thus seen to be multifaceted in nature, including in the guise of overlapping and mutually reinforcing functions. The fivefold classification utilized in this chapter serves to place in comparative perspective the terms of engagement. Constraint and opportunity, and in particular the forms of territorial initiative, the cross-currents (in constitutional reform) of continuity and change: once again matters are writ large in the case of Wales, including by reason of its situation as a national region, in the big player that is the United Kingdom.

The formal legal weakness of the devolutionary scheme is clearly illustrated in the lack of EU-orientated legislative space made available to the Assembly. The approach of central government appears overly cautious, in view of the many good reasons for substantive domestic uniformity irrespective of the local source of legislative power, more especially in the case of England and Wales. As an example of the way in which the regional entity is corralled by law inside the Single Market the scale of the threatened sanction in the GM seeds affair could scarcely be bettered.

'Partnering' is apt to appear something of a fetish in the new territorial polity. More particularly, in the early stages of the Objective 1 programme for west Wales and the Valleys, the approach may be said to have taken on a momentum of its own, above and beyond the formal legal requirements. There is obviously much that is valuable here, not least in terms of more energizing at the local level. It is, however, important not to lose sight of the associated dangers of administrative overload and fragmentation. In this respect, the auguries are not all good.

The concept of the national region is an especially valuable one. Conveying a suitably contemporary sense of multiple identities, it serves to highlight the strong measure of interdependency between the territorial and central tiers of government in the light of expanded modalities of supranational ordering. Concurrency and complexity of EU responsibilities and obligations; political and administrative liaison, cooperation and coordination; and cross-currents of decentralization and re-centralization: far from a 'withering away', such is the reinvention of the Union state. In the event, the devolved administration has reason to be encouraged, with constitutional practice under the important EU Concordat proving generous to Wales in such matters as attendance at the Council of Ministers. A different but related point: the special advantages of (cultural) identity available to the national region in the territorial competitive struggle are splendidly shown here.

The speedy emergence of Wales as a lobbying and networking region demonstrates a major channel of opportunity for the new territorial polity. Once again, the local phenomenon epitomizes a powerful contemporary trend in comparative public administration in the guise of paradiplomacy. An expanded web both of bilateral and multilateral connections now ranges beyond the more obvious economic and cultural linkages to the articulation of a regional voice in EU constitutional and administrative affairs. A window on Europe, as well as a window on Wales, this aspect of the territorial engagement is distinctly liberating.

The pressures will surely persist for 'constitutional regions' in particular to play a less submerged role in the formal European construction, most obviously in the context of enlargement. Wales, it may be noted however, is not a Flanders! A moderate stance on regional constitutional advancement sits well with the strong and continuing dependency on Whitehall encapsulated in the scheme of executive devolution. So also, a distinct local preference for flexibility in relevant political and administrative arrangements has special resonance in the context of the debate on 'the future of Europe'. Values of pluralism and diversity or weighting to the national and subnational levels, an EU constitutional framework for organic change, a mix and match of codification and convention: Europe it should hardly need saying has many futures.

In conclusion, the formal constitutional dispensation represented by the Assembly may be unnaturally weak, but this should not be allowed to obscure the broader patterns of external territorial engagement. Wales in the United Kingdom in Europe: it is a rapidly expanding world.

Devolution, Courts and Lawyers

The future is likely, I think, to bring increased devolution of legal services . . . But this administrative devolution is unlikely . . . to weaken the strong centralised character of the law itself, which has been such a marked feature of the English common law from the beginning, unless – and this is the wild card – the somewhat limited political devolution now enacted for Wales were to progress to fuller-blooded devolution on the Scottish model, or to an even greater degree of autonomy.

Lord Bingham (first Lord Chief Justice of England and Wales)[1]

An inevitable consequence of devolution is that Wales will develop its own body of public law. It stands to reason that this should evolve through the courts in Cardiff rather than in London.

Winston Roddick (Counsel General to the National Assembly)[2]

Much has been heard in recent years of so-called 'Legal Wales'.[3] In terms of the historical development – the life of the law in this little country – the term usefully points up the important role of legal actors in sustaining the sense of a distinctive or national identity in the unpromising conditions of a court system indistinct from that of England. In turn, what in the light of national devolution is seen as 'the rise of Legal Wales' refers to a bundle of developments: a repatriation of elements of administration of justice and some 'Welshifying' of the legal profession, as well as the growth of indigenous law making. Straddling the public and private sectors, and serving to highlight a series of issues ranging from the use of Welsh in court proceedings to the role and contribution of legal services in the local economy, the phenomenon can in fact be seen as one of the many processes of devolution.

Two features deserve a special emphasis. The first one concerns what I have called 'the rebirth of Welsh legal history'. In suitably Arthurian fashion, the rise of Legal Wales may be seen not as an act of creation but as a reawakening after centuries of slumber.[4] The pervasive sense of a 'submerged' legal history is after all the more poignant in view of the outstanding legal achievement, even on a European scale, that was the famous Welsh codification under Hywel Dda at the end of the first millennium.[5] Secondly, the rise of Legal Wales is a leading example of the catalytic or powerful 'spill-over' effects of national devolution. The fact of changes in the administration of justice being driven is the more noteworthy precisely because this is not a field of devolved functions.

This chapter deals with five main aspects. The first one obviously is the role – and rapid expansion – of the new legal branch of the Assembly: the Office of the Counsel General (OCG). As well as reflecting and reinforcing a general infusion of legal considerations and techniques in the conduct of government, the establishment of this office is seen to epitomize the *ad hoc* or piecemeal character of the institutional development in Welsh devolution.

The role of the OCG has not been given sufficient prominence in the public discussion of the workings and accomplishments of the Assembly. As regards the internal dynamics, the interplay between the Counsel General and the elected office-holders is in fact one of the defining relationships of the Assembly. So also, in terms of the policy outputs and general decision-making, the OCG has quickly taken on the classical dual function of the government lawyer: facilitating, as in the production of new legislation; and constraining, as in advice on the threat posed by judicial review.[6] Not only is this a task that can be approached more or less cautiously, but it is also one that takes on a special importance in the case of Wales precisely because of the novelty and complexity of the scheme of executive devolution. The office is seen to cast a long shadow.

Developments in the judicial machinery comprise the second main aspect, and in particular the novel legal procedures that have been introduced in the context of devolution. These obviously include the arrangements for handling so-called 'devolution issues', which are part of a reworked judicial architecture for the Union state, and which further reflect the peculiar territorial history of close integration with England. As indicated, however, the opportunity has also been taken to facilitate the conduct of litigation in Wales, including in public law matters generally. To this effect, senior judges in Wales will be shown as actively involved in furthering the cause of territorial constitutional development.

The potential for, and remarkable lack of, public law challenges to the devolved administration is the subject of the third section. From the ordinary domestic principles of judicial review to the risen tide of Community legal obligations, and on through the new vistas of litigation opening up in consequence of the Human Rights Act 1998, the infant body is born into a world of legal demands from many sources. The mistake is to assume that this will easily translate into legal proceedings in the particular conditions of small-country governance that are constituted by the so-called Welsh 'devolution settlement'. A combination of factors – historical and professional for example, and to do with the prevailing system of 'indirect administration' and 'partnership working' – will be seen pointing firmly in the opposite direction. It may sound odd, but the comparative absence of legal conflict is a major distinguishing feature of what I have called 'a new administrative law of Wales'.[7]

Intersecting with devolution in the UK programme of constitutional reform,[8] matters of human rights law and policy could be expected to feature prominently in the new model Wales. Although Assembly Members themselves have shown limited interest, serious efforts have been made to 'mainstream' such considerations into the Welsh policy-making process, typically following in the footsteps of central government. A subject for the fourth section, this then is an excellent example of official and lawyerly creativity in the rendering of the new Welsh polity. Looking forwards, a specialist agency is readily envisaged, with of course a major element of 'Welshifying'.

The general idea of devolution as a catalyst, including for important groups in civil society, is pursued in the final section. In the life of the law in Wales, the energizing and mobilizing element of national devolution entails such features as new specialist associations and reworked forms of networking inside the profession, as well as increased pressures for, and a substantial element of, decentralization of legal services. There are here the beginnings of a symbiotic relationship: the related dynamics whereby developing local legal expertise not only feeds on, but also contributes to, the broad devolutionary process.

A relevant concept is what I call 'the eternal triangle' of politics, public law and administration. However ill formed, a distinctive Welsh polity is in the course of construction, which further involves flanking developments in the structures and processes of public administration ('staffing matters'[9]). Specifically rendered in terms of the integration of England and Wales, the judicial part of the constitutional framework can hardly be immune from pressures for change in such conditions. Jurisprudence, including 'the English common law', is after all only one element in a functioning system or 'body of public law'. A push is given to an old cause, that of distinctively Welsh institutions and offices in the legal system.

'For Wales see England' (and London)

History speaks volumes in this context. Inexorably, one is drawn back to the centuries-long process (not an event!) of burgeoning Anglocentrality, reflected and brutally reinforced by the Edwardian Conquest. As the indigenous Welsh law 'became increasingly moribund, an element which had been central to Welsh identity was lost'.[10] It was a development effectively confirmed by the so-called 'Act of Union' 1536, the implementation of which meant sweeping away in the words of the statute the 'sinister usages and customs' regulating life in Wales. That modern historians see this both as a fine example of 'colonial cultural policy', and the necessary instrument 'of the gains accruing from a growing participation in a whole complex of institutions that . . . included common law',[11] brilliantly conveys the great sense of ambivalence in the Welsh condition.

Then there is the fact that Wales, unlike Scotland and (Northern) Ireland, did not retain a separate system of courts but shares one with England. The last vestiges were removed in 1830 with the abolition of the Court of Great Sessions, which organized into four circuits covering Wales with Chester had since Tudor times exercised original common law, equity and criminal jurisdiction. It was one of a famous series of utilitarian reforms to justice associated with Lord Brougham. In the words of the historian, 'the Welsh had lost a system that was decentralised; it had been sacrificed on the altar of legal uniformity'.[12]

A general trend of administrative centralization in the legal system was being inaugurated. After 1830 Wales was joined in the circuit system that had operated in England, but especially with the establishment of the Commercial Court in 1895 specialist legal work was increasingly done in London. Notably, and in contrast to the so-called 'awakening of Wales' in other walks of life, the great port that was Cardiff failed to obtain special concessions as a provincial court centre at the height of its prosperity.[13] Such a pattern of development would obviously do little for the cause of a viable or vibrant 'Legal Wales'. It was only in recent years that the trend began to be reversed in favour of Lord Bingham's 'administrative devolution', as with the establishment of a Chancery Court for Wales based in Cardiff in 1989.

Viewed in retrospect, another turning-point was the successful defence of the Wales and Chester Circuit against the threat of abolition in the 1960s. As a small circuit, it was naturally vulnerable to a Royal Commission chaired by the arch-rationalizing agent of the time, Dr Beeching. In the event, one of the chief arguments with which the Beeching Commission was confronted was the constitutional possibility of Welsh devolution.[14] Suffice it to add that the continued existence of the circuit is today threatened in another way. Such is the historical paradox of this 'cross-border' construction, a talisman of an earlier age, in a context of national devolution and increasing legal differentiation within the circuit.

The issue concerning Wales in the legal system that typically excited controversy was the treatment of the language.[15] It could hardly have been otherwise in view of the infamous 'language clause' of the 'Act of Union', English the only medium of the courts and those using Welsh not to receive public office, which for some four centuries would cast a shadow over Wales.

Let us not gloss over the considerable resistance that was encountered when in the modern period the case was made for change. The Welsh Courts Act 1942 for example was a pale reflection of the original proposals,[16] allowing the use of the Welsh language only if a person would otherwise be disadvantaged. It would take another generation before the situation was altered by the Welsh Language Act 1967, which ventured an unrestricted right to use Welsh in the courts. Pride of place, however, goes to the recognition of a cultural right in the Welsh Language Act 1993, which established the general principle that the English and Welsh mediums are to be treated on a basis of equality in the conduct of public business and the administration of justice.[17] What remained of course was to reinvent Welsh as a 'living language of the law', the task now begun under the auspices of the devolution statute. Suffice it to add that from a low base the incidence of the use of Welsh in the courts appears to be growing.[18]

Particular reference should also be made to the institutional development in terms of public law. On the one hand, this is the sphere in which the Assembly has its competencies. On the other hand, within the legal system, nothing has been more centralized than the special machinery for dealing with issues of constitutional and administrative law. By which is meant, formerly, the so-called 'Prerogative Orders' and exercise of jurisdiction by the 'Divisional Court' (of Queen's Bench); and, more recently, 'the Application for Judicial Review' and assignment of cases on the so-called 'Crown Office List'.[19]

In the years following the failure of Welsh devolution in 1979, this feature of the legal system was accentuated by reason of two related developments. One is the significant increase in the scale and intensity of judicial review of public authorities familiarly associated with this period. The other is the famous case of *O'Reilly v Mackman*,[20] where a rigid public/private law divide was asserted, to the effect of prioritizing the procedural ambit of the judicial review machinery and so encouraging the further channelling of cases to the Royal Courts of Justice in London. In terms of the development of Legal Wales, this public law monopoly was a pernicious one, operating to denude the territory of relevant legal specialization. Reflecting and reinforcing this feature, it was standard Welsh Office practice to look to the Inns of Court in London for the expert sources of advice. Again, in view of the lack of local visibility, it comes as no surprise to learn that Wales was producing very little by way of judicial review: only thirty or so cases a year involving the Welsh Office, many concerning planning matters.[21]

In summary, as many distinguished contributions in the Anglo-Welsh tradition serve to confirm,[22] there has been in Wales no lack of native genius for the law. However, a strong historical legacy, conditions have conspired against a firm local legal grounding for the public law project that is Welsh devolution. One reason why the rise of Legal Wales is so striking – and significant – is the comparatively low base or starting-point.

1. LEGAL SHADOW: THE OFFICE OF THE COUNSEL GENERAL

The constitutional dimension

A minimalist approach to the provision of in-house legal services for the Assembly was on offer in the devolution White Paper. In fact, it represented an extravagant version of partnership with Whitehall, being all at one with the limited devolutionary model of 'Welsh Office plus'. Close consultation between the Assembly and Whitehall would not only serve to minimize the risk of disputes between them. But also: 'The Attorney General and the Solicitor General will continue to serve Wales and England. Any disputes about the Assembly's use of its powers will be referred to the Law Officers.'[23]

The matter had simply not been thought through. A basic constitutional issue was raised, that of conflict of interest or confusion of legal roles. How could the law officers, part of the machinery of central government, properly continue to serve the devolved administration in such disputes? In the event, in the language of officials a 'reappraisal' quickly took place behind the scenes, by which is meant abandonment of the policy in the light of an internal departmental report commissioned by the Welsh Office into the needs of the Assembly for legal services.[24] The Legal Secretariat to the Law Officers (LSLO) accepted that the Assembly should not be so reliant.

Such is the backdrop to one of the first appointments made on behalf of the Assembly, that of chief legal adviser. Or rather of Counsel General to the Assembly, as the first appointee Winston Roddick QC – has preferred to be known. The change of nomenclature is once again significant, signalling both the novelty of the post and a determination on the part of Mr Roddick to secure the status of the new legal branch, or what now became known as the Office of the Counsel General (OCG). In the words of the official documentation:

> The Counsel General is independent from UK Government Departments and independent of the Law Officers of the Crown. He fulfils for the Assembly the role of providing authoritative advice in the same way that the Law Officers provide this for the UK Government. He is the senior legal adviser on all legal issues relating to the Assembly's powers. He is the final source of authoritative legal advice to the Assembly across the full range of its responsibilities for Wales and its input via the [Wales Office] into primary legislation in England.[25]

Things, however, are not so simple, since there is no provision in the GWA for this office and because Mr Roddick is a civil servant (accountable directly to the Permanent Secretary). Formal recognition – such as it is – derives from the fact that the OCG is mentioned in the Ministerial Code and made the recipient of service of any legal proceedings to which the Assembly is a party.[26] The Counsel General and his office thus represent neither the traditional central government model of the department legal adviser (with linkage to Treasury Counsel etc.), nor the classical Westminster model of the law officer (as predicated on democratic legitimacy or a ministerial appointment). In terms of UK constitutional theory and practice, the OCG is thus a peculiar part of a strange anatomy.

Personal factors take on extra importance in this context. A forceful character, Mr Roddick has brought to the job over thirty years of experience at the Bar, on topics ranging from planning and local government to complex criminal law litigation. It would have been stranger still had many of the representatives in the new fledgeling institution not gone in awe of the man and his office.

What can now be called 'the rise of the OCG' is at the heart of the rise of Legal Wales. More especially, this feature reflects and reinforces the distinctive official force of national devolution. The Counsel General has continued to navigate a more high-profile path, so further building up the status. Wales has thus gained a virtual law officer to go with its virtual parliament:

> Another important aim of the Office of the Counsel General is to enhance its reputation and standing, together with that of the Assembly, in Wales and beyond . . . This helps to ensure that the Assembly remains closely involved with the main local, national and international players within the new constitutional framework of which it is a part.[27]

In terms of the internal architecture, the reach of the OCG is a touchstone of the strength of the corporate view of the Assembly. Once again it is not surprising that the Counsel General should have so emphasized this aspect, given the position of the legal branch at the centre of things. In Mr Roddick's words, 'When I give advice, the interest I am required to serve in doing so is that of the Assembly as a whole.'[28] At one and the same time, the monolithic approach to legal services sits comfortably with the formal design of the devolution statute and was always liable to cause friction inside this national representative institution.

An independent legal adviser in the Presiding Office, dedicated legal support for the all-party subject committees; such flanking developments to the OCG have thus been welcomed as significant measures in the shift towards a more parliamentary 'face' for the Assembly.[29] Turning the argument round, the continuing growth of the OCG is largely as an instrument of the Welsh Assembly Government: and naturally so, with the gradual development of more distinctive policies at territorial level and the rise of indigenous law making. Legal staffing matters!

A multifaceted role

The OCG has featured prominently in the pages of this book, as befits the multifaceted role that the lawyers now play in the structures and processes of devolved administration. The work is usefully categorized in terms of five main functions.

The first element obviously is the core advisory work. As the official documentation puts it: 'advice should always be sought wherever new policy is under consideration . . . Lawyers should . . . be informed and involved at the earliest possible stage.'[30] This function, however, takes on an added dimension in view of the 'new, complex and immensely challenging legal and constitutional environment'[31] in which the Assembly is operating. So too, the policing role of the Counsel General – if necessary personal audiences with ministers in cases of *vires* problems – can be seen as especially important.

As one would expect, the OCG has also adopted a policy in matters of 'high importance' and where the legal arguments are 'finely balanced' of seeking counsel's opinion from the independent Bar. Especially in view of the stresses and strains inside the corporate body this is accepted to be a useful way of securing legitimacy, as well as expertise.[32]

Then there is the function of law making for Wales. Correctly, the OCG has adopted as a cardinal principle the holistic view that the primary and secondary legislative processes should be considered in tandem. 'The Assembly has no power to enact primary legislation. Nonetheless primary legislation is very much part of its business.' By definition, the efficient and effective operation of the office is critical to the performance of this expanded role, which clearly calls for close collaboration with the policy divisions as well as Parliamentary Counsel and the Wales Office. Credit where credit is due: its first major organizational test on the legislative side, the office successfully coped with the great volume of orders demanded by reason of foot and mouth disease.[33] The fact, however, that two years into devolved government OCG was having to remind policy divisions of its position as 'a key point of reference in relation to the Assembly's interest in any Bill'[34] is another sign that all has not been well.

The management of Assembly litigation – threatened and otherwise – typically involves instructing external solicitors and where necessary nominating counsel. An important innovation here is the selection by the Counsel General of certain barristers as standing counsel to the Assembly. The arrangements reflect and reinforce the constitutional development of the office, being modelled on the panel of counsel appointed by the law officers to act in UK government litigation.

The Counsel General also has the important role behind the scenes of mediating legal norms, negotiation and settlement, in the new sphere of intergovernmental relations. This is the aspect highlighted by the soft law system of concordats, with its strong emphasis on non-judicial or alternative dispute resolution.[35] As indicated, Mr Roddick has placed a special premium on fostering good relationships with high-ranking government lawyers in the key UK departments. The elite Government Lawyers Liaison Committee has provided a convenient forum.

Last but not least, the OCG has an important leadership role in terms of 'Legal Wales'. For example, the pioneering work on bilingual drafting is part of a more general concern with the rebirth of the Welsh language as a living language of the law.[36] Nor is it surprising to learn that the Counsel General's panel is a product of the Wales and Chester Circuit. It is all part of a policy of encouraging Welsh lawyers – the sense of devolution as serious legal business.[37] The office has also made something of an effort in the field of education and training. While much of the focus has been on raising legal awareness among Assembly staff and Members, there are also the beginnings of a local networking role – conferences, presentations, public lectures etc. This should flourish now.[38]

Legal branch

According to the official guide, 'the volume of the legal work is immense'.[39] The availability of legal resources was thus identified as a key pressure point in the devolved administration, with the OCG attracting substantial extra resources in a very short time.[40] The legal branch initially comprised some twenty lawyers, with some ten administrative support staff. A year on and the complement included thirty-three solicitors and barristers, as well as twenty or so translators, administrators and secretaries. Meanwhile, the annual office budget had increased to well over £2 million.[41] Two years more and the staff complement included forty-eight lawyers.[42]

This represents a major infusion of law in the conduct of territorial government. Once again, however, it is not simply a question of numbers. The broader cultural connotations for the office of a vigorous policy of recruiting from outside the Government Legal Service and from inside Wales should not be underestimated. Whether the many new young recruits from private practice stay the course remains to be seen.

Figure 17 shows how the office has been divided into eight main teams of lawyers, with line management via the three Assistant Counsel General. Essentially arranged around the portfolios of ministers, the six subject area teams have been subject to substantial reordering, with only the Agriculture team remaining largely intact.

Take for example the joint Social Care/CSIW Team. Reflecting the changed sense of priorities in the Assembly, the social care element has been carved from the more traditional designation of 'health and social services'.

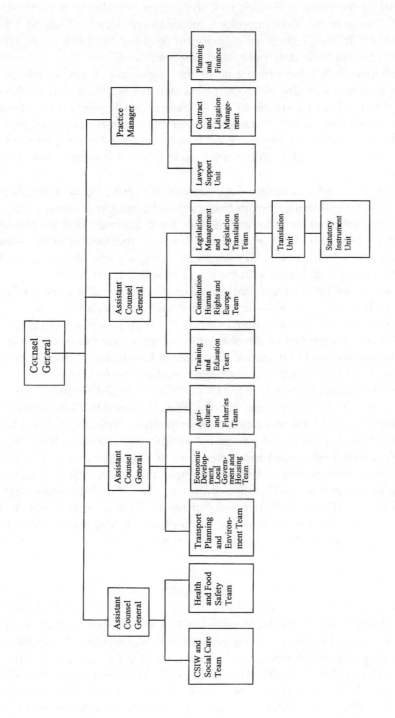

Figure 17: Office of the Counsel General – organizational structure (September 2002)

Meanwhile the work in relation to CSIW – Care Standards Inspectorate for Wales – reflects the first important prosecutorial function gained by the Assembly.[43] It thus represents a quantum leap for the office – in a most sensitive area of regulatory policy and practice.

Then there is the important role of the Legislation Team, which clearly marks the break with the Welsh Office. As well as LMU (Legislation Management Unit), which continues to try to ensure that legislation is processed effectively and efficiently through the Assembly's numerous procedures, the team now includes a highly specialist translation unit. Looking forward, the profile of the team will no doubt continue to grow, as Assembly law making grows.

By far the most interesting development, however, is the emergence of what may be called the constitutional affairs team. On the one hand, this serves as a valuable reminder of the many legal demands that are placed on the infant Assembly. On the other hand, it is a touchstone of the general political and administrative development, being a piece of machinery that would have been unthinkable in the days of the Welsh Office.

More concretely, this team marks an expanding spread of expertise in the OCG, with recruitment increasingly geared towards specialists in such cross-cutting fields as EU law and human rights.[44] It is all part of a tooling-up, and one that reflects the fact of devolution in an age of supranational ordering. Another major aspect of the work is freedom of information, which, especially in light of the bold public messages conveyed by the Assembly cabinet, is a very ready source of referrals to the OCG.[45] Not, it should be stressed, that the OCG does all the legal work for the Welsh Assembly Government: the contracting out of legal services is a major feature. Typically, a distinction is drawn between the core and non-core Assembly legal work. External service providers thus do the bread and butter work that arises from any government department – employment law for example or conveyancing – subject of course to monitoring and quality control by the office.[46] In freeing up the Assembly lawyers for their key tasks of legal advice on policy matters and legislative drafting, the arrangement further serves to underscore the scale of the lawyerly input in devolved administration.

Getting real

Future historians will no doubt see what I have described as the rise of the OCG as only a beginning. The expansion has begun from an exceptionally low base, precisely because of the 'topping and tailing' mentality of the old territorial department. Looking forward, the development of the OCG will be an essential litmus test for the ongoing allocation of functions to the Assembly. What is considered an 'immense' volume of work is not in fact a huge amount when viewed in the light of devolved government elsewhere in the Union. It would be strange indeed if the office looked the same in five or ten years' time, and it will change again should there be Assembly powers of primary legislation.

There is some more unfinished constitutional business. The symbolism of the Office of Counsel General, a distinctively Welsh institution in a legal system generally indistinct from that of England, should not be discounted. The appropriate next step is statutory recognition of a role and position akin to Counsel General, perhaps on the model familiar in the Commonwealth of an official, with a view to underpinning the attributes of authority and independence. A virtual law officer: it is time once again to get real.

2. JUDICIAL MACHINERY

'Devolution issues'

The establishment of a special juridical regime for handling 'devolution issues' is a common feature of the devolutionary schemes in Scotland, Wales and Northern Ireland. At the apex of the system is the Judicial Committee of the Privy Council. But what in the Welsh context is a 'devolution issue'?

The GWA has delivered a fourfold classification. Designed in grid-like fashion, this encompasses the different sources (domestic and otherwise) of legal obligations, and catches both acts and omissions of the Assembly.[47] 'Devolution issue' thus means a question:

- whether a function is exercisable by the Assembly
- whether a proposed or purported exercise of a function by the Assembly is within its powers (including by virtue of the requirements to comply with Community law and Convention rights)
- whether the Assembly has failed to comply with a duty imposed upon it, including complying with obligations under Community law
- whether a failure to act by the Assembly is incompatible with any of the Convention rights

This formulation is clearly predicated on the Welsh constitutional fundamental of the corporate body. It is different from the one in the Scotland Act, which must deal separately with the formally established legislative and executive branches of (parliamentary) government.[48]

'Devolution issues' thus appear to have a broad ambit in Wales. The legislative function is clearly encompassed, whether it is an issue of compliance of Assembly orders with the domestic law of *ultra vires*, Community law or Convention rights. Similarly, the collective exercise of decision-making functions by Assembly Members is engaged: most notably in the realm of planning appeals given the distinctive committee arrangements that obtain there,[49] as also the historical predominance of planning matters in judicial review cases originating in Wales. A question that has been raised is whether 'the Assembly' as a statutory term should be read to mean only the elected Assembly, so as to exclude from 'devolution issues' the exercise under the system of delegated functions of executive and administrative powers.[50] To which the answer is surely not, by reason both of the formal, legal character of the corporate body, and the huge field of government authority in Wales that would then be exempted.

The second category of case, whether the exercise of a function is 'within the powers' of the Assembly, is likely to be the most important. The question is whether the only issue involved is the scope of express limitation of legal competence – so-called 'narrow *ultra vires*' – or whether the implied obligations generally associated with judicial review, the exercise of statutory powers rationally and without procedural impropriety for example, are also included. Once again, the wide reading is the natural one, fitting both with the first category of case – focused directly on express limitation – and the classical doctrinal view of an undifferentiated law of *ultra vires*.[51]

Recycling the Judicial Committee

Why the Judicial Committee for Wales? Why target special procedures on what in the case of the Assembly will be subordinate legislation? A choice of the House of Lords and ordinary procedure would have fitted the unity of the English and Welsh legal system.[52] Effectively, however, the matter was predetermined. Not only was there an example to hand, the earlier use of the Judicial Committee in the case of Northern Ireland. There were also Scottish sensitivities, centred on historical resistance to a role for the House of Lords in Scots criminal appeals, as well as the constitutional objection to part of the UK Parliament adjudicating on the division of legislative competence.[53] To which was added the natural pull of symmetry, a concern on the part of the UK government to establish a standard form of jurisdiction in devolution issues. Paradoxically then, the development can be seen to illustrate the junior status of Wales among the countries of the Union. 'For Wales see Scotland (and Northern Ireland).'

Viewed in historical perspective, there is fine irony in recycling the Judicial Committee, with its associations with empire and jurisdiction over dependent territories. It hardly squares with New Labour rhetoric of modernization. There have thus been major pointers here, along with others in the broader process of constitutional reform such as human rights legislation, to a formally established supreme court for the United Kingdom (as has in fact now been proposed by central government).[54]

Special jurisdiction

The special jurisdiction is designed to allow for public or official advocacy in cases touching on the legal and constitutional position of the new form of territorial government. A devolution issue would generally be expected to arise in the course of ordinary litigation and so a trigger mechanism is provided by notice requirements, on the one hand to the Attorney General (representing the UK government), and on the other to 'the Assembly' (for which read the OCG). A different but related point: since devolution issues encompass a new form of constitutional litigation, the need for authoritative rulings is prioritized. As well as choosing to be joined as parties or to leave matters well alone, 'the Assembly' and the Attorney General may refer the issue direct to the Judicial Committee ('fast-track procedure'). Again, these privileged parties may so refer devolution issues that are not the subject of court proceedings (so-called 'abstract' review). Suffice it to say that it is an unusual feature in Britain, where the courts, in accordance with both the adversarial tradition and a subsidiary constitutional role, have generally insisted on 'concrete' or *a posteriori* review arising out of an ordinary lawsuit.[55]

Alternatively, the court or tribunal hearing the matter can refer a devolution issue that arises to a higher court. A complex hierarchy of reference powers has thus had to be created. In essence, references from the magistrates' courts go to the High Court, those from the County Court and High Court to the Court of Appeal, and those from the Court of Appeal (and even from the House of Lords) to the Judicial Committee.[56] There is an evident potential here for protracted litigation: not forgetting the possibility along the way of a reference in Community law to the European Court of Justice in Luxembourg (on which system the new domestic procedure is loosely modelled).

Two features serve to underscore the special nature of the procedural regime. The first one concerns the potential for (Welsh) devolution issues to arise in proceedings begun in any of the legal jurisdictions constituted in the Union. The GWA, like the other devolution statutes, establishes a series of parallel procedural processes or systems.[57] The twist in the tale in the case of national devolution to Wales is once again the absence of an equivalent 'national' legal jurisdiction. 'Proceedings in England and Wales' are a single category for the purpose of the devolution legislation.

The second feature involves so-called 'prospective overruling', or the potentially wide-ranging consequences of a successful challenge to an exercise of the law-making function. Should a court or tribunal decide that the Assembly did not 'have the power to make' subordinate legislation, it is empowered to remove or limit 'any retrospective effect of the decision', or suspend 'the effect of the decision . . . to allow the defect to be corrected'. Innocent third parties can thus be protected.[58]

The judicial architecture of devolution further demonstrates a strong brand of dualism, the interplay of special with general court procedures.[59] On the one hand, many matters that might be considered relevant are apparently excluded, including much of the interpretation of primary (Westminster) legislation in relevant fields. On the other hand, it was not intended to restrict 'any other rights in law' to challenge the exercise of functions by the Assembly.[60] Judicial review and ordinary civil action can operate here both as first vehicle for 'devolution issues' and as separate avenue of redress. For would-be litigants, this is a veritable jungle.

In fact a judicial practice note, timed to coincide with the empowerment of the Assembly, has produced a strong steer in the direction of the ordinary court process of determination and appeal. In exercising the discretion whether to refer a case, relevant factors for the lower court would be 'the delay . . . and additional costs that a reference might involve', as well as 'the importance of the devolution issue to the public in general'.[61] The way was thus being paved for the establishment of a broad category of cases seen to involve what are only 'technically' devolution issues, for example in the most litigated realm of planning law.

Speaking more generally, a remarkable amount of professional time and effort has gone into developing this new procedure in Wales. Arcane procedural points have been ventilated, and no doubt stored for future use, in the way that only lawyers can. Much has also been left for fine-tuning in the light of experience, not least via the other Celtic lands.[62] Yet thus far, all this activity behind the scenes stands in inverse proportion to the number of important cases that have been generated in Wales, which at the end of the first term of the Assembly stood at precisely zero.[63]

Revivification: two elements

Yet this, emphatically, is not the whole story. Associated with, or more strictly piggybacked on, the need to elaborate the special juridical regime of the devolution statute, important procedural steps have now been taken to combat the historical legacy in the legal system of extravagant Anglocentricity. In the long view, in inaugurating many of these developments, the original practice note will thus be seen to have a broader significance than at first appears.

Given the centuries of discrimination founded on language, the arrangements that are made in the legal system for the use of Welsh have a strong symbolic as well as practical content. Extended to 'devolution issues' is a liberal regime concerning practical requirements of notification, etc., for the use of the language, which – once again in the wake of devolution – now applies both in the Crown courts and civil courts. So also, a constitutional innovation in UK domestic law, provision is made for appointing a Welsh-speaking judicial assessor to assist the court should the need arise for comparison in light of the statutory principle of equal status of the two languages in Assembly instruments.[64]

As a distinguishing feature of 'Legal Wales', the 'ancient tongue' is in fact now being actively supported in the local system of administration of justice. Special mention may here be made of an influential yet little known body, the Lord Chancellor's Standing Committee for the Welsh Language, first established in 1999. Its official purpose is 'to ensure that various bodies concerned with the administration of justice in Wales adopt the same policies towards the Welsh Language and the implementation of the Welsh Language 1993'.[65] Reflecting the cross-cutting nature of the subject, the membership has quickly expanded beyond the senior judges in Wales and OCG to include representatives from the police and Crown Prosecution Service and the Legal Services Commission in Wales, as well as the magistracy and tribunal service.

The suitably bland description – 'a vehicle by which to minimise costs and difficulties and ensure that proper and uniform policies are in place' – disguises the fact that this is no passive advisory body. Better to convey the flavour, initiatives include a project on standardization of Welsh legal termin-ology, a review of the use of Welsh in the criminal justice system, and supervising the development of bilingual IT packages as part of a general programme of computerization in the civil courts. Setting this in the wider political and administrative context, such initiatives – notably taking place in a non-devolved sphere of state activity – sit comfortably with the Welsh Assembly Government's own visionary policy for a bilingual Wales.[66]

A second vital dimension to the local revivification in terms of practice and procedure, the legal establishment in Wales under the effective leadership of Sir John Thomas as Presiding Judge on the Wales and Chester Circuit has lobbied successfully for an administrative decentralization of judicial review proceedings. It stands in turn as a 'Trojan horse' for the evolution – in the Counsel General's words – of Wales's 'own body of public law . . . through the courts in Cardiff' (and other local centres).

The key point is the expansive coverage: where the claim for judicial review or any remedy sought involves:

(1) a devolution issue arising out of the Government of Wales Act 1998; or (2) an issue concerning the National Assembly for Wales, the Welsh executive, or any Welsh public body (including a Welsh local authority) (whether or not it involves a devolution issue).[67]

The model is a facilitative one, in the sense that applicants can choose to lodge cases in Cardiff or (as formerly) at the Crown Office in London. But where a case is heard is of course a matter for the courts. That various judicial review cases have now been heard at local centres in Wales is to this effect the sign of things to come. Suffice it to add that planning cases involving the Assembly, as also public law-type cases emanating from magistrates' courts in Wales ('case stated'), have now been brought firmly inside the decentralized system.[68]

Once again, it is a mistake to think in terms of a sudden rush of cases. Especially in the new and complex field of human rights for example, the Bar in London is not suddenly about to lose its competitive edge. Nonetheless, with national devolution the policy is clear: at one level, the idea so typical of 'Legal Wales' of local legal machinery serving to stimulate the demand for, and supply of, local legal expertise, and at another level of bringing administration of justice – together with government – 'closer to the people'.[69]

In the event, the local policy has been caught up in a more general move ahead of implementation of the Human Rights Act 1998 to streamline judicial review procedures and underpin judicial specialization and expertise in public law.[70] 'The Crown Office List is dead, long live the Administrative Court!' For present purposes, the local nomenclature – 'the Administrative Court in Wales' – is once again significant. It strikes an appropriate balance in this case between, on the one hand the basic constitutional fact of the unity of the English and Welsh legal system, and on the other hand the greater recognition now afforded the local geopolitical entity in the light of national devolution.

3. JUDICIAL REVIEW AND THE ASSEMBLY

As a creation of Parliament, the Assembly is subject to the ordinary domestic principles of judicial review. Whatever the topic, whatever the technique, the devolved administration must be able to demonstrate statutory authority in the exercise of functions. As a law-maker, the Assembly is the more vulnerable to court challenge precisely because it is only empowered to make subordinate legislation. In turn, the issue is raised of the intensity of judicial review of Assembly Orders. That is to say, a new variant on an old constitutional favourite: the proper relation of decision-making by elected bodies with the rule of law.

The scope for uncertainty is neatly illustrated by a case that has sometimes been mentioned in this context: *Kruse v. Johnson*.[71] Double-edged, it contains an argument for benevolent interpretation or judicial deference and a broad formulation of 'unreasonableness' as a ground of review. And what, it may reasonably be asked, is the precise relevance of a Victorian case dealing with the validity of local government by-laws to contemporary judicial review and the National Assembly for Wales? As every common lawyer knows, with something so novel as (Welsh) devolution, there are precedents, and there are precedents.

Review and empowerment

The task of judicial interpretation is liable to be complicated by reason both of constitutional and legal constraints and administrative and political realities. Let us suppose for example that the Welsh Assembly Government shows substantial legislative initiative using the myriad of transferred powers in pre-devolution statutes. The familiar concept of 'Parliament's intention' would make it difficult for the courts to show greater flexibility towards the Assembly than is the standard practice with central government departments. A further pull from across 'the border' becomes evident: the sense that judicial approaches can only diverge so far inside the unitary legal system that is England and Wales. Turning the argument round, in cases where secondary legislation at variance with England is challenged, the express provision in the GWA for the different exercise of functions in Wales is seen to give some but only some protection.[72]

'Every Bill a devolution Bill': the way in which post-1999 statutes are drafted with reference to the Assembly will clearly be a vital factor. A practice of broad delegation would itself permit a more flexible judicial approach. Conversely, circumstances in which tight restrictions were imposed on secondary legislative powers, say in a situation of 'cohabitation' with a Conservative government in London, could provide a severe test for the court system. This in fact is another good reason for the development of clear and accepted principles to govern the ongoing allocation of functions in executive devolution.

What, it may be asked, of the situation in Welsh executive devolution regarding 'Henry VIII clauses'? Let us suppose – in view of increased pressures in the Assembly for more generous grants of powers – that there is a major new move in this direction. Demands by interested parties for a close form of judicial scrutiny could then easily be envisaged. This again is one reason why the hypothetical constitutional model of 'quasi-legislative devolution' may be considered unappealing.

What I have called 'the Welsh difference' also raises some intriguing possibilities. As well as operating to ground the many cross-cutting themes in the local policy map, the general legal precepts relating to equality of opportunity, sustainable development and bilingualism clearly have a potential as pegs supporting legal action against the Assembly. Although for example 'the equality clause' is not user-friendly for the individual litigant, and in particular would not necessarily nullify a decision of the Assembly in a case of non-compliance, it may help to generate favourable conditions for some innovative forms of challenge. Reference need only be made to the various documents that now specify Assembly policies in the general field;[73] to the established ground in judicial review of failure to take into account relevant considerations; and to the many concentrations of socio-economic deprivation that continue to disfigure Wales.

Speaking more generally, the fact that the judicial architecture of devolution presents a formal symmetry should not be allowed to obscure a real substantive asymmetry that derives from the differing nature and extent of the constitutional allocation of functions. Welsh executive devolution and Scottish legislative devolution, for example, present the judiciary with qualitatively different tasks.

Relevant here is the idea of interpreting basic constitutional documents in a liberal and progressive manner, in contrast to the strong literalism classically associated with the ordinary (English) canons of statutory construction. The senior Scottish judge Lord Hope has spoken of the Scotland Act as 'a living instrument', it being 'for the judges to breathe life into the bare bones of the statute', including of course in relation to the division of competencies.[74] In the case of Wales, 'breathing life' into the general Transfer of Functions Orders is an improbable judicial function. The very listing of individual statutory sources of authority militates against bold new interpretative approaches.

A case for deference

There clearly is an argument that by the nature of the institutions the courts should afford the 'Assembly' less deference – or in the language of international law a smaller 'margin of appreciation' – than the 'Parliament'.[75] Nonetheless, this being national devolution in the guise of the first democratically elected and accountable government of one of the countries of the Union, one would expect the courts to give a green light, so respecting the decisions of the Assembly unless they can clearly be demonstrated to be unlawful.

To this end, ideas of the devolved administration acting 'wholly unreasonably', or (perhaps) 'disproportionately', should generally be put on hold; and especially so, given the many competing demands or complex and polycentric nature of the matter, in respect of the devolved administration's major task of resource allocation.[76] Again, while there is a lack of Westminster-style 'parliamentary privilege' or immunity from suit covering internal workings or procedures, one may reasonably expect the good sense of the judiciary to prevail in such sensitive matters of constitutional regulation and control.

A pointer in this general direction: as an Act of Parliament, the GWA has now been said to enjoy a particularly high status alongside other 'constitutional statutes' such as the Human Rights Act 1998. To this effect, so-called 'implied repeal' (via a later statute) is not in fashion.[77] Again, judicial deference may be a familiar idea in the litany of common law, but it is also undergoing something of a rebirth in Britain, in the form of a clearly articulated concept for preserving to policy-makers and law givers substantial freedom of manoeuvre, especially with regard to 'Convention Rights'.[78] Experience teaches that this approach may well be read across into other situations, not least national devolution.[79]

A lack of practice

As so often in constitution-building, it is what has not happened that is most significant. Stipulating precise contours to the so-called 'zigzag' of powers, performance of the classical constitutional role of control of abuse of power: the judiciary has been prevented from contributing directly to the shaping of the Welsh devolutionary development during these vital formative years. Courts, after all, do not self-start.

In this respect, Wales and Scotland are like chalk and cheese, the many challenges to the new Scottish institutions especially on the grounds of breach of Convention Rights being well documented.[80] And for once, the obvious explanation, the basic asymmetry in terms of competencies between the two devolutionary schemes, rings true. The functions of the Assembly being more limited, there is much less to attack. Where the Scottish cases have been heavily concentrated, general criminal law and process, is the chief area where the Assembly lacks jurisdiction.

Nor can the historical legacy, or lack of a tradition of Welsh public law, simply be wished away. The contrast with Scotland, where a confident and established local legal profession was in place prior to devolution, is very great. Matters have been compounded not only by the complex character of the Welsh scheme, so hard to get to grips with, but also by the lack in Wales of an open constitutional debate prior to the devolution legislation, which would surely have helped to promote a general legal interest. A litigation explosion in the wake of the Assembly and the establishment of the Administrative Court in Wales: it was never going to happen.

One can scarcely ignore the role of internal checks, and in particular the regulatory or policing role in this small body in the formidable person of the Counsel General. Nowhere, it is confidently suggested, are the *vires* of sub-ordinate legislation checked more thoroughly than in Wales, this being a natural product of the model of executive devolution. Mr Roddick, after all, has not been paid to take risks. Turning the argument round, the greater danger is an excessive caution in the OCG, such that the potential in devolution for innovative developments in law and policy is unduly circumscribed.

The early Welsh experience further confirms the central place in the UK devolutionary development of informal legal process, the extended opportunities for compromise, negotiation and settlement between administrations.[81] The devolved administration in general, and the OCG in particular, has simply not been in the game of resorting to courts – 'a litigation strategy' – with central government. More especially in the conditions of Labour Party hegemony, it would have been extraordinary – bizarre even – had this been otherwise.

There is still more to it than this. Historically strongly geared towards protection of the individual, judicial review commonly operates at the interface between public bodies and citizens or private entities. Whereas – the system of indirect administration – much of what the Assembly does involves the conduct of relationships with service providers or other intermediary organizations; the local authorities and the quangos, the NHS trusts and the voluntary sector, etc. As every administrative lawyer knows, such conditions can tend to militate against litigation, since a party may well lose more by disrupting the relationship through going to court than by compromising on a particular issue.[82]

Especially so, it may be said, in the local conditions of national devolution. Not only is going to court an expensive option, an obvious source of criticism in this economically disadvantaged 'region' of the UK. But it is also a brave or foolhardy body that bites the Assembly hand that feeds it. The devolved administration may lack primary legislative powers, but the fact of its alternative policy levers such as the power of the purse, together with the symbolic capital that attaches to the elected body of the people of Wales, is apt to play strongly in this context.[83]

And then there is the prevailing ideology of partnership working. Collaboration and inclusiveness, the rhetoric anyway of 'shared ownership' of policy development and implementation: at root, this stands for a political and administrative culture antithetical to a burgeoning local practice of intra-state litigation. A classic case of law and small-country governance: such it may be said is the chilling effect on judicial review of 'the closeness of Wales'.

Not, it should be stressed, that everything is set in stone. Take the fact that the devolved administration was at first slow to be creative, but in terms of 'made in Wales' policies is now picking up speed. Surprising as it may appear to the general reader, some major legal challenges will be a mark of the political and administrative maturation of the new democratic institution: a case of stretching its muscles and – one hopes – rattling vested interests. Again, to the extent that the devolved administration becomes more 'hands on' or involved in the direct exercise of powers, as for example is suggested with the abolition of the regional health authorities,[84] so the prospect of challenge by individuals and pressure groups may become less remote.

Politically incorrect it may be, but a dose of public law litigation from time to time should not be seen as unhelpful, being another useful antidote to excessive inbreeding in this little country,[85] and the necessary pill for a constructive contribution by the 'third branch of government'. The constrictive effects of a peculiar historical legacy in the law will surely wane over time, and the more quickly because of the movers and shakers of Legal Wales. Putting to one side the question of legislative devolution, which would necessarily operate to quicken the pace, an important catalyst for a more vibrant local legal culture should be the Human Rights Act. Now that it has been fully implemented in Wales, it will serve to spread, in key areas such as family and criminal law, a greater awareness of public law techniques.

4. DEVOLUTION AND HUMAN RIGHTS

General considerations

The need – when fulfilling any of the functions – for compliance with the Convention Rights now incorporated in UK domestic law courtesy of the Human Rights Act 1998 has obviously been a special concern of the Assembly's lawyers. Along with the other devolved administrations, the Assembly has in fact been something of a guinea pig, being so constrained from the very moment of empowerment,[86] ahead of general implementation of the HRA in October 2000.

Let us keep in mind the rich and diverse nature of what is entailed in 'bringing rights home'.[87] The HRA comes with many years of jurisprudence attached: the rulings of the European Court (and Commission) of Human Rights. At the same time, the European Convention is officially interpreted as 'a living instrument': one that is sensitive to changes in social conditions and mores for example.[88] Important is the role for courts in the United Kingdom not as mere conduits but as creative participants in the promotion and elaboration of a reworked culture of human rights. In the words of the statute, domestic courts and tribunals 'must take into account' – and so effectively can push beyond – Strasbourg rulings.[89]

Then there is the way in which this most profound constitutional development is designed to be reconciled with traditional doctrine in the form of parliamentary sovereignty. Central to this is the two-staged process established in the HRA for dealing with challenges to legislation.[90] All legislation must now be interpreted and given effect as far as possible compatibly with the Convention rights. Where this proves impossible, a court may quash or disapply subordinate legislation, or if it is a higher court make a declaration of incompatibility for primary legislation, so allowing the minister to make a remedial order to amend the legislation to bring it into line with the Convention rights.[91]

The interesting question is also raised of the extent to which the courts in general, and the Judicial Committee in particular, will allow different approaches to human rights questions within the devolved territories and how far they will seek to impose uniformity.[92] There is further the clear expectation of comparative borrowings and influences, especially from the leading common law jurisdictions, courtesy of the Internet.[93] The way in which a little country like Wales is subject to, and made part of, broad contemporary developments associated with the rise of supranational ordering or so-called globalization of law is highlighted here.

Local twists and possibilities

Perhaps it hardly needs saying: there are some particular twists in the case of Welsh executive devolution. One of the difficult situations with which the HRA must deal is where a public authority is required to act by statute in a certain way but doing so is incompatible with a Convention right. A public body in this position will not be said to be acting unlawfully, and in particular the validity, operation and enforcement of any subordinate legislation so made is not affected.[94] The potential relevance for the Assembly of this exception will be readily appreciated. Of course, it would be effectively sidestepped if central government were to move to broad framework legislation as a means of empowering the devolved administration.

A key issue obviously is the 'match' between the articles of the European Convention now incorporated in domestic law and – first – Assembly competencies and – second – the roles and responsibilities of the many other agencies and authorities that go to make up the emergent system of Welsh governance. Some of the rights in question may appear to have little to do with local practice; the relevance of others is more immediately apparent. But such is the expansive interpretation in the case law, and further the cross-cutting or 'horizontal' character of certain of the rights, that it is hard to overstate the potential scale of their application, here as elsewhere.

Education is a good illustration. The starting-point is Article 2 of the First Protocol to the Convention since this deals directly with the right to education, including in terms of teaching in conformity with the religious and philosophical convictions of parents. Other general provisions, however, may also be relevant, such as Article 3 (freedom from inhuman or degrading treatment), historically important in relation to corporal punishment; and Article 8 (right to respect for private and family life), hugely potent[95] and bearing for example on the language of education. Then there is Article 6 (right to a fair trial), the most frequently invoked provision of the Convention, relevant for example to school exclusions. To this catalogue might be added Article 9 (freedom of thought, conscience and religion), Article 10 (freedom of expression) and Article 14 (prohibition of discrimination).[96]

The theme can be pursued in various ways.[97] Take for example the fortunes of the Welsh language, hugely sensitive not least because of the historic wrong perpetrated against a minority population in the Union, or what would now be regarded as a flagrant breach of human rights. Turning the argument round, challenge by monolingual English speakers is no longer fanciful, and has to be carefully navigated, in the adoption of worthwhile policies in the realm of land use planning etc.[98] Then there is the way in which human rights policy and practice is generally intertwined with the social and economic condition of the country. At one and the same time, there is rich potential in Wales for a radical cutting edge, such are the patterns of deprivation and high dependency on core public services like health care, and evident problems of legal access and mobilization. The fact of a Children's Commissioner for Wales, which opens up new vistas of human rights protection, itself serves to highlight this aspect.[99]

Suffice it to add that intriguing questions are raised about the legal and political responsibility of (a form of meso-government) like the Assembly for securing compliance with Convention rights of those bodies that it funds and in respect of which it commonly has a regulatory function.[100] For interest groups etc. engaging in campaigning litigation, attempting to draw the devolved administration into disputes about service delivery etc. is an obvious tactic, one that no doubt the OCG will stoutly resist. Indirect administration versus creative mixes of legal and political leverage in the new Welsh polity: watch this space!

Three sources of law

Enough has also been said to illustrate the general scope for synergies in the case of Welsh devolution and human rights. Cross-cutting themes in the law: it would be strange indeed if 'the Welsh difference' of legal precepts on equality, language and sustainable development was somehow to be pigeon-holed, so as not to lock up together with developments under general human rights law on such matters as discrimination and environmental protection. Perhaps however the point deserves a special emphasis in the light of some recent observations from one of the leading judges in the field, Lord Justice Sedley:

> An important aspect of the reorientation of the United Kingdom's constitution towards a culture of human rights is that it draws upon not one but two new sources of law. One is the pervasive Human Rights Act 1998; the other is the

overarching European Convention on Human Rights. The two will be largely but by no means entirely co-extensive.[101]

Wales, however, demonstrates a third new source, the devolution statute or what I have called the Assembly's 'written constitution'.[102] Such is the product of the close interaction of the general themes of universality and locality, which today finds tangible expression in the rise of supranational ordering and domestic or internal subsidiarity.[103] Put another way, a culture of human rights derived from more than a couple of sources is emblematic of the contemporary dynamics of constitutional change in the United Kingdom.

'Mainstreaming'

Turning to the administrative process, it clearly is one measure of success that no successful cases have yet been taken against public authorities in Wales since full implementation of the HRA. Considerable efforts have been made behind the scenes to ensure that human rights considerations are drawn into the official mainstream, from policy-making to decision-taking, and on into service delivery. The approach fits both with the positive obligations that public authorities now have to ensure respect for human rights, and with the declared aim of the UK government that 'an awareness of the Convention rights permeates our government and legal systems at all levels'.[104]

In the case of the Assembly, this has involved close collaboration between the appropriately named PEP, the Public Administration, Equality and Public Appointments Division, and the Human Rights Task Force established by the Home Office in London, which has disseminated the core guidance for public authorities.[105] A prototype, it may be said, of intergovernmental cooperation and coordination in the new devolutionary age. The expert lawyers in the OCG have once again played a central role, including via an Assembly Human Rights Project Board that has linked in senior managers. The importance of the task – effectively promoting a mind-set of human rights – has itself been underscored by the scale of change in the local civil service in the wake of devolution.

The key instrument has been another Assembly Action Plan, one in this case similar to those devised for central government departments. It represents a classic mix of legal, promotional, networking and educational functions:

- To ensure that Assembly legislation, practices and procedures are consistent with the Convention rights and not likely to lead to legal challenge on human rights grounds
- To ensure all staff are aware of the implications of the Convention rights for their

work – particularly where this involves establishing policies or making decisions that affect individuals
- To ensure that public authorities which the Assembly funds or sponsors are aware of the implications of the HRA for their work and the action they need to take to ensure compliance with the Act
- To ensure that private and voluntary bodies are aware of the HRA and its implications for them when they are carrying out public functions
- To contribute within Wales to UK-wide efforts to promote public awareness of the significance of incorporating the European Convention into domestic law, especially among young people.[106]

In this regard, the proactive work of the OCG deserves a special emphasis.[107] One of the first actions was a wide-ranging review of legislation and procedures in conjunction with administrators in policy divisions and Whitehall colleagues, to identify areas potentially vulnerable to challenge, it then being a case of risk assessment by the Project Board. A second major element, also clearly signalled in the Action Plan, is the emphasis laid on spreading the gospel across the length and breadth of Wales. Various events, explicitly designed 'to promote a wider understanding of the [HRA] and of the values it enshrines',[108] have been organized for local government, the voluntary sector and others.

Institutional gaps

So far, so good: but is there not a case for publicly designated machinery to promote the cause of human rights in Wales? On the one hand, the devolved administration has clearly recognized the need to work on the local civic culture. At the same time, however, the OCG in particular can only do so much. On the other hand, issues of general human rights policy and practice have not featured prominently in the political discourse of the Assembly, being in fact the more notable by their absence in debates in plenary and in questions to ministers.[109] There are also degrees of 'mainstreaming': surprising as it may seem, promotion of human rights has not featured alongside other cross-cutting themes in the Welsh Assembly Government's overarching policy framework or *mappa mundi*.[110]

The institutional development could either take the classical 'parliamentary' form of an Assembly committee, or else involve the creation of a statutory agency akin to the pre-existing equality commissions, an idea which the UK government has been considering, and which in turn raises the issue of geographical remit.[111] And of course, looking forwards, any substantial move to legislative devolution would give the argument additional impetus.

The case for a standing committee was highlighted in evidence to the recent Assembly Review of Procedure.[112] 'Respect for, and promotion of, human rights should be a major feature of the new Welsh polity. Such matters are too important to be left to the lawyers.' On the basis that there was already a surfeit of committees, the proposal was for a 'Committee on Equality of Opportunity and Human Rights'. This would both 'expand on the work of the existing committee on equality of opportunity and provide a firm institutional focus in the Assembly for questions of human rights policy and practice in Wales'. In turn there would be 'a useful source of synergies', equality being a key aspect of human rights, as well as 'a useful source of democratic legitimacy for the new representative institution', including by reason of some lively discussion. 'Nothing', it was argued, 'could be more appropriate' for a body officially charged in the devolution White Paper with being 'a modern, progressive, and inclusive democratic institution'.[113]

It was not to be. Comfortable with what it was doing, the existing committee exercised a veto, citing potential overload and a blurring of focus.[114] The argument that 'as a cross-cutting issue, human rights affected the work of all Assembly committees and there was no requirement to have a committee on the subject', was somewhat less convincing, not least given the equality committee's own role and status![115] There remains a gap in the local political coverage.

Attention naturally focuses on the related question: whether a local 'constitutional space' between purely governmental and non-governmental institutions could usefully be filled by a human rights commission with duties and powers of reviewing and advising, promoting and litigating, in the cause of human dignity etc. For its part, the Welsh Assembly Government has been notably lukewarm, including in evidence to the Westminster Parliament's prestigious Joint Committee on Human Rights. 'There does not appear to be (as yet) a substantial body of political opinion in Wales in favour of a Human Rights Commission.'[116] Evidently, this came as something of a shock to the many distinguished members of the Wales Public Law and Human Rights Association, who might be thought to know something about the matter. In fact, said a blistering memorandum to the Joint Committee, not only had the devolved administration failed to take soundings, but also there was a powerful case for a Wales-only human rights commission. Correctly, since raising public consciousness is a prime task for any such body, the official argument was stood on its head.[117]

At first sight, this may appear a storm in a teacup. The affair, however, has a wider constitutional significance, going to the heart of the role of the devolved administration in representing the people of Wales to the UK Parliament and central government authorities. The basic failure of communications is the more striking here in light of the wide range of consultations that the devolved administration has undertaken in relation to other kinds of policy development. It has to be said: this was a textbook example of how not to proceed as 'a voice for Wales'. And the question has at least to be raised: how often has this happened in the confidential dealings that constitute intergovernmental relations?

Turning to the substance of the matter, the arguments have been nicely balanced.[118] A distinct and growing policy agenda addressing the scope and delivery of services of Welsh public authorities; different considerations of scale, culture and political priority; an increasing manifestation of Welsh 'state machinery: a stand-alone human rights commission for Wales would sit comfortably with these general traits. Yet it is an exaggeration to say, as does the Wales Public Law and Human Rights Association, that 'the worst scenario would be the creation of a Commission for England and Wales while Scotland and Northern Ireland have their own commissions'.[119] To reiterate, there will be many good reasons why post-devolution separate Welsh bodies or agencies are not established, a case of 'horses for courses'.[120] Here, the fact that Wales shares a legal, court and penal system with England presents a strong argument for a cross-border construction – as the Joint Committee has now recognized.[121]

A strong Welsh arm – 'the human rights commission in Wales' – is then the minimum requirement, not least to secure a local profile and give people in Wales a proper sense of ownership, and for developing close links with such agencies as the Welsh Language Board and the Children's Commissioner.[122] Of course it is just possible that financial considerations have served to tip the balance. Why, it may be asked inside the devolved administration, pick up the bill for a Wales only body when 'a single commission with an office in Wales would be likely to be more cost-effective'?[123]

5. LEGAL SOCIETY: TOWARDS A WELSH LEGAL ORDER

The rise of Legal Wales has only just begun. As such the development hardly equates with the thriving professional and intellectual life that one encounters in 'Legal Scotland', let alone in 'Legal London'. Naturally, in a country as small as Wales, many of the new initiatives have a tiny (if influential) clientele, and are severely constrained by lack of resources. Nor can one leave out of account the professional sense of the devolutionary scheme as a set of developments 'in public law', as against 'the bread and butter work' of family and crime, personal injury etc. Early survey findings that for many lawyers in Wales the Assembly is largely an irrelevance were only to be expected.[124]

Speaking more generally, the potential for apathy or resistance among various sections of the profession in Wales to an increasing sense of 'national' legal identity should not be underestimated. Take for example the impact of law firms as economic enterprises, which belatedly is now being recognized as a vital ingredient in the maintenance and growth of the Welsh economy.[125] One pragmatic argument for maintaining the unity of the English and Welsh legal system concerns the competitive position of those larger firms based in

Cardiff which supply packages of (commercial) services on both sides of 'the border'.

The speed and reach of the rise of Legal Wales is nonetheless a remarkable phenomenon. One way of looking at this is in terms of creating and animating a local civil society, previously identified as one of the many processes of Welsh devolution.[126] The constitutive and energizing effects that are entailed thus take many forms, as befits the fact that litigation is only a part of 'the world of the law'. The OCG may be at the centre actively promoting the development, but it is necessarily a complex and expanding web of new initiatives and associations. The rise of Legal Wales is then a flag-bearer for a more general set of developments increasingly visible across many walks of Welsh life, and has a special importance in terms of delineating Wales, being closely related to the political and administrative developments directly associated with the Assembly.

A different but related point: the rise of Legal Wales points up the powerful constraints associated with 'the strong centralized character of the law' and the greater sense of legal pluralism that is a natural product of the devolutionary process. Looking forwards, it would be foolish to think that all this reconstituted activity in Wales will have no knock-on effects back into the design and formal structures of the legal system. The dynamics are apt to be mutually reinforcing, including in terms of the continuing rise of Welsh 'state' or governmental machinery.

From decentralization to 'a legal voice for Wales'

'For Wales see England': this historical trend of administrative centralization in the legal system has now been reversed.[127] The arrival on the scene of the Administrative Court in Wales is part of a wider institutional reorientation, one that extends considerably beyond the strict parameters of the fields of devolved functions. It may, for the historical reasons explained, be a truism, but nonetheless – in the words of the Counsel General – 'the administration of justice in Wales is closer to the people now than at any other time during the nineteenth and twentieth centuries'.[128]

'Welshifying': there is a basic parallel here with what has been happening with some of the quangos or administrative agencies.[129] The creation of local 'branches', predicated upon the England and Wales paradigm, is thus one way forward. Some prestigious courts have been ripe for this treatment, first and pre-dating the Assembly the Chancery Court, and second in the guise of the vital commercial facility that is now the Mercantile Court in Wales. A variation on a theme, the Employment Appeals Tribunal now sits regularly in Wales, and there are also visitations by the high and mighty Civil and Criminal Divisions of the Court of Appeal. To this extent, the unitary legal system – and the Lord Chancellor's Department in particular – may be said to have responded flexibly to the changed political and administrative landscape in Wales, 'another step' in Lord Bingham's words 'towards recognising Wales as a proud, distinctive and successful nation'.[130] At the same time, there are pointers here to further and more substantial change, a broader development of truly indigenous legal institutions.

The Bar and the solicitors, in the guise respectively of the Wales and Chester Circuit and the Law Society (Office) in Wales, obviously have a pivotal role to play in what I have called 'the rebirth of Welsh legal history'. In the case of the society, the local organization has already become more distanced from London, and has also been strengthened, including with the aim of promoting effective liaison with the devolved administration. Together with the local groupings represented collectively by the Associated Law Societies of Wales, the office has taken the lead in the mundane but vital matters of professional (re-)education and training in the light of devolution.[131]

The emergence of new professional and networking organizations is seen as a litmus test of the legal and political changes. Founded in 1999, the Wales Public Law and Human Rights Association brings together judges, practitioners and other specialists on a regular basis. The aims are to promote both education and research and 'expertise amongst lawyers practising within Wales' in the relevant fields.[132] The association may be expected to grow as the Assembly grows.

Other examples can be given. A Welsh branch of the Society of Labour Lawyers was created in 2000, with the idea of sub-groups designed to shadow Assembly cabinet portfolios and provide input.[133] Recognition of the need for a dedicated Welsh perspective, or the strong potential for novel legal and political linkages in the new territorial polity, is shown clearly here. Then there is the rapid formation of professional groups such as the Wales Commercial Lawyers Association and the Welsh Personal Injury Lawyers Association. The very fact that here the substantive law is generally outwith Assembly powers or jurisdiction serves to reinforce the broad meaning of the rise of Legal Wales. Different again, the newly founded Welsh Legal History Society marks an enriching of cultural and intellectual life in the wake of the Assembly. Notably the aim is 'to make good [a] deficit': no Welsh equivalent of the famous Selden Society in England or Stair Society in Scotland. 'There is in the later history of law in Wales much which is distinctive and ought to be brought to light.'[134]

One of the very first things that an emergent jurisdiction needs is a reliable and up-to-date digest of the (devolved) powers and in particular of the laws that are made in the exercise of those powers. All the more so, it may be said in the case of Wales, by reason on the one hand of the patchwork or 'zigzag' of powers stretched across the various fields of devolved functions, and on the other hand of a natural pull in commercial legal publishing towards London. In the event, the devolved administration having been slow to grasp this particular nettle, the vacuum has been filled by 'Wales Legislation on-line', produced from Cardiff University under the direction of the former senior legal adviser to the Welsh Office, David Lambert. In his words, 'nothing can be left to chance – every aspect has to be verified'.[135] Perhaps it is fortunate then that Welsh devolution has coincided with the arrival of the Internet! Not, it may be said, that this is a wholly technical exercise, the not so subliminal message being the extreme complexity and general awkwardness of a constitutional scheme premised on specified and effectively unplanned powers.[136] Few would be converted by it to the cause of executive devolution.

A general forum for legal discussion and exchange of information is also important. So it is pleasing to record the establishment in 2001 of the *Wales Law Journal*, courtesy of the Department of Law at Swansea. A chief aim is 'to explain new Welsh law and the way in which it may be or is implemented by the National Assembly and public authorities in Wales'. According to the editor,

> lawyers, policy and business advisers, administrators and law enforcers . . . need to be informed of developments in law and policy, how these fit within the wider aims of the National Assembly . . . and how they relate to the position elsewhere in the UK, Europe and the wider world.[137]

It is not surprising to learn of flanking developments in the academic world. Founded in 1901, the Department of Law at Aberystwyth has a long and distinguished history, not least in Welsh legal studies.[138] The arrival on the scene of a new Centre for Welsh Legal Affairs shows yet again, however, the general energizing effects of national devolution. In turn, a determination 'to be outward looking and not parochial' – effectively a concept of 'Wales in the legal world' – needs to be vigorously asserted. A chief aim is 'to explore whether there is a distinct Welsh perspective on general legal questions within the common legal system of England and Wales and to ensure that Welsh legal developments are placed in the wider context of developments at the UK, European and international levels'.[139]

But what, it may be asked, of a general coordinating role, machinery for promoting strategic and joined-up thinking in the light of national devolution? Precisely this has been developed with the creation in 2002 of the Standing Committee on Legal Wales (SCLW), under the chairmanship of the Counsel General. SCLW draws together representatives from very many of the relevant constituencies: from the senior judiciary to the local professional associations, and on through the universities to official bodies like the Council on Tribunals, and further, from the major firms of solicitors in Wales to – significantly – the WDA.

The new body is clearly intended to be proactive, its purpose being 'to provide a forum for the discussion and formulation of views and proposals for action on issues affecting the administration of justice, the teaching and researching of law and the provision of legal services as they affect Wales'. More particularly, it can be seen as a 'legal voice for Wales', both inside and outside the territory. Evidently, important lessons have been learned, including from the local communications breakdown over a human rights commission in Wales. A series of lobbying and networking functions is specified:

- to coordinate responses to consultations on such matters by the Assembly or the UK government
- when considered appropriate, to make representations on such matters to the Assembly, the UK government or any other relevant body
- to promote the interests of the legal community in Wales.

Soon no doubt we will be hearing of 'Team Legal Wales'. There is much to be done, not least in breaking down the established patterns of parochialism in favour of a more 'national' approach. An integrated strategy for the location of the many lower-tier courts and tribunals that sit in Wales, not simply with a view to saving costs, but in light of the demography in the cause of local access to justice, is one obvious example.[140]

And then there is the realm of law and the local economy. At one and the same time, the legal services sector makes an important financial contribution, currently generating 1 per cent of Wales's GDP, and typically lags behind the rest of the UK.[141] More especially, the economics of professional services in large parts of Wales is now seen to be deeply problematical: which itself reflects and reinforces the depressing patterns of socio-economic deprivation concentrated in the rural areas. Fitting well with the strong general theme in Welsh devolution of economic development, there are clear pointers here to a more joined-up approach to legal services, predicated on involvement by the WDA etc., even perhaps a 'national' action plan. There may be no magic solution, but the rise of Legal Wales already has the considerable benefit of casting a fierce light on such matters.

The next frontier

The idea of (re-)establishing in a context of 'national devolution' distinctive Welsh judicial offices and bodies is not novel. It was part of the old Liberal demand, as in the Government of Wales Bill 1914, which together with legislative devolution and general territorial powers of taxation envisaged a Welsh Division of the High Court.[142] In fact, an even bolder scheme surfaced in the context of the 1919/20 Speaker's Conference, which envisaged for Wales a Chancellor, Court of Appeal, High Court and Law Officers of its own, as also a distinct Welsh Bar. Naturally, it foundered along with the proposal for legislative devolution, having previously encountered stiff opposition from the Lord Chancellor's Department.[143]

By way of contrast, it is characteristic of the limited scheme of devolution effected by the GWA that ministers saw no need to legislate for the judicial power, other than in terms of constraints on Assembly powers and 'devolution issues'. Indeed, an associated titular change, the reinvention of the Lord Chief Justice of England as Lord Chief Justice of England and Wales, betrays a certain historical irony: belated recognition at the very moment of national devolution! According to Lord Bingham, it was 'insulting' to the Welsh 'that they should play no part in the title of the Lord Chief Justice'.[144]

Criticism of the current situation has not been slow to surface, including from local practitioners. Even before a case was decided, reference was being made to 'the innate prejudices of the judiciary', or to judges likely to view as 'suspect . . . anything which makes different provision in Wales from that for England'.[145] This represents a novel dimension to an old argument: a post-devolutionary spin on what has been called in 'Old Labour' circles 'the politics of the judiciary'.[146]

The matter can be presented in different ways. What can be described as 'the John Bull argument' may sound bizarre, but it serves also as a useful warning. A pretence that no serious issue of judicial identity arises in conditions of national devolution bears the hallmark of classic unionist error. One does not have to visualize a case of direct action in the name of Wales to appreciate the point.[147] Perception does not always accord with practice, least of all in sensitive issues of constitutional law and policy.

There will surely be an increasing demand for judicial specialization in Welsh public law: in the words of Mr Justice Thomas, an understanding of 'the particular problems of Wales (and therefore the rationale of decision making)'.[148] The creation of distinctive judicial offices for Wales can also be seen as a natural progression of the current judicial policy, made evident in the procedural rules on devolution issues etc., of encouraging local legal practice by the promotion of local legal machinery.

Reference was made to 'the eternal triangle' of politics, public law and administration. The concept serves to point up the basic problem of 'fit' with the legal system in post-devolutionary Wales. Having regard to the increasing sense of administrative and political diversity, and further, heightened awareness of cultural and linguistic factors, there is thus seen to be a missing piece in the jigsaw. So-called 'peak institutions', better to secure the visibility and authority and ultimately the legitimacy of the law and legal system inside Wales, are of the essence of the matter. In this respect, the judicial architecture too is unfinished constitutional business.

An obvious first step is the (re-)establishment of the Office of Chief Justice of Wales.[149] This would involve general responsibilities for the effective and efficient operation of the courts in Wales, a pivotal role in the conduct of public law litigation inside the country, and a partnership role with the senior judiciary in England concerning the general workings of the English and Welsh legal system. It would effectively build on – and solidify – the current role of the senior Presiding Judge of the Wales and Chester Circuit.[150] More especially, the office would reflect and reinforce the representational function for law and justice in the new 'national' polity.

Remarkable as it may seem to the general reader, there is at the time of writing no Welsh judge sitting in the House of Lords, let alone – in contrast both to Scotland and Northern Ireland – an established rule to this effect. Notwithstanding the unity of the English and Welsh legal system, this represents old-fashioned thinking in the conditions of national devolution. Again, one of the few advantages of the Judicial Committee is the flexibility in terms of court composition. With membership extending to those who hold or have held 'high judicial office' there is increased scope for territorial representation.[151] But given the authoritative recognition of Wales as one of the four countries of the Union, a practice of including judges with strong Welsh connections on panels hearing disputes involving the Assembly can only be considered necessary but insufficient.[152] An established Welsh seat on the putative replacement in 'devolution issues', the 'Supreme Court': it should hardly need saying now.[153]

Once again in the words of Mr Justice Thomas, 'Wales and the legal profession in Wales does derive very substantial benefits from [the] unitary system', for example on behalf of its 'export-orientated' law firms.[154] As well as a highly developed criminal justice system, linked in turn to the current organization of the police on an England and Wales basis,[155] one can hardly overlook the market position of 'English law', extraordinarily influential across the commercial world, the instrument of choice in many international contracts. Developing and nurturing indigenous institutions; active involvement in this 'single legal market': why, it may be asked, should this little country, one with a comparative low GDP in UK terms, not seek to enjoy the best of both worlds?

It was only a matter of time before the old Liberal demand resurfaced. No longer is the development of a Wales Division of the High Court, with 'the full range of . . . jurisdiction for all first instance and review cases arising wholly within Wales and including Mercantile, Chancery and Family cases', a fanciful idea.[156] And with a national president, directly responsible for improving the speed and quality of justice in Wales, and operating to secure the local sense of judicial legitimacy: the case, it may be said, grows stronger by the day.

To this effect, the implications of national devolution for the court structure, and so in turn the local organization of the profession, and in particular the provision of legal services including outside Wales, now demands active and serious consideration at the highest levels. In fact, an instructive model for the conditions of small-country governance lies close to hand, in the guise of the Justice (Northern Ireland) Act 2002. Organization of a separate judicial system for a devolved territory: if this is considered too great a step for Wales then there remains much that can be read across, for example as regards new institutions a Law Commission, and formal involvement of the devolved administration in the judicial appointments process.

Looking forwards, this obviously is an area where the prospect of legislative devolution casts a long shadow. As the Liberals in 1914 clearly recognized, a basic reform of the local judicial architecture – effectively a Welsh legal jurisdiction – is in the face of such major political change the next frontier. Turning the argument round, members of the Kilbrandon Commission gave as one reason in favour of a lesser form of devolution to Wales the non-existence of a Welsh legal system.[157] So it would be a fine historical irony: the enhancement of the one pointing the way to the creation of the other. Suffice it to add that the juxtaposition of two primary law-makers and an undifferentiated legal system would be constitutionally unique. A federal principle, it is not!

CONCLUSION – LIVING WITH THE LAWYERS

For the legal anthropologist or sociologist Wales is currently one of the most interesting of places. How could it be otherwise in conditions, on the one hand, of the emergence of a distinctive 'national' polity, and on the other hand, of a differently conceived legal architecture, in the guise of the essential unity of the English and Welsh legal system?

Another paradox of Welsh devolution is illustrated: a model of government – executive devolution – highly dependent on legal skills, tools and techniques, and the historical legacy of a local vacuum or stunted tradition of public law inside the territory. It is one of the ways in which Wales of the three Celtic lands was the least prepared for devolution.

The lack of legal challenges to the Assembly is an important pointer, not least to the emergence of a distinctive Welsh form of political and administrative culture, reflecting and reinforcing what I have called 'the closeness of Wales'. Such litigation will no doubt begin to emerge, especially if Wales gains legislative devolution, but one should not assume the exact same patterns and practices as for example in England. Again, the situation of the law in Wales brilliantly illustrates the contemporary interaction of the forces of universality and locality. The HRA in particular serves not only to constrain the scope of Assembly operations but also in aid of establishing a vibrant tradition of public law inside the territory.

Among the many processes of devolution, the rise of Legal Wales is one of the more significant. At one and the same time, it is seen to be founded on and increasingly ranging far beyond the formal transfer of powers to the Assembly. From the development of the OCG to cleverly worked procedural changes and relocation of courts in favour of local legal business, and on through a proper respect for Welsh as a living language of the law to a general enrichment of local legal society: the evidence is all around.

As an important part of the devolutionary experience, living with the lawyers will often be uncomfortable. Yet the rise of 'Legal Wales' is in so many ways a healthy development. Law is a cultural artefact and local legal institutions have a significant role to play in the development and sustenance of a vibrant civil and political society. Making good the deficiency will be a complex challenge, not least in view of the strong centripetal force long associated with the unity of the English and Welsh legal system. Nonetheless, the creation of truly indigenous institutions – real not virtual – should move quickly now up the official agenda.

In conclusion, national devolution both works to generate, and to be properly grounded requires, a distinctive legal culture. Viewed in light of the overarching constitutional and political development Lord Bingham's 'administrative devolution' is a dull and uninspiring vision. A thousand years on from the great codification of Welsh law, it is time once again in the law to take Wales seriously.

15

Towards a Devolution Settlement

One day, the number of people who say 'Thank God we live in Wales' will exceed
the number who say 'What has the Assembly ever done for us?' We are laying the
foundations now. If we apply ourselves with faith in our future, that day will dawn.

Rhodri Morgan[1]

As Deep Throat might have said, 'Follow the institutional growth.' By this is
meant not simply the increasing scale of the local administrative apparatus, so
apt in Wales to cause much gnashing of teeth, but more importantly the
raising of inner capacities, an emergent sense in official circles of greater
confidence and creativity, and – yes – of constitutional understanding. Cut
some slack under a scheme of executive devolution founded on a democratic
act of choice, the Welsh in the words of their remembrancer have gaily set
about producing their own 'artefact'.[2] The metamorphosis of the National
Assembly from corporate body to 'virtual parliament' stands at the heart of
this development.

Consistent with the strong ongoing dynamics of the situation, this last
chapter wears a dual character, an introduction as well as conclusion. At the
time of writing, attention naturally focuses on the work of the Richard
Commission, which clearly represents another stage in the continuing saga of
Welsh devolution. Much is up for grabs, and the commission should be of the
first importance in setting the parameters of the future constitutional
advancement of Wales. At the same time, it cannot be the only show in town.
Such is the logic of the many processes of devolution.

Let us beware the future, in the form of a revisionist history. The original
design and rapid development of the new Welsh structures of government are
no great triumph of socialist planning or calculation. The scheme of executive
devolution was grievously holed from the outset, but the exact manner and
speed of its sinking has not been foretold in the stars, nor indeed is its replacement ship of state. The smooth passage of 'devolution by evolution' may be a
suitable fairy story for the children. But a potent mix of blood, sweat and tears
– unforeseen events – and of the calm and patient processes of building up
Welsh governmental institutions and a civic culture more accurately gives the
flavour.

1. AN INTERIM CONSTITUTION

Truly, in the long journey of Welsh devolution, the Assembly as presently constituted cannot be the final destination. It is seen in this book as the centrepiece of an interim constitution, one that demonstrates too many sources of instability to endure, and also one that has allowed the groundwork to be laid for further political advancement. In suitably provocative fashion, the title of this chapter serves to highlight the lack of a 'devolution settlement' properly so called, and the practical steps which may now be taken to remedy this basic constitutional deficiency.

Bringing government closer to the people

With a view to the Welsh constitutional development to be, let us first pull together some of the existing strands. The very fact of devolution may now be accounted a positive experience, one that has already served to generate and release new potentials, and to broaden horizons not least in terms of the place of Wales in the world. It is a trite conclusion, but one that, given the peculiar history of this little country including as England's 'first colony', is nonetheless worth repeating. There is no going back.

Equally, it does not do to airbrush from history the fact of an unduly slow start, as demonstrated by the style and substance of devolved government under Alun Michael ('Welsh Office plus'). Nor, one is tempted to add, a certain touching *naïveté* about the capacities of government – devolved or otherwise – to deliver rapid and substantial improvements in complex policy environments like public health. Hard lessons have still to be learned, including the importance in the public eye of the formal conduct of proceedings. Looking forward, a greater ambition in policy development, allied to a firmer grasp of the practical realities of public administration, will be a sure sign of the maturation of the new system of Welsh governance at the political level.

Attention naturally focuses on the scope or otherwise of policy divergence, and rightly so in the democratic life of the country. Strictly speaking, devolution may be about the choice (or otherwise) of diversity, but 'made in Wales' policies are a key measure of the so-called 'devolution dividend'. The First Minister's annual report for 2001–2 serves to make the point. Entitled *Delivery*, in true propaganda style it made much of a limited number of headline stories, the usual examples of Assembly Learning Grants and lower prescription charges, and on through free entry to museums and experiments with finance for small enterprises to the local restriction on testing in schools.[3]

In suitably paradoxical fashion, this very political edge also serves to obscure the true scale of local policy development. It is not simply that these are early days and that a more appropriate test would be two full terms, or that while the room for manoeuvre may be small the changes are cumulative. Reference must also be made to the overarching or strong cross-cutting themes that have characterized the Welsh policy map or *mappa mundi*;[4] and further, to significant programmes of reform in subject areas like health and education where the devolved administration very much needs 'to (be seen to) make a difference'. Emphatically, one need not don political colours, or indeed approve of a particular policy agenda, to recognize that something more general and profound is happening here under the rubric of national devolution. The Permanent Secretary may be quoted:

> The forensic interest that 60 elected Members attuned to the needs of Wales have applied to the policy process has resulted in a range of innovative initiatives which simply could not have been introduced (at least in terms of their range and originality) under the former Welsh Office arrangements. I confidently predict that if this process continues, in 10 years time the Assembly will be seen to have delivered a step change in the quality and relevance of policy making and delivery . . . in Wales.[5]

Again, it does not devalue the many and powerful forces of convergence and uniformity to point up two key sources of policy diversity. The 'power of the purse' has featured prominently in this book, not least by reason of the local control vested through the block and formula system. Successive Assembly budgets illustrate for example how the targeting of resources on local patterns of socio-economic deprivation is now being accentuated as part of a distinctive Welsh policy agenda, a case in point being the 'Communities First' programme.[6]

Secondly, a feature easily missed is the capacity of the devolved administration 'to be different by doing the same'; that is to say, opt out of a Whitehall reform agenda. An emergent strand of 'made in Wales' policies, the retention of more traditional Labour policies in fields like health and education – no foundation hospitals for example – in the face of developments in England exemplifies this form of divergence.[7] At the same time, the potential for conflict by reason of the horizontal division of powers in executive devolution is clearly signalled here.

What, it may be asked, of the ideological gloss? Representing the dominant Labour interest, Rhodri Morgan has spoken of the 'clear red water' between 'the way in which things are being shaped in Wales and the direction being followed at Westminster'. A metaphor, that is, for greater emphasis on universality as a guiding principle of public provision, and on a heightened Welsh sense of 'community'; with a corresponding distrust of the kind of 'market' solutions familiarly associated with 'New Labour'. By way of illustration, the First Minister would include practical measures like free school milk and bus passes for the elderly in 'a new set of citizenship rights' for the people of Wales.[8]

Although the scale and the direction of the development are clearly open to dispute, the underlying message should not be lightly dismissed. It would be strange indeed if the principles of social justice commonly associated with the radical political traditions of Welsh society did not come rapidly to the fore under the auspices of national devolution: even in the face of a restricted policy-making framework. Less deferential, more in tune with the condition of Wales: in this sense too, things have moved on from the days of Alun Michael.

As befits the constitutional and administrative aspects, a special emphasis is laid in this book on the different ways of working and, more especially, on the quest for new and improved techniques of governance for this little country. From the insistence on precepts of transparency and integrity to a close form of audit, and on through the 'parliamentary' routines of statements, questions and debates to an entire system of subject committees (howsoever oversold), the basic idea of official life 'in the goldfish bowl' – democratic accountability – cannot be gainsaid. So also the greater accessibility of devolved government: even if it does not always feel like this in the fastness of north Wales.

Animating civil society is no easy task, not least in view of a territorial history of parochialism and fragmentation. As the case of the lawyers serves to illustrate, however, new Welsh-focused organizations and groupings are beginning to appear, more autonomous.[9] Indicative of an enhanced sense of local national identity post-devolution, the development has obvious potential in helping to make good the historical legacy of a substantial policy-making vacuum in Wales. Presented in this book as one of the many processes of devolution, a classic illustration of the knock-on effects of the formal re-allocation of powers, the creation and mobilization of a strong civic capacity is now rightly a concern of the Welsh Assembly Government. As for the lawyers, it would be foolish to overlook the part they may play in promoting further constitutional development, both in terms of the judicial architecture etc. and more generally. Collectively speaking, 'Legal Wales' is a not insignificant interest group!

Another recurring theme in this book is 'the closeness of Wales', and more especially the many advantages of flexibility and adaptability that now accrue in the conditions of small-country governance. Notable features include the innovative machinery for partnership particularly with local government, and the harnessing (and not the 'bonfire') of the quangos. 'Doing things differently': a distinct preference for more informal or collaborative techniques of regulation etc. is also identified – the 'Welsh way'.[10] Process and product being so often intertwined, the significance of this in the conduct of public business should not be underestimated. Juxtaposed with the continuing pull of a strong 'cross-border' paradigm, not least inside the legal system, it is one of the reasons why I have talked of (overlapping) administrative laws of England and Wales.

Let us not get carried away. Not only has the devolved administration still to make good on some of the rhetoric, for example in FOI,[11] but also fashionable techniques of governance like partnership working have their own pitfalls and could usefully be applied more carefully in Wales. Nor – dare one say it – is inclusiveness a sure recipe for responsible and effective government. Looking forward, it is time to right a cardinal error in the original design, and formally accept that as in many other little jurisdictions around the world the people of Wales are quite capable of combining the virtues of parliamentary government with ample opportunities for democratic access, consultation and participation.

Lack of constitutional vision

The fact that Welsh devolution shows many good points should not now obscure the way in which the basic constitutional product has been prejudiced by the original form or process of delivery. It is not simply that Wales has once again been treated as a second-class member of the Union. The central role of autochthonous development post-devolution is itself largely explained by the lack of constitutional vision – and insularity – shown at the outset.

Turning in on itself, and so achieving internal party compromise at the expense of informed public discussion, the dominant Labour interest has thus been seen taking Wales out of the mainstream of comparative constitutional development. The 'strange anatomy' that resulted, in part as a consequence of legislative and administrative attempts to retrieve the situation via a hybrid 'cabinet and committee' model, is not exactly easy to explain, as the author has found to his cost! This feature also fits with the retarded development of a local tradition of public law; or – more harshly – with a general sense of constitutional *naïveté* in the Welsh body politic. Only a country, one is tempted to say, with so little tradition of talking about these issues could have ended up with this particular scheme of executive devolution.

The original decision-making process is also emblematic of a continuing failure in Welsh devolution to engage with the mass of the people. This is not to overlook the many consultation exercises on particular policy proposals, let alone the many practical difficulties in promoting a genuine sense of popular engagement and enthusiasm. There is, however, the quality of a self-fulfilling prophecy to circling the wagons in self-referential fashion and not promoting an open and robust debate about where devolution is supposed to be leading in Wales. Speaking more generally, local politicians should look in the mirror in the face of low turnout in Assembly elections.[12] Where, it may be asked, is the passion in Welsh devolution?

The rush job of 1997–9 can be said to have broken a logjam, creating for Wales a national democratic institution after a century and more of devolutionary rumblings. Constitutionally as well as politically speaking, however, it is now seen prolonging the agony. In the event, it did not take long for the basic internal architecture to implode, with the pieces then having to be reassembled in the form, first, of an independent Presiding Office, and, second, the self-styled Welsh Assembly Government. To reiterate, the strong role for autochthonous constitutional development has been necessary and very valuable. Yet scarce political and administrative energies have had to be redirected, an unfortunate side effect. In similar vein, the collective failure of the Welsh Labour Party to think through the legal and administrative implications of the original proposals is highlighted in the continuing controversy over the basic design of Assembly competences. Why, otherwise, is there a Richard Commission?

Sources of instability

Likewise, the many structural and procedural advances that have been made, not least in dealing with some severe teething problems, cannot disguise the more general or systemic difficulties of the particular form of devolution applied to Wales. Constitutionally speaking, this is shown to be a flimsy construction, one that demonstrates an excessive or abnormal dependency on political and administrative good will. 'Executive devolution in a cold climate': what happens when the biting east wind blows?

To quote Rhodri Morgan, the prospect of political 'cohabitation' with Westminster is 'the $64 trillion question . . . of the robustness of the settlement'.[13] On the one hand, it is easy to exaggerate the dangers, and so postulate some grand form of constitutional crisis founded on the twin elements of no obligation on Westminster to enact primary legislation for the Assembly and the historical fact of limited electoral support for the Conservatives in Wales. As the comparative experience in so many other systems of divided competencies serves to remind us, there no doubt would be a major element of accommodation, not least with a view to maintaining the health of the Union. On the other hand, it does not do to dismiss the matter as essentially speculative and so of little account in the current constitutional equation.[14] A proper constitutional 'risk assessment' thus serves to highlight the extra difficulties prone to arise from the horizontal division of powers in executive devolution and the associated political and administrative rigidities. A recipe in the conditions of political cohabitation for the efficient and effective governance of Wales, and further for clear lines of democratic accountability and authority, the scheme of executive devolution is not.

In turn, the imposing spectre of 'cohabitation' should not obscure the propensity of the Welsh scheme to generate tensions and inefficiencies even in the political conditions of (presumably Labour) Party hegemony. Such in fact is the constitutional message implicit in Rhodri Morgan's vision of 'clear red water'. As the devolved administration becomes better equipped and more experienced, and naturally seeks more 'Welsh' solutions, so the inherent limitations of a fragmented process of law making are liable to be increasingly exposed, notwithstanding the efforts at developing the idea of a legislative 'partnership'.

Given all the competing demands, why should Welsh business take high priority in the UK government's legislative programme? There is much to be said for relieving Parliament of the chore of providing for the domestic affairs of this little country, while at the same time reducing the scope for delay and disappointment on the part of local actors that is inherent in the Westminster legislative 'bottleneck'. One product of the political and administrative 'grit' associated with the scheme of executive devolution, the sheer tedium for London is in fact another reason why the so-called 'devolution settlement' lacks stability.

Again, the official comparison with the bidding strength of a Whitehall department, whereby the Assembly may reasonably hope to secure one or two Wales-only Bills a year, now appears a false analogy. At one and the same time, it reflects the backward-looking view of the Assembly as a substitute for the Secretary of State for Wales – 'Welsh Office plus' – and glosses over the fact of the multi-functional character of devolved administration, the spanning of the jurisdiction of several Whitehall departments. Precisely because the Welsh Assembly Government is now picking up steam, the general requirement to go cap in hand to Westminster is not very practical or efficient and effective. 'Piggybacking', personal experience teaches, is a somewhat exhausting activity.

Nor can one overlook the jigsaw of Assembly powers;[15] and in particular, the way in which a classically British form of muddling through in the subsequent primary legislation affecting Wales has served to reinforce a 'triumph of particularity' in the original transfer of functions order. A suitably subversive thought: if from within the government machine one had wished to wreck executive devolution, most obviously with a view to securing legislative devolution for Wales, then it is hard to think of a better way of going about it. What, it may be asked, is the constitutional magnetism of such a prosaic and – save for a chosen few – incomprehensible allocation of powers? Answer: it repels.

The impact of no primary legislative power in terms of a restricted policy-making framework is a political and administrative issue that will run now.

Constitutionally speaking, however, it is also seen to have the adverse effect of locking up or inhibiting democratic energies and potentials, as demonstrated by the particular sense of aimlessness that attaches to the 'theatre' of the Assembly in plenary session. Then there are the dynamics of constitutional and political status, most obviously the continuing pull for a greater degree of symmetry with Scotland, as also the need to ensure that Wales's 'voice' is heard loud and clear in the cacophony of 'regional' voices in Europe. Internal dissatisfaction, not least on the part of many AMs, and external considerations: this is another potent combination.

Of course if this were English 'regional' devolution, things would look rather different. It is, however, a qualitatively different species – national devolution – and there is little point in pretending otherwise. The more so, it may be said, in light of the many actions of the Welsh Assembly Government that work to accentuate this feature; from particular 'made in Wales' policies to the lessons in flag-waving that now characterize Welsh paradiplomacy. Building a 'national' representative institution and creating and pursuing policies premised in a familiar phrase on 'the particularity of Wales'; and continuing to operate on the basis of secondary legislative status: constitutionally speaking, this does not stack up, not least for those of us who are happy unionists.[16]

A lessening sense of Welsh identity in the wake of devolution is hardly to be expected.[17] Meanwhile, recent surveys of public attitudes are indicative, first, of widespread apathy about the Assembly ('what has the Assembly ever done for us?'); and, second, of growing support for a more generous 'devolution settlement', as well as a dramatic decline in the 'no devolution' camp.[18] At one and the same time, such findings sit comfortably with much comparative data, not least the strong sense of disillusionment with the more familiar forms of political process, and serve to highlight both the slow start and general sense of unfinished business in the local constitutional development. Another related theme in this book is the strong element of make-believe that has surrounded the Assembly from its inception, now encapsulated in the imagery of 'a virtual parliament'. The people of Wales, it would appear from the findings, are not so easily fooled.

Let us be clear. The road to a proper devolution settlement for Wales, robust and user-friendly, and one that in the guise of legislative devolution seeks to maximize the advantages of small-country governance as part of the constitutional 'family' of the Union state, will not be easy. Sooner or later, however, it will be travelled, such that the current 'interim constitution' is effectively consigned to the dustbin of Welsh history. Much obviously depends on happenings inside the Welsh Labour Party; and in particular whether – following on the period 1979–97 – another political purgative is required, in the form of a period of 'cohabitation'. In terms of the governance of Wales, however, it makes eminent sense to lance the boil.

Building up . . . and moving on

The novel political and administrative demands of devolution are shown in this book driving forward the powerful autochthonous constitutional development. More especially, it is the practical and pragmatic concerns of policy development and implementation – 'check against delivery' – that underpin the rapid emergence of a governmental apparatus in microcosm. Friction at the heart of the administrative machine has been viewed as part of this process. The 'old' Welsh Office being considered no longer fit for purpose, a little bureaucratic revolution has been unleashed, the flagship of which is the new Executive Board.[19]

So it is that the tectonics of institutional and administrative change assume importance, this being an excellent example in comparative public administration of constitution-building in secret or in silence. At one and the same time, there is much pepping up, especially in terms of a more policy-orientated administrative culture, and official preparation – conscious or otherwise – for the next main phase in the devolution project.

Looking to the interstices of Welsh cabinet government for example, or to the 'Welshifying' of administrative agencies and the pursuit of novel forms of 'partnership' arrangement, reveals both a deepening and widening of official potentials and a measure of cultural adaptation as part of small-country governance.[20] Alongside the *de facto* split in the Assembly architecture, a natural precursor to primary legislative powers, this more general and diffuse development conspires to give the political idea of executive devolution for Wales an increasingly dated air. Effectively, it is being outflanked.

Again, looking forwards, the Richard Commission has raised the issue: 'could the administrative machine cope with a further transformation?' In one sense, this is a non-question. What in the history of the home civil service suggests that things would not be managed, by hook or by crook? But further, the short history of the Assembly now yields more than enough examples of official creativity to admit of only one answer to the Commission's question: which perhaps helps to explain why it has been asked.

Take the Assembly lawyers, who themselves have shown considerable ingenuity in going against the grain of the statute in the cause of the internal architecture. Whereas the OCG was not properly equipped in 1999, it should now be able to acquire the capacity to make primary legislation within a reasonable time frame, building in turn on the growing experience of secondary law making for Wales, and of inputs into Wales-only Bills etc. at Westminster.[21] The Office of Parliamentary Counsel might even be prevailed upon to help.

From the standpoint of the local civil service, 'a further transformation' in the guise of primary powers should also be measured against the series of 'transformations' in the last few years. From Welsh Office to National

Assembly, and on through to the Welsh Assembly Government: a bureaucracy that can navigate this also appears sufficiently adaptable and resourceful to meet the challenge in prospect.

Confirmation, if it is needed, comes from an impeccable source. The evidence to the Richard Commission presented on behalf of the local civil service by the Permanent Secretary, Sir Jon Shortridge, can be boiled down to two essential points. First, according to the canon of civil service neutrality, the Permanent Secretary could not possibly express a view on the desirability or otherwise of legislative devolution for Wales. Second, were the Richard Commission minded to go down that route, however, then he would like to reassure the members that the local administrative apparatus would be up to the task.[22] Well, there's a thing!

2. ENTER THE RICHARD COMMISSION

First promised in October 2000 as part of the coalition agreement of Labour and the Liberal Democrats, the Independent Commission on the Powers and Electoral Arrangements of the Assembly was eventually established in July 2002. Officially 'free from any influence from either the Welsh Assembly Government or the Assembly as a whole',[23] it has been asked to report by the end of 2003, in light of the evidence of the Assembly's first term.

The composition of such bodies is always a useful clue.[24] As well as Lord Richard, the chairman and leading Labour peer, there are four 'independent' members, selected – as one would expect in the new model Wales – through the public appointments process. A substantial record of public service in Wales – the quangos and local government – is the common feature here. Emblematic of a limited local tradition, expertise in public law is the more notable by its absence. Each of the four political parties represented in the Assembly also has its own nominee. AMs, however, have effectively been barred from sitting, on the basis that this is a commission reporting to the Assembly. Real local heavyweights, a Dafydd Wigley perhaps (from Plaid Cymru), are also notable by their absence. It suffices to add that there is a strong element of continuity, two of the members having also sat on the Standing Orders Commission for the Assembly.

The potential for disagreement – dissenting opinions – must be factored into the equation. There will no doubt be great concern to achieve consensus among the 'independent' members, especially in view of likely division among the party nominees. The spectre at the feast is the Kilbrandon Commission. Viewed in historical perspective, the basic division a generation ago between those recommending legislative devolution for Wales and those favouring executive devolution has done little more than muddy the waters. A key test of the Richard Commission is whether it provides a broad clarity of vision.

To whom must the report be addressed? As well as the Welsh Assembly Government in particular and the Assembly at large, the answer clearly is the people of Wales, and further, assuming that the commission is disposed to be more than minimalist and so recommends replacement or significant amendment of the devolution statute, Westminster and Whitehall. This then would be a classic case of 'voice for Wales' – the power of the pen backed up presumably by (a majority of) the Assembly – with no implied commitment, constitutional or otherwise, on the part of UK ministers to act. Turning the argument round, a notable feature is what has not happened: a review appointed jointly and in unison by the Assembly and central government. Perhaps it is worth adding that the memorandum of evidence tabled on behalf of the UK government says little of substance; a case, in truly *Yes, Minister* style, of no hostages to fortune.[25]

Whatever happens, the basic constitutional arrangements discussed in this volume will obtain for a few years yet. Starting with the Commission, eighteen months from appointment to report is a leisurely time frame, as well as being one – conveniently or otherwise – that has stretched across the second set of Assembly elections.[26] Add in a UK general election (manifesto commitments), the parliamentary proceedings on 'the Wales Bill', and new Assembly elections, as also a possible referendum and changes to the Assembly electoral system, and one could be thinking of 2008 for a scheme of legislative devolution to come on stream.

Not just 'an affair of the elite'

Viewed in historical perspective, the Welsh devolutionary development is now aptly described in the famous phrase as 'an affair of the elite'. A reference, it is perhaps worth stressing, not simply to the governors of the Welsh Labour Party, but also to the close political and professional ranks that now frequent Cardiff Bay. Another key test then of the Richard Commission is the public process in which it engages: the steps taken to canvass the views of a broad spectrum of individuals and organizations across Wales; and, further, to promote a substantial public dialogue on the case for major reform. A popular face of this kind represents a vital source of legitimacy, not least as and when it comes to persuading London.

The very fact of the inquiry represents a significant advance on the closed practices of constitution-making for Wales that have predominated hitherto. As one would expect, the commission has set about taking evidence from Welsh Assembly Government ministers and officials and the Presiding Office, the local political parties, the UK government and other devolved administrations, public authorities like local government and the police, and leading individuals and organizations in Welsh civil society. At the time of writing, nine months into proceedings, there is already a mound of paper.

Nonetheless, one need not be an advocate of some kind of 'national convention'[27] – more broadly based and wide-ranging – to recognize a somewhat muted and old-fashioned approach to public involvement at the vital early stage of the deliberations when ideas are formed and major parameters established. By way of example, the commission's key scoping paper and public appeal for evidence – 'issues and questions for consultation' – had virtually nothing to say about possible options, and very little about how the present devolutionary scheme operates and its perceived shortcomings.[28] A potent vehicle for focused and informed participation it was not. Again, bizarre as this may seem, the commission did not have prior to the ending of the public consultation on powers an operational website. So much, when it comes to the crunch and the future governance of Wales is in issue, for local claims to world leadership in 'electronic democracy'!

Perhaps it is worth adding that 'resources' is risible by way of an official explanation. In fact, this aspect of the commission's work jars the more strongly in view of the detailed consultation paper originally issued by the National Assembly Advisory Group – 'have your say on how it will work' – and the freely available information on the altogether more tedious Assembly Review of Procedure. Again, an interactive resource of the type now familiar in European governance – not just original sources and document archive, but on through comparative materials and research findings to online consultation and an electronic forum for civil society – why, it may be asked, was this such a fantastical proposition for Wales?

Poor start: terms of reference

Turning to the substance, the terms of reference relating to Assembly powers deserve to be quoted in full:

The Commission should consider the sufficiency of the Assembly's current powers, and in particular

- whether the Assembly's powers are sufficiently clear to allow optimum efficiency in policy-making;
- whether both the breadth (*i.e. the range of issues over which it has control*) and the depth (*i.e. the capacity to effect change within those issues*) of the Assembly's powers are adequate to permit integrated and consistent policy-making on issues where there is a clear and separate Welsh policy agenda;
- whether the mechanisms for UK Government policy-making as regards Wales, and the arrangements for influence by the Assembly on these, are clear and effective, and in particular whether they correct any apparent shortcoming from the previous item;
- whether the division of responsibility between the Assembly and the UK

> Government places inappropriate constraints on Whitehall policy-making, both on matters over which the Assembly has control and otherwise.
>
> The Commission should consider any possible financial implications arising from the implementation of its proposals.

A clear product of haggling inside the devolved administration, the formulation reeks of official concerns. Against the background of a zigzag of powers, it is all put in terms of policy-making, with no mention for example of the constitutional or citizenship values of transparency and intelligibility. In turn, this represents a significant test of the Richard Commission's independence of mind. In deliberations on the future governance of Wales, a technocratic concept such as 'optimum efficiency' should not be allowed to crowd out a basic democratic principle like accountability.[29]

The general admonition to 'consider the sufficiency of the Assembly's current powers' was predictable on two fronts: as an obvious starting-place, and as a clear political steer. So typical of much in Welsh devolution, the concern not 'to frighten the horses' is communicated strongly here. Constitution-building shrouded in detail: it will also be seen linking forward to the particular methodology or way of proceeding adopted by the Richard Commission.

To pursue the theme, there are an unwarranted number of ambiguities and imperfections. By way of illustration, 'a clear and separate Welsh agenda' is an eminently contestable concept: one that is liable not only to divide the political parties but also in the case of different policy portfolios to change over time. *The Learning Country* is an admirable example. To anticipate the argument, what are considered 'adequate' powers today may be little more than a snapshot in view of the (growing) momentum of devolved govern-ment. As prevention is proverbially better than cure, so a good dose of prospective or forward-looking constitutional development – fixing powers in advance – can be seen here as more 'efficient' than the ongoing allocation of powers via primary legislation ('every bill a devolution bill').

Turning to the exercise of 'a voice for Wales', the formulation begs the question of what is 'the Assembly'. From extravagant version of the corporate body to a 'virtual' parliament: the ministers and the representatives at large are not exactly equally placed in the 'arrangements for influence'. Whether – or more accurately in what circumstances – 'they correct any apparent shortcoming' in the devolved powers admits in turn of different answers. Turning the argument round, on what evidential basis is the Richard Commission to determine 'whether the mechanisms for UK Government policy-making as regards Wales . . . are clear and effective'?

The reference to 'inappropriate constraints on Whitehall policy-making' is difficult to follow. Constraint on central government is of the essence of the constitutional policy of devolution, both in terms of the allocation of functions and the agreed practices of consultation etc. in intergovernmental relations, and further in the evident potential for policy 'slop-over'. It may appeal in certain quarters, but the idea of little Wales somehow exercising an undue influence over UK ministers under the scheme of executive devolution is best described as fanciful. Suffice it to add that the Wales Office, appearing here on behalf of the UK government, effectively declared itself nonplussed.[30]

In summary, this is another poor start in Welsh devolution. In turn, one key test of the Richard Commission is the extent to which the members choose to depart from the official specification, and more especially to add to it. In view of the powerful autochthonous development, the fate of the corporate body will be seen as the most obvious appendage.

Methodology – 'chasing a receding bus'

In the words of the commission, it 'is keen to take a very practical approach – focusing on detailed examples of how things work at the moment and how they could be improved. It intends to base its conclusions on evidence of the practical implications of the powers currently delegated to the Assembly.'[31]

Who, it might be asked, could object? Standing for modification in the light of experience, the methodology can be said to fit with the strong pragmatic and evolutionary bent in Welsh devolution. Again, it serves to highlight the political realities; the fact that reform is not in the gift of the commission, or indeed of the Assembly. Perhaps it is worth adding that with a view to winning the favour of UK ministers, for example on behalf of legislative devolution, one would expect to see considerable stress on the positive aspects of the current constitutional scheme, as well as on the sources of instability etc. Rubbing noses in it is not always the most persuasive of tactics!

Surprise, surprise: the Secretary of State for Wales has underscored the general theme. According to Peter Hain, 'any case for primary legislation amending the Welsh devolution settlement so soon after it was established would . . . have to demonstrate very clear, practical improvements in delivery of public services to the people of Wales'.[32]

But let us look more closely. This kind of 'very practical approach' is onerous and time-consuming and, further, is naturally susceptible to a failure to see the wood for the trees. It is then worth recording that the Richard Commission has no dedicated team of researchers or commissioned research programme, and no special advisers to assist in the vital tasks of clearing the ground, formulating the awkward questions and modelling the various constitutional alternatives. Provided instead with a tiny civil service secretariat, this independent commission has been left very dependent on official lines of advice and information. To this effect, asking individuals and organizations to write in with their personal experiences of dealing with the devolved administration[33] is no substitute for a serious methodology of evidence-based decision-making.

Attention naturally focuses on the evidence of Assembly ministers and officials. Behind the scenes Lord Richard has been busy orchestrating this, with the aim of building up a detailed picture in respect of each policy portfolio. Indeed, a little cottage industry has developed inside the devolved administration, tasked with answering questions like: 'are there areas of policy where responsibilities are divided between the Assembly and White-hall in ways which have (a) worked well (b) presented practical problems?'[34] True to form, the resulting product is for the most part determinedly unexceptional: very much a case of 'nuts and bolts'. An ignoble thought perhaps, but in the period immediately preceding Assembly elections how frank and open would one expect ministers to be?

Again, given the nature of the subject matter, the Assembly cabinet could not be expected to speak with one voice in the conditions of partnership government. Whereas in the initial submissions Labour colleagues generally adhered to the line of little by way of a pinching shoe, the Liberal Democrat element gave the impression of feeling more constrained.[35] This in turn is a valuable clue. The attempt by the Richard Commission to generate evidence-based recommendations cannot disguise the chief role in the constitution-building process of political judgement. How could it be otherwise, especially in the case of national devolution?

These are early days, not least for determining 'the practical implications of the powers currently delegated to the Assembly'. A simple exposé of the method, vital testimony cannot be given concerning executive devolution in the conditions of political 'cohabitation'. It is also well to remember that these ministers are relatively inexperienced. Not only is the legal constraint involved in the scheme of executive devolution liable to be felt more keenly in some policy portfolios than in others,[36] but it is also apt to feature less prominently in a formative period when the new institution is finding its feet. Looking forwards, it is a fact of political life that the devolved administration will develop greater ambitions in the pursuit of local policy priorities: as the short history of the Welsh Assembly Government itself serves to highlight. To this effect, the Richard Commission has the responsibility not to go for 'a quick fix' but to look at the matter more long-term, with a view to ensuring that the devolved administration is not unduly constrained now and in the years to come. As every parent knows, with shoe-size it is best to be generous.

Put another way, it is no criticism to say of the devolved administration of today that it is not the devolved administration of tomorrow. Indeed, such is the logic of the wide-ranging programme of structural and organizational reform now put in place by the Permanent Secretary, as also his confident prediction of a step change in policy-making and delivery in the medium term. Put simply, in following its 'very practical approach', the Richard Commission must beware chasing a receding bus.

This is not to advocate some abstract exercise in constitutional imagination, far removed from the mundane realities of executive devolution etc. To make an impact, the commission's recommendations have got to be grounded in fact, as well as being workable and realistic. At the same time, for the reasons explained, it does not do to be too prosaic. Another key challenge or test of the Richard Commission is identified: a judicious blending of present and future, of the administrative, political and legal, and – yes – constitutional practice and theory. Especially with a view to 'selling' major reform, to proceed otherwise is to risk short-changing Wales.

Tiny footnote?

Reading the runes is never easy. It would in fact be classic inquiry-type methodology for the Richard Commission to (be seen to) start cautiously and then to broaden out or become emboldened. Again, the more that the members look at comparative constitutional experience, the more likely it is that a different form of devolutionary scheme will be recommended. Such is the logic of the argument made in earlier chapters concerning insularity in the original decision-making process.

It is important to keep in mind here the scale of the autochthonous development. In one respect – the rise of a system of parliamentary government – the Richard Commission is being asked to do little more than tick the box: to deliver the formal death warrant of the corporate body. In fact, one of the most striking features of the commission's early work is the extent of the departure from the official terms of reference. Questions of internal architecture and working arrangements have been given priority along with those of powers and electoral arrangements; and rightly so, in the cause of a more rounded or holistic approach to constitution-building for Wales.

But further, the role of autochthonous development in preparing the ground for a scheme of legislative devolution can scarcely be ignored. To reiterate, from 'virtual' parliament to a real one exercising primary powers: it will not appear such a great leap for Wales. And the more so, it may be said, in view of the various hoops and obstacles – instabilities – that are now seen to exist in the present constitutional dispensation. Suffice it to add that eighteen months is a long time to labour for a tiny footnote in Welsh history. One is entitled to expect a major contribution.

3. OF PRIMARY POWERS ETC.

Declaring oneself in favour of legislative devolution for Wales is the easy part. Primary powers may be 'the big issue',[37] but all at one with the retarded development of a distinctive public law tradition there has been a noticeable lack of concrete proposals. Courtesy of the Richard Commission it is now time to help put this right.[38]

The wheel in one sense has come full circle. The simplistic dichotomy between 'legislative' and 'executive' devolution was seen in the Introduction to this book to have bedevilled the constitutional debate in Wales. The emphasis there was on the existence of different or competing models of executive devolution; the scope both for development and conflict inside the broad framework of the GWA that has now been more than amply demonstrated in the short history of the Assembly. So too, it is important now to think in terms of alternative models of legislative devolution, more or less generous, complete or phased. There is once again a rich tapestry of choice for Wales under the general rubric.

But further, the standard dichotomy is apt to imply that legislative devolution and executive devolution are mutually exclusive. In fact, for reasons that will be explained, one can expect to see not only a mixed system of primary and secondary competencies for Wales, but also one in which the secondary competencies or strictly ministerial powers feature prominently. To this effect, the Richard Commission has had more on its plate than is commonly imagined: not just 'whether', or even 'how much' legislative devolution, but also how to integrate the different kinds of legal power in a proper devolution settlement for Wales.

Perhaps it is worth adding a word about possible nomenclature in the event of a generous slice of primary powers. Generally understood, and suitably high in status, the official title of 'Welsh Parliament' would have much to commend it. Then again, the nomenclature of 'National Assembly for Wales' would properly reflect the strong element of continuity in the devolutionary development, and is itself hardly antithetical to the idea of legislative devolution. What one would expect to see however, on the basis of a proper form of parliamentary government or separate set of ministers drawn from and accountable to the representative institution, is a 'Welsh Executive'.

Scottish itinerary

On the principle of not reinventing the wheel, the obvious starting-point is Scotland. The Scotland Act 1998 and associated instruments provide much of the legal technology that is required to sustain an effective scheme of legislative devolution as illustrated in figure 18. As well as modification to take account of local conditions, this can now be fine-tuned in the light of experience, a distinct benefit for Wales.

Naturally there are many 'jagged edges' in Scottish devolution.[39] As well as the full panoply of 'general reservations' to central government, such as the constitution and public service, and defence and foreign affairs, Schedule 5 to the Act contains a much longer list of 'specific reservations'. Relevant topics range from financial and economic matters to home affairs, and on through social security and employment to trade and industry and energy. Meanwhile, Schedule 4 protects certain enactments from modification by the Scottish Parliament, not least the chief provisions of the devolution statute (local entrenchment). Nonetheless, and especially for those of us brought up on Welsh devolution, it is the basic simplicity of the model that shines through, as premised on the twin categories of 'devolved' and 'reserved' functions. And the more so, it is important to add, because of the pro-devolutionary presumption that power passes unless reserved, which is designed to promote clarity and stability.[40]

Assuming then a major tranche of primary powers, certain features are natural candidates for inclusion in a 'Wales Act'. The battery of devices for securing constitutional compliance by the Parliament, for example by means of the prior scrutiny of Bills, has already been mentioned. To this effect, some of the provisions would be entirely new for Wales, not least the ringing declaration that legislative devolution 'does not affect the power of the Parliament of the United Kingdom to make laws for Wales',[41] while others would effectively be retreads from the GWA. A different but related point: parliamentary draftsmen would no doubt read across the interpretative guidance to courts contained in the Scotland Act, a limiting provision officially designed to enable the judges to give effect to the Parliament's legislation, wherever possible, rather than invalidate it.[42] Legislative devolution, Welsh actors would do well to remember, is also about the legal tools and techniques associated with the transfer of powers.

The matter can be taken forward in several ways. First, the main 'horizontal' restrictions on devolved competencies – territorial limitation, EU obligations, Convention Rights – obviously would apply in Wales irrespective of the style of further empowerment. However, under a suitably generous model, one would also expect to see them grouped Scottish-style around the core concept of the 'legislative competence' of the national representative body.[43]

Secondly, the kind of constitutional flexibility that is shown in the allocation of legislative powers to Scotland would need to be replicated for Wales. To this effect, primary powers can be added or taken away by (ministerial) Order in Council, in either case with the consent of the Parliament as well as Westminster.[44] At first sight this may appear unexceptional, machinery for the transfer of minor matters or administrative fine-tuning in the light of

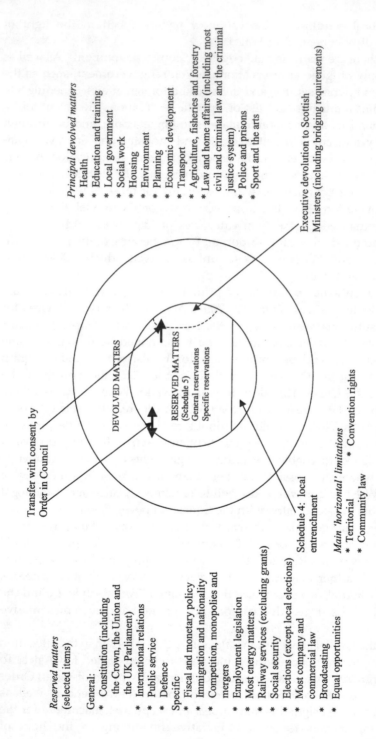

Reserved matters
(selected items)

General:

* Constitution (including
  the Crown, the Union and
  the UK Parliament)
* International relations
* Public service
* Defence

Specific

* Fiscal and monetary policy
* Immigration and nationality
* Competition, monopolies and
  mergers
* Employment legislation
* Most energy matters
* Railway services (excluding grants)
* Social security
* Elections (except local elections)
* Most company and
  commercial law
* Broadcasting
* Equal opportunities

Transfer with consent, by
Order in Council

DEVOLVED MATTERS

RESERVED MATTERS
(Schedule 5)
General reservations
Specific reservations

Schedule 4: local
entrenchment

Main 'horizontal' limitations
* Territorial   * Convention rights
* Community law

Principal devolved matters

* Health
* Education and training
* Local government
* Social work
* Housing
* Environment
* Planning
* Economic development
* Transport
* Agriculture, fisheries and forestry
* Law and home affairs (including most
  civil and criminal law and the criminal
  justice system)
* Police and prisons
* Sport and the arts

Executive devolution to Scottish
Ministers (including bridging requirements)

++ For the avoidance of doubt the models used in this chapter for Scottish and Northern Ireland devolution are designed for comparative purposes,
with a view to Welsh constitutional development. Many local complexities are passed over.

Figure 18: Legislative devolution in Scotland – reserved and devolved powers

experience. Yet it could so easily have a special resonance in the case of Wales, as one of a number of techniques by which the Assembly grows into legislative maturity. Perhaps hopefully, however, the idea that the new representative body should 'crawl' before it 'walks', and so begin with primary powers in only a few areas such as housing, local government and education, or even aspects of them, will be regarded as too restrictive.[45]

Thirdly, and proceeding on the basis of parliamentary government, with powers conferred separately on the National Assembly and the 'Welsh Executive',[46] following the Scottish example and allowing for different ambits or scale of coverage would be of critical importance. To explicate, the Scotland Act works from a simple starting-point, by initially equating the 'devolved competence' of ministers to the 'legislative competence' of the Parliament.[47] In other words, the areas on which it is competent for the Parliament to legislate – health for example – are the areas within which the ministers can exercise their powers, including the making of subordinate legislation. Flexibility however has once again been factored into the model, via a general power to transfer additional functions to Scottish ministers by Order in Council, as also to rework UK functions as concurrent ones or subject to consent or consultation requirements.[48] In the event, this form of 'decoupling' is no minor matter. Reflecting the many demands and complexities of multi-layered governance, the devolution White Paper clearly signalled the intention of Whitehall to transfer extensive executive powers to Scottish ministers, as shown now across a wide range of functions, for example in relation to the police, transport and energy.[49]

Returning to Wales, the matter once again has a particular significance. By reason of the narrower core of 'legislative competence' that the National Assembly is likely to inherit, a corralling of ministers' powers inside the boundary would severely curtail Welsh devolution. Effectively, much 'width' would have been traded for some more 'depth'. So also the powerful 'England and Wales' administrative paradigm suggests a generous use of the Scottish-style power to develop concurrent powers and consent provisions for the benefit of the Assembly: what I have called 'bridging provisions'.

The Richard Commission, it may be supposed, and certainly the Welsh Labour Party, will not go for 'the full Monty' of the Scottish model. Nonetheless, with a view to some form of legislative devolution for Wales, some vital lessons have been gleaned here, including the concept of a mixed system of legislative and executive devolution.

Northern Ireland excursion

Now let us journey to Belfast. The Northern Ireland Act 1998 contains not two but three categories of primary legislative power, as illustrated in figure 19. The

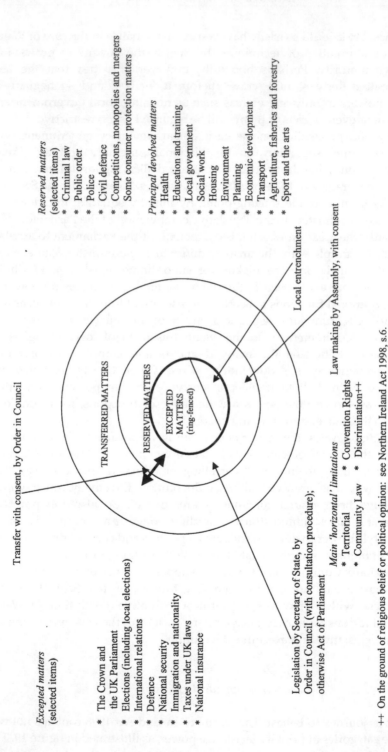

Excepted matters
(selected items)

* The Crown and
  the UK Parliament
* Elections (including local elections)
* International relations
* Defence
* National security
* Immigration and nationality
* Taxes under UK laws
* National insurance

Transfer with consent, by Order in Council

TRANSFERRED MATTERS

RESERVED MATTERS

EXCEPTED
MATTERS
(ring-fenced)

Local entrenchment

Law making by Assembly, with consent

Legislation by Secretary of State, by
Order in Council (with consultation procedure);
otherwise Act of Parliament

Main 'horizontal' limitations

* Territorial   * Convention Rights
* Community Law   * Discrimination++

++ On the ground of religious belief or political opinion: see Northern Ireland Act 1998, s.6.

Reserved matters
(selected items)

* Criminal law
* Public order
* Police
* Civil defence
* Competitions, monopolies and mergers
* Some consumer protection matters

Principal devolved matters

* Health
* Education and training
* Local government
* Social work
* Housing
* Environment
* Planning
* Economic development
* Transport
* Agriculture, fisheries and forestry
* Sport and the arts

Figure 19: Legislative devolution in Northern Ireland – excepted, reserved and transferred powers

'excepted matters' listed in Schedule 2 of the Act broadly mirror the 'reserved matters' of the Scottish legislation as the things of UK-wide concern that are for central government.[50] Notably, however, this first main category is also ring-fenced, in the sense of no power of transfer by Order in Council. An Act of Parliament would be necessary. As regards the second category – the 'reserved matters' listed in Schedule 3 – these in fact are matters on which the Assembly can legislate, but only with the consent of the Secretary of State and Westminster.[51] Turning this round, the devolution statute retains in part the (much-criticized) method whereby the Secretary of State can legislate for reserved matters by way of Order in Council, although subject now to consultation with the Assembly.[52] The third category of 'transferred matters', where the Assembly enjoys full primary powers, comprises all other matters. As one would expect, this is more narrowly drawn than its functional equivalent of 'devolved matters' under the Scotland Act.

Attention naturally focuses on the distinctive middle category, where flexibility is a crucial element. By means of an Order in Council, and with the consent of the Assembly, any reserved matter can be made a transferred matter, and vice versa.[53] Perhaps it hardly needs saying that this relates to the 'peace process' in Northern Ireland, whereby such sensitive and vital matters as public order and policing, as well as the criminal law, can be the subject of transfer if things go well; a significant inducement.[54] Yet there is more to it than this. It may be for example that a reserved matter is not envisaged as suitable for transfer. Placing such a matter in this category preserves the flexibility for the Assembly to legislate on it, which may be useful say in relation to 'cross-cutting issues', as also to transfer parts of it, if for example administrative circumstances change.

From a Welsh perspective, the general idea of a flexible intermediate category is one that could be read across. Building on the practical experience of making subordinate legislation, as also of inputs into the law-making process at Westminster, and constructed on the basis of the Assembly expanding into new or additional areas, there would thus be established another framework for organic change. To this effect, allowing the Assembly to make particular pieces of statute law would give Members and officials the opportunity to acquire the skills and refine the procedures necessary for drawing up, processing and implementing primary legislation in these fields.

To adapt the famous saying: legislative devolution is visualized here 'as a process, not an event'. Effectively a 'map' would be provided of the areas that over time the Assembly could be expected to colonize for the purposes of exercising primary law-making powers. In turn, during what would then be 'phased' or 'rolling' devolution, one could envisage generous use of framework legislation, with a view to thickening up Assembly competencies in the relevant fields, as also special efforts at enhancing the policy-making capacity etc. of the relevant parts of the local administrative machine. To summarize, if (as may well be the case) the powers-that-be consider that full-sized legislative devolution is too much for the Assembly to swallow all at once, then Northern Ireland too offers up some useful comparative lessons in constitutional design.

'For Wales see Wales'

In tune with the sense of autochthonous development that has infused this volume, one would envisage a model of legislative devolution for Wales that is sensitive both to the historical factors and (emergent) forms of local political culture, while not being too hidebound by the practical experience of executive devolution. More especially, let us hope that the Richard Commission does not spend so much time dotting the i's and crossing the t's that it too fails to articulate a clear sense of constitutional vision.

This concern has a very practical dimension. As every public lawyer knows, one of the great traps when constitution-building is to be overly prescriptive. One need look no further than the Scotland Act 1978, which in seeking to divide powers into watertight compartments, and in striving (list-style) after legal certainty, set out a rigid and highly complex scheme. In contrast, and not least in the contemporary conditions of multi-layered governance, as characterized by overlapping competencies and innovative techniques of administration, what is wanted for Wales is a designedly more flexible arrangement, one that is robust because it is more supple.

A prime concern must be to identify those areas of public policy where Wales could usefully enjoy a substantial legislative space, so allowing for greater sensitivity to local conditions. Perhaps then it is not surprising to find the idea of the differential impact of primary powers featuring prominently in the official evidence to the commission.[55] The varying importance of legislation as an implementation tool across the different policy portfolios clearly is a major consideration, including for the purpose of a 'phased' approach to a scheme of legislative devolution.

It is, however, important not to lose sight of the parallel need for a manageable and generally comprehensible constitutional arrangement. This is not to advocate a simplistic form of coordinate jurisdiction, a devolutionary analogue to so-called 'layer-cake federalism',[56] in the sense of a few basic dividing lines. Rather, the argument reflects the contemporary history of Welsh devolution, the way in which, in 'an affair of the elite', official concerns have been prioritized over the idea of 'a people's constitution'. By this is meant a set of arrangements more in tune with the radical political traditions of Wales, in the sense of being tolerably clear and understandable to the local electorate, more especially as regards basic lines of accountability and responsibility. Concurrency of powers is often a vital element, not least these days in the face of the European Union, but the would-be constitution-maker for Wales should beware sowing unnecessary confusion.

As a way of approaching the task, the sketching of a broad constitutional design, one which establishes general parameters and identifies chief parts of the machinery, has much to commend it. To this effect, in line with much comparative experience, the provision of ample space for organic growth and development inside a (newly established) robust framework – the idea of a viable Welsh 'constitution' as a living law – is of the essence of the matter. With a view to allowing local actors to breathe more freely, it is time now to reverse one of the chief paradoxes of Welsh devolution:[57] no longer weak powers and great legal paraphernalia, but more legislative autonomy and less statutory fuss.

For the less brave-hearted

Designed from the viewpoint of the less brave-hearted, figure 20 charts one possible way forward. Pinning colours to the mast, this is not the author's preferred option, which – as discussed below – is a single and generous constitutional instrument premised on a sustainable settlement and generally clear lines of political responsibility and accountability from the outset.

Incorporating ideas from Scotland and Northern Ireland, this 'mark I' model tailors local constitutional advancement to increasing political and administrative capacities – a major theme of this volume – and so picks up on the familiar refrain (at least in Welsh Labour Party circles) of 'walking before running'. To this effect, it highlights the narrow equation in so much of the contemporary public discussion in Wales of 'legislative devolution' with 'the Scottish model'; and, further, the way in which a creative use of constitutional technique can help to calm local fears of legal and administrative indigestion. Put simply, the design explodes the idea that in the name of good governance it is premature for Wales to adopt a brand of legislative devolution.

- *'Reserved matters'*

The core list of reserved matters presents little difficulty. With minor exceptions, perhaps related to the language, it is idle at this stage of the constitutional development to reckon on a Welsh scheme of legislative devolution that does not entail the catalogue of general and specific reservations set out in the Scotland Act 1998. That is to say: not only the classic state functions like defence and international relations, or the complex web of 'the welfare state' that is social security, but also a great swathe of the regulatory activities that characterize modern government, such as employment legislation and consumer protection. Nor is a Welsh law of treason seriously in prospect!

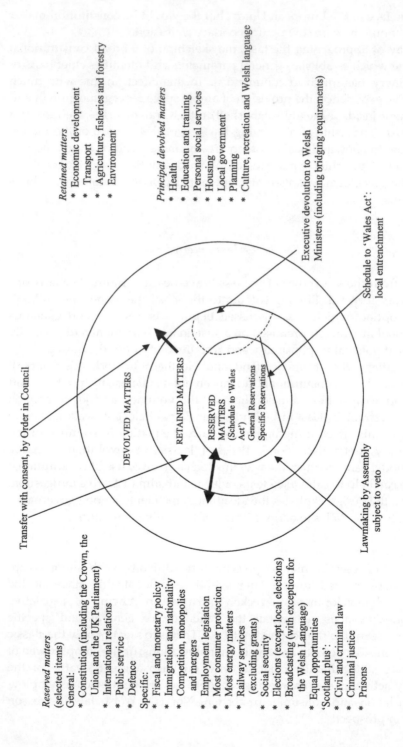

Figure 20: 'Mark I' legislative devolution for Wales – reserved, retained and devolved powers

The key issue is the additions to the catalogue. The overarching unity of the legal system of England and Wales has to be factored into the equation. Reflecting a particular territorial history, so different in this regard from Scotland, matters of general civil and criminal law are natural candidates for inclusion in an expanded Welsh list of reserved matters. Why, it may be asked, would Wales wish to opt out of such a highly developed form of jurisdiction?[58] A different but related point: perhaps one day the Assembly government will wish to have responsibility for the prisons, as also for the criminal justice system at large. Now and for the foreseeable future, however, there are many more immediate priorities.

The by now familiar devolutionary machinery of transfer with consent by Order in Council should clearly be available for the purposes of administrative adaptation and fine-tuning. Meanwhile, the further development of institutional machinery for 'cross-border' workings in ways that promote greater sensitivity to local conditions – what I call 'voices for Wales'[59] – is seen here as an integral part of the central government element in the constitutional design. From the 'Benefits Agency in Wales' to Assembly-sponsored appointees on particular UK quangos, with a little administrative imagination there is so much that can be done to thicken the idea of 'bringing government closer to the people' in the reinvented Union state. In this sense too, devolution is not just about law-making powers.

The issue also arises of local entrenchment, the preservation of certain fundamentals in the new 'constitution' of Wales. A 'Wales Act' that devolved broad legislative competence, including in a phased way, could thus be expected to follow 'the Celtic cousins' by guarding against modification by the Assembly of measures like the European Communities Act 1972 and the Human Rights Act 1998, as well as its own chief provisions.[60] Take Assembly elections for example, presupposing at least an element of proportional representation. A vital constitutional guarantee, given Labour Party dominance in Wales, the devolved legislature would be explicitly denied the powers to change the electoral system.[61]

- *'Devolved matters'*

One would not expect to see the devolved matters specified on the face of a 'Wales Act'. A useful exercise in constitutional symmetry, Wales should be treated as no different in this regard from Scotland and Northern Ireland, the presumption being that – unless stated otherwise – powers pass. This sits comfortably with the doctrine of parliamentary sovereignty, since Westminster can reclaim residuary powers which acquire UK significance, and further with the idea of evolutionary development which infuses the model, the sense that Wales should now enjoy the fruits of flexibility and room for growth.

As for possible subject areas, the Richard Commission does not have far to look. The original schedule of fields of devolved competencies in the GWA rounds up the usual suspects.[62] Health and Education and Training head the list. Both areas are seen to be at the heart of distinctive Welsh policy-making post-devolution, linked in turn to novel Wales-only provisions in primary legislation. A peculiar demography and entrenched patterns of disadvantage, and in the case of education a considerable history of Welsh policy-making, points firmly in the direction of greater diversity and adaptation to local conditions, over and above what Assembly ministers currently contemplate.[63] Primary legislative powers, to underpin the administrative room for manoeuvre and obviate the need for reliance on Westminster, and more especially – including from a Labour viewpoint – to provide a constitutional guarantee of the traditional principles of the NHS in Wales, can be seen as a natural development here.

Legislative devolution of this kind suggests not only a 'deepening' of devolved competencies but also a 'widening', with additional items being made Assembly responsibilities on the basis of the subject area classification. In turn, the issue is raised of specific reservations, which no doubt the Richard Commission will have to grapple with on a case-by-case basis. By way of example, there clearly are good arguments for devolving powers relating to the pay and conditions of teachers as part of an integrated framework of educational policy in Wales, a point highlighted by the kerfuffle on this topic in the days of Alun Michael.[64] But will they prove sufficient to carry the day?

What, it may be asked, of areas such as housing and personal social services? Once again, full statutory powers would sit comfortably with the basic constitutional ideas of responsibility and accountability on this major interface of the citizen and the administration. In the First Minister's words, 'check against delivery'. But there is more to it than this. The practical experience of devolved government can now be said to have greatly strengthened the argument, by demonstrating the increased potential for flexible and responsive approaches to policy development and implementation that range across departmental lines. Health and housing for example: it is now of the essence of the emergent forms of Welsh governance that such matters run together as part of an overarching theme like social inclusion. Better to secure a rounded development of what I have called the Welsh Assembly Government's policy map or *mappa mundi*, a blocking-up of formal legal powers across the more traditional categories of public administration is thus seen as a useful next step.

Another leading candidate for inclusion in the list of devolved matters is introduced. Local government in Wales is seen today as the principal delivery agent of Assembly policies across a broad swathe of public service provision, including by reason of more traditional Labour policies in fields like education and housing. From this it follows that the devolved administration now funds local government expenditure to a very considerable extent, as well as being engaged with the principal authorities at many different levels.[65]

But further, the partnership-style relations of this democratically elected tier with the new devolved administration are seen at the heart of a distinctive form of political and administrative culture now emergent in 'the new model Wales'. For its part, in the face of this autochthonous development, Westminster appears increasingly remote.

Full primary powers, constructed with a view to the Assembly establishing and reworking relevant legal frameworks in close dialogue with local government, can thus be seen as a valuable tool, one which reflects and reinforces the many administrative advantages of flexibility in this little country. In fact, on the constitutional front, many of the key items already fall within Assembly jurisdiction: internal structures, electoral arrangements and boundaries, etc. One would now expect to see full legal integration as part of – and recognition for – a new and distinctive system of Welsh governance.

Planning is a more difficult case. For the purpose of a fully mature scheme of legislative devolution, it clearly should come within the purview of transferred matters as a prime field for greater sensitivity and understanding of local conditions. If 'bringing government closer to the people' does not entail land use, what is it for? Supposing however that the powers-that-be were minded to go for a phased scheme, then this subject area could sensibly be assigned along with local government, where there are very close administrative connections, or left with the environment and transport etc. as one of the 'retained matters'. On balance, and factoring into the equation the weight of experience that the local civil service has in this particular field, as well as the contemporary significance of statutory reform as illustrated in the Planning and Compulsory Purchase Bill,[66] it is listed here as a devolved matter. In this case, the Welsh Assembly Government already is jogging.

Meanwhile, items such as 'culture, recreation and Welsh language' speak for themselves. Fingered in an earlier age by the Kilbrandon Commission,[67] it is inconceivable that a scheme of legislative devolution for Wales would not include them. If the Assembly cannot be trusted with full legislative responsibilities for such matters, which bear so directly on the 'particularity' or national identity of Wales, what sensibly can it do?

- *'Retained matters'*

Turning to the possible intermediate category, the novel terminology of 'retained matters' is deliberately chosen. At one and the same time, it leaves 'reserved matters' as the functional Welsh equivalent to reserved matters in the Scotland Act, and conveys the spirit of the classification as a 'map' of prospective devolutionary developments and/or facility for Assembly statute-making subject to veto by Westminster.[68] Again, while the model clearly draws inspiration from Northern Ireland, the terminology carefully marks the difference.[69]

Turning to the substance, a cluster of matters can be identified which could sensibly be made the subjects of retained powers. The orientation is distinctively economic in flavour, in contrast to the front-line service provision for the people of Wales that predominates in the category for immediate transfer under the phased model. A different but related point: the EU dimension figures prominently here. To anticipate the argument, along with other forms of secondary powers, the category of retained powers would accommodate the use by the putative 'Welsh Executive' of the important function of implementation of EU obligations that arises from the designation of the devolved administration under the European Communities Act 1972. The phased model, it is worth repeating, is about 'walking' and not retrenchment or 'sitting back'.

Economic development is the archetypal case. As a policy area, it is seen to be of the essence of the Welsh devolutionary development, a chief motor of constitutional change.[70] But further, it reflects and reinforces the importance of alternative policy levers in the effective conduct of governance. Looking to the legal base, economic development powers in Westminster legislation are classically drafted in broad terms. A range of administrative activity is authorized – grants etc. – with comparatively little in the way of subordinate law-making powers. In practice, since the economic development powers have generally been transferred to or made exercisable by the Assembly in respect of Wales, the chief constraint is the need for compliance with the overarching (EU) regulatory framework on state aid.[71]

To this effect, for those preferring to 'walk' first with a view to building up legislative and administrative experience, economic development does not cry out for the immediate grant of general primary powers. Of course there may be particular items where a measure of Assembly statute law would be useful; on the basis of the phased model this would be possible with the acquiescence of Westminster. After all, if the standard of intergovernmental relations is generally as good as Assembly ministers say, the potential for conflict is more imagined than real. It is then worth emphasizing that the technique would have the considerable practical merit of bypassing the logjam that is the UK government's legislative programme.

Then there is the closely related field of transport. As well as the power of the purse, planning functions and in particular secondary powers of strategic direction feature prominently here. It should also be recognized that this is a particularly challenging policy area for the devolved administration, not least by reason of the many 'cross-border' connotations associated with a geographical and historical context of predominantly 'east–west' links. As illustration, the recent establishment of a 'Wales and the Borders' rail passenger franchise is a textbook example of both the scope and demand for new organizational patterns and service priorities in the light of national devolution, and the need for proper representation and protection of interests in England.[72]

This is not a legislative competence that Whitehall will let go easily, and for understandable reasons. The fact that at the time of writing there are no published proposals to implement the Assembly's request for a Passenger Transport Bill[73] allowing the creation of a Wales passenger transport executive may also be taken to illustrate the sensitivities. In this context, bringing transport under the rubric of retained powers can be seen as a way of establishing a more genuine 'legislative partnership', a formal framework for a maturing political and administrative culture post-devolution of give-and-take, as the Assembly gains in experience.

Legislative 'space' is seen in especially short supply in the field of agriculture, fisheries and forestry. As the saga of GM seeds reminds us, EU requirements are never far away.[74] Again, by the nature of these sectors, the law making is not only subject to the strong pull of uniformity, but also tends to be geared towards the regulatory end of the spectrum, a feature sadly highlighted by the mass of Assembly subordinate legislation in relation to foot and mouth disease.[75] So in this sphere particularly, primary legislative powers may be considered a less pressing priority than certain key executive powers transferable by other means. Indeed, it is in the area of rural affairs that the concept of 'retained matters' may be said to come into its own, since particular local requirements should be capable of being accommodated via the special facility for Assembly statute-making.

Much the same can be said of the environment as a policy area, which tends in any case to be very closely related in Wales with rural issues. In fact, the way in which the EU dimension is likely to take on increased importance here as an effective source of devolved powers, in view of the fashion at supra-national level for strengthened techniques of decentralized governance,[76] must be a chief consideration for the Richard Commission. Often it may not be primary powers but designation for the purpose of a 'framework directive' that is the holy grail for the devolved administration in the guise of Euro-style 'regional' government.

Let us be clear. Wales is seen starting in 1997 from a long way back, constitutionally, legally and administratively. In seeking to accommodate this historical fact, the idea of a stepped approach needs to be cast firmly in the positive mould of building up official strengths, as distinct from the view that Wales – the Assembly – somehow has 'to prove itself' in order to win further constitutional advancement. 'Liberty does not descend to a people. A people must raise themselves to liberty. It is a blessing that must be earned before it can be enjoyed.' Wales deserves better in 2003 than the devolutionary equivalent of the condescending words famously inscribed on the colonial architecture of New Delhi in the twilight of empire.

Going direct

So much for the lesser alternative of phased legislative devolution: there are in fact many good reasons for going direct. The vagaries of political life can scarcely be ignored: if legislative devolution for Wales cannot be implemented smoothly and effectively in the conditions of Labour Party hegemony, when could it be? Then there is the issue of administrative timing. As an allowance for building up official strengths, a transitional period of, say, ten years should be more than sufficient. Alternatively, however, the leisurely timetable associated with the Richard Commission could now be turned to advantage, with the aim of ensuring that the relevant business structures and processes are in place for an entire scheme of legislative devolution.

Considerations of constitutional design point firmly in this direction. The concept of legislative space, at root the idea that the new devolved polity is able to develop its own policy agenda according to its own priorities and values, obviously is an elastic one. From time to time, difficult questions are bound to arise as to whether the Assembly has jurisdiction to legislate on particular matters differently from Westminster. But these are liable to be more pronounced the more narrowly the devolved primary powers are expressed. The wider the range of powers, and the more broadly they are drawn, the less likely that constitutionally enervating boundary disputes are likely to arise. A cleaner and more generous cut – a constitutional design premised on reducing the legislative grit in the political and administrative system – should appeal to the happy Welsh unionist.[77]

A new and positive dimension must be factored into the equation, courtesy of the Welsh Assembly Government. The genuine effort that is being made to take advantage of the conditions of small-country governance, including by reference to all-embracing cross-cutting themes ('the Welsh difference') and to more informal techniques of governance ('the Welsh way'), is a recurring theme in this volume. Clearing away undergrowth, in the form of an unnecessarily tangled web of legal provisions, with the aim of allowing ministers, members and officials to get on with the job in hand, can in turn be seen as a sensible bit of horticulture. Lawyers, it is worth remembering, are rarely heroes.

Take for example the bundle of responsibilities that comes under the headings of the environment, planning and transport. Integrated frameworks of 'joined-up government', which range across many facets of life in Wales, and also entail creative forms of so-called 'partnership working', are a touchstone of postmodern governance under the rubric of sustainable development. There is already a good local story to tell here, and the early devolution of primary legislative powers in these overlapping subject areas clearly would have the benefit of helping to maintain the momentum. Especially, it may be said, if the devolved administration continues to aspire to be a world leader in this most contemporary aspect of comparative public administration.

The status of the Assembly is another important factor here. Given the evident struggle to win the hearts and minds of the people of Wales, going direct has much to commend it in terms of public perception and the general health of the new Welsh polity. A 'real' not a 'virtual' parliament: there would thus be the maximum incentive for popular engagement from the outset. Again, it is worth keeping in mind the fast-moving constitutional and administrative developments in Europe. Wales has been seen punching above its weight, so playing an active role in regional networks alongside more powerful actors like Scotland, let alone Catalunya.[78] There inevitably is, however, a question of positioning.

- *Twin categorization*

'Mark II' legislative devolution for Wales: a more straightforward model would do the job, based Scottish-style on the twin categorization of 'reserved' and 'devolved' matters. The 'retained' matters in the phased Mark I model would thus be subsumed in the general category of Assembly legislative competence. The twin flexibilities of provision for transfer of primary powers and for decoupling ministerial powers (in reserved matters) would again be a major component of the system.

Testament of experience

Turning to the potential statutory outputs, the practical experience of devolution serves once again to strengthen the case for a broad allocation of legislative competence. Attention naturally focuses here on the Westminster bottleneck and the mixed fortunes of Assembly bids for new primary legislation.[79] At the same time, from education to passenger transport and land use planning, and on through audit and the ombudsman to specific (Welsh) items like Sunday licensing, there is already enough to illustrate the growing capacity to initiate and develop proposals for primary legislation. Again, looking forward, the sense in which the legislative freedom to innovate works to generate new ideas is a standard lesson of comparative constitutional development. One does not have to be dewy-eyed about Welsh 'inventiveness' to reckon that much the same will happen at home.

An obvious reference point is the list of Acts of the Scottish Parliament. Naturally some of them, for example on the abolition of feudal tenure, have a strictly Scottish connotation; or otherwise involve matters which would clearly be reserved matters in the case of Wales, such as marriage law and sexual offences, or the jurisdiction of the International Criminal Court.[80] Other titles serve, however, to highlight the greater sense of political purpose and

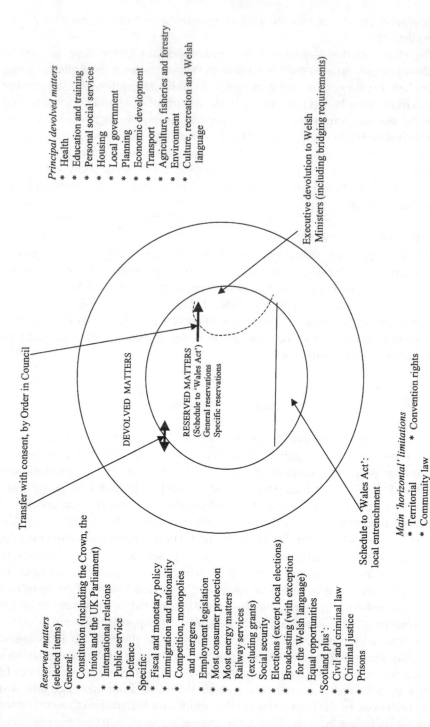

Figure 21: 'Mark II' legislative devolution for Wales – reserved and devolved powers

Reserved matters
(selected items)
General:
* Constitution (including the Crown, the Union and the UK Parliament)
* International relations
* Public service
* Defence
Specific:
* Fiscal and monetary policy
* Immigration and nationality
* Competition, monopolies and mergers
* Employment legislation
* Most consumer protection
* Most energy matters
* Railway services (excluding grants)
* Social security
* Elections (except local elections)
* Broadcasting (with exception for the Welsh language)
* Equal opportunities
'Scotland plus':
* Civil and criminal law
* Criminal justice
* Prisons

Schedule to 'Wales Act':
local entrenchment

Main 'horizontal' limitations
* Territorial   * Convention rights
* Community law

Transfer with consent, by Order in Council

DEVOLVED MATTERS

RESERVED MATTERS
(Schedule to 'Wales Act')
General reservations
Specific reservations

Executive devolution to Welsh Ministers (including bridging requirements)

Principal devolved matters
* Health
* Education and training
* Personal social services
* Housing
* Local government
* Planning
* Economic development
* Transport
* Agriculture, fisheries and forestry
* Environment
* Culture, recreation and Welsh language

democratic involvement that legislative devolution could reasonably be expected to bring to Wales. As well as the Budget (Scotland) Acts, the hallmark of a more mature polity, general reforming legislation in the guise of a Housing Act and a Transport Act can be singled out. To which may be added such diverse measures as an Education (Disability Strategies and Pupils' Records) Act, a Regulation of Care Act, and a Local Authorities (Tendering) Act. This is not Assembly-style 'watching the paint dry'![81]

Another notable feature is a cluster of Scottish statutes concerned with improving and developing the governmental infrastructure; ranging from public finance and accountability to public appointments, and on through the financing of the police and fire services to the ombudsman and the Scottish Qualifications Authority. Suffice it to note that parallel statutory developments in the Assembly would fit with the ongoing drive to enhance the local administrative apparatus and ensure fitness for purpose in 'the closeness of Wales'.[82] Again, the statute book in Scotland contains much that is low-key in character, involving the type of pragmatic and limited measure closely attuned to local conditions that can so easily get lost in the corridors of the metropolis. Illustrations include a National Parks Act, a subject not unimportant in Wales, and legislation on the national galleries, bridge tolls and fish conservation. No doubt Welsh statutes would often be in similar vein, as befits the fact of small-country governance. The very practical dimension to legislative devolution, which tends to be obscured in the high-level constitutional debate, is communicated strongly here.

'Wales's other Parliament' – super-Sewel

Much of the current constitutional debate in Wales proceeds on a false assumption: namely, that having primary law-making functions means exercising them. Westminster need not strain at a generous transfer of powers because the fact is that an Assembly government worth its salt is not going to try to legislate across the board. This, in turn, is another consideration in favour of the Mark II model.

The well-known Sewel Convention developed for Scotland, whereby Whitehall acts on the basis that Westminster 'would not normally legislate with regard to devolved matters except with the agreement of the devolved legislature',[83] is seen here as an essential element in the continuing dynamics of Welsh devolution. That is to say: not only as a protective measure, but also as a major tool for the efficient and effective conduct of legislative business, and further as an important piece of machinery underpinning Welsh constitutional advancement. 'Walking before running', or growing into the part: Sewel would allow a Welsh parliament and government that were properly clothed with primary legislative powers to do precisely this.[84]

To explicate, Westminster legislation for devolved matters in Scotland has been far more frequent than was originally envisaged. In the first three years of its existence, the Scottish Parliament agreed almost as many 'Sewel motions' seeking its consent to such legislation as it enacted bills.[85] The reasons are not difficult to understand. First, there is the strength of the pull towards uniformity in the devolution settlement. The sources of which range from electoral expectations to reliance on UK bodies for the purposes of administration, and on through subject matter that does not lend itself to different regulatory regimes to the need to give effect to international – including EU – obligations. Second, this form of legislative piggybacking may be convenient or attractive to the devolved administration in various ways, including a reliance on central government's unique policy-making capacity, avoiding disruption to the local legislative programme, and more effective 'judge-proofing' (via the doctrine of parliamentary sovereignty). 'Labour in power' in London and (in coalition) in Edinburgh obviously is another factor.

There are powerful echoes here in the law making for Wales under the scheme of executive devolution.[86] But further, one would expect to see the general effect magnified in the case of legislative devolution for Wales. It is not simply that Wales lags far behind Scotland in terms of local developmental capacities. The exceptionally strong geopolitical concept that is 'England and Wales' – a 'pull towards uniformity' unparalleled inside the United Kingdom – could also find free expression in Sewel motions, most obviously in the early years of a putative Welsh parliament.

The point is worth pursuing. In evidence to the Richard Commission, Sir Jon Shortridge has indicated that were the Assembly 'to settle down' to producing no more than four or five important pieces of primary legislation a year, then the local civil service would have the capacity to cope without much further enhancement.[87] As a filtering mechanism, a way of allowing local actors to concentrate on what seem to them to be the real areas of priority, Sewel would come into its own here.

An ever-present danger in the debates on Welsh devolution, and especially at the current stage of constitutional development, is too much emphasis on formal legislative powers. A recurrent theme in this book is the significance of the 'Welsh way', as epitomized in a creative use of alternative policy levers or techniques of governance. Once again, in the words of the Permanent Secretary, 'I would hope that the acquisition of primary legislative powers would not "squeeze out" too much of the administrative and policy ingenuity which is a feature of the present Assembly.'[88] Sewel can also help in this respect.

Then there is the political dimension. Some day, the Welsh Labour Party may learn to appreciate its good fortune. Legislative devolution coupled with Sewel: from the viewpoint of the dominant political force in Wales this could even be described as 'win–win'. Clear blue water or political cohabitation with London

– do your own thing; Labour hegemony – Sewel if you want to. The trick then is to be clear about the use and non-use of the local 'legislative space': to target resources, most obviously on the making of distinctive 'made in Wales' statutes, a category liable to expand in the light of growing policy ambition.[89]

'Super-Sewel' or a strong recourse to Westminster as 'Wales's other parliament': the idea also shows the famed flexibility of the British constitution to good advantage. Precisely because of parliamentary sovereignty, Sewel allows for effective forms of coordination and collaboration – legislative partnership[90] – that are typically more difficult to achieve in federal systems of divided competencies. Members of the Commission should thus take note of the splendid paradox: the way in which a more generous allocation of power to Wales can now be accommodated by reason of the constitutional quality of devolution – in the old phrase – as 'power retained'.

Executive powers: phoenix from the ashes

Legislative devolution, it is well to remember, is not only about primary powers. In fact, implicit in such a scheme for Wales is a major boost to the pre-existing form of law-making activity that is Assembly general subordinate legislation. In particular, and highlighting the interplay of Welsh devolution with the strong administrative paradigm of 'England and Wales', central government has been seen making many regulations applying to Wales in matters of health and education,[91] now identified as the leading candidates for legislative devolution. To the extent that secondary legislative powers follow primary ones, by which is meant the substitution of a unitary competence for the present (highly) fragmented one, local subordinate law-making activity could thus be expected to increase considerably, if only to keep up with England.

'Executive devolution is dead.' 'Long live executive devolution!' Turning the argument round, the Richard Commission could usefully scour the series of Scottish transfer of functions orders with a view to determining which ministerial powers should be allocated to Wales in respect of other reserved functions. In addition, that is, to the many ministerial powers that would remain devolved in those subject areas not yet covered by a scheme of phased legislative devolution ('retained matters'), should that approach command acceptance.

Indeed, what may now be described as the tripartite model of 'decoupling' of executive functions, whereby the outright transfers, the concurrent powers, and the consent or veto and consultation requirements, are listed in successive columns in the Scottish transfer orders, would come into its own here. Take the regulation of the medical professions, previously identified as an important source of central government regulations applying to Wales in the field of health, and also the subject of specific reservation in the Scotland Act.[92] Instead of legislative devolution, or indeed direct subordinate legislative activity by the Assembly in much of this field, one could envisage a creative use of consent provisions etc., so facilitating uniformity while underscoring the authority of the Assembly, most obviously in the official discussions with Whitehall.

It is important to keep in mind that the Scottish-style transfers of functions to ministers operate in one direction.[93] So used in the event of legislative devolution to Wales, they would not hit at the policy made evident in the original Assembly transfer of functions order of limiting the use of consent provisions etc. in favour of the UK government.[94] As a rule of thumb, central government can be left here to its own devices.

As part of a general clean-up exercise, one would expect to see some important anomalies rectified, with a view to allowing Welsh ministers to pursue coherent and rounded policies. Many examples could be given, but two that are topical at the time of writing will suffice. Bizarre as it may seem, the Assembly has not had powers of direction and guidance over the Strategic Rail Authority (SRA) in relation to services in Wales, being relegated instead to the status of a statutory consultee. To quote the all-party Welsh Affairs Select Committee, 'the Assembly cannot pursue an effective integrated transport policy without further powers'.[95] Courtesy of the transfer of functions orders, the Scots in contrast have had their act together, aided by additional resources from 2004 for the funding of local services.[96] To push home the point, this is not a question of legislative devolution, but rather a classic illustration of the mixed system of legislative and executive devolution that now obtains 'north of the border'. The provision and regulation of railway services except for certain grants etc. is thus specifically reserved under the devolution statute.[97]

As every visitor to mid-Wales knows, 'wind farms' are the fashion of the moment. Decision-taking powers for the major projects, those generating fifty-plus megawatts of electricity, currently remain with the UK government. In the anodyne language of officials, this 'raises issues when the Welsh Assembly Government tries to implement a coherent policy on renewable energy'.[98] Whereas energy matters are generally reserved under the devolution statute, the relevant executive powers have been in the hands of Scottish ministers since the dawn of the Parliament.[99]

Secondly, with the development of a primary legislative competence, central government objections to the Assembly exercising broad forms of Henry VIII powers to repeal and amend Westminster statutes would be further undermined. No longer could it be seriously argued for example that the important powers arising under the Regulatory Reform Act 2001 to remove redundant legislation or legislation which imposes unnecessary burdens on businesses etc. should be denied the Assembly. On the basis, that is, of 'equivalence' to the making of new primary legislation and so of 'inconsistency' with the so-called 'devolution settlement'.[100]

The current position is that the Assembly must be consulted on any regulatory reform order that extends to Wales and such an order can be made only with the agreement of the Assembly.[101] It thus illustrates the type of bridging requirements that one would expect to see developed more generally for a 'Welsh Executive', as well as constituting a suitable case for transfer into the category of powers exercised by Welsh ministers, in the event of a 'devolution settlement' worthy of the name. To this effect, primary powers by the Assembly, phased or otherwise, should now be recognized as providing a major opportunity for the qualitative enhancement of devolved secondary powers.

Thirdly, substantial powers for Welsh ministers may be justified in some new areas, by which is meant fields of government activity other than the fields of devolved functions mentioned in the GWA. The policing function is an obvious illustration. A striking feature of the internal political and administrative development, the Welsh Assembly Government has been seen in this book moving rapidly to develop contacts and exercise influence in this sphere under the rubric of cross-cutting themes such as community safety and social inclusion.[102] Funding, which involves the Assembly in channelling grant from central government to the four police forces in Wales, and in controlling their Council Tax precepts, is then the visible element of what is an increasingly large iceberg of working relationships involving both ministers and officials inside the territory. In short, the case for additional powers sits comfortably here with the more holistic approach to policy development and implementation currently being pursued by the devolved administration.

At the same time, however, this is a game of high constitutional stakes. Coinciding with national devolution, there has in fact been a very considerable centralization of the police service in England and Wales, with local forces increasingly under the thumb of the Home Office. Such is the era of a 'National Criminal Justice Board' and a 'National Policing Plan', as also of enhanced New Public Management techniques applied to the police, the familiar paraphernalia of standards, targets and league tables that are centrally driven. The fact that the Assembly is not mentioned in the governing legislation, the Police Reform Act 2002, says much.

The Richard Commission has the nice task of squaring the circle. By reference, that is, to the democratic imperative on the devolved administration to make a difference, not least 'on the streets', and the lack of a secure legal framework for doing so, a situation which in turn raises significant issues of responsibility and accountability in the new Welsh polity. Not forgetting the customary leech-like quality of the Home Office, which no doubt extends to primary legislative power over the police in England and Wales. Politically more feasible, a transfer of functions to Welsh ministers could usefully be targeted on issues of operational policing, for example in the guise of a 'National Policing Plan for Wales' sensitive to local conditions, as also questions of organizational structure such as the 'fit' with the other emergency services.[103] Meanwhile, the general training and back-up services could sensibly continue to be organized on an England and Wales basis, for the standard reasons of economies of scale and cross-fertilization of ideas;[104] as also, if only to placate the police themselves, their pay and conditions. The Richard Commission will need however to keep in mind the financial implications of such transfers of powers, and in particular the coverage of any consequential amendment under the famous 'Barnett' formula.

Enough has been said to show that executive devolution is destined to be a significant part of the constitutional settlement for Wales. To reiterate, legislative and executive devolution are not mutually exclusive, and a mixed system which pays proper regard to the need for political, legislative and administrative space for the new Welsh polity, while respecting the evident demands of geography and history, is now seen as the way forward. Care must be taken, however, not to reinvent the past, in the guise of a particularistic or excessively piecemeal approach to the allocation of executive functions, a requirement that demands especially of the Richard Commission a degree of conceptual rigour, as well as a strong dose of constitutional creativity.

4. CONSTITUTION-BUILDING – RELATED ASPECTS

So much for powers: especially in view of past events, there is now an evident need for a broader and more holistic or integrated approach to constitution-building for Wales. More especially, there is the question of knock-on effects in terms of the Assembly architecture in the light of substantial primary powers. Some elements of redesign would effectively be inescapable – predetermined – while the case for others would be greatly strengthened. Others again may be thought compelling irrespective of a scheme of legislative devolution.

Let us focus on certain key aspects that are likely to focus prominently in the public discussion. As well as substantive matters like composition and electoral arrangements and the basic internal design of the Assembly, not forgetting the idea of a tax-varying power, it is appropriate to consider the process of delivery, in the guise of a possible referendum.

Composition: not just bricks and mortar

The Richard Commission finds itself architecturally challenged. After many hiccups, the plans are now proceeding for a gleaming new Assembly Building in Cardiff Bay – with space for eighty Members. The original headcount under the Wales Act 1978 thus appears likely to come to fruition! Turning the argument round, a very practical obstacle has been placed in the way of the Richard Commission being expansive. And so is the Welsh constitutional development officially structured and confined: by bricks and mortar.

In typically prosaic fashion, the commission has been asked to consider 'whether the size of the Assembly is adequate to allow it to operate effectively within a normal working week, and without placing undue pressure on Members'.[105] Notwithstanding the local preference for a long recess, the commission should heed the problems of overload that are associated with a large committee system in a little body. Rightly, it has been argued, some of the pretensions about the contribution of the subject committees in the original design have now been abandoned, but there remains more than enough for the Members to do. Some key aspects of their role have thus been shown to be underdeveloped, most obviously in the realm of legislative scrutiny and inputs. An expansion of the democratic arm of the Assembly is justifiable under current conditions.

To expand the point, the internal momentum in favour of a more parliamentary 'face' for the Assembly points firmly in this direction. More and more, the Welsh Assembly Government is seen to be increasing its capacities, not simply in terms of formal legal powers, but also through staff development and growth, a greater experience in, and willingness to pursue, the exercise of policy autonomy. An expanded pool of Members, on the one hand to provide political and strategic leadership in the pursuit of cabinet government; and, on the other hand, to serve in the vital backbench role – scrutiny and influence, individual and collective forms of representation, – fits once again with this underlying trajectory. Nor should one overlook the need to provide an adequate training ground – and ample opportunities – for the next generation of senior Assembly politicians. As a way of testing the argument for greater numbers, taking evidence on the workload of AMs is once again necessary but insufficient.

Viewed in this light, the move to legislative devolution is not the necessary condition of a larger Assembly. Equally, however, a substantial dose of primary law-making powers may be said to demand it, given the innate constitutional and political importance of the task, as well as the increased workload. Especially, it is important to say, since Assembly legislative process would not only be replacing the House of Commons, including in the form of the special arrangements for scrutinizing primary legislation affecting Wales, but also the (revamped) Upper Chamber of Parliament, with its historic revising role.[106] To this effect, the empirical truth that government usually gets its way should not obscure the importance of the debating and legitimating functions in a new constitution of Wales.

Perhaps it hardly needs saying: there is no 'correct' size for a parliament or assembly.[107] As well as the functions and powers and jobs to be done, there are

some more intangible factors to consider, such as the scope for 'representativeness' and the avoidance of the danger of too much dependence on
officials, and – yes – public perceptions or the standing of the (new)
democratic institution. Let it be boldly proclaimed. Wales in the United
Kingdom in Europe: constitutionally speaking, this 'National Assembly'
could do with a size of composition more worthy of the name.

Electoral arrangements – breaking the link

As well as the size of the Assembly membership, and its implication for the
electoral system, the Richard Commission has been asked to consider: 'The
adequacy of the Assembly's electoral arrangements, and in particular . . .
whether the means of electing the Assembly, including the degree of
proportionality, adequately and accurately represents all significant interests
in Wales.'[108]

At one and the same time, this is a clear steer in favour of some form of
proportional representation, reflecting the genesis of the commission in the
partnership agreement between Labour and the Liberal Democrats, and begs
many questions, including the meaning of 'all significant interests'
(inclusiveness).

It is worth keeping in mind some constitutional facts of life. The design of
electoral systems is pleasantly open to the law of unexpected consequences.
How voters will respond to rearrangements is – emphatically – not a given, as
indeed the Welsh Labour Party discovered to its cost in the first Assembly
elections. Again, very different outcomes in seats can emerge from the same
popular division of the vote, according to the choice of electoral model.
Whereas the future history of Assembly elections cannot be guaranteed, it can
in part be engineered. A different but related point: the relevant recommendations of the Richard Commission will be the subject of animated debate
in those metaphorical 'smoke-filled rooms'. What clearly has changed are the
rules of engagement, not least the prior fact of an element of proportional
representation, even if one that was artificially curtailed in the interest of the
dominant party.[109]

How then should matters proceed, assuming an increase in the size of the
Assembly? From a constitutional viewpoint, some major considerations need
to be factored into the equation. First, there is the unwritten assumption
underlying the devolution statute, whereby the electoral system is one that
not only brings all the principal political parties inside the tent, but also
involves a genuine element of electoral competition, such that the dominant
party can reasonably expect to win a majority but may not.[110] To reiterate, this
may be accounted a healthy element in the new Welsh democracy, effectively
establishing sharp lines of political incentive and electoral accountability. One

would not wish to see a radical departure from it. The balance of party advantage produced by the electoral design is not only important for the professionals in Cardiff Bay.

Second, a reduction in the number of Welsh MPs is one of the more probable consequences of legislative devolution, and as a matter of constitutional principle rightly so. How could it be otherwise, given that the creation of the Scottish Parliament has been seen to necessitate a reduction in the number of Scottish MPs to the English level of representation, so leaving Wales as the only country of the Union 'over-represented' at Westminster in population terms? The famous 'West Lothian question', or perhaps in the local idiom the 'Blaenau Gwent' one, may be accounted astringent enough without rubbing things in! With the official electoral quota or target constituency size in Wales moving from 55,000 to 70,000, it would mean not 40–2 Welsh MPs (depending on an ongoing Westminster redistribution), but 32–4. On the one hand, this may be helpful in 'selling' an increase in AMs to a sceptical public, a trade-off or saving on the additional cost. On the other hand, it is seen to complicate the task of constructing the electoral arrangements for a larger Assembly.

Third but related, the design feature of 'coterminosity' rears its head; that is to say, the precept, currently embedded in the devolution statute,[111] that the boundaries of the parliamentary constituencies and the Assembly constituencies should be either identical, or at least not inconsistent, with each other. Constitutionally speaking, there are good reasons for this, most obviously in terms of the avoidance of confusion for voters and of overlapping forms of constituency representation, as well for the political parties in relation to their organization. Typically, it also made good practical sense in the rush to deliver Welsh devolution, so avoiding the need for the lengthy processes of creating new constituencies associated with the independent Boundary Commission.

Then again, coterminosity should not be regarded as set in stone. It is in fact being abandoned in Scotland, at least on a temporary basis, with a view to preserving the composition of the Parliament, which would otherwise reduce along with the number of Scottish representatives at Westminster.[112] Although the context of any reform in Wales would be different, a constitutional precedent will therefore exist for 'breaking the link' or decoupling the two electoral systems: UK and territorial. Presumably, if the Scots can cope, then so can the Welsh.[113]

As every student of government knows, 'representation' and 'representativeness' are slippery concepts. For present purposes, they cover an array of (competing) objectives or criteria for the selection of an appropriate electoral system. Notwithstanding its 'very practical approach', the Richard Commission has to juggle with factors like the importance of linkages between the electorate and local representative(s), and the need for adequate representation for the less populous areas.[114] Fortunately, the task need not be as daunting as perhaps it sounds. Much of the requisite conceptual and policy analysis is already available in Wales, courtesy of the Sunderland Commission on local government electoral arrangements.[115]

With a view to teasing out the possibilities, let us start with an expansive scenario. There are good arguments for an electoral system premised on around 100 members, for reasons to do with underlying constitutional values and the ease of design, as well as internal capacities. The fact that this is also an unlikely option, for cogent reasons of establishment cost and associated political sensitivities, serves in turn to highlight the many practical constraints, or the strong sense here of constitution-building as 'the art of the possible'.

To explicate, there would be continuity in terms of the Additional Member System (AMS).[116] In place of the current settlement of forty constituency members and twenty additional members elected via regional lists, the scenario would allow for 64–8 constituency members 'balanced' by 32–4 additional members, as premised on the (reduced) number of Welsh MPs in the face of legislative devolution. There could then be smaller constituencies, with the parliamentary ones being divided into two by the Boundary Commission for Assembly purposes. At one and the same time, therefore, the scenario permits both constituency links and an element of proportional representation, maintenance of the general political balance in the original design of the electoral system, respect for the idea of coterminosity, and a further element of 'bringing government closer to the people'. It is also worth placing in comparative perspective. Whereas in Wales there are currently 48,400 constituents per AM, in Scotland the relevant figure is 39,300, and in (the special circumstances of) Northern Ireland it is 15,600. On the basis of 100 and 80 AMs, the figures would be 29,040 and 36,300 respectively. What I have labelled 'an expansive scenario' is not fantastically bold.

Turning the argument round, the scenario usefully points up the difficulties in traversing the terrain to eighty members; assuming, that is, coterminosity. One of the major options clearly is adaptation of the AMS system. On the basis of a redistribution of parliamentary seats, this might entail 64–8 constituency representatives and 12–16 additional members. But this would mean changing the ratio between the two categories from 2:1 to 4:1 and more, a recipe for perpetual Labour majorities and a huge contrast to Scotland (9:7). Considerations of inclusivity apart, why on earth would the other political parties buy into it? Alternatively, of course, one might have 32–4 constituency members and 46–8 additional ones. But not only would this be impossible for Labour to countenance, since such a scheme would discriminate powerfully against the dominant party, it would also turn AMS on its head. Indeed, in the (unwanted) scenario of no legislative devolution, and so of no diminution in the parliamentary constituencies, even a 40/40 split of constituency and list seats would be a harsh pill for Labour to swallow.

No doubt (Labour) voices will be heard in favour of 'first past the post' (FTPT). One idea currently doing the rounds is for forty constituencies, each electing one man and one woman. It is perhaps best described as 'a fig leaf' of a proposal! Naked ambition, in this case for enduring Labour Party hegemony in Wales, is not so easily disguised.[117]

Let us keep in mind the democratic basis on which the devolution referendum was fought and won: 'The electoral system will . . . ensure fair representation for all areas and parties.' FTPT in other words would jar not only with the remit of the Richard Commission, but also – and more importantly – with the message of the White Paper as originally presented to the people of Wales. Again, the fact that a unicameral system has been seen to necessitate AMS for the Scottish Parliament as a kind of 'check and balance' is highly significant. Why should an Assembly in Wales armed with primary powers be treated differently?

This brings us to Single Transferable Vote (STV), notably the favoured option of the Sunderland Commission. Each of the 32–4 parliamentary constituencies could be put together with its next-door neighbour, so creating 16–17 Assembly constituencies, each of which would return 4, 5 or exceptionally 6 members according to population size, thus giving a grand total of around 80 members. STV in other words is technically feasible.

The politics, however, are apt to prove a trifle more difficult! As the internal party debates of the 1990s serve to remind us, the Welsh Labour Party is not exactly in love with STV.[118] And understandably so, since STV would not only be a shot in the dark, the exact consequences of it being very difficult to model, but also most likely to prevent one party from ever gaining a clear majority. The comrades, it may be suggested, are not about to vote for the likelihood of coalition government.

So proceeding on the basis that one must cut one's cloth and run with eighty members, it is time to consider breaking the link with the parliamentary constituencies. Freed from the constraint of coterminosity, an appropriate solution would be in the order of 48–52 constituency members and 28–32 additional members, as dictated by the pull of the current balance of party advantage versus the case for edging towards the greater measure of proportionality operating in Scotland. At one and the same time, therefore, the constituency link would be preserved, the size of the Assembly increased to the (apparently) magic number, and an electoral arithmetic produced with which the different party interests could reasonably be expected to engage.

Let us be clear. This is an untidy option, and so not something to be recommended with enthusiasm. But it can also be said to be the best available option, bearing in mind the various constitutional considerations, the history of the matter, and ultimately the need for political acceptance and democratic legitimacy. It will do.

Internal architecture – into the mainstream

The original concept of a single corporate body exercising its functions on behalf of the Crown always was dubious. As a product of the choice of executive devolution, the strict idea of 'substitution' for the Secretary of State for Wales, it jarred with the vital deliberative role of the new representative institution. The introduction and increasing pursuit of cabinet government, whereby the executive functions are treated as the responsibility of a designated part of the Assembly, has made it even more difficult to justify.

In one sense, this no longer matters very much given the scale of the 'hollowing out' inside the corporate shell; the *de facto* constitutional development that is epitomized by the rise of the Presiding Office as a distinct entity. The concept is seen, however, to retain a certain nuisance value, while continuing to offend basic constitutional ideas of the separation of functions, as in the overarching roles of the Permanent Secretary and Counsel General. Meanwhile, the paper creation that is the 'Welsh Assembly Government' can only go so far in aiding public sensibilities of the local political lines of responsibility and accountability. In short, irrespective of the case for primary legislative powers, it is time that the corporate body was put out of its misery.[119]

Retention of the corporate body and conferral of primary legislative powers hardly bears thinking about. It would be constitutionally dubious, to say the least, to speak of the Assembly acting 'on behalf of the Crown' when exercising such powers. Meanwhile, an element of farce, the Assembly in enacting primary legislation would have solemnly to delegate to itself the powers of subordinate legislation. Direct statutory authority for ministers in the devolution legislation, in place of the clumsy and artificial device that is the chain of internal delegations currently necessitated by the Assembly's corporate nature, is the obvious solution.

In any case, why retain such a strange anatomy? Happily, what I called 'the extravagant version of the corporate body' is now exploded. The contours of a system of parliamentary government have been firmly etched, and in this sense too there is no going back. The Richard Commission should not now repeat the basic error of seeing inclusiveness as a value that cannot be taken sufficiently seriously inside a more conventional constitutional framework. The fact of small-country governance can operate to great advantage here. Much can also be done around the edges of the formal design – committees, etc. – to promote collaborative ways of working.

There is also an issue of standing or status, the way in which this strange anatomy is apt to sell Wales short. Why, if the Assembly is to have primary legislative powers, deny it the familiar accoutrements of parliamentary government? In an age of political and economic integration on the grand scale, there is much to be said for being, and under the auspices of national devolution being seen to be, in the mainstream of comparative constitutional development. By all means be distinctive, but why look odd?

The general theme can be pursued in various ways. Formal enshrining in the 'Wales Act' of a separate branch of government drawn from and accountable to the 'parliament' would obviously be at the heart of the constitutional design. That is to say: a legally designated 'Welsh Executive', headed by the First Minister and otherwise consisting of cabinet ministers and a law officer, a number of junior ministers, non-ministerial office-holders, and staff who would be members of the home civil service.[120]

In turn, one would expect to see the basic canon of collective ministerial responsibility written into the statute, as in Scotland.[121] It is also important to remember that as part of 'the pursuit of cabinet government' in Wales conventional arrangements of individual and collective ministerial responsibility already have been imported from Scotland, by way of protocol.[122] There would be an appropriate match here with the new legal arrangement.

Secondly, with the cracking of the corporate shell, the way would be open to a separate parliamentary service of the type that exists not only in Edinburgh and Belfast but also across much of the Commonwealth and in Europe. The dual character of the *de facto* constitutional development – internal, pragmatic reform and the laying of the groundwork for another stage in Wales's constitutional development – is once again demonstrated here. The fact not only of a risen Presiding Office, but also of a revamped House Committee with responsibilities akin to the House of Commons Commission, can now be seen heralding formal statutory provision. How better to 'tidy things up', while setting in stone the key attributes of independence and tailored professional skills?

Primary legislative powers; further institutional growth: the two so clearly go hand in hand. All part of the maturation of a polity, there would inevitably be additional demands made on the local administrative apparatus, involving such matters as ministerial correspondence and dealings with interest groups, as well as the more obvious items of internal policy development and legal technique. No doubt there is great fun to be had with the minutiae of the costings. But further, in the competitive struggle for extra resources in the face of legislative devolution, the putative 'parliamentary service' needs to be given first priority. It is not just a matter of more 'sitting days' or even of more AMs. With a view to enhancing the quality of scrutiny and debate – that is to say, the very lifeblood of a new form of Welsh representative democracy – proper support services are essential. The extra input that the House of Lords supplies as a revising chamber must also be factored into the equation here.

Thirdly, the committee system clearly requires some redesign for the purpose of primary legislative powers. The way forward lies through the subject committees; the development of a truly multidimensional approach to scrutiny – policy, legislation, and administration – coupled with the occasional 'big inquiry'. By the time that primary powers pass, steps should have been taken to ensure that these committees have considerable experience in dealing – at one remove – with primary legislation affecting Wales, as well as with Assembly Orders. Turning the argument round, what is not required is the dual paraphernalia of standing committees and select committees on the Westminster model: costly and cumbersome. Viewed in comparative constitutional perspective, a more integrated and flexible design so clearly fits the conditions of small-country governance.

Cutting what I termed 'the umbilical cord', and so allowing these committees to breathe free of the political leadership currently provided by the minister, is again the natural concomitant. So also, with the corporate body gone, the wholly artificial provisions relating to 'accountability in fields' and thus to the subject committees' responsibilities can be swept away, so facilitating a full and balanced coverage of ministerial portfolios for the purposes of scrutiny. A different but related point: following the Scottish example, one would expect these all-party committees to have the right of legislative initiative.[123] As a way of dealing with non-contentious legislation, and further of promoting the committees as an important forum of public involvement and creativity, there is much to be said for this. It further reflects the general concern to underscore the democratic legitimacy of the Assembly as a representative institution in the case of primary legislative powers.

Speaking more generally, one would expect to see less statutory pre-scription of the internal processes of the Assembly.[124] An agreed and free-standing set of standing orders, 'entrenched' as at present on the basis of the special two-thirds majority for amendment, should generally be sufficient to protect minority interests, while avoiding many of the procedural rigidities in the GWA that have plagued local actors. A more respectful approach on the part of Westminster to this legislature, such matters should essentially be left to the elected representatives of the new 'national' polity. It is time to unburden Wales here.

Tax-varying power: paper tiger

In the words of the Scottish Constitutional Convention,

> In the Western democracies all principal levels of national and local government have powers over taxation. While the Parliament's income will principally be based on totals of expenditure set at UK level, the power to vary the rate of tax is vital if the Parliament is to be properly accountable.[125]

For its part, the Richard Commission has specifically raised the issue of tax-varying power in the case of Wales.[126]

Much ink has been spilt on 'the devolution of taxation'. Especially with a view to helping people feel more 'connected' to their taxes and to public spending – 'bringing government closer to the people' in the fiscal sense – there is a respectable constitutional case for Wales (and Northern Ireland) converging on the Scottish model and so gaining some revenue-raising power. There are some potential gains in terms of promoting local account-ability – the need to take into account the wishes of the electorate, the requirement to justify spending decisions – as also in enriching the lifeblood of the new form of territorial politics via an expanded set of policy choices. Turning the argument round, the constitutional design feature of 'represen-tation without taxation' is sometimes seen as tending to political irrespon-sibility and conflict, whereby central government is made the permanent scapegoat for all local budgetary difficulties.[127]

Nor should the principle of a modest tax-varying power be denigrated. The ability of the Parliament to resolve in favour of changing the basic rate of income tax applicable in Scotland by up to 3p in the pound is hardly a serious challenge to the highly centralized and unified control over public expen-diture and taxation traditionally enjoyed by HM Treasury.[128] Nonetheless, because of the importance of the scope of the margins in government budgeting, it has been seen to stand for a significant degree of financial autonomy.[129] The variation allowed does not have to be very large as a proportion of the territorial budget to make the (democratic) choice a significant one.

Constitutionally speaking, an Assembly tax-varying power would sit comfortably with legislative devolution. Self-evidently it is no prerequisite, but given that the process of primary legislation almost inevitably involves public spending consequences, it is not impossible to conceive of circum-stances in which a defined and limited power of this kind might serve to grease the novel wheels of Welsh statute making. Indeed, in this sense, a reserve or residual power – in the jargon of policy analysis a useful extra 'arrow' for coping with specific and local demands of law making in the conditions of small-country governance – itself appears unexceptional. A different but related point: one does not to have to be a Welsh separatist to recognize the symbolic importance to the National Assembly of a revenue-raising power. From 'virtual' to 'real' parliament: as a matter of formal constitutional design, why, it may be asked, deny this body of elected representatives of the people of Wales a democratic choice available in Scotland?

Legally speaking, what is in prospect here is a Welsh Consolidated Fund. The 'Wales Act' would thus make provision for any additional tax paid by Welsh taxpayers to be paid into the Fund, and vice versa. As a kind of 'manner and form' entrenchment, the detailed provisions in the Scotland Act which seek to protect the Parliament against changes to the Income Tax Acts that would have a significant impact on the tax-varying power could also be usefully read across.[130]

But what, it may be asked, of the block and formula system? In the event, one of the more arresting features of the official evidence is the way in which the Richard Commission has been warned off this most sensitive terrain. 'The evaluation of the arrangements for political devolution should not be distracted by the very separate considerations of financial distribution.'[131] Nonetheless, because of the basic dependency of the Assembly on the system, and further the practical measure of autonomy now familiarly associated with 'the power of the block', a public consultation on the tax-varying question only makes sense when set in this wider context.

In fact, the system is now seen to draw much of the sting of the argument but not to meet it entirely. As successive budgets increasingly show, the devolved administration does have genuine responsibility for making choices about the nature of public spending in Wales, rather than simply administering public spending decisions reached by central government (a financial take on the constitutional model of 'Welsh Office plus').[132] There may be powerful cross-currents – convergence and divergence or 'made in Wales policies' versus the 'cross-border' pull of uniformity – but local accountability is not exactly lacking in 'the power of the block', as the occasional fractious dispute in plenary simply serves to illustrate.[133] Then again, in the last resort, the Assembly is unable to vary the total budget, given its lack of taxing power, and therefore lacks financial independence. To reiterate, it is not just the conditions of political cohabitation but also of massive financial largess which have so far given the devolved administration an easy ride.

At the same time, the constitutional sense that tax-varying power would be an appropriate addition, even another fundamental for a National Assembly or parliament worthy of the name, should not disguise the strict constraints and limitations concerning the practical exercise. It is not simply that the Scots – benefiting from the block and formula system – have so far declined to explore this virgin territory. Many comparative studies of 'state' or 'regional' finance in federal systems highlight a marginal policy impact and a minimal effect on local autonomy of the existence of a formal, legal capacity for revenue-raising.[134]

Typically, this feature is liable to be accentuated in the case of Wales. A fragile local economy, bumping along at 80 per cent of UK GDP despite the best efforts of the Welsh Assembly Government, is not the most obvious target for additional revenue-raising, which is effectively what it would be in view of the constellation of local political forces. Again, a possible yield of £400 million to £500 million is a considerable sum, but not only is this increasingly dwarfed by the scale of Assembly budgeting under the UK system of territorial finance; it also raises the harsh spectre of 'tax competition', classic-ally involving the relocation of private investment and human resources, when set in the context of a very integrated, long border with England. The political and social aspect of the Welsh condition, whereby so much in public life is measured by reference to a powerful neighbour, is also apt to play strongly here. In short, the local potential for electoral suicide is not alone in suggesting something of a rarity.

Suffice it to add that leading figures in the Welsh Assembly Government like Rhodri Morgan and Edwina Hart have been notably lukewarm about having a tax-varying power. Indeed, their evidence on the point was not exactly helpful to the Richard Commission, a case of politicians 'hedging bets' ahead of the prospect of primary powers versus the more holistic approach – a constitutional package for the future – which a body like the commission might reasonably be expected to adopt.[135] For its part, in making recommendations, the commission should resist the temptation to kick the issue into touch.

To summarize: there is, constitutionally speaking, much to be said for an Assembly tax-varying power as part of a more general scheme of legislative devolution. At the same time, for particular reasons of geography, history and economics, this is not a matter worth dying in the ditch for, including in the current phase of Welsh political and administrative development. 'Paper tiger': nowhere in fact in the local constitutional construction is the distinction between having a power, and exercising it, likely to be more clearly drawn.

Why not let the people decide? Given that the electors of Scotland were afforded a separate referendum vote on the UK government's proposal for a tax-varying power, it is hard to see the basis on which a similar demand could be resisted in Wales. This constitutional precedent could now be turned to good advantage as a way of resolving matters, whereby the voters of Wales would be asked the question in the wake of a no doubt very public discussion of the virtues of principle and pragmatism. It would not hobble a scheme of primary powers should the popular answer be 'no'. And such a contemporary reworking of the radical traditions of Wales might just have the considerable benefit of breathing some excitement into the new 'national' polity.

Referendum: ask the people

But what, it may be asked, of a referendum on the issue of primary powers and a 'real', not a 'virtual' parliament? Not only are there no hard and fixed rules governing this issue, courtesy of an unwritten constitution and the doctrine of parliamentary sovereignty, but also there is no immediately comparable precedent. Rhodri Morgan may be quoted: 'the greater the change, the greater the likelihood that you would see a referendum as being required'.[136]

This bears on a political dilemma for those seeking to advance the cause of Welsh legislative devolution. How on the one hand to sell the concept to the people of Wales by reference to good works, when on the other hand the devolved administration is constrained by a lack of power in performing them? Breaking out of this apparent 'catch-22' of the local constitutional and political process demands not only more evolutionism, but also some good (chapel-like) creationism, the new opportunities presented in a constitutionally imaginative and confident way. The emergent sense in public attitudes to Welsh devolution that 'if done 'tis best done properly' should be regarded as an encouraging sign.

There are in fact good pragmatic arguments for holding a second – or strictly speaking, third – Welsh devolution referendum. A decision not to allow the people of Wales to vote on such proposals would itself be a recipe for controversy. And it risks blighting the successor body, the perceived lack of the consent of the people being a potential source of instability, a breeding ground for cynicism, or a blot on the democratic legitimacy of the institution.

Following the successful precedent of 1997, it would no doubt be a pre-legislative referendum. So as a way of convincing the UK government, and of easing the parliamentary path of the 'Wales Bill', there is also merit in the tactic. The Assembly, it is perhaps worth adding however, is legally constrained in forcing the issue. Under the terms of the devolution statute, an attempt to go it alone with a referendum on legislative devolution, as distinct from asking Westminster to provide for a poll, could immediately be challenged on the ground of *ultra vires*.[137]

Of course it may be argued that 'the big decision' was taken in 1997, such that matters can now proceed simply on the settled constitutional basis of 'devolution'. 'No clear break': the phased or Mark I model of legislature devolution for Wales may in turn have a particular appeal for the powers-that-be in this context. But to say that having voted on 'the principle', the people of Wales need not be consulted again on the 'details', does not square with the way in which the matter was originally presented to them in the devolution White Paper. It was a specific proposition: a scheme of executive devolution that involved a detailed package of proposals.[138] Nor does it do to distort the message: 'Parliament will continue to be the principal law maker for Wales.'[139]

One of the less pleasing themes in this book is Welsh devolution as 'an affair of the elite'. To say that people on the whole would not understand these things is patronizing, a sentiment fundamentally at odds with the devolutionary project of 'bringing government closer to the people'. Inconvenient it may be for the local movers and shakers, but notwithstanding the evolutionary development to what I have termed 'a virtual parliament' it must be recognized that legislative devolution in any serious sense is qualitatively different. Put simply, if the people of Wales cannot be convinced of the virtues of legislative devolution in open debate and secret ballot, then it is not worth the candle.

CONCLUSION: WALES DELINEATED

Future historians of Wales will marvel at many of the happenings described in this book. As an example of making a mountain from a constitutional molehill, the Welsh devolutionary development could scarcely be bettered. Likewise, when viewed in comparative perspective, it is the modesty of the continuing search for a tolerably efficient and robust form of devolved government, one that combines the virtues of small-country governance with adherence to, and mutually beneficial collaboration in, the Union state, that is so striking.

Many of the problems discussed in this volume stem not from devolution as such, but from the brand of devolution applied to Wales. Horizontal division and scattergun approach to powers; the strange anatomy of the corporate body; difficulties of administrative and political 'fit', especially with the UK legislative process: at times, the current constitutional scheme resembles nothing so much as an obstacle course for local actors. In turn, from spotting holes and filling them to cutting down fences, it is the scale of the autochthonous response and development that shines through.

The interplay between the practical impulse to make the best of it, and the concern to change things for the future, stands at the heart of this protracted exercise in constitution-building. Nods and winks, as well as internal tensions: the two sets of dynamics are not mutually exclusive. Whatever else it does, the Richard Commission cannot settle the argument in favour of executive devolution. Especially in view of the many sources of instability associated with the existing scheme, a more imaginative approach is now required: a constitutional game plan that in building on established strengths is essentially forward-looking, and so does not hark back once again to the 1970s.

Two alternative ways forward have been plotted in this chapter. Each design seeks to combine the lessons of comparative experience (from Scotland and Northern Ireland) with a careful regard for local conditions or the 'particularity' of Wales, including in terms of a history of close integration with England. At the heart of this approach is the idea of a mixed system of legislative and executive devolution: a solid core of primary powers or what used to be called 'Home Rule', and – reflecting the parallel demands for territorial autonomy and 'cross-border' collaboration – an expanded periphery of ministerial powers. Making good use of Westminster – the Sewel Convention – is also an important element, a tangible expression not only of the pressures for uniformity and convergence, but also of a constitutional sense of partnership, in the Union state.

The lesser alternative of 'phased' legislative devolution is designedly more cautious and calculating. Predicated on the triple classification of 'reserved', 'devolved' and 'retained' matters, it is both grounded in the pre-existing fields of devolved functions and would effectively prioritize the devolution of powers in major fields of front-line services. To this effect, the new 'Welsh Executive' would be in a position to (be seen to) 'make a difference'. The second design involving an entire scheme of legislative devolution is more conventional in character, and as such, constitutionally speaking, is clearly preferable. But further, in providing ample scope for innovative and rounded approaches, it has been seen sitting comfortably with the trajectory of policy-making and delivery demonstrated by the Welsh Assembly Government. The sheer pace of change, first in making good on the historical legacy of the Welsh Office, and second in the increasing pursuit of the positive opportunities for diversity that are now available under the auspices of an 'interim constitution', also points firmly in this direction.

The battle to drag Wales more into the mainstream of comparative constitutional development has been fought in many ways since 1997, consciously and otherwise. In the cause of the Dragon, two other dragons have had to be vanquished or at least anaesthetized: an older chap ('Welsh Office plus'), and a quirky character (the corporate body). A secure system of parliamentary government for national devolution; a set of institutions which in view of the conditions of small-country governance is sufficiently accessible and responsive, and also serves to enhance the voice of Wales in the United Kingdom in Europe: it should hardly need saying.

In conclusion, the way in which the constitutional and political argument is now framed is important. At the end of the last millennium, a question typically asked was 'why legislative devolution for Wales?' At the beginning of a new millennium, the more appropriate question – and answer – is 'why not?' A devolution settlement worthy of the name is in fact a constitutional development waiting to happen. And it will then be a case, not of *Delineating Wales*, but of *Wales Delineated*.

Postscript

For the convenience of the reader, it is appropriate to record the results of the second Assembly elections, and their immediate consequence, the type of single-party government under Labour's First Minister Rhodri Morgan that was originally envisaged in the design of the so-called 'devolution settlement'. Naturally, there are important pointers here to the future course of constitutional, political and administrative development under the general rubric of *Delineating Wales*.

Table 20: Results of second Assembly elections – May 2003

	Labour	Plaid Cymru	Conservatives	Liberal Democrats	Other
Constituency seats (40)	30 (+3)	5 (–4)	1 (n/c)	3 (n/c)	1 (+1)
Additional Members from regional lists (20)	0 (–1)	7 (–1)	10 (+2)	3 (n/c)	0 (n/c)
Total (60)	30 (+2)	12 (–5)	11 (+2)	6 (n/c)	1 (+1)
% vote in constituencies	40.0	21.2	19.9	14.1	4.8
% vote in electoral regions	36.6	19.7	19.2	12.7	11.8

Turnout: 38%
n/c = no change

Labour thus recouped its most surprising losses in 1999,[1] in the three south Wales 'heartland' seats of Islwyn, Llanelli and the Rhondda, as well as gaining an additional north Wales constituency (Conwy). These successes were in part offset by the loss of Wrexham to John Marek, the former Labour MP now separated from the Party, and – via the operation of the d'Hondt formula – of the Party's only list seat (originally held by Alun Michael). The major losers clearly were Plaid Cymru, a fact promptly marked by the resignation of the Party's leader Ieuan Wyn Jones. It is also worth a special emphasis in view of the continuing constitutional debate. Just as the report from the Richard Commission loomed, so the nationalists' voice in the Assembly was sorely weakened.

Labour representatives naturally claimed a great victory. The dominant party of government in Wales had been returned with an increased representation. It may be noted, however, that this result was no better for Labour than the 'worst case scenario' in the electoral arithmetic behind the devolution statute.[2] To this effect, a healthy competitive discipline in the new Welsh polity may well be here to stay. As the First Minister would have it: 'check against delivery.'

Not, it must be said, that the electorate crowded to the poll. At one with a general theme of this volume – a failure on the part of the local political elite properly to engage the people of Wales in the devolutionary project – the turnout was significantly down, both on the original devolution referendum (50.1 per cent) and the first Assembly elections (46.2 per cent). More food for thought for the Richard Commission, this trend will no doubt fuel the continuing constitutional debate over the empowerment of the Assembly, a mark in different eyes of no great case for change and of a need for greater political, legal and administrative relevance.[3] The basic fact of the instabilities associated with the current devolutionary scheme refuses, however, to go away.

A world record should not go unremarked. Wales now boasts the first legislature to be – in Rhodri Morgan's phrase – 'perfectly balanced between men and women'.[4] Indeed, women are in a majority both in the ranks of the governing party and in the Assembly cabinet. Less trumpeted is the continued absence of AMs from the ethnic minorities. Inclusiveness in the guise of representativeness in the new model Wales: 'Now you see it, now you don't.'

In the circumstances it clearly suited Labour Members to support the re-election of Lord Elis Thomas as Presiding Officer, whereby the Party now has a bare working majority in the Chamber. By the narrowest of margins, John Marek has also been returned as Deputy Presiding Officer.[5] In turn, as a chief pole of authority in the Assembly, the Presiding Office is likely to continue to explore the further reaches of the current constitutional framework. What I called 'a powerful triumvirate' at the top of the Office has been re-formed.[6]

Highlighting the change from coalition government to Labour rule is the absence from the new Cabinet formation of the post of Deputy First Minister. At the same time, the basic canon of collective and individual ministerial responsibility is now well established in the Welsh system of devolved government.[7] The internal separation of roles along the lines of parliamentary government – one-party rule – hardly portends retrenchment. Whether, given the precise arithmetic, single-party government can be effectively sustained for the statutory four-year period prior to the next Assembly Elections remains to be seen, of course.

WELSH ASSEMBLY GOVERNMENT – MAY 2003[8]

Cabinet

- *First Minister – Rhodri Morgan.* Responsible/Accountable for: exercise of functions by the Assembly Cabinet; policy development and the coordination of policy, the relationships with the rest of the UK, Europe and Wales abroad; the maintenance of open government; staffing/civil service.
- *Minister for Finance, Local Government and Public Services – Sue Essex.* Responsible/Accountable for: budgeting and managing the finances of the Government; the development of the strategic approach to the delivery of public services; and local government.
- *Minister for Assembly Business – Karen Sinclair.* Responsible/Accountable for: managing the business of the Government in the Assembly; and acting as chief whip to the Government's supporters in the Assembly.
- *Minister for Social Justice and Regeneration – Edwina Hart.* Responsible/Accountable for the Government's programme for regenerating the communities of Wales, in particular those suffering the greatest disadvantage: including Communities First, anti-poverty initiatives, the social economy, the voluntary sector, community safety and relations with the police, the fire service, drug and alcohol abuse, youth justice, housing; equality.
- *Minister for Health and Social Care – Jane Hutt.* Responsible/Accountable for Health and NHS Wales; social services and social care; food safety.
- *Minister for Economic Development – Andrew Davies.* Responsible/Accountable for innovation and enterprise; industrial policy and business support; inward investment; promotion of indigenous companies and regional development; transport; energy; tourism; strategic coordinating responsibility for ICT; structural funds.
- *Minister for Education and Life-Long Learning – Jane Davidson.* Responsible/Accountable for schools; further education and skills development; higher education; youth services; careers service.
- *Minister for Environment, Planning and Countryside – Carwyn Jones.* Responsible/Accountable for the environment and sustainable development; town and country planning; countryside and conservation issues; agriculture and rural development including forestry and food production.
- *Minister for Culture, the Welsh Language and Sport – Alun Pugh.* Responsible/Accountable for arts, libraries and museums, sport and recreation, the languages of Wales.

Deputy Ministers

- *Economic Development and Transport – Brian Gibbons.*
- *Health and Social Care – John Griffiths.*
- *Social Justice – Huw Lewis.*

Officially described as 'the cutting edge of the new administration',[9] the major innovation is the Social Justice and Regeneration portfolio. Clearly in tune with the radical political traditions of Wales, the development is also emblematic of the more flexible cross-cutting approaches to policy formulation and implementation, which have been seen characterizing the local post-devolutionary modes of small country governance.[10] Constitutionally speaking, it fits with the idea of expanding horizons on the part of the devolved administration, given that many of the relevant areas will involve a shared responsibility with Whitehall and Westminster. This, in turn, is fertile territory for the mixed system of primary and secondary competencies for Wales envisaged in this book. National devolution driven forward once again by a very practical concern to (be seen to) 'make a difference': watch this space!

As the Assembly's first re-elected First Minister, the last word belongs to Rhodri Morgan:[11]

> Over the coming four years, we will turn the vision of a healthier, wealthier and smarter Wales into reality . . . As we continue [the] work of economic improvement, the main theme of this new administration will now be that of anti-poverty and anti-inequality action . . . We must recreate and reinvigorate the sense of social solidarity that served Wales well during hard times, so that it also serves us during more prosperous times.

Let us see.

Notes

Introduction

[1] A. Michael, *The Dragon on our Doorstep: New Politics for a New Millennium in Wales* (Aberystwyth: Institute of Welsh Politics, 1999).

[2] A summary of the results of the second Assembly Elections, in May 2003, and the major consequence, single-party government under Labour's Rhodri Morgan, is given in the Postscript. Particular updating references appear elsewhere in the book.

[3] Most obviously in relation to Scotland: see generally V. Bogdanor, *Devolution in the United Kingdom* (Oxford: Oxford University Press, 1999).

[4] D. Robertson, *Dictionary of Politics*, 2nd edn. (London: Penguin, 1993), p. 135.

[5] B. Anderson, *Imagined Communities: Reflections on the Origin and Spread of Nationalism* (London: Verso, 1991).

[6] As in H. Kearney, *The British Isles: A History of Four Nations* (Cambridge: Cambridge University Press, 1989). See also in this context, B. Crick (ed.), *National Identities: The Constitution of the United Kingdom* (Oxford: Blackwell, 1991).

[7] As brilliantly chronicled by J. Davies, *A History of Wales* (London: Allen Lane, 1993).

[8] J. Osmond, *New Politics in Wales* (London: Charter 88, 1998), p. 7. See further, for discussion in the context of the devolution referendums held in 1997, B. Taylor and K. Thomson (eds.), *Scotland and Wales: Nations Again?* (Cardiff, University of Wales Press, 1999).

[9] G. Williams, *When was Wales? A History of the Welsh* (London: Black Raven, 1985), p. 304.

[10] L. Sharpe (ed.), *The Rise of Meso Government in Europe* (London: Sage Publications, 1992).

[11] *A Voice for Wales*, Cm. 3718 (1997), paragraph 2.1.

[12] *Scotland's Parliament*, Cm. 3658 (1997); Scotland Act 1998. See generally, N. Burrows, *Devolution* (London: Sweet & Maxwell, 2000).

[13] GWA, s. 22(2) and Schedule 2. See below, chapter 2.

[14] Especially in GWA, ss. 21–2: see below, chapter 2.

[15] National Assembly for Wales (Transfer of Functions) Order 1999, SI 1999 no. 672.

[16] GWA, s. 1(2).

[17] *A Voice for Wales*, above, n. 2, paragraph 4.1.

[18] A. Giddens, *The Third Way* (Oxford: Polity Press, 1998).

[19] Welsh Office press release, 27 November 1997. See generally, P. Chaney, T. Hall and A. Pithouse (eds.), *New Governance – New Democracy? Post-Devolution Wales* (Cardiff: University of Wales Press, 2001).

[20] R. Davies, *Devolution: A Process not an Event* (Cardiff: Institute of Welsh Affairs, 1999), p. 7.

[21] *A Voice for Wales*, above, n. 2, paragraph 3.1.

[22] Welsh Labour Party and Welsh Liberal Democrats, *Putting Wales First: A Partnership for the People of Wales* (Cardiff: Welsh Labour Party and Welsh Liberal Democrats, October 2000), pp. 3, 22.

[23] Davies, *Devolution: A Process not an Event*, above, n. 20, pp. 9, 15.

[24] *Western Mail*, 30 September 1999. See in similar vein, P. Murphy, *Devolution: The View from Whitehall and Torfaen* (Cardiff: Welsh Governance Centre, 2002). And see further below, especially chapter 15.

[25] Michael, *The Dragon on our Doorstep*, above, n. 1, p. 11.

[26] Speech to Welsh Labour Party Conference, 25 March 2000. See also R. Morgan, *Variable Geometry UK* (Cardiff: Institute of Welsh Affairs, 2000).

[27] R. Rhodes, 'The new governance: governing without government' (1996) 44 *Political Studies* 652; and see generally, J. Pierre (ed.), *Debating Governance: Authority, Steering and Democracy* (Oxford: Oxford University Press, 2000); also, L. Salamon, *The Tools of Government: A Guide to the New Governance* (Oxford: Oxford University Press, 2002).

[28] G. Marks, 'An actor-centred approach to multi-level governance' (1996) 6 *Regional and Federal Studies* 20.

[29] R. Rhodes, 'The hollowing out of the state: the changing nature of the public service in Britain' (1994) 65 *Political Quarterly* 138.

[30] See now J. Hopkins, *Devolution in Context: Regional, Federal and Devolved Government in the European Union* (London: Cavendish, 2002).

[31] R. Rawlings, 'Concordats of the constitution' (2000) 116 *Law Quarterly Review* 257; and see below, chapter 12.

[32] R. Rawlings, 'Living with the lawyers' (1999) (2) *Agenda: Journal of the Institute of Welsh Affairs* 32.

[33] In the so-called Acts of Union 1536 and 1543. See below, chapter 1.

[34] R. Hazell (ed.), *Constitutional Futures: A History of the Next Ten Years* (Oxford: Oxford University Press, 1999).

[35] See further below, chapter 12.

[36] As discussed in chapter 12.

[37] R. Rawlings, 'The new model Wales' (1998) 25 *Journal of Law and Society* 461.

[38] R. Rawlings, 'The shock of the new: devolution in the United Kingdom', in E. Riedl (ed.), *Aufgabenverteilung und Finanzregimes im Verhältnis zwischen dem Zentralstaat und seinen Untereinheiten* (Baden-Baden: Nomos, 2001).

[39] R. Hughes, *The Shock of the New: Art and the Century of Change*, 2nd edn. (London: Thames and Hudson, 1991).

[40] R. Rawlings, 'Taking Wales seriously', in T. Campbell, K. Ewing and A. Tomkins (eds.), *Sceptical Essays on Human Rights* (Oxford: Oxford University Press, 2001).

Chapter 1

[1] Lord Irvine, *The Government's Programme of Constitutional Reform* (London: Constitution Unit, 1998), p. 4.

[2] See for example in the Scottish setting, T. Nairn, *After Britain: New Labour and the Return of Scotland* (London: Granta, 1999); and for general discussion in the present context, R. Fevre and A. Thompson (eds.), *Nation, Identity and Social Theory: Perspectives from Wales* (Cardiff: University of Wales Press, 1999).

[3] L. Colley, *Britons: Forging the Nation, 1707–1837* (New Haven: Yale University Press, 1992), p. 374.

[4] N. Davies, *The Isles: A History* (London: Macmillan, 1999), p. 371.

[5] J. Davies, *A History of Wales* (London: Allen Lane, 1993), p. 161.

[6] See now G. Williams, *Wales and the Reformation* (Cardiff: University of Wales Press, 1997); also, G. Williams, *Renewal and Reformation: Wales c. 1415–1642* (Oxford: Oxford University Press, 1993).

[7] R. Davies, *The Revolt of Owain Glyn Dŵr* (Oxford: Oxford University Press, 1995), 158. See also, E. Henken, *National Redeemer: Owain Glyndŵr in Welsh Tradition* (Cardiff: University of Wales Press, 1996).

[8] Davies, *The Isles,* above, n. 4, p. 434.

[9] W. Llewelyn Williams, *The Making of Modern Wales* (London: Macmillan, 1919), p. 16.

[10] G. Williams, *When Was Wales? A History of the Welsh* (London: Black Raven, 1985).

[11] K. Morgan, *Rebirth of a Nation: Wales, 1880–1980* (New York: Oxford University Press, 1981); K. Morgan, *Modern Wales: Politics, Places and People* (Cardiff: University of Wales Press, 1995).

[12] D. Williams, *The Rebecca Riots* (Cardiff: University of Wales Press, 1955) is a seminal work.

[13] K. Morgan, *Wales in British Politics, 1868–1922*, 3rd edn. (Cardiff: University of Wales Press, 1991); and see for an earlier overview, D. Williams, *A History of Modern Wales*, 2nd edn. (London: John Murray, 1977).

[14] *Devolution Conference: Letter from Mr Speaker to the Prime* Minister, Cm. 692 (Session 1919–1920).

[15] See, in this regard, J. Kendle, *Ireland and the Federal Solution: The Debate over the United Kingdom Constitution, 1870–1921* (Ontario: McGill–Queen's University Press, 1989).

[16] See now, D. Hopkin, D. Tanner and C. Williams (eds.), *The Labour Party in Wales, 1900–2000* (Cardiff: University of Wales Press, 2000).

[17] R. Davies, *Devolution: A Process not an Event* (Cardiff: Institute of Welsh Affairs, 1999), 8.

[18] J. Jones, 'The Parliament for Wales Campaign 1950–1956' (1992) 16(2) *Welsh History Review* 207. See further, R. Merfyn Jones and I. Rhys Jones, 'Labour and the Nation' in Hopkin, Tanner and Williams (eds.), *The Labour Party in Wales 1900–2000*, above, n. 16.

[19] V. Bogdanor, *Devolution in the United Kingdom* (Oxford: Oxford University Press, 1999), p. 153.

[20] A. Butt Philip, *The Welsh Question: Nationalism in Welsh Politics 1945–1970* (Cardiff: University of Wales Press, 1975), p. 316; see also D. Davies, *The Welsh Nationalist Party 1925–1945: A Call to Nationhood* (Cardiff: University of Wales Press, 1983).

[21] L. McAllister, *Plaid Cymru: The Emergence of a Political Party* (Bridgend: Seren, 2001), p. 211.

[22] E. John, *Wales: Its Politics and Economics* (Cardiff: Welsh Outlook Press, 1919), p. 43. The Bill did not proceed beyond First Reading.

[23] Eventually rejected in *Local Government in Wales*, Cmnd. 3340 (1997); and see for discussion, J. Trice, 'Welsh Local Government Reform' (1970) *Public Law* 277.

[24] Morgan, *Rebirth of a Nation*, above, n. 11, p. 391.

[25] *Report of the Royal Commission on the Constitution, 1969–1973*, Cmnd. 5460 (1973); see also *Democracy and Devolution: Proposals for Scotland and Wales*, Cmnd. 5732 (1974).

[26] As chronicled by D. Foulkes, J. Barry Jones and R. Wilford (eds.), *The Welsh Veto: The Wales Act 1978 and the Referendum* (Cardiff: University of Wales Press, 1983).

[27] I. Gowan, 'Government in Wales in the twentieth century', in J. Andrews (ed.), *Welsh Studies in Public Law* (Cardiff: University of Wales Press, 1970).

[28] *Report of the Royal Commission on the Constitution, 1969–1973*, above, n. 25, paragraph 385.

[29] Ibid., paragraph 335.

[30] D. Balsom, 'The three Wales model', in J. Osmond (ed.), *The National Question Again: Welsh Political Identity in the 1980s* (Llandysul: Gomer Press, 1985).

[31] See for a suitably critical account, D. Williams, 'Wales and legislative devolution' (1975) *Cambrian Law Review* 80.

[32] *Report of the Royal Commission on the Constitution, 1969–1973*, above, n. 25, paragraph 1123. In the case of Scotland, eight commissioners supported legislative devolution.

[33] D. Williams, 'The devolution of powers from central government', in D. Miers (ed.), *Devolution in Wales: Public Law and the National Assembly* (Cardiff: Wales Public Law and Human Rights Association, 1999), p. 5.

[34] R. Davies, *Devolution: A Process Not An Event*, above, n. 17, p. 6.

[35] J. Lloyd, *Establishing the Assembly* (Wales Public Law and Human Rights Association Lecture, November 2000).

[36] Lord Elis-Thomas, *A New Constitution for Wales?* (Cardiff: Welsh Governance Centre, 2000).

[37] As explained in chapter 2. There are of course many more specific innovations.

[38] *A Voice for Wales*, Cm. 3718 (1997), paragraph 1.4.

[39] HM Treasury, *Public Expenditure: Statistical Analyses 1997/8*, Cm. 3601 (1998), table 7.7. See further below, chapter 2.

[40] J. Kellas and P. Madgwick, 'Territorial ministries: the Scottish and Welsh offices', in P. Madgwick and R. Rose (eds.), *The Territorial Dimension in United Kingdom Politics* (London: Macmillan, 1982), p. 29. See also, D. Griffiths, *Thatcherism and Territorial Politics: A Welsh Case Study* (Aldershot: Avebury, 1996); and for an insider's view, Sir Wyn Roberts, *Fifteen Years at the Welsh Office* (Aberystwyth: National Library of Wales, 1995).

[41] See generally, D. Balsom, 'Political developments in Wales 1979–1997', in J. Barry Jones and D. Balsom (eds.), *The Road to the National Assembly for Wales* (Cardiff: University of Wales Press, 2000).

[42] Bogdanor, *Devolution in the United Kingdom*, above, n. 19, p. 194.

[43] See now, J. Evans, *The Future of Welsh Conservatism* (Cardiff: Institute of Welsh Affairs, 2002).

[44] See for discussion, J. Barry Jones, 'Changes to the government of Wales 1979–1997' in Barry Jones and Balsom (eds.), *The Road to the National Assembly for Wales*, above, n. 41. And see below, chapter 10.

⁴⁵ J. Osmond, 'Re-making Wales', in J. Osmond (ed.), *A Parliament for Wales* (Llandysul: Gomer, 1994).

⁴⁶ See for details, K. Morgan and E. Roberts, *A Guide to Quangoland* (Cardiff: Cardiff University, 1993); also now K. Morgan and G. Mungham, *Redesigning Democracy: The Making of the Welsh Assembly* (Bridgend: Seren, 2000), chapter 2.

⁴⁷ K. Morgan, *Democracy in Wales: From Dawn to Deficit* (Cardiff: BBC Wales, 1995), pp. 1, 6.

⁴⁸ See generally, M. Loughlin, *Legality and Locality: The Role of Law in Central–Local Government Relations* (Oxford: Clarendon Press, 1996).

⁴⁹ Welsh Local Government Association, *Local Democracy in Wales: The Implications of a Welsh Assembly* (Cardiff: Welsh Local Government Association, 1997), p. 16. And see further below, chapter 10.

⁵⁰ J. Barry Jones and R. Wilford, 'Implications: two salient issues', in Foulkes, Barry Jones and Wilford (eds.), *The Welsh Veto: The Wales Act 1978 and the Referendum*, above, n. 26.

⁵¹ Morgan and Mungham, *Redesigning Democracy: The Making of the Welsh Assembly*, above, n. 46, p. 45. See also J. Bradbury, 'Conservative governments, Scotland and Wales: a perspective on territorial management', in J. Bradbury and J. Mawson (eds.), *British Regionalism and Devolution* (London: Regional Studies Association, 1997). And see generally now, Hopkin, Tanner and Williams (eds.), *The Labour Party in Wales, 1900–2000*, above n. 16.

⁵² J. Griffiths, 'Introduction', in H. Edwards, *Hewn from a Rock* (Cardiff: Western Mail Ltd, 1967).

⁵³ R. Griffiths, *Turning to London: Labour's Attitude to Wales 1898–1956* (Cardiff: Y Faner Goch, 1978); K. Morgan, *Modern Wales: Politics, Places and People* (Cardiff: University of Wales Press, 1995), chapter 24.

⁵⁴ A. Thomas, 'Wales and devolution: a constitutional footnote?' (1996) 4 *Public Money and Management* 21 at 24.

⁵⁵ An extreme example is P. Hain, 'A Welsh Third Way?' *Tribune* (1999).

⁵⁶ Davies, *Devolution: A Process not an Event*, above, n. 17, p. 4.

⁵⁷ See for example, A. Thomas, 'The moment of truth: Labour's Welsh Assembly proposals in practice' (1996) 30 *Regional Studies* 694; and R. Deacon, 'New Labour and the Welsh Assembly: "preparing for a new Wales" or updating the Wales Act 1978?' (1996) 30 *Regional Studies* 689.

⁵⁸ Quoted in J. Griffiths, *Pages from Memory* (London: Dent, 1969).

⁵⁹ Davies, *Devolution: A Process not an Event*, above, n. 17, pp. 5–6. See also now, idem, *Evidence to the Richard Commission* (December 2002).

⁶⁰ *Scotland's Parliament: Scotland's Right* (Edinburgh: Scottish Constitutional Convention, 1995).

⁶¹ Under the auspices of the Campaign for a Welsh Assembly: see J. Osmond, 'Re-making Wales', in J. Osmond (ed.), *A Parliament for Wales* (Llandysul: Gomer Press, 1994). See further, Parliament for Wales Campaign, *Power to the People of Wales* (Cardiff: 1997).

⁶² Notably Williams, 'Wales and legislative devolution', above, n. 31; see latterly, R. Hazell, *An Assembly for Wales* (London: Constitution Unit, 1996).

⁶³ As documented in B. Taylor and K. Thomson (eds.), *Scotland and Wales: Nations Again?* (Cardiff: University of Wales Press, 1999).

⁶⁴ Morgan and Mungham, *Redesigning Democracy: The Making of the Welsh Assembly*, above, n. 46, p. 99.

65 See for details, L. McAllister, 'The Welsh devolution referendum: definitely, maybe?' (1998) 51 *Parliamentary Affairs* 149.

67 Welsh Labour Party, *A Statement on the Future of Local and Regional Government in Wales* (Cardiff: Welsh Labour Party, 1990).

68 Welsh Labour Party, *Shaping the Vision: A Report on the Powers and Structure of the Welsh Assembly* (Cardiff: Welsh Labour Party, 1995), pp. 4–5. See also Welsh Labour Party, *Preparing for a New Wales* (Cardiff: Welsh Labour Party, 1996). The different features are discussed elsewhere in this volume.

70 HM Treasury, *Principles to Govern Determination of the Block Budgets for the Scottish Parliament and National Assembly for Wales*, Dep. Paper 3s/5621 (December 1997); and see below, chapter 2.

72 *A Voice for Wales*, Cm. 3718 (1997); a sentiment echoed word for word in the preface to the Scottish White Paper, *Scotland's Parliament*, Cm. 3658 (1997).

73 R. Hazell, 'Reinventing the constitution: can the state survive?' (1999) *Public Law* 84 at 102. And see House of Lords Select Committee on the Constitution, Fourth Report: *Changing the Constitution: The Process of Constitutional Change* (HL 69, Session 2001–2).

74 New Labour, *Because Britain Deserves Better* (London: Labour Party, 1997), p. 33.

75 *Rights Brought Home: The Human Rights Bill*, Cm. 3782 (1997), paragraph 2.23.

77 R. Davies, 'The economic case for a Welsh Assembly' (1996) (2) *Welsh Democracy Review* 6, pp. 6–7.

79 Welsh Assembly Government, *A Winning Wales: The National Economic Development Strategy of the Welsh Assembly Government* (January 2002).

80 S. Rokkan and D. Urwin, 'Introduction: centres and peripheries in western Europe', in S. Rokkan and D. Urwin (eds.), *The Politics of Territorial Identity: Studies in European Regionalism* (London: Sage, 1982).

81 See now, N. Walker, 'Beyond the unitary conception of the United Kingdom constitution?' (2000) *Public Law* 384.

82 M. Keating, 'What's wrong with asymmetrical government?' (1998) 8 (1) *Regional and Federal Studies* 195 at 205.

83 The First Minister has been known to wax lyrical in this regard: R. Morgan, *Variable Geometry UK* (Cardiff: Institute of Welsh Affairs, 2000).

84 See for pungent criticism, K. Sutherland (ed.), *The Rape of the Constitution?* (Thorverton: Imprint Academic, 2000).

85 Keating, 'What's wrong with asymmetrical government?', above, n. 82, p. 195.

86 See, for general overviews, R. Hazell (ed.), *The State and the Nations: The First Year of Devolution in the UK* (London: Constitution Unit, 2000); and R. Hazell (ed.), *The State of the Nations 2003: The Third Year of Devolution in the UK* (London: Constitution Unit, 2003).

87 As enshrined in the statute: Scotland Act (henceforth SA) 1998, ss. 44–58. This is not to overlook the various internal difficulties: see B. Winetrobe, *Realising the Vision: A Parliament with a Purpose – an Audit of the First Year of the Scottish Parliament* (London: Constitution Unit, 2001).

⁸⁸ *The Belfast Agreement*, Cm. 3883 (1998); Northern Ireland Act 1998; and see B. O'Leary, *The British-Irish Agreement: Power-Sharing Plus* (London: Constitution Unit, 1998). The work of the Northern Ireland Assembly is currently suspended.

⁸⁹ As developed under strand three of the Agreement. There is an informative website: *www.british-irishcouncil.org*

⁹⁰ Department of Transport, Local Government and the Regions, *Your Region, Your Choice: Revitalising the English Regions*, Cm. 5511 (2002). See also the Regional Assemblies (Preparations) Act 2003.

⁹¹ See in the local context, R. Hazell, *The Dilemmas of Devolution: Does Wales have an Answer to the English Question?* (Cardiff: Welsh Governance Centre, 2001). And see generally C. Jeffery and J. Mawson (eds.), *Devolution and the English Question* (London: Regional Studies Association, 2002).

⁹² M. Keating, *The New Regionalism in Western Europe: Territorial Restructuring and Political Change* (London: Edward Elgar, 1998); M. Telo (ed.), *European Union and New Regionalism: Regional Actors and Global Governance in a Post-hegemonic Era* (Aldershot: Ashgate, 2001).

⁹³ See for example, J. Barry Jones and M. Keating (eds.), *The European Union and the Regions* (Oxford: Clarendon, 1995); and (for a more sceptical view), P. Le Gales and C. Lequesne (eds.), *Regions in Europe* (London: Routledge, 1998).

⁹⁴ R. Rawlings, 'Law, Territory and Integration: A View from the Atlantic Shore' (2001) 67(3) *International Review of Administrative Sciences* 479. See also, J. Loughlin (ed.), *Sub-National Democracy in the European Union: Challenges and Opportunities* (Oxford: Oxford University Press, 2001).

⁹⁵ J. Barry Jones, 'Welsh Politics and Changing British and European Contexts' in J. Bradbury and J. Mawson (eds.), *British Regionalism and Devolution: The Challenges of State Reform and European Integration* (London: Regional Studies Association, 1997).

⁹⁶ As discussed in chapter 11. See also J. Gray and J. Osmond, *Wales in Europe: The Opportunity Presented by a Welsh Assembly* (Cardiff: Institute of Welsh Affairs, 1997).

⁹⁷ See below, especially chapter 5.

⁹⁸ See National Assembly Advisory Group (NAAG), *National Assembly for Wales: A Consultation Paper* (April 1998), paragraph 1.3.

⁹⁹ As explained below.

¹⁰⁰ NAAG, *Recommendations* (August 1998); and see for general discussion, L. McAllister, 'The new politics in Wales: rhetoric or reality?' (2000) 53 *Parliamentary Affairs* 591.

¹⁰¹ See for detailed discussion below, chapter 3.

¹⁰² For details see M. Laffin and A. Thomas, 'Designing the National Assembly for Wales' (2000) 53 *Parliamentary Affairs* 557.

¹⁰³ GWA, ss. 50–1.

¹⁰⁴ Issued in the form of a letter to Gareth Wardell, the Chair of the commissioners (August 1998). See further below, chapter 3.

¹⁰⁵ See below, especially chapter 3, on the special architectural features designed to promote transparency etc. in the new model Wales.

¹⁰⁶ Ron Davies, *House of Commons Debates*, vol. 302, col. 676 (8 December 1997); and see for further details, R. Deacon, 'How the additional member system was buried and then resurrected In Wales' (1997) 34 *Representation* 219.

¹⁰⁷ GWA, ss. 2–7 and Schedule 1.

¹⁰⁸ Whereby the first additional member is identified by taking the number of

constituency seats won by each party in the region, adding one (so providing 'the divisor'), and dividing the number of each party's list votes in the region. The calculation is then repeated for the second to fourth additional members, factoring in any additional member seats allocated in previous rounds.

[109] An aspect pursued in R. Rawlings, 'The new model Wales' (1998) 25 *Journal of Law and Society* 461; see also L. McAllister, 'The road to Cardiff Bay: the process of establishing the National Assembly for Wales' (1999) 52 *Parliamentary Affairs* 634.

[110] *A Voice for Wales*, Cm. 3718 (1997), paragraph 4.3, and for further details, Annex C. The minimalist approach is prescribed in the legislation (GWA, Schedule 1, paragraph 8) and so unless altered will govern future reviews by the Boundary Commission.

[111] In contrast that is to the Sainte-Lague formula, which uses as divisors odd numbers beginning at 1. See for (an accessible) discussion of the variants of AMS, T. Mackie and R. Rose, *The International Almanac of Electoral History*, 3rd edn. (London: Macmillan, 1990).

[112] Where the Parliament has been established with 73 constituency Members and 56 additional Members. See further, P. Dunleavy, H. Margetts and S. Weir, *Devolution Votes: PR Elections in Scotland and Wales*, Democratic Audit Paper no. 12 (Colchester: Democratic Audit, September 1997), chapter 3.

[113] GWA, s. 3; and see Welsh Labour Party, *Shaping the Vision*, above, n. 68, paragraph 7.5.

[114] In the fall of Alun Michael: see below, chapter 4.

[115] D. Melding, 'The Conservative Party's shy and muted campaign', in Barry Jones and Balsom (eds.), *The Road to the National Assembly for Wales*, above, n. 41, p. 73.

[116] Committee on Standards in Public Life, *The Funding of Political Parties in the United Kingdom*, Cm. 4057–1 (1999). There were also complaints of voter confusion. See further J. Barry Jones, 'The referendum: a flawed instrument', in Barry Jones and Balsom (eds.), *The Road to the National Assembly for Wales*, above, n. 41.

[117] Most notably in terms of the shift towards a cabinet-style form of administration: see below, chapter 3.

[118] See for an anecdotal account, L. Andrews, *Wales Says Yes: The Inside Story of the Yes for Wales Referendum Campaign* (Bridgend: Seren, 1999). See generally, L. McAllister, 'The Welsh devolution referendum: definitely, maybe?' (1998) 51 *Parliamentary Affairs* 149.

[119] Yes for Wales Steering Committee, *Aims of the Campaign* (1997), p. 1.

[120] R. Davies, 'Preface' in Taylor and Thomson (eds.), *Scotland and Wales: Nations Again?*, above, n. 63, p. xviii.

[121] R. Wyn Jones and D. Trystan, 'The 1997 Welsh referendum vote' in Taylor and Thomson (eds.), *Scotland and Wales*, above, n. 120.

[122] G. Evans and D. Trystan, 'Why was 1997 different?', in Taylor and Thomson (eds.), *Scotland and Wales*, above, n. 120, p. 112. See also D. Balsom, 'The referendum result', in Barry Jones and Balsom (eds.), *The Road to the National Assembly for Wales*, above, n. 41.

[123] R. Wyn Jones and D. Trystan, *Scotland and Wales*, above, n. 121, p. 90.

[124] See to this effect (in the context of the ensuing Assembly elections), R. Wyn Jones and D. Trystan, 'Turnout, participation and legitimacy in the politics of post-devolution Wales', in P. Chaney, T. Hall and A. Pithouse (eds.), *New Governance – New Democracy? Post-Devolution Wales* (Cardiff: University of Wales Press, 2001).

[125] Melding, 'The Conservative Party's shy and muted campaign', above, n. 115, p. 76.

[126] Chronicled by J. Barry Jones, 'Labour pains', in Barry Jones and Balsom (eds.), *The Road to the National Assembly for Wales*, above, n. 41.

[127] See for detailed analysis, D. Balsom, 'The first Welsh general election', in D. Balsom (ed.), *The Wales Yearbook 2000* (Cardiff: HTV, 2000); also L. McAllister, 'Changing the landscape? The wider political lessons from recent elections in Wales' (2000) 71 (2) *Political Quarterly* 211.

[128] However, as summarized in the Postscript, the story of the 2003 Assembly Elections was very different.

Chapter 2

[1] Welsh Office Devolution Unit, *A Guide to the Government of Wales Act 1998* (1998).

[2] There is an obvious parallel here with the other UK devolutionary schemes, but the idea plays differently in Wales precisely because of (the weaker form of) executive devolution. See further below.

[3] See to this effect, K. Patchett, 'The new Welsh constitution: the Government of Wales Act 1998', in J. Barry Jones and D. Balsom (eds.), *The Road to the National Assembly for Wales* (Cardiff: University of Wales Press, 2000).

[4] R. Rawlings, 'Concordats of the constitution' (2000) 116 *Law Quarterly Review* 257; and see below, chapter 12.

[5] L. Smith, *Quangos: Not so much a 'Bonfire' More a Damp Squib* (Brynmawr: 2002).

[6] See below, chapter 11.

[7] GWA, ss. 126–8 and Schedules 13–14.

[8] GWA, ss. 111–12 and Schedules 9–10.

[9] GWA, ss. 90–6.

[10] See below, chapter 6.

[11] As discussed in chapter 9, there are some particular statutory provisions.

[12] GWA, s. 113 and Schedule 13. And see below, chapter 10.

[13] GWA, ss. 114–15.

[14] See on the parallel development 'north of the border', G. Clark, 'Scottish devolution and the European Union' (1999) *Public Law* 504.

[15] GWA, ss. 29, 106(7) and 106(1) respectively. Matters are detailed in chapter 13.

[16] GWA, Schedule 3, paragraph 5.

[17] Discussed further in chapter 14.

[18] Wales Act 1978, ss. 34–5. See also on the parallel development in Scotland, N. Burrows, 'Unfinished business: the Scotland Act 1998' (1999) 62 *Modern Law Review* 241.

[19] Assuming, that is, the failure of political and administrative negotiations. See further below, chapter 12.

[20] See also on this aspect, A. Sherlock, 'The establishment of the National Assembly for Wales' (1999) 5 *European Public Law* 42.

[21] See for general discussion, C. Williams, 'Operating through two languages', in J. Osmond (ed.), *The National Assembly Agenda* (Cardiff: Institute of Welsh Affairs, 1998).

²²   GWA, ss. 47, 122.

²³   See below, especially chapters 6 and 14.

²⁴   GWA, s. 121. And see K. Bishop and A. Flynn, 'The National Assembly for Wales and the promotion of sustainable development: implications for collaborative government and governance' (1999) 14 *Public Policy and Administration* 62.

²⁵   See National Assembly, *A Sustainable Wales – Learning to Live Differently* (2000) and *How We are Learning to Live Differently* (March 2002).

²⁶   GWA, s. 120(1). See also s. 48 (the Assembly to have due regard to equal opportunities in the conduct of its business). Workings are currently under review: Assembly cabinet statement, 'Revising the Assembly's sustainable development scheme', 24 June 2003.

²⁷   Race Relations Act 1971, s. 71; *Wheeler v Leicester City Council* [1985] AC 1054; also *R v Lewisham LBC ex parte Shell UK Ltd* [1988] 1 All ER 938.

²⁸   See below, chapter 7. And see now, P. Chaney and R. Fevre, *An Absolute Duty: Equal Opportunities and the National Assembly for Wales* (Cardiff: Institute of Welsh Affairs, 2002).

²⁹   In this respect the approach fits with the (EU) Charter of Fundamental Rights, agreed at Nice in December 2000, Official Journal 2000/C 364/01 (Article 21, non-discrimination).

³⁰   Patchett, 'The new Welsh constitution', above, n. 3; and see above, pp. 11–13 (the concepts of strict executive devolution and quasi-legislative devolution).

³¹   See for example, N. MacCormick, 'Is there a constitutional path to Scottish independence?' (2000) 53 *Parliamentary Affairs* 721.

³²   This is not to overlook for example the contemporary claim to 'self-determination' asserted by Plaid Cymru. See for a useful comparative discussion, M. Walters, 'Nationalism and the pathology of legal systems: considering the Quebec succession reference and its lessons for the United Kingdom' (1999) 62 *Modern Law Review* 371.

³³   In addition, that is, to post-legislative challenge in the courts on the basis that an Act of the Parliament is not law. See Scotland Act 1998, ss. 28–37; and N. Burrows, 'Unfinished business: the Scotland Act 1998' (1999) 62 *Modern Law Review* 241.

³⁴   There is also the historical precedent of s. 75 of the Government of Ireland Act 1920: 'the supreme authority of the Parliament of the United Kingdom shall remain unaffected and undiminished over all persons, matters and things'. See further, B. Hadfield, 'Political process: peace process?' (1998) *European Public Law* 451.

³⁵   Backed up by the new court procedures involving the Judicial Committee of the Privy Council. The details are discussed in chapters 8 and 14.

³⁶   Ron Davies, *House of Commons Debates* (Hansard), vol. 302, col. 685 (8 December 1997).

³⁷   Discussion of the Assembly's powers to implement EU laws and policies is reserved to chapter 13 ('Wales in Europe').

³⁸   GWA, ss. 27–8; and see further below, chapter 11.

³⁹   GWA, s. 40; a type of provision familiar from local government.

⁴⁰   This is not to overlook the scope for boundary disputes ('devolution issues'); see below, chapter 14. And see in respect of excepted matters, Scotland Act 1998, Schedule 5.

⁴¹   See above, p. 5.

⁴²   See Schedule 2 of the Wales Act 1978, some twenty-five pages long.

⁴³   R. Rawlings, 'The new model Wales' (1998) 25 *Journal of Law and Society* 461.

⁴⁴ See above, chapter 1.

⁴⁵ Quoted in V. Bogdanor, *Devolution in the United Kingdom* (Oxford: Oxford University Press, 1999), p. 258; and see for general discussion, D. Lambert, 'The Government of Wales Act – an Act to be ministered in Wales in like form as it is in this realm?' (1999) 30 *Cambrian Law Review* 60.

⁴⁶ *Report of the Royal Commission on the Constitution, 1969–1973*, Cmnd. 5460 (1973), paragraph 828. And see further below, chapter 9 ('Rawlings principles').

⁴⁷ See further D. Lambert, 'A voice for Wales – the National Assembly for Wales', in T. Watkin (ed.), *Legal Wales: Its Past, Its Future* (Cardiff: Welsh Legal History Society, 2001); also, A. Sherlock, 'A Wales of bits and pieces' (2000) 6 *European Public Law* 193.

⁴⁸ C. Harlow and R. Rawlings, *Law and Administration*, 2nd edn. (London: Butterworths, 1997), chapters 6–7.

⁴⁹ Win Griffiths, *House of Commons Debates* (Hansard), vol. 304, col. 860 (20 January 1998)

⁵⁰ See further below, chapter 8.

⁵¹ Welsh Office, *Make Your Mark on Wales* (April 1999), p. 2.

⁵² D. Lambert, 'The Government of Wales Act', above, n. 45, p. 63.

⁵³ See generally, T. Daintith and A. Page, *The Executive in the Constitution: Structure, Autonomy and Internal Control* (New York: Oxford University Press, 1999).

⁵⁴ Made under the Ministers of the Crown Acts 1964 and 1975.

⁵⁵ For example the rate support grant provisions of the Local Government Act 1974.

⁵⁶ National Assembly for Wales (Transfer of Functions) Order 1999, SI 1999 No. 672, made under s. 22 of the GWA.

⁵⁷ Welsh Office Devolution Unit, *Technical Guide to the Transfer of Functions Order* (November 1998), p. 5. The Unit also produced a so-called 'popular version': *Making the Difference in Wales: A Guide to the Powers of the National Assembly for Wales* (October 1998).

⁵⁸ The National Assembly for Wales (Transfer of Functions) Order 2000, SI 2000 no. 253 (patriation of functions mainly in the realm of European regulations; repatriation of powers under the mental health legislation). See for later examples, The National Assembly for Wales (Transfer of Functions) Orders, SI 2000 no. 1829; SI 2000 no. 1830 and SI 2001 no. 3679.

⁵⁹ With some limited flexibility in respect of cross-border bodies and English border areas. See further GWA, Schedule 3, paragraph 3.

⁶⁰ The definition of concurrency as set out in the *Technical Guide*, above, n. 57, p. 2.

⁶¹ See for important practical examples the approval requirements in Schedule 3 of the Welsh Development Agency Act 1975. Article 5 and Schedule 2 of the Order also made provision – typically in the sphere of public appointments – for the obverse situation of ministerial functions exercisable only with the consent of, or after consultation with, the Assembly.

⁶² D. Lambert, 'A comparison between the office of the Secretary of State for Wales and the National Assembly for Wales', in D. Miers (ed.), *Devolution in Wales: Public Law and the National Assembly* (Cardiff: Welsh Public Law and Human Rights Association, 1999), p. 23.

⁶³ Destructive Imported Animals Act 1932, ss. 3, 5 and 8.

[64] Transfer of Functions (Wales) Order 1969, SI 1969, no. 388, Article 3 and Schedule 2.

[65] D. Miers and D. Lambert, 'Law making in Wales: Wales legislation online', (2002) *Public Law* 663.

[66] Non-attributable interview, February 2000.

[67] See on the management and control of water resources, GWA, Schedule 3, paragraph 6.

[68] Powerfully expressed in evidence from the Law Society to the Assembly Review of Procedure (February 2002): see below, chapters 8–9.

[69] See below, chapter 15 (the commission's terms of reference).

[70] Lord Elis-Thomas, 'National Assembly, a year in power?' (Aberystwyth: Institute of Welsh Politics, 2000).

[71] See below, chapters 10–11.

[72] K. Patchett, 'The central relationship: the Assembly's engagement with Westminster and Whitehall', in J. Barry Jones and J. Osmond (eds.), *Building a Civic Culture: Institutional Change, Policy Development and Political Dynamics in the National Assembly for Wales* (Cardiff: Institute of Welsh Affairs and Welsh Governance Centre, 2002).

[73] R. Davies, 'The tools for the job' (1996) 4 *Agenda: Journal of the Institute of Welsh Affairs* 18, pp. 19, 21.

[74] *A Voice for Wales*, Cm. 3718 (1997), paragraph 3.39. See to this effect, P. Silk, 'The Assembly as a legislature', in J. Osmond (ed.), *The National Assembly Agenda*, above, n. 21.

[75] See below, chapter 3 for elaboration of this concept.

[76] Non-attributable interview, March 2002.

[77] R. Hazell and R. Cornes, 'Financing devolution: the centre retains control', in R. Hazell (ed.), *Constitutional Futures: A History of the Next Ten Years* (Oxford: Oxford University Press, 1999).

[78] Scotland Act 1998, ss. 73–5. The case for a Welsh equivalent is discussed in chapter 15.

[79] See for example D. Bell and A. Christie, 'Finance – the Barnett formula: nobody's child?', in A. Trench (ed.), *The State of the Nations 2001* (Thorverton: Imprint Academic, 2001), p. 135; and for discussion in the local context, G. Bristow and A. Kay, 'Spending autonomy in Wales', in Barry Jones and Osmond (eds.), *Building a Civic Culture*, above, n. 72.

[80] Welsh Assembly Government, *A Winning Wales: The National Economic Development Strategy of the Welsh Assembly Government* (January 2002), p. 20.

[81] C. Thain and M. Wright, *The Treasury and Whitehall: The Planning and Control of Public Expenditure, 1976–1993* (Oxford: Clarendon Press, 1995), p. 307.

[82] HM Treasury, *Funding the Scottish Parliament, the National Assembly for Wales and the Northern Ireland Assembly: A Statement of Funding Policy* (March 1999), paragraph 1.

[83] For the avoidance of doubt, this discussion proceeds from a Welsh perspective. There are of course adaptations, most obviously for the Scottish tax-varying power.

[84] The standard account is D. Heald, 'Territorial public expenditure in the United Kingdom' (1994) 72 *Public Administration* 147.

[85] See below, chapter 6 (the Assembly's budget-setting process).

[86] HM Treasury, *Needs Assessment Study – Report* (1979). See further, House of

Commons Treasury Select Committee, *Second Report: The Barnett Formula* (HC 341, Session 1997–8); and for the UK government's response, Treasury Committee, *Fourth Special Report: Government Response to Second Report* (HC 619, Session 1997–8).

[87] See for the procedural details, HM Treasury, *Funding the Scottish Parliament, the National Assembly for Wales and the Northern Ireland Assembly*, above, n. 83, especially paragraph 11.

[88] GWA, ss. 90–103. Further provisions relating to the Assembly's finances were inserted in the GWA by the Government Resources and Accounts Act 2000.

[89] GWA, s. 101. Major change however is in the offing; see below, chapter 11 (draft Wales (Audit) Bill).

[90] As explained in another context: Scottish Affairs Committee, *The Operation of Multi-layer Democracy* (HC 460–1, Session 1997–8), p. xiv. See further below, chapter 12.

[91] GWA, s. 81 merely requires the Secretary of State to detail and explain estimated payments.

[92] Win Griffiths, quoted at (1998) 3 *Welsh Democracy Review* 18. See further, *House of Commons Debates* (Hansard), vol. 305, cols. 863–95 (3 February 1998); and *House of Lords Debates* (Hansard), vol. 591, cols. 1387–90 (9 July 1998).

[93] See below, chapter 12.

[94] (Assembly) Economic Development Committee, *The Barnett Formula* (July 1999), as derived from the 1998 CSR. See now HM Treasury, *Statement of Funding Rules* (3rd edn., 2002).

[95] See for discussion of these paradigms, below, chapters 9–11.

[96] Welsh Office, *Departmental Report 1999* (1999).

[97] The words of R. Davies, 'The economic case for a Welsh Assembly' (1996) 2 *Welsh Democracy Review* 6, at 6–7.

[98] Source: HM Treasury, *Public Expenditure Statistical Analysis 1999/2000* (2000). The miscellaneous item includes the costs of the central administration of the Office of the Secretary of State for Wales.

[99] R. Ross Mackay, *The Search for Balance: Taxing and Spending across the United Kingdom* (Cardiff: Institute of Welsh Affairs, 2001), pp. 39, 43, 49.

[100] Cm. 3718 (1997), paragraph, D. 12.

[101] Cm. 3658 (1997), paragraph 7.7.

[102] The kind of model operating for example in Australia: see for comparative discussion, I. McLean, 'A fiscal constitution for the UK', in S. Chen and T. Wright, *The English Question* (London: Fabian Society, 2000). See also now, House Of Lords Select Committee on the Constitution, *Devolution: Inter-institutional Relations in the United Kingdom*, HL 28, 2002–3; and – a cool one, *Government Response*, Cm. 5780/2003.

[103] Alistair Darling, *House of Commons Debates* (Hansard), vol. 301, col. 1080 (27 November 1997).

[104] The promise might even be argued to raise a 'legitimate expectation', justiciable in the courts. See below, chapter 14 for discussion of this doctrine in the context of the concordats.

[105] Key elements of the initiative are discussed in chapter 13. See, R. Rawlings, 'Law, territory and integration: a view from the Atlantic shore', (2001) 67 (3) *International Review of Administrative Sciences* 479.

[106] HM Treasury, *Funding the Scottish Parliament, the National Assembly for Wales and the Northern Ireland Assembly*, above, n. 82, pp. 5–6.

[107] See for further details, National Assembly for Wales, *Objective 1 Funding* (February 2000); also G. Bristow and N. Blewitt, *Unravelling the Knot: The Interaction of UK Treasury and European Union Funding for Wales* (Cardiff: Institute of Welsh Affairs, 1999).

[108] We return to the saga in chapter 4.

[109] Bell and Christie, 'Finance – the Barnett formula', above, n. 79, p. 147.

[110] See for example, P. Williams, *The Case for Replacing the Barnett Formula* (Cardiff: Plaid Cymru, April 2002); *Official Record*, 7 May 2002 (minority party debate).

[111] See *Official Record*, 16 July 2002.

[112] Full resource budgeting basis, net of depreciation.

[113] HM Treasury, *Public Expenditure: Statistical Analysis 2001–2002* (Cm. 5101, 2001)

[114] *Official Record*, 16 July 2002 (Minister of Finance, Edwina Hart).

[115] *Western Mail*, 18 April 2000.

Chapter 3

[1] J. Shortridge 'Equipped for the future' (February 2000) *Overview Magazine* 6.

[2] R. Davies, 'We need a coalition of ideas' (2000) 4 *Agenda: Journal of the Institute of Welsh Affairs* 27 at 29, 31.

[3] This is a recurring theme in the evidence to the Assembly Review of Procedure (February 2002): see below, chapter 7.

[4] D. Williams, 'Wales, the law and the constitution' (2000) 31 *Cambrian Law Review* 51 at 58

[5] W. Roddick, *Crossing the Road* (Cardiff: The Law Society, 1999), pp. 1–2.

[6] Reference was made to s. 33 of the GWA ('a voice for Wales'): see above, chapter 2.

[7] See further below, chapter 14.

[8] GWA, s. 1(3).

[9] W. Roddick, *The Challenge of the Welsh Assembly* (London: University College London, 1998), p. 2. The projected death of the corporate body in the face of legislative devolution is discussed in chapter 15.

[10] R. Davies, *Devolution: A Process not an Event* (Cardiff: Institute of Welsh Affairs, 1999), p. 15.

[11] M. Mitchell, *Standing Orders: A New Political Culture for the National Assembly for Wales* (London: Charter 88, 1998), p. 3.

[12] See above on the role of NAAG, chapter 1. And see further, M. James, 'The Assembly at work', in J. Osmond (ed.), *The National Assembly Agenda* (Cardiff: Institute of Welsh Affairs, 1998). The strong Scottish influence has also been noted.

[13] National Assembly Advisory Group (NAAG), *Recommendations* (1998), paragraph 1.13.

[14] A theme further developed in chapter 8 in the context of Assembly law making.

[15] National Assembly Advisory Group, *National Assembly for Wales: A Consultation Paper* (1998), paragraph 3.5.

[16] *A Voice for Wales*, Cm. 3718 (1998), especially chapter 4, 'The Assembly at work'.

[17] See below, especially chapter 10.

[18] Clauses 52–8 of Bill 88 of 1997–8.

[19] There are certain similarities here with the devolutionary model established for Northern Ireland: see R. Wilford and R. Wilson, *A Democratic Design? The Political Style of the Northern Ireland Assembly* (London: Constitution Unit, 2001).

[20] See for general discussion in this context, R. Hazell, *An Assembly for Wales* (London: Constitution Unit, 1996), chapter 6.

[21] *House of Commons Debates*, vol. 309, col. 536 (25 March 1998).

[22] As explained in later chapters, some important powers cannot be delegated.

[23] The government resisted attempts to entrench a cabinet system in the devolution legislation: *House of Lords Debates*, vol. 590, cols. 369–71 (3 June 1998).

[24] Ron Davies, *House of Commons Debates*, vol. 309, col. 538 (25 March 1998).

[25] See further below, chapter 4.

[26] GWA, section 34.

[27] See to this effect Ron Davies, *House of Commons Debates*, vol. 309, col. 574 (25 March 1998).

[28] Welsh Office, *Devolution and the Civil Service: Staff Guidance* (1998), paragraph 14. And see further below.

[29] In the guise of the Scottish Parliamentary Corporate Body: see Scotland Act 1998, s. 21 and Schedule 2.

[30] *House of Commons Debates*, vol. 309, col. 562 (25 March 1998).

[31] Ibid. And see below, chapter 15 (in the context of the Richard Commission).

[32] NAAG, *Recommendations* (1998), paragraph 4.6.

[33] See further below, chapter 4.

[34] Clause 79, and see *House of Commons Debates*, vol. 309, cols. 721–35 (26 March 1998).

[35] GWA, s. 53(4). The Freedom of Information Act 2000 is discussed below.

[36] See further, on the competing constitutional models, chapter 4.

[37] This follows the recommendations of the National Assembly Advisory Group.

[38] See also the Postscript to the book, for the shape of the cabinet following the 2003 Assembly elections.

[39] We return to these points in the next chapter.

[40] National Assembly, *Cabinet Responsibilities – Statement by the First Secretary* (29 June 1999).

[41] Cabinet Secretariat, *Responsibilities of the National Assembly for Wales and the Assembly Cabinet* (February 2000), 1

[42] See above, chapter 2.

[43] *Official Record*, 21 July 1999.

[44] Cabinet Secretariat, above, n. 41.

[45] Welsh Labour Party and Welsh Liberal Democrats, *Putting Wales First: A Partnership for the People of Wales* (Cardiff: Welsh Labour Party and Welsh Liberal Democrats, October 2000).

[46] The argument is elaborated in chapter 15 in the context of the Richard Commission.

[47] See *Official Record*, 17 October 2000.

[48] Standing Orders Commissioners, *Draft Standing Orders Submitted to the Secretary of State* (January 1999), paragraph 2.4.

[49] Welsh Office, *Standing Orders of the National Assembly for Wales* (April 1999), p. 72.

[50] See *Official Record*, 18 May and 16 June 1999.

[51] Welsh Liberal Democrats, *The National Assembly in Deadlock: Is There a Better Way Forward for Wales?* (Cardiff: Welsh Liberal Democrats, November 1999).

[52] National Assembly, *Discharge of Functions under the Government of Wales Act: Delegations and Accountability* (1999), paragraph 6.

[53] See further below, chapter 6.

[54] See for illustration, *Official Record*, 14 December 1999 (delegation of functions under the Food Standards Act 1999).

[55] *Official Record*, 17 May 2000 (delegation of functions under the Structural Funds Regulations 2000), SI 2000 no. 906.

[56] *Official Record*, 27 March 2000. The role of the subject committees is discussed in chapter 7.

[57] See below, especially chapter 11.

[58] In true 'hybrid' fashion, the Assembly cabinet is classified as a committee in the devolution statute (s. 56: 'the executive committee'). This need not detain us here.

[59] The regional committees are discussed in chapter 7.

[60] Not that the Welsh approach begins to equate with the route followed in Northern Ireland: see generally Wilford and Wilson, *A Democratic Design? The Political Style of the Northern Ireland Assembly*, above, n. 19.

[61] See for example section 57(8) on subject committees. For the avoidance of doubt, the cabinet or 'executive committee' is exempt from the principle.

[62] As recommended by NAAG, the standing orders have specified a range of seven–eleven Members, e.g. for the subject committees. See generally, NAAG, *Recommendations*, above, n. 13, s. 5.

[63] For the sake of completeness, there are also quasi-judicial Planning Decision Committees, tasked with determining important planning cases that have been referred to the Assembly for decision, and a Public Appointments Committee, charged with scrutinizing relevant processes. They too need not detain us.

[64] M. Evans, 'A constitutional perspective', *Submission to Assembly Review of Procedure* (May 2001).

[65] It also enjoys a somewhat shadowy existence, being one of the few Assembly committees to meet in private.

[66] Evans, 'A constitutional perspective', above, n. 64.

[67] NAAG, *Recommendations*, above, n. 13, s. 5.

[68] Formerly the European Affairs Committee: see below, chapter 13.

[69] This matter would resurface in the Assembly Review of Procedure.

[70] The concept is discussed in this volume especially in the context of human rights: see below, chapter 14.

[71] See GWA, section 54(2); and Standing Orders Commissioners, *Draft Standing Orders Submitted to the Secretary of State*, above, n. 48, Preface.

[72] But not before controversy over an attempt by the First Minister to appoint Michael German as Chair of the European and External Affairs Committee: see further below, chapter 4. Under standing orders the appointment ('of a Minister') was in the gift of the Assembly *qua* Assembly.

[73] The Legislation Committee, discussed in chapter 8 under the rubric of law making, has thus been able to have a Liberal Democrat Chair notwithstanding coalition or 'partnership government'.

[74] Whereby the subject committees would have exercised day-to-day executive responsibilities: see above, p. 90.

75 Chamber Wales, FSB and CBI Wales, *Submission to Assembly Review of Procedure* (March 2001).
76 NAAG, *Recommendations*, above, n. 13, paragraphs 5.7, 5.12.
77 The precise formulation has now been altered in the light of the Assembly Review of Procedure: see further below, chapter 8.
78 GWA, ss. 74–5 and Schedule 5.
79 The practical workings are examined in chapter 7.
80 See below, chapter 8, on the initial design of Assembly law-making procedures.
81 Panel of Chairs, *Submission to Assembly Review of Procedure* (May 2001), p. 5.
82 *Official Record*, 7 December 1999.
83 See for general discussion, below, chapter 7.
84 J. Osmond, 'The enigma of the corporate body', in J. Barry Jones and J. Osmond (eds.), *Inclusive Government and Party Management* (Cardiff: Institute of Welsh Affairs, 2001).
85 See especially, Report of the Hansard Society Commission, *The Challenge for Parliament – Making Government Accountable* (London: Hansard Society, 2001). The argument is buttressed now by a reduction of subject committee meetings in the light of single-party Labour rule in the Assembly: see further below, chapter 7.
86 See further below, chapter 7, on the operation of this dynamic.
87 R. Morgan, *Check against Delivery* (Aberystwyth: Institute of Welsh Politics, 2000).
88 Most notably perhaps, the wide-ranging report of the Culture and Education and Lifelong Learning Committees, *Our Language: Its Future* (June 2002).
89 *A Voice for Wales*, above, n. 16, paragraph 1.24.
90 *First Report of the Committee on Standards in Public Life*, Cm. 2850 (1995).
91 GWA, ss. 69–71.
92 GWA, s. 72.
93 NAAG, *Recommendations*, above, n. 13, paragraphs 6.18–6.24.
94 Standing Orders Commissioners, *Draft Standing Orders*, above, n. 49, Preface. The concept of fire-watching is discussed further in chapter 11 in the context of the Welsh Administration Ombudsman.
95 National Assembly, *Code of Conduct for Assembly Secretaries* (May 1999).
96 See for details, National Assembly Committee on Standards of Conduct, *Annual Report 2000–2001* (November 2001).
97 Ibid.; and see below, chapter 7.
98 *A Voice for Wales*, above, n. 16, paragraphs 4.27, 4.31.
99 GWA, s. 70(1–3).
100 See for further details, National Assembly, *Publication Scheme* (October 2002).
101 *Your Right to Know: The Government's Proposals for a Freedom of Information Act*, Cm. 3818 (1997); and see, P. Birkinshaw, *Freedom of Information: The Law, the Practice and the Ideal*, 3rd edn. (London: Butterworths, 2001). The Act is still some years away from full implementation.
102 Whether the public interest in maintaining the exemption outweighs the public interest in disclosing the information: see Freedom of Information Act 2000, ss. 35–6.
103 National Assembly, *Code of Practice on Public Access to Information*, 1st edn. (1999).
104 *Official Record*, 30 January 2001.
105 First Secretary, *Statement on Freedom of Information* (March 2000).

[106] National Assembly, *Guidance to Staff: Publication of Cabinet Papers* (June 2001). Likewise, papers of the Assembly Administration's 'Executive Board' are made available; see further below, chapter 5.

[107] National Assembly, *Code of Practice on Public Access to Information*, 2nd edn. (2001).

[108] National Assembly, *Code of Practice on the Provision of Information to Assembly Members* (May 1999), paragraph 1.4.

[109] See for example *Official Record*, 2 May 2002 ('inclusive government').

[110] As discussed in the following chapter. No doubt the advent in 2003 of single-party rule will further underline this trend.

[111] *Western Mail*, 19 August 2002.

[112] First Secretary, *Statement on Freedom of Information* (March 2000).

[113] J. Shortridge, *Greater Openness and Access to Information – Memorandum to Staff* (March 2000).

[114] See below, chapter 9. Confidentiality is itself a key theme of the intergovernmental system of concordats: see below, chapter 12.

Chapter 4

[1] Lord Elis-Thomas, *National Assembly: A Year in Power?* (Aberystwyth: Institute of Welsh Politics, 2000).

[2] *Official Record*, 22 May 2001.

[3] To which may now be added single-party government with a bare working majority; see below, Postscript.

[4] *Western Mail*, 10 February 2000.

[5] *Official Record*, 14 February 2002 (Assembly Review of Procedure).

[6] R. Rawlings, *Towards a Parliament – Three Faces of the National Assembly for Wales* (Swansea: University of Wales, 2002); reprinted in 15 *Contemporary Wales* (2002) 1.

[7] See above, pp. 11–13.

[8] See above, chapter 3.

[9] R. Morgan, *Check against Delivery* (Aberystwyth: Institute of Welsh Politics, 2000).

[10] See in this vein, A. Michael, *The Dragon on our Doorstep: New Politics for a New Millennium in Wales* (Aberystwyth: Institute of Welsh Politics, 1999).

[11] See A. Thomas and M. Laffin, 'The first Welsh constitutional crisis: the Alun Michael resignation' (2001) 16 *Public Policy and Administration* 18.

[12] See above, chapter 1.

[13] R. Davies, 'We need a coalition of ideas' (2000) 4 *Agenda: Journal of the Institute of Welsh Affairs* 27 at 28.

[14] *Official Record*, 12 May 1999.

[15] See further, K. Morgan and G. Mungham, *Redesigning Democracy: The Making of the Welsh Assembly* (Bridgend: Seren, 2000), Postscript.

[16] Pre-sixteen Education Secretary Rosemary Butler: see *Official Record*, 7 December 1999. And see below, especially chapter 7.

[17] Welsh Labour Party, *Working Hard for Wales* (1999). And see by way of contrast, the party's manifesto for the second Assembly Elections: Welsh Labour Party, *Working together for Wales* (2003).

[18] See below, chapter 8.

[19] *Official Record*, 23 November 1999. See also M. German, *The National Assembly in Deadlock: Is There a Better Way Forward for Wales?* (Cardiff: Welsh Liberal Democrats, 1999).

[20] See below, chapter 4, in the context of the Welsh Assembly Government.

[21] See for example, *Official Record*, 19 May 1999.

[22] Food Safety Act 1990, especially ss. 16, 48.

[23] The Agriculture and Rural Development Committee; see for details, J. Barry Jones, 'Driven by events', in J. Barry Jones and J. Osmond (eds.), *Inclusive Government and Party Management* (Cardiff: Institute of Welsh Affairs, 2001).

[24] *Official Record*, 15 September 1999.

[25] In addition, that is, to the Presiding Officer and the Deputy Presiding Officer.

[26] National Assembly Advisory Group, *Recommendations* (1998), p. 29.

[27] *Official Record*, 29 June 1999.

[28] Directive 90/220. See further below, chapter 13.

[29] *Official Record*, 24 May 2000.

[30] *Official Record*, 19 October 1999.

[31] *Western Mail*, 14 October 1999.

[32] *Official Record*, 2 November 1999.

[33] See to this effect, M. James and G. Mathias, 'Coping with the fixed term' (2000) 4 *Agenda: Journal of the Institute of Welsh Affairs* 32.

[34] See on the political background, Morgan and Mungham, *Redesigning Democracy: The Making of the Welsh Assembly*, above, n. 15.

[35] See above, chapter 2.

[36] Laffin and Thomas, 'The first Welsh constitutional crisis: the Alun Michael resignation', above, n. 11. See also *Western Mail*, 16 February 2000.

[37] Alun Michael, letter to Lord Elis-Thomas, 9 February 2000; and see *Western Mail*, 3 January 2001.

[38] See above, chapter 3. The classic common law authority is *Huth* v. *Clark* (1890) 25 QBD 391.

[39] See above, p. 101.

[40] *Official Record*, 9 February 2000.

[41] Late efforts by Alun Michael to construct a coalition with the Liberal Democrats had been rebuffed, in light of the continuing difficulty over Objective 1: see Morgan and Mungham, *Redesigning Democracy: The Making of the Welsh Assembly*, above, n. 15.

[42] National Assembly, *Votes and Proceedings* (9 February 2000).

[43] *Official Record*, 15 February 2000.

[44] Rhodri Morgan, speech to the Welsh Labour Party, quoted in Morgan and Mungham, *Redesigning Democracy: The Making of the Welsh Assembly*, above, n. 15.

[45] Rhodri Morgan, *Variable Geometry UK* (Cardiff: Institute of Welsh Affairs, 2000), p. 12.

[46] *Western Mail*, 10 February 2000.

[47] See generally J. Osmond, 'A constitutional convention by other means: the first year of the National Assembly for Wales', in R. Hazell (ed.), *The State and the Nations: The First Year of Devolution in the UK* (London: Constitution Unit, 2000).

[48] *Official Record*, 15 February 2001.

[49] See above, chapter 2.

[50] M. Marinetto, 'The settlement and process of devolution: territorial politics

and governance under the Welsh Assembly' (2001) 49 *Political Studies* 306. See further, A. Cole and A. Storer, 'Political dynamics in the Assembly: an emerging policy community', in J. Barry Jones and J. Osmond (eds.), *Building a Civic Culture: Institutional Change, Policy Development and Political Dynamics in the National Assembly for Wales* (Cardiff: Institute of Welsh Affairs and Welsh Governance Centre, 2002).

51 Michael, *The Dragon on our Doorstep*, above, n. 10.

52 Davies, 'We need a coalition of ideas', above, n. 13.

53 Lord Elis-Thomas, *National Assembly: A Year in Power?*, above, n. 1.

54 A second aspect, considered in chapter 8, is a revamp of Assembly law-making practice and procedure.

55 See Welsh Assembly Cabinet, *Minutes* (13 March 2000); also Lord Elis-Thomas, *Reviewing a Democratic Body* (Cardiff: Institute of Welsh Affairs, 2001).

56 Office of the Presiding Officer, *Corporate Plan 2001–2002*, paragraph 1.

57 GWA, s. 34; and see above, chapter 3.

58 GWA, s. 40.

59 GWA, s. 85(1).

60 Lord Falconer of Thoroton, *House of Lords Debates*, vol. 590, col. 941 (9 June 1998).

61 See C. Harlow and R. Rawlings, *Law and Administration*, 2nd edn. (London: Butterworths, 1997), chapter 8.

62 R. Rawlings, 'Concordats of the constitution' (2000) 116 *Law Quarterly Review* 257. And see further below, in the context of 'concordats' and intergovernmental relations, chapter 12.

63 National Assembly, *Arrangements for Making the Office of the Presiding Officer More Independent* (September 2000), 1.

64 Ibid.

65 Welsh Labour Party and Welsh Liberal Democrats, *Putting Wales First: A Partnership for the People of Wales* (Welsh Labour Party and Welsh Liberal Democrats, October 2000).

66 Quite the reverse: see below, especially chapter 7.

67 *Official Record*, 10 October 2001.

68 Office of the Presiding Officer, *Service Level Agreement with Financial Planning Division* (October 2000). Further reform of the House Committee is discussed below.

69 See now for further details, W. Roddick, *Evidence to the Richard Commission* (December 2002). We return to the general topic of Assembly legal services in chapter 14.

70 See *Official Record*, 29 February 2000.

71 See for details, Presiding Office, *Annual Report 2001–2002* (September 2002).

72 GWA, s. 98

73 National Assembly, *Accounting Officer Agreement between the Principal Accounting Officer of the National Assembly for Wales and the Clerk to the Assembly* (September 2000), paragraph 7.

74 National Assembly, *Agreement between the Permanent Secretary and the Assembly Clerk on the Transfer of Personnel Functions delegated to the Office of the Presiding Officer* (November 2000).

75 National Assembly, *Service Level Agreement for the Provision of Services to the Office of the Presiding Officer by Internal Audit Services* (September 2000), paragraph 1.

76 GWA, s. 54(2)(b); and see further below (separation project mark II).

77 See below, chapter 6.

78   See for general details, Presiding Office, *Annual Report 2001–2002*.

79   The PO and DPO cannot be from the same political party: GWA, s. 52(3).

80   *Official Record*, 19 October 2000. And see the Postscript to this book.

81   See on the procedural 'routing' of Assembly legislation, below chapter 8. Following the 2003 Assembly Elections, an opposition AM is to chair the Business Committee: see *Official Record*, 13 May 2003.

82   National Assembly, *Clerk to the National Assembly for Wales: Information for Candidates* (December 2000).

83   Office of the Presiding Officer, *Corporate Plan 2000–2001*, paragraph 1.5. See further below, chapter 7.

84   Presiding Office, *Annual Report 2000–2001*, p. 13.

85   Office of the Presiding Officer, *Corporate Plan 1999–2000*, paragraph 3; Office of the Presiding Officer, *Corporate Plan 2000–2001*, paragraph 2.

86   *Assembly Review of Procedure* (February 2002), paragraphs 6.10, 6.20, and 9.8.

87   Previously the more notable by their absence: see below, chapter 8.

88   *Official Record*, 18 December 2002; and see Business Committee minutes 3 December 2002.

89   See above, p. 93.

90   Especially in terms of 'accountability' (GWA, s. 56(3)); see above, p. 92.

91   Assembly standing orders, as amended.

92   See above, p. 96. The theme is pursued in chapter 15.

93   GWA, s. 56; and see above, chapter 3.

94   See further below, chapter 5 ('Staffing Matters').

95   National Assembly, press release, 16 October 2000.

96   Welsh Labour Party and Welsh Liberal Democrats, *Putting Wales First: A Partnership for the People of Wales*, above, n. 65, part III(1).

97   Assembly Cabinet, *Protocol for Partnership Government in the Assembly* (October 2000).

98   Scottish Labour Party and Scottish Liberal Democrats, *The Scottish Coalition Agreement* (Edinburgh: Scottish Labour Party and Scottish Liberal Democrats, 1999); and see P. Goldenberg, 'The Scottish Coalition Agreement' (1999) 20 *Amicus Curiae* 4.

99   *Protocol*, above, n. 97, paragraph 1.7.

100   V. Bogdanor (ed.), *The Blackwell Encyclopaedia of Political Science* (Oxford: Blackwell, 1991).

101   GWA, s. 56(7),

102   *Protocol*, above, n. 97, paragraph 3.10.

103   Ibid., paragraph 3.11.

104   Ibid., paragraph 4.3.

105   Ibid., paragraph 4.6.

106   A. Storer and M. Lang, *Institutional Evolution: The Operation of the Welsh Executive* (Cardiff: Welsh Governance Centre, Working Paper no. 5, 2001).

107   Naturally, tensions between the two parties came increasingly to the fore in the run-up to the 2003 Assembly Elections; see J. Osmond (ed.), *Dragon Takes a Different Route* (Cardiff: Institute of Welsh Affairs, 2002).

108   Welsh Labour Party and Welsh Liberal Democrats, *Putting Wales First: A Partnership for the People of Wales*, above, n. 65, part III(1).

109   See especially *Assembly Review of Procedure* (February 2002), chapter 2 and Annex IV (Assembly Cabinet guidance note, *The Role of Deputy Ministers*).

110   *Protocol*, above, n. 97, paragraph 5.7.

[111]   Huw Lewis, press release, 12 April 2001.

[112]   R. Morgan, *Check against Delivery*, above, n. 9, pp. 3, 8.

[113]   R. Wyn Jones and R. Scully, *Public Attitudes to the Devolution Settlement in Wales* (Aberystwyth: Institute of Welsh Politics, 2002).

[114]   *Western Mail*, 21 November 2000. See further below, chapter 6.

[115]   Welsh Assembly Cabinet, *Programme for Government* (November 2000).

[116]   National Assembly, *Improving Health in Wales – NHS Plan* (January 2001); and see further below, chapter 11.

[117]   The product of which is discussed in chapter 10.

[118]   After a slow start: see below, chapter 8.

[119]   Welsh Assembly Government Strategic Policy Unit, *Serving Wales – A Policy Map* (March 2002).

[120]   National Assembly, *Communities First: Guidance for Local Authorities* (May 2002), p. 10.

[121]   See on the general policy development, Welsh Assembly Government, *Planning: Delivering for Wales* (January 2002).

[122]   National Assembly, *A Better Wales* (1999).

[123]   National Assembly, *Plan for Wales 2001* (September 2001), Foreword; and see *Official Record*, 25 October 2001.

[124]   Welsh Assembly Government, *Appointment of Non-executive Directors to the Executive Board* (July 2002), p. 4.

[125]   See further below, chapter 5.

[126]   National Assembly, *The Learning Country* (September 2001).

[127]   See below, especially chapters 8–10. See also chapter 7 (role of the subject committee).

[128]   As for example in the case of Welsh Assembly Government, *A Winning Wales: The National Economic Development Strategy of the Welsh Assembly Government* (January 2002).

[129]   *Official Record*, 18 April 2002.

[130]   Morgan, *Check against Delivery*, above, n. 9, p. 5.

[131]   Assembly Cabinet, *Cabinet Sub-committees* (May 2001).

[132]   Details of the membership, meetings, etc. are available on the Assembly cabinet web site: *http://www.wales.gov.uk/organicabinet/index.htm*

[133]   GWA, s. 55.

[134]   See below, chapter 13.

[135]   As discussed in cabinet: see minutes, 12 March 2001.

[136]   See Assembly cabinet statement, *Cabinet Changes* (18 June 2002).

[137]   The reshuffle also marked the return to the cabinet of DFM Michael German – after a long lay-off by reason of police investigation. The Liberal Democrats' Jenny Randerson had been serving as 'acting' DFM.

[138]   See further below, especially chapter 10 ('the Welsh way').

[139]   See below, chapter 11. It can now also be seen signposting the way to a 'Social Justice and Regeneration' cabinet portfolio: see below, Postscript.

[140]   GWA, s. 57(4); see above, chapter 3. The dispute was metaphor for continuing tensions surrounding the existence of the coalition government: see especially, *Official Record* 18 June 2002.

[141]   *Official Record*, 2 July 2002. The provisions have now been amended: *Official Record* 5 November 2002.

¹⁴² M. Evans, 'A constitutional perspective', submission to the *Assembly Review of Procedure* (February 2002). This is not to suggest that such confusion is unknown in more conventional constitutional systems such as Scottish devolution.

¹⁴³ Following Scottish precedents: see *Assembly Review of Procedure* (February 2002), chapter 2.

¹⁴⁴ See further *Official Record*, 8 January 2002 and 12 February 2002 (Presiding Officer's rulings).

¹⁴⁵ National Assembly, *Guide to the Identity to be used by Individual Offices, Groups and Departments* (March 2002).

¹⁴⁶ *Links Dolenni* (Assembly newsletter), 1 March 2002.

¹⁴⁷ See for example, P. Craig, *Public Law and Democracy in the United Kingdom and the United States of America* (Oxford: Clarendon, 1990).

¹⁴⁸ Preferably, I suggest, by referendum: see below, chapter 15.

Chapter 5

¹ House of Lords Select Committee on the Constitution, *Devolution: Inter-institutional Relations in the United Kingdom – Minutes of Evidence* (HL 147, Session 2001–2002), p. 233.

² National Assembly Peer Review, *Looking for the Route Map* (February 2001), p. 12.

³ R. Rawlings, 'Concordats of the constitution' (2000) 116 *Law Quarterly Review* 257.

⁴ See above, p. 98.

⁵ *Carltona Ltd v Works Commissioners* [1943] 2 All ER 560.

⁶ See for discussion, *House of Commons Debates*, vol. 309, col. 788 (26 March 1998).

⁷ National Assembly, *Delegation of Statutory Functions to Assembly Staff* (May 1999), paragraph 4.

⁸ See above, p. 99.

⁹ National Assembly, *Delegation of Statutory Functions*, above, n. 7, paragraph 17.

¹⁰ GWA, s. 98. The Permanent Secretary has been assigned general responsibilities for Assembly staff under the Civil Service (Management of Functions) Act 1992.

¹¹ The theme is elaborated in R. Rawlings, 'Living with the lawyers' (1999) 2 *Agenda: Journal of the Institute of Welsh Affairs* 32.

¹² This is not to overlook the greater separation of official roles associated with the ongoing constitutional trajectory of the Assembly.

¹³ National Assembly, *Protocol for Relationships between Assembly Members and Assembly Staff* (May 1999), paragraph 3.

¹⁴ *Official Record*, 14 September 2000.

¹⁵ *Western Mail*, 11 November 2000.

¹⁶ J. Shortridge, 'Equipped for the future' (February 2000) *Overview Magazine* 6.

¹⁷ Welsh Office, *Departmental Report*, Cm. 3915 (1998).

¹⁸ J. Shortridge, *Evidence to the Richard Commission* (December 2002).

¹⁹ See for details, National Assembly Peer Review, above, n. 2.

²⁰ See above, chapter 1.

²¹ See below, chapter 11.

²²   M. Laffin, 'The engine room', in J. Barry Jones and J. Osmond (eds.), *Building a Civic Culture: Institutional Change, Policy Development and Political Dynamics in the National Assembly for Wales* (Cardiff: Institute of Welsh Affairs and Welsh Governance Centre, 2002).

²³   See above, chapter 2.

²⁴   See further below, chapter 10.

²⁵   See below, chapter 10.

²⁶   National Assembly, *Improving Health in Wales: A Plan for the NHS with its Partners* (January 2001).

²⁷   As discussed in chapter 13.

²⁸   A theme developed in chapter 11.

²⁹   See below, especially chapter 8.

³⁰   See below chapter 14, for more detailed discussion of the rise of the OCG.

³¹   Rachel Lomax, quoted in M. Laffin and A. Thomas, 'New ways of working: political–official relations in the National Assembly for Wales' (2001) 21(2) *Public Money and Management* 45 at 50. And see generally, House of Commons Welsh Affairs Select Committee, *The Welsh Office's Organisational Preparedness for the National Assembly – Minutes of Evidence* (HC 166-i, Session 1998–1999).

³²   L. Paterson and R. Wyn Jones, 'Does civil society drive constitutional change?', in B. Taylor and K. Thomson (eds.), *Scotland and Wales: Nations Again?* (Cardiff: University of Wales Press, 1999), p. 169.

³³   R. Morgan, *Check against Delivery* (Aberystwyth: Institute of Welsh Politics, 2000), pp. 6–7.

³⁴   See for the detailed facts and figures, Welsh Office, *Departmental Report* (1998), above, n. 17.

³⁵   See for general discussion, Laffin and Thomas, 'New ways of working', above, n. 31.

³⁶   Morgan, *Check against Delivery*, above, n. 33, p. 4.

³⁷   See for example, R. Parry and A. Jones, 'The transition from the Scottish Office to the Scottish Executive' (2000) 15(2) *Public Policy and Administration* 53.

³⁸   See for a valuable discussion of the Scottish experience, A. Brown, J. Curtice, K. Hinds, D. McCrone, A. Park, L. Paterson and P. Surridge, *New Scotland, New Politics* (Edinburgh: Edinburgh University Press, 2001).

³⁹   J. Davies, *Developing the Functions of the Assembly* (Cardiff: Plaid Cymru, 2000), p. 8.

⁴⁰   R. Lomax, *Preparing for the Assembly* (Cardiff: Institute of Welsh Affairs, 1997), p. 2; see further, J. Osmond, *The Civil Service and the National Assembly* (Cardiff: Institute of Welsh Affairs, 1999).

⁴¹   Shortridge, 'Equipped for the future', above, n. 16, 7.

⁴²   UK Cabinet Office, *Modernising Government*, Cm. 4310 (1999). And see R. Parry, 'Devolution, integration and modernisation in the UK Civil Service' (2001) 16 *Public Policy and Administration* 53.

⁴³   See now for critical analysis, M. Barzelay, *The New Public Management: Improving Research and Policy Dialogue* (Berkeley: University of California Press, 2001).

⁴⁴   See for example, R. Silcock, 'What is e-government?' (2001) 54 *Parliamentary Affairs* 88.

⁴⁵   National Assembly, *Appointment of Non-executive Directors to the Executive Board* (July 2002).

⁴⁶ See for an introduction, British Quality Foundation, *The Model in Practice: Using the EFQM Excellence Model to Deliver Continuous Improvement* (London, 2000); and see generally, K. Zink, *Total Quality Management as a Holistic Management Concept: The European Model for Business Excellence* (London: Springer-Verlag, 1998).

⁴⁷ Assembly Executive Board, *Delivering Better Government – EFQM Action Plan 2002–2003.*

⁴⁸ National Assembly, *Delivering Better Government Newsletter* (December 2000).

⁴⁹ National Assembly, *Cymru Ar-lein – Online for a Better Wales* (November 2001).

⁵⁰ National Assembly, *Appointment of Non-executive Directors*, above, n. 45.

⁵¹ Ibid.

⁵² See for example, Assembly Cabinet, *Minutes* (19 June 2000).

⁵³ Separate arrangements have applied in the case of the Northern Ireland departments.

⁵⁴ House of Lords Select Committee on the Constitution, above, n. 1, p. 281. The committee itself has recommended retention of a single home civil service: HL 28, Session 2002–3, chapter 5.

⁵⁵ Welsh Labour Party and Welsh Liberal Democrats, *Putting Wales First: A Partnership for the People of Wales* (Cardiff: Welsh Labour Party and Welsh Liberal Democrats, October 2000), p. 23.

⁵⁶ See now, House of Lords Select Committee on the Constitution, above n. 1, *Memorandum by Lord Elis-Thomas.*

⁵⁷ J. Shortridge, *Evidence to the Richard Commission* (December 2002).

⁵⁸ As discussed in chapters 10–11.

⁵⁹ See below, chapter 7.

⁶⁰ Assembly Cabinet, *Minutes* (3 December 2001).

⁶¹ National Assembly, *Review of Senior Corporate Management Functions* (July 2001), appendix 6.

⁶² See for details, A. Storer and M. Lang, *Institutional Evolution: The Operation of the Welsh Executive* (Cardiff: Welsh Governance Centre, Working Paper no. 5, 2001).

⁶³ GWA, s. 121; and see above, chapter 2.

⁶⁴ Storer and Lang, above, n. 62.

⁶⁵ Welsh Assembly Government, *Strategic Policy Unit* (February 2002).

⁶⁶ See below, chapter 10.

⁶⁷ See above, p. 149.

⁶⁸ National Assembly, *Appointment of Non-executive Directors to the Executive Board* (July 2002).

⁶⁹ National Assembly Executive Board, *Memorandum on the Governance of the Executive Board and its Committees* (November 2001).

⁷⁰ National Assembly, *Transforming the Management Board* (August 2001), p. 2.

⁷¹ Report from the National Assembly Peer Review, above, n. 2, p. 3.

⁷² National Assembly, *Review of Senior Corporate Management Functions* (July 2001), paragraph 3.3.

⁷³ We return to this point in chapter 15, in the context of the Richard Commission.

Chapter 6

[1] *Final Report of the Assembly Review of Procedure Group* (February 2002), paragraph 3.2.

[2] The work of subject committees etc. is considered in the next chapter, together with the internal stock-take that was the Assembly Review of Procedure. Assembly law making – in the guise of delegated or subordinate legislation – is examined in chapter 8.

[3] See above, chapter 2.

[4] See for biographical detail, D. Balsom (ed.), *Wales Yearbook 2002* (Cardiff: HTV, 2002).

[5] See further below, chapter 15 (a point of criticism of the narrow terms of reference of the Richard Commission).

[6] National Assembly Advisory Group, *Recommendations* (1998), section 4. The decision-making body that is the Parliamentary Bureau of the Scottish Parliament is very different: see for an overview, B. Winetrobe, *Realising the Vision: A Parliament with a Purpose* (London: Constitution Unit, 2001).

[7] See below, chapter 8.

[8] See further below.

[9] Likewise in the Labour administration folllowing on the May 2003 Assembly Elections: see Postscript.

[10] Ibid.

[11] See for example, Business Committee, Minutes, 12 June 2001 (use of statements as opposed to motions).

[12] The Scottish Parliament also has a separate Procedure Committee.

[13] See above, chapter 3 (the hierarchy of rules).

[14] Relations (in the Business Committee) have been visibly more fraught in the first months of single-party Labour rule, following on the May 2003 elections: see further below.

[15] NAAG, *Recommendations* (1998), paragraph 4.1.

[16] Review Secretariat, *Analysis of Staff Responses* (February 2001), p. 1.

[17] Rhodri Morgan, letter to Lord Elis-Thomas, 5 July 2002.

[18] This is not to overlook the general deliberative capacity of the Assembly that arises under the (statutory) rubric of 'A Voice for Wales': see below.

[19] The characterization is borrowed from Winetrobe, *Realising the Vision*, above, n. 6, p. 130.

[20] *Final Report of the Assembly Review of Procedure Group* (February 2002), paragraph 3.2.

[21] Now jealously guarded: see ibid., paragraph 3.19.

[22] Assembly Review Secretariat, *Plenary Business* (January 2001) and *Plenary Business: Further Issues* (February 2001).

[23] *Final Report of the Assembly Review of Procedure Group* (February 2002), paragraph 3.7.

[24] *Official Record*, 15 March 2001.

[25] See *Official Record*, 12 April 2000.

[26] *Final Report of the Assembly Review of Procedure Group* (February 2002), paragraph 3.5

[27] See *Official Record*, 29 October 2002.

[28] Welsh Assembly Government, *First Minister's Report August 2001–July 2002* (October 2002); and see *Official Record*, 30 October 2002.

[29] See *Final Report of the Assembly Review of Procedure Group* (February 2002), paragraph 4.12. And see generally below, chapter 8.

[30] The Legislation Committee for example is a notable omission.

[31] Presiding Office, *Annual Report 2001–2002*, p. 3.

[32] See above, chapter 2.

[33] *With Respect to Old Age: Long Term Care – Rights and Responsibilities*, A Report by the Royal Commission on Long Term Care (the Sutherland Commission), Cm. 4192-I (1999); and Community Care and Health (Scotland) Act 2002. See also Health and Social Care (Northern Ireland) Act 2002.

[34] See *Official Record*, 16 May 2002 ('the Older Person's Strategy').

[35] *Official Record*, 21 May 2002.

[36] See further below, and also chapter 11 (Children's Commissioner).

[37] See for practical illustration *Official Record*, 30 October 2002 (First Minister's annual report).

[38] See above, chapter 4.

[39] See generally, Presiding Office, *Guidance on Assembly Questions* (July 2001).

[40] So also emergency debates: see for practical illustration, *Official Record*, 18 April 2002 (Wales European Centre).

[41] See above, chapter 3.

[42] See *Official Record*, 12 June 2001 (carers).

[43] See *Final Report of the Assembly Review of Procedure Group* (February 2002), paragraphs 3.8–3.11.

[44] See further below, chapter 9.

[45] The (competing) lists are made available on the Assembly web site.

[46] Epitomized in successive debates on the minister's business statements: see for example, *Official Record*, 17 June 2003.

[47] Culminating in an unseemly squabble over seating arrangements, which came to be defused (in classic Welsh fashion) by setting up a committee: see *Official Record*, 18 July 2003.

[48] These rules would have involved the Assembly assenting to order-making by the Secretary of State: see for explanation, below, chapter 8.

[49] The phraseology is borrowed from N. Burrows, *Devolution* (London: Sweet & Maxwell, 2000).

[50] See for discussion of the block and (Barnett) formula system, above, chapter 2.

[51] Whereas in the case of Assembly law making the GWA is notably prescriptive: see below, chapter 8.

[52] *A Voice for Wales*, Cm. 3718 (1997), paragraphs 4.9, D.9.

[53] A. Michael, *The Dragon on our Doorstep: New Politics for a New Millennium in Wales* (Aberystwyth: Institute of Welsh Politics, 1999), p. 3.

[54] *A Voice for Wales*, above, n. 52, paragraph 1.22.

[55] National Assembly Advisory Group, *Recommendations* (1998), paragraphs 4.1, 7.7.

[56] Standing Orders Commissioners, Draft Standing Order 20.1.

[57] *Official Record*, 1 December 1999.

[58] National Assembly, *A Better Wales* (July 1999).

[59] M. German, *Silent Earthquakes: Reforming Politics from Within* (Cardiff: Institute of Welsh Affairs, 2000), p. 3.

[60] See *Official Record*, 1 December 1999.

[61] *Official Record*, 8 February 2000.

[62] Business Committee, *Note on Changes to Standing Order 19* (May 2000); *Official Record*, 23 May 2000. And see for illustration of the flexibility, the emergency rural recovery package announced in response to foot and mouth disease: National Assembly, press notice, 26 July 2001.

[63] See for example, National Assembly, *Commissioning Paper for the 2001 Budget Planning Round* (June 2001).

[64] See for practical illustration, Education and Lifelong Learning Committee, *Initial Consideration of Budget Priorities* (June 2001).

[65] *Official Record*, 18 October 2001.

[66] Ibid.

[67] See above, chapter 2.

[68] See *Official Record*, 26 October 2000 (draft budget): *Official Record*, 7 December 2000 (final budget).

[69] See for discussion, below, chapters 10–11.

[70] See *Official Record*, 18 October 2001; and for details, G. Bristow and A. Kay, 'Spending autonomy in Wales', in J. Barry Jones and J. Osmond (eds.), *Building a Civic Culture: Institutional Change, Policy Development and Political Dynamics in the National Assembly for Wales* (Cardiff: Institute of Welsh Affairs and Welsh Governance Centre, 2002).

[71] *Official Record*, 6 November 2002. And see further below, chapter 11.

[72] V. Bogdanor, *Devolution in the United Kingdom* (Oxford: Oxford University Press, 1999), p. 235.

[73] See above, chapter 2 (constraints on financial autonomy).

[74] *Official Record*, 18 October 2001.

[75] K. Morgan, 'The new territorial politics: rivalry and justice in post-devolution Britain' (2001) 35 *Regional Studies* 343.

[76] *Official Record*, 28 March 2000.

[77] For example, D. Reynolds, 'Education funding gap grows' (2000) 4 *Agenda – Journal of the Institute of Welsh Affairs* 7.

[78] See below, chapter 7.

[79] See *Official Record*, 2 May 2002.

[80] Assembly Cabinet, *Statement on the Comprehensive Spending Review*, 16 July 2002.

[81] In contrast to the case of associated regulatory mechanisms: see below, chapter 11.

Chapter 7

[1] *Official Record*, 12 July 2000.

[2] Assembly Review of Procedure, minutes, 30 January 2002.

[3] See above, chapter 3.

[4] S. Arnstein, 'A ladder of citizen participation' (1969) 35 *Journal of the American Institute of Planners* 216. The topmost 'rungs', delegated power and citizen control, are far beyond the reach of these (advisory) committees.

[5] The wide range of subject committee responsibilities was noted in chapter 3.

[6] *Final Report of the Assembly Review of Procedure Group* (February 2002), paragraph 6.9.

[7] See for details, Economic Development Committee, *Annual Report 2000–2001* (May 2001).

[8] Environment, Planning and Transport Committee, *Policy Review of Public Transport* (December 2001). And see now for a particularly good overview by a subject committee Chair: Richard Edwards, *Evidence to the Richard Commission* (December 2002).

[9] See for discussion, J. Barry Jones, 'Driven by events', in J. Barry Jones and J. Osmond (eds.), *Inclusive Government and Party Management* (Cardiff: Institute of Welsh Affairs, 2001); J. Barry Jones, 'Politics and crisis management', in J. Barry Jones and J. Osmond (eds.), *Building a Civic Culture: Institutional Change, Policy Development and Political Dynamics in the National Assembly for Wales* (Cardiff: Institute of Welsh Affairs and Welsh Governance Centre, 2002).

[10] See especially, Agriculture and Rural Affairs Committee, *Policy Review of Rural Diversification* (March 2001).

[11] M. Evans, 'A constitutional perspective', *Submission to Assembly Review of Procedure* (May 2001).

[12] Typically promoted by the dominant Labour interest, see Welsh Assembly Government media briefing, 10 June 2003.

[13] Jocelyn Davies, quoted in J. Osmond, 'Constitution building on the hoof', in Barry Jones and Osmond (eds.), *Building a Civic Culture*, above, n. 9, p. 78.

[14] Labour Group, *Submission to the Assembly Review of Procedure* (May 2001), paragraph 1.

[15] *Final Report of the Assembly Review of Procedure Group* (February 2002), paragraphs 6.10, 6.14.

[16] Ibid., paragraph 6.2.

[17] See for details, Assembly Review Secretariat, *Summary of Consultation Responses* (July 2001).

[18] See further below, chapter 10. The cabinet has led the way, with an expedited programme of ASPB reviews.

[19] As illustrated below, in the context of education policies.

[20] *Official Record*, 14 February 2002 (Cynog Dafis).

[21] A point elaborated in chapter 15.

[22] See for example, National Assembly, *Review of Primary Care Strategy* (2001). See also, Kirsty Williams, *Evidence to the Richard Commission* (December 2002).

[23] See generally, D. Egan and R. James, 'Open government and inclusiveness', in Barry Jones and Osmond (eds.), *Building a Civic Culture*, above, n. 9.

[24] Post-Sixteen Education and Training Committee, *Taking Forward the Recommendations of the Education and Training Plan* (December 1999).

[25] See *Official Record*, 1 February 2000. There have, however, been some notable organizational problems with the design: see below, chapter 11.

[26] See for further details, D. Egan and R. James, 'A promising start', in *Inclusive Government and Party Management* (Cardiff: Institute of Welsh Affairs, 2001).

[27] Education and Lifelong Learning Committee, *Policy Review of Higher Education* (January 2002); and see *Official Record*, 22 January 2002.

[28] See most notably, Sir David Williams, *The University of Wales: A Review of its Membership, Structures and Modus Operandi* (Cardiff: University of Wales, May 2002).

[29] Welsh Assembly Government, *Reaching Higher* (March 2002).

[30] By virtue of the Assembly's proposed 'Education (Miscellaneous Provisions) (Wales) Bill'; see below, chapter 9.

[31] Education Act 1986 and Teachers' Pay and Conditions of Service Act 1991.

[32] National Assembly, press release, 1 March 2000.

[33] See above, chapter 4 (the fall of Alun Michael).

[34] Education and Lifelong Learning Committee, minutes of meetings, 17 May 2001 and 13 June 2001.

[35] See *Official Record*, 14 June 2001.

[36] Committee Secretariat, *Issues arising from Panel of Chairs Meetings* (July 2001).

[37] Culture and Education and Lifelong Learning Committees, *Our Language: Its Future* (June 2002).

[38] See above, chapter 1.

[39] GWA, ss. 32, 47; and see further below.

[40] *Our Language: Its Future*, above, n. 37, Chairs' Foreword.

[41] *Official Record*, 9 July 2001 (Delyth Evans and Helen Mary Jones).

[42] *Our Language: Its Future*, above, n. 37, paragraph 7.1.

[43] Ibid., paragraph 7.3.

[44] Ibid., paragraph 2.1.

[45] Ibid., paragraph 3.22.

[46] GWA, s. 32; see above, chapter 2.

[47] Welsh Language Act 1993, Preamble. See further below, chapter 14 ('Devolution, Courts and Lawyers').

[48] *Our Language: Its Future*, above, n. 37, paragraphs 9.1–9.8.

[49] See above, Introduction ('The Rebirth of Welsh Legal History').

[50] *Our Language: Its Future*, above, n. 37, Chairs' Foreword.

[51] Ibid.

[52] Welsh Assembly Government, *Bilingual Future: A Policy Statement* (July 2002), Foreword.

[53] Welsh Assembly Government, *Iaith Pawb* (November 2002).

[54] Welsh Assembly Government, *Welsh Language Scheme* (October 2002) (replacing the Welsh Office scheme).

[55] See for example, Junior Minister, Win Griffiths, *House of Commons Debates*, vol. 305, col. 798 (2 February 1998).

[56] *House of Commons Debates*, vol. 307, cols. 754–84 (2 March 1998).

[57] *House of Lords Debates*, vol. 591, col. 811 (1 July 1998).

[58] *House of Commons Debates*, vol. 309, cols. 708–13 (26 March 1998).

[59] GWA, s. 61.

[60] The general principle of party political balance in Assembly committees was noted in chapter 3.

[61] NAAG, *Recommendations* (1998), paragraph 5.24.

[62] *Final Report of the Assembly Review of Procedure Group* (February 2002), Annex vi; *Official Record*, 14 February 2002.

[63] Review Secretariat, *Making the Most of Regional Committees* (Assembly Review of Procedure, June 2001), paragraph 17.

[64] See most laudably, South East Wales Regional Committee, *Annual Report 2001–2002* (May 2002).

[65] See for chapter and verse, K. Hollingsworth, 'Connecting with wider Wales', in Barry Jones and Osmond (eds.), *Building a Civic Culture*, above, n. 9.

[66] South West Wales Regional Committee, *Annual Report 2000–2001*, paragraph 6.

[67] See for details, Presiding Office, *Annual Report 2001–2002*.

[68] See for example North Wales Regional Committee, *Annual Report 2001–2002* (May 2002).

[69] NAAG, *Recommendations* (1998), paragraph 5.23.

[70] Review Secretariat, *Making the Most of Regional Committees*, above, n. 63.

[71] Ibid.

[72] North Wales Regional Committee, *Annual Report 1999–2000*, paragraph 2.

[73] Review Secretariat, *Making the Most of Regional Committees*, above, n. 63, paragraph 9.

[74] *Official Record*, 28 June 2000 (Gareth Jones, first Chair of the committee).

[75] Review Secretariat, *Making the Most of Regional Committees*, above, n. 63.

[76] *Final Report of the Assembly Review of Procedure Group* (February 2002), paragraphs 7.5–7.8.

[77] *Final Report of the Assembly Review of Procedure Group* (February 2002), paragraph 7.16.

[78] As part of the general drive to modernize local bureaucratic structures: see above, chapter 5.

[79] See further below, chapter 15.

[80] GWA, ss. 48, 120.

[81] Committee on Equality of Opportunity, *Annual Report 2001–2002* (June 2002), paragraphs 3, 5.

[82] See for a detailed account, P. Chaney and R. Fevre, *An Absolute Duty: Equal Opportunities and the National Assembly for Wales* (Cardiff: Institute of Welsh Affairs, 2002).

[83] See Welsh Assembly Government, *Second Annual Equality Report* (2001).

[84] See further below, chapter 10 (systematic exclusion of ethnic minorities from the political life of Wales); as also, the Postscript.

[85] See above, chapter 2.

[86] Chaney and Fevre, *An Absolute Duty: Equal Opportunities and the National Assembly for Wales*, above n. 82, p. 22. See also, L. Clements and P. Thomas, 'Human rights and the Welsh Assembly' (1999) 136 *Planet* 11.

[87] National Assembly for Wales, *Lifting Every Voice* (March 2001).

[88] See above, chapter 5.

[89] See for details, Equality of Opportunity Committee, *Annual Report 2001–2002* (May 2002).

[90] See: *www.winningourbusiness.wales.gov.uk*

[91] The case is put by Chaney and Fevre, *An Absolute Duty: Equal Opportunities and the National Assembly for Wales*, above, n. 82.

[92] Cm. 3718 (1997), paragraph 4.36.

[93] Review Secretariat, *Staff Comments* (February 2001).

[94] Audit Committee, *Annual Report 1999–2000*, paragraph 2.2.

[95] See GWA, ss. 60, 90–100; and see above, chapter 2. As previously explained, the Comptroller and Auditor General (at Westminster) also retains jurisdiction: GWA, s. 101.

[96] Audit Committee, *Annual Report 1999–2000*, paragraph 3.23.

[97] *Official Record*, 31 October 2000 (Janet Davies).

[98] K. Hollingsworth, 'A reputation for probity', in Barry Jones and Osmond (eds.), *Building a Civic Culture*, above, n. 9.

[99] See below, chapter 10.

[100] See for details, Hollingsworth, 'A reputation for probity', above, n. 98.

[101] See *Official Record*, 1 March 2001.

[102] Audit Committee, *Accommodation for the National Assembly for Wales* (May 2001).

[103] Audit Committee, *Report on Clinical Negligence in the NHS in Wales* (August 2001).

[104] This is not to overlook the issue of fiscal accountability associated with a lack of taxing powers: see above, chapter 2.

[105] See above, chapter 3, on the initial design.

[106] D. Woodhouse, *Review of the Standards of Conduct Regime of the National Assembly for Wales* (Committee on Standards of Conduct, 2002).

[107] See for details, Committee on Standards of Conduct, *Annual Report 2000–2001* (November 2001). Five complaint investigations were conducted in the first two years, all involving allegations of the misuse of Assembly stationery.

[108] See for details, Committee on Standards of Conduct, *Review of Members' Interests – A Consultation Paper* (July 2000).

[109] Listed by Woodhouse, above, n. 106, paragraph 2.2.

[110] Ibid., paragraph 2.3.2.

[111] See further, O. Gay, 'The regulation of parliamentary standards after devolution' (2002) *Public Law* 422.

[112] See Committee on Standards of Conduct, *The Role of and Access to the Assembly's Independent Adviser on Standards of Conduct* (March 2000); Committee on Standards of Conduct, *Complaint Procedure for Dealing with Complaints against Assembly Members* (July 2000).

[113] European Convention on Human Rights, Article 6. A special requirement to register membership of the freemasons has been another obvious target for legal challenge. It has also now come home to roost politically speaking: see *Official Record*, 13 November 2002 (resignation of the committee Chair over a failed attempt at reform).

[114] See Woodhouse, above, n. 106, paragraph 2.3.2.

[115] In the guise respectively of a standards commissioner and an Assembly ombudsman: see for details, O. Gay, above, n. 111.

[116] Woodhouse, above, n. 106, paragraph 4.2.

[117] *Final Report of the Assembly Review of Procedure Group* (February 2002), Annex ii: and see *Official Record*, 12 July 2002 (announcement of the review).

[118] *Final Report of the Assembly Review of Procedure Group* (February 2002), Annex ii.

[119] See especially chapter 9 (principles to be adopted in government Bills affecting the Assembly).

[120] See for further details, J. Osmond, 'Constitution building on the hoof', in Jones and Osmond (eds.), *Building a Civic Culture*, above, n. 9, 78.

[121] Chamber Wales, Federation of Small Businesses and CBI Wales, *Assembly Review of Procedure – Written Evidence* (March 2001), p. 1.

[122] Welsh Conservative Group, *Submission to the Assembly Review of Procedure* (April 2001); Plaid Cymru, *Response to the Assembly Review of Procedure Consultation* (May 2001).

[123] Rhodri Morgan, letter to Lord Elis-Thomas, 5 July 2002.

[124] *Final Report of the Assembly Review of Procedure Group* (February 2002), paragraph 1.3.

[125] As discussed in chapters 8–9.

[126] *Final Report of the Assembly Review of Procedure Group* (February 2002), chapter 10: and see *Official Record*, 14 February 2001.

[127] Assembly Review of Procedure, minutes of meeting, 31 October 2001; and see above, chapter 4.

[128] In the guise of the joint secretariat: J. Osmond, 'Constitution building on the hoof', in Jones and Osmond (eds.), *Building a Civic Culture*, above, n. 9, p. 78.

[129] See for illustration, M. Evans, 'A constitutional perspective', *Submission to Assembly Review of Procedure* (May 2001).

[130] See on the consequential amendments to standing orders, *Official Record*, 11 June and 5 November 2002.

[131] See for practical illustration, Welsh Liberal Democrats, *Submission to Assembly Review of Procedure* (January 2001).

[132] See above, chapter 1.

Chapter 8

[1] *Final Report of the Assembly Review of Procedure Group* (February 2002), paragraph 5.1.

[2] See for an insider's account, D. Lambert, 'The Government of Wales Act – an Act for laws to be ministered in Wales in like form as it is in this realm?' (1999) 30 *Cambrian Law Review* 60.

[3] House of Commons and House of Lords Joint Select Committee on Statutory Instruments, *Twenty-Seventh Report* (HC 33-xxvii, Session 1997–8), Appendix 1; HMSO Archives (1998).

[4] As discussed in chapter 2.

[5] See above, chapter 5.

[6] See for discussion in the local context, P. Silk, 'The Assembly as a legislature', in J. Osmond (ed.), *The National Assembly Agenda* (Cardiff: Institute of Welsh Affairs, 1998).

[7] *A Voice for Wales*, Cm. 3718 (1997), paragraphs 3.39, 4.22–4.23.

[8] R. Davies, 'The tools for the job' (1996) 4 *Agenda – Journal of the Institute of Welsh Affairs* 18 at 19.

[9] See above, p. 70.

[10] W. Roddick, *Evidence to the Assembly Review of Procedure* (June 2001); as discussed in J. Williams, 'The Assembly as a legislature', in J. Barry Jones and J. Osmond (eds.), *Building a Civic Culture: Institutional Change, Policy Development and Political Dynamics in the National Assembly for Wales* (Cardiff: Institute of Welsh Affairs and Welsh Governance Centre, 2002).

[11] *Final Report of the Assembly Review of Procedure Group* (February 2002), paragraph 5.4. This is not to overlook the extent to which Assembly legislation is driven from elsewhere: see further below.

[12] See further below, especially chapter 10 ('the Welsh way').

[13] As demonstrated in the official evidence to the Richard Commission: see further below, chapter 15.

[14] See for a classic study, E. Page, *Governing by Numbers: Delegated Legislation and Everyday Policy-Making* (Oxford: Hart, 2001). And see further below.

[15] GWA, s. 58(6); and see further below, chapter 11. The Assembly's power to make subordinate legislation implies a power to amend or revoke existing subordinate legislation: Interpretation Act 1978, s. 14.

[16] GWA, ss. 42, 44.

[17] The scope for 'private member's legislation', in the guise of forcing a

minister's hand, is discussed below. As one would expect, the right of financial initiative is expressly reserved to the Administration: GWA, s. 68.

[18] GWA, ss. 64–8.

[19] Andrew Davies, *Official Record*, 24 May 2000.

[20] National Assembly Advisory Group (NAAG), *Recommendations* (1998), paragraph 7 and Annex B.

[21] GWA, s. 67; NAAG, *Recommendations* (1998), paragraph 7.1.

[22] The exceptions being expressly targeted on 'the particular circumstances' of the case: GWA, s. 66(4). See further below.

[23] GWA, s. 65.

[24] A classic technique being the provision of (at best) 'boiler-plate reasons' for non-application of the technique: see for practical illustration, Business Committee (1 February 2001) (food additive regulations). See further *Official Record*, 28 January 2002 (NHS structural reforms).

[25] See *Official Record*, 26 November 2002.

[26] The published minutes of the Business Committee are replete with examples.

[27] See further below for the relevant statistics.

[28] Under GWA, s. 67(1).

[29] GWA, s. 58(4).

[30] *Memorandum from the Leader of the House*, House of Commons and House of Lords Joint Select Committee on Statutory Instruments, *Twenty-Seventh Report* (HC 33-xxvii, Session 1997–8). See generally on the work of the JCSI, Page, *Governing by Numbers*, above, n. 14.

[31] GWA, s. 58(5).

[32] See for general discussion, R. Rawlings, 'Scrutiny and reform: Assembly lawmaking and the role of the Legislation Committee', in J. Barry Jones and J. Osmond (eds.), *Inclusive Government and Party Management* (Cardiff: Institute of Welsh Affairs, 2001).

[33] See above, chapter 7, for the parallel argument relating to financial scrutiny and the audit function ('bringing it home').

[34] Legislation Committee, *Oral Evidence to the Richard Commission* (December 2002) (Mick Bates)

[35] Ibid.

[36] *Final Report of the Assembly Review of Procedure Group* (February 2002), paragraph 8.11. The primary responsibility of course is that of the OCG, as discussed in chapter 14.

[37] Rawlings, 'Scrutiny and reform', above, n. 32. And see further below.

[38] Via a 'memorandum of corrections' laid before the Assembly: see further below.

[39] Legislation Committee, *Annual Report 2001–2002*, p. 17.

[40] General issues of devolution and human rights are considered in chapter 14.

[41] Chronically Sick and Disabled Persons Act 1970, s. 21.

[42] Leading on to a reworking of the regulations: see *Official Record*, 20 June 2000.

[43] *Final Report of the Assembly Review of Procedure Group* (February 2002), paragraph 8.12.

[44] Legislation Committee, *Evidence to the Richard Commission* (December 2002).

[45] In particular the School Standards and Framework Act 1998 and the Local Government Act 1999. See for a more detailed account, Rawlings, 'Scrutiny and reform', above, n. 32.

[46] See above, chapter 4.

[47] So occasioning a peculiarly fractious Assembly debate: *Official Record*, 21 March 2000.

[48] To the extent of a claim that almost 600 pieces of legislation had 'gone missing': *Western Mail*, 20 March 2000.

[49] As discussed in chapter 6.

[50] A feature emphasized by various parties to the proceedings: see *Official Record*, 24 May 2000.

[51] See above, chapter 5.

[52] The internal architecture of the OCG is explored in chapter 14.

[53] *Official Record*, 23 May 2000.

[54] See *Official Record*, 27 June 2000.

[55] Involving notice by only three Members: see for practical illustration, *Official Record*, 4 July 2000.

[56] See above, chapter 7.

[57] See especially Legislation Committee, *Annual Report 2000–2001* (summary of submission to Assembly Review of Procedure).

[58] *Official Record*, 10 October 2000.

[59] GWA, s. 22(4): see above, chapter 2.

[60] Assembly cabinet, *Minutes*, 4 June 2001.

[61] See above, chapter 4.

[62] Williams, 'The Assembly as a legislature', above, n. 10, p. 9.

[63] See for practical illustration *Official Record*, 26 June 2001 (composite motion covering such diverse matters as food regulation, valuation for rating, and NHS charges).

[64] *Official Record*, 19 and 21 June 2001; and see below, chapter 10 (implementation of the Local Government Act 2000).

[65] *Official Record*, 19 June 2001.

[66] See *Official Record*, 6 March 2001 (resolution instructing the minister) and 18 July 2002 (approval of the Town and Country Planning (Use Classes) (Amendment) (Wales) Order 2002, SI 2002 no. 1875 (W.184)); and *Official Record*, 2 May 2002 (defeated motion).

[67] Andrew Davies, *Evidence to Assembly Review of Procedure* (June 2001).

[68] *Final Report of the Assembly Review of Procedure Group* (February 2002), paragraphs 5.11–5.12.

[69] A matter discussed in chapter 14. And see generally, Lord Prys Davies, 'The legal status of the Welsh language in the twentieth century', in G. Jenkins and M. Williams (eds.), *'Let's do our Best for the Ancient Tongue': The Welsh Language in the Twentieth Century* (Cardiff: University of Wales Press, 2000).

[70] See E. Roberts, 'The Welsh Church, canon law and the Welsh language', in N. Doe (ed.), *Essays in Canon Law* (Cardiff: University of Wales Press, 1992).

[71] GWA, ss. 66(4), 120. And see above, chapter 2 ('the Welsh difference').

[72] See for an instructive parallel, Welsh Language Board, *National Assembly Dictionary of Procedural Terms* (1999).

[73] R. Macdonald, 'Legal bilingualism' (1997) 42 *McGill Law Journal* 119 at 159. See also, R. Bergeron, 'Co-drafting: Canadian experience of the creation of bilingual legislation in a bijural system', in J. Jones (ed.), *The Law Making Powers of the National Assembly for Wales* (Cardiff: Law Society in Wales, 2001).

[74] Office of the Counsel General, *The Office of the Counsel General* (2001), paragraph 15.

[75] See above, chapter 7.

[76] As a distinguishing feature of so-called 'Legal Wales': see below, chapter 14 ('Devolution, Courts and Lawyers').

[77] P. Godin, 'The New Brunswick experience: the practice of the English common law in the French language' (2001) 1 *Wales Law Journal* 40.

[78] Office of the Counsel General, *Bilingual Lawmaking and Justice* (2001).

[79] Ibid., paragraph 15.

[80] See for example, Seminar Report, *The Welsh Language and the Legal Process in Wales* (2001) 1 *Wales Law Journal* 9.

[81] See for details, Legislation Committee, *Annual Reports 1999–2000, 2000–2001.*

[82] GWA, s. 66(4).

[83] Legislation Committee, *Annual Report 2000–2001*, p. 3.

[84] Office of the Counsel General, *The Office of the Counsel General* (2001), paragraph 15.

[85] GWA, s. 122(2). It is a matter of regret that this power has not yet been used.

[86] Office of the Counsel General, *Eisteddfod Presentation* (2002), p. 2.

[87] Office of the Counsel General, *Bilingual Law Making and Justice*, paragraphs 10, 15.

[88] Ibid., paragraph 15.

[89] As defined in terms of Wales-only statutory instruments: see above.

[90] D. Miers, 'Law making', in J. Osmond and J. Barry Jones (eds.), *Birth of Welsh Democracy* (Cardiff: Institute of Welsh Affairs, 2003).

[91] Lord Morris, *The Development of Welsh Political Institutions over Fifty Years* (Pontypridd: University of Glamorgan, 2001).

[92] W. Roddick, 'Doing business with the Assembly: defining the parameters and utilising the opportunities' (2002) 1 *Wales Law Journal* 305 at 308. The figures quoted are as subsequently amended by the OCG.

[93] Ibid.

[94] Early examples are the Education (Out-turn Statements) Wales Regulations 2000, SI 2000 no. 1717 (W.117) and the Education (Education Standards Grants) (Wales) Regulations 2000, SI 2000 no. 834 (W.32).

[95] M. Navarro, *The Statutory Instruments Systems within the Context of Devolution* (Cardiff: Plaid Cymru, 2002) 3.

[96] Ibid., p. 4.

[97] As signalled early on in the brouhaha over performance-related pay: see above, chapter 4.

[98] Motor Vehicles (Tests) (Amendment) Regulations 2001, SI 2001 no. 1648, Public Service Vehicles (Conditions of Fitness, Equipment, Use and Certification) (Amendment) Regulations 2001, SI 2001 no. 1649 and Goods Vehicles (Plating and Testing) (Amendment) Regulations 2001, SI 2001 no. 1650; made under the Road Traffic Act 1998.

[99] See especially now, W. Roddick, *Evidence to the Richard Commission* (December 2002).

[100] The procedural breakdown for the first full term was standard-185; accelerated-209; extended-12; and executive-291.

[101] Source: Presiding Office. The exception that proves the rule: in mid-December

2002 the Conservatives tabled no fewer than 116 amendments to a single commencement order by way of protest over the handling of a particular piece of legislative business: see *Official Record*, 17 December 2002.

    102 Lord Prys Davies, *The National Assembly: A Year of Laying the Foundations* (Cardiff: Law Society in Wales, 2000). And see above, chapter 5.

    103 See to this effect, Lord Elis-Thomas, *Evidence to the Richard Commission* (December 2002), p. 10.

    104 *House of Lords Debates*, vol. 611, cols. 818–19 (29 March 2000).

    105 See further below, chapter 9.

    106 Including from the author: R. Rawlings, *Evidence to the Assembly Review of Procedure* (March 2001).

    107 K. Patchett and R. Rawlings, *Further Evidence to the Assembly Review of Procedure* (May 2001), p. 7.

    108 On the ground of 'failure to fulfil statutory or other legal requirements': see *Final Report of the Assembly Review of Procedure Group* (February 2002), paragraphs 8.7–8.11.

    109 D. Lambert and W. Roddick, *Joint Legal Opinion for the Assembly Review of Procedure* (March 2001).

    110 Primary legislation raises its own particular problems of consultation for the subject committees, as discussed in chapter 9.

    111 *Official Record*, 5 November 2002. And see for general discussion of so-called 'co-legislation' between the Assembly and Westminster below, chapter 9.

    112 *Final Report of the Assembly Review of Procedure Group* (February 2002), paragraph 5.5.

    113 Ibid., paragraph 5.4, Business Committee, *Protocol for the Management of General Subordinate Legislation Proposed by the Welsh Assembly Government* (March 2003).

    114 Source: Presiding Office.

    115 See further below, chapter 11 (NHS reorganization in Wales).

    116 Health and Social Services Committee, *Minutes*, 29 May 2002, 19 June 2002 and 17 July 2002.

    117 Select Committee on Modernization of the House of Commons, First Report: *The Legislative Process* (HC 190, Session 1997–8). And see further below, chapter 9 (particular relevance in the context of Welsh executive devolution).

    118 *Protocol for the Management of General Subordinate Legislation Proposed by the Welsh Assembly Government* (March 2003), paragraph 8.

    119 Cabinet and Constitution Unit, *New Guidance on Using the Executive Procedure* (December 2002).

    120 *Protocol for the Management of General Subordinate Legislation Proposed by the Welsh Assembly Government* (March 2003), paragraph 12 (Business Committee to review operation of the protocol in nine months' time).

    121 *Final Report of the Assembly Review of Procedure Group* (February 2002), paragraph 5.7.

    122 See for example, Lord Elis-Thomas, *Evidence to the Richard Commission* (December 2002). The argument is pursued in the next chapter.

    123 See further below, chapter 15.

Chapter 9

[1] R. Morgan, *Memorandum by the Welsh Assembly Government* (October 2002), House of Lords Select Committee on the Constitution, *Devolution: Inter-Institutional Relations in the United Kingdom* – Evidence (HL 147, Session 2001–2), paragraph 14.

[2] Richard Commission, *The Powers of the National Assembly for Wales: Issues and Questions for Consultation* (November 2002), p. 4.

[3] See below, chapter 13, for the parallel argument in the EU context.

[4] As predicted in R. Rawlings, 'The new model Wales' (1998) 25 *Journal of Law and Society* 461.

[5] The general system of IGR is discussed in chapter 12.

[6] K. Patchett, *The Assembly's Engagement with Westminster and Whitehall* (Cardiff: Institute of Welsh Affairs, 2002).

[7] Welsh Affairs Select Committee, *The Primary Legislative Process as it Affects Wales* (HC 79, Session 2002–3), paragraph 3; and see now, *Government Response* (HC 989, Session 2002–3).

[8] K. Patchett, *Developing a Partnership Approach to Primary Legislation between Westminster and the National Assembly* (Cardiff: Institute of Welsh Affairs, 2002).

[9] The latter aspect is also pursued in chapter 12.

[10] R. Rawlings, 'Quasi-legislative devolution: powers and principles' (2001) 52 *Northern Ireland Legal Quarterly* 54.

[11] Under GWA, s. 29 and European Communities Act 1972 s. 2(2); this method is discussed in chapter 13.

[12] For example, the Government Resources and Accounts Act 2000: see above, chapter 2.

[13] T. Daintith and A. Page, *The Executive in the Constitution: Structure, Autonomy and Internal Control* (Oxford: Oxford University Press, 1999); and see also in a parallel context, J. Croft, *Whitehall and the Human Rights Act 1998* (London: Constitution Unit, 2000).

[14] As discussed further in chapter 12.

[15] And now on occasion from the Assembly: see below, p. 295.

[16] Welsh Affairs Select Committee, *The Primary Legislative Process as it Affects Wales – Evidence*, above, n. 7, paragraph 96.

[17] See below, chapter 11.

[18] Welsh Affairs Select Committee, *The Primary Legislative Process as it Affects Wales – Evidence*, above, n. 7, paragraph 171.

[19] As discussed by K. Patchett, 'The New Constitutional Architecture', in J. Osmond and J. Barry Jones (eds.), *Birth of Welsh Democracy* (Cardiff: Institute of Welsh Affairs 2003).

[20] See to this effect, D. Melding, *The Unitary State: As Dead as Queen Anne* (Cardiff: Welsh Governance Centre, April 2002).

[21] As discussed in the local context by Rhodri Morgan and Secretary of State for Wales Peter Hain, Welsh Affairs Select Committee, *The Primary Legislative Process as it Affects Wales – Evidence*, above, n. 7.

[22] See for example, *Official Record*, 12 March 2003 (David Melding). And see now, for an insider's view, S. McCann, 'Permissive powers are good for the Health Service' (2002) 2 *Wales Law Journal* 176.

[23] See below, chapter 11.

[24]   *Official Record*, 13 March 2003.

[25]   The Commonhold and Leasehold Reform Act 2002, which has minor differences for Wales, is a good example.

[26]   J. Owen Jones, 'Welsh Scrutiny for Welsh Bills' (2002 (1)) *Agenda – Journal of the Institute of Welsh Affairs* 35.

[27]   Select Committee on Modernisation of the House of Commons, First Report, *The Legislative Process* (HC 190, Session 1997–8).

[28]   R. Cook, *Memorandum submitted by the Leader of the House of Commons* (December 2001), Select Committee on Modernisation of the House of Commons, *Modernisation of the House of Commons: A Reform Programme for Consultation* (HC 440, Session 2001–2), paragraph 18.

[29]   See further below, chapter 11 (The rise of Welsh 'state' machinery).

[30]   See Welsh Affairs Select Committee, *The Draft National Health Service (Wales) Bill* (HC 959, Session 2001–2), and *Government Response* (HC 1215, Session 2001–2); and Welsh Grand Committee, *Proceedings*, 16 July 2002. The work of the two committees – a 'parliamentary voice' for Wales – is discussed generally in chapter 12.

[31]   Health and Social Services Committee, *Minutes*, 29 May 2002; *Official Record*, 18 July 2002.

[32]   *Final Report of the Assembly Review of Procedure Group* (February 2002), paragraph 4.9.

[33]   *Official Record*, 14 February 2002. We will return to the point in the context of the recent WASC report.

[34]   Welsh Assembly Government, *Children and Adult Mental Health Strategies* (September 2001).

[35]   Health and Social Services Committee, *Minutes*, 17 February 2002.

[36]   *Official Record*, 19 December 2000.

[37]   R. Davies, 'In search of attitude' (Memorandum, December 2000).

[38]   *Official Record*, 19 December 2000.

[39]   *Official Record*, 12 March 2003 (Carwyn Jones and Cynog Dafis).

[40]   D. Lambert, 'A comparison between the Office of the Secretary of State for Wales and the National Assembly for Wales', in D. Miers (ed.), *Devolution in Wales: Public Law and the National Assembly* (Cardiff: Welsh Public Law and Human Rights Association, 1999), p. 63.

[41]   See for details, Lord Prys Davies, *The National Assembly: A Year of Laying the Foundations* (Cardiff: Law Society in Wales, 2000).

[42]   See on the background, Welsh Affairs Select Committee, Second Report: *The Transport Bill and its Impact on Wales* (HC 287, Session 1999–2000); and for the responses of the UK government and the National Assembly for Wales, Welsh Affairs Select Committee, *Fifth Special Report* (HC 497, Session 1999–2000).

[43]   See further below, chapter 11.

[44]   See above, chapter 6.

[45]   As discussed in chapter 11.

[46]   See *Lost in Care – The Report of the Tribunal of Inquiry into the Abuse of Children in Care in the Former County Council Areas of Gwynedd and Clwyd since 1974* (The Waterhouse Report) (HC 201, Session 1999–2000); see further below, chapter 11.

[47]   See *Assembly Record*, 4 July 2000.

[48]   Welsh Affairs Select Committee, *The Primary Legislative Process as it Affects*

Wales – Evidence, above, n. 7, 64, paragraph 5.8. The issue of 'Henry VIII' clauses is pursued below.

⁴⁹   Children's Commissioner for Wales Act 2001, especially s. 4.

⁵⁰   Welsh Affairs Select Committee, *The Primary Legislative Process as it Affects Wales – Evidence*, above, n. 7, paragraph 171.

⁵¹   *Official Record*, 19 December 2000. The resolution reinforced an earlier one in favour of a 'flexible' devolution of functions in primary legislation affecting Wales: see *Official Record*, 2 February 2000.

⁵²   *Official Record*, 12 December 2000.

⁵³   *Official Record*, 11 July 2000.

⁵⁴   The Joint Ministerial Committee et al.; see below, chapter 12.

⁵⁵   Peter Hain, Welsh Affairs Select Committee, *The Primary Legislative Process as it Affects Wales – Evidence*, above, n. 7, paragraph 142.

⁵⁶   Wales Office, *Memorandum by the UK Government to the Richard Commission* (October 2002), paragraph 17.

⁵⁷   See Welsh Assembly Government press release, 17 July 2003 (agreement on the 'broad principles').

⁵⁸   House of Lords Select Committee on the Constitution, Second Report: *Devolution: Inter-institutional Relations in the United Kingdom* (HL 28, Session 2002–3), paragraph 123.

⁵⁹   *Memorandum by the Welsh Assembly Government* (May 2002), House of Lords Select Committee on the Constitution, above, n. 1, paragraph 17.

⁶⁰   Office of the Deputy Prime Minister, *Devolution Guidance Note No. 4 (The Role of the Secretary of State for Wales)* (January 2003), paragraph 10.

⁶¹   Ibid., paragraph 4; *Concordat between the Cabinet of the National Assembly for Wales and the Wales Office* (January 2001), paragraph 4.

⁶²   The reorganization is discussed in chapter 12.

⁶³   R. Morgan and P. Hain, Welsh Affairs Select Committee, *The Primary Legislative Process as it Affects Wales – Evidence*, above, n. 7, paragraph 144. The general theme is pursued in chapter 12.

⁶⁴   Ibid.

⁶⁵   This aspect is also addressed in chapter 12.

⁶⁶   Office of the Deputy Prime Minister, *Devolution Guidance Note No. 9 (Post-Devolution Primary Legislation Affecting Wales)* (January 2003), paragraph 8.

⁶⁷   Ibid., paragraph 5.

⁶⁸   Ibid., Annex.

⁶⁹   Ibid., paragraph 7.

⁷⁰   GWA, s. 33; as discussed in chapter 2.

⁷¹   *Devolution Guidance Note No. 9*, above, n. 66, paragraph 1.

⁷²   Welsh Affairs Select Committee, *The Primary Legislative Process as it Affects Wales – Evidence*, above, n. 7, 64, paragraph 2.2.

⁷³   Ibid., paragraph 35. It is said to be 'current practice': *Government Response*, above, n. 7, p. 3.

⁷⁴   *Concordat between the Cabinet of the National Assembly for Wales and the Wales Office* (January 2001), paragraph B.5; *Devolution Guidance Note No. 9*, above, n. 66 (version of October 2002).

⁷⁵   GWA, s. 41; and see above, chapter 2.

⁷⁶   See for details, McCann, 'Permissive powers are good for the Health Service', above, n. 22.

[77] *Concordat between the Cabinet of the National Assembly for Wales and the Wales Office*, above, n. 74, paragraph B.5.

[78] *Devolution Guidance Note No. 9* (version of January 2003), above, n. 66, paragraph 8.

[79] See below, chapter 15.

[80] *A Voice for Wales*, Cm. 3718 (1997), paragraph 3.38.

[81] GWA, s. 31.

[82] GWA, s. 33; see above, chapter 2.

[83] See *Official Record*, 26 November 2002.

[84] *Official Record*, 2 February 2000.

[85] *Official Record*, 19 December 2000.

[86] *Concordat between the Cabinet of the National Assembly for Wales and the Wales Office*, above, n. 74, paragraphs B6–B7.

[87] *Official Record*, 12 March 2003.

[88] See further below, chapter 11 (ELWa).

[89] See above, p. 280 (Carwyn Jones).

[90] *Final Report of the Assembly Review of Procedure Group* (February 2002), paragraph 4.8.

[91] *Official Record*, 22 January 2002.

[92] J. Griffiths, *Official Record*, 12 March 2003.

[93] See for details, *Official Record*, 11 April 2000. The procedure extends to considering how the Assembly might use the powers conferred: see above, chapter 8.

[94] *Official Record*, 11 December 2002.

[95] See above, chapter 8.

[96] *Final Report of the Assembly Review of Procedure Group* (February 2002), paragraph 4.10.

[97] Richard Edwards, *Evidence to the Richard Commission* (November 2002).

[98] Kirsty Williams, *Evidence to the Richard Commission* (November 2002).

[99] Ibid.; and see above, chapter 6.

[100] No doubt the Scottish experience will prove influential here: see further below, chapter 15.

[101] *Assembly Review of Procedure*, paragraph 4.2

[102] This aspect is discussed generally in chapter 12.

[103] *Assembly Review of Procedure*, paragraphs 4.13; 6.6

[104] Ibid., paragraph 4.10.

[105] Wales Office, press release, 3 December 2001.

[106] Lord Elis-Thomas, Oral Evidence to the Richard Commission (December 2002).

[107] Lord Elis-Thomas, *Evidence to the Richard Commission*, 10.

[108] See further below, chapter 12.

[109] T. Mullen, 'Scottish Parliament legislation 1999–2002' (2003) 9 *European Public Law* 179.

[110] As expressed in the case of Scotland in the so-called 'Sewel Convention' whereby Westminster legislates on devolved matters by agreement: see below, chapter 15 ('Super-Sewel').

[111] See for detailed analysis, Wales Legislation On-Line: *www.wales-legislation.org.uk*.

[112] See *Official Record*, 12 March 2003.

[113] See Welsh Assembly Government, *Planning: Delivering for Wales* (January 2002); the general theme is pursued in chapter 11 in the context of the NHS.

[114] *Official Record*, 12 March 2003 (Carwyn Jones).

[115] Welsh Affairs Select Committee, *The Primary Legislative Process as it Affects Wales – Evidence*, above, n. 7, 6.

[116] Ibid, Evidence, paragraph 6. (See also, for a telling argument to similar effect, Law Society of England and Wales, *Evidence to the Assembly Review of Procedure* (2001).)

[117] Ibid., *Evidence*, paragraph 101.

[118] Ibid., paragraph 17.

[119] *Government Response*, above, n. 7, pp. 1–2.

[120] Welsh Affairs Select Committee, *The Primary Legislative Process as it Affects Wales*, above, n. 7, paragraphs 18–21.

[121] R. Rawlings, 'Quasi-legislative devolution: powers and principles', above, n. 10.

[122] Following discussion between the Parliamentary Counsel Office and the Counsel General: see Welsh Affairs Select Committee, *The Primary Legislative Process as it Affects Wales*, above, n. 7, paragraph 29.

[123] See now for practical illustration, Explanatory Memorandum on the Health and Social Care (Community Health and Standards) Bill, Annex C.

[124] Welsh Affairs Select Committee, *The Primary Legislative Process as it Affects Wales*, above, n. 7, paragraphs 22–4; also *Government Response*, above, n. 7, p. 2.

[125] Ibid., paragraph 6.

[126] Ibid., paragraphs 37, 41.

[127] Ibid., paragraphs 46–7.

[128] Welsh Affairs Select Committee, *The Primary Legislative Process as it Affects Wales*, above, n. 4, paragraphs 48, 52.

[129] *Government Response*, above, n. 7, pp. 3–4.

[130] In marked contrast to the recent report of the House of Lords Select Committee on the Constitution, which may be criticized for excessive stargazing. See below, chapter 12.

[131] Lord Elis-Thomas, *Evidence to Richard Commission* (December 2002).

[132] A familiar theme in the UK in the context of central–local relations.

[133] *Memorandum by the Welsh Assembly Government*, House of Lords Select Committee on the Constitution, above, n. 1, paragraph 17.

[134] See above, p. 11–13.

[135] C. Harlow and R. Rawlings, *Law and Administration* (Butterworths, 2nd edn. 1997), especially chapter 6.

[136] N. Barber and A. Young, 'The rise of prospective Henry VIII clauses and their implications for sovereignty' (2003) *Public Law* 122. See for judicial confirmation of the prospective effect, at least in the case of so-called 'constitutional statutes' such as the European Communities Act 1972, *Thoburn v. Sunderland City Council* (2002) 1 *Weekly Law Reports* 247.

[137] Barber and Young, ibid. Less condescendingly, the statutes can be presented in terms of an alternative method of creating primary legislation: see for example, N. Burrows, *Devolution* (London: Sweet and Maxwell, 2000).

[138] Famously expressed in the Report of the Committee on Ministers' Powers (the Donoughmore Committee) (Cmnd. 4060, 1932): see also, G. Rippon, 'Henry VIII Clauses' (1989) 10 *Statute Law Review* 205.

[139] As also – a point of potential significance in the devolutionary context – 'whether they subject the exercise of legislative power to an inappropriate degree of parliamentary scrutiny'.

[140] GWA, ss. 27–8; as discussed in chapter 11.

[141] Welsh Affairs Select Committee, *The Primary Legislative Process as it Affects Wales – Evidence*, above, n. 7, paragraph 77.

[142] See further below, chapter 15. Another striking example is provided by the Electronic Communications Act 2001, s. 8.

[143] Wales Office memorandum, above , n. 48.

[144] W. Roddick, *Evidence to the Richard Commission* (December 2002).

[145] Welsh Affairs Select Committee, *The Primary Legislative Process as it Affects Wales – Evidence*, above, n. 7, paragraph 163. But see further below chapter 13, on the design of the relevant 'designation orders'.

[146] Ibid.

[147] Ibid., paragraph 24 (Lord Elis-Thomas).

[148] See above, chapter 2.

[149] There is in fact a rough equivalence with the special safeguards applied by Parliament in the case of Regulatory Reform Orders.

[150] See in relation to this, GWA s. 44(2) and (4).

[151] Welsh Affairs Select Committee, *The Primary Legislative Process as it Affects Wales – Evidence*, above, n. 7, paragraph 35.

[152] Ibid., paragraphs 156, 160.

[153] Lord Elis-Thomas, *Evidence to the Richard Commission* (December 2002).

[154] R. Rawlings, 'Quasi-legislative devolution: powers and principles', above, n. 121.

[155] As discussed in chapter 2.

[156] See, for example, the Learning and Skills Act 2000 (allocation to the Assembly) and the Local Government Act 2000 (key powers of commencement for the Secretary of State).

[157] Welsh Affairs Select Committee, *The Primary Legislative Process as it Affects Wales – Evidence*, above, n. 7, paragraph 27.

[158] *Assembly Review of Procedure*, paragraph 4.4; and see *Official Record*, 14 February 2002.

[159] *Assembly Review of Procedure*, annex V ('Principles to be adopted in Government Bills Affecting the National Assembly for Wales').

[160] Above, p. 294.

[161] See below, chapter 15.

[162] Peter Hain, *Oral Evidence to the Richard Commission* (March 2003).

[163] Community Care (Delayed Discharges Etc.) Bill, clause 12(6).

[164] Community Care (Delayed Discharges Etc.) Act 2003, s. 16 (Assembly can make any regulations that the Secretary of State has power to make in relation to England).

[165] GWA, s. 22(4): see above, chapter 2. The approach also finds echoes in the subsequent primary legislation: see for example, Regulatory Reform Act 2001, s. 1(5).

[166] So establishing a Welsh equivalent of the famous Sewel convention in relation to Scotland: see below, chapter 15. Some functions have reverted to central government post-devolution: see above, chapter 2.

[167] Education Act 2002, ss. 105(6) and 107. See also s. 214 (the concept of Henry VIII-type implementing powers by reference to the purposes of the legislation).

[168] Education Act 2002, ss. 84(6) and 86.

[169] See, for example, Commonhold and Leasehold Reform Act 2002 and Community Care (Delayed Discharges Etc.) Act 2003

[170] Lord Elis Thomas, *Evidence to the Richard Commission* (December 2002).

[171] Welsh Affairs Select Committee, *The Primary Legislative Process as it Affects Wales – Evidence*, above, n. 7, paragraph 129. Nor has the Counsel General been enthused: W. Roddick, *Evidence to the Richard Commission* (December 2002).

[172] Lord Elis Thomas, *Evidence to the Richard Commission* (December 2002).

[173] D. Lambert and S. Beasley, *Evidence to the Richard Commission* (March 2003).

[174] GWA Schedule 2; see above, chapter 2.

[175] Welsh Affairs Select Committee, *The Primary Legislative Process as it Affects Wales – Evidence*, above, n. 7, paragraph 162.

[176] *A Voice for Wales*, Cm 3718 (1997), paragraph 3.37.

[177] Welsh Affairs Select Committee, *The Primary Legislative Process as it Affects Wales – Evidence*, above, n. 7, paragraph 160.

[178] Council Directive 1999/31/EC ('the landfill directive'). See also the White Paper, *Waste Strategy 2000: England and Wales*, Cm. 4693 (2000), and Welsh Assembly Government, *Wise about Waste – National Strategy for Wales* (June 2002).

[179] Select Committee on Delegated Powers and Regulatory Reform, *Second Report: Waste and Emissions Trading Bill*, HL 20, Session 2002–3, paragraph 21.

[180] Ibid., annex 3, paragraph 172.

[181] See below, chapter 12.

[182] R. Rawlings, 'Quasi-legislative devolution: powers and principles', above, n. 154.

[183] Rhodri Morgan, letter to Lord Elis Thomas, 18 November 2002.

[184] Welsh Affairs Select Committee, *The Primary Legislative Process as it Affects Wales – Evidence*, above, n. 7, paragraph 155.

[185] Ibid., paragraph 128.

[186] House of Lords Select Committee on the Constitution, *Devolution: Inter-Institutional Relations in the United Kingdom*, above, n. 58, paragraph 124; *Government Response*, Cm. 5780 (2003), paragraph 21.

[187] It has a certain capacity to amuse: see Peter Hain, *Oral Evidence to the Richard Commission* (March 2003).

[188] *Government Response*, above, n. 7, p. 5.

[189] Welsh Affairs Select Committee, *The Primary Legislative Process as it Affects Wales – Evidence*, above, n. 7, paragraph 151.

[190] *Government Response*, above, n. 7, p. 6.

[191] Ibid.

[192] Welsh Affairs Select Committee, *The Primary Legislative Process as it Affects Wales – Evidence*, above, n. 7, paragraph 151.

Chapter 10

[1] National Assembly, *Local Government Partnership Scheme* (2000), paragraph 1.3.

[2] *Western Mail*, 4 February 2002.

[3] G. Williams, *When was Wales? A History of the Welsh* (London: Black Raven, 1985), p. 304.

⁴ R. Rhodes, *Control and Power in Central–Local Government Relations* (Aldershot: Ashgate, 1999).

⁵ D. Walker, *Living with Ambiguity: The Relationship between Central and Local Government* (York: Joseph Rowntree, 2000).

⁶ See for example, C. Scott, 'Analysing regulatory space: fragmented resources and institutional design' (2001) *Public Law* 329.

⁷ See above, chapter 2.

⁸ M. Loughlin, *Legality and Locality: The Role of Law in Central–Local Government Relations* (Oxford: Clarendon, 1996).

⁹ See above, especially chapter 2.

¹⁰ A. Michael, *The Dragon on our Doorstep: New Politics for a New Millennium in Wales* (Aberystwyth: Institute of Welsh Politics, November 1999), p. 8.

¹¹ See further for a legal analysis, W. Roddick, 'Doing business with the Assembly: defining the parameters and utilising the opportunities' (2002) 1 *Welsh Law Journal* 306.

¹² See for general discussion, B. Dicks, T. Hall and A. Pithouse, 'The National Assembly and the voluntary sector: an equal partnership?', in P. Chaney, T. Hall and A. Pithouse (eds.), *New Governance – New Democracy? Post-devolution Wales* (Cardiff: University of Wales Press, 2001). And see National Assembly, *Voluntary Sector Scheme* (June 2000); also *Official Record*, 25 April 2002 (minority party debate).

¹³ As discussed in the next chapter.

¹⁴ G. Boyne, P. Griffiths, A. Lawton and J. Law, *Local Government in Wales* (York: Joseph Rowntree, 1991). Compare M. Loughlin, *Legality and Locality*, above, n. 8.

¹⁵ Welsh Local Government Association, *Local Democracy in Wales: The Implications of a Welsh Assembly* (1997), p. 16.

¹⁶ Welsh Office, *Local Voices: Modernising Local Government in Wales*, Cm. 4028 (1998), paragraph 1.19.

¹⁷ See, to the same effect, M. Laffin, G. Taylor and A. Thomas, *A New Partnership? The National Assembly for Wales and Local Government* (York: Joseph Rowntree, 2002). And see below, chapter 12, for discussion of the concept of comity in the context of central–territorial relations.

¹⁸ See above, chapter 1.

¹⁹ *Local Voices*, above, n. 16, pp. vii, 72.

²⁰ National Assembly, *Local Government Partnership Scheme* (2000), paragraph 5.1; and see *Official Record*, 11 July 2000.

²¹ Department of Environment, Transport and the Regions, *Modernising Local Government: In Touch with the People*, Cm. 4014 (1998).

²² *Local Voices*, above, n. 16, chapter 3.

²³ Ibid., paragraphs 1.23–1.25, 8.2.

²⁴ Local Government Act 2000, Part I.

²⁵ *Local Voices*, above, n. 16, paragraphs 8.32–8.33.

²⁶ Local Government Act 2000, Part III; *Third Report of the Committee on Standards in Public Life: Standards of Conduct in Local Government in England, Scotland and Wales*, Cm. 3702 (1997).

²⁷ Above, chapter 8.

²⁸ This principle notably informs the Council of Europe's *European Charter of Local Self Government* (European Treaty Series no. 122, opened for signature on 15 October 1985, entered into force on 1 September 1988), now ratified by the UK government.

²⁹ See above, chapter 6.

³⁰ The lowest tier of Welsh local government (some 750 town and community councils) lies beyond the scope of this discussion.

³¹ Sources: *Wales Yearbook 2002* (Cardiff: HTV, 2002); Report of the Commission on Local Government Electoral Arrangements in Wales (Sunderland Committee), *Improving Local Democracy in Wales* (July 2002).

³² National Assembly, *Local Government Partnership Scheme* (July 2000), paragraph 2.2. And see above, chapter 2.

³³ See above, n. 2. And see for an excellent general discussion, O. O'Neill, *A Question of Trust* (Cambridge: BBC Reith Lectures 2002).

³⁴ National Assembly, press release, 19 February 2002.

³⁵ A. Thomas, 'Realising partnership: relations between the Assembly and local government', in J. Barry Jones and J. Osmond (eds.), *Building a Civic Culture: Institutional Change, Policy Development and Political Dynamics in the National Assembly for Wales* (Cardiff: Institute of Welsh Affairs and Welsh Governance Centre, 2002).

³⁶ The theme is traced in subsequent chapters, in the context both of government agencies and of civil society.

³⁷ For further detail, see Laffin, Taylor and Thomas, *A New Partnership? The National Assembly for Wales and Local Government*, above, n. 17.

³⁸ See above, chapter 4.

³⁹ Assembly Learning Grants, as established in the wake of an Assembly-sponsored investigation: T. Rees, *Investing in Learners: Coherence, Clarity and Equity for Student Support in Wales*. See further (on this watered-down version of Scottish policy) below, chapter 15.

⁴⁰ A. Edwards, *Stating the Difference* (Cardiff: Churches' National Assembly Centre, 2002).

⁴¹ This is further underscored by the election manifesto, Welsh Labour Party, *Working together for Wales* (2003).

⁴² J. Adams and P. Robinson, *Devolution in Practice: Public Policy Differences within the UK* (London: Institute of Public Policy Research, 2002).

⁴³ *Western Mail*, 4 February 2002.

⁴⁴ *Official Record*, 19 March 2002.

⁴⁵ National Assembly, *The Learning Country* (September 2001).

⁴⁶ Welsh Assembly Government, *Freedom and Responsibility in Local Government* (March 2002), p. 25.

⁴⁷ See for details, National Assembly, *Wales Programme for Improvement: Guidance for Local Authorities* (January 2002).

⁴⁸ Under the auspices of the Health and Social Care (Community Health and Standards) Bill, currently before Parliament.

⁴⁹ R. Andrews, G. Boyne, J. Law and R. Walker, *A Comparison of Local Authority Performance in England and Wales* (Cardiff: Local and Regional Government Research Unit, 2002); and see National Assembly, press release, 31 January 2002.

⁵⁰ As shown in the provisions of the Health and Social Care (Community Health and Standards) Bill. Notably, reviews and investigations of Welsh NHS bodies will be undertaken by a Healthcare Inspectorate Unit for Wales: see Wales Office, press release, 12 March 2003.

⁵¹ *Official Record*, 16 July 2002.

⁵² GWA, s. 113 and Schedule 11; and see above, chapter 2.

⁵³ National Assembly, *Local Government Partnership Scheme* (December 2000), paragraph 2.1.

⁵⁴ *House of Commons Debates*, vol. 305, col. 932 (3 February 1998).

⁵⁵ See generally M. Loughlin, *Legality and Locality*, above, n. 8.

⁵⁶ See generally National Assembly, *Annual Reports of the Local Government Partnership Scheme 2000–2001, 2001–2002* (June 2002); also *Official Record*, 4 July 2002.

⁵⁷ In conjunction with standing orders: see National Assembly, *Protocol for the Handling of Partnership Council Business by the Joint Secretariat* (September 2000).

⁵⁸ See for details, Welsh Assembly Government, *Freedom and Responsibility in Local Government* (March 2002). And see below, chapter 11.

⁵⁹ See Welsh Assembly Government and Welsh Local Government Association, *Narrowing the Gap in the Performance of Schools* (October 2002); *Official Record*, 19 November 2002.

⁶⁰ As promised in the economic plan, Welsh Assembly Government, *A Winning Wales* (January 2002).

⁶¹ *Western Mail*, 31 May 2002.

⁶² See below, chapter 12. And see further on the role for expanded policy networks and professional associations, Laffin, Taylor and Thomas, *A New Partnership? The National Assembly for Wales and Local Government*, above, n. 17.

⁶³ Welsh Assembly Government, *Freedom and Responsibility in Local Government* (March 2002), p. 31.

⁶⁴ Welsh Assembly Government, press release, 19 February 2002.

⁶⁵ The Welsh approach should, however, not be confused with the 'Policy Service Agreements' negotiated individually by councils in England with a view to achieving greater flexibility in service budgets. See generally, P. Vincent Jones, 'Central–local relations under the Local Government Act 1999 – a new consensus?' (2000) 63 *Modern Law Review* 84.

⁶⁶ Partnership Council, *Policy Agreements – Relationships with Other Forms of Performance Information* (June 2000), p. 1; and see further, Partnership Council, *The Concept of Policy Agreements* (February 2000).

⁶⁷ Welsh Local Government Association, *Policy Agreements between Local Authorities and the National Assembly for Wales – The New Framework* (December 2000), p. 1. And see further below, on the concept of community leadership (and planning).

⁶⁸ C. Harlow and R. Rawlings, *Law and Administration*, 2nd edn. (London: Butterworths, 1997), especially chapter 5.

⁶⁹ M. Power, *The Audit Explosion* (London: Demos, 1994); E. Fisher, 'Drowning by numbers: standard setting in risk regulation and the pursuit of accountable public administration' (2000) 20 *Oxford Journal of Legal Studies* 109.

⁷⁰ See for further details, Laffin, Taylor and Thomas, *A New Parnership? The National Assembly for Wales and Local Government*, above, n. 17.

⁷¹ Welsh Local Government Association, *Policy Agreements between Local Authorities and the National Assembly for Wales – The New Framework* (December 2000), p. 1.

⁷² Welsh Assembly Government, *Freedom and Responsibility in Local Government* (March 2002), p. 31.

⁷³ Ibid., p. 1.

⁷⁴ Department of Local Government, Transport and the Regions, *Strong Local Leadership – Quality Public Services* (Cm. 5327, December 2001).

⁷⁵ Local Government Act 2000, s. 4; National Assembly for Wales, *Preparing Community Strategies* (December 2001).

⁷⁶ Welsh Assembly Government, *Freedom and Responsibility in Local Government* (March 2002), p. 11.

⁷⁷ Ibid., pp. 23–4; and see above, chapter 5.

⁷⁸ Ibid., chapter 9. And see for the consultation, National Assembly, *Simplifying the System* (September 2000).

⁷⁹ See for details, Chartered Institute of Public Finance and Accountancy (CIPFA), *Code of Practice on Prudential Borrowing* (2002).

⁸⁰ Welsh Assembly Government, *Freedom and Responsibility in Local Government* (March 2002), p. 4.

⁸¹ Ibid., p. 6.

⁸² See for example, Audit Commission, *Changing Gear: Best Value Annual Statement 2001* (September 2001).

⁸³ Welsh Assembly Government, *Freedom and Responsibility in Local Government* (March 2002), p. 15.

⁸⁴ See for details, ibid., p. 17.

⁸⁵ Welsh Local Government Association, *The Future of Public Services in Wales* (October 2001).

⁸⁶ Welsh Assembly Government, *Freedom and Responsibility in Local Government* (March 2002), p. 17.

⁸⁷ Ibid., p. 1.

⁸⁸ Report of the Commission on Local Government Electoral Arrangements in Wales (Sunderland Committee), *Improving Local Democracy in Wales* (July 2002).

⁸⁹ Welsh Labour Party and Welsh Liberal Democrats, *Putting Wales First: A Partnership for the People of Wales* (October 2000), p. 17.

⁹⁰ Report of the Commission on Local Government Electoral Arrangements in Wales (Sunderland Committee), *Improving Local Democracy in Wales* (July 2002), p. 17.

⁹¹ Ibid., p. 46.

⁹² Ibid., p. 18.

⁹³ Ibid., p. 58.

⁹⁴ See *Official Record*, 19 March 2003.

⁹⁵ See above, chapter 1; and see further below, chapter 15.

⁹⁶ See for a classic discussion of the concepts, A. Birch, *Representative and Responsible Government: An Essay on the British Constitution* (London: Allen & Unwin, 1977).

⁹⁷ Report of the Commission on Local Government Electoral Arrangements in Wales (Sunderland Committee), *Improving Local Democracy in Wales* (July 2002), p. 47.

⁹⁸ Edwina Hart, Welsh Assembly Government cabinet statement, 19 March 2003.

⁹⁹ Ibid., p. 57.

¹⁰⁰ See now, D. Balsom, 'A report destined for the long grass' (2002) (2) *Agenda – Journal of the Institute of Welsh Affairs* 28.

¹⁰¹ See above, chapter 6.

¹⁰² See further, for the parallel argument in respect of central government, below, chapter 12.

Chapter 11

[1] House of Lords Select Committee on the Constitution, *Devolution: Inter-Institutional Relations in the United Kingdom – Evidence* (HL 147, Session 2001–2), Q.1021).

[2] See above, chapter 1.

[3] C. Harlow and R. Rawlings, *Law and Administration*, 2nd edn. (London: Butterworths, 1997), especially chapter 5.

[4] G. Majone, 'The rise of the regulatory state in Europe' (1994) 17 *West European Politics* 77.

[5] C. Hood and C. Scott, 'Bureaucratic regulation and New Public Management in the United Kingdom: mirror-image developments?' (1996) 23 *Journal of Law and Society* 321.

[6] M. Power, *The Audit Explosion* (London: Demos, 1994).

[7] See for practical illustration, *Official Record*, 9 July 2002 (the Welsh Assembly Government's response to the Communications Bill).

[8] See now for practical illustration, the question of the design of a Human Rights Commission (below, chapter 14).

[9] *A Voice for Wales*, Cm. 3718 (1997), paragraph 3.11 and Annex B. And see for a detailed breakdown, Constitution Unit, *An Assembly for Wales* (London, 1996), Appendix A.

[10] See on this point, the complaint of the anti-devolutionist: L. Smith, *Quangos: Not so much a 'Bonfire' – More a Damp Squib* (Brynmawr: 2002).

[11] Cabinet Office, *Devolution Guidance Note 9: Post-devolution Primary Legislation Affecting Wales* (January 2001), Annex.

[12] See generally, D. Oliver, *Government in the United Kingdom: The Search for Accountability, Effectiveness and Citizenship* (Milton Keynes: Open University Press, 1991); also, R. Mulgan, ' "Accountability": an ever expanding concept?' (2000) 78 *Public Administration* 555.

[13] R. Ashworth, G. Boyne and R. Walker, 'Devolution and regulation: the political control of public agencies in Wales', in P. Chaney, T. Hall and A. Pithouse (eds.), *New Governance – New Democracy? Post-devolution Wales* (Cardiff: University of Wales Press, 2001).

[14] *Official Record*,10 May 2000.

[15] See now National Assembly, *Code of Practice for Ministerial Appointments to Public Bodies* (June 2002); and *Official Record*, 25 June 2002.

[16] GWA, ss. 74–5.

[17] See above, chapter 6.

[18] See for practical illustration, National Assembly Audit Committee, *The Arts Council for Wales: Centre for Visual Arts* (May 2002).

[19] K. Hollingsworth, 'A reputation for probity', in J. Barry Jones and J. Osmond (eds.), *Building a Civic Culture: Institutional Change, Policy Development and Political Dynamics in the National Assembly for Wales* (Cardiff: Institute of Welsh Affairs and Welsh Governance Centre, 2002), p. 102.

[20] GWA, s. 74 and Schedule 5.

[21] *Official Record*, 10 May 2000.

[22] See to this effect, J. Osmond, 'Emergence of the Assembly government', in Barry Jones and Osmond (eds.), *Building a Civic Culture*, above, n. 19.

[23] With reference for example to clamping down on unauthorized media contacts by agency officials: see *Western Mail*, 18 January 2002.

[24] National Assembly, *Quinquennial Reviews of Executive Assembly Sponsored Public Bodies – Guidelines* (May 2000).

[25] *Official Record*, 10 May 2000 (Edwina Hart).

[26] See above, chapter 1.

[27] See K. Morgan and G. Rees, 'Learning by doing: devolution and the governance of economic development in Wales', in Chaney, Hall and Pithouse (eds.), *New Governance – New Democracy? Post-devolution Wales*, above, n. 13.

[28] Ibid.

[29] See further below, and for details, Welsh Development Agency, *Corporate Plan 2001–2002* (March 2001).

[30] See to this effect, Economic Development Committee, *Annual Report 2001–2002* (May 2002).

[31] *Official Record*, 10 May 2001.

[32] National Assembly, *First Quinquennial Review of the Welsh Development Agency* (March 2001), paragraphs 1, 10.

[33] *Official Record*, 10 May 2001 (Michael German); and see above, chapter 1.

[34] See above, chapter 9.

[35] See above, chapter 7, on the contribution of the Assembly subject committee.

[36] As provided for in the statute: Learning and Skills Act 2000, s. 48 and Schedule 5.

[37] As illustrated by *Memorandum of Understanding between the National Council for Education and Training for Wales and the Welsh Development Agency* (April 2001).

[38] National Assembly, *Remit Letter to Council for Education and Training for Wales* (January 2001).

[39] National Council for Education and Training for Wales – ELWa, *Corporate Strategy* (March 2002).

[40] Learning and Skills Act 2000, ss. 31–7.

[41] Learning and Skills Act 2000, s. 44; and see also s. 47 (power of directions) and s. 49 (power to make grants to the Council).

[42] *Official Record*, 26 March 2003.

[43] Auditor General for Wales, *National Council for Education and Training Wales – 2001/2 Accounts* (January 2003), paragraph 24. Speaking more generally, there have been various complaints of a lack of transparency in this affair, culminating in rulings by the Presiding Officer on the naming of agency staff: see *Official Record*, 18 March 2003.

[44] See generally, Audit Committee, *Additional Report on Activities to March 2003* (March 2003).

[45] See for practical illustration, D. Egan and R. James, 'Open government and inclusiveness', in Barry Jones and Osmond (eds.), *Building a Civic Culture*, above, n. 19. Latterly, Members have become a little more robust: see for example, Education and Learning Committee, 27 February 2003 (HEFCW).

[46] *ELWa: Review of Senior Structure* (the so-called 'Rawlings Report'): see Education and Lifelong Learning Committee, *Minister's Report – Annex*, 21 November 2002.

[47] See above, chapter 7.

[48] *Official Record*, 26 March 2003.

⁴⁹   See now, *Official Record*, 12 March 2003.

⁵⁰   Previously characterized as part of 'the Welsh difference': see above, chapter 2.

⁵¹   Commonly in the form of Directives: which then raise important issues of legislative implementation. See below, chapter 13.

⁵²   See Environment Agency, *http://www.environment-agency.gov.uk/aboutus/*

⁵³   P. Selznick 'Focusing organisational research on regulation', in R. Noll (ed.), *Regulatory Policy and the Social Sciences* (Berkeley: University of California Press, 1985); and see Harlow and Rawlings, *Law and Administration*, above, n. 3, chapter 10.

⁵⁴   Environment Agency Wales, *Corporate Plan Wales 2002–2003* (March 2002).

⁵⁵   Environment Agency Wales, *http://www.environment-agency.gov.uk/regions/wales/*

⁵⁶   Environment Agency Wales, *Annual Review and Forward Look* (March 2002).

⁵⁷   At Nant-y-Gwyddon; see for details A. Kay, 'Effectiveness through consensus', in J. Barry Jones and J. Osmond (eds.), *Building A Civic Culture* (Cardiff: Institute of Welsh Affairs, 2002).

⁵⁸   See *Official Record*, 19 March 2002.

⁵⁹   National Assembly, *Improving Health in Wales: A Plan for the NHS with its Partners* (January 2001).

⁶⁰   Welsh Assembly Government, press release, 7 November 2002.

⁶¹   M. Sullivan, 'Health policy: differentiation and devolution', in J. Adams and P. Robinson (eds.), *Devolution in Practice: Public Policy Differences within the UK* (London: Institute for Public Policy Research, 2002), p. 60.

⁶²   See for example, Department of Health, *The National Health Service: A Service with Ambitions*, Cm. 3425 (1996); and for discussion, K. Woods, 'Health policy and the NHS in the UK, 1997–2002', in Adams and Robinson (eds.), *Devolution in Practice*, above, n. 61. But see further below.

⁶³   National Assembly, *Improving Health in Wales*, above, n. 59, Preface.

⁶⁴   See above, chapters 9–10.

⁶⁵   *Official Record*, 19 November 2002 (Jane Hutt).

⁶⁶   See *Official Record*, 16 October 2002 (draft budget).

⁶⁷   Many difficulties are highlighted by *The Review of Health and Social Care in Wales* (June 2003), a report commissioned by the Welsh Assembly Government.

⁶⁸   See for example, G. Jones, *A Reorganisation Too Far* (Cardiff: Institute of Welsh Affairs: 2001).

⁶⁹   Welsh Assembly Government, *The New NHS Wales Functions and Structures* (July 2002), paragraph 7.1.

⁷⁰   National Assembly, *Improving Health in Wales*, above, n. 59, p. 9; and see now, Welsh Assembly Government, *The Future of Primary Care* (July 2002).

⁷¹   P. Townsend, *Targeting Poor Health* (Welsh Assembly Government, March 2002).

⁷²   Ibid.

⁷³   NHS Structural Change Programme Team, *Partnership Working* (October 2002).

⁷⁴   *Official Record*, 27 November 2001. As distinct from reorganization or set-up costs (some £15 million).

⁷⁵   National Assembly, *Improving Health in Wales*, above, n. 59, paragraphs 3.1–3.4.

⁷⁶   See above, chapter 10 (table 17).

⁷⁷   Welsh Assembly Government, *The New NHS Wales Functions and Structures* (July 2002), paragraph 4.17.

[78] See further below (the Wales Centre for Health).

[79] *Official Record*, 5 November 2002.

[80] Welsh Assembly Government, *The New NHS Wales Functions and Structures* (July 2002), paragraph 4.1. The Chief Medical Officer is also a member of the executive board.

[81] Ibid., paragraphs 4.4–4.16.

[82] See for example, *Official Record*, 28 January 2003.

[83] Assembly cabinet, statement, 21 December 2000; National Assembly, *Five Yearly Reviews of Non-Executive Assembly Sponsored Public Bodies – Guidelines* (January 2001).

[84] A point notably stressed in the (UK) pre-legislative scrutiny of the National Health Service (Wales) Bill; see above, chapter 9.

[85] See *Western Mail*, 20 March 2002. Latterly, their work has come under scrutiny by the subject committees.

[86] National Assembly, press release, 7 June 2002.

[87] National Assembly, press release, 22 August 2002.

[88] See for example, National Assembly, press releases, 27 June 2002, 5 July 2002. The related question of powers for the Assembly over police authorities in Wales is now firmly on the constitutional and political agenda; see below, chapter 15.

[89] Sir John Thomas, 'Developing legal Wales: the economy and the future of devolution', (2000) 2 *Agenda – Journal of the Institute of Welsh Affairs* 17.

[90] C. Harlow, 'Ombudsmen in search of a role' (1978) 41 *Modern Law Review* 446; also Harlow and Rawlings, *Law and Administration*, above, n. 3, chapters 12–13.

[91] *A Voice for Wales*, Cm. 3718 (1997), paragraph 4.39.

[92] See *House of Lords Debates*, vol. 590, cols. 442–5 (3 June 1998) (Lord Williams of Mostyn). Once again, the argument from symmetry – the Scots were going their own way – clearly played a part.

[93] GWA, s. 111 and Schedule 9, paragraph 14.

[94] Parliamentary Commissioner Act 1967. The Ombudsman also currently has jurisdiction in relation to freedom of information: see above, chapter 3.

[95] GWA, Schedule 9, paragraph 23; and see Assembly standing orders.

[96] GWA s. 112 and Schedule 12; and with certain modifications, for example on the use of special reports.

[97] Welsh Administration Ombudsman, *Annual Report 2000–2001* (October 2001), chapter 1. The PCA has consistently doubled up as HSC.

[98] A. Barron and C. Scott, 'The Citizen's Charter programme' (1992) 55 *Modern Law Review* 526; and see National Assembly Advisory Group, *Discussion Paper: Complaints Procedures* (1998).

[99] National Assembly, *Code of Practice on Complaints* (2001).

[100] See for details, Welsh Administration Ombudsman, *Annual Report 2000–2001*, chapter 2; and see further, Parliamentary Ombudsman, *Annual Report 2001–2002* (HC 897 (2001–2)).

[101] See for details, *Annual Report 2001–2002* (July 2002), chapter 3.

[102] Wales Office and Welsh Assembly Government, *Ombudsmen's Services in Wales: Time for Change?* (November 2002); and see *Official Record*, 12 March 2003 (bid for a 'Public Services (Ombudsman) Bill' as noted in chapter 9).

[103] GWA, Schedule 9, paragraph 27.

[104] 'Housing Ombudsman (Wales) Bill', as now incorporated in the (draft) Housing Bill.

[105] Cabinet Office, *Review of the Public Sector Ombudsmen in England* (the Collcutt Report) (April 2000).

[106] Wales Office and Welsh Assembly Government, *Ombudsmen's Services in Wales*, above, n. 102, paragraph 6.

[107] See above, chapter 9.

[108] See generally, K. Hollingsworth and G. Douglas, 'Creating a children's champion for Wales? The Care Standards Act 2000 (Part V) and the Children's Commissioner for Wales Act 2001' (2002) 65 *Modern Law Review* 58.

[109] See for example *Official Record*, 18 June 2002 (debate on establishment of the Richard Commission).

[110] Care Standards Act 2000, s. 72A (inserted by the 2001 statute). It is only in regulations that reference is made to the UN Convention on the Rights of the Child (1989), a chief inspiration of the reform.

[111] Care Standards Act 2000, s. 72B.

[112] See for details, Hollingsworth and Douglas, 'Creating a children's champion for Wales?', above, n. 108.

[113] Children's Commissioner for Wales Regulations, SI 2001 no. 2787 (W.237), Regulation 12.

[114] See *Official Record*, 7 June 2000.

[115] House of Commons Standing Committee F (23 January 2001).

[116] See above, chapter 2.

[117] Wales Office, press release, 3 April 2001.

[118] Care Standards Act 2000, s. 75A.

[119] Here in the guise of Her Majesty's Chief Inspector of Schools in Wales: see GWA, s. 104 and Schedule 6.

[120] See above, chapter 4.

[121] See for example, *Official Record*, 14 May 2002.

[122] Learning and Skills Act 2000, Part IV.

[123] Estyn, *Annual Report of Her Majesty's Chief Inspector of Education and Training in Wales, 2000–2001* (February 2002), especially chapter 4.

[124] Estyn, press release, 15 February 2002.

[125] Estyn, press release, 28 March 2002.

[126] *Western Mail*, 13 June 2002.

[127] Welsh Local Government Association, *Response to Audit Commission Draft Strategy* (September 2001).

[128] Audit Commission, *Delivering Improvement Together: Corporate Strategy 2001–2004*, p. 19.

[129] Audit Commission, *Director Wales* (June 2002).

[130] Audit Commission, *Public Services in Wales* (2002), p. 42.

[131] *Official Record*, 19 March 2002; and see above, chapter 9.

[132] Wales Office, *Draft Public Audit (Wales) Bill*, Cm. 5796 (2003).

[133] See now, for a useful preliminary analysis, Adams and Robinson (eds.), *Devolution in Practice*, above, n. 61.

[134] L. Paterson and R. Wyn Jones, 'Does civil society drive constitutional change?', in B. Taylor and K. Thomson (eds.), *Scotland and Wales: Nations Again?* (Cardiff: University of Wales Press, 1999).

[135] J. Osmond (ed.), *Education Policy Breaks Loose* (Cardiff: Institute of Welsh Affairs, 2002).

[136] Reference is here being made to so-called 'green light' and 'amber light' theories of administrative law: see Harlow and Rawlings, *Law and Administration*, above, n. 3, chapters 2–3. This is not to overlook the unity of the legal control exercised by the ordinary courts ('red light' theory) on an England and Wales basis. See below, chapter 14.

[137] This is not to overlook the critical mediating effects of supranational legal ordering (pressures for convergence inside the member state paradigm). See below, chapters 12–13.

[138] The theme is elaborated in chapter 13, in the context of European regional policy (structural funds).

Chapter 12

[1] Wales Office and Office of the Deputy Prime Minister, *Evidence to the Commission on the Powers and Electoral Arrangements of the National Assembly for Wales* (the Richard Commission) (December 2002).

[2] This factor is commonly identified as fuelling a modern growth in federal systems of intergovernmental machinery. See for example, B. Galligan, O. Hughes and C. Walsh (eds.), *Intergovernmental Relations and Public Policy* (Sydney: Allen & Unwin, 1991).

[3] The general theme is pursued in R. Rawlings, 'Concordats of the constitution' (2000) 116 *Law Quarterly Review* 257.

[4] House of Lords Select Committee on the Constitution, *Devolution: Inter-Institutional Relations in the United Kingdom* (HL 28, Session 2002–3).

[5] See generally, R. Rhodes, *Tensions in the Territorial Politics of Western Europe* (London: Cass, 1987).

[6] See for a useful overview, J. Poirier, 'The functions of intergovernmental agreements: post-devolution concordats in a comparative perspective' (2001) *Public Law* 134.

[7] Welsh Office, *Concordats* (1998), paragraph 4.

[8] *Official Record*, 7 October 1999.

[9] As discussed in chapter 13.

[10] *Memorandum of Understanding and Supplementary Agreements*, Cm. 5240 (2001). The Supplementary Agreements comprise the Agreement on the Joint Ministerial Committee and the four overarching concordats noted in the text.

[11] Poirier, 'The functions of intergovernmental agreements', above, n. 6; and see to similar effect, L. Hunter, *Managing Conflict after Devolution: A Toolkit for Civil Servants* (London: Constitution Unit, 2000). During the passage of the devolution legislation, ministers resisted attempts to create formal procedural requirements for the making of concordats: see for example *House of Commons Debates*, vol. 309, col. 617 (25 March 1998).

[12] As discussed in chapter 9; and see below in relation to the role of the Secretary of State for Wales.

[13] See for details, *Memorandum by the Cabinet Office* (February 2002), House of Lords Select Committee on the Constitution, *Devolution: Inter-Institutional Relations in the United Kingdom – Evidence* (HL 147, Session 2001–2).

[14] *Memorandum of Understanding*, above, n. 10, paragraphs 4–9.

[15] Ibid., paragraph 11. And see above, chapter 3 (category of exempt information under the Freedom of Information Act 2000).

[16] 'Bundestreue'; see for an introduction, P. Blair and P. Cullen, 'Federalism, legalism and political reality: the record of the Federal Constitutional Court', in C. Jeffery (ed.), *Recasting German Federalism: The Legacies of Unification* (London: Pinter, 1999). And see further below, in the context of parliamentary accountability.

[17] *Memorandum of Understanding*, above, n. 10, paragraphs 26–7.

[18] Ibid., paragraph 2.

[19] *Council of Civil Service Unions v. Minister for the Civil Service* [1985] AC 374.

[20] Rawlings, 'Concordats of the constitution', above, n. 3.

[21] *Official Record*, 7 October 1999.

[22] *House of Commons Debates*, vol. 307, col. 371 (27 February 1998), Written Answers, no. 5.

[23] See above, chapter 2.

[24] *Concordat between HM Treasury and Cabinet of the National Assembly for Wales* (December 1999), p. 1.

[25] See GWA, s. 123.

[26] A familiar theme in the emergent literature on IGR: see for example, A. Trench, 'Intergovernmental relations a year on', in A. Trench (ed.), *The State of the Nations 2001: The Second Year of Devolution in the UK* (London: Constitution Unit, 2001). And see further below.

[27] *Concordat between the Lord Chancellor's Department and the Cabinet of the National Assembly for Wales* (December 1999), pp. 2–3.

[28] The concordat is now with the Department of Transport, Local Government and the Regions.

[29] *Concordat between the Department of the Environment, Transport and the Regions and the National Assembly for Wales* (April 2000), pp. 1–2.

[30] Joint Ministerial Committee, *Devolution One Year On* (September 2000).

[31] *Memorandum by the Cabinet Office*, House of Lords Select Committee on the Constitution, *Devolution: Inter-institutional Relations in the United Kingdom*, above, n. 13, paragraph 1.

[32] Joint Ministerial Committee, *Devolution One Year On* (September 2000).

[33] See above, chapter 4.

[34] *Memorandum by the Cabinet Office*, House of Lords Select Committee on the Constitution, *Devolution: Inter-institutional Relations in the United Kingdom*, above, n. 13, paragraph 10.

[35] Once again this is not to overlook Northern Ireland, where 'cohabitation' with the UK government is a given. The conditions of 'party competition' are hardly comparable.

[36] *Memorandum of Understanding*, above, n. 10, paragraph 22

[37] Ibid., paragraph 23.

[38] Instructive accounts from federal systems include J. Zimmerman, *Interstate Relations: The Neglected Dimension of Federalism* (London: Praeger, 1996).

[39] Joint Ministerial Committee, *Devolution One Year On* (September 2000).

[40] National Assembly, press release, 15 June 2000.

[41] House of Lords Select Committee on the Constitution, *Devolution: Inter-institutional Relations in the United Kingdom*, above, n. 4, paragraphs 31–2.

[42] Ibid., paragraph 32.

[43]   See for further details, *Memorandum by the Cabinet Office*, House of Lords Select Committee on the Constitution, *Devolution: Inter-institutional Relations in the United Kingdom*, above, n. 13. This aspect is pursued in chapter 13 ('Wales in Europe').

[44]   R. Morgan, *Oral Evidence* (27 May 2002), House of Lords Select Committee on the Constitution, *Devolution: Inter-institutional Relations in the United Kingdom – Evidence* (HL 147, Session 2001–2), Question 816.

[45]   R. Morgan, *Memorandum by the Welsh Assembly Government* (October 2002), House of Lords Select Committee on the Constitution, *Devolution: Inter-institutional Relations in the United Kingdom – Evidence* (HL 147, Session 2001–2), paragraph 7.

[46]   R. Morgan, *Evidence to the Richard Commission* (December 2002).

[47]   E. Hart and A. Peat, *Oral Evidence to the Richard Commission* (December 2002).

[48]   *Memorandum of Understanding*, above, n. 10, paragraph 25.

[49]   *Supplementary Agreements*, Cm. 5240 (2001), Agreement on the Joint Ministerial Committee, paragraph A1.6.

[50]   House of Lords Select Committee on the Constitution, *Devolution: Inter-institutional Relations in the United Kingdom*, above, n. 4, paragraph 194.

[51]   Ibid., Summary of Recommendations (Use of Formal Mechanisms).

[52]   Many of the points are elaborated in Rawlings, 'Concordats of the constitution', above, n. 3.

[53]   House of Lords Select Committee on the Constitution, *Devolution: Inter-institutional Relations in the United Kingdom*, above, n. 4, paragraph 3.

[54]   Ibid., paragraph 20.

[55]   See for details, ibid., paragraphs 111–18.

[56]   See for example, *Official Record*, 24 October 2000.

[57]   R. Davies, 'In search of attitude' (memorandum, December 2000).

[58]   There is some useful Commonwealth experience to draw on; see R. Cornes, 'Intergovernmental relations in a devolved United Kingdom: making devolution work', in R. Hazell (ed.), *Constitutional Futures: A History of the Next Ten Years* (Oxford: Oxford University Press, 1999).

[59]   See below, chapter 13.

[60]   See, *Government's Response to House of Lords Select Committee on the Constitution, Second Report: Devolution: Inter-institutional Relations in the United Kingdom (HL 28, Session 2002–03)*, Cm. 5780 (2003).

[61]   *Memorandum by the Cabinet Office*, House of Lords Select Committee on the Constitution, *Devolution: Inter-Institutional Relations in the United Kingdom*, above, n. 13, paragraphs 2, 11.

[62]   House of Lords Select Committee on the Constitution, *Devolution: Inter-institutional Relations in the United Kingdom*, above n. 4, paragraph 2.

[63]   *Supplementary Agreements*, Cm. 5240 (2001), Agreement on the Joint Ministerial Committee, paragraph A1.8.

[64]   House of Lords Select Committee on the Constitution, *Devolution: Inter-institutional Relations in the United Kingdom*, above, n. 4, paragraph 4.

[65]   Joint Ministerial Committee, *Devolution One Year On* (September 2000).

[66]   House of Lords Select Committee on the Constitution, *Devolution: Inter-institutional Relations in the United Kingdom*, above, n. 4, paragraph 190.

[67]   Wales Office, *Devolution Guidance Note No. 4* (January 2003).

[68]   Wales Office, *Devolution Guidance Note No. 4* (original version: January 2000).

[69]   GWA, s. 76.

[70] P. Murphy, *Oral Evidence* (26 October 1999), House of Commons Select Committee on Welsh Affairs, *The Role of the Secretary of State for Wales* – Evidence (HC 854, Session 1998–9).

[71] Wales Office, *Devolution Guidance Note No. 4* (January 2003).

[72] House of Lords Select Committee on the Constitution, *Devolution: Inter-institutional Relations in the United Kingdom*, above, n. 4, paragraph 59.

[73] P. Murphy, *Oral Evidence* (15 October 2002), House of Commons Select Committee on Welsh Affairs, *The Wales Office Departmental Report 2002* – Evidence (HC 1216, Session 2001–2).

[74] R. Morgan, *Memorandum by the Welsh Assembly Government* (October 2002), House of Lords Select Committee on the Constitution, *Devolution: Inter-institutional Relations in the United Kingdom* – Evidence (HL 147, Session 2001–2), paragraph 8.

[75] See for further details, Wales Office, *Departmental Report 2002*, Cm. 5431 (2002), paragraph 2.5.

[76] P. Murphy, *Oral Evidence* (15 October 2002), House of Commons Select Committee on Welsh Affairs, above, n. 73. Presumably the same goes for Mr Murphy's successor in title, Peter Hain.

[77] Ibid.

[78] *A Voice for Wales*, Cm. 3718 (1997), paragraph 3.35.

[79] Wales Office, *Devolution Guidance Note No. 4* (January 2003).

[80] P. Murphy, *Oral Evidence* (10 April 2002), House of Lords Select Committee on the Constitution, *Devolution: Inter-institutional Relations in the United Kingdom* – Evidence (HL 147, Session 2001–2), Questions 164 and 175. And see for practical illustration, *House of Commons Debates*, vol. 352, col. 891 (28 June 2000); *Western Mail*, 5 July 2000 (hunting with hounds)

[81] See above, chapter 6.

[82] Wales Office, *Departmental Report 2001*, Cm. 5121 (2001), paragraph 1.5.

[83] Wales Office, *Departmental Report 2003*, Cm. 5928 (2003), paragraph 1.4.

[84] House of Lords Select Committee on the Constitution, *Devolution: Inter-institutional Relations in the United Kingdom*, above, n. 4, paragraph 67.

[85] Wales Office, *Departmental Report 2003*, above, n. 83, paragraph 2.3.

[86] *Concordat between the Cabinet of the National Assembly for Wales and the Wales Office* (January 2001).

[87] Ibid.

[88] *A Voice for Wales*, Cm. 3718 (1997), paragraphs 3.34–3.36.

[89] R. Hazell, *Three into One Won't Go: The Future of the Territorial Secretaries of State* (London: Constitution Unit, 2001).

[90] House of Lords Select Committee on the Constitution, *Devolution: Inter-institutional Relations in the United Kingdom*, above, n. 4, paragraph 68.

[91] UK Government press release, 12 June 2003.

[92] Wales Office press release, 13 June 2003.

[93] *Offical Record*, 17 June 2003.

[94] House of Lords Debates, vol. 649, col. 1081 (20 June 2003).

[95] See for example, R. Hazell, 'Westminster squeezed from above and below', in R. Hazell (ed.), *Constitutional Futures: A History of the Next Ten Years* (Oxford: Oxford University Press, 1999).

[96] Select Committee on Modernization of the House of Commons, Second Report: *Modernisation of the House of Commons: A Reform Programme* (HC 1168-I, Session 2001–2).

[97] House of Commons Select Committee on Procedure, Fourth Report: *The Procedural Consequences of Devolution* (HC 185, Session 1998–9), paragraph 5.

[98] House of Commons Select Committee on Procedure, First Special Report: *Government Response to the Fourth Report – The Procedural Consequences of Devolution* (HC 814, Session 1998–9).

[99] House of Commons Select Committee on Procedure, Fourth Report: *The Procedural Consequences of Devolution* (HC 185, Session 1998–9), paragraphs 2–3.

[100] Committee Office Guide, Annex A; see House of Lords Select Committee on the Constitution, *Devolution: Inter-institutional Relations in the United Kingdom – Written Evidence* (HL 147, Session 2001–2), paragraph 57.

[101] *Memorandum of Understanding*, above, n. 10, paragraphs 13–16.

[102] Ibid.

[103] B. Winetrobe, 'Inter-parliamentary relations in a devolved UK: an initial overview', in House of Lords Select Committee on the Constitution, Second Report: *Devolution: Inter-institutional Relations in the United Kingdom* (HL 28, Session 2002–3), Appendix 5.

[104] So working to insulate unionist governments in the province from scrutiny at Westminster: *House of Commons Debates*, cols. 1624–5 (3 May 1923).

[105] *House of Commons Debates*, vol. 335, cols. 21–2 (12 July 1999); and see for the background, E. Wood, *The Procedural Consequences of Devolution*, House of Commons Research Paper no. 99/85 (1999).

[106] *House of Commons Debates*, vol. 336, col. 774 (25 October 1999).

[107] House of Commons Table Office, *Responsibilities of the National Assembly for Wales: Guidance to Parliament* (1999). See further, Office of the Deputy Prime Minister, *Devolution Guidance Note No. 11 – Ministerial Accountability After Devolution* (July 2000).

[108] See now, for comparative discussion, O. Gay, 'Evolution from devolution: the experience of Westminster', in R. Hazell (ed.), *The State of the Nations 2003: The Third Year of Devolution in the United Kingdom* (Thorverton: Imprint Academic, 2003).

[109] J. Barry Jones, 'The Select Committee on Welsh Affairs', in G. Drewry (ed.), *The New Select Committees*, 2nd edn. (Oxford: Clarendon, 1989).

[110] Welsh Affairs Select Committee, First Special Report: *The Work of the Committee since Devolution* (HC 81, Session 2000–1), paragraphs 3–4.

[111] Welsh Affairs Select Committee, Third Report: *The Work of the Committee in 2002* (HC 263, Session 2002–3), paragraph 17.

[112] House of Commons Liaison Select Committee, Second Report: *Select Committees: Modernisation Proposals* (HC 692, Session 2001–2).

[113] House of Commons Standing Order 152; Welsh Affairs Select Committee, *The Work of the Committee since Devolution*, above, n. 110, paragraph 9.

[114] See for details, Welsh Affairs Select Committee, *The Work of the Committee in 2002*, above, n. 111.

[115] Welsh Affairs Select Committee, First Report: *European Structural Funds* (HC 46, Session 1999–2000); and see above, chapter 2.

[116] See, for details, Welsh Affairs Select Committee, *The Work of the Committee in 2002*, above, n. 111, paragraph 16.

[117] Study of Parliament Group, *Memorandum on Welsh Devolution* (HC 185-ii, Session 1998–9). The author was among the contributors. See also, Hansard Society, *The Consequences of Devolution* (London: Hansard Society, 1998).

[118] As discussed in chapter 9.

[119] See further, J. Bradbury, 'Conservative governments, Scotland and Wales: a perspective on territorial management', in J. Bradbury and J. Mawson (eds.), *British Regionalism and Devolution: The Challenges of State Reform and European Integration* (London: Kingsley, 1996).

[120] *A Voice for Wales*, Cm. 3718 (1997), paragraph 3.44.

[121] In the light of the introduction of debates in Westminster Hall (see for example, debate on the GWA, *House of Commons Debates*, vol. 376, cols. 91WH–116WH (5 December 2001).

[122] House of Lords Select Committee on the Constitution, *Devolution: Inter-institutional Relations in the United Kingdom*, above, n. 4, paragraph 114.

[123] Including by Plaid Cymru; see for example *House of Commons Debates*, vol. 336, cols. 606–54 (21 October 1999) and *House of Lords Debates*, vol. 313, cols. 302–3 (2 June 1998).

[124] See to this effect, K. Patchett, 'The central relationship', in J. Barry Jones and J. Osmond (eds.), *Building a Civic Culture: Institutional Change, Policy Development and Political Dynamics in the National Assembly for Wales* (Cardiff: Institute of Welsh Affairs and Welsh Governance Centre, 2002). And see above, chapter 9.

[125] See for details, Welsh Affairs Select Committee, *The Work of the Committee in 2002*, above, n. 111, paragraph 20; and see generally now, Welsh Affairs Select Committee, Fourth Report: *The Primary Legislative Process as it Affects Wales* (HC 79, Session 2002–3).

[126] Lord Elis-Thomas and J. Marek, *Oral Evidence* (27 May 2002), House of Lords Select Committee on the Constitution, *Devolution: Inter-institutional Relations in the United Kingdom* – Evidence (HL 147, Session 2001–2).

[127] As the Select Committee on the Constitution quickly discovered: House of Lords Select Committee on the Constitution, *Devolution: Inter-institutional Relations in the United Kingdom*, above, n. 4, paragraph 140.

[128] See for an admirable survey, Winetrobe, 'Inter-parliamentary relations in a devolved UK: an initial overview', above, n. 103.

[129] See above, chapter 4 (especially in relation to the role of the Assembly Clerk).

[130] *A Voice for Wales*, Cm. 3718 (1997), paragraph 3.37.

[131] UK Cabinet Office, *Devolution Guidance Note 2 – Guidance on Handling Correspondence under Devolution* (1999), paragraphs 18–19.

[132] See further Rawlings, 'Concordats of the constitution', above, n. 3.

[133] See further, Welsh Labour Party, *Evidence to the Richard Commission* (July 2003).

[134] Assuming that executive devolution lasts that long: see further below, chapter 15.

[135] See for example Lord Elis-Thomas, *Oral Evidence* (27 May 2002), House of Lords Select Committee on the Constitution, *Devolution: Inter-institutional Relations in the United Kingdom* – Evidence (HL 147, Session 2001–2).

[136] Westminster seats were vacated by AMs ahead of the 2001 general election, one example being Ron Davies.

[137] Richard Commission, *Issues and Questions for Consultation*, p. 6. The probability of a reduction in the number of Welsh MPs is discussed in chapter 15, in conjunction with aspects like 'the West Lothian Question'.

[138] At least to this extent, the experience of Scottish MPs since 1999 may prove an uncertain guide.

[139] See above, chapter 11 (the defeat of the so-called 'Hanson doctrine').

[140] See for example, *House of Lords Debates*, vol. 649, cols. 1066–1096 (Lords Morgan and Prys-Davies).

[141] Royal Commission on Reform of the House of Lords, *A House for the Future*, Cm. 4534 (2000). See also, J. Osmond, *Reforming the House of Lords and Changing Britain* (London: Fabian Society, Pamphlet no. 587, 1998).

[142] White Paper, *The House of Lords – Completing the Reform*, Cm. 5291 (2001); House of Commons Select Committee on Public Administration, Fifth Report: *The Second Chamber – Continuing the Reform* (HC 494-I, Session 2001–2), paragraph 63.

[143] House of Commons and House of Lords Joint Select Committee on House of Lords Reform, First Report: *House of Lords Reform* (HC 171, Session 2002–3); *House of Commons Debates*, vol. 399, cols. 152–238, 4 February 2003.

Chapter 13

[1] Cm. 3718 (1997), paragraphs 3.46, 3.52.

[2] Ibid., paragraph 2.25.

[3] It was first introduced in R. Rawlings, 'Cymru yn Ewrop', in P. Craig and R. Rawlings (eds.), *Law and Administration in Europe* (Oxford: Oxford University Press, 2003).

[4] H. Holm and G. Sorensen, *Whose World Order? Uneven Globalisation and the End of the Cold War* (Oxford: Westview Press, 1995), p. 1. See for an accessible overview, R. Holton, *Globalisation and the Nation-State* (Basingstoke: Macmillan, 1998).

[5] M. Keating and H. Elcock, 'Introduction: devolution and the UK state' (1998) 8 (1) *Regional and Federal Studies* 1 at 5. See also, M. Keating, *The New Regionalism in Western Europe: Territorial Restructuring and Political Change* (London: Edward Elgar, 1998).

[6] A. Giddens, *Runaway World* (London: Profile, 1999).

[7] See for a valuable corrective, J. Loughlin (ed.), *Sub-national Democracy in the European Union: Challenges and Opportunities* (Oxford: Oxford University Press, 2001).

[8] See for example, M. Telo (ed.), *European Union and New Regionalism: Regional Actors and Global Governance in a Post-hegemonic Era* (Aldershot: Ashgate, 2001).

[9] T. Christiansen, 'Territorial politics in the European Union' (1999) 6 *Journal of European Public Policy* 349; C. Jeffery, 'Sub-national mobilization and European integration: does it make any difference?' (2000) 38 *Journal of Common Market Studies* 1.

[10] R. Davies, 'The economic case for a Welsh Assembly' (1996) (2) *Welsh Democracy Review* 6.

[11] See for details, the Welsh Assembly Government's strategic plan, *A Winning Wales: The National Economic Development Strategy of the Welsh Assembly Government* (January 2002).

[12] The discussion in this section is elaborated in R. Rawlings, 'Law, territory and integration: a view from the Atlantic shore' (2001) 67 *International Review of Administrative Sciences* 479.

[13] A. Michael, *The Dragon on our Doorstep: New Politics for a New Millennium in Wales* (Aberystwyth: Institute of Welsh Politics, November 1999).

[14] Welsh European Task Force, *The National Assembly for Wales and the European Union* (1998), p. 3. And see, E. Balls and J. Healey, *Towards a New Regional Policy: Delivering Growth and Full Employment* (London: Smith Institute, 2000).

[15] National Assembly Advisory Group, *Recommendations* (1998), paragraph 5.13.

[16] Welsh European Task Force, *The National Assembly for Wales and the European Union* (1998).

[17] L. Gwilym, *The Ineffectiveness of the National Assembly's European Affairs Committee* (Plaid Cymru research paper, 2000); J. Barry Jones, 'Searching for a role: the Committee on European Affairs', in J. Barry Jones and J. Osmond (eds.), *Inclusive Government and Party Management* (Cardiff: Institute of Welsh Affairs, 2001).

[18] See especially *Official Record*, 27 June 2000 (debate on the committee's first annual report).

[19] Committee on European Affairs, *Options for Future Committee Activity* (April 2001).

[20] Committee on European Affairs, *Annual Report 2000–2001*, pp. 2, 6.

[21] See for details, ibid., p. 8. And see further on the phenomenon of 'asymmetrical scrutiny' in Scotland and Wales, C. Carter, 'Democratic governance beyond the nation state: third-level assemblies and scrutiny of European legislation' (2000) 6 *European Public Law* 429.

[22] Committee on European Affairs, *Annual Report 1999–2000*, p. 4.

[23] Committee on European Affairs, *Options for Future Committee Activity* (April 2001); *Final Report of the Assembly Review of Procedure Group* (February 2002), chapter 8. And see J. Barry Jones, 'Wales in Europe: developing a relationship', in J. Barry Jones and J. Osmond (eds.), *Building a Civic Culture: Institutional Change, Policy Development and Political Dynamics in the National Assembly for Wales* (Cardiff: Institute of Welsh Affairs and Welsh Governance Centre, 2002).

[24] Assembly Review of Procedure, *Committee on European Affairs* (February 2001). See now, Committee on European and External Affairs, *Annual Report 2001–2002* (May 2002).

[25] See *Official Record*, 30 October 2001.

[26] Ibid.

[27] Committee on European Affairs, *Options for Future Committee Activity* (April 2001).

[28] Committee on European and External Affairs, *The Extended Remit – Beyond Europe* (March 2002).

[29] *House of Commons Debates*, vol. 384, col. 1071 (2 May 2002). See especially on the difficulties of forging greater global recognition, Welsh Affairs Select Committee, *First Report: Wales in the World: The Role of the UK Government in Promoting Wales Abroad* (HC 38, Session 2000–1).

[30] Committee on European Affairs, *Annual Report 1999–2000*, Preface.

[31] Discussion of the impact of human rights considerations is reserved to chapter 14.

[32] Article 249 EC Treaty.

[33] Council Regulation 1260/1999, Article 8.

[34] See *Memorandum of Understanding and Supplementary Agreements*, Cm. 5240 (2001).

[35] F. Aldecoa and M. Keating (eds.), *Paradiplomacy in Action: The Foreign Relations of Sub-national Governments* (London: Frank Cass, 1999).

[36] See for example, J. Hopkins, *Devolution in Context: Regional, Federal and Devolved Government in the European Union* (London: Cavendish, 2002), chapter 5; also, N. MacCormick, *Democracy at Many Levels: European Constitutional Reform* (European Convention Paper 298/02, 2002).

[37]   See for example, A. Dashwood, 'The limits of European Community powers' (1996) 21 *European Law Review* 113.

[38]   The standard usage as coined in the German context: see U. Bullmann, 'The politics of the third level' (1996) 6 *Regional and Federal Studies* 3.

[39]   European Commission, *White Paper on Governance*, COM (2001) 428.

[40]   As signalled in the Treaty of Nice (Declaration no. 23) and the subsequent Laeken Declaration, *The Future of the European Union*, SN 273/01. See on the local perspective, European and External Affairs Committee, *Convention on the Future of Europe* (March 2003).

[41]   House of Lords Select Committee on the Constitution, *Devolution: Inter-institution Relations in the United Kingdom*, *Evidence* (HL 147, Session 2001–2), Memorandum by the Welsh Assembly Government, paragraph 30.

[42]   Welsh Office, press release, 20 February 1998.

[43]   GWA, s. 29. Central government retains concurrent powers to make subordinate legislation for the purpose of implementing Community obligations: GWA, Schedule 3, paragraph. 5.

[44]   European Communities (Designation) (no. 3) Order 2001, SI 2001 no. 3495.

[45]   See for details *www.wales-legislation.org.uk*

[46]   Statutes such as the Agriculture (Miscellaneous Provisions) Act 1968, Animal Health Act 1981 and Food Safety Act 1990 feature prominently here as vehicles for the transposition of EU obligations; see for practical illustration, Welfare of Farmed Animals (Wales) Regulations 2002, SI 2002 no. 1898 (W.99).

[47]   Tir Gofal (Amendment) (Wales) Regulations 2001, SI 2001 no. 423 (W.17); Organic Farming Scheme (Wales) Regulations 2001, SI 2001 no. 424 (W.18).

[48]   See above, chapter 8.

[49]   *Francovich and Bonifaci v Italy*, Cases C-6/90 and C-9/90 [1991] *European Court Reports* I-5357. Notwithstanding, that is, restrictive interpretations in the subsequent case law. And see below on EU penal competence and the internal or domestic transfer of sanction.

[50]   House of Lords Select Committee on the Constitution, *Devolution: Inter-institution Relations in the United Kingdom*, Evidence (HL 147, Session 2001–2), Memorandum from the Welsh Assembly Government by Rhodri Morgan, paragraph 28. Especially, it may be noted, in a field like agriculture.

[51]   *EU Concordat*, paragraph B4.17, see *Memorandum of Understanding and Supplementary Agreements*, Cm. 5240 (2001).

[52]   European Commission, *White Paper on Governance*, COM (2001) 428 at 4; and see now European Commission, *Report on European Governance* (2003).

[53]   *Assembly Proceedings*, 17 January 2001. The Assembly's detailed response to the White Paper is discussed below.

[54]   GWA, s. 106. See further below, chapter 14 on the special court machinery established for dealing with 'devolution issues'.

[55]   Article 10 EC Treaty: A. Dashwood, 'The European Union and the National Assembly', in D. Miers (ed.), *Devolution in Wales* (Cardiff: Wales Public Law and Human Rights Association, 1999), p. 60.

[56]   Articles 211, 226 EC Treaty; and see for discussion of the competing modalities, R. Rawlings, 'Engaged elites: citizen action and institutional attitudes in Commission enforcement' (2000) 6 *European Law Journal* 4.

[57]   See above, chapter 4.

[58]   *Official Record*, 23 October 2001.

[59] *EU Concordat*, paragraph B4.25; see *Memorandum of Understanding and Supplementary Agreements*, Cm. 5240 (2001). See further, Memorandum by the Cabinet Office, Select Committee on the Constitution, *Devolution: Inter-Institutional Relations in the United Kingdom*, HL 147, session 2001/2.

[60] Jocelyn Davies (Plaid Cymru), *Official Record*, 23 October 2001. See now, Genetically Modified Organisms (Deliberate Release) (Wales) Regulations 2002, SI no. 3188 (W.304), 2002.

[61] Case C-387/97 *Commission v Greece* [2000] *European Court Reports* I-5047. In accordance with its responsibility under Article 228 EC Treaty to propose a sanction, the Commission had suggested a daily rate of some EUR 25,000.

[62] See for discussion M. Theodossiou, 'An analysis of the recent response of the community to non-compliance with Court of Justice judgements' (2002) 27 *European Law Review* 25.

[63] See further on this type of approach, which is epitomized by so-called 'Quebec Inc.', M. Keating, 'Stateless nation building: Quebec, Catalonia and Scotland in the changing state system' (1997) 3 *Nations and Nationalism* 689.

[64] Welsh European Task Force, *The National Assembly for Wales and the European Union* (1998), p. 1.

[65] Available at: *www.betterwales.com*

[66] See above, chapter 4.

[67] Welsh Assembly Government, *A Winning Wales: The National Economic Development Strategy of the Welsh Assembly Government* (January 2002), p. 1.

[68] See generally, I. Bache, *The Politics of European Regional Policy* (Sheffield: Sheffield University Press, 1998); and for a legal perspective, J. Scott, 'Regional policy: an evolutionary perspective', in P. Craig and G. de Burca (eds.), *The Evolution of EU Law* (Oxford: Oxford University Press, 1999).

[69] A familiar theme in the literature: M. Keating, 'Is there a regional level of government in Europe?', in P. Le Gales and C. Lequesne (eds.), *Regions in Europe* (London: Routledge, 1998).

[70] See K. Morgan and A. Price, *The Other Wales* (Cardiff: Institute of Welsh Affairs, 1998).

[71] The territory also derives a measure of support under Objective 2 (areas in difficulty and undergoing socio-economic change) and Objective 3 (human resource development). See further, G. Jones, *A Guide to European Funding in Wales 2000–2006* (Cardiff: Institute of Welsh Affairs, 2001).

[72] National Assembly for Wales, *Single Programming Document: The Economic and Social Regeneration of West Wales and the Valleys* (April 2000).

[73] Ibid., 2.

[74] Commissioner Michel Barnier, *Inforegio Newsletter* (October 1999).

[75] Council Regulation 1260/1999, Article 8; J. Sutcliffe, 'The 1999 reform of the structural funds regulations: multi-level governance or renationalization?' (2000) 7 *Journal of European Public Policy* 290.

[76] L. Hooghe (ed.), *Cohesion Policy and European Integration: Building Multi-level Governance* (Oxford: Oxford University Press, 1996). See also J. Scott, 'Law, legitimacy and EC governance: prospects for "partnership" ' (1998) 36 *Journal of Common Market Studies* 175.

[77] For discussion see A. Evans, 'Regionalist challenges to the EU decision-making system' (2000) 6 *European Public Law* 377.

78   GWA, ss. 120, 121 ('the Welsh difference'); M. Bauer, 'The EU's "partnership principle": still a sustainable governance device across multiple administrative arenas?', 80 *Public Administration* (2002) 769

79   Council Regulation 1260/1999, Article 35.

80   As elaborated in Commission Regulation 438/2001.

81   See for details, Welsh European Funding Office, *Making European Funds Work in Wales* (Cardiff, 2001). The local and regional groups also follow the model of tripartite equal representation.

82   For discussion see L. McAllister, 'Devolution and the new context for public policy-making: lessons from the EU structural funds in Wales' (2000) 14 *Public Policy and Administration* 38. See also Welsh Affairs Select Committee, *First Report: European Structural Funds* (HC 46, Session 1999–2000).

83   See now Audit Committee, *European Union Structural Funds – Maximising the Benefits for Wales* (December 2002).

84   A. Thomas, 'Sharpening the cutting edge of economic governance' (2001) 4 *Agenda – Journal of the Institute of Welsh Affairs* 24; also J. Bachtler, 'Objective one: a comparative assessment', 15 *Contemporary Wales* (2002) 30.

85   Late in the day, the Assembly cabinet has begun to move in this direction (less partnership, a more 'streamlined' approach): Welsh Assembly Government press release, 23 June 2003.

86   House of Lords Select Committee on the Constitution, *Devolution: Inter-institutional Relations in the United Kingdom, Evidence* (HL 147, Session 2001–2), memorandum by the Welsh Assembly Government, paragraph 25.

87   The jurisprudence of the European Court of Justice is notably fierce in this respect. *Commission v Italy* [1992] 2 CMLR 353 and *Commission v Italy* [1994] *European Court Reports* I-1 are classic authorities.

88   J. Poirier, 'The functions of intergovernmental agreements: post-devolution concordats in a comparative perspective' (2000) *Public Law* 134.

89   *A Voice for Wales*, Cm. 3718 (1997), paragraphs 3.46–3.56.

90   *Scotland's Parliament*, Cm. 3658 (1997), chapter 5.

91   See *House of Commons Debates*, vol. 305, cols. 772–4 (2 February 1998).

92   See above, chapter 6.

93   House of Lords Select Committee on the Constitution, memorandum by the Welsh Assembly Government, above, n. 86, paragraph 25.

94   *Memorandum of Understanding and Supplementary Agreements*, Cm. 5240 (2001), paragraph 17.

95   R. Rawlings, 'Concordats of the constitution' (2000) 116 *Law Quarterly Review* 257. See also, A. Scott, 'The role of concordats in the new governance in Britain: taking subsidiarity seriously?' (2001) 5 *European Law Review* 21.

96   Concordat on EU Policy Issues, paragraph B1.4, see *Memorandum of Understanding and Supplementary Agreements*, Cm. 5240 (2001). The concordat is here following the White Paper formulation: see *Scotland's Parliament*, Cm. 3658 (1997), paragraph 54.

97   *Official Record*, 7 October 1999.

98   Article 203 EC Treaty. A useful comparative analysis is A. Cygan, 'Scotland's Parliament and European affairs: some lessons from Germany' (1999) 24 *European Law Review* 483.

99   EU Concordat, paragraph B3.12, see *Memorandum of Understanding and Supplementary Agreements*, Cm. 5240 (2001).

[100] Ibid., paragraph B3.14.

[101] We return to this point in the context of discussion on 'the future of Europe'.

[102] House of Lords Select Committee on the Constitution, above, n. 4, paragraphs 185–6.

[103] Committee on European Affairs, *Assembly Representation in Brussels* (October 1999).

[104] See for details, Wales European Centre, *Annual Report 2001/2002*; and see for comparison in terms of the pre-devolutionary development, D. Hughes, *Wales European Centre 1991–1999: A Retrospective* (Wales European Centre, Brussels, 1999).

[105] See J. Goodburn, *A Representative Office for the Scottish Executive in Brussels* (Scottish Office, 1998). As Goodburn observes (at p. 13), the success of regional offices in Brussels is 'almost impossible to quantify in any objective manner', not least because of the range and diversity of contacts.

[106] See further, Rawlings, 'Law, territory and integration', above, n. 12.

[107] Wales European Centre, *Business Plan 2000–2003*, p. 5. See also Welsh European Centre, *Wider and Deeper: The Next Intergovernmental Conference and the Implications for the 'Lobbying' Region* (Brussels, 2000).

[108] Wales European Centre, *Moving East: What Enlargement Means for Wales* (Brussels, 1999); Wales European Centre, *EU Enlargement and the Implications for Wales* (Brussels, 2000).

[109] Wales European Centre, *Engaging Wales: A Draft Strategy for Wales in the Enlarged European Union* (Brussels, 2001), p. 5.

[110] Ibid., p. 10.

[111] See further, J. Barry Jones, 'Wales in Europe', in Barry Jones and Osmond (eds.), *Building a Civic Culture*, above, n. 23.

[112] As well as some of the small Baltic states: see for details, European and External Affairs Committee, Minutes February–March 2002.

[113] *Official Record*, 18 June 2002 (Michael German).

[114] Wales European Centre, *Moving East: What Enlargement Means for Wales* (Brussels, 1999), Annex 1.

[115] Wales European Centre, *EU Enlargement and the Implications for Wales* (Brussels, 2000).

[116] Provided the arrangements do not affect the conduct of international relations or prejudice UK interests: see *Concordat on International Relations* in *Memorandum of Understanding and Supplementary Agreements*, Cm. 5240 (2001) at paragraph D4.7.

[117] Ibid., paragraph D4.16.

[118] *EU Concordat* in *Memorandum of Understanding and Supplementary Agreements*, Cm. 5240 (2001), paragraph B4.27.

[119] House of Lords Select Committee on the Constitution, *Devolution: Inter-institution Relations in the United Kingdom* (HL 28, Session 2002–3), paragraph 179.

[120] Committee on European Affairs, *International Relations and the Profile of Wales* (March 2000).

[121] Wales has had a series of collaborative programmes with Ireland under this cross-border rubric. Details are available from Welsh European Funding Office, the current managing authority, see *http://www.wefo.wales.gov.uk/*

[122] See *Official Record*, 4 March 2003. The decisional process has itself a subject of fierce political controversy ('who said what to whom?'): see for example *Official Record*, 16 April 2002.

[123] *Official Record*, 2 May 2002.

[124] See generally now, A. Sloat, *Scotland in Europe: A Study of Multi-level Governance* (Berne: Peter Lang, 2002).

[125] House of Lords Select Committee on the Constitution, memorandum by the Welsh Assembly Government, above, n. 86, paragraph 24.

[126] See for details, Co-ordination Committee of RegLeg, *The Regions with Legislative Power in the Framework of the Next Institutional Reform of the EU* (submission to the Constitutional Convention) (September 2002).

[127] Committee on European and External Affairs, *European Regions with Legislative Powers* (March 2002). Despite its name, the network includes (directly elected) regional governments with power to legislate or 'to take significant executive decisions'.

[128] See for a general overview, J. Kottman, 'Europe and the regions: sub-national entity representation at community level' (2001) 26 *European Law Review* 159.

[129] J. Jones, 'The Committee of the Regions, subsidiarity and a warning' (1997) 22 *European Law Review* 313.

[130] *Political Declaration by the Constitutional Regions of Bavaria, Catalonia, North-Rhine Westphalia, Salzburg, Scotland, Wallonia and Flanders* (May 2001). And see Colloquium of the Constitutional Regions, *Reinforcing the Role of the Constitutional Regions in Europe* (February 2001).

[131] In the event, there is regional representation through CoR and (indirectly) via a Contact Group of Regional and Local Authorities.

[132] Under Article 230 EC Treaty; see further, Case T-214/95 *Het Vlaamse Gewest (Flemish Region) v Commission* [1998] *European Court Reports* II-717; Case T-609/97 *Regione Puglia v Commission* [1998] *European Court Reports* II-4051.

[133] Second Presidential Conference of the Regions with Legislative Power, *Towards the Reinforced Role of the Regions with Legislative Power within the European Union* (Liège, November 2001).

[134] For his part, the Assembly First Minister has recorded his 'broad agreement and enthusiasm' for the general approach and aspirations expressed at Liège: *Response from the First Minister of the Welsh Assembly Government to the Liège Resolution* (November 2001).

[135] Welsh Assembly Government Cabinet Paper, *The Regional Dimension of European Governance* (January 2002).

[136] Emilia-Romagna et al., *Common Declaration on European Governance* (Brussels, March 2002).

[137] See *Official Record*, 17 January 2002.

[138] See especially European Parliament, Constitutional Affairs Committee, *Report on the Commission White Paper on European Governance*, Doc. A5-0399/2001 final (PE 304.289); also D. Wincott, 'Looking forward or harking back? The Commission and the reform of governance in the European Union' (2001) 39 *Journal of Common Market Studies* 897.

[139] The fact that the document proceeded on the basis of the treaties (and thus assumed a lack of constitutional 'fit' with the rise of the regions) is only a partial explanation.

[140] Commission Communication, *A Framework for Target-Based Tripartite Contracts*, COM (2002) 709 final.

[141] Commission Communication, *Towards a Reinforced Culture of Consultation and*

Dialogue, COM (2002) 704 final. See also, Commission, *Report on European Governance* (2003).

¹⁴² See for elaboration, LSE Study Group on European Administrative Law, *Taking Governance Seriously* (2002): available at *www.europa.eu.int/comm/governance/contributions/*

¹⁴³ *Response from the First Minister*, above, n. 134, pp. 2–4.

¹⁴⁴ See P. Hain, *Europe and the Regions* (Convention Paper 526/03, 2003); Assembly Cabinet, *Written Statement*, 6 February 2003. In the event, the draft constitution signals a modest advance in terms of the constitutional position of the regions, formally recognizing their competencies in several places: see for the local reaction, *Official Record*, 18 June 2003.

¹⁴⁵ The heterogeneity of Euro-regions obviously is a formidable obstacle, as illustrated now in the proceedings of the Convention. See for example, Praesidium, *The Regional and Local Dimension in Europe* (Convention Paper 518/03, 2003).

¹⁴⁶ Rhodri Morgan, *Assembly Proceedings*, 17 January 2002. The touchstone typically is attendance at the Council of Ministers. See also Welsh Assembly Government, press release, 14 November 2002 (speech by the First Minister to the presidents of Regions with Legislative Power).

¹⁴⁷ See *Official Record*, 19 December 2000.

Chapter 14

¹ Lord Bingham, 'The future of the common law' (1999) 18 *Civil Justice Quarterly* 203, 213.

² 'Law Wales' supplement, *Western Mail*, 28 February 2000.

³ See most notably, Sir John Thomas, 'Legal Wales: its modern origins and its role after devolution: national identity, the Welsh language and parochialism', in T. Watkin (ed.), *Legal Wales: Its Past, Its Future* (Cardiff: Welsh Legal History Society, 2001); also, I. Davies, *The Challenge of Legal Wales* (Cardiff: Law Society in Wales, 2001); and J. Williams, 'Legal Wales', in J. Osmond and J. Barry Jones (eds.), *Birth of Welsh Democracy* (Cardiff: Institute of Welsh Affairs, 2003).

⁴ W. Roddick , 'Doing business with the Assembly: defining the parameters and utilising the opportunities' (2002) 3 *Welsh Law Journal* 306, 311. See in similar fashion, D. Watkin Powell, *The Law in Wales: Yesterday, Today and Tomorrow* (Cardiff: Associated Law Societies of Wales, 1998).

⁵ See for the standard edition, D. Jenkins, *The Law of Hywel Dda* (Llandysul: Gomer, 1986).

⁶ See for the leading discussion in the context of central government, T. Daintith and A. Page, *The Executive in the Constitution: Structure, Autonomy and Internal Control* (Oxford: Oxford University Press, 1999), chapter 9.

⁷ See above, chapter 11.

⁸ See above, chapter 1.

⁹ See above, chapter 5.

¹⁰ J. Davies, *A History of Wales* (London: Allen Lane, 1993), p. 168.

¹¹ N. Davies, *The Isles* (London: Macmillan, 1999), p. 493; G. Williams, *Wales and the Reformation* (Cardiff: University of Wales Press, 1997), p. 399.

[12] M. Ellis Jones, '"An invidious attempt to accelerate the extinction of our language": the abolition of the Court of Great Sessions and the Welsh language' (1998) (19) 2 *Welsh History Review* 226, 263.

[13] See for details, Sir John Thomas, 'Legal Wales', above, n. 3. And see above, chapter 1.

[14] Royal Commission on Assizes and Quarter Sessions (the Beeching Commission), *The Reorganisation of the Courts in England and* Wales, Cmnd. 4153 (1969).

[15] See generally R. Lewis, *Cyfiawnder Dwyeithog (Bilingual Justice)* (Llandysul: Gomer, 1998).

[16] Lord Prys Davies, 'The legal status of the Welsh language in the twentieth century', in G. Jenkins and M. Williams (eds.), *'Let's do our Best for the Ancient Tongue': The Welsh Language in the Twentieth Century* (Cardiff: University of Wales Press, 2000); and see for practical illustration, *R v Merthyr Tydfil Justices ex p Jenkins* [1967] 1 *All England Law Reports* 636.

[17] Within the borders of Wales: see *Williams v Cowell* [2000] 1 *Weekly Law Reports* 187. This is not to suggest that all issues are resolved; see for example, G. Parry, 'Random selection, linguistic rights and the jury trial in Wales' (2002) *Criminal Law Review* 805.

[18] Sir John Thomas, 'The legal implications of Welsh devolution', in D. Miers (ed.), *Devolution in Wales: Public Law and the National Assembly* (Cardiff: Wales Public Law and Human Rights Association, 1999).

[19] See generally, C. Harlow and R. Rawlings, *Law and Administration*, 2nd edn. (London: Butterworths, 1997), chapter 16. And see further below, 'the Administrative Court'.

[20] [1983] 2 *Appeal Cases* 237.

[21] Sir John Thomas, 'The legal implications of Welsh devolution', above, n. 18.

[22] See D. Seaborne Davies, *Welsh Makers of English Law* (Cardiff: BBC, 1967); also J. Andrews (ed.), *Welsh Studies in Public Law* (Cardiff: University of Wales Press, 1970).

[23] *A Voice for Wales*, Cm. 3718 (1997), paragraph 3.43.

[24] The 'Woolman Report': see for extracts, W. Roddick *Evidence to the Richard Commission* (December 2002).

[25] National Assembly, *The Office of the Counsel General* (April 2001), paragraph 2. See also W. Roddick, *Crossing the Road* (Cardiff: Law Society in Wales, 1999).

[26] See further below.

[27] National Assembly, *The Office of the Counsel General* (April 2001), paragraph 7.

[28] *Western Mail, Law Supplement*, 28 February 2000.

[29] See above, chapters 4 and 7–8.

[30] National Assembly, *The Office of the Counsel General* (April 2001), paragraph 8.

[31] OCG home page – *http://www.wales.gov.uk/organiocg/index.htm*

[32] National Assembly, *The Office of the Counsel General* (April 2001), paragraph 12.

[33] See above, chapter 8.

[34] National Assembly, *The Office of the Counsel General* (April 2001), paragraphs 19, 24.

[35] See above, chapter 12.

[36] See further below.

[37] R. Rawlings, 'Living with the lawyers' (1999) 2 *Agenda – Journal of the Institute of Welsh Affairs* 32.

38 See further below, especially with regard to human rights.
39 National Assembly, *The Office of the Counsel General* (April 2001), paragraph 1.
40 See above, chapter 5.
41 S. Allen, 'Getting assembled' (2000) 97(11) *Law Society Gazette* 30.
42 W. Roddick, *Evidence to the Richard Commission* (December 2002).
43 Under the auspices of the Care Standards Act 2000. It also accounts for six of the extra lawyers in post at the end of 2002.
44 See to this effect, S. Allen, 'Getting assembled', above, n. 41.
45 See above, chapter 3.
46 See further, V. MacCallum, 'Land of our lawyers' (2000) 34(12) *Law Society Gazette* 35.
47 GWA, Schedule 8, paragraph 1.
48 Scotland Act 1998,
49 See above, chapter 3.
50 Sir John Thomas, 'The legal implications of Welsh devolution', above, n. 18.
51 *Anisminic Ltd v Foreign Compensation Commission* [1969] 2 *Weekly Law Reports* 163; *Council of Civil Service Unions v Minister for the Civil Service* [1985] *Appeal Cases* 374. This is not to overlook the burdensome requirements that may be involved if something is labelled a 'devolution issue': see below.
52 See to this effect, D. Williams, 'Devolution: the Welsh perspective', in J. Beatson, C. Forsyth and I. Hare (eds.), *Constitutional Reform in the United Kingdom: Principles and Practice* (Oxford: Hart, 1998).
53 C. Boyd, 'Parliament and courts: powers in disputes resolution', in T. St. J. Bates (ed.), *Devolution to Scotland: The Legal Aspects* (Edinburgh: T. & T. Clark, 1997).
54 Department for Constitutional Affairs, *Constitutional Reform: A Supreme Court for the United Kingdom* (consultation paper 11/03. July 2003). The Government provisionally favours the transfer of 'devolution issues' from the Judicial Committee to the new court.
55 See for discussion, Sir John Laws, 'Judicial remedies and the constitution' (1994) 57 *Modern Law Review* 213.
56 See for details, P. Craig and M. Walters, 'The courts, devolution and judicial review' (1999) *Public Law* 274. For the provisions outlined in the text, see GWA, Schedule 8, paragraphs 3–11, 29–31.
57 See on Scotland and Northern Ireland respectively, GWA, Schedule 8, Parts III and IV.
58 GWA, s. 110.
59 Instructive in this context are the workings of the Government of Ireland Act 1920; see H. Calvert, *Constitutional Law in Northern Ireland* (London: Stevens, 1968), chapter 15.
60 According to the official Notes on Clauses published with the Devolution Bill.
61 Practice Note (Devolution Issues: Wales) [1999] 3 *All England Law Reports* 466.
62 Typically, however, the devolution issue cases arising in Scotland have concerned criminal justice: for example *Brown v Stott* (2001) 2 *Weekly Law Reports* 817. And in Northern Ireland, see G. Anthony, 'Public law litigation and the Belfast Agreement' (2002) 8(3) *European Public Law* 401.
63 Unless one counts the minor legal controversy in *South Wales Fisheries Committee v National Assembly for Wales* (2001) EWHC Admin 1162 (quashing of a poorly drafted Assembly Order).

⁶⁴   GWA, s. 122. No doubt comparative legal practice would be drawn on in reconciling texts, most obviously in Canada: see for example, P. Godin, 'The New Brunswick experience: the practice of the English common law in the French language' (2001) 1 *Wales Law Journal* 40.

⁶⁵   Lord Chancellor's Standing Committee for the Welsh Language, *Second Annual Report* (February 2002), p. 3.

⁶⁶   See above, chapter 7.

⁶⁷   Civil Procedure Rules, Part 54 Practice Direction, paragraph 3.1.

⁶⁸   Lord Chancellor's Department, *Note for Guidance: The Administrative Court in Wales* (July 2001).

⁶⁹   As explained below, the local development in judicial review is part of a more general trend of repatriation of legal proceedings to Wales. It is also the leading element in a wider decentralization of public law work.

⁷⁰   See for a useful overview, T. Cornford and M. Sunkin, 'The Bowman Report, access and the recent reforms of the judicial review procedure' (2001) *Public Law* 11.

⁷¹   [1898] 2 *Queen's Bench* 91; considered by D. Williams, 'The devolution of powers from central government', in Miers (ed.), *Devolution in Wales*, above, n. 18.

⁷²   GWA, s. 42, and see above, chapter 2.

⁷³   Beginning with the strategic plan, National Assembly, *A Better Wales* (1999); see above, especially chapter 7.

⁷⁴   Lord Hope, 'Judicial review of Acts of the Scottish Parliament' (1999) 263 *SCOLAG* 107; drawing in turn on the constitutional experience of independent Commonwealth countries and in particular the Canadian federal system.

⁷⁵   See further, B. Winetrobe, 'Scottish devolved legislation and the courts' (2002) *Public Law* 31. This in turn is not to equate the Scottish Parliament with Westminster: *Whaley v Lord Watson* (2000) *Scots Law Times* 475.

⁷⁶   See especially, *Nottinghamshire County Council v Secretary of State for the Environment* [1986] *Appeal Cases* 240.

⁷⁷   *Thoburn v Sunderland City Council* (2002) 1 *Weekly Law Reports* 247.

⁷⁸   See for example *International Transport Roth v Secretary of State for the Home Department* (2002) 1 *Common Market Law Reports* 52; and for discussion, J. Jowell, 'Judicial deference and human rights: a question of competence', in P. Craig and R. Rawlings (eds.), *Law and Administration in Europe* (Oxford: Oxford University Press, 2003).

⁷⁹   See now for practical illustration, *Adams v Lord Advocate, Times Law Reports*, 8 August 2002 (the Scottish Parliament and foxhunting). It should be stressed, however, that the legal position is very fluid.

⁸⁰   C. Himsworth, 'Rights versus devolution', in T. Campbell, K. Ewing and A. Tomkins (eds.), *Sceptical Essays on Human Rights* (Oxford: Oxford University Press, 2001). See most notably, *Anderson, Doherty and Reid v Scottish Ministers* (2002) 3 *Weekly Law Reports* 1460.

⁸¹   See above, chapter 12 (intergovernmental relations).

⁸²   Harlow and Rawlings, *Law and Administration*, above, n. 19, chapter 16.

⁸³   See to this effect, T. Shellens, 'The importance of public law challenges in Wales' (2001) 1 *Welsh Law Journal* 64.

⁸⁴   See above, chapter 11.

⁸⁵   See above, chapters 10–11.

⁸⁶   By virtue of GWA, s. 107: see above, chapter 2.

[87] *Rights Brought Home: The Human Rights Bill*, Cm. 3782 (1997); and see generally, S. Grosz, J. Beatson and P. Duffy, *Human Rights: The 1998 Act and the European Convention* (London: Sweet & Maxwell, 2000).

[88] See the classic authority of *Marckx v Belgium* (1979–80) 2 *European Human Rights Reports* 330.

[89] Human Rights Act 1998, s. 2(1); and see the leading case of *R (Anderson) v Secretary of State for the Home Department* (2002) 4 *All England Law Reports* 1089.

[90] Human Rights Act 1998, ss. 3–4; and see especially, *Re S, Re W* [2002] 2 *Appeal Cases* 291.

[91] Human Rights Act 1998, s. 10.

[92] An issue much discussed in the context of Scotland: see for example Himsworth, 'Rights versus devolution', above, n. 80.

[93] See for recent illustration in the guise of the common law, *Porter v Magill* (2002) 1 *All England Law Reports* 465.

[94] Which once again opens up the possibility of a declaration of incompatibility as regards the governing statute: see Human Rights Act 1998, ss. 3–4, 6; also GWA, s. 107(4).

[95] See for an instructive example, *Johansen v Norway* (1997) 23 *European Human Rights Reports* 33.

[96] See further, A. Bradley, 'Scope for review: the Convention right to education and the Human Rights Act 1998' (1999) 4 *European Human Rights Law Review* 395.

[97] See further, R. Rawlings, 'Taking Wales seriously', in T. Campbell, K. Ewing and A. Tomkins (eds.), *Sceptical Essays on Human Rights* (Oxford: Oxford University Press, 2001).

[98] See above, chapter 7 (the vision of 'a bilingual Wales'). There has long been scope for development in the Convention jurisprudence: see especially *Belgian Linguistic Case* (1968) 1 *European Human Rights Reports* 252.

[99] See above, chapter 11. Reference was made to the UN Convention on the Rights of the Child.

[100] L. Clements, 'Devolution in Wales and the human rights implications', *Legal Action* (July 1999), 20; and see generally on the rich heritage of campaigning litigation in Britain, C. Harlow and R. Rawlings, *Pressure through Law* (London: Routledge, 1992).

[101] S. Sedley, 'Foreword', in Grosz, Beatson and Duffy (eds.), *Human Rights*, above, n. 87.

[102] See above, chapter 2. This is not to overlook the contribution of Community law, now underscored by the EU Charter of Fundamental Rights, agreed at Nice in December 2000 (*Official Journal* 2000/C 364/01).

[103] See especially chapter 13 (Wales in Europe).

[104] Human Rights Task Force, *A New Era of Rights and Responsibilities* (Home Office, 2000), p. 4.

[105] Ibid.; PEP has now been subdivided: see above, chapter 5.

[106] National Assembly, *Human Rights Act Implementation: Action Plan* (January 2000).

[107] The incorporation of human rights considerations into Assembly law making was discussed in chapter 8.

[108] National Assembly cabinet, statement, 7 August 2002.

[109] See by way of exception, *Official Record*, 21 November 2000 and 14 December 2000 (ministerial statements on the HRA).

[110] See above, chapter 4.

[111] See on the background, S. Spencer and I. Bynoe, *A Human Rights Commission: The Options for Britain and Northern Ireland* (London: Institute of Public Policy Research, 1998). A Human Rights Commission was established in Northern Ireland in 1999, as part of the peace process.

[112] See *Final Report of the Assembly Review of Procedure Group* (February 2002), paragraph 8.5. The evidence came from the author.

[113] *A Voice for Wales*, Cm. 3718 (1997), paragraph 4.1.

[114] National Assembly Committee on Equality of Opportunity, Minutes, 26 June 2002.

[115] See above, chapter 7.

[116] Joint Select Committee on Human Rights, *Twenty Second Report: The Case for a Human Rights Commission: Interim Report* (HL 160, Session 2001–2002), Appendix 30.

[117] Ibid., Appendix 31. And see K. Williams, 'Failure to bring rights home: the need for devolved human rights commissions' (2003) 2 *Wales Law Journal* 244.

[118] L. Clements and S. Spencer, 'A Human Rights Commission in Wales?' (2001)(1) *Welsh Law Journal* 131.

[119] Joint Select Committee on Human Rights, *The Case for a Human Rights Commission*, above, n. 116, Appendix 31, paragraph 4; the Scots having now pre-empted the British option by choosing to go their own way.

[120] See above, chapter 11.

[121] Joint Select Committee on Human Rights, *Sixth Report: The Case for a Human Rights Commission* (HL 67-1, Session 2002–2003).

[122] See in this vein, National Assembly cabinet, statement, 7 August 2002.

[123] Joint Select Committee on Human Rights, *The Case for a Human Rights Commission*, above, n. 116, Appendix 30, paragraph 4.

[124] M. Barnard and D. Bindman, 'The dragon has landed', *Law Society Gazette*, 26 May 1999.

[125] Seminar Report, 'The courts, the legal profession and the economy: the challenges and opportunities of Legal Wales' (2002) 1 *Wales Law Journal* 240. And see further below.

[126] See above, chapter 11.

[127] There are of course other more general centralizing tendencies, as is shown in the Courts Bill currently before Parliament.

[128] W. Roddick, 'Doing business with the Assembly: defining the parameters and utilising the opportunities' (2002) 1 *Wales Law Journal* 306, p. 311.

[129] See above, chapter 11.

[130] Quoted in W. Roddick, 'Doing business with the Assembly', above, n. 128, p. 310; and see to similar effect, Mr Justice Thomas, 'Legal lines through the devolution settlement' (2002) 2 *Agenda – Journal of the Institute of Welsh Affairs* 17.

[131] See especially, Law Society in Wales, *Our National Assembly: The Legal Brief* (Cardiff, 1999).

[132] Wales Public Law and Human Rights Association, *Constitution* (September 1999).

[133] *Western Mail*, 'Law Wales' supplement, 28 February 2000.

[134] Welsh Legal History Society, *Prospectus* (October 1999).

[135] *www.wales-legislation.org.uk*. And see D. Miers and D. Lambert, 'Law making in Wales: Wales legislation on-line' (2002) *Public Law* 663.

[136] See above, chapter 2.

[137] J. Jones, 'Editorial' (2001) 1 *Wales Law Journal* 7. This is not to overlook the well-established *Cambrian Law Journal*, based at Aberystwyth.

[138] See especially, Andrews (ed.), *Welsh Studies in Public Law*, above, n. 22.

[139] Centre for Welsh Legal Affairs, *Aims and Remit* (April 2000).

[140] Sir Stephen Richards, *The Court System in Wales: Challenge and Change* (Aberystwyth: Centre for Welsh Legal Affairs, 2001).

[141] J. Price, 'The Welsh economy and professional services' (2002) 1 *Welsh Law Journal* 236.

[142] See for text and explanation, E. John (ed.), *Wales: Its Politics and Economics* (Cardiff: The Welsh Outlook Press, 1919). And see for an early contemporary variant, Parliament for Wales Campaign, *Power to the People of Wales* (1997).

[143] See for details, Sir John Thomas, *Legal Wales*, above, n. 3.

[144] *The Times*, 3 August 1998.

[145] K. Bush, 'Legislative powers of the National Assembly' (1998) 2 *Triban* 1, 6.

[146] J. Griffith, *The Politics of the Judiciary* (London: Fontana, 1997).

[147] As famously in modern Welsh history, in the case of the RAF bombing school: D. Jenkins, *A Nation on Trial: Penyberth, 1936* (Caernarfon: Welsh Academic Press, 1998).

[148] Sir John Thomas, 'The legal implications of Welsh devolution', above, n. 18, p. 18.

[149] Abolished along with the Courts of Great Session in 1830: see above.

[150] Power to alter such judicial titles is a notable feature of the current Courts Bill.

[151] GWA, Schedule 8, paragraph 33; and see for discussion in the Scottish context, A. O'Neill, 'Judicial politics and the Judicial Committee: the devolution jurisprudence of the Privy Council' (2001) 64 *Modern Law Review* 603.

[152] Precedent exists despite the absence of separate Welsh courts: see for example *Morris v Crown Office* (1970) 1 *Weekly Law Reports* 792.

[153] The recent consultation paper from the Department for Constitutional Affairs, *Constitutional Reform: A Supreme Court for the United Kingdom*, above, n. 54, is lukewarm in this regard.

[154] Sir John Thomas, *Legal Wales*, above, n. 3, p. 161.

[155] Which is itself a testing ground for the work of the Richard Commission: see further below, chapter 15.

[156] Lord Carlile, *The Evolution of Devolution* (Criccieth: 2002), p. 15. See also now, Sir Roderick Evans, *Legal Wales – Some Thoughts for the Future* (Cardiff: Lord Morris of Borth-y-Gest lecture, 2002).

[157] *Report of the Royal Commission on the Constitution, 1969–1973* Cmnd. 5460 (1973), paragraph 1151. The argument in the text assumes a substantial slice of legislative devolution as against tinkering at the edges; see further below, chapter 15.

Chapter 15

[1] *Official Record*, 13 June 2002.

[2] See above, p. 3.

[3] Welsh Assembly Government, *Delivery: First Minister's Report 2001–2002* (October 2002), p. 1.

[4] See above, chapter 4.

[5] J. Shortridge, *Evidence to The Richard Commission* (December 2002).

⁶ See above, chapter 6; and for chapter and verse, Churches' National Assembly Centre, *Stating the Difference* (Cardiff, 2002).

⁷ See above, especially chapter 11.

⁸ R. Morgan, *Western Mail*, 11 December 2002.

⁹ See above, chapter 13.

¹⁰ See above, chapters 10–11.

¹¹ See above, especially chapter 3.

¹² See further the Postscript to this volume.

¹³ This is not to overlook controversial features like the fiscal constitution (Barnett formula etc.).

¹⁴ See to this effect, P. Murphy, *Devolution: The View from Whitehall and Torfaen* (Cardiff: Welsh Governance Centre, 2002).

¹⁵ See also now, Welsh Labour Party, *Evidence to the Richard Commission* (July 2003). At one and the same time, the topic of legislative devolution is carefully avoided, and the lack of clarity in the existing arrangements is highlighted in the submission.

¹⁶ See for illustration, Lord Griffiths, *A Conservative Agenda for Wales* (Aberystwyth: Institute of Welsh Politics, 2002); and in contrast, Welsh Conservatives, *Evidence to the Richard Commission* (February 2003).

¹⁷ See for a useful comparative analysis, J. Curtice, *Devolution, the Union and Public Opinion*, reported in House of Lords Select Committee on the Constitution, Second Report: *Devolution: Inter-institutional Relations in the United Kingdom* (HL 28, Session 2002–3), paragraphs 70–85.

¹⁸ R. Wyn Jones and R. Scully, *Public Attitudes to the Devolution Settlement in Wales* (Aberystwyth: Institute of Welsh Politics, 2002).

¹⁹ See above, chapter 5.

²⁰ See above, chapters 4 and 10–11.

²¹ W. Roddick, *Evidence to the Richard Commission* (December 2002).

²² J. Shortridge, *Evidence to the Richard Commission* (December 2002). And see to the same effect, the evidence from the Counsel General.

²³ As stated in the terms of reference: see on the establishment of the commission, *Official Record*, 18 April 2002 and 20 June 2002.

²⁴ See for details of the individual members, National Assembly, press release, 31 July 2002.

²⁵ Wales Office, *Memorandum by the UK Government to the Richard Commission* (October 2002): it thus bears no repetition here.

²⁶ In fact, the commission agreed to the Welsh Labour Party presenting its evidence after the elections.

²⁷ As was suggested recently by Plaid Cymru: see *Official Record*, 4 March 2003.

²⁸ Richard Commission, *The Powers of the National Assembly for Wales: Issues and Questions for Consultation* (November 2002). The commission could not say but that it had been warned: K. Patchett, *The Commission on the Powers and Electoral Arrangements of the National Assembly for Wales: Issues and Methodology* (Cardiff: Institute of Welsh Affairs, 2002).

²⁹ The early signs here have been encouraging: see Richard Commission, *The Powers of the National Assembly for Wales: Issues and Questions for Consultation* (November 2002), p. 2.

³⁰ Wales Office, *Memorandum by the UK Government to the Richard Commission* (October 2002), paragraphs 18–20.

[31] Richard Commission, *The Powers of the National Assembly for Wales: Issues and Questions for Consultation* (November 2002), p. 2.

[32] Peter Hain, *Evidence to the Richard Commission* (March 2003); and see to similar effect, P. Murphy, *Devolution: The View from Whitehall and Torfaen*, above.

[33] Ibid.

[34] See for practical illustration, *Evidence to the Richard Commission* (December 2002).

[35] See especially Michael German, *Evidence to the Richard Commission* (November 2002).

[36] A theme pursued below, in the context of proposals for legislative devolution.

[37] Ron Davies, *Evidence to the Richard Commission* (October 2002). The more thoroughgoing constitutional possibilities of (Welsh) independence and (UK) federalism are emphatically not on the agenda of the Richard Commission.

[38] The material in the following section has been presented to the Members: R. Rawlings, *Evidence to the Richard Commission* (May 2003).

[39] See for detailed legal analysis, C. Himsworth and C. Munro, *The Scotland Act 1998* (Edinburgh: W. Green, 2nd edn., 2000).

[40] A familiar argument in the literature: see for example, Constitution Unit, *Scotland's Parliament: Fundamentals for a New Scotland Act* (London: Constitution Unit, 1996), chapters 3–4. And see Scotland Act 1998, s. 29 (legislative competence).

[41] As adapted from Scotland Act 1998, s. 28(7).

[42] Scotland Act 1998, s. 101 (and related provisions); see also Northern Ireland Act 1998, s. 83.

[43] Scotland Act 1998, s. 29.

[44] Scotland Act 1998, s. 30 and Schedule 7.

[45] See for this scenario, Lord Elis-Thomas, *Evidence to the Richard Commission* (December 2002). And see further below.

[46] The terminology is also borrowed from Scotland. And see below, on the putting to rest of the corporate body.

[47] Scotland Act 1998, s. 54.

[48] Scotland Act 1998, s. 63 and Schedule 7.

[49] *Scotland's Parliament*, Cm. 3658 (1997), paragraph 2.7, and see especially, Scotland Act 1998 (Transfer of Functions to the Scottish Ministers etc.) Order 1999, SI 1999 no. 1750 (the original one).

[50] See for detailed comparison, B. Hadfield, 'The nature of devolution in Scotland and Northern Ireland: key issues of responsibility and control' (1999) 3 *Edinburgh Law Review* 3. The tripartite categorization – see Northern Ireland Act 1998, s. 4 – derives originally from the Government of Ireland Act 1920.

[51] Northern Ireland Act 1998, ss. 8, 15.

[52] Northern Ireland Act 1998, s. 85: it otherwise has to be done by Act of Parliament.

[53] Northern Ireland Act 1998, s. 4. Cross-community support is required for the Assembly resolution.

[54] See generally to this effect, B. O'Leary, *The British–Irish Agreement: Power-sharing Plus* (London: Constitution Unit, 1998).

[55] A point notably stressed by the Permanent Secretary: J. Shortridge, *Evidence to the Richard Commission* (December 2002).

[56] There is a massive literature. But see now, for discussion in the local context,

M. Laffin, G. Taylor and A. Thomas, *Options for Change* (Pontypridd: University of Glamorgan, 2002).

[57] See above, chapter 2.

[58] As discussed in the previous chapter.

[59] See above, especially chapter 11.

[60] See for example Northern Ireland Act 1998, s. 7.

[61] From proportional representation to 'first past the post': the (early) history of Stormont serves as a warning.

[62] GWA, Schedule 2: see above, chapter 2.

[63] See especially, Jane Davidson, *Evidence to the Richard Commission* (December 2002).

[64] See above, chapter 4.

[65] See above, chapter 11.

[66] See above, chapter 9.

[67] *Report of the Royal Commission on the Constitution, 1969–1973*, Cmnd. 5460 (1973), chapter 24.

[68] A watered-down version of the Northern Ireland arrangements, whereby an Assembly Bill was made subject to negative resolution procedure prior to being presented for Royal Assent, would help to limit the likelihood of dispute between the UK government and the devolved administration.

[69] There would of course be no power for the Secretary of State to legislate for Wales on 'retained matters'.

[70] See above, especially chapter 1.

[71] As the minister has quickly discovered: Andrew Davies, *Evidence to the Richard Commission* (December 2002). See also above, chapter 12 (concordat on financial assistance to industry).

[72] See for the background, Welsh Affairs Select Committee, *Transport in Wales* (HC 205, Session 2002–3).

[73] See above, chapter 9.

[74] See above, chapter 13.

[75] See above, chapter 8.

[76] See above, chapter 13.

[77] And see for the parallel argument – development of legislative 'principles' in the context of executive devolution – above, chapter 9.

[78] See above, chapter 13.

[79] See above. chapter 9.

[80] See for discussion in the local context, R. Hazell, 'Multi-level governance', in J. Osmond and J. Barry Jones (eds.), *Birth of Welsh Democracy* (Cardiff: Institute of Welsh Affairs, 2003). For obvious reasons, the legislative record of the Northern Ireland Assembly is less instructive.

[81] See above, chapter 6 (the 'hollow core' of plenary).

[82] See above, especially chapter 11.

[83] *Memorandum of Understanding and Supplementary Agreements*, Cm. 5240 (2001), paragraph 13.

[84] One could even envisage 'general' Sewel motions, whereby Parliament would legislate on subject areas of devolved competencies until the Assembly was ready to become involved: in effect, another form of 'phased devolution'.

[85] A. Page and A. Batey, 'Scotland's other parliament: Westminster legislation about devolved matters in Scotland since devolution' (2002) *Public Law* 501. And see

Scottish Executive, *The Sewel Convention: Procedural and Practical Issues* (January 2003).

[86]   Not least in the EU context: see above, chapter 13.

[87]   J. Shortridge, *Evidence to the Richard Commission* (December 2002).

[88]   Ibid.

[89]   This is not to overlook the need to protect the position of the devolved parliament in the Sewel process, for example, via a special 'scrutiny reserve': see, House of Lords Select Committee on the Constitution, Second Report: *Devolution: Inter-institutional Relations in the United Kingdom* (HL 28, Session 2002–3), paragraphs 126–34.

[90]   As distinct from the nascent form of 'co-legislation' in the current scheme of executive devolution: see above, chapter 9.

[91]   See above, chapter 8.

[92]   Scotland Act 1998, schedule 5, section G.

[93]   With the caveat that new requirements of agreement or consultation can be imposed on powers transferred or made concurrent under such an order: Scotland Act 1998, s. 63(3).

[94]   If with limited success: see above, chapter 2.

[95]   Welsh Affairs Select Committee, *Transport in Wales* (HC 205, Session 2002–3), paragraph 38; a view reflected in the 'Passenger Transport Bill' proposed by the Assembly.

[96]   See especially Scotland Act 1998 (Transfer of Functions to the Scottish Ministers) Order 1999, SI 1999 no. 1750; also, Scotland Act 1998 (Transfer of Functions to the Scottish Ministers) Order 2001, SI 2001 no. 954.

[97]   Scotland Act 1998, Schedule 5, s. E2; also Scotland Act 1998 (Modifications of Schedule 5) Order 2002, SI no. 1629, 2002.

[98]   See Andrew Davies, *Evidence to the Richard Commission* (December 2002), especially Annex 2. The powers are contained in ss. 36–7 of the Electricity Act 1989.

[99]   Scotland Act 1998, Schedule 5, section D1; Scotland Act 1998 (Transfer of Functions to the Scottish Ministers) Order 1999, SI 1999 no. 1750.

[100]   The official explanation: see Andrew Davies, *Evidence to the Richard Commission* (December 2002). And see above, chapter 9.

[101]   See for practical illustration, *Official Record*, 29 January 2003.

[102]   See above, chapter 11. Culminating in a new cabinet portfolio of 'Social Justice and Regeneration': see Postscript.

[103]   See UK Government White Paper, *Our Fire and Rescue Service*, Cm. 5808 (2003), which contains plans to devolve responsibility for fire-fighting and fire safety issues to the Assembly. The ambulance service obviously is already devolved.

[104]   See for example, above, chapter 11 (the Environment Agency).

[105]   *Terms of Reference for the Richard Commission* (June 2002).

[106]   The idea of an upper Chamber of a Welsh 'Parliament' need not detain us here.

[107]   See for a valuable comparative survey, P. Norton (ed.), *Legislatures and Legislators* (London: Ashgate, 1998); also, P. Wijesekera and D. Reynolds, *Parliaments and Governments in the Next Millennium* (London: Commonwealth Parliamentary Association and Cavendish Publishing, 1999).

[108]   Richard Commission, *Electoral Arrangements of the National Assembly for Wales: Issues and Questions for Consultation* (March 2003).

[109]   See above, chapter 1.

[110] See above, chapter 1.

[111] GWA, Schedule 1, paragraph 1 ('The Assembly constituencies shall be the parliamentary constituencies in Wales'). The Richard Commission's consultation on electoral arrangements has focused directly on this aspect.

[112] Scotland Act 1998, Schedule 1.

[113] The setting up of an independent commission into issues caused by different boundaries for Holyrood and Westminster not before but after the event may itself be considered to send a powerful message: see *House of Commons Debates*, cols. 859–873 (18 December 2002) (Secretary of State for Scotland, Helen Liddell).

[114] See Richard Commission, *Electoral Arrangements of the National Assembly for Wales*, above, n. 108, paragraphs 19–20.

[115] See above, chapter 10.

[116] This is not to exclude the possibility of fine-tuning; for example, to prevent dual candidature (constituency and regional list).

[117] In the event, the Party's evidence to the commission is more nuanced: not directly advocating FTPT, but noting 'serious deficiencies' in the current system.

[118] As illustrated in the policy document, Welsh Labour Party, *Shaping the Vision: A Report on the Powers and Structure of the Welsh Assembly* (Cardiff: Welsh Labour Party, 1995): see above, chapter 1. Along with the Liberal Democrats, the nationalists have called for STV: Plaid Cymru, *Evidence to the Richard Commission* (February 2003).

[119] In the sense explained in chapter 4: replacement by a parliamentary corporate body.

[120] See for the parallel arrangements, Scotland Act 1998, Part II.

[121] Provision for parliamentary resolution of no confidence in the Executive; see above, chapter 4 for the different arrangement under the GWA.

[122] See above, chapter 4.

[123] See generally, P. Lynch, 'The committee system of the Scottish Parliament', in G. Hassan and C. Warhurst (eds.), *The New Scottish Politics: The First Year of the Scottish Parliament and Beyond* (Norwich: Stationery Office, 2000). See also, in the local context, Charter 88, *Standing Orders: A New Political Culture for the National Assembly for Wales* (London: Charter 88, 1998).

[124] See above, especially chapter 2. Wales could usefully draw lessons here from the Scottish experience (including in terms of restrictive provisions in the devolution statute).

[125] *Scotland's Parliament. Scotland's Right* (Edinburgh: Scottish Constitutional Convention, 1995), p. 27.

[126] Richard Commission, *The Powers of the National Assembly for Wales: Issues and Questions for Consultation* (November 2002), 3. And see especially, Welsh Liberal Democrats, *Evidence to the Richard Commission* (February 2003).

[127] A familiar theme in the lore of central–local government relations; and see generally, in this context, V. Bogdanor, *Devolution in the United Kingdom* (Oxford: Oxford University Press, 1999).

[128] As discussed in chapter 2.

[129] Commission on Taxation and Citizenship, *Paying for Progress: A New Politics of Tax for Public Spending* (London: Fabian Society, 2000), chapter 9.

[130] Scotland Act 1998, s. 76.

[131] Edwina Hart, *Evidence to the Richard Commission* (December 2002), p. 2.

[132] See further, for discussion of taxing power in terms of the concepts of decentralization of administration and of choice, L. Blow, J. Hall and S. Smith, *Financing Regional Government in Britain* (London: Institute of Fiscal Studies, 1996).

[133] As discussed in chapter 6.

[134] See for example, J. Hopkins, *Devolution in Context: Regional, Federal and Devolved Government in the EU* (London: Cavendish, 2001), chapter 9.

[135] See also Edwina Hart, *Memorandum by the Minister for Finance, Local Government and Communities, National Assembly for Wales*, House of Lords Select Committee on the Constitution, *Devolution: Inter-institutional Relations in the United Kingdom* – Evidence (HL 147, Session 2001–2),

[136] *Official Record*, 18 April 2002.

[137] See especially GWA, s. 36 (provision for poll specifically tied to exercise of Assembly functions).

[138] A point notably stressed by the ministerial architect: Ron Davies, *Evidence to the Richard Commission* (October 2002).

[139] *A Voice for Wales*, Cm. 3718 (1997), paragraph 3.37.

Postscript

[1] See above, chapter 2 (table 2).

[2] See above, chapter 2 (even counting Dr Marek's constituency as a 'Labour' seat).

[3] Once again this is not to overlook the broader comparative trends or general sense of 'disconnection', including now in the case of the Scottish Parliament (turnout of 49%, down 9%).

[4] *Official Record*, 7 May 2003.

[5] Ibid.

[6] Including the Clerk to the Assembly; see above, especially chapters 4 and 9 (internal architecture and primary legislation affecting Wales).

[7] Notwithstanding the formal demise of the *Protocol for Partnership Government* laying out much of the framework: see above, chapter 4.

[8] See *Official Record*, 13 May 2003.

[9] Ibid. (Rhodri Morgan).

[10] As illuminated in the Welsh Assembly Government's policy map or *mappa mundi*: see above, chapter 4.

[11] *Official Record*, 20 May 2003 ('State of the Nation' debate).

Index of Statutes

Index